Finland
Russia
Estonia
Latvia
Lithuania
Byelarus
Poland
Ukraine
Moldova
Hung.
Romania
Georgia
2
3
4
5
Bulgaria
Greece
Turkey
Kazakhstan
Mongolia
Uzbekistan
Turkmenistan
Kyrgyzstan
Tajikistan
N. Korea
S. Korea
Japan
Cyprus
Syria
Lebanon
Israel
Iraq
Azerbaijan
Armenia
Afghanistan
China
Iran
Jordan
Bhutan
Nepal
Pakistan
Egypt
Kuwait
Qatar
Saudi Arabia
U.A.E.
Oman
India
Taiwan
Myanma
Laos
Hong Kong
Chad
Sudan
Yemen
Djibouti
Bangladesh
Thailand
Vietnam
Philippines
Cent. Afr. Rep.
Ethiopia
Somalia
Sri Lanka
Kampuchea
Brunei
Malaysia
Maldives
Uganda
Kenya
Rwanda
Zaire
Burundi
Singapore
Papua New Guinea
Indonesia
Tanzania
Solomon Islands
Seychelles
Malawi
Comoros
Angola
Zambia
Mozambique
Vanatu
Zimbabwe
Botswana
Madagascar
Mauritius
Australia
W. Samoa
Swaziland
South Africa
Lesotho
New Zealand

PRINCIPLES OF MARKETING

A GLOBAL PERSPECTIVE 2ND EDITION

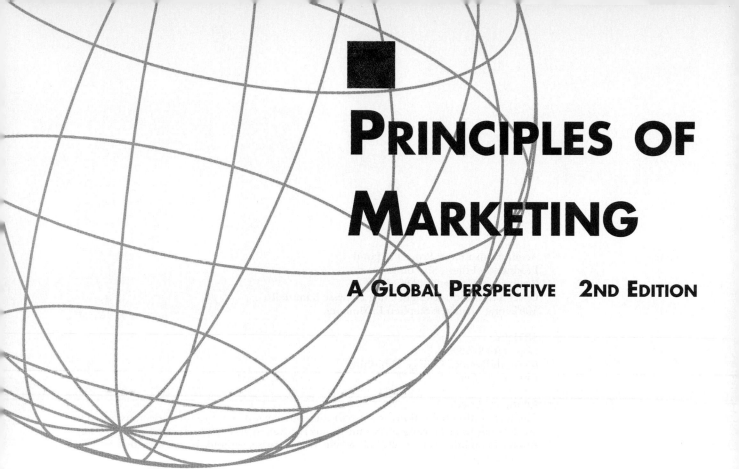

PRINCIPLES OF MARKETING

A GLOBAL PERSPECTIVE 2ND EDITION

RICHARD J. SEMENIK
Professor of Marketing
The University of Utah
David Eccles School of Business
Salt Lake City, Utah

GARY J. BAMOSSY
Professor of Marketing
Vrije Universiteit
Amsterdam, The Netherlands

SOUTH-WESTERN College Publishing

An International Thomson Publishing Company

Acquisitions Editor: Robert B. Jared
Production Editor: Sharon L. Smith
Production House: Bookmark
Cover and Interior Design: Craig LaGesse Ramsdell
Marketing Manager: Stephen E. Momper

SB71BA

1 2 3 4 5 6 7 KI 0 9 8 7 6 5 4

Printed in the United States of America

Library of Congress Cataloging-in-Publication Data

Semenik, Richard J.
Principles of marketing: a global perspective / Richard J. Semenik, Gary J. Bamossy. – 2nd ed.
p. cm.
Includes bibliographical references and index.
ISBN 0-538-83913-9
1. Marketing–Management. I. Bamossy, Gary J., 1949. II. Title.
HF5415.13.S437 1995
658.8—dc20 94-22222
CIP

International Thomson Publishing Company

South-Western College Publishing is an ITP Company.
The ITP trademark is used under license.

To my parents, Augustine and Joseph who showed me the value of hard work.

To my daughter Andi, who showed me the value of having fun.

To my wife Molly, who showed me how much she cares by putting up with me while this book was being written.

RJS

Voor Joost en Lieke

liefs, Papa

PREFACE

Oh no!! Not another revised principles of marketing book! As authors, we have been most gratified by the reception to the First Edition of *Principles of Marketing: A Global Perspective.* Faculty who have used and read the book have reviewed it with such comments as "the Semenik and Bamossy book is like a breath of fresh air," and "I found the text written at a more 'intellectual level' than the competition." With respect to the global perspective sections that conclude each chapter: "Much better than integrating global/international material in 'very small tidbits' throughout the chapters."*

There is no doubt about it, the First Edition was a major departure from other texts on the market. We took a bold step to expand the parameters in the principles course. Comments from faculty, students, corporate executives, and reviewers have helped us create an even stronger and more appealing text in this, the Second Edition of *Principles of Marketing: A Global Perspective.* We have added more traditional material where it was needed and pushed the parameters even further when we were encouraged to do so.

In this era of global, digitized, interactive business environments, students need a bold, contemporary, and lively treatment of the principles of marketing. With this new edition, we give you the newest, most up-to-date and relevant concepts and examples in the principles of marketing and the global challenges facing marketing managers.

HOW THIS BOOK IS (STILL) DIFFERENT

The First Edition of *Principles of Marketing: A Global Perspective* was conceived to be different from any other principles text on the market. Some of the features we built into the conception of the text have worked so well in the classroom that we have retained them in this Second Edition. Specifically, three features make this treatment of marketing unique, and, we believe, better:

1. **Global Perspectives**. Every chapter in the textbook concludes with a six to ten page section titled "Global Perspectives," which raises the essential issues and chal-

*A full set of reviewers' comments is available upon request.

lenges of global marketing related to the chapter topic. This is not a superficial "box" treatment or a sentence or two marked with a couple of foreign flags. Contained in these sections is concise coverage of the unique considerations facing marketing decision makers in the global context. From the fundamentals of comparative advantage and competitive interdependence to gender bias in global personal selling, the critical, contemporary topics of global marketing are covered. Global issues are covered in a way that an understanding of global challenges, topic by topic, is accomplished. These global sections are highlighted with the colorful "sidebars" you see on the edge of the page here. This way, students will readily recognize that the topics on these highlighted pages relate specifically to the global context.

Of equal importance to the content in this area is the person who wrote the material. Gary Bamossy is an American-trained Ph.D. in marketing and is Professor of Marketing at the Vrije Universiteit in Amsterdam. He lives and teaches in the dynamic European setting, and has consulted with major multinational corporations like Apple Computer-Europe, American Express, Heineken, and KLM-Royal Dutch Airlines.

2. **A Macro-Micro-Macro Sequence of Presentation**. The overall format of the book is designed to cover the principles of marketing in a macro-micro-macro format. Section 1: Foundations of the Marketing Process (Chapters 1 and 2), treats the macro topics of marketing in business and society and analyzing the environment for decision making. Section 2: Analyzing Markets and Buyer Behavior (Chapters 3 to 6), continues the macro orientation to marketing and covers marketing research, consumer and business market analysis, and consumer and business buyer behavior. The topics in Sections 1 and 2 span the totality of the functional areas of marketing and provide a macro orientation to the process.

Section 3: Operationalizing the Marketing Process: The Marketing Mix (Chapters 7 through 15), adopts a micro (organizational) perspective and provides comprehensive coverage of the functional areas of marketing divided into four parts. Each part focuses on one of the marketing mix variables: Part One: product development, management, and strategies; Part Two: pricing objectives, methods, and strategies; Part Three: communications processes, mass communication, personal selling, and integrated marketing communications; and Part Four: developing channels of distribution, retailing, wholesaling, and physical distribution.

After these micro operational aspects are firmly established, the text returns to a macro perspective once again. Section 4: Managing the Marketing Process (Chapters 16 and 17), establishes the contemporary view of marketing management in both the domestic and global context. Chapter 16 covers the principles of marketing management as they have developed and evolved over the last several decades. Chapter 17 then provides an interpretation of global issues and challenges of managing the marketing process within and across international market settings. Section 5: Special Aspects of the Marketing Process, concludes the final macro perspective. Here, marketing in service and not-for-profit organizations is covered in detail (Chapter 18). Finally, since students have now been exposed to all aspects of the marketing process and operations, the critical issues related to social, ethical, and environmental aspects of marketing are presented.

3. **Concise Treatment of Topics**. In the Second Edition, we have continued our dedication to a concise and straightforward treatment of topics. Our colleagues told us that they cannot tolerate books that use 24 chapters and 900 pages to cover the principles of marketing. Instructors and students have told us how much they appreciate the fact that we can cover all the topics in the principles of marketing in just 19 chapters and in less than 700 pages. This includes both the principles and the global perspectives sections. But, this concise coverage doesn't mean we left out topics. We continue to provide coverage of many topics that most principles books overlook: semantic product design, the virtual corporation and re-

engineering, qualitative research methods (including the "emic" and "etic" perspective on cross cultural research), gender bias in international personal selling, and value pricing strategies to name a few.

HOW THIS EDITION IS NEW

Feedback from faculty has led us to make some significant changes in the Second Edition. Most conspicuously, we have added a bit more tradition to the sequence of coverage. The five sections of the text now follow an order of presentation common in principles text. This is highlighted in Section 3 which relies on a 4Ps organization in which each of the marketing mix variables is featured in a separate section with a separate set of chapters. Also, strategic planning is introduced much earlier in the text with full treatment of procedures and a marketing plan in Chapter 2.

One of the new features of the text that recurs as a theme through several chapters is an emphasis on "value." Beginning in Chapter 1 with a discussion of how customer satisfaction is based on consumers' perceptions of "value" and continuing through consumer buying behavior (Chapter 6), product development (Chapter 7), pricing (Chapter 9), and distribution (Chapters 13 to 15), value is a featured concept that reflects one of the key corporate challenges of the 1990s.

This edition of the book is also slightly longer than the First Edition because we have added numerous graphic displays of conceptual material. We found many opportunities where providing students with a visual representation greatly enhanced the discussions of complex concepts. And, the entire book has been produced in color as a means to deliver the text material in a stylish and appealing way.

We have continued the tradition of the First Edition by including more new and different topics than most principles texts. Topics like co-branding strategy, value pricing strategies, strategy implications of product classifications, integrated marketing communications, the virtual corporation, and the horizontal corporation are a few of the unique topics you will find presented in this edition.

Principles of Marketing: A Global Perspective was conceived to be different and better: the factors listed above serve to accomplish those goals. As you read through the text, you will find that the features that make this book different and better are fundamental and pervasive. We did not just add little boxes of information or tack on ancillary material—we wrote a fundamentally different principles of marketing book.

ACKNOWLEDGEMENTS

No book is written without the aid of a large number of people. The reviewers of both the First and Second Editions of this text provided useful insights that were directly incorporated into the text. The timeliness, coverage, and quality of this book was greatly enhanced by these dedicated academics and marketing practitioners:

Ronald J. Adams
University of North Florida

Thom Belich
St. Cloud State University

S. Tamer Cavusgil
Michigan State University

Janeen Costa
University of Utah

David A. Cohen
Northern Arizona University

Catherine Cole
University of Iowa

C. Anthony di Benedetto
Temple University

William M. Diamond
SUNY Albany

Haiko Emanuel
Lairve Holland, B.V.

Fred van Eenennaam
Vrije Universiteit, Amsterdam

Sevgin Eroglu
Georgia State University

Ruud Fontijn
Vrije Universiteit, Amsterdam

David J. Good
Central Missouri State University

Peter Gordon
Southeast Missouri State University

Bruce H. Johnson
Gustavus Adolphus College

Wouter Koetzier
Unilever B.V.

Kenneth Lord
SUNY Buffalo

Nancy Ryan McClure
Eastern New Mexico University

Ronald E. Michaels
Indiana University

Robert A. Mittelstaedt
University of Nebraska

David Morris
University of New Haven

Gordan L. Patser
University of Northern Iowa

Eric Pratt
New Mexico State University

Joseph B. Shapiro
University of Maryland
University College
European Division

Bob E. Smiley
Indiana State University

Michael Tan
Moret, Ernst & Young
Management Consultants
The Netherlands

Jerry Thomas
San Jose State University

Daniel Wardlow
San Francisco State University

James F. Wenthe
Georgia College

Many people at South-Western Publishing deserve recognition. Randy Haubner and Scott Person dedicated themselves to making sure this Second Edition was initiated in a timely manner. They have, from the beginning, shared our vision of a different and challenging text. Steve Momper picked up the mantel from the marketing side. It was great to watch his enthusiasm grow as we neared completion of the project. Sue Ellen Brown started us in production and Sharon Smith provided us with guidance through the final stages. Craig LaGesse-Ramsdell patiently put up with our endless suggestions to come up with a beautiful design for the book. Finally, senior administration has not only been supportive but actually involved. We both want to thank Tim McEwen and Mark Hubble.

We enjoyed writing this Second Edition of *Principles of Marketing: A Global Perspective.* The methods for presenting principles combined with global perspectives is an approach we considered carefully. Students and instructors alike have found this treatment of great value. We want to thank students, instructors, and practitioners for their feedback in helping us prepare this edition. We also want to thank them for the way they continue to teach us about the discipline of marketing.

Richard J. Semenik
The University of Utah

Gary Bamossy
Vrije Universiteit, Amsterdam

Brief Contents

SECTION 1
FOUNDATIONS OF THE MARKETING PROCESS

SECTION 2
ANALYZING MARKETS AND BUYER BEHAVIOR

SECTION 3
OPERATIONALIZING THE MARKETING PROCESS: THE MARKETING MIX

Part Three
Promotional Decisions 321

Part Four
Distribution Decisions 433

SECTION FOUR
MANAGING THE MARKETING PROCESS

SECTION FIVE
SPECIAL ASPECTS OF THE MARKETING PROCESS

Contents

Section 1 Foundations of the Marketing Process 1

cDonald's
McDonald's

Dreyer's

PART TWO PRICING DECISIONS 280

PART THREE PROMOTIONAL DECISIONS 321

PART FOUR DISTRIBUTION DECISIONS 433

13 Channels of Distribution 433

14 Retailing and Retailing Strategy 466

thés
petits
déjeuner
céréales
Nestlé
Cheerios

SECTION ONE

FOUNDATIONS OF THE MARKETING PROCESS

1

Marketing in Business and Society

AFTER STUDYING THIS CHAPTER, YOU WILL UNDERSTAND THAT:

1. Marketing is a complex activity that is both a business function and a broad social and economic process.
2. Marketing serves an important role and purpose within business organizations from large multinational corporations to small not-for-profit organizations.
3. Marketing also serves important roles and purposes in an economy and throughout a society.
4. The marketing concept is a philosophy of business that focuses on customer satisfaction.
5. A global perspective on marketing in business and society requires knowledge of the nature of competition and interdependence in a changing world order.

What happened to General Motors (GM), IBM, and Sears? In 1963, General Motors controlled 51 percent of the U.S. automobile market; IBM had just launched its new *System/360* line of computers, which would redefine the nature of computer applications worldwide; Sears dominated U.S. retailing with annual sales that were larger than the combined sales of its four closest competitors. Each of these companies was perched at the top of its respective industry, and yet each managed to somehow squander that vaunted position. By 1992, General Motors share of the U.S. automobile market had slipped to just 35 percent, IBM's mainframes were considered oversized and obsolete, and Sears had been surpassed in merchandise sales by two retailers that didn't even exist thirty years earlier. These three pinnacles of U.S. commerce had combined losses for the year of $32.4 billion!

What had happened? Most analysts agree that the scenario is familiar and can be seen in many organizations—from large multinational firms to small family-run businesses: these companies failed to adapt their products and services to changes in the marketplace. Or, put another way, they failed to adjust their marketing programs to reflect changes in the complex and dynamic environment within which they were doing business. In fact, they were so out of touch with their markets that one analyst referred to them as "dinosaurs."[1] Sears ignored the eminent rise of capable discounters such as Kmart and Wal-Mart. GM was slow to respond to the market's demand for small, stylish, fuel-efficient cars and brought competitive models to the market much too late. Finally, IBM failed to invest in new miniaturization technology and saw computing power move away from its mainframe machines to small, desktop (and then laptop) microcomputers. Today, each firm is making sweeping changes in their marketing programs and redesigning the way they develop, sell, and deliver products and services. By 1993, GM, Sears, and IBM had all registered quarterly profits. GM has undertaken several marketing strategies to change performance. New versions of the mid-size *Lumina* and a reincarnation of the popular *Monte Carlo* nameplate are two strategies the firm hopes will attract more buyers. IBM's profitability is somewhat suspect, however. While the firm registered a small profit at the end of 1993, total revenues actually *decreased.* Most of IBM's profits came from restructuring and cost cutting rather than marketing improvements. It remains to be seen if IBM's marketing activities, including new products like the *ThinkPad* portable computer and the firm's alliance with Apple Computer and Motorola to develop the *PowerPC* processor chip, will pay off in the market.

Marketing Is Both a Business and a Societal Process

Stories about huge corporations like GM, IBM, and Sears are good examples of how marketing is essential to corporate success. But marketing isn't just a business process, it's a societal process as well. And, marketing isn't just for giant companies—all types and sizes of organizations can benefit from marketing.

As a business process, marketing is a wonderfully diverse and exciting part of every business from the large multinational, industrial conglomerate to the

Marketing evolves in a society to provide efficient and effective satisfaction of citizens' needs. Here, ancient meets modern as a Chinese peasant uses a traditional distribution method while the billboard proclaims the wonders of the modern PC.

small, not-for-profit service organization. Marketing people are responsible for the design of a product, pricing it, promoting it, making sure it is available to customers, and ensuring customer satisfaction after a purchase is made. In a unique way, marketing challenges businesspeople to leave no stone unturned, no source of information untapped in the search for market opportunities. The diversity of marketing, as you will learn, is invigorating. Marketing people help design products, study what consumers like and don't like, and get involved in preparing advertising, just to name a few of the activities. If you like math, you can design sales forecasting models; if you like psychology, you can analyze consumer behavior and try to understand why consumers buy certain products. Marketing is also invigorating because a business depends on marketing to generate sales: it is the life-blood of an organization.

Marketing is also a societal process. Citizens in every society have wants and needs. Many of those wants and needs can be satisfied with goods and services. What is required, then, is an efficient and effective way to distribute the goods and services produced by a society to the citizenry. Through activities related to efficient distribution and exchange processes marketing serves to satisfy the needs of the society and its individual members.

This chapter will identify the role and purpose of marketing in business and society. Throughout this book the emphasis for our study of marketing will predominantly be on the individual business organization. However, marketing, more than any other business discipline, is affected by societal change and, in turn, affects the daily lives of people in a society. Therefore, the effects of marketing on society, and vice versa, will also be examined.

A Formal Definition of Marketing

At the outset, we need a formal and workable definition of marketing. Before we do that, though, it is worth taking a moment to dispel some myths and common misconceptions about what marketing is and what it does.

To dispel these myths and misconceptions, let's begin our definition of marketing with a discussion of *what marketing is not.* Marketing is *not advertising.* Although advertising is a very conspicuous and valuable tool of marketing, it is only one of marketing's responsibilities. Marketing is *not selling.* Again, much of marketing decision making and implementation deals with selling products and services, but marketing is much more broad and complex than selling alone. Marketing is *not simply common sense.* After a well-conceived marketing strategy is clearly articulated, the claim is often made that it was all "just common sense." Such a claim is hard to defend in the face of the harsh realities of the market. For example, in spite of billions of dollars spent each year on marketing research to identify products and services with high market potential, more new products fail than succeed. Firms that are highly successful in developing and marketing products, such as Merck, Honda Motors, and The Limited Stores, maintain large marketing staffs and *still* spend hundreds of millions of dollars a year on outside experts like marketing consulting firms and advertising agencies to help them cope with the complexities of marketing decisions. Finally, think about the number of times you've heard someone say (or maybe you've even said this yourself on occasion), "Why didn't I think of that! I could have made a million dollars!"

Well, the reason most of us "didn't think of that" is because marketing analysis and decision making are complex and go far beyond simple common sense and intuition. Marketing requires careful analysis of a dynamic environment, highly integrated planning, and precise implementation of activities. With this in mind, a formal definition of **marketing** is:

The process of planning and executing the conception, pricing, promotion, and distribution of ideas, goods, and services to create exchanges that satisfy individual and organizational objectives.[2]

The implications of this definition are far reaching. First, the definition specifies that marketing is a *process of planning and executing.* That is, marketing represents a series of integrated decisions *and* activities. Second, marketing assumes a wide range of responsibilities related to the *conception, pricing, promotion, and distribution* of ideas, goods, and services. These responsibilities of marketing are referred to as the **marketing mix** and will be discussed in detail in the next section. Third, the definition emphasizes that marketing relates to not just tangible products, but also to a full range of market offerings to serve human needs and wants that includes *ideas, goods, and services.* When political candidates run for office, for example, they are really marketing their political ideas and plans for the future. Finally, marketing activities are designed to provide *satisfaction* to individuals and organizations. When satisfaction is increased, then marketing has functioned to provide greater value to customers. It is this element of satisfaction in the definition of marketing that exemplifies the modern day philosophy of marketing in enlightened and sophisticated organizations.

Armed with this definition of marketing, we can move on to a discussion of what specific activities are carried out by marketing people in individual organizations and those that relate to marketing as a societal process as well.

Marketing in Business Organizations

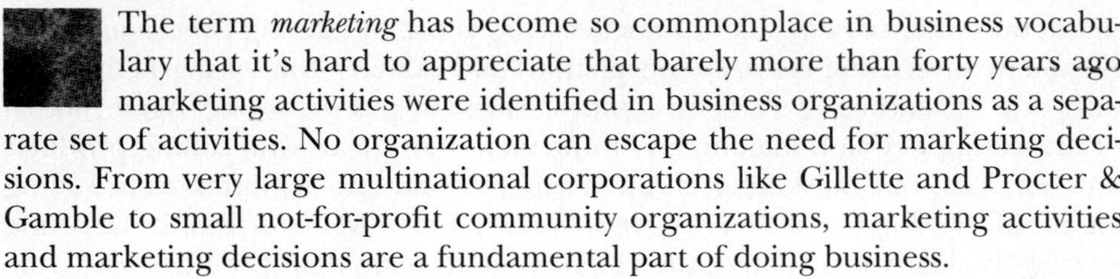

The term *marketing* has become so commonplace in business vocabulary that it's hard to appreciate that barely more than forty years ago marketing activities were identified in business organizations as a separate set of activities. No organization can escape the need for marketing decisions. From very large multinational corporations like Gillette and Procter & Gamble to small not-for-profit community organizations, marketing activities and marketing decisions are a fundamental part of doing business.

Some firms will have large marketing staffs and invest millions of dollars in marketing while others will do no planning whatsoever and make marketing decisions in a panic. Regardless of an organization's approach to marketing decision making, there are two separate but related aspects of marketing within an organization: marketing mix decisions and revenue generation.

The Role of Marketing in Business Organizations: Marketing Mix Decisions

The marketing mix refers to the four primary areas of decision making in marketing—product decisions, pricing decisions, promotional decisions, and place (or distribution) decisions. The marketing mix is also frequently referred to as the **Four Ps,** a description first used by E. Jerome McCarthy in the early 1960s. Marketing mix decisions describe the role marketing plays within an individual organization. Every decision and action associated with marketing in an organization will relate to product, pricing, promotion, or distribution. When Ford Motor Company invested over $6 billion in the new *Mondeo* automobile line, a major product line extension occurred and the product area of the marketing mix was being managed. When Apple Computer revamped the pricing of its three primary computers, a major pricing strategy was implemented. The marketing mix will be described and discussed in greater detail in Chapter 2 when aspects of strategic planning and the decision-making environment are considered. For now, recognize that the marketing mix defines the **role of the marketing** function within organizations.

The Purpose of Marketing in Business Organizations: Revenue Generation

The range of activities carried out in a typical business organization can be categorized into one of four traditional business areas: accounting, finance, management, and marketing. Accounting involves keeping track of the firm's funds. Accounting personnel set payroll procedures, provide budget summaries, adhere to federal, state, and local tax mandates, and administer a variety of other activities to ensure that the organization's fiscal matters are in order. Finance personnel ensure that assets earn a target return on investment and otherwise manage the debt structure of an organization. The purpose of management in an organization includes creating and implementing personnel policy and procedures, human resource management issues, and overseeing production and operations.

So far, we have described an organization that would need many different people performing many different and very important tasks. There is, however, one glaring omission in the description of all these business activities: revenue generation. Some part of the organization must be responsible for generating revenue. In the absence of revenue, not much will happen.

Just as accounting, finance, and management fulfill fundamental purposes in the organization, the **purpose of marketing** is to generate revenue.* No other part of the organization has this primary mandate. In the words of the highly regarded management consultant and scholar Peter Drucker, "Marketing and innovation produce results: all the rest are 'costs'."[3] As such, the marketing function shoulders an important responsibility. The people who fill various marketing positions in an organization are responsible for a broad range of activities designed to generate sales and therefore revenues for the firm. As alluded to in the introduction to this chapter, marketing activities in the firm are highly integrated and systematized to cultivate markets and compete effectively within those markets to generate sales.

Marketing decision makers must also understand the purpose of marketing in the context of the entire organization. The goal is not just to successfully generate revenue but to generate revenue in a way that is consistent with corporate policy and overall objectives of the organization. Figure 1-1 illustrates how an organization's objectives and policy are guiding principles in the development of marketing planning, strategy, and tactical implementation, which leads to revenue generation.

Corporations pursue objectives within carefully stated goals, or mission statements, to effectively use scarce human and financial resources. This corporate statement of direction, as it is embodied in policies and objectives, ultimately sets the direction for all marketing activities as well. For example, the marketing activities of Procter & Gamble, the $30 billion packaged-goods giant, are directed by the following statement of corporate objective made by the organization's chairman and chief executive officer:

Globalization has special meaning within Procter & Gamble. It means that we will continue to change from a U.S.-based business that sells some of its products in international markets into a truly world company, a company that thinks of everything it does—including development of products—in terms of the entire world. We will increasingly plan for growth of our business, and our technology investments, on a worldwide basis.[4]

As an example of Procter & Gamble's commitment to globalization, the firm acquired *Oil of Olay* beauty fluid. With new product design and strategic world planning by Procter & Gamble, *Oil of Olay* realized a 60 percent increase

*In not-for-profit organizations, marketing fulfills the role of revenue generation when fundraising activities are undertaken or performances and events earn revenue for the organization. Otherwise, marketing activities are focused on efficient and effective allocation of resources and servicing of client/patron needs. The adaptation of marketing in the not-for-profit context will be fully developed in Chapter 18.

FIGURE 1-1
The Purpose of Marketing in Organizations: Revenue Generation

in sales worldwide in 1990. Figure 1-2 demonstrates how the revenue generating purpose in marketing *Oil of Olay* in global markets fits into overall corporate planning at Procter & Gamble. Procter & Gamble's *corporate objectives and policies,* such as globalization of market opportunities, would be translated through its *strategic business units* (e.g., the Skin and Beauty Care Division) to the marketing planning, strategy, and tactical implementation.

This example of Procter & Gamble's broad corporate objectives as carried out in the marketing of *Oil of Olay* highlights the relationship between the specific purpose of marketing in an organization and overall corporate planning. We will change our emphasis now from marketing in the business organization to issues related to marketing in society.

Marketing in Society

While the emphasis of our study of marketing will be on marketing activities and decisions within the individual business organization, it is important to identify the role and purpose of marketing in society. Marketing serves important roles and purposes relative to a society's needs because the flow of goods and services is an inescapable activity in any societal setting. In some cases, the flow of goods and services is minimal, as in primitive hunting and gathering societies. Or it may be highly complex, as in the case of modern mass production and mass consumption societies based on free enterprise economic systems. Regardless of the level of complexity, marketing has both economic and social roles and purposes in a broad societal sense.

The Economic Role of Marketing in Society

Both within an economy and between economies, people learn that they can gain much by engaging in **exchange**, that is, trading goods and services for either money or other goods and services. Ultimately, parties that exchange

FIGURE 1-2
Procter & Gamble's Corporate Policy and the Purpose of Marketing

Economies of scale occur when a good is produced in large quantities. The effect of economies of scale is lower cost for each item produced. Here, Tootsie Pops are manufactured in large quantities to keep the costs low.

will acquire better goods and services and these goods and services will often cost *less* than if each party tried to make the items themselves. One of the benefits of exchange is that people get better products at lower cost.

Two factors explain these economic benefits of exchange. First, when people concentrate on the production of a particular good, they gain skill and expertise that may be superior to all others who try to make the same good. This is known as the effect of *specialization*. The second factor producing economic benefits of exchange is known as economies of scale. *Economies of scale* occur when a particular good is produced in large quantities and, because of this large-scale production, the fixed costs of production of each item are reduced. In turn, this lowers the cost of the item and can result in a lower price.

The marketing process makes an important contribution to bringing about exchange between parties and thus helps bring about specialization and economies of scale. The conception of goods, pricing them, promoting them, and distributing them (recall these factors from the definition of marketing) directly relate to the process of exchange. In the absence of some mechanism for exchanging goods that are produced, neither the specialization nor the economies-of-scale effects of exchange would be realized.

The idea of exchange is essential to appreciating the **economic role of marketing** conceptually, but we can find concrete evidence as well. Over the last one hundred years, the number of people employed in the wholesaling and retailing sectors (which directly bring about exchange in a modern setting) of the U.S. economy has increased twelvefold, while the number engaged in production has only tripled. By 1994, more than half of the gross domestic product of the United States was generated by businesses such as these.

The basic issue to be understood here is that exchange serves an important role in an economy by providing goods and services effectively and efficiently. The demand for goods and services is fostered by the collective marketing efforts of many organizations, and the economy is stimulated and grows. Marketing, then, plays an integral role in an economy by facilitating exchange.

THE ECONOMIC PURPOSE OF MARKETING IN SOCIETY

In the broad perspective, economists point out that the overall **economic purpose of marketing** in a society is to bring about **satisfaction**. This satisfaction is referred to in economic terms as **utility**. The entire marketing system works to create four types of utility: *form utility, time utility, place utility,* and *possession utility* (see Illustration 1-1).

Form utility is created when a product (or service) is provided to a buyer in a form that is both useful and useable. Wood is converted to furniture. Cotton is processed into clothing. Oil is refined into gasoline. When raw materials are processed into a useable form through the design and product planning efforts of the marketing function, form utility (satisfaction) is created. **Time utility** refers to the satisfaction gained from having a product available at the time at which it is desired. Marketing decisions related to product storage and inventory as well as to production scheduling combine to create time utility. A grocery store that stays open 24 hours a day is providing its customers with time utility because the store's products are available to buyers at any time they might be desired.

Place utility is the satisfaction customers receive when a product is located where they want it. The convenient location of products in retail outlets creates place utility for consumers. The ultimate example of place utility in modern exchanges is the use of toll-free 800 phone numbers by firms, such as L. L. Bean, Eddie Bauer, and other catalog merchants or by computer services, such as Prodigy. With direct telephone and computer access, products and services can be purchased from the convenience of the customer's home or office.

ILLUSTRATION 1-1
Marketing in a society helps create utilities that contribute to consumer satisfaction

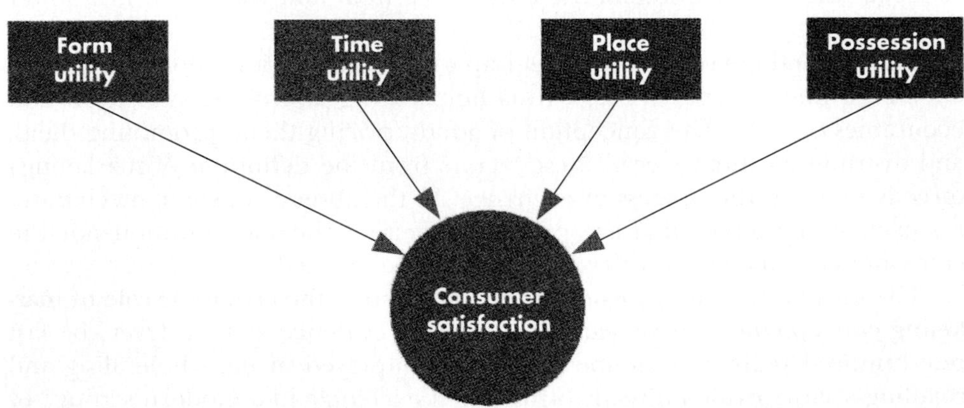

ILLUSTRATION 1-2
Catalog merchants like L.L. Bean increase consumer satisfaction by providing place utility: Purchasing conveniently from home or office.

Finally, **possession utility** relates to that broad economic purpose for marketing where consumers can acquire the satisfaction of product as quickly as possible. That is, the marketing system works in such a way that consumers can "possess" a product and begin to benefit with few hassles. Providing credit and financing, delivery, installation, and other associated services to consumers that allow for immediate possession are the best examples of activities that create possession utility.

These economic concepts of utility are essential to the process of providing for the needs and wants of a nation's citizens. As marketing strategies are designed to bring about these utilities for consumer satisfaction, then marketing directly contributes to the process as well. A compelling example of how important marketing activities are to creating satisfaction through these utilities was reflected by the state of the economy in the former Soviet Union in the early 1990s. The fundamental processes of marketing existed in this economy in the most limited ways and citizens were facing starvation due to severe shortages of meat, milk, potatoes, bread, and other basic goods. The crucial state distribution channels had collapsed into chaos. Shops were empty and shelves were not being replenished. Simply, an essential part of the marketing system had failed and utilities were not being created.

THE SOCIAL ROLE OF MARKETING IN SOCIETY

In discussing the **social role of marketing** in a society, we are really looking at marketing in its most favorable light and considering only those aspects of marketing that can have a beneficial effect on society. In general, the social role of marketing can be stated quite simply: to ensure the success and availability of products and services that are satisfying to members of a society. The negative effects and abuses in marketing (of which there are several) will be discussed in Chapter 19 in the context of social issues.

The social role served by marketing has several dimensions. First, marketing activities can promote *innovation.* Innovation is an activity that not only provides new and better products to satisfy customers and earn revenues for firms but also benefits society as a whole. New pharmaceuticals and labor-saving devices are examples. While products like these certainly result from the efforts of medical and engineering science, their success and survival in the marketplace is a result of proper marketing. A second dimension of the social role of marketing is to produce a *greater variety and choice of products and services.* As more products and services are made available, then individuals are more likely to find items suited to their unique needs and desires.

Third, the marketing process performs the function of *information provision.* Consumers are informed of products and services available through the promotional activities of marketing. The effect is reduced search time associated with acquiring goods, which in turn reduces the cost of exchange. Reducing the cost of exchange subsequently increases the satisfaction associated with the exchange.

Finally, some firms are accepting an *environmental* role in the production and distribution of goods and services. Some manufacturers and marketers have become sensitized to air, water, and solid-waste pollution problems facing the world. As such, firms can address these problems in all phases of their marketing activities.

THE SOCIAL PURPOSE OF MARKETING IN SOCIETY

The **social purpose of marketing** in a society can be stated directly as the responsibility to *deliver a standard of living to society.* Marketing encompasses those activities that deliver to society the discoveries of scientists and the inventions of entrepreneurs. No other social or business activity fulfills the need for design, pricing, information provision (promotion), and physical delivery (distribution) of the output of society. As such, marketing performs an important social purpose. The discovery of new drugs and electronic marvels would lie useless in laboratories without some mechanism to deliver them to society.

Certainly not every product and service conceived in the economic system and delivered to society through the marketing process has made a significant impact on the history of humanity. Admittedly, much of what comes through the system is frivolous and trivial. That does not change the fact that the *function of marketing* itself is essential in order for a society to take advantage of that which is significant and important. The process must be in place for discoveries to survive and to enhance the well-being of citizens.

Marketing, considered in this broad fashion, is both an economic and social phenomenon and force. As stated at the outset, some process must evolve in an economic setting for a society to deal with the efficient and effective creation and disposition of goods and services. The activities that have evolved to serve these economic and social needs have come to be know as marketing.

So far, we have defined marketing and described the role and purpose of marketing in organizations and in the economy and society (this is summarized in Table 1-1). The satisfaction provided to customers by marketing activities has been a recurring theme throughout the chapter. At this point, we will turn our attention to a philosophy of marketing that has emerged from an emphasis on satisfaction as a guiding principle: the marketing concept.

THE MARKETING CONCEPT

The **marketing concept** is a business philosophy that states that the fundamental purpose of a business is to serve the wants and needs of customers. Perhaps the most direct and forceful expression of this business philosophy comes once again from Peter Drucker, who said, " [marketing] is first, a central dimension of the entire business. It is the whole business seen from the point of view of its final result, that is, from the customer's point of view."[5]

Despite the intuitive appeal of the marketing concept and the thinking of scholars such as Drucker, it is a philosophy that took literally centuries to evolve. Many treatments of the evolution of marketing describe four twentieth-century orientations for marketing practice: the production orientation, the product orientation, the sales orientation, and finally, the marketing orientation, which includes the marketing concept.

TABLE 1-1
The Role and Purpose of Marketing in Business and Society

Marketing in Business	Marketing in Society
Role: Marketing mix decisions • Product • Price • Promotion • Distribution	Economic role: Exchange • Specialization • Economies of scale Social role: Ensure success and availability of products • Innovation • Greater variety and choice • Information provision • Environmentalism
Purpose: Revenue generation	Economic purpose: Satisfaction • Form utility • Time utility • Place utility • Possession utility Social purpose: Deliver a standard of living

Anecdotal evidence suggests that firms throughout this century have emphasized production and aggressive sales over customer satisfaction; little fundamental evidence supports this however. A more insightful and well-researched portrayal of the evolution of marketing, and ultimately the marketing concept, is provided by modern-day marketing historians. This well-documented view of the **evolution of marketing** suggests the following chronology:

1. *The Era of Antecedents* A long gestation period for marketing that began in Britain in the 1500s and in Germany and North America during the 1600s. Production and transportation were primitive and 75 to 90 percent of the population were self-sufficient. The beginnings of capitalism were evident and facilitating mechanisms—banks, stock exchanges, paper money—began to emerge. The first versions of distributive institutions also emerged in the form of fixed retail shops, advertising, warehouses, and traveling salespeople.
2. *The Era of Origins* Starting in Britain in 1750 and in the United States and Germany around 1830, this era included the onset of the Industrial Revolution. Vast improvements in production and transportation coupled with urbanization of the population produced the origins of mass markets. Promotion of all types was evident, and products were being designed to appeal to potential buyers. Competition also intensified greatly.
3. *The Era of Institutional Development* Dating from 1850 in Britain and 1870 in the United States and Germany, most of the major institutions and many of the modern marketing practices first appeared during this era. Advertising, marketing research, better physical distribution, and expanded retailing were all being used to stimulate demand for mass production.
4. *The Era of Refinement and Formalization* This era dates from the 1930s to the present. Marketing practice has continued to develop with the most important refinements taking place in retailing, physical distribution, and market analysis. It is during this period that marketing activities have become formally recognized in organizations and marketing concepts formally articulated.[6]

But the marketing concept is more than just part of the next iteration of the evolution of marketing. It also represents a way of doing business on a daily basis. At American Express, resources are marshalled to understand the preferences of its card members and potential card members. The firm runs surveys annually to test and refine new marketing ideas. They know which features—automatic car-rental insurance, 24-hour phone lines for service, free product warranties—make a difference to customers. It breaks the card-carrying market into groups based on income and lifestyle and then pitches services to each—limousine pickup at airports for its "platinum" card members, extra travel insurance for security-conscious senior citizens, and magazine discount rates for students.[7] Every aspect of the firm's operations is scrutinized to ensure that customer needs are being satisfied.

Firms need to be somewhat visionary in their implementation of the marketing concept to satisfy customers in a timely fashion because consumers are really only good at expressing their current rather than future needs.[8] If a firm successfully uses the marketing concept as a way of doing business, it has the base for building a long-term market and generating fierce loyalty among its customers. Coca-Cola learned of the fierce loyalty of *Coke* drinkers when it tried to replace the original formula *Coke* with *New Coke.* The upheaval caused by long-time *Coke* drinkers forced Coca-Cola to reintroduce the traditional formula as *Coke Classic* at considerable expense and some embarrassment. Is it worth it to generate loyalty among customers? According to studies by the Boston consulting firm Forum Corporation, keeping a current customer typically costs about one-fifth as much as acquiring a new one.[9]

Given all the potential benefits of successfully implementing the marketing concept in a firm, is the marketing concept prevalent among organizations as a business philosophy? Honestly, the answer has to be *no* because it is difficult to introduce the marketing concept throughout an organization. If a firm truly wants to commit to the marketing concept and the orientation of complete customer satisfaction, then the following steps must be taken:

1. **Top management must define the purpose of the entire organization as customer satisfaction.** It does no good to delegate customer satisfaction only to the marketing department. Every department in an organization ultimately has contact with the customer one way or another. If the accounting department does not respond quickly to customer billing inquiries or if the personnel department treats potential employees rudely, then the marketing concept is not being implemented.
2. **Customer satisfaction needs to be defined in specific and precise terms.** The definition of customer satisfaction needs to be explicitly stated in precise terms that can guide the actions of all parts of the organization. The marketing department can identify and define a customer satisfaction opportunity, but top management must specify its implementation in the context of the firm's overall strategy.
3. **Upper-level management must ensure a commitment to the marketing concept.** Such an assurance can be accomplished through formal discussion (such as corporate meetings), in the reward system, and through a visible pattern of management decisions. At American Express, "heroic moments" in customer service—like the employee who hand-delivered a replacement card to a stranded customer at Logan airport in the middle of the night—are immortalized in a series of *Great Performers* booklets distributed to all 45,000 travel-service employees worldwide.[10]

The value of successfully focusing on customer satisfaction through the marketing concept is manifest in superior competitive prowess and long-term market success. Firms that are sincerely focused on customer satisfaction work hard to completely understand their customers' needs and design products and procedures to satisfy those needs as completely as possible. But a philosophy of business that encompasses the marketing concept and its guiding principle of customer satisfaction seems difficult and unattainable. Let's turn our attention now to the realities of providing satisfaction in the marketplace by discussing how firms actually implement the marketing concept and try to satisfy their customers' desires.

Customer Satisfaction: Bringing the Marketing Concept to Life

The concept of satisfaction has been identified as integral to marketing in business and society. Providing customer satisfaction, however, involves more than simply philosophizing. Many firms have successfully implemented the marketing concept by focusing the efforts of the entire firm on customer satisfaction:

- Broderbund is a small software-design company whose products dominate the list of leading software programs designed to increase productivity and provide entertainment to home computer users. You probably know this firm for its popular *Where in the World is Carmen Sandiego?* program. The firm's success is captured in a simple statement, "Identify a need and turn it into a product."[11]
- General Electric pursues customer satisfaction through what it calls the QMI system—Quick Market Intelligence. The QMI system is designed to break down the boundaries between GE and its customers and "allows the entire company to understand, to sense, to touch the changing desires of the customer, and to act on them in almost real time." [12]
- Matsushita Electric, the Japanese electronics maker, pursues the marketing concept by defining customer satisfaction in terms of quality products at the lowest possible price. This firm's version of the marketing concept is expressed by its president: "The purpose of an enterprise is to contribute to society by supplying goods of high quality at low prices in ample quantity. Profit comes in contribution to society."[13]
- The Four Seasons hotel chain has installed a computer system that stores information about each guest's unique needs. For example, does the guest require a nonallergenic pillow or request a special rare tea?[14]

Numerous firms in the United States and globally are committed to the *concept* of customer satisfaction. But how does a firm go about operationalizing a concept that is intangible and philosophical? The way this concept can be actualized is by realizing that *a firm must provide more satisfaction to customers than the costs it asks those customers to incur to acquire the product or service.*[15] Very simply, a firm has to realize that consumers will choose the alternative in the market that seems to hold the most potential for satisfying the consumer's need. And, consumers have to believe that the satisfaction in that alternative *is greater than* the costs they perceive to be incurred in acquiring that alternative. Such an orientation by consumers can be stated as a simple inequality:

The satisfaction customers perceive in a product >
The costs customers perceive to acquire the product
(> means "is greater than")

If a firm is unable to maintain this inequality with respect to the products and services it markets, then it gives consumers no reason to continue to purchase its products rather than those of a competitor.

To create such a result, however, the firm must understand the dimensions of satisfaction and cost *from the customer's point of view.* Is it possible to define satisfaction and cost in such a way that a single definition makes sense for firms as diverse as Broderbund, GE, Matsushita Electric, and Four Seasons? The answer, believe it or not, is *yes,* because consumers pursue fundamental dimensions of satisfaction and perceive fundamental costs associated with acquisition regardless of the product or service.

THE DIMENSIONS OF CUSTOMER SATISFACTION AND COST

In order for firms like Broderbund, GE, Matsushita, and Four Seasons to successfully deliver on the promise of providing satisfaction to customers in a way that exceeds the customers' perceptions of cost, there must be dimensions of customer satisfaction and cost around which daily business operations can be built. The following are the dimensions of satisfaction and cost that allow for operationalizing the marketing concept expressed as the inequality Customer Satisfaction > Costs of Acquisition:

Customer Satisfaction	**>**	**Costs of Acquisition**
Functional satisfaction		Monetary costs
Emotional satisfaction		Time costs
Benefits of use satisfaction		Risk costs
		Opportunity costs
		Anxiety costs

Customer Satisfaction

It is crucial for a firm to recognize some universal bases for consumer's assessment of satisfaction. The dimensions listed under customer satisfaction represent the different kinds of satisfaction customers might expect from a product or service. **Functional satisfaction** relates to those tangible attributes of a product or service that can be measured in some standardized fashion. Examples of tangible attributes include the fuel economy of an automobile, the watts-per-channel output of a stereo receiver or the on-time performance of an airline company. Price, warranty, and performance features are other prominent functional features on which product satisfaction can be judged. Many household consumers and most industrial buyers emphasize these criteria in their evaluation of products.

A totally different type of customer satisfaction is emotional. **Emotional satisfaction** is linked to status, prestige, security, or any other benefit that is intangible and not measurable in a standardized way. Literally thousands of products are valued for their symbolism and, therefore, emotional satisfaction. Consider the value of the BMW nameplate or a Rolex watch. If mere transportation or time-keeping accuracy (i.e., functional satisfactions) were the only buying motives in the marketplace, then the $46,500 BMW *540i* or the $21,000 gold Rolex watch would not exist. But such products do exist because emotions play a significant role for some consumers with regard to satisfaction sought in some product categories.

But, functional and emotional factors alone do not explain all the possibilities for seeking satisfaction. **Benefits of use satisfaction** relates to the value gained from owning and using a product or service. Benefits of use satisfaction

Consumers often seek satisfaction based on the functional features of a product. This Cadillac advertisement highlights functional features.

is perhaps most prevalent as a motive in the purchase of computer equipment, especially microcomputers. The average microcomputer buyer couldn't care less about the functional features of a microcomputer—the microprocessor, bits, bytes, ram, rom, or the bus system of a particular micro. Nor does the typical buyer presume that the purchase of a micro will suddenly elevate her or him in social status and prestige (or any other emotional basis for buying). However, the benefit of information and data handling or the ability to have a computer at home and interface with computers at work are all benefits of ownership and use that form a substantial basis for satisfaction.* It is just such a benefit-of-use approach that has distinguished the appeals made to consumers by Dell Computer versus Compaq. Dell has always concentrated on the benefits to consumers of direct distribution and after-sale service as a way to deliver satisfaction to consumers. Compaq, on the other hand, has concentrated on building leading-edge technology into its computers and focuses on the functional characteristics of the machines.[16]

*In the majority of instances, benefits-of-use satisfactions are a by-product of and are derived directly from the functional features of a product. However, since consumers typically do not deduce the benefits-of-use values directly from individual functional features, the benefits-of-use satisfaction forms a separate category.

A firm must recognize the difference among different forms of satisfaction potentially being sought by consumers. If the firm misjudges the basis upon which its product or service is being evaluated, it may choose the wrong basis upon which to develop and execute the elements of the marketing mix. Consider the Four Seasons hotel chain and its attempt to attract customers. What if Four Seasons erroneously concludes that customers want larger rooms with couches and tables (functional features) when, in fact, what customers prefer in their accommodations is pleasant ambience and spectacularly decorated lobbies (emotional criteria for satisfaction). Operating under the wrong premise, Four Seasons would tout its large rooms and customers would ignore the chain because it apparently does not provide the features (decor) that are desired. Proper understanding of the range and possibilities of satisfaction provides the firm with the basis to assess the customer. In response, it can design its market offering to appeal to customer desires, which is the essence of the marketing concept and customer satisfaction.

Costs

In the *customer satisfaction* > *cost* inequality, remember that costs in this context have nothing to do with the costs incurred by the organization (such as production or delivery costs). Rather, costs here refer to **costs of acquisition** facing the *consumer*. In any exchange, the buyer faces a variety of potential costs. Recognition of the full range of acquisition costs from the customer's perspective is essential for the firm.

Monetary costs are the most obvious costs associated with acquisition. These are the dollar and cents, (or pounds and pence or francs and centimes) the customer is asked to pay for the product or service. Monetary costs are not the only costs considered by customers. Think about the last time you shopped at a 7-11 or Circle K convenience store. All of us know that every product in a convenience store is available just down the street at a grocery store for as much as 40 percent less. Then why is it that millions of consumers a day shop at convenience stores? *Time and convenience costs* are important costs to consumers. These are also precisely the types of costs that can often be avoided at the 7-11 or Circle K convenience store. Consumers are willing to pay more in monetary costs for the benefit of parking close to the door, quickly finding the items they want, and usually not having to stand in line to check out. All of these benefits to shopping at convenience stores reduce a type of *cost of acquisition*: time and convenience. Other time and convenience factors considered by consumers include store hours, store location, parking ease, speed of delivery, use of credit cards rather than cash or financing. Think about a situation in which one airline is notorious for putting callers on hold for long periods when they phone in to book a flight. That cost of acquisition (the inconvenience of being put on hold) might be enough of a deterrent for customers to avoid dealing with the airline. Similarly, the retail outlet with "Low, Low Discount Prices!" that is located twenty-five miles from the nearest metropolitan area might be perceived as "too costly" to shop at by consumers.

It may seem odd to specify *risk* as an acquisition cost, but it can be the driving force in many consumer and business decisions. Consumers perceive various types of risk in purchasing goods and services—financial risk (overpaying for an item), social risk (being criticized by peers for a purchase), psychological risk (an item is inconsistent with self-image), performance risk (the product fails to achieve the desired results), or physical risk (the threat of bodily harm). As an example of financial and performance risk, think about your own decision to buy a microcomputer. What if you saw an ad that read, "We're ABC Computer Company. We're new on the market, but our machines cost 10 percent less than IBM's computers." Would you take the risk of saving $200.00 or $300.00 on a $3000.00 purchase? Many consumers will forgo the monetary cost savings to reduce the risk costs of acquisition—by dealing with a reputable supplier, manufacturer, or retailer or by purchasing a well-known and well-established brand name, the perception of risk can be reduced. This was clearly indicated in a recent study of computer buyers who said they would pay up to $295.00 more for well-known computer brands to avoid lesser-known brand names.[17] Consumers will use a variety of techniques to reduce risk, such as gathering more information about products, buying the most popular or most well-known brand, or buying the smallest quantity available.

Opportunity costs of acquisition simply refers to the fact that if a consumer chooses the product or service of one company, then he or she has foregone the opportunity to buy and own the product or service of another. This cost of acquisition highlights the competitive nature of trying to provide satisfaction to customers. Organizations must recognize that consumers have a variety of choices in every product and service category. If the firm is fortunate enough to attract a customer, then that customer has given up the opportunity to be served by a competing firm. There is a broader context with regard to this cost as well. One of the opportunity costs a customer incurs in making a purchase is forgoing the chance to spend that money in a totally different way. For example, a new car could just have easily been an expenditure for a trip to Europe, or a new stereo the opportunity cost of purchasing stocks and bonds. The firm must appreciate just how diverse consumer opportunity costs are in order to be sensitive to this cost of acquisition. This concept of *indirect competition* will be discussed more fully in Chapter 2.

Finally, to varying degrees, consumers experience *anxiety costs* in acquisition. Anxiety in the decision-making process is referred to as *cognitive dissonance.* This particular factor may strike you as quite odd. Isn't anxiety some sort of psychological or personality problem? Actually, it is a very normal human reaction to making a decision in a variety of life circumstances including product decision making. While anxiety can occur both before and after a purchase decision, it is the anxiety after the decision that is most directly related to acquisition costs. The issue of anxiety in consumption decision making will be discussed more fully in Chapter 6, but for now you should recognize that anxiety associated with acquisition represents a cost to consumers just as much as the other factors. If a consumer buys a product or uses a service and feels a large amount of anxiety, this not only represents a cost to the consumer but it detracts from the satisfaction the consumer experiences (i.e., affects the *satisfaction* > *cost* inequality). If the anxiety is strong enough, that consumer may feel the cost (anxiety) is too great to repeat the purchase again in the future. For example, consider a situation in which you bought a stereo for $1200 on your already tight student budget. After the purchase, you struggle with the guilt of spending that much money on stereo equipment as opposed to saving it for future school needs. You might forever associate the discomfort of that decision with the manufacturer or retailer of the equipment. As such, the firms involved in providing the product may lose you as a customer forever.

Creating Value Through Customer Satisfaction

The reason the specific factors in this *satisfaction* > *cost* inequality are so critical to the marketing concept is because when consumers perceive satisfaction to be greater than costs of acquisition, then consumers believe that a firm is offering superior value. **Value** in the minds of consumers is, in reality, that perception of greater satisfaction than cost. This value perception is argued to be the reason behind the renewed success of the Chevrolet *Cavalier*. By adding valued features like ABS brakes and cutting the price by 6 percent, the *Cavalier* actually outsold Ford's highly successful *Taurus* for several months.[18] And, this example shows that firms need to realize that they can increase value for consumers by either increasing the satisfaction a product offers or by reducing the costs of acquisition. Firms of all sorts, from Mercedes-Benz to McDonalds, are changing product design and pricing strategy to appeal to consumers on a value basis.[19] This relationship is depicted in Illustration 1-3. So, firms as diverse as Broderbund, Versatec, Matsushita Electric, and Four Seasons can all consider either increasing the satisfaction of their product/service or reducing costs incurred by their customers to provide satisfaction and truly operationalize the marketing concept.

Structure for Marketing Activities

In modern industry, a basic structure exists within which marketing activities take place. In this section, we will take a quick look at the structure and participants in the marketing process. Figure 1-3 portrays this **structure of marketing activities** beginning with the primary producers and service providers and progressing through a variety of participants until the ultimate consumer is served.

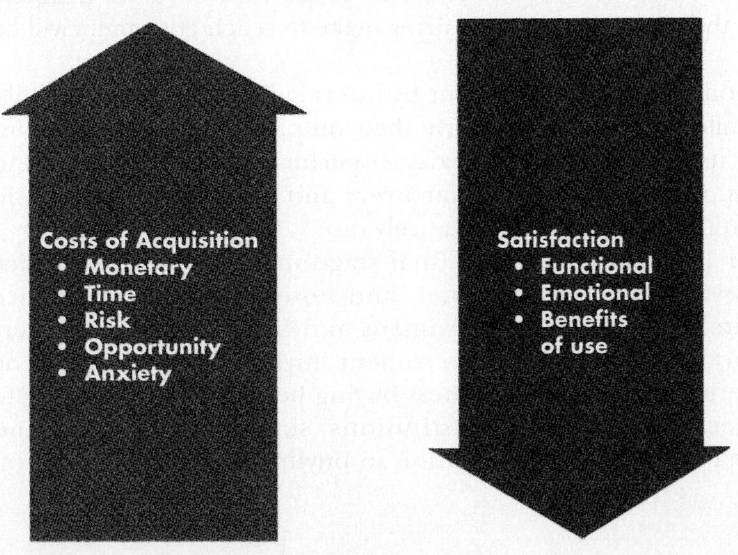

ILLUSTRATION 1-3
Inverse Effects of Changes in "Costs" on Satisfaction

FIGURE 1-3
Structure for Marketing Activities

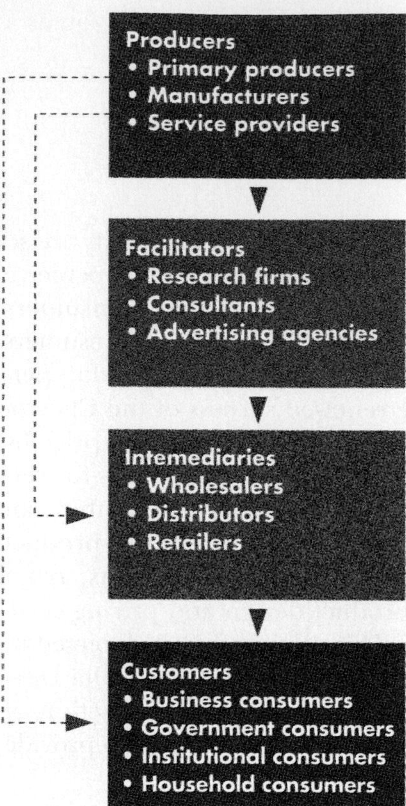

The structure shown in Figure 1-3 simply portrays the flow of activities and participants from the manufacturing level through the consumption level. Firms that manufacture products or provide services may or may not enlist the services of facilitators (research firms, consultants, and advertising agencies) that deal directly with intermediaries. Similarly, some firms will choose to deal directly with customers and skip the intermediary level as well. Figure 1-3 shows these alternative routes on the left side of the figure. As we progress through the text, the alternative choices firms make to reach customers will be discussed fully.

The distribution process is carried out by intermediaries: wholesalers, distributors, and retailers. Firms need to have their output distributed and delivered to the final user. Intermediaries exist to perform the distribution and delivery activities. On occasion, manufacturers and primary producers do their own distribution although this is relatively rare.

The customer level represents the final stage in the structure. Notice that business, government, institutional, and household consumers are identified separately. The reason government and institutional consumers are listed as separate groups is that government buying procedures may be substantially different from typical business buying behavior so that separate recognition is necessary. Similarly, institutions, such as universities and many hospitals, have a different orientation to buying because of their not-for-profit status.

Studying the Global Perspective

One of the important and distinguishing features of this book is that it highlights and explores the principal issues in marketing from a global perspective. After considering the universal principles of marketing related to a particular aspect of marketing (as we have just done with marketing in business and society), each chapter of the book will conclude with a five-to-eight-page section of Global Perspectives related to the chapter topic. As you can see, the section that follows here is "Marketing in Business and Society: A Global Perspective." These Global Perspective sections highlight the unique considerations of marketing in the global context for every topic in marketing. Much of what constitutes the principles of marketing are applicable in the global perspective. However, adaptations and reinterpretations of principles will be raised in these final sections. You will learn that adopting a global perspective with regard to the principles of marketing is essential for successfully analyzing worldwide marketing issues.

Each time the text material turns to the "Global Perspective," the globe icon (shown in the following section) will appear in the margin and the edges of the pages will be marked with colorful sidebars. This indicates that global perspectives are being considered. The material in these sections places basic principles in a global context to provide a truly contemporary treatment of the principles of marketing.

Marketing in Business and Society: A Global Perspective

As the title of this text states, the principles and practice of marketing must be considered from the global perspective. Markets for many goods and services are global, rather than local, regional, or national in scope. Within the past three decades, information and technological accessibility have made the world a single, global competitive environment. Financial institutions, multinational corporations, and a variety of market intermediaries are wired to worldwide communications networks that operate 24 hours a day. As traditional military and political alliances between nations become relatively less important and new alliances are forged, new market opportunities are created and new competitive challenges appear on the horizon.

This globalization of markets and competition must be understood, however, on two distinct levels. On the one hand, globalization provides individual firms with new market opportunities. This is the business level of activity within which firms establish marketing objectives and marketing mix strategies to pursue revenue generation in international markets. On the other hand are the broad societal roles and purposes discussed earlier in this chapter, which represent the broad social and economic effects of the marketing process. These global factors need to be considered for their effect on the process of marketing.

In the pages that follow, we will consider both of these business and social/economic aspects of marketing from a global perspective. In general, marketing principles and concepts are widely applicable. However, the envi-

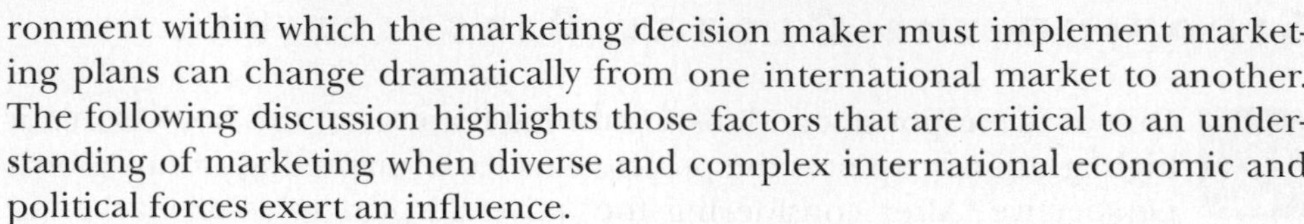
ronment within which the marketing decision maker must implement marketing plans can change dramatically from one international market to another. The following discussion highlights those factors that are critical to an understanding of marketing when diverse and complex international economic and political forces exert an influence.

MARKETING IN SOCIETY: A GLOBAL PERSPECTIVE

The economic and social roles and purposes of marketing that were discussed earlier in this chapter apply to the global market situation as well. These roles and purposes are fundamental to the *process* of marketing and do not change from market to market. What does change is the *context* within which these roles and purposes manifest themselves. Adopting a global perspective of societal marketing issues requires an understanding of two key international economic factors related to marketing. These factors are *comparative advantage* and *type of economic system.*

Comparative Advantage

Comparative advantage as an aspect of global business was most clearly articulated by David Ricardo in 1817.[20] He posited that all nations would benefit from trade, which would allow individual countries to specialize in producing goods that they are best suited to produce (because of talents, raw materials, or unique conditions in the nation). These nations would then trade with each other. By doing so, each trading nation would gain or increase satisfaction through the exchange. Comparative advantage focuses on the *tradeoffs* that countries make in global trading arrangements. Countries will forego the opportunity to produce some things for which they have little or no comparative advantage in order to produce and trade those things for which the country does have a comparative advantage. This concept is important in terms of understanding, explaining, and predicting trading patterns between nations. The United States, for example, has a comparative advantage worldwide in its talent and technology for producing aircraft and a natural resource advantage in producing certain chemicals. As such, the United States is a net exporter of these items worldwide.

The concept of comparative advantage affects the broad economic role of marketing in society related to exchange. When a country has a comparative advantage worldwide in producing a certain item, then the processes of marketing are able to function to facilitate exchange with other countries. The country with comparative advantage has an item of value to offer the world, and the marketing process will function to bring about the effective exchange for that item. A more recent theoretical departure from comparative advantage as a framework for explaining world trading patterns is the notion of **competitive advantage,** which argues that globalization and technological change have made traditional ways of gauging comparative advantage, such as the costs of labor and raw materials, less important. When assessing a particular country's competitive advantage, what matters are the abilities to innovate and to develop clusters of competitive companies in particular industries. Throughout the global sections of the text, examples of both analytical frameworks will be given to illustrate strategic choices made by countries and by companies.

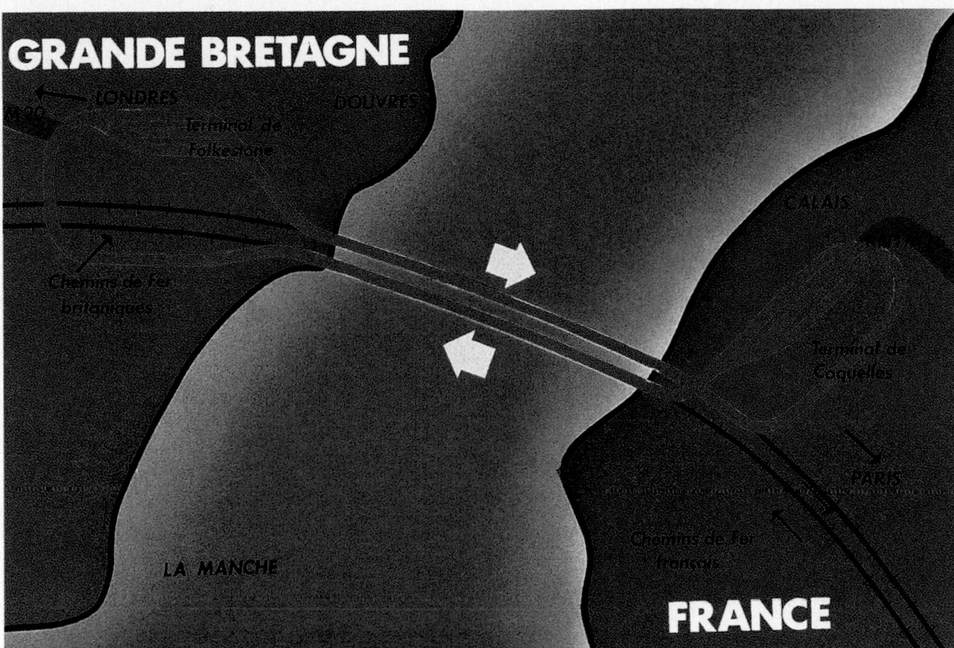

The "Chunnel" connecting France with England is an example of modern technology facilitating exchange between countries.

Types of Economic Systems

All societies ultimately adopt an economic system through which the needs of its members are served. An **economic system** is a set of mechanisms though which scarce resources are allocated to produce goods and services and then to distribute those goods and services to members of a society. Nations adopt and operate economic systems based on the objectives of their political leaders. In general, economic systems worldwide can be classified as either planned economies or market-driven economies.

Planned economies are systems that are rigidly controlled by the government. Government leaders and organizations decide what will be produced, when it will be produced, the quantity that is produced, and where the goods are distributed. Government planners estimate the needs for goods and services and mandate their production, price, and distribution with respect to what is good for society as a whole rather than what might be satisfying to individuals within the society. The result is that the variety of goods and services in planned economies tends to be quite limited. Historically, planned economies have also tended to limit the supply of available goods. Much of what we know as marketing does not exist or exists in a limited form in planned economies. Product innovation, market research, branding, personal selling, and advertising are not prevalent or integral in planned economies. The former Soviet Union and China were the most visible examples of planned economic systems throughout most of the twentieth century. Government leaders in both of these economies have begun to adopt mechanisms typifying market-driven systems.

Market-driven economies are systems that operate on the premise that market forces will result in the most efficient allocation of scarce resources. Prices for goods and services are determined by the classic relationship between supply and demand. As more of an item is demanded by consumers in a society, that item can command a higher price. The goods and services produced in market-driven economies are determined by producers' estimates of demand for particular goods and services. If a producer believes an item will attract consumers and can be sold at a profit, it gets produced. Market-driven systems tend to provide citizens with a greater variety of choices and better quality products than planned economies due to the effects of competition. Because competitors in market-driven economies are searching for advantage, the utilities that create customer satisfaction are more readily identified than in planned economic systems. Providing utility can create a strong competitive advantage.

All market-driven economies have an element of government intervention, which typically involves the provision of roads, schools, waste disposal, and water management; most governments exert significant control over these services. Additionally, governments will establish regulations related to business practices designed to promote fair competition and safe products. Market-driven economies exhibit the full complement of marketing activities with branding, advertising, and extensive distribution systems being the most prevalent. Certainly, some of the most visible and dramatic examples of business activities related to becoming an efficient market-driven economy are taking place in the former Soviet Union and much of eastern Europe. The "marketization" efforts under way in these economies to move from decades of planned economic systems to market-driven systems will be tremendously challenging and will profoundly influence the political, economic, and social lives of the citizens.

The economic and social roles and purposes of marketing are affected depending on the economic system operating in a country. Exchange of value within the economy, the potential for utilities to be created, innovation, product variety, and information provision, and delivering a standard of living are all more possible in the context of market-driven economies than in planned economies. Some of these roles and purposes of marketing are irrepressible and will be in evidence in even the most rigidly controlled economies. However, the full potential of the marketing process is realized only when market mechanism are allowed to function freely as they are in the market-driven economic systems.

MARKETING IN BUSINESS ORGANIZATIONS: A GLOBAL PERSPECTIVE

The role and purpose of marketing within a business organization remain the same when a global perspective is adopted. As firms venture beyond their home borders, the marketing role of making marketing-mix decisions still needs to be undertaken. Firms will develop strategies and tactics to execute the marketing mix in international markets. Further, the basic marketing purpose in the global context is to generate revenues for an organization. While the principles are not new or different, the differences among nations and markets can be great, and the global marketer needs to understand how foreign countries and how people in different markets will likely respond to marketing strategies and tactics.

The process of generating revenues may be more complex in the global business context. More often, tradeoffs need to be made by internationally oriented companies in order to account for the uniqueness and complexities of decision making in different international markets. For example, in order to gain efficiencies from economies of scale, companies doing business in the United States typically choose to standardize production and marketing as much as possible. In doing so in international markets, however, such standardization could compromise the effectiveness of the marketing-mix variables designed to generate revenue. This is true because differences among consumers in international markets do not allow the marketing of a standardized product in each of those markets. For example, the fragrance of *Oil of Olay* is reformulated for most of the fifteen countries within which it is distributed based on women's preferences in those markets. Other corporate-level considerations such as spreading investment risks, managing foreign currency exchange risks, or concentrating on a particular market region at the expense of others in order to gain market penetration will also influence micromarketing tactics of the firm pursuing global opportunities. Generally speaking, standardization of marketing practices is more likely to take place for global business products and services, while adjustments in the marketing mix occur more frequently for consumer products and services.

Competition and Interdependence

Within the highly dynamic world order, two dominant market forces continue to set the basic agenda for world business: **competition and interdependence.** These sometimes conflicting but always interrelated forces provide an underlying framework for micromarketing. As companies try to develop and sustain competitive advantage in the global marketplace, they constantly do so within a framework of competition, negotiations, and to some extent, cooperation with and dependence upon their trading partners. The successful completion in late 1993 of the Uruguay round of the General Agreement on Tariffs and Trade (GATT) talks to reform and enlarge world trade provides a striking example of the notions of competition and interdependence in global trade. At the broad social/economic level, agreements relating to such rules of trade as *voluntary export restraints* and *dumping* (selling products abroad at prices well below the domestic market price) will have a significant effect on a number of countries' balance-of-trade figures. At the level of the individual business organization, new rules relating to the deregulation of selling services globally and more strict rules protecting intellectual property rights (such as patents, copyrights, and trademarks) will provide new market opportunities and increase the likelihood of profits for thousands of individual firms who operate globally or wish to operate globally. In the clear majority of cases, gains that companies achieve are the result of executing superior marketing strategies in highly competitive environments. The point is, however, that international trade and the marketing strategies associated with cultivating that trade often take place in an environment where a number of interrelated issues are at stake—not all of which have to do with head-to-head competition between companies.

Finally, a discussion on competition and interdependence in the global economy of the 1990s must necessarily consider the evolution of the new world order. On the one hand, the triad blocks of Asia, North America, and Europe are consolidating their global positions through strategic trade alliances. 1993 witnessed the passage of the Uruguay round of GATT, the

North American Free Trade Agreement (NAFTA), and the first birthday of the European Union. On the other hand, the end of the cold war and the increasing transnational nature of the global economy is fostering a borderless future in which the traditional sovereign powers of nations are fading as the century draws to a close. Regional trading blocks, such as *Mexamerica, Greater South China,* and *Eastcentraleurope* will all flourish and function beyond the confines of national borders. This **economic regionalism** will alter the regulatory powers of nation states and ultimately change the nature of competition.[21]

What makes the challenge of marketing in a global context so interesting is having to direct marketing activities at the individual business level (product, price, promotion, and distribution) in an uncontrollable and complex international environment so that marketing and revenue objectives for a firm are achieved. Even though marketing principles and concepts are widely applicable, the environment can change dramatically from one market or country to another. While the beginning of this chapter argues that marketing is both a business and a societal process, we would add that within the context of international marketing a new dimension of understanding cultural processes is critical to successful management.

Key Terms and Concepts

Marketing
Marketing mix
Four Ps
Role of marketing in organizations
Purpose of marketing
Exchange
Economic role of marketing
Economic purpose of marketing
Utility
Form utility
Time utility
Place utility
Possession utility
Social role of marketing
Social purpose of marketing
Marketing concept
Evolution of marketing
Functional satisfaction
Emotional satisfaction
Benefits of use satisfaction
Costs of acquisition
Value
Structure for marketing activities
Comparative advantage
Competitive advantage
Economic system
Competition and interdependence
Economic regionalism

Questions and Exercises

1. What is marketing? What is the relationship between marketing and advertising? Between marketing and selling?
2. What are the components of the marketing mix?
3. What is the primary purpose of marketing within an organization? What other part of an organization serves the same purpose as the marketing function?
4. Discuss the economic purpose of marketing using the economic concept of "utility." Describe an experience you have had where the marketing system provided you with "time utility."
5. What social role can the marketing process play with regard to the natural environment?
6. What is the "marketing concept?" Why is it a logical way of doing business?
7. Consumers consider a variety of "costs" when deciding to purchase an item. Describe a circumstance where you didn't buy the lowest price item available because you perceived a "cost" other than monetary in doing so.

8. If a firm wants to increase the satisfaction customers get from using the firm's product or service, there are two basic ways satisfaction can be increased. What are those two ways?
9. Describe the relevance of "comparative advantage" and the nature of "economic systems" to understanding marketing in the global perspective.
10. How are competition and interdependence related to marketing activities on a global basis?

REFERENCES

1. Carol J. Loomis, "Dinosaurs?" *Fortune* (May 3, 1993): 36–42.
2. Definition by the American Marketing Association in *Marketing News* (March 1, 1985): 1.
3. Peter F. Drucker. *People and Performance: The Best of Peter Drucker on Management.* New York: Harper's College Press, 1977, 90.
4. The Procter & Gamble Company 1990 Annual Report, Cincinnati: The Procter & Gamble Co., 1990, 5.
5. Quotes taken from Peter F. Drucker, op. cit., 89 and 91 respectively.
6. This conceptualization of the evolution of marketing is taken from Ronald A. Fullerton, "How Modern Is Modern Marketing? Marketing's Evolution and the Myth of the 'Production Era'," *Journal of Marketing,* 52, no. 1 (January 1988): 108–125. This portrayal of the evolution of marketing is also strongly suggested by the History of Marketing Thought Association.
7. John Paul Newport, Jr., "American Express: Service that Sells," *Fortune* (November 20, 1989): 80–94.
8. Franklin S. Houston, "The Marketing Concept: What It Is and What It Is Not," *Journal of Marketing* 50, no. 2 (April 1986): 81–87.
9. Patricia Sellers, "Getting Customers to Love You," *Fortune* (March 13, 1989): 38.
10. The bases for successful implementation of the marketing concept within an organization were adapted from H. Michael Hayes, "Another Chance for the Marketing Concept?" *Business* (January–March 1988): 10–18.
11. Andrew Kupfer, "Identify a Need, Turn a Profit," *Fortune* (November 30, 1992): 78–79.
12. *General Electric Company, Annual Report.* General Electric Company, Fairfield, CT, 1992, 4.
13. Michael Hayes, *Business,* op. cit., 14.
14. Patricia Sellers, *Fortune,* op. cit., 40.
15. The concept of "satisfaction and cost" as a basic orientation by consumers was first proposed by Weldon Taylor and Roy T. Shaw, Jr. in *Marketing: An Integrated Analytical Approach,* 2d ed. Cincinnati: South-Western Publishing Co., 1969, 30.
16. Kyle Pope, "For Compaq and Dell, Accent Is on Personal in the Computer Wars," *The Wall Street Journal* (July 2, 1993): A1, A8.
17. Kyle Pope, "Computers: They're No Commodity," *The Wall Street Journal* (October 15, 1993): B1.
18. Joseph B. White, "GM, Pitching Value, Scores Cavalier Upset," *The Wall Street Journal* (May 1, 1993): B1, B8.
19. *See* Oscar Suris, "Mercedes-Benz Tries to Compete on Value," *The Wall Street Journal* (October 20, 1993): B1; and Patricia Sellers, "Look Who Learned about Value," *Fortune* (October 18, 1993): 75.
20. David Ricardo, *On the Principles of Political Economy and Taxation,* New York: E. P. Dutton, 1948.
21. Fred C. Bergsten, "The Rationale for a Rosy View," *The Economist* (September 11, 1993): 59–62. *See also* "Across the Rio Grande," *The Economist.* (October 9, 1993): 69–70.

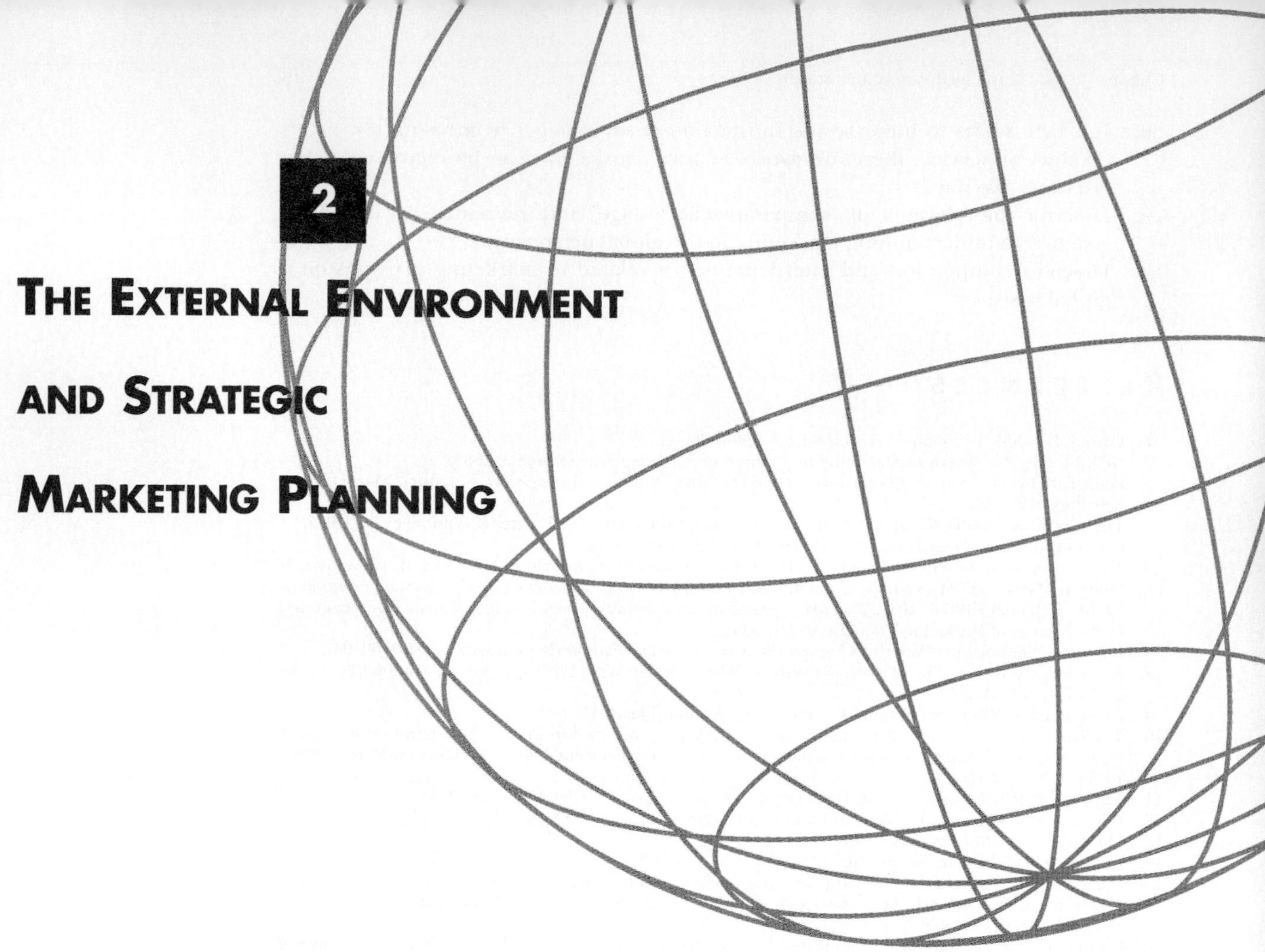

2

The External Environment and Strategic Marketing Planning

AFTER STUDYING THIS CHAPTER, YOU WILL UNDERSTAND THAT:

1. Firms must identify changes in the external, uncontrollable environment and respond quickly with effective marketing strategies.
2. Factors in the external environment—demographic trends, social and cultural trends, economic conditions, political/regulatory environment, technological change, competitors, and the natural environment—present both marketing opportunities and threats to firms.
3. Decisions made with respect to the marketing mix, market segmentation, and a marketing plan are the strategic planning tools firms can use to successfully respond to the external environment.
4. Unconscious references to one's own cultural values, experiences, and knowledge—known as Self Reference Criteria—are obstacles to effective strategic marketing planning with a global perspective.
5. Strategic marketing planning with a global perspective requires an orientation wherein the firm continually seeks out worldwide opportunities for coordination and concentration of marketing strategies.

Sales in Europe are down over 20 percent. Sales in the United States are down almost 10 percent. Overall corporate losses for the year stand at $579 million. How would you like to be the firm that's the proud owner of these numbers? Well, the firm that crafted this performance in the first half of 1993 was none other than Mercedes-Benz! One of the most prestigious corporate names in the entire world. But, those were, indeed, the less than impressive numbers Mercedes-Benz turned in. The reason Mercedes-Benz experienced such poor performance is that the firm ignored strong signals from the external environment—those factors in business, the economy, and society that shape demand—which clearly indicated Mercedes-Benz products would have difficulty competing. By ignoring the signs in the external environment, the firm did not respond with strategic marketing planning that could have combated the decline in revenue and profit.

What were those strong signals in the external environment that Mercedes-Benz appears to have ignored? First, buyers entering the luxury car market in the early 1990s held a different attitude about what constituted luxury. These buyers, members of what is referred to as the baby boom generation, grew up in the late 1960s and early 1970s driving "muscle cars": stiff riding, high horse power land rockets. As baby boomers tastes matured and mellowed into the 1990s, they still were seeking high performance, but comfort and style became important as well. Japanese auto manufacturers Honda (*Acura*), Nissan (*Infiniti*), and Toyota (*Lexus*), all correctly read this change in luxury car buyers' attitudes and took market share from Mercedes-Benz as well as from BMW and Audi.

Second, beyond the luxury car market, the overall market for vehicles in the United States (the largest market in the world), was showing growth in three distinct areas: light trucks, minivans, and four-wheel-drive sport utility vehicles categories, in which Mercedes-Benz has no competitive entries. Third, at the outset of the 1990s, a broad and fundamental shift in attitudes towards wealth and status seeking was taking place. Traditional icons of status, such as Mercedes-Benz, were caught in a backlash that reduced demand for its cars. Finally, the economic environment did not work in favor of Mercedes-Benz. While U.S. families were contemplating saving for retirement and children's college education, the decline in the value of the dollar to the German Mark caused an increase in the price range of Mercedes-Benz cars to $40,000 for the lowest-priced model to over $100,000 for the *SEL* line.

Several changes in the external environment—demographic trends, social trends, and economic conditions—all combined over time to severely compromise Mercedes-Benz' ability to market cars and generate revenue. But the new President and CEO of the company, Helmut Werner, has initiated strategic marketing plans to respond to these external environment changes. Mercedes-Benz will introduced a new C-class of luxury cars in 1994 priced from $29,000 to $34,000, which is actually less than the price of the Japanese luxury models. The firm is developing a minivan likely to be built in its newly announced U.S. plant. Finally, a super small, highly efficient "city car" is in the works targeted for the Japanese market.[1]

In Chapter 1, we learned that the ultimate purpose and role of marketing within an organization is to generate revenue by providing satisfaction in the marketplace. This chapter will consider the challenge of marketing in fulfilling that role: providing satisfaction in the marketplace by making decisions in an environment filled with uncontrollable influences on the organization's performance. Just as Mercedes-Benz has discovered the need to respond to social and economic changes, so too must every organization, large and small alike, identify and respond to a variety of external environment influences affecting its ability to generate revenue and satisfy customers. Every organization from a giant multinational to a small mom and pop grocery must be sensitive to the cues from the environment that signal opportunities for success and threats to existence. This chapter will first consider the forces in the external environment that challenge the very existence of organizations. Then, factors *within* the organization itself will be considered that represent the marketing response to those forces.

The External Environment: Uncontrollable Variables

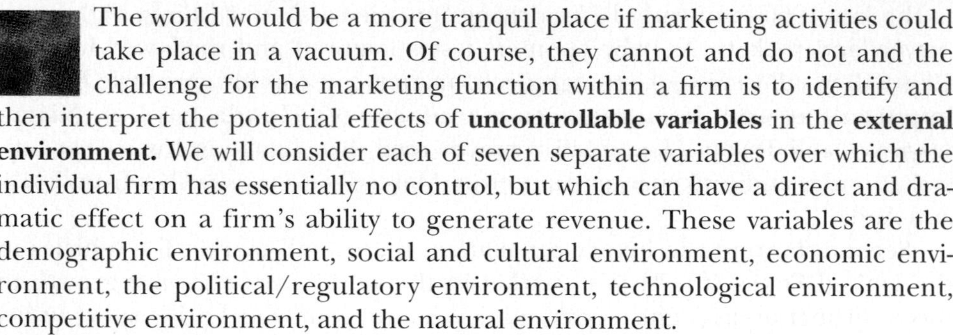

The world would be a more tranquil place if marketing activities could take place in a vacuum. Of course, they cannot and do not and the challenge for the marketing function within a firm is to identify and then interpret the potential effects of **uncontrollable variables** in the **external environment.** We will consider each of seven separate variables over which the individual firm has essentially no control, but which can have a direct and dramatic effect on a firm's ability to generate revenue. These variables are the demographic environment, social and cultural environment, economic environment, the political/regulatory environment, technological environment, competitive environment, and the natural environment.

The Demographic Environment

Demographics are objective population characteristics such as age, gender, marital status, occupation, and size of household. The **demographic environment** is of critical importance to marketers and strategic marketing planning because population characteristics affect markets and markets produce revenue. Further, accurate information on the demographic environment allows marketers to make inferences regarding behavior, thus providing a basis for predicting future consumption patterns. An important caution here, however, is that demographic descriptors are, at best, indirectly related to behavior. That is, while many 20 year olds engage in similar behaviors, there is great diversity in the behavior of any particular demographic group.

Five critical dimensions of the demographic environment are population size, age distribution, geographic distribution, household composition, and the ethnic population. These five population factors translate into market potential. *Population size* in a country is affected by the birthrate, death rate, and net immigration. In the United States, the population size in 1993 was approximately 260 million people. The birthrate over time in the United States has shown dramatic variation as has the number of births. The number of births in the United States in recent history peaked in the late 1950s and early 1960s at approximately 4.3 million. This was the height of the baby boom. From that time, births have declined steadily to a low of 3.1 million in 1975. Then, the baby boom "echo" began to occur. This echo of baby boomers having their own children produced approximately 3.8 million births in 1988 and 1989. Births again began to decline at that point. A total population in the United States of just over 280 million people is expected in the year 2010.[2]

The growth of total population in the United States is shown in Figure 2-1. Broad-based population growth statistics relate directly to the demand for housing needs over a 15- to 20-year period, which is a critical statistic for marketers. Population growth also means household formation. And household formation means an explosion in demand for consumer goods—from bathroom fixtures and lawnmowers to kitchenware and toothpaste. Marketers are dependent on population growth and the consumer spending it represents for an estimate of future market potential and revenues.

Age distribution is a refinement of the simple population size statistic. The composition of a population based on age provides more insights for marketers. In the United States, age distributions have been changing dramatically over the last several decades. Since 1900, the percentage of Americans over 65 has tripled from 4.1% of the population to 12.6% in 1990, and the absolute number of people in this age category increased 10 times from 3.1 million to 31.5 million. Similarly, barring any radical changes in birthrate trends, the proportion of the population under 25 will continue to decline through the year 2000. Table 2-1 and Figure 2-2 show population trends and age distribution patterns for the United States from 1970 projected through the year 2010. This skewing of the age distribution in the population of the United States has occurred for several reasons. First, changes in childbearing behavior in the 1970s created a trough, or decline, in the population group under age 25. Second, lifestyle changes and advances in medical care have increased life expectancies. Add to this the large size of the population cohort born between 1945 and 1960 (the baby boom), and the population is aging.

Descriptions like these related to the age distributions within a population are very important to marketers in evaluating long-term market trends. The

FIGURE 2-1
U.S. Population Growth

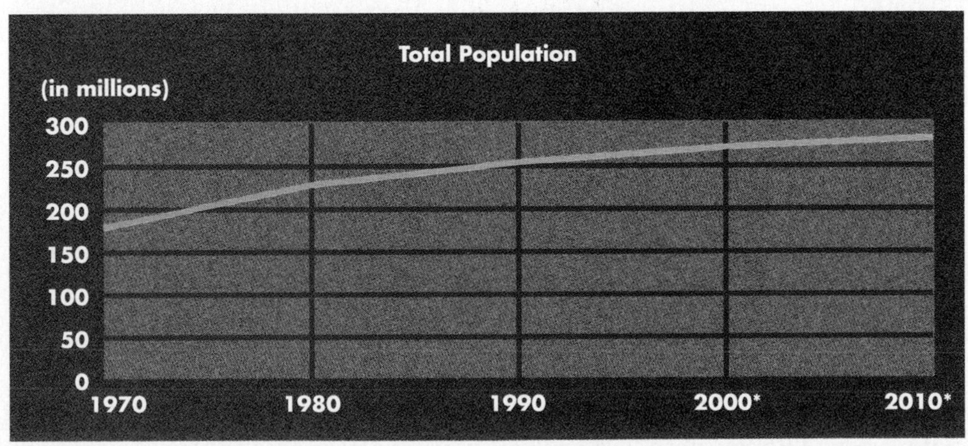

*Estimate

Source: U.S. bureau of the Census, *Statistical Abstract of the United States* (Washington, D.C.: U.S. Government Printing Office, 1990, 1992), Tables 18 and 20 respectively.

TABLE 2-1
Total Population and Age Distribution of Population in the United States 1970–2010

Age	1970	1980	1990	2000*	2010*
< 5	8.4%	7.2%	7.4%	6.3%	6.0%
5–17	25.7	20.8	18.2	18.2	16.2
18–24	12.1	13.3	10.4	9.4	9.6
25–34	12.4	16.5	17.5	13.8	13.3
35–44	11.2	11.4	15.1	16.4	13.2
45–54	11.3	10.0	10.2	13.9	15.3
55–64	9.1	9.4	8.5	9.0	12.5
65–74	6.1	6.9	7.3	6.8	7.4
>75	3.7	4.4	5.3	6.2	6.5
Total population in millions:	180	227	255	268	282

*Estimate

Source: U.S. Bureau of the Census, *Statistical Abstract of the United States* (Washington, D.C.: U.S. Government Printing Office, 1990 and 1992): Tables 18 and 20.

products and services desired by the over-65-years-old age group will represent a large and growing market in the year 2000 and beyond. The demands for vacation homes, recreational products, and medical products are expected to grow dramatically as this group continues to grow. Conversely, the 35- to 49-years-old group will shrink dramatically as baby boomers pass through that category. This is the population group that has traditionally contributed the most to consumer spending for automobiles, luxury goods, travel, and entertainment. The expectation is that these product markets will realize a general contraction in demand. Recognizing the size of a population group based on age provides marketers with important information for mid- and long-term planning. Consumer products firms like Kellogg, Procter & Gamble, and Frito-Lay will track age statistics and alter their product mix and distribution strategies over time based on the information.

The *geographic distribution* of the population provides yet another perspective. Strategic marketing planning is greatly affected by the concentration of certain populations within geographic areas. The location of distribution outlets and advertising media schedules will change based on information about population densities and population dispersion. Figure 2-3 shows current population distribution in the United States and how population distributions have changed since 1970.

Aside from the importance of the sheer numbers of consumers within a geographic region, certain parts of the United States, such as southern Florida and Arizona, have attracted older consumers and a population of that segment of society that is much higher than in other parts of the country. Similarly, the population of the United States shows migration and birthrate patterns whereby parts of the country are losing population and other parts are gaining population. The southern and western states are gaining population at four to five times the rate of the northeast and midwest and are expected to do so through the year 2000. The biggest percentage gains will be in Nevada, Utah,

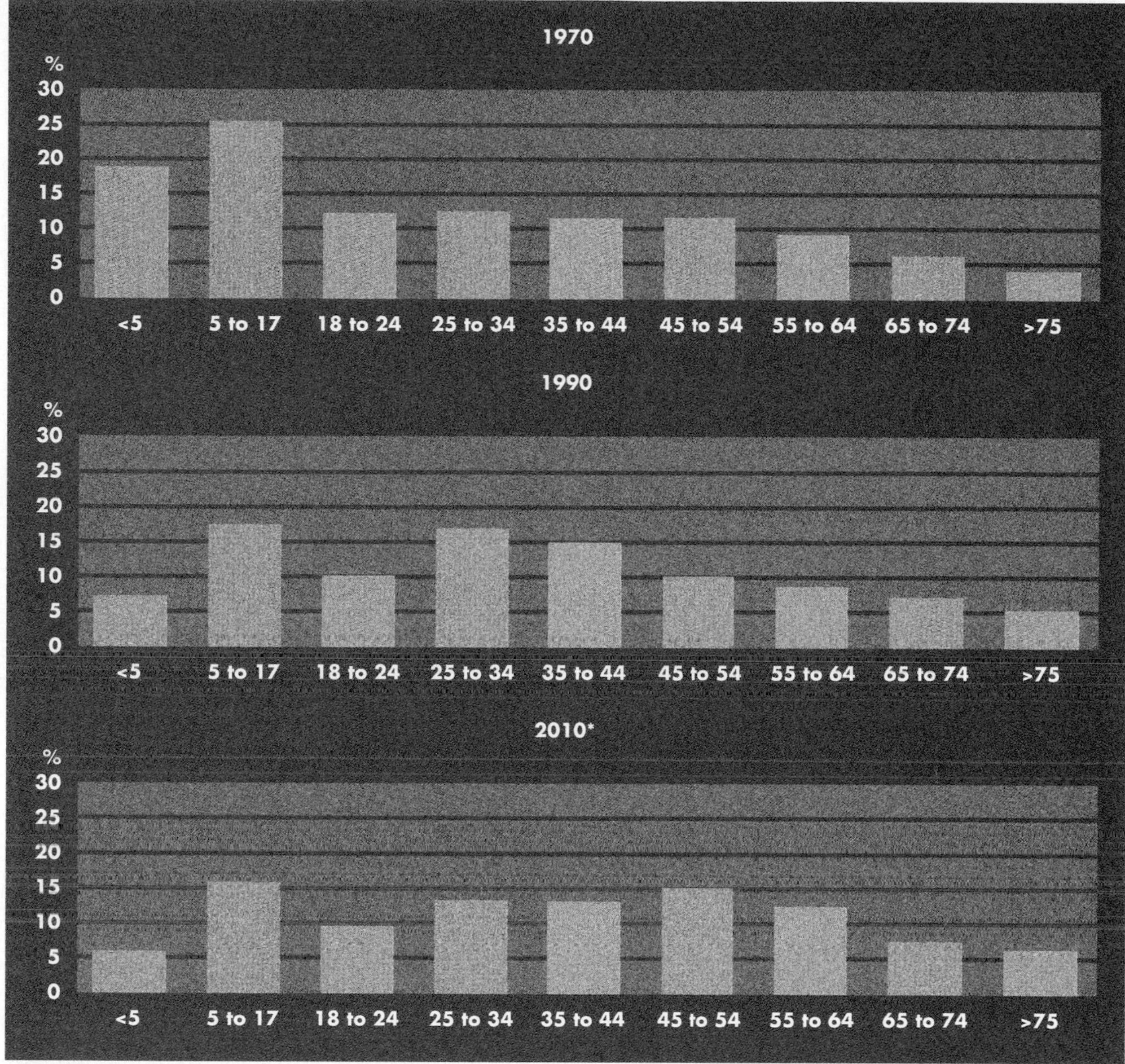

*Estimate

Source: U.S. Bureau of the Census, *Statistical Abstract of the United States* (Washington, D.C.: U.S. Government Printing Office, 1990 and 1992): Tables 18 and 12 respectively.

FIGURE 2-2
Age Distribution of U.S. Population

Arizona, Florida, and Texas. The largest percentage losses will be in New York, Washington, D.C., Michigan, and Massachusetts.[3]

As patterns like these are identified, firms must adjust marketing plans to reach the customers that represent primary markets. All aspects of the marketing mix are affected. As more people live in the relatively warm climates of the south and west, fewer cold-weather products and more warm-weather products

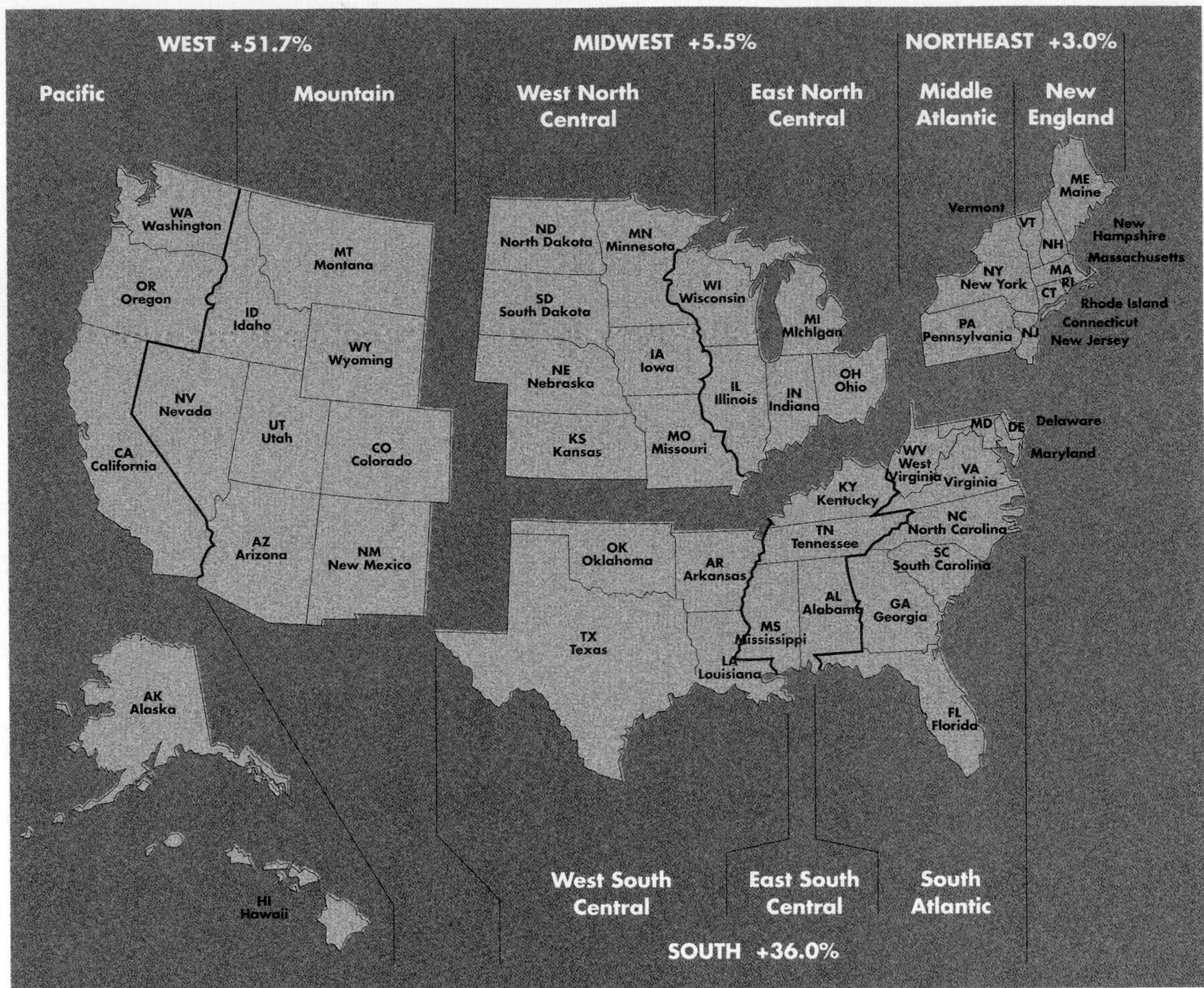

Source: U.S. Bureau of the Census, *Statistical Abstract of the United States* (Washington, D.C.: U.S. Government Printing Office, 1990).

FIGURE 2-3
Regional Population Change 1970–1990

will be needed. Think of a typical southern versus northeastern household and the different products each would need: sunscreen, light shirts and jackets, and air conditioners versus snow tires, snowblowers, large-capacity furnace systems, and Sorel boots. Aside from climate-related differences, different regions in the country have demonstrated different purchase behavior patterns as well: movie attendance, alcoholic beverage consumption, and imported versus domestic product preference all vary by region of the country. As such, marketers must carefully track population movements for future marketing strategies.

Household composition has been changing and evolving over the last three decades. With changes in marital behavior, childbearing behavior, divorce rates, and home ownership, household composition is very different today than in generations past. People are choosing not to marry, or to marry later, and to have children later. Consider the data in Table 2-2, which demonstrates

TABLE 2-2
Household Composition in the United States 1970–1991

	1970	1980	1991	percentage change 1970–1991
Average number of persons	3.14	2.76	2.63	(16.2%)
Number of households (in millions):				
Total	63.4	80.7	94.3	48.7%
1 Person	10.8	18.3	23.6	118.5%
Families	55.5	59.5	66.3	19.4%

Source: Adapted from U.S. Bureau of the Census, *Statistical Abstract of the United States* (Washington, D.C.: U.S. Government Printing Office, 1992): Table 56.

how household composition has evolved dramatically in the short period of time from 1970 through 1991. Single person households rose during this period from about 17 percent to nearly 25 percent of total households by 1991. Conversely, the average size of a household has shrunk from 3.14 persons in 1970 to 2.63 persons in 1991. Dual breadwinner households where both spouses work have risen dramatically over the same period.[4]

As the data in Table 2-2 dramatically demonstrate, the traditional household with a male and female spouse present and children living at home has become a bit of American history. The effect on marketing planning is dramatic when household composition changes. Different goods and services are demanded based on the number and type of individuals who comprise a household. Auto makers struck gold in the late 1980s and early 1990s with the creation of the minivan. The need for this product emerged from the baby-boomer segment needing transportation that could accommodate several small children. In a related sense, a small family needs a smaller home, which greatly affects home building and the scope of products needed.[5]

Ethnic population also affects marketing planning and decision making in that different ethnic groups demonstrate different behaviors and preferences in the consumption process. For example, African-American consumers are more likely to try new and highly visible products, and Spanish-speaking Americans have been shown to be more traditional and demonstrate greater brand loyalty in their purchase decisions. Brand-loyal consumers are so important to marketers that firms such as Frito-Lay and Borden have completely separate marketing plans and marketing managers for areas of the country with large Hispanic populations.

As of 1990, the population of the United States was approximately 80 percent white. Various ethnic groups comprise significant proportions of the population with African-Americans representing 12.1 percent, Hispanics 9 percent, and Asians 2.9 percent. Of greater importance is that ethnic groups are growing much faster than the general population. From 1980 to 1990, the Asian population more than doubled, Hispanic residents increased over 50 percent, and the African-American population grew 13.2 percent. During the same decade, the white population increased only 6 percent.[6] This means that over the next few decades the ethnic composition of the United States will be very different than it is currently. Similarly, world population gains are greatest in underdeveloped countries. Again, over time, the ethnic composition of the world will change dramatically and so too will market demands based on ethnic influences.

THE SOCIAL AND CULTURAL ENVIRONMENT

One of the most important and most difficult external environmental factors to gauge is the **social and cultural environment**. The social and cultural environment is related to the broad-based values evident in a society. In recent history, changes in such social and cultural values have spawned multibillion dollar industries in the United States. The value placed on health and fitness, which began to emerge as a cultural value in the United States in the late 1960s and carried through the 1980s, gave rise to the health food industry, the spa and fitness center industry, as well as a huge boost to the outdoor recreation industry. Just think of the number of different products that have either been introduced over the last 20 years or have been altered to comply with this social and cultural trend: dietary supplements such as vitamins, spa and fitness centers, aerobic workout centers, fitness clothing (Reebok and L.A. Gear didn't exist 15 years ago!), home fitness equipment, high-fiber cereals, outdoor equipment and clothing retailers such as REI, and weight loss centers. Conversely, other products have lost favor because of the health and fitness trend: cigarettes, alcoholic beverages, and foods high in fat and cholesterol have all lost sales over the same period.

Social and cultural trends evolve slowly but have an enormous affect on the collection of goods and services prevalent in a society. Consider several of these trends that have shaped the demand for goods and services in the United States over the last 30 years:

- *Changes in the Family.* Over the last thirty years, the nature of the family has changed dramatically. Increased divorce rates (more than doubled from 1960 to 1990) and the demise of the traditional family to the point where nonfamily households are growing faster than family households (see Table 2-2) . These changes affect values and life orientations.
- *Changing Sex Roles.* Related to the changes in the family are changes in sex roles. As more females enter the job market, the nature of their roles in the household has also changed. More males are doing shopping, housecleaning, and providing childcare within the home. Similarly, services for various household tasks traditionally performed by the female are being purchased, such as housecleaning and childcare services.
- *Emphasis on Health and Fitness.* As discussed earlier, this social and cultural trend has created multibillion dollar industries. From nutrition supplements to health and beauty spas, Americans and more recently Europeans, are placing more value on healthy lifestyles. This particular value may be manifesting itself as a concern for the environment.
- *The Importance of Time.* The culture in the United States places enormous importance and value on time itself. As one writer put it, the decade of the 1980s was "the decade in which time has come to rival money as the commodity people crave most."[7] Fast food chains, convenience stores, one-stop shopping, and extended shopping hours are all

manifestations of how much value consumers place on time. Products from microwave ovens to frozen foods prepared in the microwave all relate to this cultural value. One of the more recent products to emerge from the fascination with time is the cellular phone. While this product relates to efficiency in a corporate setting, more and more people see it as a way to get work done more quickly so as to increase leisure time.

- *Sensitivity to the Natural Environment.* Air pollution, water pollution, and solid waste disposal problems have sensitized individuals and organizations to the effects consumption of products is having on the natural environment. In 1990, a variety of firms were already engaging in what is referred to as "green marketing": appealing to consumers with "environmentally friendly" products or packaging. Even the federal government has embarked on a rigorous plan for using products that are energy efficient or made from recycled materials.[8]
- *Attitudes toward Wealth and Status Seeking.* Some analysts are beginning to think that the "borrow and spend" decade of the 1980s is creating a new attitude as the United States heads into the 1990s. One perspective suggests that "an age of inconspicuous consumption may well be arriving. Practicality, prudence, and need will gain in shoppers' minds at the expense of status, chic, and luxury."[9] Another analyst suggests that a revolt may be brewing against the rich and that we are headed for the "post affluent" society[10]—an attitude that may create a resurgence in the emphasis on the family.

THE ECONOMIC ENVIRONMENT

Several factors in the **economic environment** affect the ability of firms to successfully generate revenue. Fundamental features of the economy, such as gross domestic product (GDP), interest rates, and inflation, influence the ability (and desire) of both household and industrial consumers to spend. Some industries are more sensitive to economic conditions than others. Traditionally, the automobile industry (and other durable goods industries), tourism, and housing suffer the most if economic conditions sour. Conversely, basic consumer packaged goods, pharmaceuticals, and some industrial categories suffer little from a general slowdown in demand. Of the enormous number of economic statistics available, the most useful for firms to monitor are household income and spending patterns, inflation and the consumer price index, and consumer confidence.

Household Income and Consumption Patterns

A level of specificity greater than GDP relates to household income and spending patterns. Since all consumption is driven by household consumption (to be discussed in greater detail in Chapter 4), the income characteristics and spending patterns of households provides valuable information regarding economic conditions. Economists use income and consumption patterns to predict both short- and long-term features of the economy. During a recession, consumer spending tends to contract dramatically thus impacting the revenue performance of firms. In late 1990 and early 1991, economists carefully tracked consumer income (after taxes and adjusted for inflation), consumer spending, and consumer savings rates in an attempt to assess the severity of the recession in the United States at that time.

A more long-term perspective using household income and consumption patterns identifies trends in spending patterns. Figure 2-4 illustrates the trend in the proportion of personal income that is spent on durable and nondurable goods versus services since 1970. If you ever doubted that the United States

FIGURE 2-4
Personal Consumption of Goods and Services in the United States

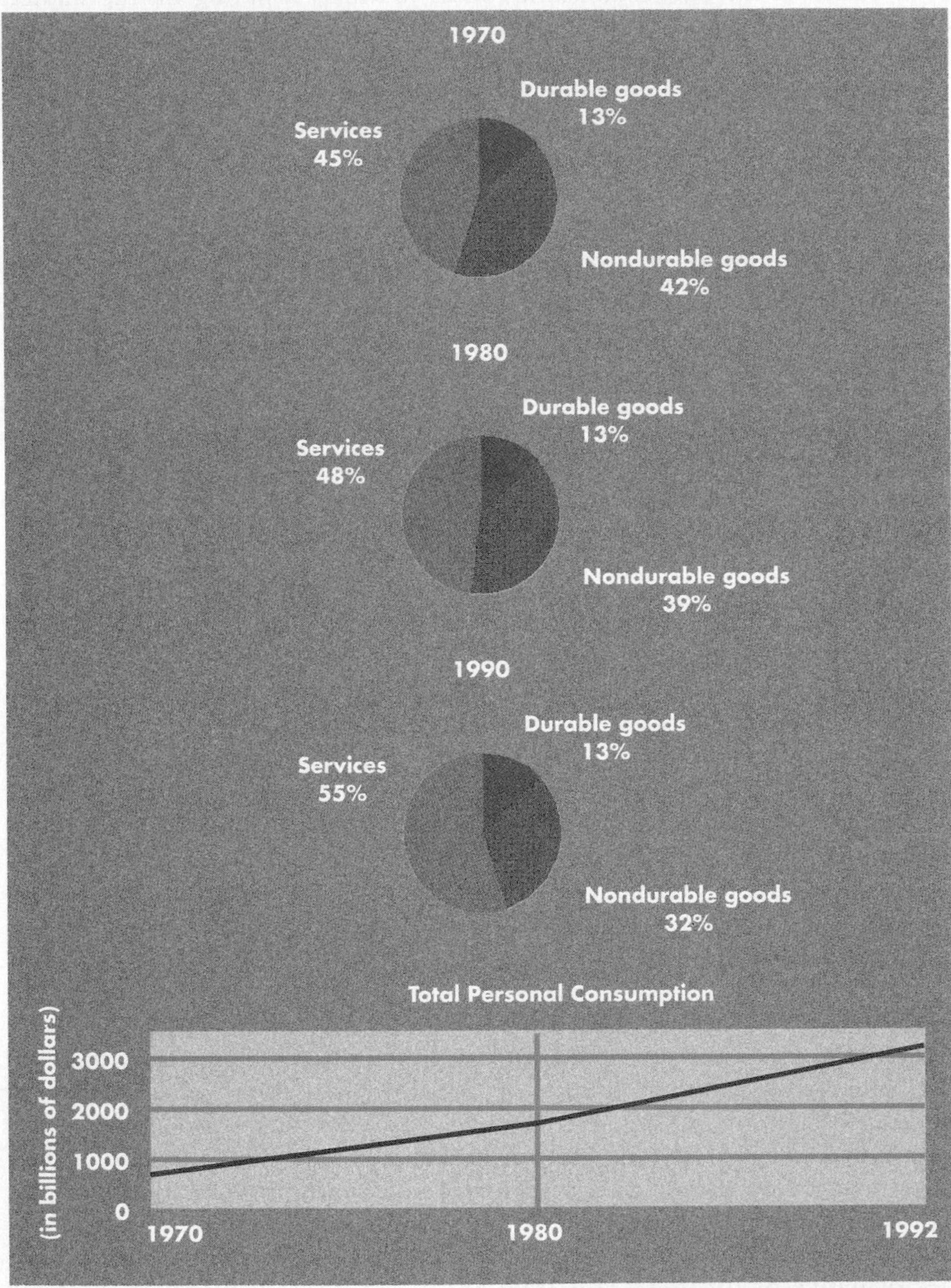

Source: U.S. Bureau of the Census, *Statistical Abstract of the United States* and Bureau of Economic Analysis, *Survey of Current Business* (Washington, D.C.: U.S. Government Business Office, 1992): Tables 681 and 1 respectively.

was a service economy, this information should remove those doubts. Since 1970, services have grown from 45 percent of personal consumption spending to 55 percent in 1990. The information in Figure 2-4 shouldn't be interpreted to mean that durable or nondurable goods businesses are dying. The growth in both of these areas since 1970 (not adjusted for inflation) has been a healthy 500 percent! What the personal consumption data do suggest, however, is that over that time period a greater proportion of individual income has been spent on services rather than goods, thus signaling a more rapid growth in the services sector of the economy. Firms will track such trends in an attempt to take advantage of and participate in growth areas in the economy with new products or services.

Inflation and the Consumer Price Index

When prices move higher due to inflation, consumer and industrial purchasing power are eroded. *Inflation* is defined as "a time of generally rising prices for goods and factors of production."[11] Information about inflation is reported by the U.S. Department of Labor Statistics via the Consumer Price Index (CPI). The CPI measures prices of items in a representative market basket of goods and is published monthly. When we hear news reports about the "rate of inflation," what the media are typically reporting is the percentage change in the CPI from month to month. Figure 2-5 displays the movement of the CPI since 1970.

During periods of high inflation most consumers and industrial buyers are unable to purchase as much in quantity or in quality from period to period. This creates a "dampening" effect, and while corporate revenues may show increases from quarter to quarter, those increases may be due simply to price increases rather than volume increases. Growth of this sort is superficial rather than real.

Consumer Confidence

A much more short-term, volatile, and highly impactive element of the economic environment is *consumer confidence.* This psychological measure identifies consumers' general optimism toward the economy, primarily, and the state of affairs, generally, in the United States. Measures of consumer confidence are reported by two sources: The Commerce Department of the federal government through the Conference Board and the University of Michigan's Institute for Social Research. The Conference Board Index uses 1985 consumer confidence as a base year indexed at 100. In recent years, the measure has fluctuated from 120 in 1988 to a low of 54 in early 1991. The effect of consumer confidence manifests itself quickly throughout the economy. When confidence drops, consumers restrain their credit card spending and delay purchases, particularly of durable goods. When optimism rises, individuals open up their pocketbooks and start to spend. Such changes show up in revenues of firms almost immediately. And, marketers respond by adjusting their strategies related to inventory levels, pricing tactics, and new product introductions. As an example, during the recession of 1991–1992, Ford and General Motors increased "discounts on just-introduced 1992 models, bowing to slow sales and flagging consumer confidence."[12]

Firms also monitor other related elements of the economic environment, such as interest rates, cost-of-living index (by area), savings rate, and borrow-

FIGURE 2-5
Annual Percent Change in Consumer Price Index, 1970–1988

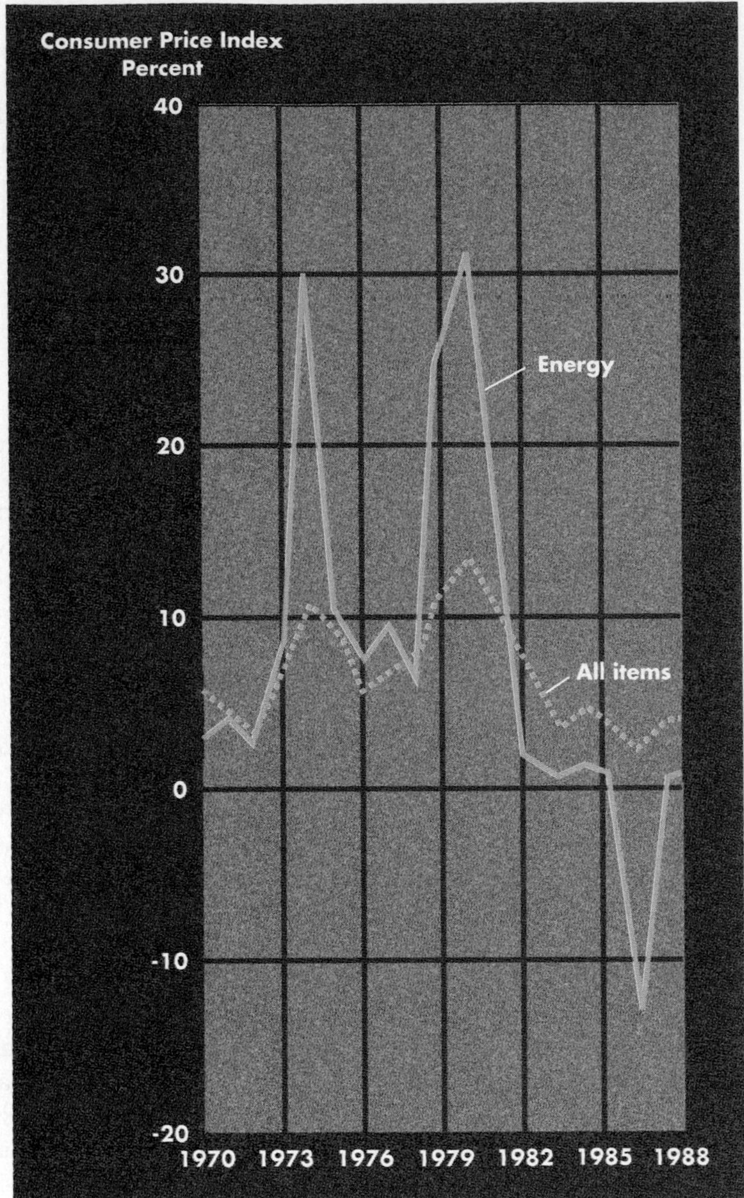

Source: Adapted from material provided by the U.S. Bureau of the Census.

ing patterns. By carefully monitoring the elements of the economic environment, firms can prepare for both downturns in the economy and periods of expansion by adjusting their operations to reflect these influences.

THE POLITICAL/REGULATORY ENVIRONMENT

Effects of the **political and regulatory environment** come from both government and nongovernment sources. Numerous restrictions have been imposed on marketing practices over the last one hundred years by both federal and state governments. The federal agencies that have the most direct effect on marketing practices are the Federal Trade Commission (FTC), the Food and

Drug Administration (FDA), and the Federal Communications Commission (FCC). The FDA and FTC are highly active in regulating marketing activities. The FDA has recently proposed that sun screen manufacturers provide more specific information on their labels to inform consumers of the effectiveness of the lotions.[13] The FTC has conducted an extensive investigation of diet-program companies to verify the advertising claims these firms have been making about the efficacy of their programs and products.[14] Figure 2-6 lists the major federal laws affecting marketing decisions.

Individual states are also active in legislation that affects marketing activities. A recent example is the stringent new air-pollution standards in California, which go well beyond federal Clean Air Act specifications. Automakers are scrambling to redesign engines and emission controls to comply with these new standards.[15] Auto manufacturers really have no choice but to comply with the regulations. The 1.7 million cars and trucks sold per year in California represent a market larger than all but seven nations worldwide! What kind of marketing strategies will the automakers come up with to comply? Chrysler plans to build as many as 100,000 vehicles per year that will run on methanol. GM is taking a completely different approach. It has stepped up the research and development on the first ever mass-produced electric car, the *Impact,* which the firm hopes to introduce by the mid-1990s.

Regulation of marketing practices, however, does not have to be legislated or even political. A variety of nongovernmental bodies exert an influence on individual firms or entire industries. Most prominently, consumers, industry associations, and the media all have informal regulatory powers. Consumers exert a regulatory influence on firms when broad-based sentiment in the market changes purchase behavior. A recent example is the segment of consumers who are aware of dolphins being trapped in tuna nets and insist on buying

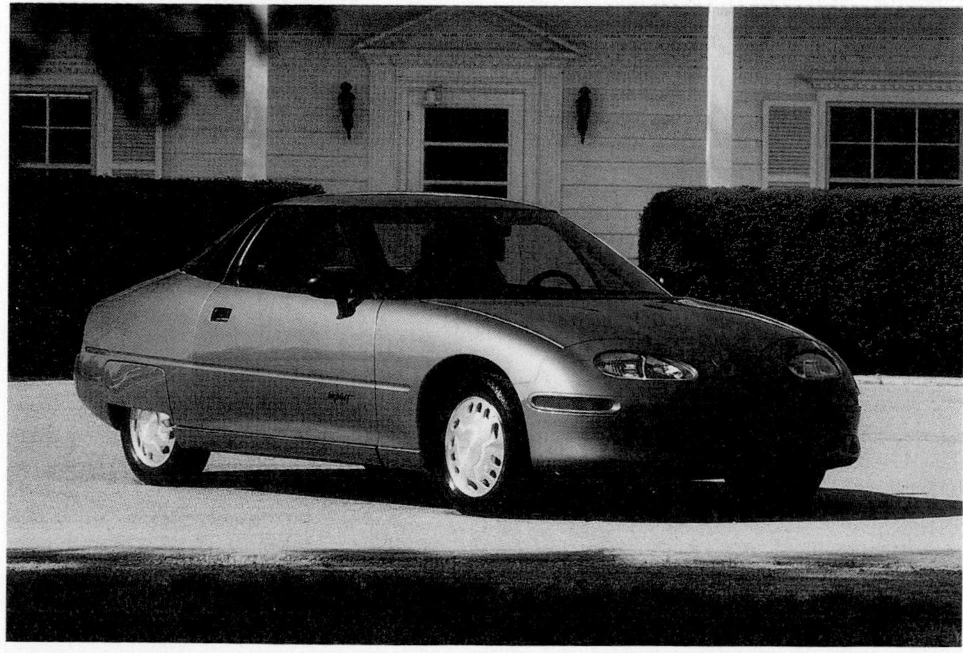

General Motors is developing this electric car, the Impact, in anticipation of more stringent air pollution regulations.

FIGURE 2-6
Major Federal Regulations Affecting Marketing Practices

Sherman Antitrust Act (1890)
Prohibits contracts, combinations, or conspiracies that restrain interstate trade. Makes it illegal to monopolize or attempt to monopolize any part of interstate trade or commerce.

Federal Trade Commission Act (1914)
Prohibits unfair methods of competition and (by the addition of the Wheeler-Lea Amendment of 1938) unfair or deceptive acts or practices deemed harmful to consumers.

Clayton Act (1914)
Supplemented the Sherman Antitrust Act and defined more precisely certain prohibited practices regarding price discrimination, tying clauses, exclusive dealer agreements and stock ownership in directly competing companies where the effect may be to substantially lessen competition.

Robinson-Patman Act (1936)
Amendment to the Clayton Act that makes it illegal to discriminate between buyers in price or terms of sale for commodities of like quality and quantity. Prohibits brokerage fees except to independent brokers. Forbids promotional allowances or provisions of services except on "proportionately equal" terms. This regulation was brought on by differential practices by manufacturers trying to win the business of large chain store operations.

Child Protection Act (1966)
Prohibits the sale of toys and articles deemed hazardous to children.

Fair Packaging and Labeling Act (1967)
Requires accurate and fair labels and containers. Requires manufacturers to include on the label the contents of the package, identity of the manufacturer, and amount contained in the package.

Consumer Credit Protection Act (1968) (encompassing Truth in Lending Act)
Requires full disclosure of the cost of credit and loans.

National Environmental Policy Act (1970)
Directs federal agencies to consider the impact on the environment of all activities. Environmental Protection Agency controls the antipollution programs for noise, air, land, and water.

Consumer Product Safety Act (1972)
Set up the Consumer Product Safety Commission to issue and enforce safety standards for consumer products.

Equal Credit Opportunity Act (1975)
Prohibits credit discrimination based on sex or marital status.

Magnuson-Moss Warranty Act (1975)
Sets forth requirements for full and limited express warranties.

Toy Safety Act (1984)
Gives the federal government the authority to recall toys discovered to be dangerous or hazardous.

Nutrition Labeling and Education Act (1990)
Requires uniformity in nutrition labeling of food products and establishes strict rules for health claims and nutritional attributes of food products.

Children's Television Act (1990)
Limits the minutes of advertising allowable during television programs for children. Limits are 10.5 minutes per hour on weekends and 12 minutes per hour on weekdays.

canned tuna that is warranted to be "dolphin free." Sunkist Tuna is now repackaged and the "dolphin free" warranty is emblazoned across the can. The consumer movement toward more environmentally sound products is an example of consumer sentiment that may have a broad-based affect on manufacturers' marketing practices in the form of recyclable packaging, for example. McDonalds has recently switched back to paper packaging in an effort to reduce solid waste disposal and use recycled paper. Of course, McDonalds takes the opportunity to inform consumers of this change as a way to appeal to prevailing consumer sentiment regarding environmental issues.

Another nongovernment organization that has regulatory influence is the Council of Better Business Bureaus. The National Advertising Division (NAD) of the Council has the most influence on firms. This division handles complaints from companies regarding advertising practices of competitors and acts as an arbiter between firms. Recent issues brought before the agency include a Ford Motor Co. complaint against Chevrolet for statements made in its truck advertising.[16] Ford's complaint was that Chevy's advertising claim "America's Favorite Pick-up" is misleading to consumers. Ford offered statistics that showed Ford trucks outsold Chevy during the preceding nine months. Chevrolet's response was that the ad didn't claim superiority for *all* pick-ups but rather for the *S-15* model featured in the ad. The NAD offers firms an opportunity for voluntary resolution of disputes, thus avoiding lawsuits.

The broadcast and print media are powerful regulators of marketing practices of firms. If a media organization deems an advertisement questionable in terms of truthfulness or good taste, it can refuse to run an ad. Nutri/System, Inc. ran straight into this form of regulation after several lawsuits were filed against the company alleging health hazards associated with its products. In the months that followed the lawsuits, the firm prepared ads strongly asserting the safety of the Nutri/System program and its products. All the major television networks, however, refused to run the ads because they were concerned that the health and safety claims in the proposed ads were unsubstantiated.[17]

The fundamental issue regarding the political and regulatory environment is that firms need to remain apprised of any regulation, state or federal, that may directly affect their marketing practices. Additionally, however, organizations must be sensitive to nongovernmental and nonlegislative restrictions that may be imposed on business activities. Consumers, industry associations, and media organizations, depending on the prevailing political climate, can exert an influence on a firm or an entire industry equal in strength to formal legislation.

THE TECHNOLOGICAL ENVIRONMENT

Firms have ridden the waves of new technology to the heights of success and to the depths of bankruptcy. Advances in the **technological environment** can either bolster the fortunes of a firm or, literally, put it out of business. Dozens of Fortune 500 companies have emerged in the last two decades because of market opportunities created by advances in technology—Intel (computer processors), Novell (computer networking), and Amgen (bio-technology) are examples. These firms were founded on and flourished in new technology.

Other firms, however, have been left behind. For two decades, Data General Corp. was a potent competitor in the computer industry. But in the early 1980s, it failed to get into the PC business and stayed exclusively in the minicomputer market. In retrospect, the chairman and co-founder recognizes the lack of participation in PC technology as a mistake and claims that "few companies are able to participate in the next wave of technology because they are blinded by the business at hand."[18]

This statement by the former leader of Data General Corp. highlights the challenge of monitoring the external technological environment. If opportunities and threats in the technological environment are not identified quickly and accurately, a firm can miss opportunities for revenue growth or, in the worst case, see its revenues lost to firms with competitive advantages stemming from new technology.

The decade of the 1990s may prove to be one of the most dramatic in terms of technological change and the effect such change has on corporations. High-profile megamergers, such as the multibillion dollar cable company agreements promise to make the information superhighway a reality. Everything businesses and consumers have known about communication will give way to computer-driven data and video access to any programming or information source.[19] The much discussed information arena is just one area of change, though. Less conspicuous underlying technology will also change society in the years ahead. "Optoelectronics," the combining of light and electricity, will affect quality and productivity in medicine, transportation, and manufacturing by providing instantaneous information never before available.[20]

Technological advances like these don't just affect the corporate marketing strategy of the firms involved in the technology. Technology affects society, and as it does it affects behavior in that society. When basic human behavior changes, consumption behavior invariably changes and a wide range of firms are affected. If the information superhighway makes it feasible for people to work in offices at home rather than traveling to work, then consumption of and demand for automobiles, gasoline, fast food, clothing, and a variety of other work-related products will change. A long-term and visionary perspective of technology and its impact is essential.

THE COMPETITIVE ENVIRONMENT

Emerson Electric, led by Chuck Knight, is known as a *killer competitor.* Killer competitors are firms whose strategies are insightful, intelligent, and aggressive. Every industry has its killer competitors: Wal-Mart in retailing, Procter & Gamble in packaged goods, and Anheuser-Busch in the brewing industry. "In the businesses they're in, they amass crushing market share. Then they amass some more."[21] Even if a firm is oblivious to all the external factors discussed to this point, it is typically aware of what its competitors are doing. And among the sophisticated giants, competition is carefully scrutinized: Ford monitors Chevrolet, Miller Brewing Co. keeps an eye on Anheuser-Busch, Coke battles Pepsi, and Burger King has wars with McDonald's. There is no room for complacency when it comes to monitoring the activities of competitors. What is

New technology presents opportunities for new products for many firms.

less obvious, though, is that threats in the **competitive environment** come from both **direct competition** and **indirect competition.**

The salty snack-food market—chips, nuts, and pretzels—is an example of fierce direct competition. The industry leaders are Frito-Lay and Borden. But with over $10 billion in annual revenue at stake, new and formidable competitors have entered the market: Procter & Gamble, Anheuser-Busch, and Keebler are now part of the snack food fray. With every *one percent of market share* in salty snacks worth over $100 million, it's not surprising these marketing powerhouses are after part of the market. The new entries prompted the vice president of Borden to say, "We consider this a snack war."[22] To combat the competitive challenge, Borden has altered its marketing strategies by rolling back prices and increasing promotional expenditures by as much as 25 percent.

Consider the somewhat different circumstances in which United Airlines competes with a small technology firm called PictureTel and Pepsi competes with Maxwell House coffee. These are examples of indirect competition. The threats of such competition are many times more difficult to monitor. In what way does United compete with PictureTel? As communication technology becomes more sophisticated and reliable through the use of computers, firms may choose to forgo the expense of physically sending (via air travel) company representatives to remote locations for meetings. Instead, firms will hold "teleconferences" using computers and satellite communications links. [23] Similarly, Pepsi wants to crack the huge morning beverage market with its *Pepsi A.M.*

brand. While coffee still dominates the morning beverage market, morning consumption of soft drinks has increased to 4 percent of the total market. Morning consumption of soft drinks represents 15 percent of all soda sales or a whopping $6 billion in soft drinks in industry sales.[24] Coffee makers need to take note of this incursion by new, different, and indirect competitors.

THE NATURAL ENVIRONMENT

The final environmental element that needs to be mentioned is the physical, or **natural, environment** itself. That is, the weather or natural environmental forces over which firms have no control. For the years 1988 through 1993, the businesses and households in the United States suffered over $93 *billion* in losses from weather events such as Hurricane Andrew in Florida and the midwestern floods in the summer of 1993.[25] Aside from direct losses, if inclement weather accompanies a major holiday, auto retailers can anticipate reduced customer traffic. Airlines and outdoor entertainment facilities are likewise adversely affected by uncooperative weather. Summer recreation areas, national parks, and ski resorts are totally dependent on favorable weather conditions to attract customers and, therefore, to generate revenues. Hundreds of firms in the Los Angeles area had to cope with the devastating effects of the 1994 earthquake. Firms can only hope to react quickly and positively to natural environmental phenomena.

The main issue is that vigilant assessment of external environmental factors must be a primary input to strategic marketing planning. Since the external environmental factors are uncontrollable, a firm can only hope to quickly detect changes and adjust its marketing activities to be consistent with or combat the effects. The next section discusses how firms can conduct their strate-

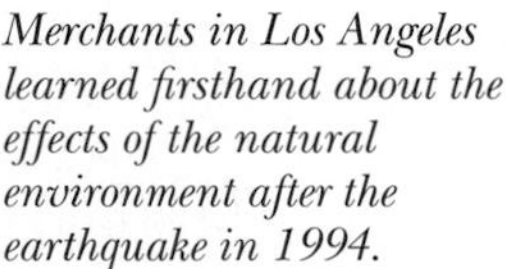

Merchants in Los Angeles learned firsthand about the effects of the natural environment after the earthquake in 1994.

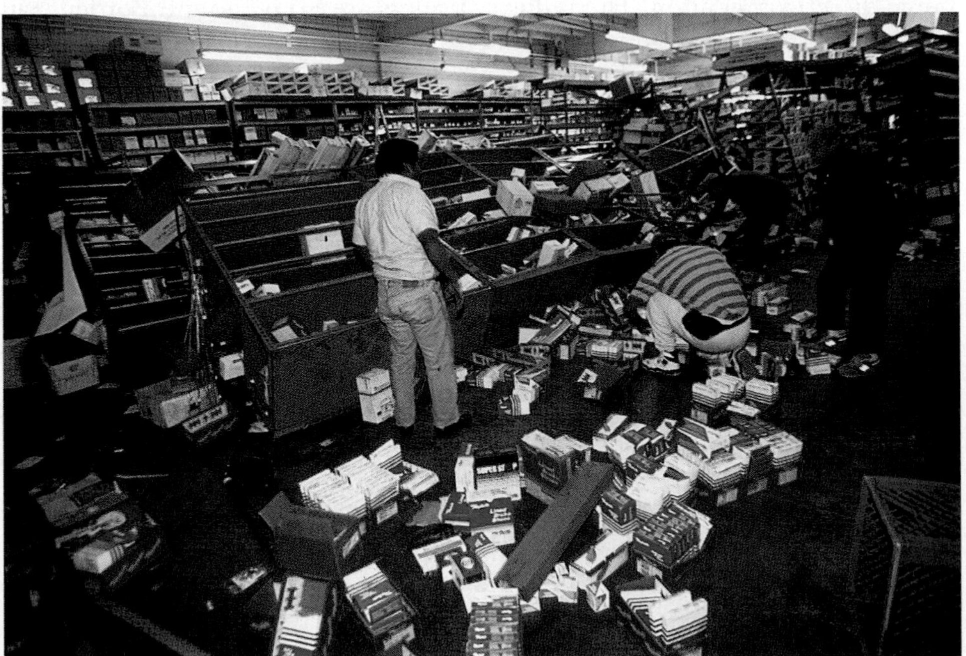

gic marketing planning in a way that allows quick and effective reactions to the influences of the external environment.

RESPONDING TO THE EXTERNAL ENVIRONMENT: STRATEGIC MARKETING PLANNING

The challenges and threats from the external environment are dynamic, formidable, and potentially devastating to a firm. As such, firms must be prepared to respond to these uncontrollable forces. Strategic marketing planning allows firms to respond to changes in the external environment. The tools of strategic marketing planning are the marketing mix, market segmentation and target marketing, and the marketing plan. Figure 2-7 shows the tools of strategic marketing planning as a way to respond to environmental forces.

THE MARKETING MIX

In Chapter 1, we learned that every firm must use the four Ps of marketing (product, price, promotion, and place) as a way to pursue the goal of generating revenue. When different emphasis among the four Ps is considered in the very specific context of strategic planning, then the firm's **marketing mix** is being determined. That is, the mix of strategy elements that constitutes the

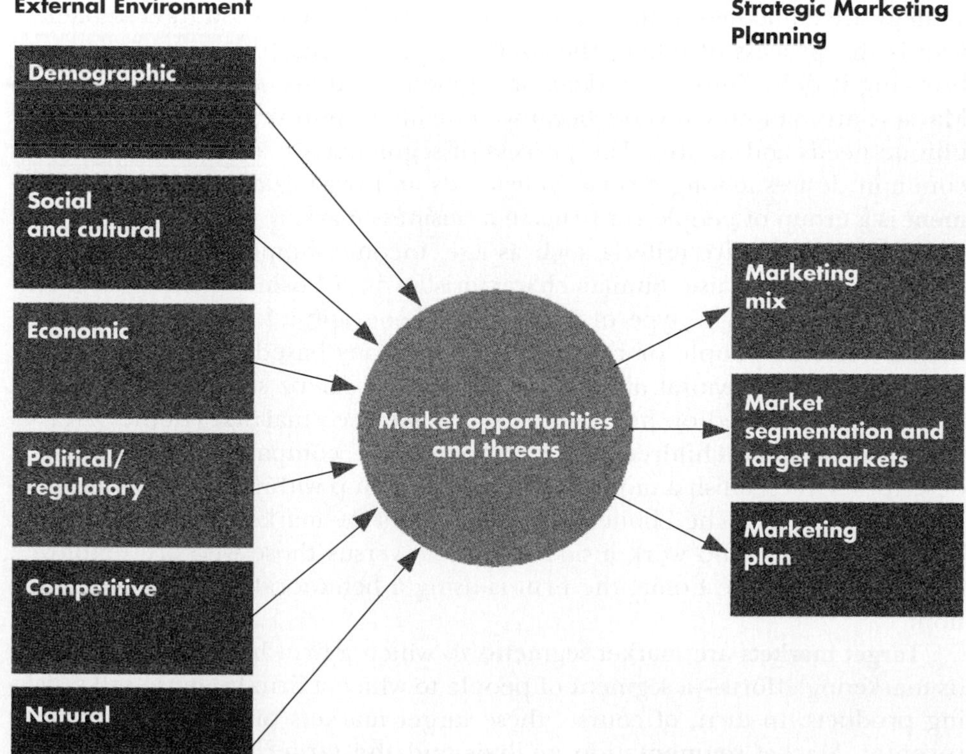

FIGURE 2-7 *The Tools of Strategic Marketing Planning Used to Respond to the External Environment*

most effective response to factors in the external environment. Recall those changes in the environment that negatively affected Mercedes-Benz' performance: demographic changes, social and cultural trends regarding wealth and status, and competitive challenges from Japanese luxury cars. Mercedes-Benz is now responding to these changes with strategic marketing planning by altering its marketing mix. The first step is to *re-mix* the variables (i.e., change the emphasis among the four Ps). First, the new C-class sedans will be priced less than comparable Japanese models. Second, the vehicles will have more responsive engines and transmissions. Third, Mercedes-Benz is developing a minivan and a "city car" to compete in faster-growing segments of the market. Mercedes-Benz is using the product and pricing variables to respond to the external environment. Mercedes-Benz could have chosen to emphasize the promotion variable or distribution variable as well. If a new ad campaign or change in dealer operations had been initiated, then the promotional and distribution variables in the marketing mix would have been affected.

It is important to recognize the role that the marketing mix plays in strategic marketing planning. Regardless of the source of the challenge—demographic, social/cultural, economic, political/regulatory, technological, competitive, or natural—changes in the marketing mix provide a firm with a fundamental basis for response.

MARKET SEGMENTATION AND TARGET MARKETS

Of all the strategic marketing planning tools that provide the firm with a basis for responding to the external environment, none is more important than market segmentation and target marketing. Effective and efficient marketing strategy are embodied in these two closely related decisions. **Market segmentation** is the process of taking the total heterogeneous (diverse) market and breaking it down into submarkets or segments that are more homogeneous. Markets are naturally diverse because individuals and organizations all have unique needs and desires. The process of segmentation seeks to discover the common desires among diverse individuals and organizations. A **market segment** is a group of people (or firms in a business market) identified according to specific descriptive criteria such as age, income, home ownership, or frequency of product use. Similar characteristics in a business market segment would be size of firm, type of industry, or geographic location. Market segments describe people or business organizations based on either physical descriptors or behavioral dimensions. If Mercedes-Benz segments the market for luxury cars based on marital status and age (i.e., married couples over 45 years old with two children living at home), the company is using physical descriptors to establish a more homogeneous group within the entire automobile market. When The Limited Stores segments the market for clothing based on those women who work inside the home versus those who are employed full-time outside the home, the firm is using a behavioral basis for segmentation.

Target markets are market segments to which a firm has decided to direct its marketing efforts—a segment of people to which a firm hopes to sell satisfying products. In turn, of course, these target markets provide the firm with revenue. Market segmentation analysis and the target markets which ulti-

emerge are of critical importance in dealing with the external environment. When a firm carefully segments the market and understands all the potential target markets, several benefits result. The firm can more efficiently deploy its limited resources and more quickly respond to changes in the environment.

Chapter 4 and Chapter 5 will go into great detail regarding the criteria and procedures used in operationalizing market segmentation in both the consumer and business markets. It must be recognized that market segmentation is one of the essential means by which firms focus their limited resources in response to influences from the external environment.

THE MARKETING PLAN

The **marketing plan** is the document that guides a firm's marketing efforts. A sound marketing plan must be in place to implement marketing activities. Many different formats are appropriate for a good marketing plan. The important thing is that a plan focuses the company's marketing effort on a well-defined target market and considers the effects of the external environment. The components of a good marketing plan are: situation analysis, assessment of opportunities and threats, statement of objectives, strategies, tactics, forecasts, and evaluation. Figure 2-8 outlines the components of a good marketing plan.

FIGURE 2-8
Components of a Marketing Plan

1. **Situation Analysis**
   a. External environment assessment
   b. Target market identification
2. **Assessment of Opportunities and Threats**
   a. Market factors
   b. Company factors
3. **Identification of Objectives**
   a. Sales volume in dollars and (product) units
   b. Total profit and profit margin
   c. Geographic market coverage
   d. Market share
   e. Revenue growth projections
4. **Strategies**
   a. Product: differentiation, competitive advantage
   b. Price: market position
   c. Promotion: theme, media choice, sales force deployment, promotions
   d. Distribution: coverage, channels
5. **Tactics**
   a. Activities to operationalize strategies
6. **Evaluation**
   a. Achievement of objectives
   b. Effectiveness of strategies
   c. Effectiveness of tactics

Situation Analysis

The first phase of a marketing plan provides the so-called lay of the land for management to consider. A **situation analysis** will first provide information on the current and future state of the external environmental factors discussed in this chapter: demographic, social/cultural, economic, political/regulatory, technological, competitive, and natural. Note that the information on the external environment considers current *and* future conditions. It is important that a firm recognize both long- and short-term conditions. Next, the target market is described: current size of market, growth projections, consumer (or organizational) characteristics, and buying behavior. Here a firm tries to assess the current status (for an existing product) or the projected status (for a new product).

Assessment of Opportunities and Threats

A situation analysis would provide some insights regarding opportunities and threats for a product, but the assessment undertaken here is more focused on the market itself and a firm's unique capabilities. Here, a firm will state **opportunities and threats** based on an assessment of market factors such as consumption trends in the product category, competitors' strengths and weaknesses, and other factors specifically affecting the target market. With regard to an assessment of opportunities and threats related to company factors, here the organization has to make an honest assessment of its product superiority or inferiority, production capabilities, management, and salesforce potential related to cultivating the target market. Thus, an assessment of company factors can be thought of as an appraisal of strengths and weaknesses within the firm.

Identification of Objectives

Objectives are concise statements outlining what is to be accomplished by the firm in key areas during specified time periods. This phase of the marketing plan requires that the firm make projections related to total revenue and unit sales, anticipated total profit and profit margin per unit, geographic market coverage, market share objectives (total and by region), and revenue growth projections. The firm must establish realistic objectives for performance in these categories. Objectives with low probability for achievement confound the resource allocation process and destroy motivation and morale within the organization.

Strategies

Strategies are plans of action designed to accomplish objectives. Here the firm lays out the strategies in each area of the marketing mix that will allow it to pursue objectives for revenue, profits, and market share. In the product area, a statement of competitive differentiation and competitive advantage will be included as well as the basis for the product's appeal to consumers. In the pricing area, a justification of price level is provided along with projections for dollar and unit sales at different price levels. The promotional area will state strategies with regard to the emphasis placed on advertising, personal selling, and sales promotions (discounts, coupons, etc.) within the marketing program. Finally, a statement of method of distribution to achieve the volume objectives is included as well as the basis for choice of wholesalers and retailers. It is important to realize that strategies can be both proactive and reactive. *Proactive strategies* are those conceived to take advantage of market opportunities that present themselves. *Reactive strategies* are those that combat challenges from external environment forces.

Tactics

Tactics are specific activities undertaken to pursue strategies. A firm must specify areas of responsibility and timetables for implementation. For example, it is this part of the marketing plan that would identify quarterly production schedules in the product area, media schedules for the advertising element of promotion, and the program for delivering products to retail outlets.

Evaluation

A firm will generate data relative to the achievement of objectives in order to get an **evaluation** of success or failure of the marketing plan. A firm must have data on total revenue, unit sales, profit, profit margin, and other factors listed in the area of objectives. However, evaluations based on these broad measures alone do not provide detailed enough information to take corrective action if objectives are not being met. The firm must therefore have information on activities associated with each aspect of the marketing mix. In this way, if objectives are not being achieved, the firm can turn to an evaluation of product, price, promotion, and distribution activities in an effort to detect where the problems lie. The evaluation stage highlights the need for accurate and comprehensive information regarding the external environment and how such influences may affect execution of marketing mix activities.

The External Environment and Strategic Marketing Planning: A Global Perspective

While it is still too early to draw conclusions, it's reasonable to speculate that historians will regard the 1990s as one of the most politically, socially, and economically turbulent decades in modern history. Radical political and market changes in eastern Europe, the economic integration of the European Union, the emerging growth and power of markets in the Asian Pacific, continuing political turmoil in the Middle East, and changes in the economic and competitive strengths of North America are all events that create a highly dynamic and often unpredictable environment for strategic planning. If ever there was a period that challenged managers and students of business to cultivate and develop a worldview for planning and decision making, that period seems to be now.

The approach we will take in this Global Perspectives section is to understand the *process* of how to identify important factors from the external environment and formulate a strategic response to those factors using marketing tools. We will not specifically identify differences between various global markets here. Those differences will be identified in global perspectives sections in later chapters. The critical first step for international marketers is to acquire a

global perspective for analyzing the external environment in order to make effective decisions and compete successfully in the worldwide arena.

Global marketing and **global companies** are terms that will be used throughout this text to describe a company's international orientation and approach to international markets. More often than not, it is large, multinational corporations that offer the most clear examples of a global marketing orientation. Corporations of large multinational status reflect the company's ability to exploit strengths gained in one nation or market in order to establish a position in other nations or markets. Figure 2-9 shows which countries house most of the world's 500 largest companies. Table 2-3 lists the world's 20 largest companies ranked by sales and number of employees. While company size does influence the extent to which managers can exploit opportunities worldwide, large size is not a necessary precondition to operate globally, nor is size alone sufficient to be a globally successful firm.

What is necessary for international marketing managers is a **global perspective**, that is, a strong orientation toward nondomestic markets. It is a global perspective of doing business that allows a midsize company like the Swedish firm IKEA to successfully operate over 120 retail furniture stores in 24 different countries.[26] Facing mature markets at home, IKEA's strategy of competing in the midpriced furniture market involves insightful application of all elements of their marketing mix.

By sourcing raw materials globally (eastern Europe and the former Soviet Union provide much of the wood used in IKEA's products) and by designing all its furniture for low-cost manufacture and distribution, the company is able

FIGURE 2-9
Countries with the Most Companies among the 500 Largest in the World

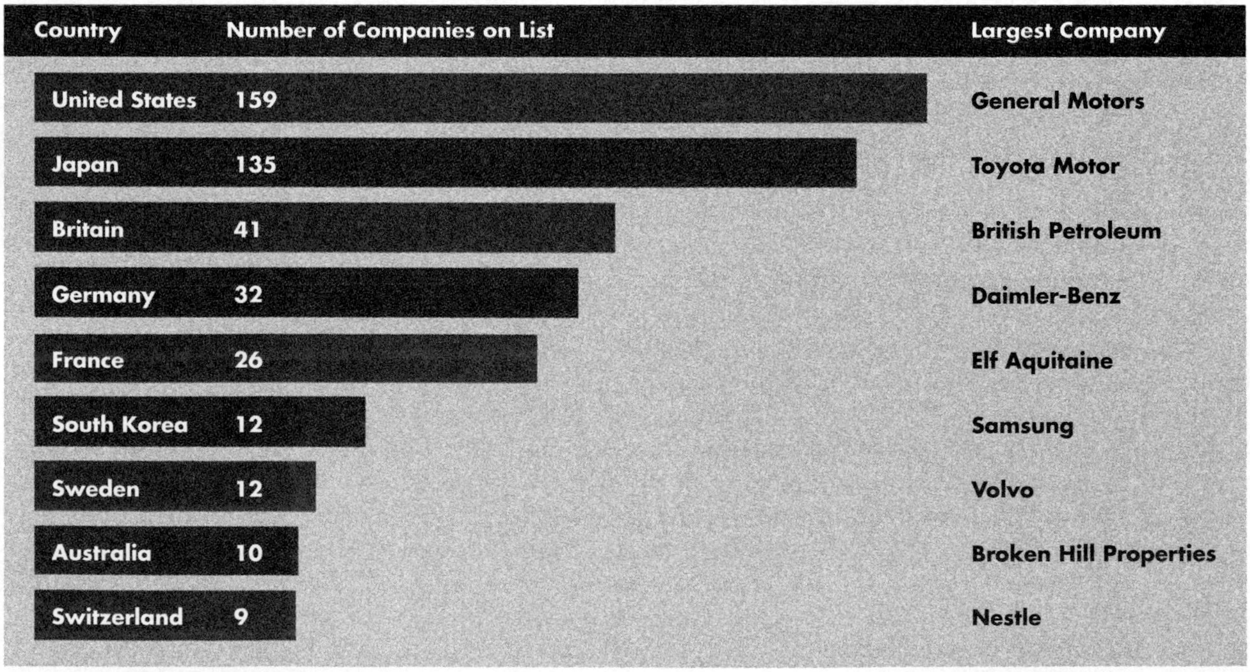

Country	Number of Companies on List	Largest Company
United States	159	General Motors
Japan	135	Toyota Motor
Britain	41	British Petroleum
Germany	32	Daimler-Benz
France	26	Elf Aquitaine
South Korea	12	Samsung
Sweden	12	Volvo
Australia	10	Broken Hill Properties
Switzerland	9	Nestle

Source: *Fortune* (July 26, 1993) 188.

TABLE 2-3
The 20 Largest Companies in the World

Company	Sales (in millions)	Employees
General Motors, U.S.	133,621.9	710,800
Ford Motor, U.S.	108,521.0	322,200
Exxon, U.S.	97,825.0	91,000
Royal Dutch/ShellGroup, Britain/Netherlands	95,134.4	117,000
Toyota Motor, Japan	85,283.2	109,279
Hitachi, Japan	68,581.8	330,637
Int'l. Business Machines, U.S.	62,716.0	267,196
Matsushita Electric Indus., Japan	61,384.5	254,059
General Electric, U.S.	60,823.0	222,000
Daimler-Benz, Germany	59,102.0	366,736
Mobil, U.S.	56,576.0	61,900
Nissan Motor, Japan	53,759.8	143,410
British Petroleum, Britain	52,485.4	72,600
Samsung, S. Korea	51,345.2	191,303
Philip Morris, U.S.	50,621.0	173,000
IRI, Italy	50,488.1	366,471
Siemens, Germany	50,381.3	391,000
Volkswagen, Germany	46,311.9	251,643
Chrysler, U.S.	43,600.0	128,000
Toshiba	42,917.2	175,000

Source: *Fortune* (July 25, 1994) 143.

to offer a product mix of high-quality furniture at exceptional value. This basic strategy has allowed IKEA to be highly successful in penetrating segments of middle- to upper-middle class consumer markets in a number of industrialized countries, as well as in Hungary and Poland, which represent emerging consumer markets with high pent-up demand for quality home furnishings. Further savings come from the company's ability to shift a variety of cost burdens to the consumer by eliminating many of the utilities (discussed in Chapter 1) which the marketing system can provided. Payment is made at a central location, and then the consumer picks up the merchandise from a separate distribution area or selects it personally from warehouse shelves. IKEA does not deliver or install, but all furniture is designed to be assembled with one allen-type wrench. These price-reducing activities are not seen as obstacles by large segments of the furniture buying public and actually appeal to consumers from a variety of countries. This allows IKEA to standardize much of their pricing strategies and their store formula worldwide.

While offering little in terms of after-sales service, the marketing strategists at IKEA are nonetheless very much in tune with the shopping behavior of their customers. Recognizing that buying furniture is typically a high-involvement shopping activity for people in all countries and that many customers have

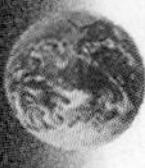

IKEA, a Swedish furniture retailer, has a global perspective and operates stores in 24 different countries.

little or no expertise in judging standards for furniture quality, IKEA grades its furniture according to Swedish testing board standards and labels each piece of furniture based on these standards. This practice reduces the risk for consumers while exploiting the generally held favorable attitudes that consumers have about the integrity of Swedish furniture. It also helps to establish a reputation for consistency and quality for IKEA internationally. This positive association of perceived high-quality furniture originating in Sweden gives IKEA a competitive edge since they have to compete with Asian manufacturers who also have access to all the technology, capital, and labor needed to produce (or quickly copy) stylish home furniture.[27] In terms of distribution, IKEA's approach is to strategically locate their large retail outlets in areas with high automobile access. In Holland, a country that has the highest per-capita expenditures in Europe for household furnishings, IKEA has five outlets each located by major freeway exchanges that form a triangle whereby 75 percent of the country's 15 million people can reach an IKEA store within forty minutes.

In recognizing the growing trend of increasing demand for quality home furnishings at reasonable prices, and by understanding the high degree of commonality in consumers' criteria and buying behaviors across countries with respect to furniture, IKEA has been able to effectively compete in markets that had been typically characterized as mature or stagnant. Using a global orientation for doing business, the company is able to develop more revenues and profits, offer more to customers, and ultimately be more competitive than if they had remained a domestic-oriented company. IKEA's strategic thrust for the 1990s and beyond is in the Middle East, Asia, and the Pacific Rim. The discussion of developing consumer markets in Chapter 4 will give you a clear indication of why these regions are the next target markets for IKEA.

OBSTACLES TO THE DECISION-MAKING PROCESS

Much of this chapter has been devoted to explaining the value of trying to understand the uncontrollable external environment in which firms operate so that they can develop and implement effective responses. In domestic markets, the reaction to much of the impact of the uncontrollable variables on the marketer's activities is fairly automatic. That is, the experiences we have gained throughout a career and a lifetime have become comfortable and second nature. Our unconscious reference to our own cultural values, experiences, and knowledge serve as a basis for guiding our behavior, selecting and evaluating information, and making decisions. When confronted with facts, managers react either spontaneously or in some reasoned fashion, but almost always within the context of knowledge assimilated over a lifetime and based on meanings, values, symbols, and behaviors that are relevant to our own culture.

This **self-reference criterion (SRC),** the unconscious reference to one's own cultural values, experiences, and knowledge as a basis for decisions, is one of the primary obstacles to success in decision making with a global perspective. The key to successful international marketing is in understanding and adapting to the environmental differences from one market to another. A manager's SRC can prevent him or her from being aware that there are cultural differences or from recognizing the importance of those differences. This in turn can influence the evaluation of the appropriateness of a domestically designed marketing mix for a foreign market. For example, AT&T's highly successful "Reach Out and Touch Someone" advertising campaign was viewed as much too sentimental for most European audiences. Likewise, their "Call USA" campaign (aired on many European TV satellites), which was aimed at Americans doing business in Europe who needed to keep in touch with the office back in the United States, was also negatively perceived by many Europeans who were also part of AT&T's target market. The ad featured a harassed U.S. businessman whose foreign language skills were so poor (English only!) that he could barely stumble his way through a busy French hotel in order to find a telephone booth, where he was gratefully connected to an English-speaking AT&T operator. European businesspeople are typically fluent in two or three languages and have enough competence to ask for a telephone. This ad gave a negative portrayal and provided a negative association with the product offering.[28]

The most effective way to control for the negative influences that SRC can have on the international marketer's decision processes is to recognize its existence and to constantly be aware of the need to be sensitive to potential differences among markets. Granted, there will be many market situations where the similarities will be greater than the differences across cultures. Nonetheless, in order to avoid errors in business decisions, it is necessary to make a cross-cultural analysis to isolate SRC influences. The following steps are suggested as a framework for such an analysis:

1. Define the business problem or goal in domestic cultural traits, habits, or norms.
2. Define the business problem or goal in foreign cultural traits, habits, or norms. Make no value judgments.

3. Isolate the SRC influence in the problem and examine it carefully to see how it complicates the problem.
4. Redefine the problem without the SRC influence and solve for the optimum business goal situation.[29]

Notice that this approach requires an understanding of the culture of each foreign market as well as one's own culture. By following a framework like the one above, a global manager will be forced to recognize the extent to which either personal criteria or domestic market strategies are appropriate for the decisions being considered for international markets.

DEVELOPING A GLOBAL PERSPECTIVE FOR DECISION MAKING

Obviously, managers develop their SRC over a long period of time—they are not born with it. Likewise, firms are not born with a global perspective. Businesses develop this perspective with experience and knowledge as they come to rely on foreign markets for revenue-generating opportunities. In a later chapter, we will discuss the factors that influence the phases of commitment that companies have to international marketing activities over time. Right now, the focus is on the *philosophical orientation* that management can have regarding global decision making.

While a variety of approaches have been suggested to describe the global orientation that firms can have, the approach most commonly quoted is the *EPRG* schema.[30] The authors of this approach suggest that firms can be classified as having an *ethnocentric, polycentric, regiocentric,* or *geocentric* global orientation (**EPRG**) depending on the international commitment of the firm. An **ethnocentric** firm views its domestic market as most important, perhaps reacting defensively to international markets, if at all. Here, an analysis of the external global environment is either nonexistent, passive, or done for reactive rather than proactive reasons.

A **polycentric** firm sees international markets as a series of domestic or national markets, each of potentially equal value. Here, no real attempt is made at synergy between markets, but rather a decision-making approach is taken where each market is viewed separately in terms of marketing plans.

By contrast, firms with a **regiocentric** orientation do seek opportunities for coordinated and possibly concentrated marketing programs, but usually within a geographically or culturally homogeneous region. For example, a management consultant company that specializes in setting up joint venture arrangements for eastern European companies who are seeking western European production or marketing skills has a regiocentric view. Knowledge gained in one market may be adapted for developing strategies and tactics in similar market situations.

Finally, a **geocentric** firm depicts a commitment to a global orientation wherein the firm continually seeks out worldwide opportunities for coordination and concentration of marketing mix strategies and tactics. These companies develop standardized products of dependable quality to be sold to a global market, that is, the same country-market set throughout the world. The manager's responsibility is to be aware of his or her self-reference criteria during the process of analysis and decision making and how much it is affecting market (i.e., ethnocentric, polycentric, regiocentric or geocentric) orientation.

Here, analysis of the environment is comprehensive, active, and integrative. The decision-making process takes into account the complexities of global strategies with multiple corporate objectives. Minor adjustments may be made in the marketing mix in order to comply with local conditions such as legal and/or media regulations, but, otherwise, geocentric firms attempt to treat the world as one market for their offerings. For example, Coca-Cola uses *Coke Lite* as a brand name instead of *Diet Coke* in some European countries, since the word diet is restricted due to medical connotations in some cultures. Coca-Cola also uses a slightly sweeter formula for the syrup in their Middle East markets to accommodate local tastes. Otherwise, they analyze their environment (in particular their competitive environment) with the intention of developing and executing global marketing strategies.

In the chapters to come, other uncontrollable elements in the international environment, such as political and social issues, demographic and lifestyle trends, attitudes towards technology, and global competitive strategies, will be discussed in order to illustrate the special challenges of analyzing global markets and making international marketing decisions. At this point, we have established that decision making with a global perspective requires the adoption of an international orientation to marketing strategy and planning decisions.

Key Terms and Concepts

External environment
Uncontrollable variables
Demographic environment
Social and cultural environment
Social and cultural trends
Economic environment
Political/regulatory environment
Technological environment
Competitive environment
Direct competition
Indirect competition
Natural environment
Market segmentation
Market segment
Target market
Marketing plan
Situation analysis
Objectives
Strategies
Tactics
Evaluation
Global marketing
Global companies
Global perspective
Self-reference criterion (SRC)
EPRG
Ethnocentric
Polycentric
Regiocentric
Geocentric

Questions and Exercises

1. What are demographics? How are these factors used by a firm to assess future market opportunities and challenges?
2. In your opinion, what is the most important social and cultural trend affecting the nature of products and services? What future trends do you see having an effect on the types of products and services we use?
3. Discuss the difference between direct and indirect competition. Why are the risks of indirect competition often difficult for a firm to identify?
4. Give an example of direct and indirect competition for a video game manufacturer.

5. Consumer confidence in the economy and in the general state of affairs in the United States is claimed to affect consumer purchasing behavior. Describe an instance where you, personally, restricted your expenditures because you lacked confidence in the economy.
6. Define market segmentation. What is the relationship among market segmentation, market segments, and target markets?
7. Distinguish strategies from tactics as part of a marketing plan. If a firm chooses to use television advertising rather than personal selling to cultivate customers, do you think this is a strategic decision or a tactical decision?
8. In the evaluation stage of the marketing plan, the firm will use information related to revenues, unit sales, and profit margin. Is this information detailed enough to initiate corrective action if objectives are not being achieved? If so, how is corrective action initiated? If not, what other information is needed?
9. How did IKEA, the furniture retailer discussed in the chapter, use a global perspective to cultivate a worldwide market for its furniture?
10. What is a self-reference criterion? Why is it considered one of the primary obstacles to success in marketing decision making with a global perspective?

REFERENCES

1. Adapted from information found in Alex Taylor III, "Making Up for Lost Time," *Fortune* (October 18, 1993): 78–79; John Templeman, "Mercedes Is Downsizing—and That Includes the Sticker," *Business Week* (February 8, 1993): 38; Oscar Suris, "Mercedes-Benz Tries to Compete on Value," *The Wall Street Journal* (October 20, 1993): B1.
2. Information for the discussion of population size and birthrate was taken from U.S. Bureau of the Census, *Statistical Abstract of the United States* (Washington, D.C.: U.S. Government Printing Office, 1991, 1992).
3. Ibid. 1992, Table 23.
4. Ibid., Table 56.
5. Mitchell Pacelle, "More Builders Plan Low-Cost, Small Houses," *The Wall Street Journal.* (August 8, 1991): B1.
6. U.S. Bureau of the Census, *Statistical Abstract of the United States* (Washington, D.C.: U.S. Government Printing Office, 1993), Table 58.
7. Alix M. Freedman, "The Microwave Cooks Up a New Way of Life," *The Wall Street Journal* (September 19, 1989): B1.
8. Mary Beth Regan and Peter Burrows, "Uncle Sam Goes On An Eco-Trip," *Business Week* (June 28, 1993). Also, for a good discussion of this issue that includes consumer views, see David Kirkpatrick, "Environmentalism: The New Crusade," *Fortune* (February 12, 1990): 45–54.
9. Quote from *Industry Forecast,* an economic newsletter, cited in Alfred L. Malabre Jr., "Consumer Spending: From Spur to Drag," *The Wall Street Journal* (January 21, 1991): A1.
10. Anne B. Fisher, "A Brewing Revolt against the Rich," *Fortune* (December 17, 1990): 89–94.
11. U.S. Bureau of the Census, *Statistical Abstract of the United States* (Washington, D.C.: U.S. Government Printing Office, 1990): 446.
12. Gregory A. Patterson, "Ford and GM Step Up Rebates on 1992 Models," *The Wall Street Journal* (September 27, 1991): B1.
13. Rose Gutfeld, "FDA Proposes Requiring Labels to Show Effectiveness of Sunscreens, Tan Lotions," *The Wall Street Journal* (May 13, 1993): B8.
14. Jeanne Saddler, "Diet Firms' Weight-Loss Claims Are Being Investigated by FTC," *The Wall Street Journal* (March 26, 1993): B1.
15. Neal Templin, "Auto Makers Strive to Get Up to Speed on Clean Cars for the California Market," *The Wall Street Journal* (March 26, 1991): B1, B10.
16. Jacqueline Mitchell, "Ford Accuses Chevy of Telling Whoppers in Pickup Truck Ads," *The Wall Street Journal* (October 17, 1990): B8; Francine Schwadel, "Setting Standards for Advertising," *The Wall Street Journal* (September 30, 1988): 34.
17. Kathleen Deveny, "Nutri/System Is Struggling to Get TV Networks to Clear Its New Ads," *The Wall Street Journal* (April 12, 1990): B4.
18. John R. Wilke, "Data General Board Ousts Co-Founder," *The Wall Street Journal* (October 13, 1990): B1.
19. John Huey and Andrew Kupfer, "What *That* Merger Means For You," *Fortune* (November 15, 1993): 82–90.
20. John Carey and Neil Gross, "The Light Fantastic," *Business Week* (May 10, 1993): 44–50.
21. Bill Saporito, "Companies That Compete Best," *Fortune* (May 22, 1989): 36.
22. Kathleen Deveny, "Crunch Time in the Snack Industry," *The Wall Street Journal* (December 17, 1989): B1, B6.

23. Al Senia, "Video Conferencing Enters Mainstream as Prices Decline," *International Herald Tribune* (October 8, 1991): 14.
24. Michael J. McCarthy, "Test Shows That Pepsi's Rival to Coffee So Far Isn't Most People's Cup of Tea," *The Wall Street Journal* (March 30, 1990): B1, B4.
25. Michael J. Mandel, "Big Savings to Be Had from Better Weather Watching," *Business Week* (October 4, 1993): 22.
26. Adapted from Bill Saporito, "IKEA's Got 'Em Lining Up," *Fortune* (March 11, 1991): 72; and Joan Veldkamp, "Het IKEA Gevoel," *Quote* (September 1993): 63–66.
27. Telephone interview with M. C. Van den Toorn, national sales manager, IKEA B.V., Nederland, January 12, 1994; and Bill Saporito, "Where the Global Action Is," *Fortune* (Autumn/Winter 1993): 64. *See also* Noel Fung "IKEA to Find New Homes in Region," *South China Morning Post* (September 22, 1993): 3.
28. For a complete book on mistakes made by sophisticated companies in international business, see David A. Ricks, *Big Business Blunders* (Homewood, IL: Dow-Jones Irwin, 1983).
29. James A. Lee, "Culture Analysis in Overseas Operations," *Harvard Business Review* (March–April, 1966): 106–111.
30. Yorum Wind, Susan P. Douglas, and Howard V. Perlmutter, "Guidelines for Developing International Marketing Strategy," *Journal of Marketing* (April 1973): 14–23.

SECTION TWO

ANALYZING MARKETS AND BUYER BEHAVIOR

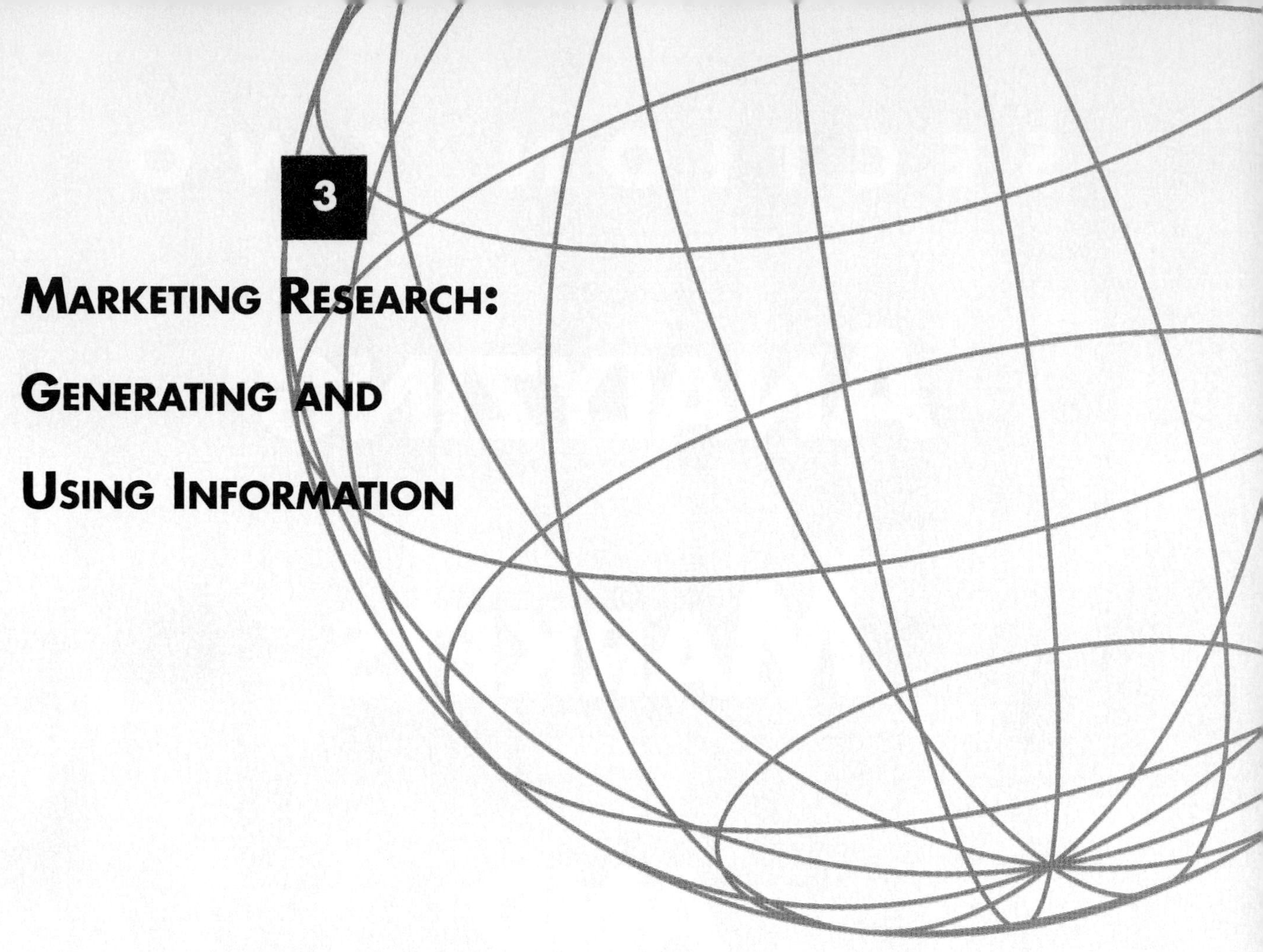

3

Marketing Research: Generating and Using Information

AFTER STUDYING THIS CHAPTER, YOU WILL UNDERSTAND THAT:

1. The role of marketing research is to generate information about the external environment for strategic marketing planning.
2. There are two types of research information available: primary (marketing research projects) data and secondary (existing data sets) data.
3. The nature and purpose of a Marketing Information System (MkIS) is to generate pertinent information on an ongoing basis.
4. Generating data through a marketing research project requires rigor in the development of the project and great care in the gathering and interpretation of data.
5. The tremendous diversity and complexity of the global environment has increased the importance and value of information generation and use in global strategic planning.

How would you like to answer 35,000 phone calls every day? How about opening 500,000 envelops in a year? Well, Dell Computer *did* answer all 35,000 calls it received in 1993 and USAA, a financial services company, *does* evaluate 500,000 mail questionnaires every year from its 2.5 million customers.[1] These highly successful firms and others, like Ford, Black & Decker, and Chris-Craft, use phone calls, questionnaires, and focus groups to generate information for use in strategic marketing planning and marketing mix decision making. In 1993, firms spent over $8.1 billion worldwide and U.S. firms spent $2.9 billion on marketing, advertising, and public relations research to better understand the external environment.[2]

A firm like Dell Computer needs information to stay successful—it holds the largest market share in the fiercely competitive $45 billion a year PC global market. Dell's chief information office was quoted as saying, "Information is a valuable competitive weapon. Our whole business system is geared to collect it."[3] Dell uses toll-free 800 numbers to provide customers with direct and convenient access to company sales representatives. As reps answer questions for current and potential customers, they type information from each call as it is taking place directly into the firm's central customer database. The database has over a million entries and is shared across departments in the company from product development to customer service. Dell strategists use the information to more efficiently target customers and more effectively design marketing programs. The system is so sophisticated it even coaches sales reps *during* a sales call. As a rep is entering information about a caller, the information system quickly offers the rep suggestions via the computer screen on what products to suggest. The system has instantaneously profiled the caller based on existing records and offered the rep hints on making a sale.

Few firms have an information system as sophisticated and efficient as Dell's, but the example highlights how powerful information can be once it is generated and used properly. Marketing research is the process through which firms generate data to improve marketing planning. Chapters 1 and 2 discussed the importance of accurately assessing customer desires in a dynamic and complex environment. Marketing research encompasses a wide range of activities employed by a firm to generate information for this purpose. A formal definition of **marketing research** is:

The systematic gathering, organizing, interpreting, and reporting of information pertinent to marketing decision making.

The Scope of Marketing Research

The need to track consumers closely and monitor influences from the external environment is reflected in the amount spent on research. During the 1980s, research expenditures grew at an annual rate of 8 percent.[4] While growth has slowed, the industry as a whole still realized over $8 billion in revenue worldwide. One marketing research firm estimates that in a single year, over 70 million Americans are interviewed in survey research.[5] More evidence of the scope of marketing research is contained in Table 3-1.

TABLE 3-1
Marketing Research Activities of 587 Companies in 1988 (1983 data provided where comparable)

Research Activities	Percentage of Firms Engaged in Activity 1988	1983
A. Business/economic and corporate research		
1. Industry/market characteristics and trends	83%	91%
2. Acquisition/diversification studies	53	73
3. Market share analysis	79	97
4. Internal employee studies (morale, communication, etc.)	54	76
B. Pricing		83
1. Cost analysis	60	
2. Profit analysis	59	
3. Price elasticity	45	
4. Demand analysis		
a. market potential	74	
b. sales potential	69	
c. sales forecasts	67	
5. Competitive pricing analyses	63	
C. Product		
1. Concept and development testing	68	76
2. Brand name recognition and testing	38	
3. Test marketing	45	59
4. Product testing of existing products	47	80
5. Package design studies	31	65
6. Competitive product studies	58	87
D. Distribution		
1. Plan/warehouse location studies	23	68
2. Channel performance studies	29	71
3. Channel coverage studies	26	
4. Export and international studies	19	49
E. Promotion		
1. Motivation research	37	47
2. Media research	57	68
3. Copy research	50	61
4. Advertising effectiveness	65	76
5. Competitive advertising studies	47	67
6. Public image studies	60	
7. Sales force compensation studies	30	60
8. Sales force quota studies	26	
9. Sales force territory structure	31	78
10. Studies of premiums, coupons, deals, etc.	36	58
F. Buying behavior		
1. Brand preference	54	
2. Brand attitudes	53	
3. Product satisfaction	68	
4. Purchase behavior	61	
5. Purchase intentions	60	
6. Brand awareness	59	
7. Segmentation studies	60	

Sources: 1988 information obtained from Thomas C. Kinnear and Ann R. Root, eds., *1988 Survey of Marketing Research* (Chicago: American Marketing Association, 1988), 43; information for 1983 obtained from Dik Warren Twedt, ed., *1983 Survey of Marketing Research*, (Chicago: American Marketing Association, 1983), 41.

Notice that the 587 companies surveyed engaged in research covering literally the full range of marketing mix decisions. The information in Table 3-1 indicates a reliance on marketing research data by many firms, but note that since 1983 it would appear that firms are not gathering as much data. In literally every category where comparable 1988 and 1983 data are available, fewer firms report conducting that particular type of research. Part of the reason is the large expense of conducting research. Also, research techniques have become so complex, that some managers are simply overwhelmed by the nature and volume of information.

Despite a decrease in research activities by some firms, however, the need for research information remains critical. The globalization of competition forces firms to respond quickly to consumer desires and competitors' activities. In fact, changes in all of the external environmental forces require that marketing strategists make precise refinements in each area of the marketing mix to have products and services consistent with desires in the marketplace. One firm that uses information for responding to customer needs is General Electric. GE maintains an "800 Center" for customer service at a cost of about $10 million a year. But the center's manager says the payback is many times that expense.[6] GE uses the feedback to redesign products, refine the distribution system, and generally fine tune the marketing mix for each product in its line. But research isn't just for huge firms like GE. The procedures and methods discussed in this chapter are readily available to the small firm as well. It isn't always necessary to spend a lot of money to acquire good information.

The Role of Marketing Research and Information

An important perspective to retain regarding the role of marketing research is that the information a firm gathers cannot be a substitute for judgment in the decision-making processes. Sophisticated data collection methods and data analysis techniques *never* provide marketing decision makers with answers to problems, per se. Rather, information can be used to *enhance* the decision-making and strategy-planning processes. Research information is by no means a guarantee that correct decisions will be made. Consider that American firms did not put the fax machine on the market even though they had the technology to do so because market research convinced them that there was no demand for such a gadget.[7] As a result, not one fax machine offered for sale today is American-made.

The **role of research** in marketing is to aid marketing decision makers in analysis, planning, implementation, and control of all phases of the marketing process. A key element of marketing decision making is risk. Risk is inescapable in the pursuit of the profit reward in the marketplace. Information gathered through research may increase the probability of a successful decision, but the information itself can never completely eliminate the risk involved. Risk may be reduced and, perhaps, better understood but not eliminated.

An important issue related to the role of marketing research is that the information generated *must be used and must be used properly*. Coca-Cola's $4 million investment and two full years of research before its introduction of *New Coke* is infamous. For whatever reason, the information Coca-Cola gathered prior to abandoning *Coke Classic* did not account for consumer reaction. While the company's research showed that most people liked the taste of *New Coke,* this research didn't account for the negative sentiment about changing a 99-year-old product. Translating information into effective action is a fine art. Figure 3-1 depicts the position of marketing research in marketing mix decision making.

Objectives of Marketing Research

So far, we have only described the role and nature of marketing research without understanding the purpose or **objectives of marketing research**. In general, marketing research and information generation will be undertaken to pursue one or more of three basic objectives: planning, problem solving, and control.

Marketing research with a **planning** objective involves taking a long-term perspective and generating information about the broad-based external environmental influences that affect a firm's ability to market products and services successfully. Examples of research with a planning objective are studies of business trends (such as those shown in Table 3-1) and social values. From Chapter 2, the study of fertility rates, home ownership rates, and overall demographic profiles provided in census data are topics researched with a planning objective.

Problem solving is perhaps the most common marketing research objective. As a firm faces a difficult issue in its marketing planning, it will many times turn to research data to specifically address the issue. Another application of problem solving has to do with operating problems that require immediate attention. Clues to their solution may be found in research information. For example, if a firm is experiencing declining market share in a region, factors such as sales force performance or competitors' activities may lead to an understanding of what changes in operations are needed to improve performance. Similarly, when a firm contemplates changing a product's package design, gathering data directly from consumers on their impressions of the proposed changes will be used in making a final decision.

Control as a research objective focuses on monitoring current operations. Even if a firm is not experiencing specific problems, it will want feedback on the status of all phases of its marketing program. A unique value of the control

FIGURE 3-1
Role of Marketing Research in Marketing Decision Making

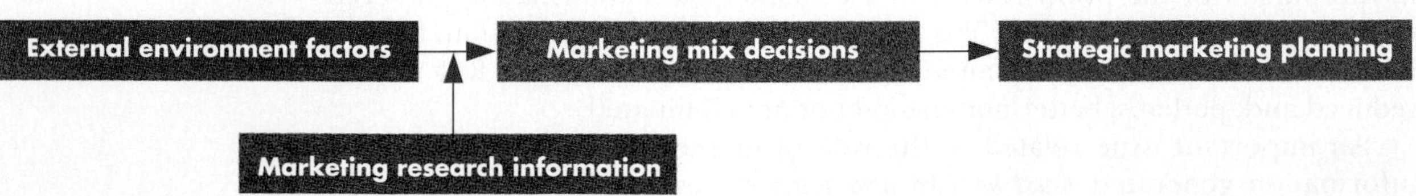

objective is that it allows strategists to more quickly identify problems when they do arise. Further, research focusing on control helps a firm assess its strengths and weaknesses across all types of marketing activities.

TYPES OF RESEARCH INFORMATION

It is important to appreciate the vast array of information available to organizations to pursue research objectives. There are two basic types of research information available to a firm: secondary data and primary data. A wealth of potentially relevant information can be obtained from existing sources. This information is referred to as **secondary data**. Secondary data is information generated for some other purpose (many times by an outside organization) that relates directly to the information needs of the firm. In contrast, **primary data** is information generated by a firm or its research company designed to provide data specific to a firm's current information needs. Such data are generated through marketing research projects, which will be discussed later in the chapter. Secondary data have the distinct advantage of being far less costly to obtain and more immediately available than primary data. Primary data, on the other hand, while almost always more expensive and time consuming to obtain, can be tailored to the current information needs of a firm. We will discuss the nature of primary data and the information it generates later in the chapter when marketing research projects are discussed. At this point, we will turn our attention to the nature and value of secondary data sources.

SECONDARY DATA SOURCES

Secondary data are abundantly available. Before a manager initiates the gathering of primary data, every available source of secondary data should be investigated. The four most prominent and useful sources of secondary data are internal sources, government sources, commercial sources, and professional publications.

Internal Sources

Some of the richest and most valuable data are available within the firm itself and are, therefore, referred to as *internal sources* of secondary data. Customer service records, warranty registration cards, letters from customers, customer complaints, gross sales figures, sales by region, sales by customer type, and the like all provide a wealth of information relating to the proficiency of company marketing practices and, more generally, changing consumer tastes and preferences. Suppliers and distributors also have valuable information about customer and competitor behavior. Finally, managers in the organization may have critical insights about the market and competitors based on past experience. In other words, information about the external environment and feedback about the effectiveness of current marketing strategies may be interpreted from common and readily available information that already exists within a firm.

Government Sources

Various government entities generate statistics on population, housing, transportation, and levels of business activity. Most prominent of the government data sources is the census of population, which has been taken in the United States every ten years since 1790. This is only one of several major government data collection efforts. Table 3-2 gives a partial listing and brief description of censuses and government surveys that are useful sources of secondary data.

Another important government source of secondary data, especially for firms selling in the business market, is the Standard Industrial Classification (SIC). It is prepared by the Bureau of the Budget, Office of Statistical Standards, and classifies types of establishments engaged in extraction, manufacturing, service, and distribution. The coding system divides the nation's businesses into broad industrial categories based on a 2-digit major group, a 3-digit industry subgroup, and a 4-digit detailed industry. Table 3-3 demonstrates how this 2-, 3-, and 4-digit classification scheme would work for classifying a furniture manufacturer. Both products and services are assigned SIC numbers. The SIC number provides uniformity in definitions and, for example, facilitates the use of data for decision making related to market segmentation and target marketing. (The use of SIC classifications for strategic decision making is discussed in Chapter 5.)

The array of published data available regarding consumers and businesses from government sources is a particularly useful starting place for small businesses. Such publications are reasonably current and many are available at public libraries, which enables the small business owner to access large amounts of information at little or no cost.

Commercial Sources

Since information is so valuable for marketing decision making, commercial data services have emerged to provide data of various types. Firms specializing in this sort of information tend to concentrate their data gathering efforts on household consumers. Table 3-4 lists some of the more prominent commercial sources of this information. These sources can provide information that is quite comprehensive and is normally gathered using high-quality research methods; typically, however, the cost of information from these sources is greater than from government sources. But, despite this greater expense, acquiring information from commercial sources is still likely to cost *less* than generating primary data (as you will learn shortly).

Professional Publications

The last type of secondary data source is professional publications, which are periodicals within which professionals with similar interests report significant information related to their fields. In marketing, there are several academic, trade, and general business publications that carry research studies and industry statistics that can be valuable sources of secondary data. It may be that precisely the information a firm needs has been reported in a recent academic, trade, or general business publication. Table 3-5 lists some of these publications. Failure to explore this resource before initiating original data collection is an untenable oversight.

TABLE 3-2
Government Sources of Secondary Data

Government Data Source	Type of Information
Census of population	This counts the population of the nation. Information can be obtained for the nation as a whole or by state, city, county, or region. Different volumes identify the citizenry by age, sex, income, race, marital status, and other demographic features. Published every ten years in years ending with a "zero."
Census of housing	Housing units are described on the basis of size, number of inhabitants, type of fuel used, number and type of major appliances, and condition and value of structures. Major urban areas are broken down by city block. Published every ten years in years ending with a "zero."
Census of manufacturers	Identifies manufacturing facilities based on output, value added, number of employees, wages, sales, and utility consumption. Census is taken every five years in years ending with "2" and "7."
Census of retail trade	Provides detailed information on retail activity including number of retail outlets, total sales and employment. Published in years ending in "2" and "7." Statistics are available for relatively small geographic areas such as counties and cities.
Census of wholesale trade	Defines wholesalers by 150 different categories. It contains information on functions performed, warehouse space, expenses, and sales volume. Census is taken every five years in years ending with "2" and"7."
Census of service industries	Identifies service providers by category and geographic area and indicates sales, employment, and number of units. Census is taken in years ending in "2" and "7."
Census of transportation	Identifies usage of three major transportation modes: passenger, truck, and bus. Twenty-four thousand households were surveyed in 1977 and information includes number of trips, number of persons taking trips, duration, means of travel, and destination. Census is taken in years ending in "2" and "7."
Survey of current business	Published monthly by the Bureau of Economic Analysis of the Department of Commerce. It provides information on general business indicators, real estate activity, commodity prices, personal consumption expenditures, and income and employment by industry. There are twenty-six hundred different series in the survey, most of which contain data on the last four years.

PROBLEMS WITH SECONDARY DATA

As advantageous as secondary data can be, they are not perfect. While these data can be diverse, comprehensive, and relatively easy to access, secondary

TABLE 3-3
Example of Standard Industrial Classification (SIC)

Category	Code	Title
Major group	25	Furniture and fixtures
Industry subgroup	251	Household furniture
Detailed industry	2511	Wood household furniture

TABLE 3-4
Commercial Sources of Secondary Data

Commercial Information Source	Type of Information
Dun and Bradstreet Market Identifiers	DMI is a listing of 4.3 million businesses that is updated monthly. Information includes number of employees, relevant SIC codes that relate to the businesses' activities, location, and chief executive. Marketing and advertising managers can use the information to identify markets, build mailing lists, and specify media to reach an organization.
Neilsen Retail Index	Neilsen auditors collect product inventory turnover data from 1,600 grocery stores, 750 drug stores, and 150 mass merchandise outlets. Information is also gathered on retail prices, in-store displays, and local advertising. Data from the index is available by store type and geographic location.
SAMI/Burke	The SAMI report is similar to the Neilsen index except that sales volume figures are based on warehouse withdrawals rather than retail sales. Furthermore, SAMI/Burke data track only food operators but do include all forms of grocery operations including "mom and pop" stores. Samscan is SAMI/Burke service that uses supermarket scanner data.
National Purchase Diary Panel	With over 13,000 families participating NPD is the largest diary panel in the United States. Families record on preprinted sheets their monthly purchases in 50 product categories. Information recorded includes, brand, amount purchased, price paid, use of coupons, store, specific version of the product (flavor, scent, etc.), and intended use.
Starch Advertisement Readership	The Starch service tracks readership of over 70,000 advertisements appearing in 1,000 consumer, farm publications, newspapers, and business periodicals. Over 100,000 personal interviews are conducted each year to determine the readership of the ads. Starch uses a "recognition" approach, which rates each ad on the extent of readership it was able to stimulate. Data on headlines, copy, and other components of an ad are also recorded.
Neilsen Television Index	The index provides estimates of the size and characteristics of the audience for television programs. Data is gathered through an electronic device attached to participating households' television sets. The device records the times the TV is on and to what channel it is tuned. Reports on viewership are published biweekly.
Consumer Mail Panel	This panel is operated by a firm called Market Facts, Inc. There are 45,000 active participants at any point in time. Samples are drawn in lots of 1,000. The overall panel is representative of different geographic regions in the U.S. and Canada, it is broken down by household income, urbanization, and age of respondent. Data are provided on demographic and socioeconomic characteristics as well as type of dwelling and ownership of durable goods.
Information Resources, Inc.	One of the leading organizations in "single source" research where all phases of a consumer's media exposure and, ultimately, purchase behavior are tracked. This firm is also recognized for its research on the impact of grocery store promotions (PromotioScan) and coupon redemption research.

TABLE 3-5
Professional Publications Containing Secondary Data

Academic Publications	Trade Publications	General Business Publications
Journal of Advertising	*Marketing News*	*Forbes*
Journal of Advertising Research	*Advertising Age*	*Fortune*
Journal of Marketing	*Chain Store Age*	*The Wall Street Journal*
Journal of Marketing Research	*Progressive Grocer Stores*	*Barrons*
Journal of Consumer Research	*Sales and Marketing Management*	*Investors Daily*
Harvard Business Review	*INFOWORLD*	*Business Week*
Journal of Health Care Marketing	*Individual Industry Trade Associations*	
Sloan Management Review		

data can occasionally be poorly suited for decision making for several key reasons:

- The information is out of date.
- The data are expressed in categories that aren't useful. For example, a firm may be interested in the total number of women in a geographic area between the ages of 18 and 25. Published secondary data may provide statistics on women who are less than 18 and from 19 to 29 years of age. This would leave the decision maker without the needed information.
- The unit of measurement may be different than the unit required for analysis. For example, secondary data sources may report income figures for individuals, families, households, or spending units in Ameri-

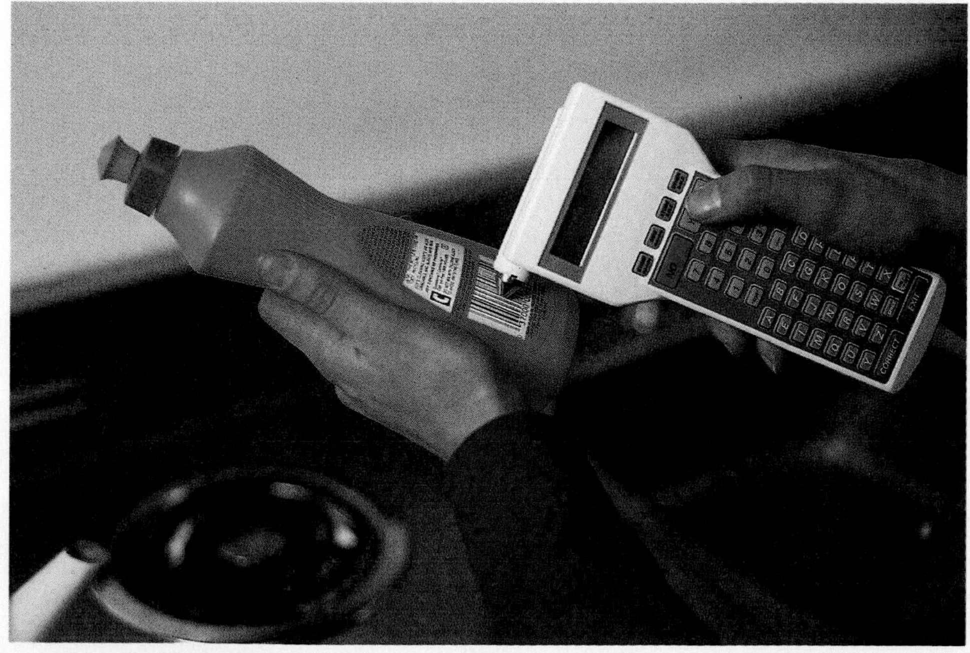

Home scanners are used by commercial research agencies to gather data on household product purchases.

can dollars, but how the firm needs the information is in German Marks.

- The source of the data may not be objective. Industry trade associations may generate and report data that make the industry look good, for example.

Generating and Managing Information: The Marketing Information System

Information in today's complex business environment is looked upon as a critical resource much like human resources (labor), capital (land, equipment, and buildings), and financial resources. This view of information as a resource means that, like other resources, information must be developed and managed. The need for information development and management in an organized and ongoing fashion has given rise to the marketing information system.

A **marketing information system (MkIS)** is a structured, interactive complex of people and machines designed to generate pertinent data on an ongoing basis from sources within and outside of the firm to aid in marketing decision making. The information generated and managed in an MkIS will be used both for current decision making and future planning.

Figure 3-2 illustrates a basic MkIS system. Note that the system begins with the identification of information sources and progresses through the use of that information to achieve important decision-making results for the organization. At this point, we will consider each phase of a typical MkIS and how it is managed to benefit marketing decision making and strategic planning within an organization.

Information Sources

Useful and pertinent information can be generated as input to an MkIS from a variety of sources. *Internal company records and activities* and *environmental scanning systems* provide the secondary data inputs to the MkIS. Within a firm that maintains an MkIS, staff will be assigned to scan data from secondary sources to identify information relevant to the firm's marketing activities. Critical to the information input to an MkIS are marketing research projects. **Marketing research projects** are those efforts by a firm to generate primary data suited to the unique information needs of decision makers. Marketing research projects, as depicted in Figure 3-2, represent a major information source. Research projects can provide the most detailed and organization-specific data that decision makers will have available. Procedures for conducting marketing research projects will be discussed in more detail later in this chapter.

Information Generated

The second phase of the MkIS, as depicted in Figure 3-2, is the specification of what type of information should be generated from secondary and primary

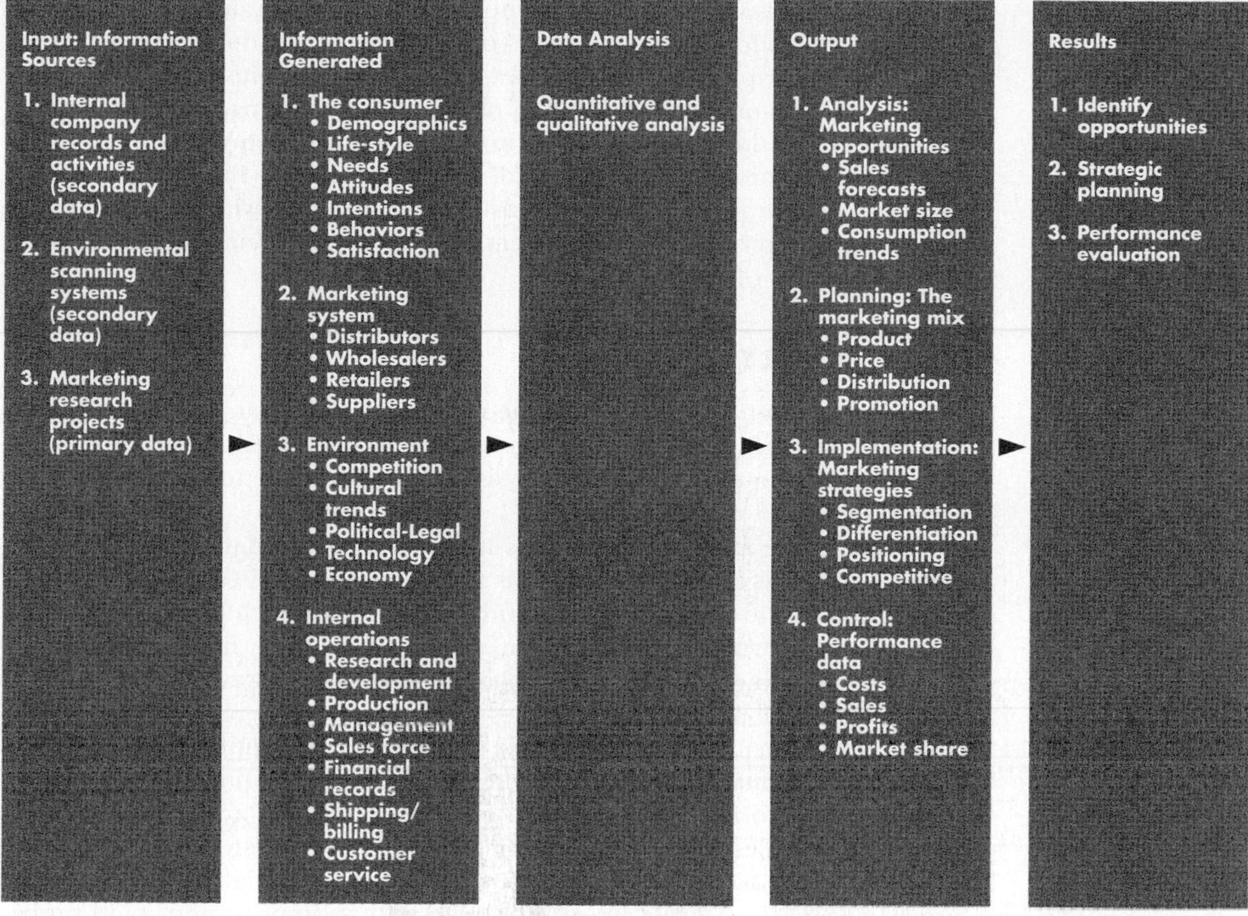

FIGURE 3-2
The Marketing Information System (MkIS)

data sources. Information about *consumers* is the crux of pertinent information. Whether a firm is selling to household consumers or is marketing to businesses, the goal of successfully and competitively providing satisfaction in the marketplace requires an understanding of consumers. Figure 3-2 identifies the types of information about consumers that firms typically find useful.

Feedback about the marketplace performance of products and services is available from the *marketing systems* employed by a firm. Distributors, wholesalers, retailers, and suppliers have direct contact with customers and competitors and can provide information that in many instances would otherwise be unobtainable. When Black & Decker was developing its *Quantum* line of power tools, the firm turned to retailers like Home Depot, Lowe's, and Wal-Mart to discover what do-it-yourselfers were looking for in moderately priced power tools.[8]

Environmental influences tracked by environmental scanning systems are factors that can affect both routine marketing activities as well as long-term planning. As we saw in Chapter 2, changes in the external environment require a response from the organization in order to produce products and services that are both satisfying to the market and competitive.

Information generated regarding *internal operations* often alerts decision makers to both problems and opportunities. As the research and development department makes new discoveries, these can be incorporated into marketing planning. Sales force performance (overall and by product line, customer group, or geographic region) provides a basis for competitive product performance. The customer service section of internal operations at Dell Computer provides one of the major sources of input to Dell's marketing information system. Even the production activities of the firm relate to marketing decision making because product design must be coordinated with manufacturing capability and production costs affect pricing strategy, margins, and profitability.

DATA ANALYSIS

Once information is generated in the relevant areas, it can be subjected to a variety of analyses. Depending upon the type of data obtained, firms can use quantitative or qualitative data analysis techniques to better understand the information.

Quantitative analysis emphasizes inspection of the data using statistical techniques. The quantitative analysis techniques listed in Table 3-6 allow a decision maker to manipulate data and try to gain as much insight as possible by viewing information in different ways. Quantitative methods have the advantage of being objective and unbiased (They may, however, be interpreted in a biased fashion). These techniques can identify subtle relationships within bodies of data that nonstatistical inspection would not identify.

Qualitative analysis of data is used when the information is generated in nonnumerical form. For example, if in-depth interviews are conducted with consumers or salespeople and the data are provided in the form of audiotaped interviews, then by necessity a more interpretive form of data analysis must be used. In some cases, firms receive information that simply cannot (and probably should not) be converted to numerical form. During the development of the *Quantum* line, Black & Decker marketing executives watched consumers use power tools, followed them to hardware stores, and asked why they liked and disliked the tools they were using. Under these conditions, analysts use their judgment and experience to interpret the data. Guidelines and methods are available for such qualitative analysis methods and interpretation.[9] Qualitative studies are often undertaken to establish a foundation for subsequent quantitative research.

TABLE 3-6
Commonly Applied Quantitative Methods in the Analysis of Marketing Data

Descriptive Analyses	Tests for Differences	Prediction and Data Reduction Analyses	Tests for Association
Frequencies (means)	Chi-square	Cluster analysis	Correlation analyses
Cross tabulation	t-test	Conjoint analysis	Regression analyses
	Analysis of variance	Discriminant analysis	
		Factor Analysis	
		Path Analysis	

While quantitative data analysis has been the hallmark of marketing research and marketing information systems, more open-ended research methods and qualitative interpretation are gaining in popularity.[10] Researchers are beginning to realize the drawbacks of quantitative techniques, which restrict respondents' answers to only those questions asked. The open-ended nature of qualitative methods lets respondents determine what is and is not important about an area of inquiry. One company using qualitative methods is American Express. The firm's president of financial services has said, "the survey can become a self-fulfilling prophecy. Open-ended questions allow customers to tell you something that is not on your list.[11]

OUTPUT

The output of an MkIS allows marketing decision makers to effectively engage in analysis, planning, implementation, and control of the activities in the marketing function. After data analysis, *analysis of market opportunities* based on the inspection of the data can be considered. With the data and its interpretation in hand, marketing decision makers can produce sales forecasts, identify and predict consumption trends, estimate present and future market size, and generally plan marketing strategies. When managers at Wendy's International examine daily receipts from the firm's nearly 1000 hamburger outlets, they can identify trends in menu items ordered by customers in different geographic regions. This information is then used to adjust inventory levels, shipping schedules, and to contemplate changes in the firm's pricing and promotional strategies. *Planning the marketing mix* is heavily dependent on MkIS output. Detecting changes in competitors' activities or customer buying habits allows the firm to adjust the four Ps accordingly for greater efficiency and effectiveness. At Pizza Hut, the carry-out and delivery outlets keep a data bank on each customer's order patterns. This allows the firm to target special promotions to customers who prefer large pizzas or regularly order multiple toppings, for example.[12]

Implementation of marketing strategy is aided by the readily available information from an MkIS. Successfully segmenting a market and positioning a brand within the market are essential marketing strategy decisions that can be severely compromised without current and pertinent information. The subtle nuances of the marketplace are too complex to fully understand without the aid of information. Procter & Gamble decided that the success of the *Cover Girl* line of makeup was diminishing. The line had been promoted for years to teenagers as "the makeup models use." Procter & Gamble decided to reposition the line to appeal to baby boomers concerned about wrinkles. The packages were redesigned, advertising was increased, and the research department set about developing a new line of skin care products.[13]

Finally, *control* is pursued through the use of various data outputs related to *performance data.* Monitoring internal operations provides cost information from production and measures of sales force success. Data related to the activities of retailers and wholesalers in the marketing system will furnish revenue numbers through which profitability can be calculated. Finally, an estimate of market share—that relative view of product sales compared to competition—can be calculated. Market share analysis is essential. Some firms have discovered, for example, that despite a 15 percent increase in product sales on an absolute basis, a product has actually lost market share during a period. This means that the overall market (and the competitors' sales) have grown even more. Information like this may signal trouble for a product.

RESULTS

The results of a well-operated MkIS should contribute to more effective marketing management decisions: identifying opportunities, strategic planning, and performance evaluation. *Identifying opportunities* in the market for introducing new products or cultivating new segments for existing products will affect the growth of a firm's revenues (recall, from Chapter 1, that this is the overall goal of the marketing function). *Strategic planning* of marketing mix variables and specific marketing strategies can be more quickly and astutely assessed with the aid of an MkIS. Finally, *performance evaluation* of the marketing system can be carried out with the aid of hard information.

INTERPRETATION AND APPLICATION

Until very recently, spread sheets and statistical reports were the only ways interpretation and application of data generation could be carried out. Analysts would pour over these reports and, combined with their background and experience, draw conclusions that would lead to marketing strategies. For many firms, this type of analysis will continue to be used. But technological advances have provided new and insightful ways to interpret the data generated by in an MkIS. One such advance is referred to as the *Geographic Information System (GIS)*. Firms like Cigna Insurance, Sears, Super Valu Stores, and The

A Geographic Information System (GIS), like this one used by Sylvania, help firms organize and interpret data from marketing information systems.

Gap now take demographic, economic, competitive, and internal corporate data and feed this data into software that converts it into digitized maps of geographic areas.[14] Theses maps, often displayed on giant screens, can help firms to visualize aspects of the market that traditional output methods fail to highlight. For example, Sylvania can present a distributor with a demographic map of the store's clientele within a ten-mile radius, color coded to indicate different bulb-buying behavior. Such GISs can be used for site location studies, sales staff support, fleet management, and other strategic planning elements related to the marketing mix. The advantage of the GIS over traditional output is that it can increase the probability that available information will get used.

Overall, an MkIS is designed to provide marketing decision makers with the information necessary to understand the nature of the market and to fulfill the responsibilities of the marketing function in discovering opportunities for revenue generation. Armed with current and reliable information, decision makers can construct an effective and efficient marketing program for the firm.

GENERATING PRIMARY DATA: THE MARKETING RESEARCH PROJECT

As Figure 3-2 indicates, one of the basic information inputs to an MkIS is primary data generated through marketing research projects initiated by a firm. In many ways, primary data are the most important data a firm can have. This is because marketing research projects generate data that are tailored specifically to a current and specific information need. When secondary data sources do not provide sufficient information, then many times a marketing research project is launched.

A **marketing research project** is defined as the generation, analysis, and interpretation of primary data from household consumers, business buyers, or members of the marketing system with the purpose of providing information for marketing decision making. Firms often do not carry out their own marketing research projects. The highly specialized skills needed to generate primary data often require the services of outside research organizations such as those listed in Table 3-4. Whether a firm has the resources to conduct its own research projects or enlists a specialty research house, a methodical, systematic approach to the project is essential. Such care is needed because marketing research projects must provide data that have reliability and validity. **Reliability** means that the information generated is accurate and that the research methods used to generate the information were not biased. A research project with high reliability would produce similar results if the study were repeated. **Validity** means that the information generated is relevant to the research questions being investigated. Another way of describing validity is to say that the "right" information was generated. To help ensure reliability and validity, a marketing research project has six steps: problem formulation, research design, sample selection, data collection, data analysis, and the research report. Figure 3-3 shows the flow of these stages. Because of the importance and complexity of marketing research projects, the proper procedures for generating information are discussed in detail now.

FIGURE 3-3
Stages in a Marketing Research Project

PROBLEM FORMULATION

Problem formulation is a statement of the purpose of a marketing research project. The purpose of the research should be stated as specifically as possible. Vague and general problem formulations will likely result in inefficiency throughout a project. Without specific direction and purpose, research projects waste time and money and can produce unusable information. For example, a problem formulation that states that a research project will be designed to "investigate the decline in sales in territory A" is not nearly as specific as stating "the performance of salespeople and competitors' activities will be investigated to determine the effect these factors are having on sales in territory A." The latter problem formulation is more specific and will direct resources for the research project more efficiently and effectively.

RESEARCH DESIGN

This stage of the marketing research project involves setting up procedures to address the research questions raised in the problem formulation. The **research design** specifies the variables that are of interest, the exact data to be collected, the sample from which the data will be gathered, the data collection methods, and the types of analyses that will be conducted. In general, the research design is the blueprint researchers will follow to carry out a project.

SAMPLE SELECTION

Sample selection is a specification of the respondents from whom data will be gathered. Since it is not feasible to gather information from every consumer or even every member of the marketing system, a sample is selected to represent the market under study. The primary issues in sample selection are *sample size* and *sample representativeness.* The issue of sample size tends to be misunderstood. Certain types of marketing research require very large samples in order to assure accuracy. Consumer panels that track product use and brand choice may maintain samples as large as 15,000 households. Complex research questions and diverse populations from which data are being gathered require large samples. Conversely, research projects with very narrowly defined research questions that rely on data from very homogeneous populations may use extremely small samples and still achieve a high degree of accuracy. The point to appreciate is that sample size requirements increase as the relevant population to be researched and the breadth of the research questions increase. Small samples can be as accurate as large samples. Therefore, the potential accuracy and usefulness of data should not be judged simply by the size of the sample.

Another key issue in sample selection is that the sample must be representative of the population of interest. We often hear about a *random sample* being used in a research study. The value of a random sample is that the researcher does not impose a personal bias on who will or will not participate in the study.

Selecting respondents for a research project in a random fashion does not ensure representativeness, however. The real issue related to representativeness has to do with choosing a sample of respondents from whom pertinent information can be obtained. In many cases, pertinent information will come from a particular segment of the population that constitutes either the current target market for a product or a segment that is being considered for targeting. This being the case, marketing researchers often can forgo the strict rigors of random sampling and rely on methods of nonrandom sampling such as convenience samples, judgment samples, or quota samples.

Answering the question of representativeness often rests with the researcher's judgment. The important point is that the sample is representative of the population on those factors specified in the problem formulation. A sample of women from a church group and another sample of women from a local PTA, for instance, may be representative of various types of women and their hair-care problems. As such, a firm interested in studying the problems women are having with hair-care products could derive an adequate and representative sample from such relatively small and nonrandom groups.

DATA COLLECTION

Data collection is the physical gathering of data through contact with respondents. Data collection is initiated after a relevant sample is selected. The five common methods for collecting primary data are surveys, experiments, focus groups, observation, and naturalistic inquiry. The most difficult tasks at the data collection stage are careful training and monitoring of staff involved in the data collection process. Poorly trained and inexperienced staff can introduce biases into the data collection process that will be manifest in inaccurate data. It is essential that a firm either carefully train its in-house staff or request complete information about staff training from the outside supplier commissioned to gather data.

Surveys

Information from surveys is collected by asking a sample of respondents questions about a variety of issues related to product or service choice and use. The areas of interest to marketers (and examples of questions in each area) that affect all areas of marketing decision making are questions concerning:

- Current states (e.g., what is your age?)
- Past behavior (e.g., what brand of catsup did you last purchase?)
- Knowledge and awareness (e.g., what brands of VCR have you seen advertised in the last six weeks?)
- Attitude (e.g., do you feel U.S.-made products are as high in quality as foreign-made products?)
- Intentions (e.g., do you plan to purchase an automobile in the next year?)

Structured questions like these are asked by using a questionnaire. The way a respondent answers can vary depending on the type of question asked. If a respondent is asked simply, "What attributes are most important to you in your choice of a grocery store?" this would allow the respondent to answer in an **open-ended** fashion. On the other hand, if the same question were asked,

"Please indicate whether each of the following attributes that describe grocery stores is (a) not important, (b) somewhat important, or (c) very important to you in the choice of a grocery store: prices, freshness of the produce, location, cleanliness of the store," this approach would constrain the respondent to a **closed-ended** set of ratings. Figure 3-4 is an example of a well-designed survey used by United Airlines that uses exclusively closed-ended questions.

FIGURE 3-4
Survey Used by United Airlines

Survey Questions

1. How many round trips have you taken during the past 12 months on all airlines?_________

2. What is your main reason for not participating in Mileage Plus? (Please check one.)
- ❑ A. I no longer fly frequently.
- ❑ B. I fly United frequently, but am unsure how to receive credit for my flights.
- ❑ C. I do not recall becoming a member of Mileage Plus.
- ❑ D. It's more convenient for me to fly a different airline.
- ❑ E. I prefer another airline's frequent flier program.

(Please continue only if you checked items D or E above.)

3. Please check the one airline you fly most frequently.
- ❑ A. American
- ❑ B. Delta
- ❑ C. TWA
- ❑ D. US Air
- ❑ E. Northwest
- ❑ F. Continental
- ❑ G. Other

4. For what reasons do you prefer to fly this carrier? (Check all that apply.)
- ❑ A. More convenient schedule or route structure.
- ❑ B. Lower airfares.
- ❑ C. Better customer service by employees.
- ❑ D. Better inflight service from flight attendants.
- ❑ E. More comfort inflight.
- ❑ F. Superior on-time departure performance.
- ❑ G. Greater arrival time reliability.
- ❑ H. Better baggage handling.
- ❑ I. Faster processing time at airports.
- ❑ J. Better club rooms.
- ❑ K. Better frequent flier program.

(Please answer the following question only if you checked item K.)

5. In what ways is the other frequent flier program better? (Please check all that apply.)
- ❑ A. Easier for me to track my miles for the flights I've taken.
- ❑ B. Recording mileage is easy, no need for flight cards.
- ❑ C. More accurate and reliable at posting flight credit.
- ❑ D. More recognition for frequent fliers.
- ❑ E. Offers better awards.
- ❑ F. Prefer their program partner airlines.
- ❑ G. Prefer their program partner hotels or car rental agencies.
- ❑ H. Easier/quicker to earn awards.
- ❑ I. Easier to understand program, better communication.
- ❑ J. Offers awards based on segments. rather than mileage flown.

Thank you for completing this survey. Please return this form in the enclosed postage-paid envelope.

Source: Reprinted with permission.

Closed-ended survey questions have the advantage of being easy to analyze and relatively quick to administer. Unfortunately, the closed-ended approach may constrain the respondents' answers to such a degree that the true issues underlying choice go undetected. Open-ended survey questions are more difficult to analyze and more time consuming to administer, but they do allow respondents to express their own views about what is important.

Surveys are regularly used by firms to monitor operations and identify new product opportunities. Surveys allow the customization of data generation according to a firm's current information needs. Surveys are also easy to administer and large amounts of data can be gathered in a short time.

Finally, a critical issue in the survey approach to data collection is the way data are gathered. Several choices are available: mail, telephone, and mall-intercept surveys. Gathering data with a *mail survey* allows a firm to gather large amounts of data at relatively low cost. Disadvantages of mail surveys are low response rates, the respondents' inability to ask for clarification of questions, and no assurance that the appropriate people complete the survey. *Telephone surveys* improve on some of the disadvantages of the mail survey by allowing the respondent to ask questions, the response rate can be improved, and data is generally gathered more quickly. The disadvantages of using the telephone are limits on the time of the interview, limits on the complexity of questions that can be asked, and interviewer bias introduced by the manner (and tone) in which questions are asked. Finally, the *mall-intercept survey* has become popular over the last ten years. Unfortunately, this method is fraught with serious problems. In this method, interviewers are stationed in shopping malls and "intercept" shoppers to administer a survey. First, interviewers tend to be poorly trained and poorly compensated. Second, shoppers may be averse to having their shopping experience disrupted. Third, mall-intercept interviewers may introduce a bias into the survey by approaching only those people who they feel comfortable in stopping. Finally, the survey is necessarily short to allow shoppers to get on with their business in the mall. In all, data gathered using the mall-intercept method is subject to a variety of threats to validity and reliability. The technique has become popular because of its low cost, but this is not a compelling reason for its use.

Experiments

An **experiment** is considered by many to be the most powerful form of data collection because it presents the opportunity to investigate potential *causes* of behaviors and beliefs. The distinguishing feature of experiments is that a researcher can manipulate variables to identify the effect of different factors on behaviors or beliefs. Unfortunately, conducting experiments in marketing is difficult due to the complexities of the external environment and the many interactions between factors that affect consumer behavior.

Experiments can be conducted in either a laboratory or in the field. Having a group of people enter a controlled environment to compare the taste of two new cake mix products and then asking them to rate each on different features like taste and moistness would be an experiment in a laboratory. The problem with laboratory experiments, however, is that it is difficult to judge whether the results obtained in an artificial setting will hold true in the real world. In a field experiment researchers would manipulate variables in a real setting to see what effect they have. For example, a researcher could change the shelf position of a product in a grocery store (from eye level to knee level, for example) and monitor sales of the product at the different positions for a two-week period. If significantly more units are sold while the product is on one shelf position than on the other, the conclusion would be that shelf position is one of the causes of a difference in sales. The potential problems with this experiment are obvious. The researcher cannot control a variety of other factors that might have caused the change in sales (for example, competitors' activities or store traffic during the experimental period).

Only under certain conditions do experiments represent good data collection opportunities in marketing. When conditions are correct, however, data from experiments can be extremely informative because of the unique cause and effect nature of the data interpretation possibilities.

Focus Groups

"Six people sitting around a table eating pizza is a party. Six people sitting around a table talking about eating pizza as market researchers watch through a one-way mirror is a focus group."[15] While this is a facetious description of focus group methodology, it is actually quite accurate. The **focus group** method of data collection brings together from 6 to 15 respondents who represent individuals the firm feels hold valuable information. In some cases, the group is asked open-ended questions about product choice criteria or use behavior, and the discussion is directed by a focus group leader. In other cases, the group may be asked to test a product (either a real product or a prototype) and the groups' reactions are audio- and videotaped for analysis. Participants are paid from $35 to $150 for their time.

The Buick Division of General Motors used focus groups to help develop the *Regal* two-door, six-passenger coupe. Twenty focus groups were held across the country and each was asked what features customers wanted in a new car. What researchers found was that customers wanted a legitimate back seat, at least 20 miles per gallon in gas mileage, and 0–60 miles-per-hour acceleration in less than 11 seconds. They wanted a stylish car, but they didn't want it to look like it "had just landed from outer space."[16] Buick engineers then set about the task of creating clay models and went back to another focus group to refine the design. Additional focus groups were then used to develop advertising for the newly created car.

For the focus group to be successful, the focus group leader (or facilitator) must be highly expert in guiding the group to useful discussions. In many cases, a particularly opinionated participant can bias the group discussion. Focus groups need to be conducted carefully and the data need to be used in the appropriate fashion.

Observation

Observation is distinguished as a data collection method in that a researcher does not communicate directly with respondents through a survey or interview but rather simply observes the behavior of individuals.

Observation can be *direct,* such as watching people in a consumption setting (like a supermarket) and recording their activities. How long do people hesitate in front of a shelf before making a purchase? What percentage of shoppers read the package contents before they purchase? Or, in an innovative approach, researchers have studied garbage in various neighborhoods to identify both categories of consumption and brand choice. Direct observation research is the most simplified and traditional version of this technique.

Recently, observation has gained much greater sophistication through the use of *indirect* observation techniques. With the advent of universal product codes (UPC) on product packages and the proliferation of cable television, research firms are now able to engage in single source research and observe the behavior of individuals and households indirectly by tracking behavior from the television set to the checkout counter.[17] **Single source research** gathers information about brand purchases, coupon use, and television advertising exposure from individual households by combining grocery store scanner data and devices attached to households' televisions, which monitor viewing behavior. Such observation data is being used to measure the effect of advertising and promotions on consumer brand purchases. Firms like Information Resources Inc., Arbitron, and Neilsen offer single source research services.

Indirect observation methods provide enormous amounts of data. However, reflective of the problem with observation data in general is the following confusing discovery made by Campbell Soup while using this method. Campbell found that viewers of the daytime serial *Search for Tomorrow* bought 27 percent more spaghetti sauce and 22 percent less *V-8 Juice* than the average household. Furthermore, viewers of another daytime serial, *All My Children*, purchased 46 percent *more V-8 Juice* than the average household. These results were highly significant statistically, but what could they possibly mean?

Herein lies the problem with data gathered through observation. Researchers can obtain objective data through observation, but the interpretation of that data is often difficult if not totally mystifying. Without communicating directly with respondents, it is not possible to probe for reasons *why* people behave the way they do. Researchers are forced to speculate about what odd combination of influences might explain results. Such was the challenge facing Campbell with the spaghetti sauce and *V-8 Juice* data.

Naturalistic Inquiry

Over the past several years, some marketing researchers have begun to question the sufficiency of traditional methods of marketing research and the data collection techniques just discussed. Issues have been raised regarding the so-called positivist (i.e., highly structured and quantitative) approach to data collection.[18] A *positivist* approach uses methods of natural science (that is, traditional scientific methods) to study phenomena. Surveys, experiments, and, to a lesser degree, observation techniques are deterministic and statistical and presume that human behaviors have a universal nature. The positivist, deterministic approach has been alleged to be problematic in research dealing with household consumers and has given rise to a variety of alternative methods.

Naturalistic inquiry is one of these alternative approaches. **Naturalistic inquiry** is described as "a more encompassing, new 'paradigm of thought and belief that draws upon substantive (rather than merely methodological) vanguard ideas from a wide variety of disciplines'."[19] When using this method, researchers do not begin the research using any particular theoretical premise within which respondents are confined. Rather, the data collection method uses qualitative techniques (such as videotape, audiotape, and photographs) to study an issue holistically. This method is felt to hold great potential for the advancement of information gathering in marketing. In reference to a recent major research effort using naturalistic inquiry, an advertising executive wrote, "The [research] turned out to be useful in the very best sense. One cannot read this volume without learning something about how real consumers make decisions about what to buy."[20]

DATA ANALYSIS

The methods of data analysis discussed in the section describing an MkIS are applicable to the data analysis stage of a marketing research project as well. Primary data generated through surveys, experiments, and observation are particularly well suited to the quantitative techniques listed in Table 3-6. When data are generated in numerical form, analysis usually starts with the descriptive methods that seek information related to who, what, where, when, how, and how often (frequencies analysis). From this basic look at the data, cross tabulation of variables is often the next useful step. From this point, additional analyses for differences or associations between variables many times depends on the sophistication of the marketing decision makers. The same is true for the even more complex techniques of discriminant analysis, factor analysis, and cluster analysis.

It is important to recognize that all of these quantitative data analysis techniques can provide a statistical test of significance, which may be important to the interpretation of the data. For example, a test that indicates that the mean response to one variable is significantly different statistically from the mean response to another variable at the ".05 level" means that the probability that the result is random (rather than real) is less than 5 percent. This can be a great aid to the decision maker in classifying what information is important and what is not. It does not mean, however, that statistical significance is a panacea for all data interpretation. Again, the ability to gain knowledge from data still depends on the decision maker's judgment.

Qualitative methods of data analysis are particularly useful when focus groups or naturalistic inquiry methods have been used as the data collection techniques. Because these techniques rely on more broad-based and open-ended methods for recording data, then a more interpretative (rather than statistical) approach to data analysis is appropriate. Again, there are well documented procedures for qualitative data analysis.

PREPARING THE RESEARCH REPORT

The final stage in the research project is preparing a **research report**. Uppermost in preparing the report is considering the audience to whom the information and its interpretation will be delivered. The purpose of a research report is to convey to the reader in a clear and explicit manner the findings and implications of the research project.

The report must present both the strong and weak points of the research. The researcher has an obligation to recognize and identify unanswered questions in the research project. The report is basically an outline and discussion of all the stages of the research project beginning with a well-articulated statement of purpose through a discussion of data analysis techniques and interpretation of results. The researcher must also be able communicate the findings effectively to managers. Many managers are only minimally versed in research methods and are interested in the "meaning" of the results.

Marketing Research: A Global Perspective

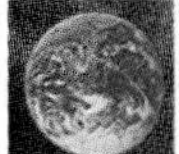

Information generation and use in the global marketplace presents unique challenges. The need for highly structured procedures and accurate information remains the same, but the context for generating that information changes. The differences in information generation and use through marketing research will be considered from a global perspective.

THE IMPORTANCE OF RESEARCH FOR GLOBAL MARKETING DECISIONS

In the decades immediately following the end of World War II, companies very often became involved with foreign markets via indirect exports, that is, filling unsolicited orders from abroad through their domestic sales organization.[21] As a consequence, international marketing research seldom needed to go beyond gathering the basics in terms of the information that was necessary to operate abroad: identifying acceptable shipping agents, bankers, insurance agents, and importers. The period from the 1960s through the 1980s witnessed a tremendous increase in the growth and activities of multinational corporations and a more deliberate focus on foreign markets. This necessitated more contact with foreign markets and a greater degree of control over operations abroad. The diversity of environments in which companies operated, coupled with the differences in marketing infrastructures that were encountered, subsequently led to an increase in the importance of gathering marketing information for strategic and tactical decision making.

Currently, large multinationals tend to view the entire world as their market. Small- and medium-sized companies everywhere feel competition from abroad, while at the same time they are becoming more and more aware of their own opportunities to export, forge joint ventures, and develop their own global niches. Consumer markets are rapidly expanding in Asia, South America, and eastern Europe. Many of the tariff and trade barriers that have hindered the flow of goods and services throughout the industrialized and industrializing world are disappearing, and new opportunities for business and consumer markets will open up. The growth of these activities serve to underscore the importance of the role of marketing research in the global context. Simply put, the tremendous competition, diversity, and complexity of the international environment increase the amount of risk inherent in the decision-making process. As stated earlier in this chapter, research provides information about the environment and generates increased understanding and the ability to cope effectively with market complexities.

THE PROCESS OF RESEARCH IN GLOBAL MARKETING STRATEGY

The *fundamental* principles and objectives of marketing research for the activities related to planning, problem solving, and control remain the same, regardless of whether the context is domestic or international. Furthermore, gathering information from secondary and primary data sources remains useful for international marketing as well. However, strategic decision making in international markets is more likely to rely heavily on secondary data sources and on management experience accumulated through operating in different countries and market environments. In terms of primary data collection, research conducted in international markets poses a number of conceptual and operational problems that do not arise, or at least not in the same magnitude, in domestic marketing research. The remaining sections in this chapter examine the types of information and the means of gathering it that can aid in developing international marketing strategies. In addition, issues relating to problem formulation, analyses, and interpretation are discussed, along with some examples of the types of mistakes that can be made due to either *missing* important sources of information or *mis-using* information that has been gathered.

Multicountry Operations

Having marketing operations in many countries implies that in addition to basic decisions relating to the countries' marketing mix, there must also be decisions relating to the *multicountry* aspects of operations. Typical issues that would require current and relevant information include: decisions relating to which countries to enter and when, how to schedule market entry, and whether to pursue similar target markets in each country. This can be more complex than it sounds, since it may be necessary to make decisions that involve a number of countries simultaneously, rather than on a country-by-country basis.

A recent example comes from a joint venture between Coca-Cola, the world's largest soft drink manufacturer, and Switzerland's Nestle, the world's largest food company. By combining Nestle's well-known trademarks with Coca-Cola's massive global distribution system, the joint venture will allow the new operating unit to bring coffee and tea products to worldwide markets much faster than either company could do alone. However, since Nestle's product offerings meet with varying degrees of success in different markets, and Coca-Cola's distribution networks are better established in some countries than in others, information regarding the timing and execution of marketing the new products will require careful analysis. For example, test marketing of Nestle's *Mocha Cooler* (a combination of coffee, chocolate, and milk in a can) and Nestle's iced coffee show strong appeal to younger consumers in the United States as an alternative to mineral water and fruit juices (typically sold in retail supermarkets). In northern Europe, the cultural values and social rituals regarding the drinking of coffee are deeply embedded, and alternatives to hot coffee are less likely to be successfully marketed via retail food outlets. In southern Europe, Coca Cola and Nestle may face a totally different set of problems since coffee and soft drinks are more likely to be competing beverage products.[22]

Country and Company Indicators

Decisions concerning the integration of country level operations on a global level require information at two different levels of analysis. First, **country indicators** need to be identified in order to assess the risks and returns likely to be associated with operating in various foreign markets. This information would be factors discussed in Chapter 2, such as the *political environment* (i.e., policies regarding foreign investment, employment, the potential influencing role of bureaucracy), the *legal and regulatory environment* (i.e., the judicial system, the role and rights of labor unions, patent and trademark laws, minimum standards for health and safety, etc.), the *economic climate* (i.e., per-capita income, inflation rates, currency exchange fluctuations), *infrastructure development* (i.e., communications, media availability, transportation systems, channels of distribution), and *general demographic, sociocultural, and life-style patterns.* Throughout the remainder of the text, examples of how and what types of information are used in analyzing these factors and their influence on marketing strategy and tactics will be presented.

The second level of information that is regularly needed in global marketing management has to do with **company performance indicators** in countries where the firm is already operating. Keep in mind that a multinational corporation has a unique ability to exploit strengths gained in one nation or market in establishing and cultivating a position in other nations or markets. Global, strategic decisions require accurate, timely, and detailed information regarding return on investment, sales growth, patterns of market share, and profitability from different product-markets or countries. Given the sophistication of computerized information systems networked throughout the world and the recent trend toward worldwide accounting firms, companies of all sizes have the capability to remain up-to-date in their global operations.

SECONDARY DATA FOR GLOBAL MARKETING

Secondary data sources are the most valuable and cost-effective means to assess the attractiveness of foreign markets about which management has little knowledge. They are regularly used in strategic planning activities to identify geographic or product markets to be screened for more in-depth consideration. They are also used to monitor changes in the global external environment. Secondary data provide a manager with a cursory evaluation of risk associated with operating in a particular market. This information can also be used to evaluate the costs of alternative operating plans and to generate forecasts of potential returns associated with entering a market. The advice given earlier in this chapter to thoroughly investigate secondary data sources before proceeding with the collection of primary data is especially applicable in the case of international markets in light of the increased magnitude of risks associated with opportunity costs or poorly executed planning.

Information Sources

Generally speaking, as a country develops economically and becomes more and more involved in international business, a greater interest in basic data and better collection methods develops. This holds true for companies in the development of their internal sources of secondary data as well. The wide variety of detailed external secondary data sources that an American marketer

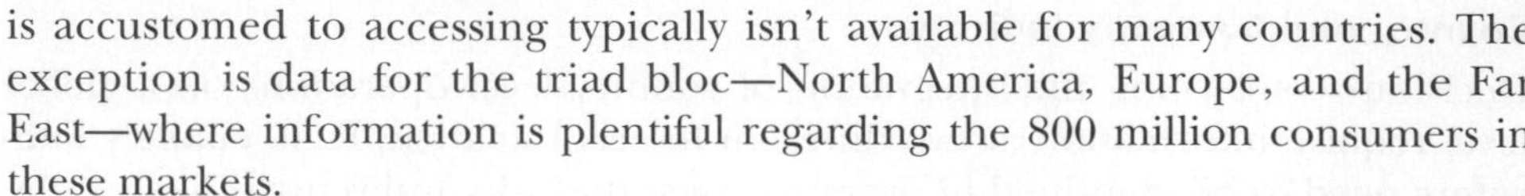

is accustomed to accessing typically isn't available for many countries. The exception is data for the triad bloc—North America, Europe, and the Far East—where information is plentiful regarding the 800 million consumers in these markets.

The basic strategy for searching external sources of secondary information is to move from the general to the specific. Sometimes, its as simple as making the right phone call to the right office in order to save a great deal of time and expense! Consider the case of a small, California-based publisher specializing in books with high technical content that was interested in having its books translated and distributed throughout Europe. Following two weeks of touring major European cities, staying in expensive hotels, and arranging unsuccessful interviews with booksellers, the publisher was asked by a Dutch publisher why he was attempting to research his options in the spring. The Californian replied that he wanted to avoid trying to interview potential contacts during the summer months, when everyone was on vacation. The Dutchman pointed out that if he had come in the fall, he could have met every important publisher in the world in a five-day period at the *Frankfurter Buch Messe* (Frankfurt Book Fair)—the world's largest book fair, which has been held every October for over 50 years and specializes in selling translation and distribution rights! A visit to any good library or Chamber of Commerce would have uncovered a copy of *The Bookseller,* the trade magazine for publishing in Europe, which would have provided him with information to save money, time, and lots of frustration!

U.S. and Foreign Government Sources

The U.S. government, and in particular the Department of Commerce and the State Department, are key sources of information about foreign markets.

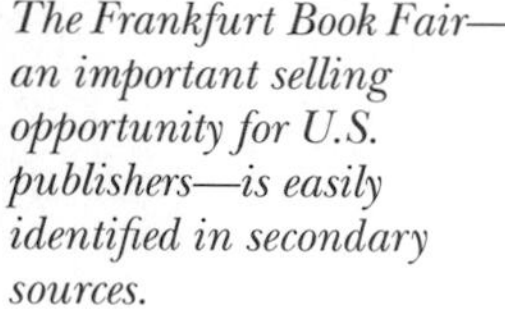

The Frankfurt Book Fair—an important selling opportunity for U.S. publishers—is easily identified in secondary sources.

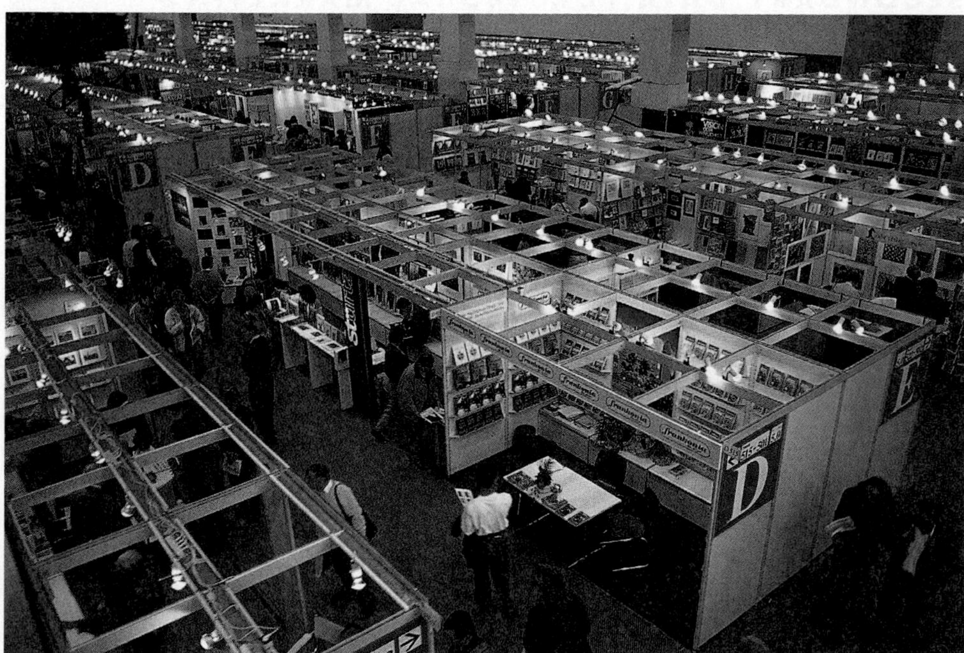

In some cases, the information is detailed and analytical (special reports) and in other cases it is more general. Within the State Department, each country that has diplomatic and trade relations with the United States is represented by a Country Desk, which is a rich source of country-specific information, such as import-export statistics, schedules regarding trade fairs, and analyses of particular industrial sectors. Foreign embassies in the United States and U.S. Embassies in foreign countries often have trade departments and commercial attaches who are responsible for facilitating the exchange of all sorts of business information. Also, the *Thomas Register of American Manufacturers* and *Exporters Encyclopedia* offered by Dun's Marketing Services provide comprehensive market information for over 200 markets on a country-by-country basis.

International Chambers of Commerce

International Chambers of Commerce have information on the products and performance of individual firms. The Netherlands Chamber of Commerce in the United States in New York City acts as a sort of matchmaker between Dutch and American companies, and one of its main functions is to provide market information. Similarly, the U.S. Chamber of Commerce in The Hague (Netherlands) has a wealth of information about U.S. firms for Dutch businesses.

Supra-National Organizations

The United Nations provides comprehensive social and economic data for over 250 different countries free of charge or for a nominal fee. Other supra-national organizations, such as the OECD (Organization for Economic Cooperation and Development) in Paris, the Pan American Union, and the EU (European Union) in Brussels all offer trade statistics and analytical market-sector studies in a number of languages (including English).

Trade, Business, and Service Organizations

These organizations are particularly good sources of information on specific products or industrial sectors. They often perform special studies and provide competitive, confidential information to subscribing members. For example, the European Currency Unit (ECU) Newsletter is published monthly and offers members information and analysis on a variety of environmental and political factors that have influence on the shaping of European Monetary Union and the acceptance of a common European currency.

Commercial Agencies

The growing information needs of companies who do business on a global level has resulted in agencies signing multinational cooperative agreements, thereby building worldwide chains of research agencies. Examples include the merging of Dun & Bradstreet with the A. C. Neilsen Company, which is now the world's largest market research firm. Another example is Young and Rubicam, an advertising agency that has developed a huge consumer data base that can monitor life-styles and trends and compare them across countries. Their "4Cs" data base—*Cross Cultural Consumer Characteristics*—contains life-style data, media habits, product-usage data, attitudes regarding a wide range of issues, and sociodemographic data for over 3500 households in each of more than 20 different countries. Much of this research is sold "as is" to clients to help frame other research projects or develop promotional strategies. Finally, a number of commercial marketing research agencies throughout the world are listed in professional directories and source guides[23].

SECONDARY SOURCES FOR STUDENTS

Read! Many libraries have specialists for certain areas of the world who can provide you with a general list of international business journals and magazines. Many libraries can also access *electronic data banks,* such as LEXIS or NEXIS, which often have flat subscription fees (one fee per year, unlimited use). Also, large libraries frequently subscribe to regional issues of periodicals, such as *The Wall Street Journal* (European and/or Asian editions) and *Business Week International. The Economist* (in particular the *Economist Intelligence Unit* publications) and *Asia Week* are excellent sources of information about European and Asian markets; they offer feature articles containing detailed analyses of products, countries, and sectors. In addition to English-language publications, magazines and newspapers, such as *Le Monde* (French) and *Frankfurter Allgemeine Zeitung* (German), are excellent publications that go well beyond the level of analysis reported in U.S. weekly news magazines.

PROBLEMS OF AVAILABILITY AND USE OF SECONDARY DATA

Three factors affect the use of external sources of secondary data for international marketing decisions: the *availability,* the *reliability,* and the *comparability* of the data. Two key problems associated with the *availability* of data continue to be (1) literally locating the relevant data, and (2) finding the kind of detail in reporting that allows for analysis and planning. Many countries simply do not have the tradition of systematically and accurately recording statistics relating to production and consumption. Even basic data on population trends and income distribution are not always available or up to date. Developing accurate forecasts and estimating market demand require good predictor variables. In many countries, such information is simply not available or recorded in such a form that analysis is impossible.

Another problem with the use of secondary data is that available data may not have the level of *reliability* necessary for confident decision making. Official statistics sometimes reflect national pride or optimism rather than reality. Tax policies can affect the accuracy of production statistics, particularly in the case where grants and export subsidies are involved. Depending on the industry in question, data can become quickly out of date. Two-year-old data regarding beer consumption in Greece may still be useful for Heineken's marketing manager, while two-year-old data regarding the use of networking software for personal computers in Germany will at best be viewed as "interesting history" for the marketing manager of Compaq.

A final problem involves the *comparability* of available data. Quite often, data are collected and reported in different categories between nations. It isn't that the data is not available, you just need to know where to look for it and then reasonably assess its usefulness for your purposes. The following checklist outlines the problems associated with the comparability of secondary data:

1. *The criteria for grouping data into statistical categories are different.* For example, the purchase of a television set in Germany is recorded in the category "recreation and entertainment," while in the United States, the same purchase falls into "furniture and household equipment."
2. *The categories in the statistics to be compared have been given different latitudes.* For example, occupational statistics in the United States may use different age categories than the same statistics in Italy.
3. *The categories are defined too broadly.* For example, if a marketer of ball bearings for ski lifts wants to determine market volume in France, production statistics won't help if they only contain a category for all metal parts in ski-lift equipment.
4. *The data come from different units of analysis.* Two data sets about the projected market potential of personal computer sales in Germany and England would not be comparable if the first data set came from distributors and the second from a survey of Electronic Data Processing (EDP) managers.[24]

PRIMARY DATA COLLECTION: CONCEPTUAL ISSUES IN CROSS-CULTURAL RESEARCH

As noted earlier in the chapter, generating primary data should provide the most specific information for either planning, problem solving, or control. As companies move more into global markets and attempt to standardize elements of their marketing mixes across countries, cross-cultural studies become more important as a method of checking the appropriateness of these activities. Ideally, a combination of useful secondary data and managerial expertise gained through experiences in product-markets will provide sufficient insight into the appropriateness of marketing strategies and tactics. However, in new market situations or in markets that are rapidly evolving, the manager's needs for information will often depend on primary data collection. International marketing managers are primarily interested in *identifying similarities,* since these offer the greatest opportunities for standardizing strategies across markets. For the international market researcher, this means finding a balance in using research methods that are universal enough to capture similarities between markets, but sensitive enough to point out important differences.

There are two basic approaches to this task. The first research approach (termed the **etic** school by cross-cultural researchers) is concerned with identifying and assessing universal attitudinal and behavioral dimensions and with developing culture-free measures that facilitate comparisons across countries. The second research approach (called the **emic** school) argues that attitudes and behaviors are unique to a culture and best understood in their own terms. This means emphasizing the particularities of each country and identifying and understanding their unique characteristics. Table 3-7 summarizes the perspectives that the etic-emic approaches bring to cross-cultural research.

As an example of this research dilemma, consider a credit card company that wants to assess the possibility of using the same promotional strategy to stimulate use of their credit card in two closely related countries, Belgium and the Netherlands. The Benelux countries (**Be**lgium, **Ne**therlands, **Lux**embourg)

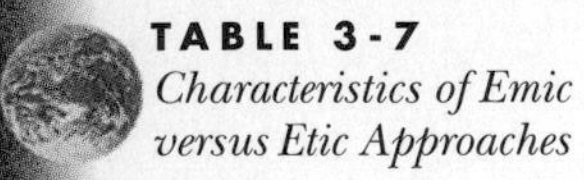

TABLE 3-7
Characteristics of Emic versus Etic Approaches

Characteristic	Emic	Etic
Perspective taken by researcher:	Studies behavior from within the system	Studies behavior from a position outside the system.
Number of cultures studied:	Examines only one culture	Examines many cultures, comparing them.
Structure guiding research:	Structure discovered by the researcher	Structure created by the researcher
Criteria used to compare behavior to the culture:	Criteria are relevant to internal characteristics	Criteria are seen as absolute or universal

Source: John W. Barry, "Introduction to Methodology" in Harry C. Triandis and John W. Berry, eds., *Handbook of Cross-Cultural Psychology* (Boston: Allyn & Bacon, Inc., 1980): 11.

are often grouped together in product markets because of their proximity, size, and long history of economic and trade cooperation. An etic approach to research would argue that identical questions regarding attitudes and behavior towards credit cards and their usage could be developed. This would involve only minor translation changes between the Dutch and Flemish speaking samples (the French-speaking sample in Belgium would insist on a French questionnaire, even if they could comprehend the Flemish version!). The etic approach would assume that both countries share sufficient cultural values to be able to respond freely and accurately to questions and the results could be compared.

The emic school's approach would be to identify deeply rooted cultural values of Calvinism in Holland (briefly, and in this context: hard work, frugality; and not spending money that is not yours are all desirable behaviors), and would take these characteristics into account in attempting to understand Dutch attitudes and behaviors toward credit cards. *Really* understanding this issue in Holland may require research techniques such as in-depth personal interviewing instead of a standard questionnaire. Given the highly similar market structure, availability of financial services, and per-capita incomes between Holland and Belgium, there must be some other, less apparent explanation as to why market penetration of credit cards in Belgium is over 80 percent, with frequent usage, while Holland's market penetration is under 40 percent, and characterized by infrequent usage.

PRIMARY DATA COLLECTION: METHODOLOGICAL ISSUES IN CROSS-CULTURAL RESEARCH

While the preceding discussion raises questions about the fundamental approach to doing cross-cultural research, there are also a number of other issues dealing with primary data collection that arise in international research. These issues are not exclusive to international research—they are issues in domestic research as well. It's just that they are more likely to be highly relevant in cross-cultural studies. Basically, these research problems concern (1) making certain you're asking the right questions to (2) the right people, (3) being certain that the respondent understands the question the same way in which the researcher thinks it is being asked, and (4) being certain that the respondent has the willingness and ability to respond. Each of these problems is discussed in the following sections.

Incorrect Problem Formulation

Any research project, domestic or global, must begin with a careful definition of the problem. The care and accuracy with which this first step is taken largely determines what follows in the research effort and the usefulness of the research results. In cross-cultural research, incorrect problem formulation typically arises when the researcher lacks sufficient cultural insights to know what important questions should be asked. When CPC International test marketed its dry *Knorr Brand* soups in the United States, results were so promising that the company felt it had a competitive product to offer. CPC had test marketed the product by serving passersby a small portion of its already-prepared warm soup. After the taste test, respondents were asked how they liked the soup and if they would be willing to buy it. The responses were positive. Sales, however, were very low once the packages were placed on grocery store shelves. Further investigation indicated that the market tests had overlooked American's tendency to avoid most dry soups. During the testing, those interviewed were unaware that they were tasting a dried soup. Had they known the soup was sold in a dry form and that preparation required 15–20 minutes of occasional stirring, they would have shown less interest in the product. Instead of only asking questions about how the soup tasted, CPC would have done well to ask consumers how they felt about preparing dry soups.[25]

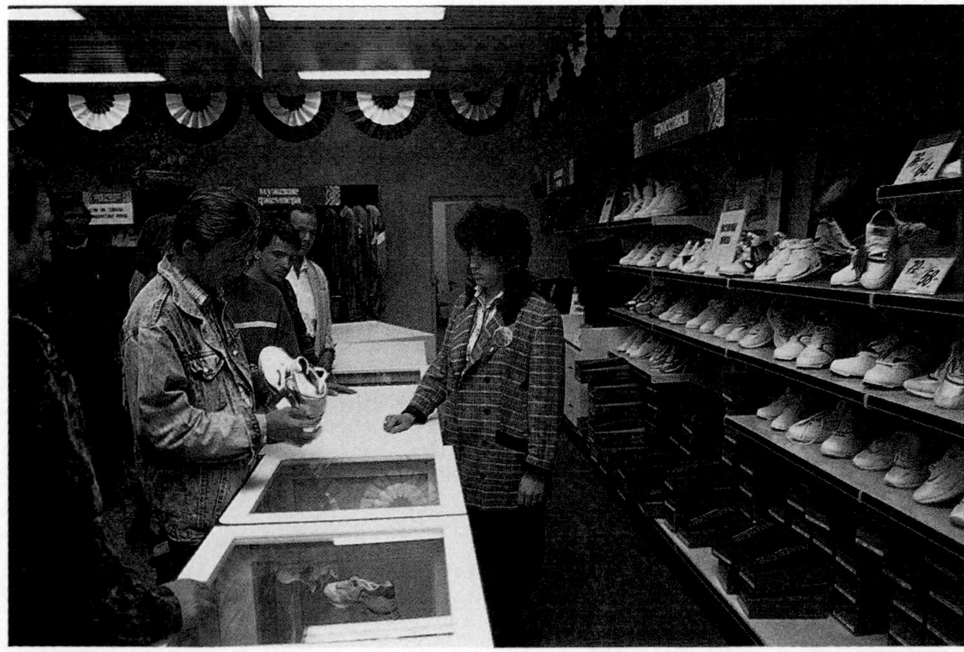

Russian consumers like these shoe store shoppers cannot handle merchandise without a clerk being present. Marketing researchers need to know these sorts of cultural differences to properly frame research questions.

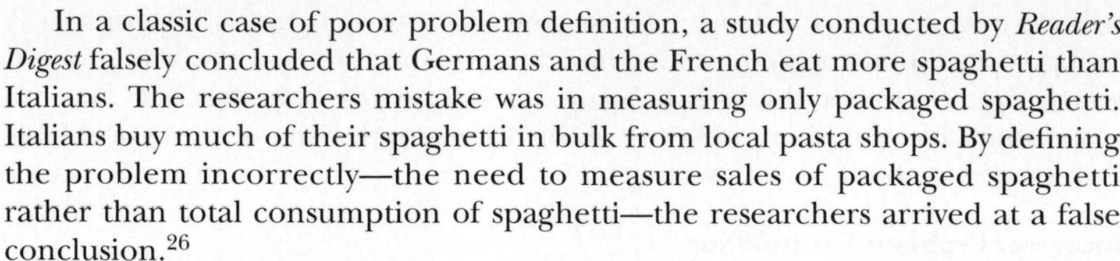

In a classic case of poor problem definition, a study conducted by *Reader's Digest* falsely concluded that Germans and the French eat more spaghetti than Italians. The researchers mistake was in measuring only packaged spaghetti. Italians buy much of their spaghetti in bulk from local pasta shops. By defining the problem incorrectly—the need to measure sales of packaged spaghetti rather than total consumption of spaghetti—the researchers arrived at a false conclusion.[26]

Proper Sampling Frame/Unit of Analysis

Sampling in field surveys presents special problems in international research. Countries differ in the amount of detailed social and economic information made available making it difficult to identify and draw meaningful samples to interview. In many countries, drawing probability samples is simply impossible. Apart from a lack of reliable sources to determine sampling frames, many survey techniques are hindered by the country's infrastructure or cultural norms regarding asking questions. If houses have no street addresses (as in many urban areas of North Africa) or if the postal system is inefficient (Italy), then mail surveys are doomed before they begin. If personally interviewing women is incorrect behavior in the respondent's country (as in many Arab lands), then the researcher will end up with responses interpreted and edited by an entirely male sample or with no responses at all. If cross-cultural research results are to be compared between countries based on a telephone survey, then the manager would do well to ask the critical question of just how comparable the samples are. In Sri Lanka, less than 3 percent of the residents (only the wealthy) have telephones. Outside of developed urban areas, such as the Greek islands or rural Portugal, fewer than 50 percent of households have telephones. Even in urban areas, telephone surveys can be a dubious technique. It is estimated that in Cairo 50 percent of the telephones can be out of service at any point in time and 75 percent of all dialed calls fail to get through on the first attempt.

Conceptual Equivalence

While it's important to ask the right questions to the right people, its equally important that the person being asked understands what's being asked of him or her! In international research some misunderstandings are simply translation errors, due to simple carelessness, multiple-meaning words, or idioms. Having personal interviews or translations of questionnaires done by local residents is one simple way to avoid these problems. One of the best techniques for ensuring correct translations is to use **back translation**. This approach requires one person to translate survey questions into the desired foreign language and then have another person retranslate the foreign version back into the original language. By comparing the two original language versions, problems in meaning and idiomatic expressions can be quickly identified.

A more subtle problem is **functional equivalence** where questions about a particular behavior are clear to both parties, but the usage contexts differ. For example, in the United States bicycles are basically used for recreation, while in the Netherlands and several developing countries, they provide a basic mode of transportation. Research about attitudes towards using bicycles would need to be clarified in each market in order for functional equivalence to exist in the comparison of responses.

Respondent Willingness/Ability to Respond

Various problems related to willingness and ability to respond arise in international research. Using locally prominent people in the research effort will often open otherwise closed doors. Overcoming suspicions regarding the purposes of carrying out the research will greatly improve the extent of cooperation received. Recognizing that a respondent's ability to articulate an answer or express an attitude toward a new product or service will depend on their ability to recognize the usefulness and value of the offering is an important first step in determining the correct research method. Imagine the difficulty of correctly measuring eastern Europeans' attitudes towards installing catalytic converters and using unleaded petrol for automobiles. On the one hand, they are painfully aware of the environmental problems that have evolved in their region over the decades since the end of World War II. On the other hand, converters and unleaded petrol represent higher acquisition costs and operating expenses for one of the most sought-after products in eastern Europe.

In the final assessment, global marketers must be willing to live with the fact that there will be situations where, regardless of exhaustive secondary and primary data collection efforts, they may be left with imperfect information. Consider the case of a large Dutch producer of infant milk powder and baby food, who recently signed a joint venture agreement with two producers in the Czech Republic. The Dutch company's initial investigation of the market showed strong brand preference for baby food products with western European names. As part of the overall business analysis for the joint venture, the company needed accurate figures on the volume of commercial baby products consumed in the past years. By combining this information with the fairly accurate data available regarding Czech birth rates, the Dutch company would be in a good position to negotiate the terms of the joint venture and make reasonable decisions regarding production investments, marketing efforts, sales, and profits. However, the production statistics provided by the two state plants (which together controlled 100 percent of the market) suggested that Czech babies must be consuming 19 kilograms of infant milk powder per year. This was difficult for the Dutch company to reconcile, since their own long history of experience in this product area showed that average yearly consumption by babies in various Western countries was only 11–12 kilos per year. After unsuccessful attempts to resolve the discrepancy through secondary data sources (the state-owned companies' accounting procedures were not always accurate; health officials knew nothing of the problem; channels of distribution were pharmacies who sold the powder at highly subsidized prices and kept no records), the Dutch firm sent a representative to Prague to research the discrepancy.

The Dutch representative spoke neither Czech nor Slovak and found personal interviews to be difficult since his respondents were not comfortable speaking German or English. He did sense that his questions were often received with resentment or perceived as a threatening experience to the interviewees. Following five months of failed efforts and false leads, he finally discovered that consumers other than mothers were coming into the pharmacies to buy the infant powder—farmers were purchasing the powder in large quantities (at subsidized prices, of course) to feed to their calves! The manager of the state-run plant, the central buyer from the state, and the pharmacists didn't find this phenomenon to be particularly interesting, nor did they have any idea about the extent of this practice. It wasn't that they were unwilling to offer the information, they simply hadn't ever thought about it or cared to investigate.

TRENDS IN GLOBAL MARKETING RESEARCH

Traditionally, the *country* has been the most common unit of analysis for global marketing research. Many multinational company subsidiaries and sales forces are still organized along regions or country lines, and performance evaluations are still often grouped according to national boundaries. Over the past three decades, these organizational structures have had an influence on the process of gathering data. While this approach was convenient, it was not always effective. One disadvantage is that this perspective encourages describing an entire country or region with a level of homogeneity that simply doesn't exist. Just as marketers recognize and exploit the climatic, social, and economic diversities between Detroit and San Francisco, global companies need to recognize and appreciate regional differences within countries as well. Northern and southern Italy are as economically, industrially, and culturally diverse as any two extremes you can find within the United States (for example, Texas and New York). Using macro economic data about consumers in eastern Europe or Spanish-speaking Latin America for anything more than a first level of analysis tends to lead to sweeping generalizations about these markets, which will be of little use in setting reasonable goals or in formulating effective strategies and tactics.

A second disadvantage of using country data for purposes of comparison is that it is a perspective that often fails to discover the best business opportunities. A **product-market perspective** describes potential markets that face similar problems, seek similar benefits, share similar life-style values, or display similar response patterns but do *not* necessarily share the same nationality. Using this approach, the marketer gains the advantage of being able to compare target markets regardless of size and geographic boundaries and cluster them into homogeneous global markets. For example, manufacturers of luxury class goods such as Rolex and Pierre Cardin target wealthy, sophisticated, highly mobile, status-conscious consumers via international print media and satellite TV, no matter what their nationality. Companies with products that have strong life-style appeal, such as Nike, Coca-Cola, and Levi-Strauss also view markets in this fashion and gather, analyze, and compare information from worldwide sources in developing their global, standardized strategies. To the extent that characteristics of the product category allow, the trend in international marketing research is toward the etic approach of gathering and using information for decision making.

KEY TERMS AND CONCEPTS

Marketing research
Objectives of marketing research
Planning
Problem solving
Control
Secondary data
Primary data
Marketing Information System (MkIS)
Marketing research project
Quantitative analysis
Qualitative analysis
Reliability
Validity

Problem formulation
Research design
Sample selection
Data collection
Survey
Closed-ended question
Open-ended question
Experiment
Focus group
Observation
Single source research
Naturalistic inquiry
Research report
Marketing research in global strategy
Country indicators
Company performance indicators
Etic
Emic
Back translation
Functional equivalent
Product-market perspective

Questions and Exercises

1. What is the role of marketing research? How does the issue of risk relate to the role research plays in marketing decision making?
2. Distinguish among planning, problem solving, and control objectives in marketing research.
3. What is the difference between secondary data and primary data? If a firm gathers data from its wholesalers and retailers using a telephone interview, are the data gathered primary or secondary data?
4. What is the differences between a marketing information system and a marketing research project? How are these two forms of information generation related?
5. Twelve consumers are brought to the headquarters of a major packaged goods firm. The firm demonstrates a new glass cleaner to these consumers and then asks them questions about the product. The session is videotaped and reviewed by a team of marketing personnel. What form of data collection did this firm use? Should the firm use quantitative or qualitative analysis to examine the data gathered from this group of consumers?
6. What is naturalistic inquiry? Why has it recently emerged as an alternative data collection technique?
7. Define reliability and validity as they relate to a marketing research project. What can be done to heighten the reliability and validity of data gathered in marketing research projects?
8. Why is marketing research so important for global marketing decisions?
9. How can a firm use company and country indicators in global marketing research?
10. What are the distinguishing features of etic and emic approaches to cross-cultural research? Describe a data collection situation where an emic approach is the proper perspective for data gathering.

References

1. Information about Dell Computer was adapted from Ricardo Sookdeo, "How to Bolster the Bottom Line," *Fortune* 128, no. 7, (Autumn 1993): 15–28. Information about USAA was adapted from Terrence P. Pare, "How to Find Out What They Want," *Fortune* 128, no. 13, (Autumn/Winter 1993): 39–41.
2. Jack Honomichl, "Some Final Musings as Jack Writes Off into the Sunset" *Marketing News* (January 3, 1994): 17.
3. Sookdeo. *Fortune,* op. cit., 18.
4. Mark Landler, "The 'Bloodbath' in Market Research," *Business Week* (February 11, 1991): 73–74.
5. Ibid., 72.
6. Brent Bowers, "Companies Draw More on 800 Lines," *The Wall Street Journal* (November 11, 1989): B1.
7. Peter F. Drucker, "Marketing 101 for a Fast Changing Decade," *The Wall Street Journal* (November 20, 1990): A16.
8. Susan Caminiti, "A Star Is Born," *Fortune* 128, no. 13 (Autumn/Winter 1993): 44–47.
9. Yvonna S. Lincoln and Egon G. Guba, *Naturalistic Inquiry Beverly Hills*: Sage Publications, 1985.
10. For discussions of this trend see Mark Landler, "The 'Blood Bath' in Market Research," *Business Week,* op. cit., and Jeffery A. Trachtenberg, "Listening, the Old-Fashioned Way," *Forbes* (October 5, 1987): 202 and 204.

11. Terence P. Pare *Fortune,* op. cit., 40.
12. Ibid.
13. Alecia Swasy, "Cover Girl Is Growing Up and Moving Out As Its New Parent, P & G, Takes Charge," *The Wall Street Journal* (March 28, 1991): B1.
14. Rick Tetzeli, "Mapping For Dollars," *Fortune* (October 18, 1993): 91–96.
15. Jeffery A. Trachtenberg, *Forbes,* op. cit.
16. Ibid., 202.
17. Kessler. *Fortune,* op. cit., 58.
18. For a good discussion of this issue see Paul F. Anderson, "On Method in Consumer Research: A Critical Relativist Perspective," *Journal of Consumer Research* 13, no. 2 (September 1986): 155–173.
19. Lincoln and Guba, *Naturalistic Inquiry,* op. cit., 44.
20. This observation was made by William D. Wells in the preface to Russell W. Belk, ed., *Highways and Byways: Naturalistic Research from the Consumer Behavior Odyssey* (Provo, UT: Association for Consumer Research, 1991): iii.
21. Warren J. Bilkey, "An Attempted Integration of the Literature of the Export Behavior of Firms," *Journal of International Business Studies* 9 (Spring/Summer 1978): 33–46.
22. Michael J. McCarthy, "Coca-Cola, Nestle Discuss Uniting to Make New Drinks," *The Wall Street Journal Europe* (December 1, 1990): 3.
23. See, for example, "1993 Directory of International Marketing Research Firms." *Marketing News* 27, no. 5 (March 1, 1993).
24. Adapted from R. Bartos, "International Demographic Data. Incomparable!" *Marketing and Research Today* (November 1989): 205–212.
25. D. A. Ricks, *Big Business Blunders: Mistakes in Multinational Marketing* (Homewood, IL: Richard D. Irwin, 1983): 129.
26. Ibid., 137.

4

THE CONSUMER MARKET: ANALYSIS, SEGMENTATION, AND PRODUCT CLASSIFICATIONS

AFTER STUDYING THIS CHAPTER, YOU WILL UNDERSTAND THAT:

1. The first step in effectively analyzing the consumer market requires an analysis of basic people and money factors.
2. Market segmentation is a fundamental and critically important strategy in developing a proper marketing mix for household consumer products.
3. Market segmentation increases the efficiency and effectiveness of a firm's operations.
4. Consumer products are classified as convenience goods, shopping goods, specialty goods, and services. These classifications help marketers develop strategic marketing plans.
5. Effective analysis of global consumer markets requires an assessment of the distribution of wealth among nations, the composition of age groups within nations, and the basic stage of economic development of each country under consideration.

Two hundred and sixty million, 94,312,000, $30,126, $1,642, 19.7 percent—these numbers are essential to understanding the consumer market. What do they mean? Two hundred and sixty million represents the population of the United States in 1992. Ninety-four million three hundred and twelve thousand was the number of households in the United States in 1991. The average family income in 1991 was $30,126 and that average household spent $1,642 on food outside the home. Finally, 19.7 percent of the U.S. population was made up of minority groups in 1990.

These numbers and hundreds of others provide the starting point for marketers in analyzing the consumer market. The goal is to understand this diverse market well enough so that strategy planning for the marketing mix can proceed effectively and efficiently. But the challenge of cultivating the consumer market goes well beyond merely tracking down some numbers. How does one begin to identify marketing opportunities among 260 million different people? Each with a unique personality, value system, and life-style? Some people live in cities, while others live in suburbs and small towns. How does the small business decide how to spend its precious funds to attract customers and then please them once they've been attracted? Firms cannot possibly come up with a single product or service to satisfy the diversity of desires in the consumer market. Rather, groups of individuals in the market who share similar values and desires can be identified and products and services can be developed specifically for them. Kraft USA recently designed a market experiment in which the firm pinpointed 30 specific grocery stores where people frequently bought items from special displays. Kraft then installed custom-made coolers in the stores. The coolers carried special flavors of cream cheese tailored to the tastes of the stores' shoppers. The result was a 147 percent increase in sales over the prior year.[1] With a similar desire to serve the well-defined customer group of families with young children, Konica USA, Inc., has introduced high-speed (ASA 400) "baby film," which, the company claims, will to bring out the very delicate skin tones of young children's faces.[2]

This is the world of consumer marketing and microsegmentation. These examples illustrate some of the ways in which firms deal with the vast diversity of the consumer market. By tracking trends through market research and marketing information systems, firms have become more knowledgeable about consumers and can develop products and services to appeal specifically to unique tastes and desires.

The **consumer market** refers to the market for goods and services purchased by individuals and households to satisfy their consumption desires. To compete effectively for the favors of household consumers, firms must try to live the marketing concept: identify and understand the needs and desires of potential customers and then respond to these needs and desires with carefully designed products and services. Chapter 2 described the way in which firms assess the broad environment. This chapter focuses specifically on a description of the way features of the population can be analyzed to better understand consumer needs and desires. Also, the process of segmentation in the consumer market will be presented in detail. This discussion includes the criteria and procedures for target marketing. Next, a classification of products destined for the consumer market is presented. These categories of products with different characteristics have different strategic implications for each marketing mix variable. The final section in this chapter will highlight critical issues related to the analysis of consumer markets from a global perspective.

CONSUMER MARKET ANALYSIS: TRACKING PEOPLE AND MONEY

In the most basic sense, the consumer market is made up of people with money to spend and a willingness to spend that money on goods and services to satisfy their needs and desires. The "people factor" of a market—population and the geographic distribution of population—represents the broadest area of analysis for market opportunities. The "money factor" relates to the amount, distribution, and expenditure patterns of income in the consumer market. Fundamentally, then, effective analysis of the consumer market depends on tracking people and money to determine the overall market potential for products and services.

TRACKING PEOPLE

People need goods and services to fulfill the needs of their daily lives. Since this is a fact of life in advanced societies like the United States, then a good starting point in analyzing the consumer market for goods is to simply understand as much as possible about the consumer population. In other words, a basic understanding of trends with regard to total population, geographic distribution, age distribution, and household composition is valuable. From the U.S. Census and other secondary data sources, it is projected that in the coming decades the United States will experience some broad-based changes:

1. *Total population* as of 1992 was approximately 260 million people and is expected to grow at a rate of less than 1 percent a year to a total of 282 million in the year 2010. During the 1980s, population increased a total of 9.8 percent. That growth rate will fall in the coming years to about 7.0 percent.
2. *Geographic distribution* of the population continues to shift to the West and South. In 1990, 12 western states contained nearly 21 percent of the population and 16 southern states had approximately 35 percent of the population. These two regions showed dramatic growth in population during the decade of the 1980s from both births and immigration. There is no indication this trend will change in the near future.
3. *Age distribution* of the population is shifting as the baby boom population cohort ages. In 1990, 31 percent of the population was over the age of 45. By the year 2000, that percentage will increase to 35.9 percent and in 2010 it is projected to be 41.7 percent.
4. *Ethnic population* in the United States was nearly 20 percent of the total population in 1990 and is expected to reach more than 30 percent of the total by the year 2010. Further, the ethnic population is much younger than the general population.

5. *Household composition* continues to change. The number of married couple households is increasing but at a slower rate than single parent, single person (currently 25 percent of the population), and nonfamily households. Family size has decreased from 3.14 persons in 1970 to 2.63 persons in 1991. Nonfamily households constitute 29.1 percent of all U.S. households compared with just 18.7 percent of such households in 1970.

Descriptors of population like these and the information shown in Illustration 4-1 are ideal for assessing the nature of the demographic environment in a broad-based and general fashion. However, as firms try to assess the potential for specific products with an eye toward serving narrowly defined segments in the market, the level of analysis needs to become more specific. As such, marketers turn to more detailed population data.

Three detailed "market area" descriptions are available to marketers from the United States government. The basic unit of market area measurement is the **Metropolitan Statistical Area (MSA)** description. The U.S. Bureau of the Census reports data on 335 MSAs in the United States. In order for a geographical area to qualify as an MSA it must have either a central city with a population of 50,000 or a general urban area of 50,000 people with a total metropolitan population of at least 100,000. The standards also provide that an MSA must include a central county in which a central city is located and there are adjacent counties where at least 50 percent of the population lives in the urbanized area. The boundaries of an MSA may actually cross state lines. A **Primary Metropolitan Statistical Area (PMSA)** is an area larger than an MSA

ILLUSTRATION 4-1
Average U.S. Household Size: Number of People, 1850–1991

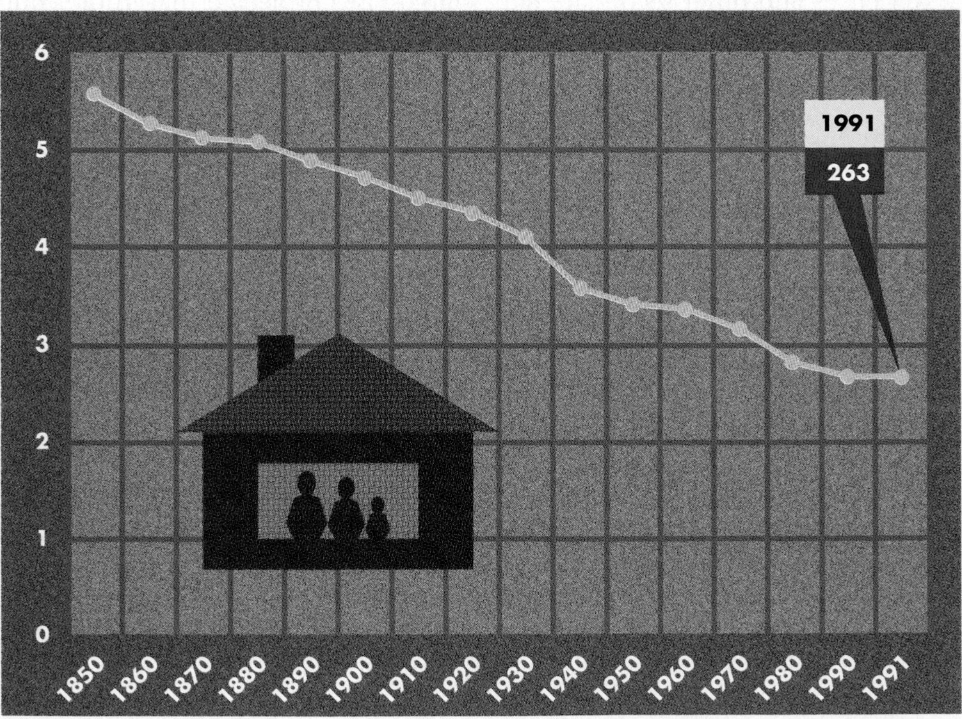

Source: U.S. Bureau of the Census.

that has a total population of one million or more people. It must also have counties with total populations greater than 100,000, a population that is at least 60 percent urban, and fewer than 50 percent of the residents commute outside the county for employment.

The largest geographical classification is the **Consolidated Metropolitan Statistical Area (CMSA).** A CMSA is referred to as a *megalopolis,* which consists of a group of PMSAs. Examples are Boston-Lawrence-Salem, Massachusetts; Chicago-Gary-Lake County, Illinois; and San Francisco-Oakland-San Jose California. Significant information including demographic characteristics, income, and housing as well as trade and manufacturing data are available about each MSA, PMSA, and CMSA. These classifications are critically important to marketers since approximately 75 percent of the U.S. population is housed in these classification areas and 80 percent of all retail sales are accounted for in these areas. Information contained in these classifications can be critical to understanding the consumer market because the data reveal total market potential and growth trends related to the people and money factors of market demand. Table 4-1 and Illustration 4-2 show how this sort of data can reveal areas of the United States where population and income growth are attractive as opposed to areas where market potential is decreasing.

Marketers can rely on government information for even more specific data that identify local neighborhood areas. Local neighborhood markets within metropolitan areas can have demographic and behavioral characteristics that vary dramatically from those of the standard MSA. Consequently, two data

TABLE 4-1
Population and Income Analysis of U.S. Counties

County (MSA)	Population Change 1970–1990	Income Change per capita 1979–1987	Persons per Square Mile 1990
High Growth Counties (MSA)			
Fayette, GA (Atlanta)	449.2%	79.2%	316
Collin, TX (Dallas–Fort Worth)	294.6	76.8	311
Gwinnett, GA (Atlanta)	387.8	76.0	815
Hernando, FL (Tampa–St. Petersburg)	494.7	66.3	211
Howard, MD (Baltimore)	202.6	81.6	743
Low Growth Counties (MSA)			
Orleans, LA (New Orleans)	–16.3%	44.5%	2,751
Cuyahoga, OH (Cleveland–Akron–Lorain)	–18.0	54.7	3,081
Wayne, MI (Detroit–Ann Arbor)	–20.8	54.7	3,438
St. Louis, MO (St. Louis)	–36.2	65.4	6,406
Washington, D.C. (Washington)	–19.8	65.0	9,883

Source: Adapted from data contained in G. Scott Thomas, "America's Hottest Counties," *American Demographics* (September 1991): 34–38.

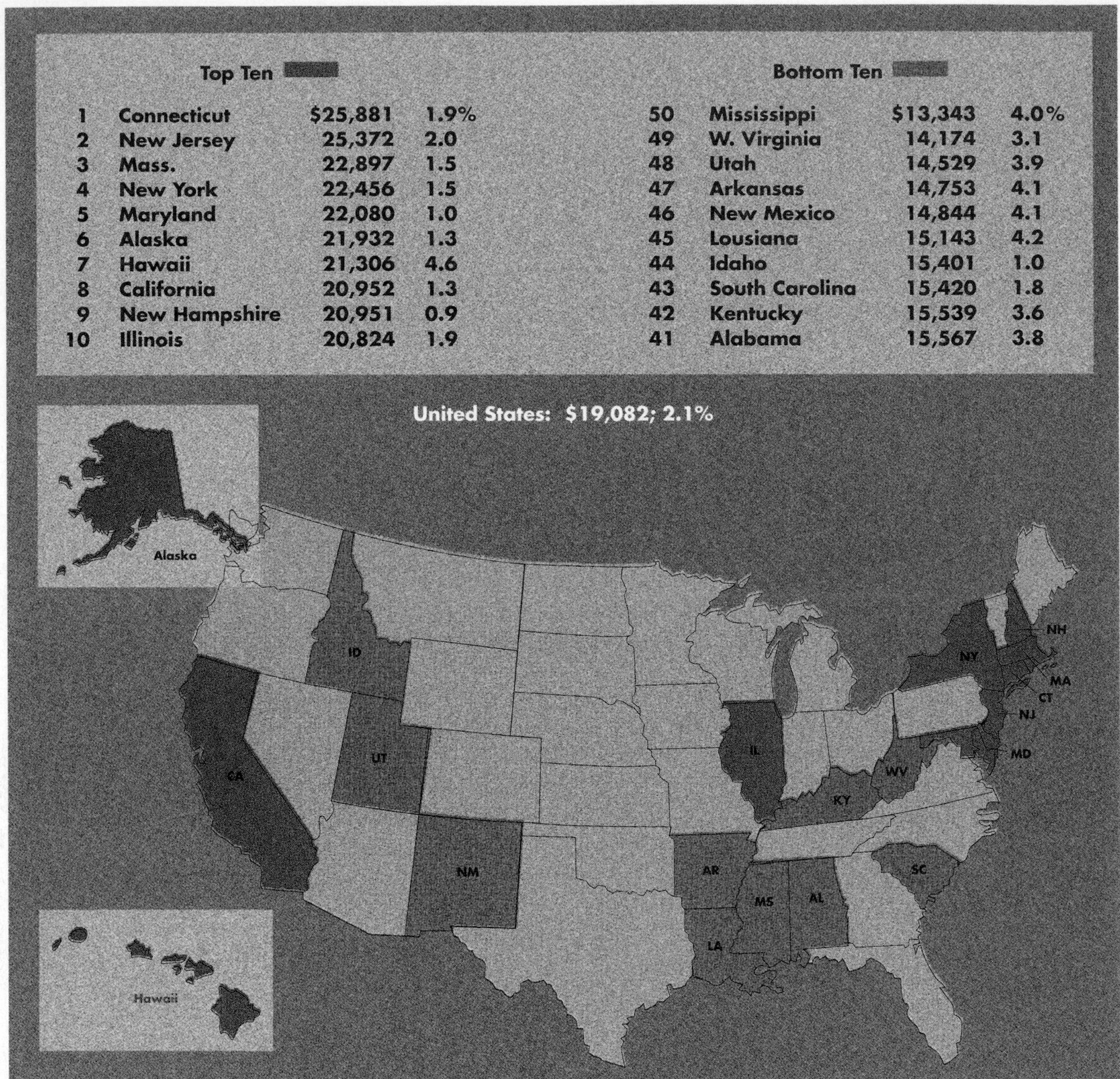

Top Ten
1 Connecticut $25,881 1.9%
2 New Jersey 25,372 2.0
3 Mass. 22,897 1.5
4 New York 22,456 1.5
5 Maryland 22,080 1.0
6 Alaska 21,932 1.3
7 Hawaii 21,306 4.6
8 California 20,952 1.3
9 New Hampshire 20,951 0.9
10 Illinois 20,824 1.9
Bottom Ten
50 Mississippi $13,343 4.0%
49 W. Virginia 14,174 3.1
48 Utah 14,529 3.9
47 Arkansas 14,753 4.1
46 New Mexico 14,844 4.1
45 Lousiana 15,143 4.2
44 Idaho 15,401 1.0
43 South Carolina 15,420 1.8
42 Kentucky 15,539 3.6
41 Alabama 15,567 3.8
United States: $19,082; 2.1%
Alaska
Hawaii
ID
UT
CA
NM
IL
KY
WV
NY
NH
MA
CT
NJ
MD
AR
MS
AL
SC
LA

Source: U.S. Commerce Department.

ILLUSTRATION 4-2
Best and Worst Personal Incomes: Top and Bottom Ten States by Per Capita Incomes in 1991 and the Annual Percentage Change from 1990.

bases are used to gather information on these smaller areas. They are data from individual census tracts and postal zip code districts. A **census tract** is an area of approximately 4,000 persons with similar demographic and income characteristics. **Postal zip code districts** often include more than one census tract. As such, there may be more diversity in these data. The census tract data is available in government documents and the postal zip code districts are available from university research bureaus or private research firms.

TRACKING MONEY

The essential element for any market to hold potential for revenue generation by a firm is money. While some barter situations are available to consumers where goods or services can be traded for other goods or services, the vast majority of corporate revenue generated throughout the world is based on money exchange. Money, in a formal analysis, is the money income consumers have to spend on goods and services. Several levels of income relevant to consumer market analysis are as follows:

1. **National income** is the nation's total income from all sources including individual income and corporate profits.
2. **Personal income** is the total annual money income received by individuals from all sources including wages, dividends, interest, business and professional income, and farm income.
3. **Disposable personal income** is the amount remaining after individuals have paid personal federal, state, and local taxes that is available for spending and saving.
4. **Discretionary income** is the amount of disposable personal income left over after paying for essentials: housing, food, clothing, installment debt, and local transportation. (Discretionary income is somewhat hard to define because affluent families have a different definition of "essential" than less affluent families.)
5. **Real income** is the purchasing power of personal income. This is what personal income will buy in goods and services. On an annual basis, if personal income increases 4 percent but the consumer price index rises 5 percent, then real income actually decreases by 1 percent.

Disposable personal income in the United States is currently between $3.5 and $4.0 trillion per year. That amount plus pension payments is the amount of money potentially available for spending on goods and services and saving. To get an idea of the nature of total income distribution in the United States, Table 4-2 shows that since 1970, the median household income has actually advanced very little (in constant dollars). The median household income increased only $1,413 (approximately 4.9 percent) in over 20 years from 1970 to 1991. Illustration 4-3 reinforces the fact that real income has changed very

TABLE 4-2
Money Income of Households (in constant 1991 dollars)

	Percentage of Households		
Money Income	**1970**	**1980**	**1991**
< $5,000	6.3%	4.8%	4.8%
$5,000–9,999	9.9	10.6	10.1
$10,000–14,999	8.7	9.4	9.4
$15,000–24,999	18.0	18.3	17.4
$25,000–34,999	19.0	16.1	15.2
$35,000–49,999	19.0	18.8	17.3
$50,000–74,999	12.8	14.7	15.4
$75,000–99,999	3.4	4.6	6.0
$100,000 and over	2.0	2.6	4.4
Median income	$28,803	$29,309	$30,126

Source: Adapted from U.S. Bureau of the Census, *Current Population Reports,* series P-60, no. 180 (Washington, D.C.: U.S. Government Printing Office 1993): Table 2: 5.

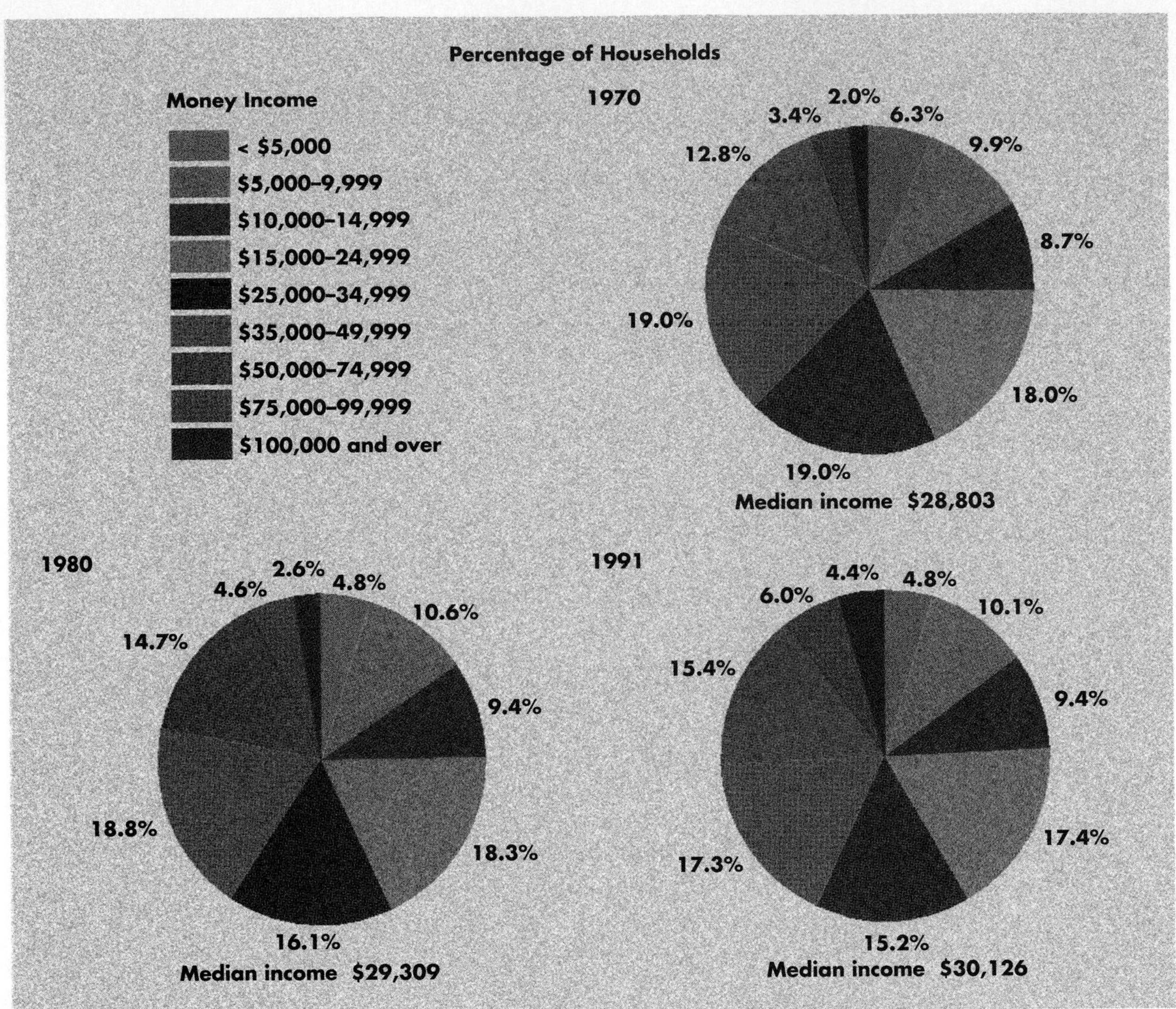

Source: Adapted from U.S. Bureau of the Census, *Current Population Reports,* series P-16, no. 180, (Washington, D.C.: U.S. Government Printing Offic 1993): Table 2: 5.

ILLUSTRATION 4-3
Money Income of Households (in constant 1991 dollars)

little over the last two decades. The majority of the gain from 1970 to 1991 was realized in the percentage of households earning more than $50,000 per year. The explanation of this change has to do largely with an increase in the number of multiple wage earner households that emerged during the decade of the 1980s.

How much of household income will be spent and by whom are questions marketers need to answer in order to identify and pursue market opportunities. A way to assess potential spending is to examine expenditure patterns among households. Table 4-3 shows expenditures by category for the average household and an upper-income household in 1991. Note that for every category listed, the upper-income household spends more dollars on an absolute basis than the average household. *But,* in only a few categories does the upper-income household spend a greater percentage than the average household. These categories are telling. Data such as these are not used for predicting

TABLE 4-3
Annual Expenditures by Household in the United States in 1991 (selected categories).

	Average Household		Upper Income Household	
	Dollars	Percent	Dollars	Percent
Total expenditures	$30,487	100.0%	$56,946	100.0%
Food—total	4,367	14.1	6,955	12.2
At home	2,725	8.8	3,841	6.7
Away from home	1,642	5.3	3,114	5.5
Alcoholic Beverages	314	1.0	564	.9
Housing—total	9,533	31.2	17,094	30.0
Shelter	5,416	17.8	9,935	17.4
Utilities	1,961	6.3	2,765	4.9
Operations and furnishings	1,252	4.1	2,589	4.6
Household services	452	1.5	1,036	1.8
Housekeeping supplies	451	1.5	768	1.3
Apparel	1,801	5.9	3,520	6.2
Transportation—total	5,235	17.2	9,443	16.6
Vehicles	2,154	7.1	4,042	7.1
Public trans.	308	1.0	666	1.2
Health care	1,523	5.1	2,137	3.7
Pension and social security	2,788	9.1	7,291	12.8
Other—Entertainment, personal care, education, charity, savings	4,999	16.4	10,535	18.5

Source: U. S. Bureau of the Census, Bureau of Labor Statistics, *Consumer Expenditure Survey 1991* (Washington, D.C.: U.S. Government Printing Office, 1992).

what *specific brands* within a product category a household is likely to purchase; rather, the data present a broad view of how households allocate their money and particularly the level of discretionary income that is available for purchases. Managers use information like this for strategic planning related to broad *product and services categories* that represent growth opportunities. The upper-income household spends a greater percentage on household furnishings and services, apparel, public transportation, pension/social security, and entertainment. These categories represent discretionary income spending. These types of data suggest to marketers that targeting upper-income households with products and services holds good potential.

The people and money factors just presented allow firms to read the demand potential in broad-based consumer product and service categories. Armed with this data, firms will then proceed to more incisive analyses to better understand different parts of the total consumer market. That is, take a heterogeneous, diverse, and generalized description of broad categories and trends and break those categories and trends into much more specific and detailed descriptions. So, if the broad analyses discussed so far suggest that households in the United States spend from 6 to 8 percent of their income on meals away from home, then managers use that information to readjust their market strategies. It is precisely this trend in U.S. households to spend more money on food away from home, which has prompted grocery stores across the country to add more pre-prepared food options within the store. For years, supermarket managers watched fast-food chains and restaurants take more and more money from their revenue. Now, store managers are adding deli counters, seating areas, and separate checkout counters where shoppers can buy prepared items to take home or enjoy in the store.[3] The success of strategies like these, though, depends on providing these products and services to the right group of consumers. The process of market segmentation is the next topic that will be discussed.

MARKET SEGMENTATION

Over the last forty years, firms have become much more sophisticated in their understanding of the consumer market and ability to develop strategic marketing plans for well-defined groups of consumers. In the 1950s, marketers defined their market as white, middle-class housewives. In the 1980s, with the aid of marketing research information, the focus sharpened to households with children where both parents worked outside the home. Today, aided by even more sophisticated research techniques, firms have been able to take market segmentation analyses to greater levels of specificity. MCI, the long-distance phone company, tracks its customer phone usage so that if an individual gets a lot of collect calls, a service representative will contact the customer directly and pitch MCI's personal 800-number service. If you tend to read books within a narrowly defined genre, Waldenbooks will send you information directly about new titles in that area.[4] While few firms are, as yet, defining market segments this precisely, market segmentation is a critical process in consumer market analysis.

Recall that **market segmentation** is the process of taking the total, heterogeneous (diverse) market and breaking it into smaller submarkets or segments that are more homogeneous (similar) in physical or behavioral characteristics that relate to the purchase of the firm's products or services. A fundamental goal of the market segmentation process is to identify consumer segments in such a way that there is a high degree of behavioral similarity *within* segments (intrasegment homogeneity) and a high degree of dissimilarity *between* segments (intersegment heterogeneity). In this way, a firm has separated the heterogeneous market into similar subsegments that are distinct from one another.

Once the firm has identified separate segments, it will choose those segments that appear to hold the greatest potential and make them **target markets:** those consumer groups to which the firm will market its products and services. The days of making a product or service that tries to be all things to all people are over. Such "chameleon" products invariably have a blurred image among consumers and consequently end up being "nothing to everyone." Further, as firms within an industry better understand the motives, needs, desires, and behaviors of consumers, products and services are being carefully refined to appeal to consumers' precise desires. The firm that does not segment the market and target specific consumer groups is often at a severe competitive disadvantage. This is not to say that some products cannot be mass marketed to broad and diverse consumer groups. The point is that a firm that can successfully identify a specific need within a group of consumers, and then develop a product specifically suited to that need, has a high probability of competitive success. The segmentation and targeting process are tied to the positioning of the firm's products in the marketing. The strategic aspects of positioning are discussed in detail in Chapters 7 and 8 in the context of product development and management.

There are several ways to proceed with market segmentation in the consumer market. Table 4-4 shows the major physical and behavioral descriptors and their subcategories, which form the bases for segmentation analysis and allow firms to identify segments that have high intrasegment homogeneity and intersegment heterogeneity. A discussion of the ways in which each of these categories of segmentation is analyzed follows.

PHYSICAL DESCRIPTORS

The broadest of all segmentation plans relies on physical descriptions (called **physical descriptors**) of consumers, which are tangible descriptions of consumers like who, what, where, and how many. With data much like those obtained from government data banks, firms can describe potential segments based on age, gender, marital status, area of residence, income, and the like. The two basic categories of physical descriptors used for segmentation analysis are geographic location and demographic characteristics.

Geographic Location

Marketers can describe consumer segments by nation, region, state (or province), city, county, or even neighborhood. As the discussion of people and money earlier in this chapter showed, firms can get large amounts of data to describe segments based on where people live. A geographic basis for segmentation will take such data and try to determine if *where* people live correlates with *what* they buy. Intuitively, we know that the market for snow tires is greater

TABLE 4-4
Principal Bases for Identifying Consumer Market Segments

Physical Descriptors	Behavioral Descriptors
Geographic location	Use characteristics
• Nation	• Volume of consumption
• Region	• Product category use
• State	• Brand use
• City/county	
• Neighborhood	
Demographic characteristics	Life-style (psychographics)
• Age	
• Gender	
• Marital status/family size	Benefits sought
• Education	
• Occupation	
• Income	

in the upper midwestern United States than in Florida, for example. But a geographic analysis and the segmentation decisions based on it can be much more sophisticated than that sort of intuition. Besides obvious climate related products, such as home heating and air conditioning, insulation, or snow tires, a number of products sell better in specific geographic regions than in others. Campbell Soup Company distributes a spicier *Nacho Cheese* soup in Texas and California than in other parts of the country, for example. H. J. Heinz Company realizes much greater sales of its *Home Style Gravy* in the northeastern United States than anywhere else in the country.[5] These are examples of geographic segments with high intrasegment homogeneity and intersegment heterogeneity. Gottschalks, a highly profitable chain of clothing stores, has followed a decidedly geographic location strategy in segmenting the market.[6] Gottschalks locates in smaller, less urban markets (population less than 100,000 residents) to avoid well-entrenched competitors like The Gap and The Limited. Differences in hobbies, entertainment preferences, and recreational activities have also been discovered based on geographic analyses. While there is no doubt of an interaction between where people live and personal characteristics (socioeconomic status, for example), the point remains that consumer use of products and services can be identified by geographic analysis and, therefore, this factor results in a useful basis for segmentation.

Demographic Characteristics

Demographics have been raised several times as a component of marketing analysis. Age, gender, education, income, family size, or ethnic background often correlate with product purchase and use. A fundamental application of demographic analysis is in market segmentation. For example, earlier discussions pointed out that demographic shifts in population result in emerging or contracting markets. As the number of single person households has increased, food marketers have responded to this segment of the market by providing "single serving" food packages, for example. If the number of persons in a household continues to decline, significant changes in the nature of housing units may result. The expansion of the Levi-Strauss line of *505 Jeans* and the introduction of *Dockers* was based, in part, on the aging of the male population in the United States. These two new lines of men's casual trousers were designed to accommodate the changing shape of the male body that comes about with age.

Firms can successfully segment the market based on demographic descriptors if those variables translate into purchase and use tendencies. Consumer electronics makers have only recently targeted female buyers with their advertising. With the realization that during 1989 women purchased 40 percent of all videocassette recorders, 41 percent of all compact disk players, and 58 percent of all console stereo systems, firms like Pioneer Electronics, Sharp Corp., and Matsushita Electric Industrial are taking note of the female segment of the market. Some marketers rely heavily on demographics for their description of the market. Radio stations have known for years that various age groups have predominant tendencies in music preferences and segment the market based on age (as well as time slot). The ultimate in demographic segmentation is the National Bicycle Industrial Co., which takes physical measurements of a person—height, weight, length of legs, length of arms, foot size—and faxes the

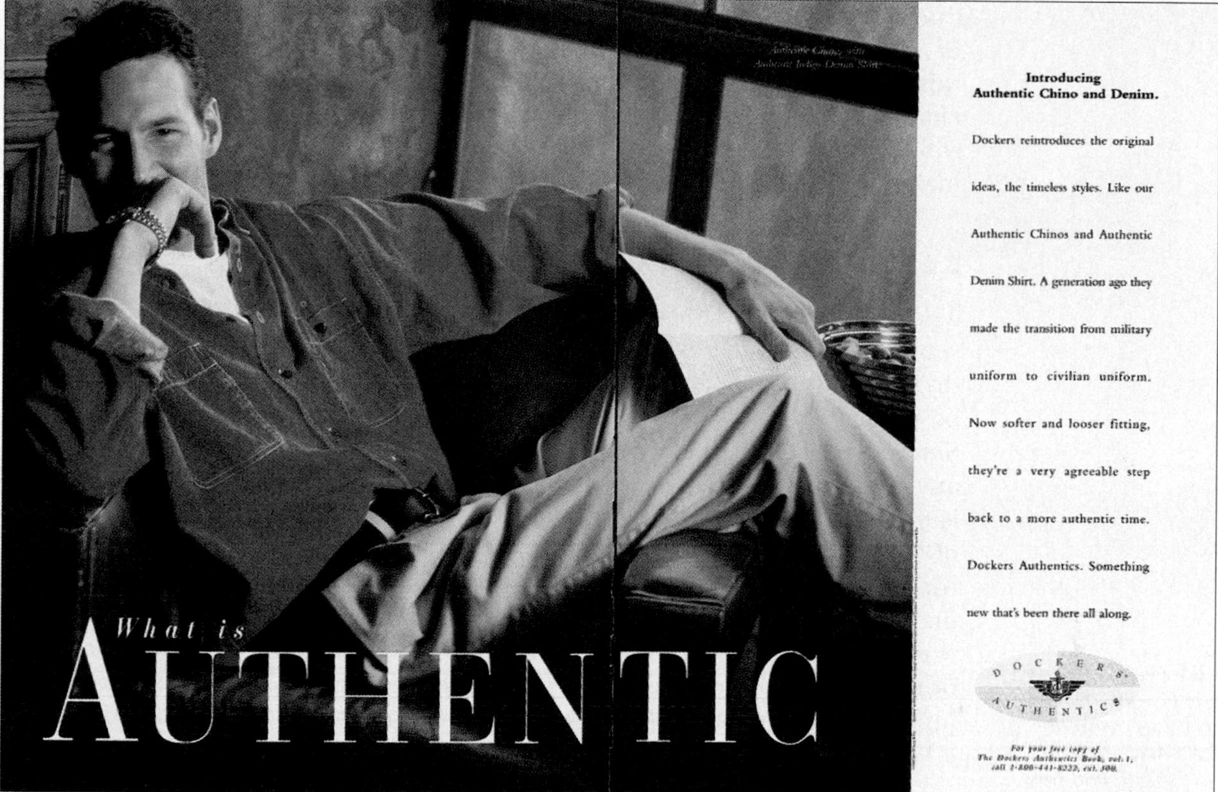

ILLUSTRATION 4-4
Levi-Strauss introduced the Docker line of men's apparel in response to the changing needs of the U.S. male population.

specifications to its custom production facility. Computers process the customer data and robots construct a truly custom-fit bicycle based on demographics. The firm can produce any of 11,231,862 variations on 18 models of racing, road, and mountain bikes in 199 color patterns and promise delivery in two weeks![7] Literally any demographic variable can be used as basis for segmentation if the factor is associated with product preference and purchase.

Income level is a demographic characteristic that often relates to product purchase and use. The data in Table 4-3 shows that more affluent families spend their money differently than the average American household. Recently, it was discovered that blue collar and other nonprofessional consumers may be more brand loyal than their wealthier counterparts. This may occur because a mistake in buying an item is more costly to these lower-income consumers, and consequently they are more likely to stick with brands that please them.[8] Creating brand loyalty is the ultimate goal of every marketer. Brand loyal customers represent a solid foundation for market share and predictable cash flow. If income is, indeed, related to brand loyalty, then its value as a segmentation factor is immense.

While demographics have traditionally been related to product purchase and use, the nature of that relationship may be changing. Aging baby boomers who fueled spectacular growth in consumer spending during the 1980s may now be restrained by the costs of raising children and credit card debt.[9] This hotly pursued segment of the population is large in size and characterized by high education and high income, but their spending habits may be changing due to their changing station in life (i.e., married with children). As such, firms like BMW, Filofax, and Liz Claiborne have had to change their appeal to this group by stressing value rather than glitz and status. For example, BMW changed its promotional theme (see Illustration 4-5) from prestige to safety with the advertising appeal, "Before you buy a safe car, you should know what makes a car safe."

BEHAVIORAL DESCRIPTORS

The physical descriptors just discussed are valuable as ways to segment the consumer market to the extent that each can be correlated with product purchase or use. Here lies a fundamental limitation of using physical descriptors as a basis for segmentation: physical states are only indirectly related to behavior. Since the ultimate goal of segmentation analysis is to identify the potential of any segment to *purchase* a product or service, then identifying behavior, per se, is the real result being sought. Because of this, marketers will turn to a variety of "life" behaviors or product use behaviors as bases for segmentation. Why then are the physical descriptors just discussed used at all? Primarily because marketers must be able to identify segments in terms of physical characteristics when planning the marketing mix. As a practical example, media organizations describe *their* markets only in terms of demographics. As such, marketers must be aware of the demographics of a segment in order to effectively and efficiently buy media time and space for promotional purposes.

ILLUSTRATION 4-5
To comply with trends in the consumer market, BMW has changed its advertising appeal from prestige to safety.

THE NAME OF THE CAR STARTS WITH A FIVE,
THE PRICE DOESN'T.
While zero-to-sixty times and top speed statistics are impressive, the BMW 525i Sedan is engineered to quicken your pulse with another set of numbers.
$34,900.*
Under the hood you'll not only find classic BMW performance, but the balanced practicality of two overhead cams, six in-line cylinders and 24 maintenance-free valves.
All of which help the compact, fuel-injected 2.5-liter engine produce 189 horsepower efficiently.
A variable valve timing system further enhances the powerplant's responsiveness. It helps improve torque at low and medium speeds, and makes idling smoother.
Of course, a high-performance engine needs a high-performance means of slowing it down.
Massive disc brakes nearly a foot in diameter and an advanced anti-lock braking system on all four wheels help prevent wheel lock-up and fading under hard braking.
Additional active safety features include an agile steering system and suspension that continuously feed road information back to you. So you can react more quickly.
Even an alarm reminds you to look out for slippery surfaces when the temperature outside dips below 37 degrees.
Passive safety comforts such as an innovative impact sensor system, front seatbelt tensioners and dual airbags inside add to your sense of security and well-being.
The rest of the interior is typical of BMW. Ten-way power front seats. Dual climate controls. And a stereo with 250 watts and ten speakers.
But these are merely facts and figures. To fully appreciate the 525i Sedan, try the following number: 1-800-334-4BMW.
*Suggested retail price for the base model 1994 BMW 525i Sedan is $34,900. Actual price will depend on dealer. Price excludes destination and handling charges, taxes, license and options. ©1994 BMW of North America, Inc. The BMW trademark and logo are registered.

The **behavioral descriptors** listed in Table 4-4, however, may provide more useful information. They identify use characteristics, life-styles, and benefits sought as a way to segment the consumer market that is more directly related to the motives for product purchase.

Use Characteristics

In many cases, the purchase and use behavior consumers display in a product class is a sufficient basis for segmenting the market. Usage can relate to three factors: volume of consumption, brand use, and product category use. *Volume of consumption* analysis segments the market into nonusers, light users, and heavy users of a product category. This sort of behavior segmentation received impetus during the 1960s when it was discovered that 15 to 17 percent of the beer drinkers accounted for 88 percent of all beer consumption and 16 percent of all buyers of canned hash consumed 86 percent of that product.[10] In many consumer product categories like these, marketers have discovered that half the consumers purchase around 80 percent of the product. What was first discovered three decades ago still holds true in contemporary markets. An analysis of the New York metropolitan market identified that heavy users of *Peter Pan Peanut Butter* were households with children headed by 18 to 54 year olds in suburban and rural areas.[11] Similar purchase behaviors by this "heavy half" of the users of a product category were discovered for cake mixes and soaps and detergents (83 percent and 75 percent respectively of these purchases by less than half of all buyers).[12] When a product category demonstrates such skewed consumption by a relatively small proportion of the market, then it makes sense for marketers to strategically design the marketing mix to appeal to these high-volume segments.

Brand use identifies those consumers who demonstrate consistent loyalty to a single brand in the market. Brand loyal consumers are of great value to marketers since it is estimated to cost five times more to attract a new customer than to retain an existing customer. Firms are conscientious in understanding the segments of the market that are loyal to their brands because of this cost factor. Another level of usage is *product category use.* This analysis identifies segments that tend to purchase a particular form of a product. For example, it is possible to segment the market for laundry detergents based on liquid versus powder users. Similarly, soft drink marketers can describe segments based on bottled versus canned soft drink purchasers. It is important to recognize the emergence of trends within a product category with regard to consumers who prefer one form of a product over another. Based on this use characteristic alone, these consumers can be targeted with marketing mix strategies.

Life-style (Psychographics)

Segmenting the market based on **life-style** (and the related underlying element of **psychographics**) draws heavily on an analysis of social and cultural trends and the values related to these trends. As people change their views of what is important and relevant in a broad cultural sense, these values affect the goods and services purchased to accompany their life-styles. Psychographics was a word coined in the 1970s to describe people's attitudes, opinions, and activities and the effect these factors have on purchase behavior.

Describing individuals based on psychographic analysis provides insights into the life-styles that psychographics promote. The application of psychographics to the practical issues of consumer market analysis was pioneered in the late 1960s by SRI International in Menlo Park, California. SRI devised what is called the *VALS* (values, attitudes, and life-styles) program for segmenting consumers into distinct life-style categories. The new *VALS-2* program is still widely used by marketers and advertising agencies to segment the consumer market. VALS-2 proposes a typology that divides consumers into nine life-styles. The groupings are based on consumers' self-images, values, aspirations, and resources (income and education) and the products they use.[13] As an example, in the "achievers" category are individuals who are higher in income and formal education. They are career and success oriented and their social activities center first on family and then on business acquaintances. An example of the application of VALS-2 is the American Express advertising theme, "Don't Leave Home Without It." This campaign is aimed at the achievers. The purpose of the campaign is to establish a position for the American Express card among people for whom projecting an image and success orientation is important.[14]

While life-style analysis can be extraordinarily valuable in identifying and understanding consumer market segments, there is some evidence that traditional approaches are beginning to fail. Some ad agencies have apparently abandoned the SRI approach claiming it is not detailed enough.[15] The failure of common life-style analysis, however, is not a matter of insufficiency on the part of SRI's VALS system or any other research approach. Rather, it would appear that the values of contemporary consumers are in a period of significant change. Modern consumers are adopting choice criteria that emphasize different values from even a decade before. Greater concern over nutrition, the natural environment, more emphasis on quality and value, and a greater distrust of manufacturers seem to be emerging values in the product choice process.[16] The life-style approach to segmentation still holds great potential. The challenge for marketers is to keep abreast of consumers' rapidly changing values and identify how these values will be translated into product and service preferences and ultimately a new system like VALS for segmentation analysis and strategic planning.

Benefits Sought

Benefit segmentation isolates consumer groups based on their desire for a particular result from owning or using a product or service. It really doesn't matter whether these consumers are young or old (a demographic basis) or what values they hold (a life-style basis). Rather, the product's ability to deliver a certain result is the overriding consideration in identifying a segment.

In Chapter 1, the marketing concept discussion of "satisfaction › cost" highlighted the benefit factor as one of the elements consumers would perceive as potentially satisfying in product purchase and use. A variety of product categories are subject to a benefits emphasis in evaluation. The value of using a financial service organization (like Dean Witter) is perceived by consumers to be related to the benefits the organization's products can provide. The benefit of a comfortable retirement or a college education fund are related to the advice financial consults give. In a classic study of benefits sought regarding fast food outlets, researchers identified a better way to measure and predict the loyalty of customers than past attempts that had used demographic and other consumer attributes.[17] Benefits sought as a behavioral basis for segmentation often cuts through much of the irrelevant information in the market and gets to the real issue: what people want.

THE VALUE OF MARKET SEGMENTATION

The value of a carefully conducted market segmentation analysis not only fosters the success of marketing efforts but also enhances performance across all phases of corporate operations. This enhancement of corporate operations is often realized in dramatic effects on the firm's efficiency and effectiveness. From human resource needs to the speed of implementing competitive strategies, a firm is able to more astutely make decisions when market segmentation has been done properly. Specifically, market segmentation analysis enhances a firm's efforts related to:

- the precise specification of marketing objectives,
- a better understanding of the needs, desires, and motives of consumers,
- a better understanding of why customers purchase and noncustomers do not,
- more efficient allocation of human and financial resources,
- the ability to assess competitive strengths and weaknesses of the firm's marketing activities,
- the ability to respond more quickly to changes in the external environment.

The reason a firm will realize these benefits is that market segmentation analysis forces an organization to focus its efforts within well-defined limits. This makes decision makers more knowledgeable and more sensitized to factors that affect a firm's operations. The effect is really one of specialization versus generalization. As the decision makers in an organization become specialists with regard to a particular group of consumers, then the ability to understand satisfaction and the means to deliver it are greatly increased. And, in turn, one of the primary roles of the marketing function discussed in Chapter 1 is served: devising an effective marketing mix.

APPLYING MARKET SEGMENT ANALYSIS

The whole purpose of market segmentation analysis is to focus the firm's marketing efforts on those segments that hold the greatest potential. That is, to identify target markets the firm can pursue with its product or service. Figure 4-1 shows the process of applying market segmentation analysis and the ultimate result of devising a marketing mix for each chosen target segment.

After a firm has carried out a market segmentation analysis using physical and behavioral descriptors, analysts will proceed with identifying the high potential target markets. This determination will be made with respect to *both* the characteristics of the segment determined from the segmentation analysis *and* the nature of the firm's product or service. Additionally, a firm will identify the potential for profit in selling to the segment, growth projections for

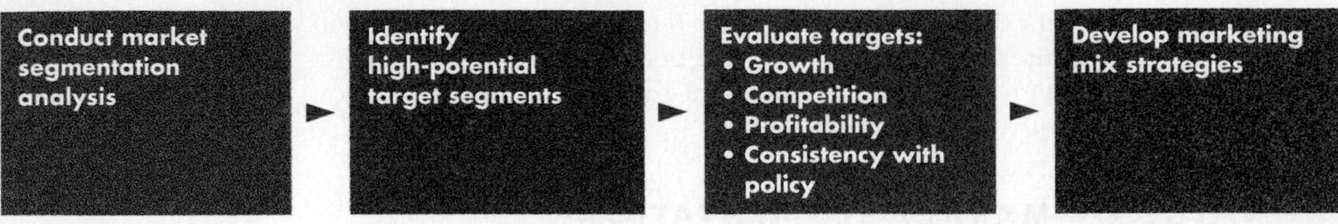

FIGURE 4-1
Applying Market Segmentation Analysis

sales within the segment, competition within the segment, and whether pursuing the segment is consistent with corporate policies and objectives. Once this series of assessments is made, decision makers turn their attention to devising marketing mix strategies that fulfill the expectations for satisfaction of consumers within the target market segments.

At this point, it is important to recognize two general but essential elements of conducting and implementing segmentation analysis. First, firms will normally use **multiple segmentation bases**. That is, rather than relying on a single descriptor such as demographics or life-style, several different factors will be used in combination. The reliance on several descriptors to define a single target market provides a much more complete profile of consumers and their desires upon which marketing mix strategies can be built. Second, firms must remain **flexible in segmenting** the market and pursuing targets. Consider the case of *Infiniti* Division of Nissan Motors. When *Infiniti* first segmented the market for its *Q45* luxury sedan, the firm anticipated that it would intercept buyers who were just moving up into the luxury car market before they bought a higher-priced European car.[18] But during the first year, Nissan discovered that nearly half the people who traded in cars to purchase the $54,000 *Infiniti Q45* were trading in Mercedes, BMWs, and other much higher-priced European sedans. Once alerted to this difference between their original segmentation plan and the actual behavior of consumers, Nissan responded to the realities of the market and produced the ad displayed in Illustration 4-6. Nissan would appear to be targeting consumers that fit both the original plan to intercept potential buyers of luxury sedans and also, by specifically identifying Mercedes and BMW in the ad, communicating to current owners of those name plates getting ready to trade-in. This advertisement by Nissan is an excellent example of a firm being flexible in its segmentation strategy and altering its marketing mix activities in response.

Market segmentation analysis is one of the fundamental underpinnings of successful selling in the consumer market. As we have seen, the ability to understand the nature of demand is greatly aided by the segmentation analysis. The next step in analyzing the consumer market is to understand the nature of different types of consumer products and the marketing requirements associated with each type.

Classification of Consumer Products

The prospect of devising a proper marketing mix for a consumer product can be confusing and intimidating. How important is a price emphasis? What sort of retail outlet should be used? Does it make sense to use coupons? These questions are all relevant and important to the

If you're thinking about a Mercedes or a BMW, this ad may steer you in a different direction.
When people compare the Infiniti Q45 performance luxury sedan with the Mercedes 300E and the BMW 735i, here's what they discover. The Q45 has a bigger engine. More horsepower. And goes from zero to sixty faster, than both the 300E and 735i.* And even with all these advantages, people are also discovering the Q45 sells for thousands less. Discover the Infiniti Q45 advantage today.
* All comparisons are based on Road & Track's Guide to the Infiniti Q45 1990.
INFINITI.
1991 Infiniti Division of Nissan Motor Corporation in U.S.A.

ILLUSTRATION 4-6
Nissan bases its advertising messages on information about target segment behavior.

marketing mix. Strategic decision making regarding issues such as these is greatly aided by the proper classification of a consumer product. The mere classification of consumer products into distinct categories does much to inform decision makers of the marketing challenges related to properly marketing to buyers in the consumer market. While there have been many classification schemes proposed for goods sold in the consumer market, a very simple description allows marketing planning to proceed swiftly: convenience goods, shopping goods, specialty goods, and services.

CONVENIENCE GOODS

Convenience goods are those consumer products that are low priced, frequently purchased, and available in many retail outlets. Examples of products in this category are toothpaste, laundry detergent, hand soap, facial tissue, bread, and margarine. Consumers tend to spend little time deliberating about which brand to purchase and perceive (due to the low cost) little risk in the decision process. These are the products that are distributed through grocery stores, drug stores, convenience stores, and discount houses. When you take your weekly trip to the grocery store, it is likely that you take a shopping list along which specifically indicates "brands" you intend to buy. It is also likely that you do not spend much time in front of the shelf before making a purchase. Consumers show some brand loyalty in this product category, but there is a degree of price sensitivity and frequent brand switching that goes on. Products that are bought on *impulse* also fall within this category. While the majority of products are planned purchases, a candy bar, chewing gum, or other small, inexpensive item (strategically located near the check-out counter) may be bought on impulse. Be aware that convenience goods derive their name *not* from features of the product related to convenience of use, but rather that these products are *convenient to acquire.*

SHOPPING GOODS

This product category derives its name from the tendency on the part of consumers to shop around for the item before purchasing. **Shopping goods** are higher priced, less frequently purchased items for which the consumer is willing to invest some time and effort in making comparisons among brands on the market. Examples of products in this category are furniture, appliances, automobiles, clothing, and electronics. In this product category, it is typical for consumers to visit several retail outlets and compare prices and features among brands. Information search in general is much higher in this product category with advertising, sales people, friends, and relatives all being sources of information. Consumers are also more prone to seek out the results of product performance tests (such as those conducted by *Consumer Reports*) in this product category than in any other. Shopping goods are also evaluated at the point-of-purchase (e.g., taking a car for a test drive or scrutinizing the picture quality of a color television set).

SPECIALTY GOODS

Specialty goods are those products that have unique characteristics and a significant group of buyers are willing to make a special purchasing effort to acquire them. A product achieves the status of a specialty good when a group of consumers *insist* on one brand to the total exclusion of others. These consumers are willing to exert extraordinary effort to locate and purchase the brand. Brand insistence, therefore, is the key distinguishing feature of a specialty good. Products that fall into this category are typically high-priced luxury items such as designer clothing and esoteric sports equipment. However, *any* brand that engenders fierce loyalty among consumers and motivates those consumers to exert extraordinary effort to acquire the item can legitimately be classified as a specialty good. The hamburger prepared and sold by the White Castle fast-food chain in the midwestern United States is not considered a specialty good by most consumers. However, large groups of midwesterners who have moved to retirement communities in Arizona and Nevada certainly do. Several groups have had the tiny, square burgers specially packed and shipped to them at considerable expense. Such behavior is classic with respect to a specialty good.

SERVICES

There is some debate as to whether services should constitute a separate category of consumer goods or whether there are service products that fall into the convenience, shopping, and specialty goods categories. Services have enough universal features that, for our purposes, a separate classification and treatment is warranted. **Services** are intangible consumer goods that are characterized by little standardization, low capitalization costs, and consumer participation in the "production" of the service. Examples are airline travel, medical and legal services, sporting events, lawn care, and tax preparation. The intangibility of consumer services is a key distinguishing feature of this category. As consumers, we know we do not take a physical, tangible item away from a service encounter. Furthermore, we do not "own" anything after a service encounter except, perhaps, a good feeling or good memories. The feature of consumer participation in the production of a service warrants some discussion. Very simply, service providers have nothing to provide unless consumers participate in the production of the service. A physician must have a client in order to make a diagnosis and provide treatment. The airlines must have passengers before their service exists and an attorney must be provided with information from clients before there is a case on which work can be done. This is a another key distinguishing attribute of the service category of consumer goods. The intangibility feature and the requirement of consumer participation represent unique and formidable challenges to marketers, as you will see in Chapter 18, which deals with the marketing of services.

An additional important distinction must be made with respect to services. Services as they are described in this section represent the "product" many organizations offer to the market for the purpose of generating revenues. Services of this type are not to be confused with the *ancillary* services that accompany many tangible products. If an auto dealer offers free oil changes for a year with every new car purchased, this is an ancillary service. If a computer manufacturer offers credit, delivery, installation, and training with every purchase, these are, again, ancillary services associated with a tangible product purchase. While services during and after the sale of a product are of enormous strategic importance, they are different from the services described here, which constitute the primary revenue generating good a firm offers to consumers.

MARKETING MIX STRATEGY IMPLICATIONS OF CONSUMER PRODUCT CLASSIFICATIONS

The simple process of putting consumer products into categories does much to inform marketing decision makers about the marketing mix strategies that will be needed for a particular product. Simple recognition that a product is a convenience good, for example, alerts marketing decision makers to the nature of consumer search behavior, the influence of price, distribution requirements, and typical strategies to be used in the promotional area. Table 4-5 identifies the consumer purchase characteristics and the primary strategic implications for the market mix variables based on the classification of consumer goods.

	Convenience Goods	**Shopping Goods**	**Specialty Goods**	**Services**
Product Examples	toothpaste bread laundry detergent	clothing home electronics automobiles	designer clothes fine china gourmet foods	tax preparation legal services air travel
Consumer Purchase Characteristics	frequent purchase little perceived risk little comparison low brand loyalty perceived homogeneity	infrequent purchase moderate perceived risk extensive comparison moderate brand loyalty perceived differences	infrequent purchase no perceived risk little comparison fierce brand loyalty perceived differences	infrequent purchase high perceived risk moderate comparison variable loyalty limited ability to distinguish differences
Marketing Mix	low price advertising "presells"	high price personal selling	high price little promotion	variable pricing advertising/personal selling
Implications	little p.o.p* judgment coupons widespread distribution large inventory	judged at p.o.p rebates selective distribution moderate inventory	no p.o.p. judgment no price discounts exclusive distribution small inventory	word-of-mouth some price cutting direct distribution no inventory is possible

*point of purchase

TABLE 4-5
Marketing Mix Strategy Implications of Consumer Product Classifications

Note from the descriptions in Table 4-5 that consumers demonstrate considerable variability in their approach to purchasing different consumer goods. As products become more costly and, in the case of services, less tangible, consumers perceive more risk in the purchase process. While the element of greater perceived risk is understandable, other differences, like differences in the amount of comparison consumers engage in, require clarification. Consumers engage in little comparison shopping for convenience goods due to their low cost, frequency of purchase, heavy advertising, and consumers' perception of similarity among brands. Conversely, shopping goods engender greater comparison shopping due to their high price, long life, and large number of product features. Specialty goods do not motivate comparison because of the brand loyalty consumers show toward these products. Services, despite the high perceived risk and infrequent purchase, are not associated with a lot of comparison shopping. The reason has to do with the intangibility of services and the professional providers in many service areas who tend not to disseminate much information. Together, these factors result in an inability on the part of consumers to make informed comparisons.

Each of these differences in consumer purchase characteristics has implications for the marketing mix. We have already discussed the differences in features among product categories. Table 4-5 shows the implications for the price, promotion, and distribution variables. Convenience goods require a low price and are "presold" through advertising. That is, mass media advertising attempts to affect a brand decision on the part of the consumer before a trip to the store. Coupons are used heavily in this category both to promote brand switching and in the case of in-package coupons to promote brand loyalty. Consumers are unable to test the product in the store (with the exception of occasional in-store sampling programs), thus the lack of point-of-purchase evaluation. Firms are required to secure distribution in a large number of different types of retail outlets and these retailers need to keep large inventories on hand.

Shopping goods are higher priced items with a large number of product features. Point-of-purchase evaluation is used in this category and requires personal selling in the promotional process. Manufacturers use rebates as a pricing technique to stimulate interest in brands and sell excess inventory. The distribution for shopping goods is more selective than for convenience goods and the inventory requirements are more moderate. Specialty goods have a much less complex marketing mix due to the brand insistence feature of this category. Since consumers are highly knowledgeable about the brand they want, there is little promotion and point-of-purchase evaluation. Further, the fierce brand loyalty on the part of consumers eliminates the need for price discounting. The distribution is exclusive and highly restricted since products in this category tend to be luxury or high prestige items. Similarly, the inventory requirements are minimal.

Services present an interesting and complex marketing mix challenge. Prices can be very low, as in the case of hair styling or lawn care services. On the other hand, the price of legal or medical services can be extremely high. Advertising is used in most service areas to make consumers aware of the availability of a service and the service provider's name. Some services, such as real estate sales, also depend heavily on personal selling. Services are further distinguished in the promotional area in that many consumers rely on word-of-mouth information from friends and relatives rather than traditional advertising media. Due to the difficulty in judging service providers discussed earlier, consumers rely on friends, relatives, and business associates for recommendations. As an example, in real estate services, 41 percent of consumers rely on the advice of friends, relatives, and business associates when choosing a real estate agent.[19] Marketers are forced to make price concessions in some service markets, like airline travel, whereas in the highly skilled professions prices are rarely cut. The most distinctive part of the marketing mix for services is distribution. Due to the consumer's participation in production, there is no distribution channel for services (consumers come to the providers) and it is literally impossible to "store" services in inventory.

As you can see, the marketing decision maker who correctly classifies a consumer product often has a solid foundation of information upon which to build marketing mix strategies. Properly classifying a product allows decision makers to concentrate on the more sophisticated and subtle elements of strategic planning, which result in potent competitive maneuvers.

Analyzing the global consumer market will be a formidable and exciting challenge in the decades to come. There are literally billions of consumers to be pursued by firms outside their own domestic markets. The process of consumer market analysis with a global perspective requires a recognition of factors that are quite different from the domestic perspective covered so far.

THE CONSUMER MARKET: A GLOBAL PERSPECTIVE

In adopting a global perspective in consumer market analysis, a company will constantly be involved in evaluating regions, or the entire world as its potential market. The extent of operating globally will depend on the company's objectives and priorities, coupled with their evaluation of the attractiveness of consumer markets throughout the world. To increase the efficient and effective selection of appropriate consumer markets, companies need to follow some systematic processes of analysis and segmentation. There is, unfortunately, no standard formula for market selection in global marketing. This is the case not only because different companies have different objectives and priorities underlying their strategic planning, but also because different markets throughout the world are so diverse, reflecting different states and rates of development.

While different companies have different approaches to selecting consumer markets, most will operate under an explicit model for analyzing markets, which can be generally represented by the process depicted in Figure 4-2.

This process suggests that firms follow three basic steps in assessing markets and that the entire process is influenced by corporate goals and priorities. The first step, *initial selection,* is a rough first cut where countries, regions, or product-markets are reviewed based on broad indicators such as level of economic development, political structure and stability, and sociocultural factors. This type of global assessment is done on a continuing basis and most often undertaken through the collection and analysis of secondary data. Assuming the market under review matches up well with corporate goals and priorities, a more thorough analysis of the market takes place. This next step is the *screening* process and is based on a detailed and rigorous analysis of the market including the nature and extent of competition, existing marketing infrastructure (i.e., channels of distribution, legal regulations affecting marketing activities, media availability, tariff and nontariff barriers, etc.), and the potential of the market (size, accessibility, growth rates, and its responsiveness to marketing effort). At this stage, companies will not only make use of available information (secondary data) but may also carry out primary research to gain more specific insights. The final step in the process is *market selection and entry,* which entails making a decision to commit resources to a specific country or market and developing strategies and tactics for market entry. The remaining sections of this chapter focus on the steps involved in analyzing and segmenting con-

FIGURE 4-2
Process for Analyzing Global Consumer Markets

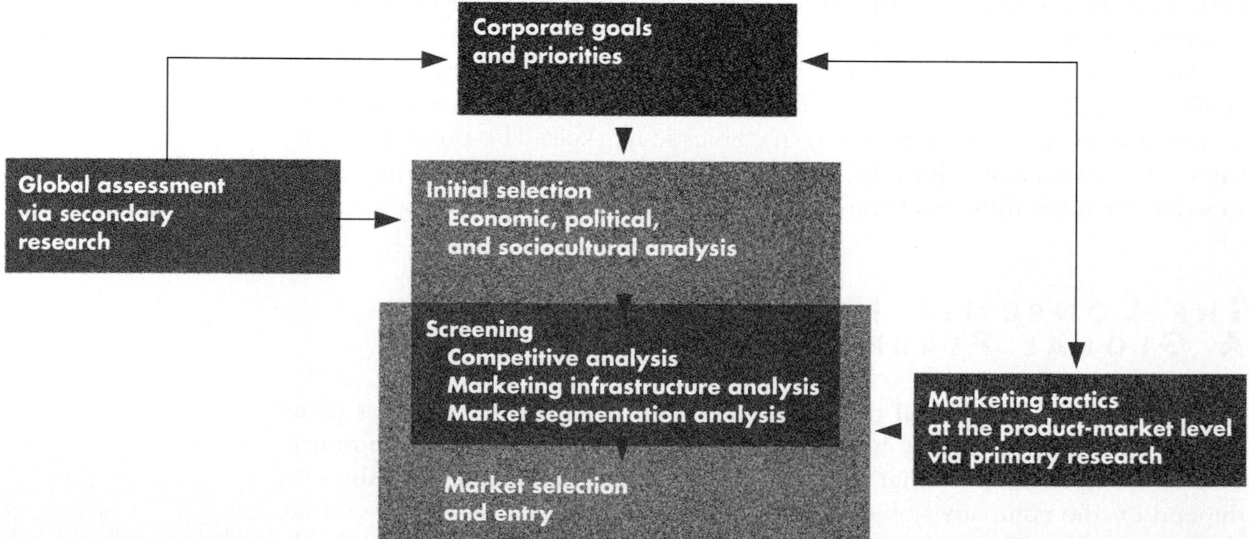

sumer markets at a global level and the complexities of developing accurate and useful analyses.

SOCIOECONOMIC ANALYSIS OF GLOBAL CONSUMER MARKETS

Global companies take a wide variety of factors into account when developing analyses for consumer markets. Geographic and political groupings are traditional bases for analyzing consumers markets. Similarly, groupings that consider the role of culture and religion on consumption patterns often form the foundation for consumer market analysis. Often, a multinational corporation's organizational structure will evolve over time in response to the geographic, social, cultural, political, and economic developments in the world. Heineken Brewing Company carries out consumer analyses of their key beer and beverage markets worldwide through a process of geographic segmentation, with operating divisions and strategic partnerships in Europe, Africa, Latin America, North America, and Asia. As consumer markets develop, they take on local partners and bottlers with knowledge of the local markets. The corporate marketing research department regularly visits these regions and attempts to integrate the local information into their corporate models of analyzing trends and demand. In Europe and the United States (Heineken's most important export market), they noted a fast-growing segment of beer drinkers who prefer a nonalcoholic beer. By virtue of their expertise in brewing nonalcoholic beer for sale in Moslem countries (a consumer segmentation approach based on cultural and religious factors), they have been able to respond quickly to this new segment.

Earlier in this chapter, "tracking people and money" was offered as an approach to analyzing consumer markets in the United States. The same sort of analysis can be applied to global markets, but with significant differences.

Consumer socialization reaches all corners of the earth. Here, Brazilian Indians gather in a village for an evening of TV in which the plight of their forest is aired.

Whether one feels good, bad, or indifferent about it, there is a highly skewed user-consumption ratio for the world's population and the world's use of resources. The **distribution of the world's wealth** provides an important global perspective for marketers. While economists predict that, throughout the remainder of the 1990s, access to technology and the freeing of world markets are favorable conditions that will lead to the poorer countries improving their wealth at a rate much faster than the industrialized countries, the fact remains that roughly 20 percent of the world's population controls 75 percent of the wealth and accounts for 75 percent of all consumption.[20] The other 80 percent of the world population divides the remaining 25 percent of the resources.

Within countries with developing market economies, this distribution is often no more equitable with as little as one-fifth of the population controlling two-thirds of the wealth and income. This pattern is referred to as *dual income distribution,* and it is an important level of analysis for the global marketer of consumer products. Figure 4-3 shows income allocations for a number of countries in developed and developing economies. Note the overwhelming majority of wealth that is controlled by the top two income groups. A ramification of the dual income distribution phenomenon is that a wide variety of consumer products and services, including luxury and fashion goods, ski vacation packages, sports cars, and consumer electronics are in high (but limited) demand in countries with low per-capita income.

In addition to the distribution of the world's wealth, the **composition of the world's age groups** is of keen interest to global marketers. While much has been written about the so-called graying and de-greening (a decrease in the number of younger aged citizens) of the population in the United States and other developed countries, the rest of the world does not follow this pattern. In the Middle East, Africa, and Latin America, roughly 40 percent of the population is currently under the age of 15![21] Increases and decreases in the proportion of the population in specific age groups are closely related to the demand for particular products and services. As fertility rates continue to increase in developing countries, new market opportunities emerge for products and services for young families and children. Similarly, as certain groups age and death rates continue to increase in countries with stable population rates, demand for consumer products and services such as health aids, health care, travel, labor for the services industries, and retirement funds will also evolve. For the global marketer, it is increases and shifts in demand from countries with high levels of economic development, coupled with the emerging demand in less developed countries (LDCs) that will likely provide the most attractive consumer market opportunities.

While the distribution of wealth and composition of age are important market factors that may influence the strategies and tactics of multinational firms, a perspective on global consumer markets that emphasizes a **country's stage of economic development,** coupled with a realistic assessment of the country's projected rate of market development (which is produced by analyzing economic and demographic trends in combination) continues to be the most common and useful approach to the analysis of consumer markets. Examining the global market on these bases allows for a structured and organized approach to analyzing the consumer market. Breaking the world's markets into three broad classes of economic development—less developed coun-

How Income Is Allocated

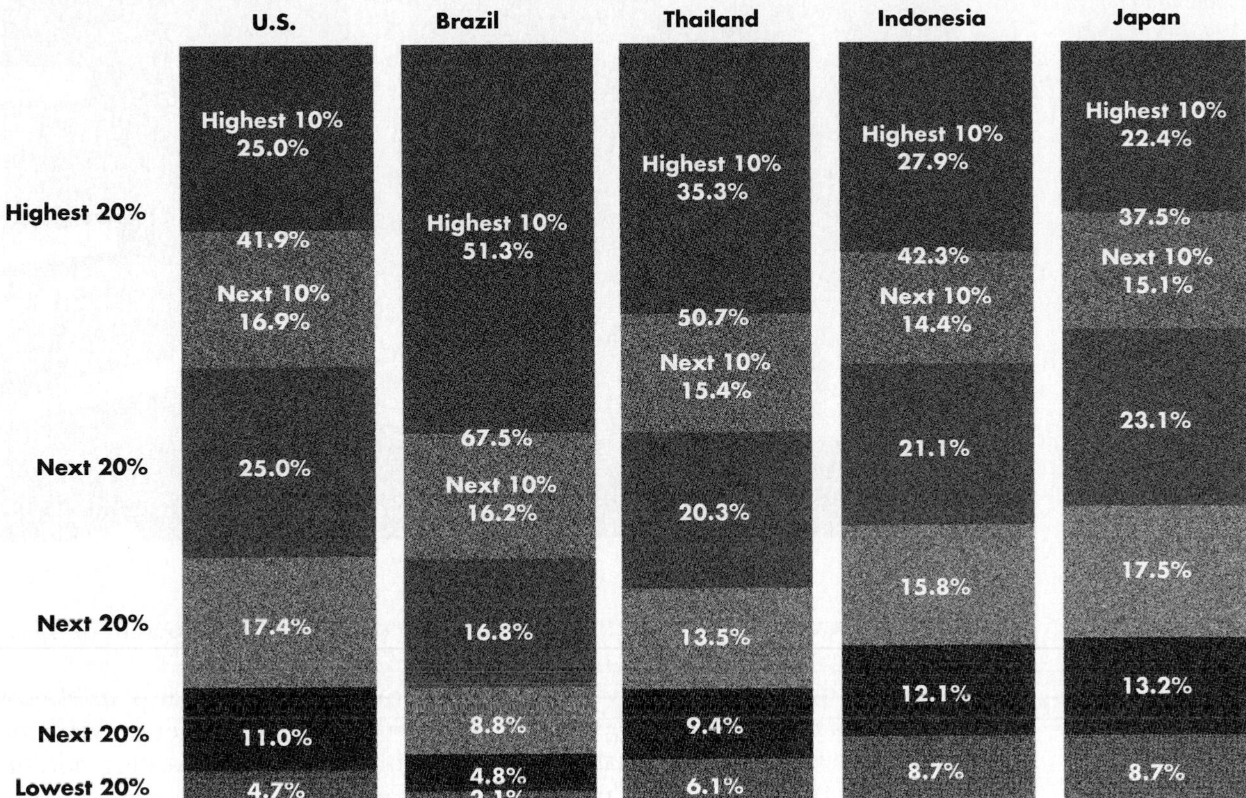

Source: Richard Sookdeo, "The New Global Consumer," *Fortune* (Autumn/Winter, 1993): 68–79.

FIGURE 4-3
How Income Is Allocated

tries, newly industrialized countries, and highly industrialized countries—provides a useful framework for analysis.

Less Developed Countries

Roughly 75 percent of the world's population live in the 94 nations that the World Bank classifies as "developing economies." Most of the world's *truly poor* countries, such as Burkina Faso, Somalia, Benin, and Sudan, are located in sub-Saharan Africa. Plagued by drought and civil wars, these nations' economies lack almost all the resources necessary for development: capital, infrastructure, political stability, and trained workers. Developing market opportunities here depends on identifying the nations' most urgent needs and developing appropriate solutions, including the organizing of financing (note the general similarities to the essence of the marketing concept, discussed in Chapter 1). It also often requires taking a long-term view of doing business, with a willingness to transfer technology, assist in infrastructure development, train workers, and cultivate relationships with local firms and key government and business individuals. Products and services with the greatest potential in these truly poor economies are typically not consumer products but tend instead to be business products such as heavy machinery for building infrastructure, agricultural equipment, basic food products, and health services. This is not to say that there is no demand for consumer products! It's just that

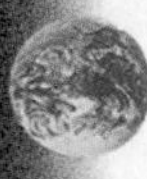

Japaanese consumer electronics are heavily price discounted throughout Asia. Rising incomes among the middle classes in many Asian countries offer new market opportunities.

the economic priorities and the projected rate of market development in these countries continues to focus on basic needs.

In contrast to the world's truly poor countries, a large number of *developing country economies* offer considerable opportunities for consumer goods marketers. Countries with a dual income distribution or with a growing middle class offer opportunities for niches, or for broader-based growth markets. Due in large part to the technological revolution of the 1970s and 1980s, the world's economies are changing more rapidly now than in any other time in history since the Industrial Revolution. India continues to emerge as one of the world's greatest suppliers of relatively low-cost labor, but labor that is highly skilled and highly educated and is in high demand. Very few nations in the world are content with pursuing an economic policy of status quo. A genuine desire for economic development and an improved standard of living have been the main ingredients in the political reforms of the former Soviet Union, eastern Europe, and other developing economies throughout the world.

Newly Industrialized Countries

It is difficult to discuss the development of newly industrialized countries strictly in terms of economic analysis, since that offers too narrow a perspective on the many marketing implications growing out of the so-called economic miracle of these countries. Tremendous economic growth in countries such as South Korea, Singapore, Hong Kong, and Taiwan have created a new middle class of consumers with radically different expectations compared to a mere decade ago. Certainly, the Asian countries of the Pacific Rim provide the most striking examples of economic and market development that will strongly influence consumer marketing opportunities throughout the 1990s. Performing at compound growth rates of 8 to 9 percent over the past three decades, many Asian nations have followed Japan in performing a feat never before seen: Combining fast growth in the early stages of economic development with an increase (rather than a decline) in income equality. Running parallel with this increase in prosperity are powerful social movements that have implications for markets and marketing: growing national populations, a dramatic shift from rural to urban living, changing family structures, and increasingly sophisticated consumers who have greater access to information than ever before. By the year 2010, an additional 400 million people will be born in the Pacific Rim region. While the current demographic profile is relatively young, within ten years 30 percent of the population in these markets will be in their 30s and 40s, the prime earning, spending, and child-rearing years. Coupled with the overall increase in population will be the shift of the population from rural to urban areas. In just 30 years, South Korea's population "flip-flopped" to 73 percent urban from 72 percent rural. By the year 2000, more than 80 percent of all South Koreans will likely live in cities.[22] This shift creates tremendous opportunities and strains on markets such as housing, transportation, energy, education, and agriculture.

While populations are increasing, the number of members in an average newly industrialized country household is declining. Extended families who once lived together under the same roof are establishing separate households (a by-product of increased education and income and changing expectations). While Asian women still have great strides to make in social emancipation, there is growing evidence that they are staying in school longer, marrying later, and entering the work force in greater numbers—trends that create and stimulate markets for consumer durables as well as demand for cosmetics, vacations, and time-saving appliances. See Figure 4-4 for an overview of some of the marketing implications regarding Asia's emerging middle class.[23] Note how the consumption emphasis changes based on the emergence of the middle class.

Finally, the unceasing and accelerating global exchange of information serves to speed these trends along. Asian consumers are heavy users of media-based information and are constantly tuned into information sources

FIGURE 4-4
The Pac Rim's Booming Buying Power

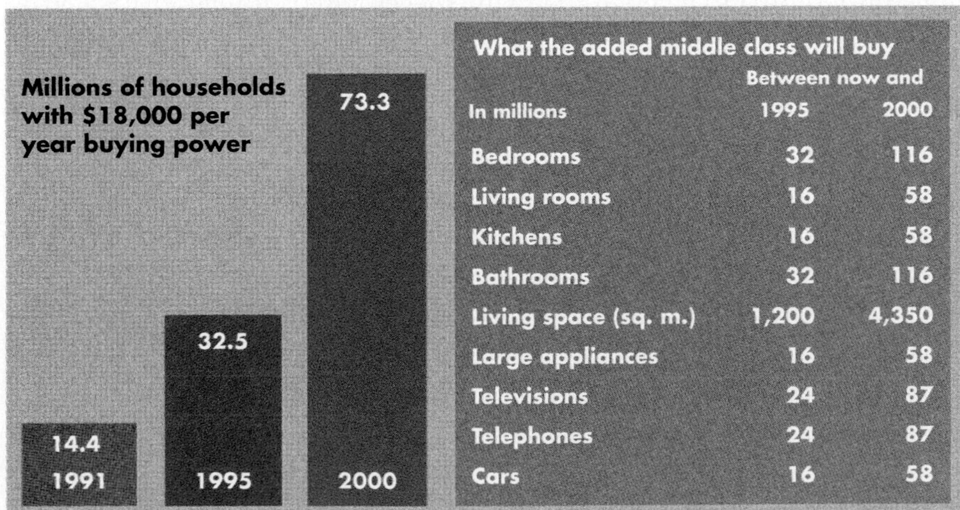

What the added middle class will buy

In millions	Between now and 1995	2000
Bedrooms	32	116
Living rooms	16	58
Kitchens	16	58
Bathrooms	32	116
Living space (sq. m.)	1,200	4,350
Large appliances	16	58
Televisions	24	87
Telephones	24	87
Cars	16	58

Source: Bill Saporito, "Where the Global Action Is," *Fortune* (Autumn/Winter, 1993): 64.

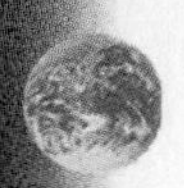

such as newspapers, radio, and TV. The latest global trends in fashion, music, and travel have shorter and shorter lag times in reaching this region of the world, thus fueling and shaping expectations. Perhaps no other region in the world offers greater opportunities for consumer product markets than does Asia in the 1990s. Companies with the ability to manage change and view rapid change as an opportunity will likely find this region of the world to be exciting, frustrating, and rewarding.

Highly Industrialized Countries

The 94 countries categorized as less developed countries accounted collectively for $2.4 trillion dollars in Gross Domestic Product in 1989. This amount is about equivalent to the GDP of the United States alone. The seven countries with the highest GDP, which include Canada, France, Germany, Italy, Japan, the United Kingdom, and the United States meet regularly (these economic summits are referred to as the meeting of the "G7" countries) to discuss issues of conflict and cooperation with respect to economic policies. While they obviously don't have complete control over global economic conditions, they do have a large influence on setting the agenda of economic agreements between themselves. Issues such as money supply, massive loans, and long-term economic priorities are discussed at these meetings. The triad of global economic competitors (the United States, western Europe, and Japan) represented in the G7 most often trade among themselves—roughly 70 percent of all their trade is among themselves.[24] Further, the companies who claim the G7 countries as their home base are also the major competitors in each others' markets. Other countries who are not part of the G7, such as Australia, New Zealand, Switzerland, and the Scandinavian countries, can also be classified as highly industrialized and have strong, competitive markets for both import and export activities.

Within this broad grouping of highly industrialized countries, the marketing focus is likely to be on more detailed analyses of the market, including the nature and extent of competition, marketing channels structure, life-style trends, and market potential and market share. Firms pursuing opportunities in highly industrialized countries would proceed with consumer market analysis in much the same way they would for consumer markets in the United States. Table 4-6 provides an example of purchasing power comparisons of upper-middle income managers from four of the world's major markets for a variety of goods, services, and consumer durables.

While information such as that in Table 4-6 provides interesting insights into how consumers in affluent markets spend their disposable income, it misses the richness of detail needed to develop effective marketing tactics within each consumer market. For example, Germans and Britains pay much higher sales tax than do Americans (14.5 percent, compared to between 5 and 8 percent in the United States); import quotas on Japanese cars in the European community raise prices about 25 percent over the U.S. level; tariff and nontariff barriers significantly influence the channels of distribution strategies for consumer electronics in France. Here again, the complex list of particulars for each market will strongly influence the process of selecting, entering, and competing in markets on a global level.

Analysis of the consumer market from a global perspective requires an appreciation of the broad range of economic and social influences that shape

TABLE 4-6
A Comparison of Upper-Middle Income Manager Households

	U.S.	Japan	Germany	Britain
Salary (U.S. dollars)	$125,000	$129,000	$133,779	$84,942
Tax rate	29.2%	32.7%	33.7%	25.4%
Percentage of after-tax income spent on:				
Alcohol & tobacco	1.8%	1.2%	1.7%	5.3%
Cars & commuting	10.0%	4.3%	8.6%	9.8%
Clothing	6.0%	8.1%	7.3%	7.3%
Food at home	8.0%	17.3%	10.3%	11.7%
Food away from home	5.5%	3.8%	4.2%	3.7%
Furnishings & household operations	6.3%	1.3%	8.6%	6.2%
Housing	17.2%	10.0%	13.2%	16.0%
Medical care	2.3%	2.3%	1.4%	0.6%

Source: Shawn Tully, "Where People Live Best," *Fortune* (March 11, 1991): 46.

market potential. In this section, we have highlighted the socioeconomic factors related to the distribution of world wealth, composition of world age groups, and stages of economic development as the bases for global consumer market assessment. In Chapter 6, Consumer and Business Buying Behavior, we will continue to refine the analysis of global consumer markets by considering factors such as global product consumption patterns and life-styles as a basis for market potential.

Key Terms and Concepts

Consumer market
Metropolitan Statistical Area (MSA)
Primary Metropolitan Statistical Area (PMSA)
Consolidated Metropolitan Statistical Area (CMSA)
Census track
National income
Personal income
Disposable income
Discretionary income
Real income
Market segmentation
Target market
Physical descriptors
Behavioral descriptors
Life-style (psychographics)
VALS
Value of market segmentation
Multiple segmentation bases
Convenience good
Shopping good
Specialty good
Services
Distribution of world wealth
Composition of world age groups
Country stage of economic development
Less developed countries
Newly industrialized countries
Highly industrialized countries

Questions and Exercises

1. The consumer market was described in the chapter as "people with money to spend who are willing to spend it." What are the specific "people" and "money" factors that relate to the overall market potential for products and services?
2. Define market segmentation. What is the relationship between the process of market segmentation and a firm's identification of a target market?
3. Why is geographic location a useful basis for market segmentation? Identify three consumer products or services for which a geographic segmentation approach would be appropriate.

4. Why are behavioral descriptors argued to be superior to physical descriptors as a basis for market segmentation?
5. For many years the VALS (values and life-styles) program was used by firms to implement life-style segmentation. In recent years, the traditional VALS approach has been abandoned by some firms. Why?
6. Explain why both the efficiency **and** effectiveness of a firm's operations are enhanced when market segmentation is properly conducted.
7. Define a "specialty good." What is the key distinguishing feature of a specialty good from other consumer products? Give an example of a specialty good.
8. How does the mere classification of consumer products into categories inform marketing decision makers about the marketing challenges associated with a particular product?
9. How are distribution of world wealth and composition of world age groups used in global consumer market analysis?
10. Why do newly industrialized countries represent such attractive consumer markets?

REFERENCES

1. Michael J. McCarthy, "Marketers Zero In on Their Customers," *The Wall Street Journal* (March 18, 1991): B1.
2. Joan E. Rigdon, "Photography Companies Focus on Niches," *The Wall Street Journal* (June 12, 1993): B1.
3. Eleena De Lisser, "Catering to Cooking-Phobic Customers, Supermarkets Stress Carryout, Add Cafes," *The Wall Street Journal* (April, 5, 1993): B1.
4. Examples taken from Kathleen Deveny, "Segments of One," *The Wall Street Journal* (March 22, 1991): B4.
5. "Marketing's New Tool," *Business Week* (January 26, 1987): 64.
6. Michael Selz, "Gottschalks Is One Retailer That Likes Tallying Sales," *The Wall Street Journal* (February 6, 1991): B2.
7. Susan Moffat, "Japan's New Personalized Production," *Fortune* (October 22, 1990): 132–134.
8. Kathleen Deveny, "Downscale Consumers, Long Neglected, Start to Get Some Respect From Marketers," *The Wall Street Journal* (May 13, 1990): B1 and B6.
9. Steve Pomper, "Where Have All the Yuppies Gone?" *Working Woman* (February 1991): 63–65.
10. Norton Garfinkle, "How Marketing Data Can Identify Your Target Audience," Address to the Eastern Regional Conference of the American Association of Advertising Agencies, 1966.
11. Data cited in Michael J. McCarthy, "Marketers Zero in on Their Customers," *The Wall Street Journal* (March 18, 1991): B1 and B6.
12. Victor J. Cook, Jr. and William A. Mindak, "A Search for Constants: The 'Heavy-User' Revisited," *Journal of Marketing* 1, no. 4 (1984): 79–81.
13. Andrew Mitchell, *The Nine American Lifestyles* (New York: Macmillan, 1983).
14. "'Inner-Directed' Is Where It's at in New Strategies," *Adweek* (May 26, 1986): 17.
15. Mark Lander, "The 'Bloodbath' in Market Research," *Business Week* (February 11, 1991): 72 and 74.
16. See Rahul Jacob, "Beyond Quality and Value," *Fortune,* Special Issue, "The Tough New Consumer." (Autumn/Winter 1993): 8–14; and Faye Rice, "How to Deal with Tougher Customers," *Fortune* (December 3, 1990): 39–48.
17. Kenneth E. Miller and Kent L. Granzin, "Simultaneous Loyalty and Benefit Segmentation of Retail Store Customers," *Journal of Retailing* (Spring 1979): 47.
18. Krystal Miller, "Nissan, Toyota Draw from BMW, Mercedes," *The Wall Street Journal* (October 3, 1990): B1.
19. *The Home Buying and Selling Process,* National Association of Realtors, (Washington, D.C.: National Association of Realtors, 1987).
20. Clive Cook, "Catching Up," *The Economist,* Special Issue, "The World in 1994" (Winter, 1993): 15–16.
21. Adapted from Richard Sookdeo, "The New Global Consumer," *Fortune (*Autumn/Winter, 1993): 68–79.
22. Ford S. Worthy, "A New Mass Market Emerges," *Fortune* (Fall 1991).
23. See Bill Saporito, "Where the Global Action Is," *Fortune* (Autumn/Winter, 1993): 64; "A Survey of Asia: A Billion Consumers," *The Economist (*October 30, 1993); "Economic Miracle or Myth," *The Economist* (October 2, 1993): 65–66.
24. *World Development Report 1985* (Washington, D.C.: World Bank, 1985): 196–197.

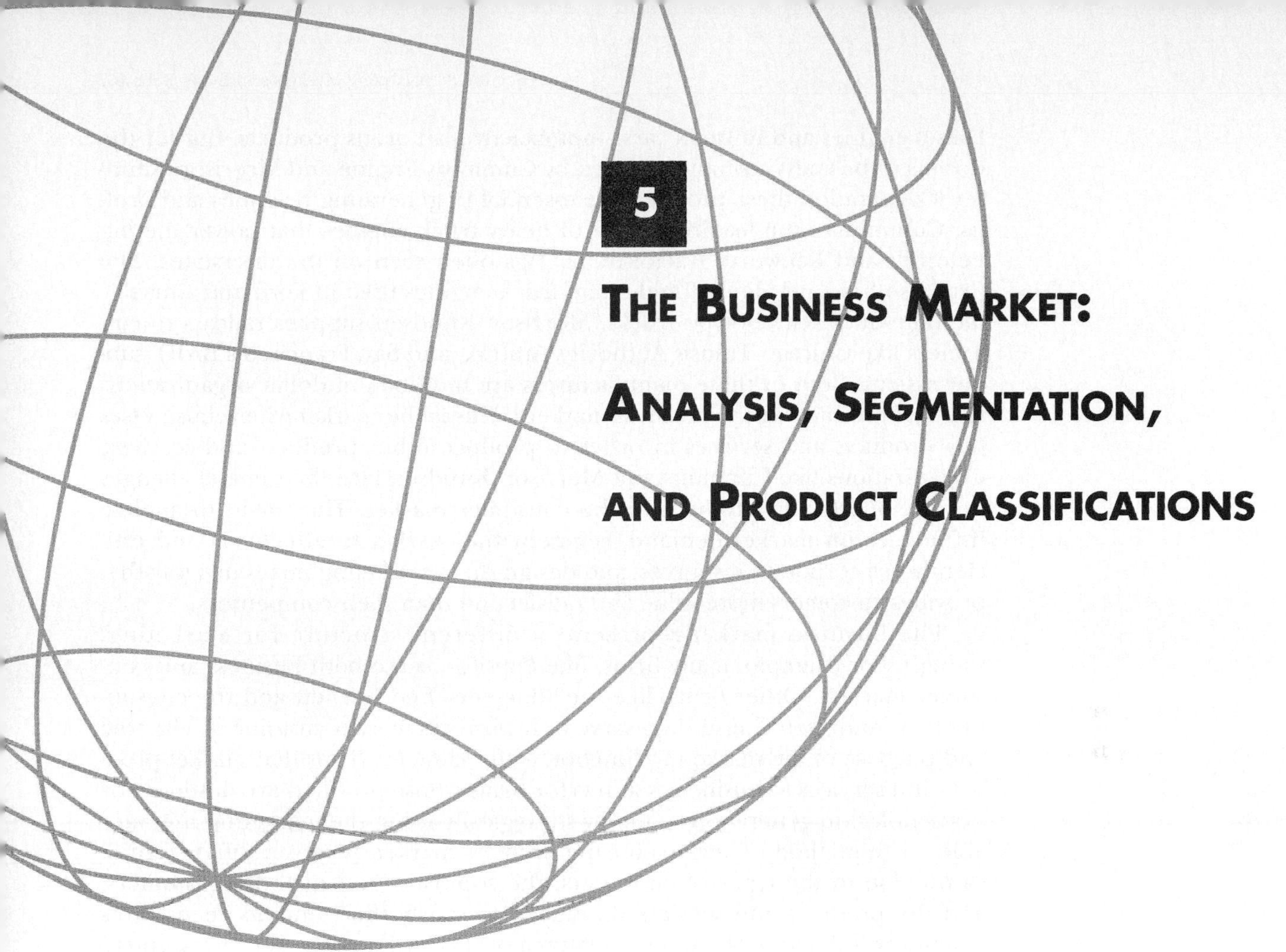

5

THE BUSINESS MARKET: ANALYSIS, SEGMENTATION, AND PRODUCT CLASSIFICATIONS

AFTER STUDYING THIS CHAPTER, YOU WILL UNDERSTAND THAT:

1. The business market has many unique features including unusual forces that shape demand and distinctive features of market transactions.
2. Business buyers are significantly different than household consumers.
3. Segmentation in the business market relies on physical descriptions of organizations and behavioral aspects of product and service use not unlike the consumer market segmentation factors.
4. The classification of business products into distinct categories allows the development of more effective marketing mix strategies.
5. Global business markets are characterized by greater complexity in the transactions process and greater diversity of transaction environments.

Diesel engines and railroad cars—not exactly glamorous products. But for the dozens of business customers served by Cummins Engine and Morrison Knudsen Corporation these products are essential to generating revenues and profits. Cummins is the leading maker of heavy truck engines that power the big Peterbilt and Kenworth tractor-trailer rigs often seen on the interstates. The firm also has a new line of mid-range truck engines used in Ford and Chrysler medium-duty delivery-type trucks. Morrison Knudsen supplies railcars to customers like Chicago Transit Authority, Amtrak, and San Francisco's BART subway system. Both of these manufacturers are multibillion dollar organizations that sell products in the business market.[1] This is the market where businesses buy products and services in order to produce other products and services. Organizations like Cummins and Morrison Knudsen face the same challenges as firms marketing products to the consumer market. They need to analyze influences on market demand, segment the market to effectively and efficiently use corporate resources, and design their marketing mixes in a way that provides customers more value and satisfaction than their competitors.

The business market represents a different structure for marketing, though. For example, many firms, like PepsiCo, serve both business and consumer markets. Other firms, like the ad agency Leo Burnett and the consulting firm Andersen Consulting, serve only business market customers. The role and purpose of the marketing function is the same for firms that market products and services to businesses as it is for firms whose products are destined for households: to generate revenue by strategically using the marketing mix variables. The method of analysis for the business market, however, differs significantly due to the types of customers, the sophistication of those customers, and the products and services developed to satisfy their unique needs. This chapter will describe the unique features of the business market, the segmentation strategies employed, and the classification of business goods that helps firms devise effective marketing mix strategies.

The Business Market Defined

Business marketing is the practice of firms selling goods and services to other businesses. This area of marketing is often referred to as the "business to business" market or the "organizational market." For our purposes, we will use the straightforward description business market. A **business market** is made up of a variety of different business and institutional buyers (like government buyers) who purchase products and services to be used in the production of goods or services or offered for resale to other businesses or household consumers. The business market is not restricted to only manufacturers of heavy equipment, however. Business goods include a vast array of large and small items. Some products are nuts, bolts, and screws used in manufacturing. Other products are manufactured for resale by retail outlets. And business services of all types are included in the classification of business goods. A simple way to clarify the scope of the business market is to realize that it involves all sales transactions *except* those sales made to household consumers.

This jet engine is one of many products that General Electric sells in the business market.

General Electric is an excellent example of a corporation that sells primarily in business markets to business and organizational users. In 1993, GE generated over $60 billion in total revenues through 13 key business operations. Of that total, nearly $50 billion in revenue was earned by providing products and services to business users. General Electric aircraft engines, medical systems, transportation systems, and other business products are as well known to corporate buyers as GE light bulbs and appliances are known to household consumers. Firms like Sony, IBM, Rolodex, and Swiss Life (business insurance) are examples of other companies that generate a large percentage of their total revenue from the business market.

Unique Features of the Business Market

The nature of the business market is significantly different than the consumer market. The factors that make the business market unique have to do with the characteristics of demand, buyers, and market transactions; geographic concentration in the market; and the distribution channels used to serve business buyers. These forces combine to make the process of strategic marketing planning quite complex. We will look at each of these factors and identify the characteristics of each that shape the nature of the business market.

Characteristics of Demand

The nature of demand for goods and services in the business market is influenced by a variety of unique forces. Remember that in the household consumer market, demand was brought about by people with money to spend and a willingness to spend it. The factors that shape demand in business markets must be clearly understood because the flow of goods and the desire for goods and services among business buyers change based on these factors.

Derived Demand

Demand for business goods is described as **derived demand.** This description is used because demand for business goods is ultimately "derived" from the demand for household consumer goods. When the demand for automobiles slackens, the demand for steel, plastic, copper, and a variety of other industrial goods deceases. If household consumer preferences in the furniture market switch from wood furniture to wicker or metal, the demand for lumber is affected. It is necessary for business goods manufacturers to carefully monitor consumption trends in the household consumer market in order to accurately predict the derived demand for their own products and services.

Inelastic Demand

Total demand for most business goods is described as **inelastic demand.** That is, the demand for business products and services is not particularly sensitive to changes in price. If attorney fees rise 10 percent in a year, a firm generally will not decrease its use of attorney services based on this increase. This is true because the price of any particular business good or service as a percentage of the finished product represents a relatively small part of the final price paid by the buyer. The cost of the machines to produce furniture or kitchen appliances, for example, is spread over many thousands of units over several years and does not contribute a great amount to the final retail price of the item. Nor would the increase in attorney fees mentioned earlier be significant to Whirlpool's pricing strategy for washers and dryers. Again, as business demand is derived from household consumer demand, a small price change in materials would not produce a marked shift in the demand for the business goods that go into the consumer product. If the price of copper used for the fabrication of automobile radiators drops, auto manufacturers are not going to buy significantly more copper unless consumers buy more cars.

While inelasticity of demand is a key feature of demand in the business market, the conclusion should not be drawn that demand is totally insensitive to price changes. Demand tends to be inelastic in the short run because manufacturers cannot make changes in production methods quickly enough to eliminate an item that may have risen in price. In the long run, however, lower-priced substitutes, such as plastic for steel in the construction of side panels in Saturn automobiles, would affect the amount of steel demanded. Also, while total demand may be inelastic, an individual supplier of materials for making telephones or appliances can capture business by making significant price concessions to individual manufacturers even though overall industry demand remains constant.

Fluctuating Demand

In the business market, large commitments of capital are necessary to expand plant capacity or replace equipment that is obsolete. If household consumer demand increases 10 or 15 percent in a product category, then business demand for production machinery may increase as much as 100 percent. Conversely, during periods of slow or declining consumer demand, manufacturers of both capital and consumer goods tend to delay expansion or machinery replacement until there is evidence that demand is recovering. The attempt to anticipate and then respond to household consumer demand create what is referred to in the business market as **fluctuating demand**. A manufacturer cannot add only part of a machine to meet the increase in household consumer demand nor can a plant easily cut production by fractional amounts should household consumer demand drop. Another contributing factor to fluctuating demand is that business firms often "speculate" about inventory levels as they anticipate future increases or decreases in demand for their output. All of these types of influences work to produce more widely fluctuating demand in the business market.

CHARACTERISTICS OF BUYERS

Buyers in the business market are significantly different from buyers in the consumer market. The nature of those differences has great impact on understanding the environment within which business marketing decisions are made.

Number and Size of Buyers

From Figure 5-1 you can see that there are approximately 5.6 million business establishments in the United States compared with over 260 million household consumers. That relatively small group of purchasers wields enormous purchasing power. Total dollar sales of business goods is roughly equal to the total dollar sales of household consumer goods. This means that there are fewer but larger buyers in the business market. This unique feature of the business market is advantageous in that buyers are more easily identified. Bose, the stereo manufacturer, can identify twenty major automobile producers to which it can try to sell its audio systems. Conversely, the attempt to market successfully to over 92 million households in the United States as potential customers is a much more formidable task. Similarly, buying power in the business market tends to be highly concentrated. In the aircraft, photo equipment, and organic fiber industries, the four largest firms produce over 70 percent of the total output. In some industries, the largest firms are massively dominant: 100 percent of canned baby food, 96 percent of disposable diapers, and 98 percent of tractor tires are manufactured by only four firms.

Another measure of size is the amount of money spent by business organizations to carry on their business. In 1992, 3M Corporation—makers of industrial chemicals, adhesives, and paper products—generated $13.8 billion in sales but *spent* $11.8 on materials and selling expenses to generate that revenue. Monsanto Company had similar expenditures: $7.7 billion in revenue and $5.8 billion in expenses. These billions of dollars in purchasing power by business products firms shape the nature of demand in the business market.

Knowledgeable Buyers

Business buyers become expert in evaluating not only products and services on the market, but also the suppliers who provide the products. In many cases,

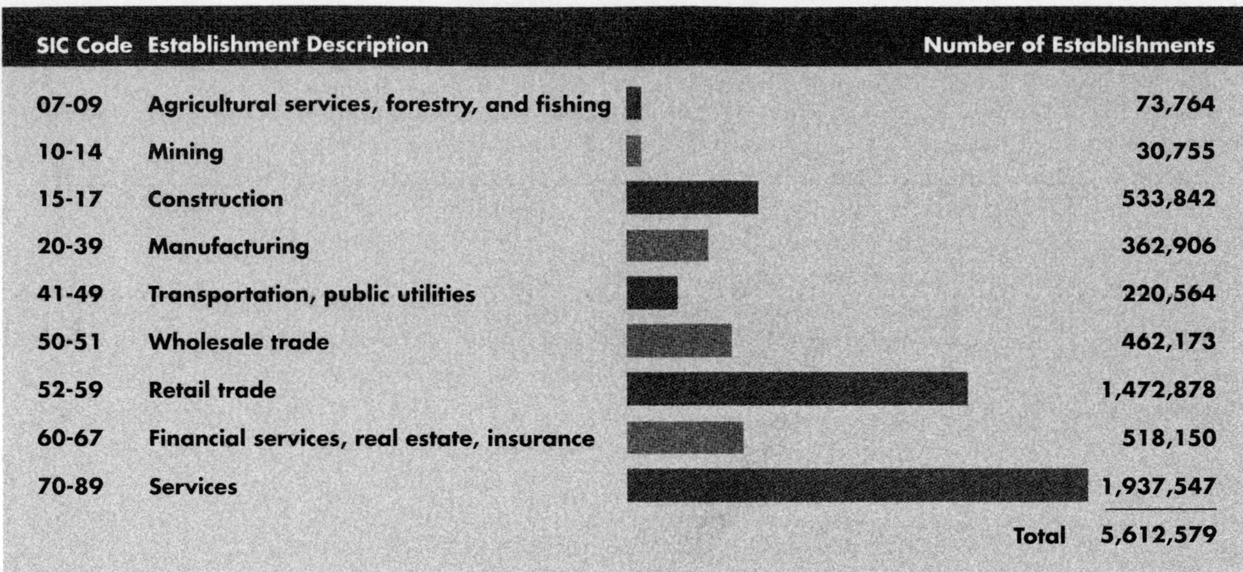

SIC Code	Establishment Description	Number of Establishments
07-09	Agricultural services, forestry, and fishing	73,764
10-14	Mining	30,755
15-17	Construction	533,842
20-39	Manufacturing	362,906
41-49	Transportation, public utilities	220,564
50-51	Wholesale trade	462,173
52-59	Retail trade	1,472,878
60-67	Financial services, real estate, insurance	518,150
70-89	Services	1,937,547
	Total	5,612,579

Source: Adapted from U.S. Bureau of the Census, *County Business Patterns, 1988, United States* (Washington, D.C.: U.S. Government Printing Office, 1990), Table 1a: 1, 2.

FIGURE 5-1
U.S. Business Establishments by Major Groups in 1988

a firm's ability to compete is only as good as the component parts that go into its products *and* the timeliness with which it can deliver those products to its buyers. This need to serve customers creates a very high level of knowledge among business buyers. Business buyers generally will also use more formalized procedures to determine their needs for goods and services than do most household consumers. This is not to say that less tangible factors do not enter the decision-making process. Business buyers do not always choose the least expensive sources of supply, for example. Because of the extreme importance of reliability and dependability in the flow of products, business buyers must avoid as much risk as possible in supply and often place high priority on the relationships that develop with sources. For example, when a producer at the ad agency Dahlin, Smith, and White contracts with a production house to prepare materials for the agency's client Intel, the quality and timeliness of the production service is more important than the cost.

GEOGRAPHIC CONCENTRATION OF INDUSTRIES

Business manufacturing is characterized by significant geographic concentration of activity. Figure 5-2 shows the percentage of *value added* in the manufacturing sector for different parts of the United States. **Value added** is a measure of the difference between the cost of materials that enter the production process in a factory and the price charged for the product at the "finished-goods" end of the process. Note that nearly 40 percent of total manufacturing value added activity is in eight states comprising the Middle Atlantic and East North Central census of manufacturing regions. Since 1982, the West region has grown considerably and as of 1987 accounted for over 17 percent of value added in manufacturing.

In addition, several industries have gravitated to different parts of the United States creating geographic concentration. The steel, rubber, and auto-

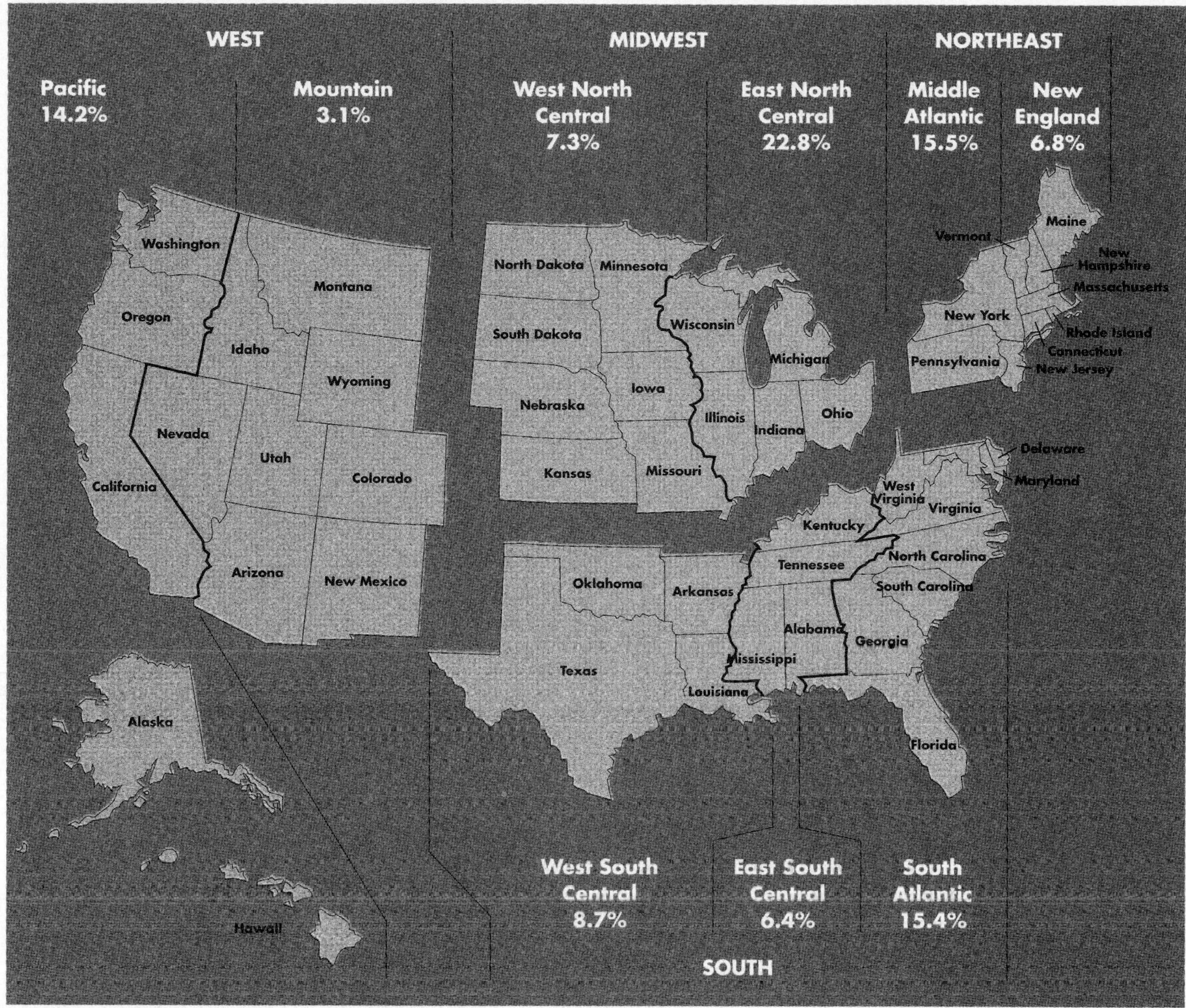

Source: Derived from U.S. Bureau of the Census, *Census of Manufactures* (Washington, D.C.: U.S. Government Printing Office, 1987) General Summary, Part 1, MC87-S-1, Figure 1 and Table G.

FIGURE 5-2
Percentage of Total Manufacturing Value Added by Census Regions and Geographic Divisions of the United States

mobile industries have been concentrated in just a few East North Central and East South Central states. The Silicon Valley in California and Route 128 in Massachusetts represent a concentration of high-technology companies. The firms that supply these concentrated industries often locate facilities near their customers to provide more rapid and reliable service. Pricing strategies can also be affected when customers are heavily concentrated in a single geographic region. These strategies are covered in Chapter 9. For now, realize that the marketing mix needed to effectively serve business markets can be greatly affected by the extent of geographic concentration.

DISTRIBUTION CHANNELS

The unique feature of distribution channels that affects the business goods market is that distribution channels for business products tend to be more direct. Since business goods and services are often designed to strict buyer specifications, supplying firms must work closely with buying firms throughout the process. If a product is custom made, the channel of distribution will not include distributors or wholesalers but rather the item will be shipped directly or actually constructed at the buyer's location. Large processing and manufacturing equipment also requires direct distribution. These items are large, bulky, and installed by the seller. If intermediaries were used in the distribution channel, the cost of shipping such a large item from location to location before it reached the buyer would be prohibitive. Finally, the reduced number of buyers and the large orders that they place also makes it feasible to distribute directly. Selling firms will find it profitable to assume the costs of distribution when there are large orders from just a few buyers.

CHARACTERISTICS OF MARKET TRANSACTIONS

Due to economic influences or because of tradition, several aspects of market transactions are unique in the business market. These distinguishable and unique characteristics are diffused buying responsibility within organizations, the interdependence that can develop between buyers and sellers, leasing rather than buying equipment, negotiation and bidding for jobs, and the "make or buy" decision.

Diffused Buying Responsibility

The typical business purchase order is signed by a purchasing agent, but that person is usually *not* the person who made the decision about what to buy. It is often not clear to those *outside* the buying firm precisely who *within* the buying firm is making the decision to buy. Production workers, research and development (R&D) staff, design engineers, or top-level executives may be the ones who determine the specifications for products. Additionally, it is common in business purchases for several different people to be involved in a single decision. This is known as **diffused buying responsibility** because multiple decision makers are involved. This aspect of business buying is also often referred to as the *buying center* concept because several people are involved in the process. Specifically, it is possible to identify as many as six different types of decision makers who may be involved in any particular business purchase decision—these are outlined in Table 5-1.

Recognizing that there are potentially different players in a context with diffused buying responsibility is critically important. If the selling firm does not target the proper individuals, then the chances of ever selling to the organization are minimal. Different members of an organization have different values and objectives in the decision-making process which may require that different selling appeals be used. Also, as separate levels of the organization become involved, the relative power of individuals at different levels will vary. Finally, as multiple decision makers are encountered, conflict resolution may be occurring within an organization. As an example of this, a clerical staff person may be the gatekeeper for all product and service information that flows to the ultimate decision makers. If the selling firm does not properly understand this individual's role and influence, its product or service may never even make it to the consideration stage.

TABLE 5-1
Potential Decision Makers Who Create Diffused Buying Responsibility in the Business Market

1. Initiator
This person first suggests that a purchase needs to be made. This person may be directly involved in operations or may be from a different part of the organization entirely, such as the home office. Also, an initiator may actually be from outside the organization. Often, outside consultants recommend the purchase of equipment or services to enhance a firm's operations.

2. User
This, of course, is the individual within the organization who ultimately uses the product. A scientist in the research and development laboratory may require a specially designed microscope or an engineer may need a high-powered computer work station. The user often establishes product specifications and submits an evaluation of product performance.

3. Decision Maker
The ultimate decision maker in an organization can literally be anyone. The user is many times the decision maker. The purchasing agent can be the decision maker. In some organizations, the president or chief executive officer may become involved as the ultimate decision maker.

4. Influencer
An influencer in a diffused buying process is someone in the organization who, because of experience or specialized expertise, exerts an influence on other members of the organization involved in the decision.

5. Buyer
This person simply places the order for the item. In most organizations, this will be a purchasing agent or the equivalent position.

6. Gatekeeper
This individual is critical to the process. Gatekeepers control the flow of information into an organization. Information about products from literature or directly from salespeople is controlled by the gatekeeper. Gatekeepers can be purchasing agents or even clerical staff in an organization.

Because of the complexity of diffused buying situations, firms like IBM have established selling teams to cope with the many decision makers involved. IBM has formed Information Systems Investment Strategies (ISIS) teams to deal with large customers like G. Heileman Brewing and Gulfstream Aerospace. The teams spend several months with customers in all levels of the organization analyzing operations and the customer's facilities. To better assess the situation, members of the team come from various technical and nontechnical backgrounds within the organization. This enables the team to deal with all types of potential participants in the buying decision because of the many skills represented on the team. One customer said of the ISIS system that it facilitated making complicated decisions and put them "into terms that senior management could understand."[2] The IBM approach focuses several levels of a buyer's organization on a decision at a single point in time, thus effectively coping with diffused buying responsibility.

While firms like IBM have plenty of staff to deploy in this complex buying situation, it's not as easy for small businesses to cope with characteristic market transactions. Small businesses normally do not have enough staff to deploy to various parts of the organization. In this case, the small business operator can best cope with diffused buying responsibility by selling directly to the user and enlisting the user's help in negotiating the complex decision-making process. Since the buyer has the most to gain from the product, then the buyer may be willing to act as a champion for the firm's product within the organization.

Interdependence of Buyers and Sellers

Because of the importance of the business purchase decision, close relationships many times develop between buyers and sellers. This is referred to as the **interdependence of buyers and sellers.** What happens in business markets is that buyers and sellers essentially form a partnership where they work closely on the design and manufacture of products or the precise nature of services to be provided. For example, sales representatives for data processing equipment must learn enough about a customer's firm to develop and install complete systems for accounting and management control. Business machine companies have specialists in supermarket organization, store layout and decor, and stock control. These specialists work closely with decision makers in the buying firm to carefully work out the details of the installation. A very important interdependence relationship develops during this process. The seller depends on the buyer to provide information regarding product performance needs. The buyer is dependent on the seller to translate those needs into actual products or services. This feature of the business market is often referred to as **relationship marketing.** Relationships between buyers and sellers in the business market become much more complex and comprehensive than most in the household consumer market. Interactions create a deeply felt trust. Buyers and sellers become partners in business rather than simply participants in a commercial exchange. The CEO of Home Depot, Inc., Bernard Marcus, spends much of his time on the road meeting with the CEOs of Home Depot's main vendors. The close ties Home Depot has developed with these of vendors allow the retailer to carry lower inventories because the vendors are willing to rapidly restock supplies. Home Depot's CEO says, "We don't believe in adversarial relationships. We need each other."[3]

Reciprocity can be an outgrowth of this close relationship between buyers and sellers. When business buyers and sellers make an effort to buy and use each others products as a demonstration of goodwill, this is referred to as **reciprocity**. This is not to say that all reciprocity arrangements are friendly. At times, buyers expect sellers to buy their own goods in return. Such expectations can be destructive and are hard to defend on ethical grounds. Whenever a buyer or seller *expects as a condition of purchase or sale* that the other party reciprocate, such coercive reciprocity is unethical and may be illegal as well.

Leasing

Leasing is a prevalent feature of business market transactions. A variety of factors contribute to the preference for leasing business equipment rather than purchasing it outright. First, the high cost of most major capital investments creates a financing problem for many firms. The lease method, however, permits payments to be made as the equipment is used. The net amount of working capital required is, therefore, reduced. (A key feature of many leases is that no cash payment is required at the outset.) Second, some equipment is technically complex and requires special servicing. Many lease arrangements also include provisions for servicing by the lessor. Third, manufacturing firms are hesitant to purchase equipment in areas where the risk of changes in technology may render the equipment obsolete in a relatively short period of time. Leasing such equipment provides a hedge against obsolescence in that short-term lease arrangements can be made. Finally, property taxes are not generally charged against leased equipment in many cases. To determine the extent to which leasing is an advantage over purchasing, the buying firm must calculate the tax advantages of depreciation that could be charged against owned equipment relative to the advantages of leasing just described. Firms marketing in the business market must be prepared to offer lease arrangements on products due to its popularity among business buyers and the potential benefits leasing accords to buyers.

Selling organizations benefit from leasing as well. They benefit from the steady cash flow that comes from lease arrangements, which can reduce the impact of cyclical declines in an industry. The seller generally also benefits from the lessee's need for supplies, parts, and service, which can contribute a substantial portion of profitable business. Finally, sellers who offer the lease option can many times attract potential customers who would otherwise not be able to afford the equipment on a purchase basis. Leasing by sellers does not offer only advantages, however. Selling firms accept the responsibility of arranging the financing for the equipment and must bear the risk and cost of obsolescence and taxes.

Negotiation and Bidding

Many exchanges in the business market are subject to **negotiation and bidding.** In negotiated contracts, price, delivery schedules, product specifications, and the responsibilities of each party are set through bargaining. While negotiations can be complex and sometimes heated, both buyer and seller benefit from the specifications that emerge from well-conducted negotiations. Also, sellers may actually benefit greatly from the process in that long-term commitments can result from negotiated contracts.

Bidding is a feature in many markets, especially when government buyers are involved. Bidding most directly affects the price component of a seller's marketing mix. Aside from government contracts, bidding has emerged in business markets where buyers perceive a high degree of homogeneity among suppliers. Examples are in the printing and automobile component parts industries. Bidding has tended to erode the profitability of suppliers in markets where the practice has become prevalent. As firms engage in *lowball* bidding (submitting a bid that is actually below costs) just to obtain business, competition becomes very price intensive. However, more sophisticated bidding procedures rely on *bundling* of services where a basic bid represents only the barest minimum product and service provision. As buyers require more precise product specifications or demand more complete service in the transaction, the bid is escalated. If, for example, a buyer requires products that are produced within very small tolerances of error, the bid is increased. If delivery times are spaced in short intervals, then again the bid would be higher. For firms that get involved in business market transactions where bidding is the basis for price determination, it is essential to have complete cost figures readily available for different levels of product and service specification.

Make or Buy Decision

At some point, business buyers need to determine whether making a product or providing its own service is more cost effective than buying the product or service from an outside supplier. Henry Ford was famous for building a business empire in which the firm bought virtually nothing. Ford Motor Company made its own glass, rubber, and steel. Ultimately, however, Ford discovered that complete independence from specialized providers was unprofitable. Firms that specialize in the production of an item often realize economies of scale and levels of quality that the nonspecialized firm simply cannot match. General Motors has gone so far as to have PPG Industries run the paint shops in some of its production plants due to the quality of PPG paints and the expertise the firm brings to the process.[4] While firms may regularly review their supplier relationships with an eye toward making rather than buying a product, only occasionally is it discovered that making the product is more cost efficient than buying from a seller who specializes. Selling firms need to be alert to situations where buyers may be considering the decision to make rather than buy in order to counter-argue the proposition and retain the business.

These unique features of the business market are critically important. The preceding discussion highlights that product development, pricing, distribution, and promotional strategies are all affected by the nature of business buyers and the way in which they carry out their market transactions. Table 5-2 provides an overview of the issues presented. But this descriptive view of the business market must proceed to more strategic issues. The process of segmentation in the business market will now be considered.

MARKET SEGMENTATION

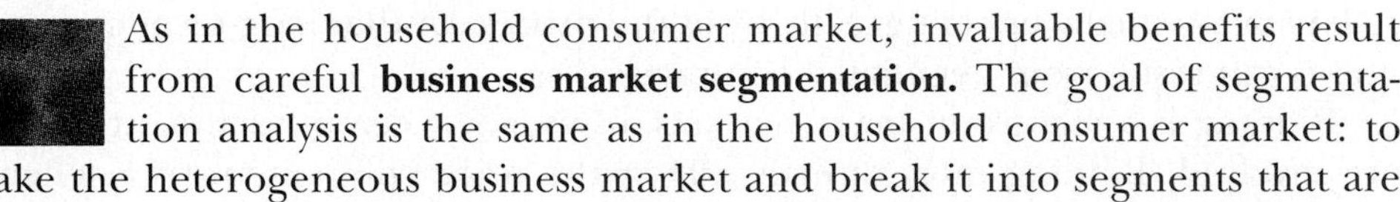

As in the household consumer market, invaluable benefits result from careful **business market segmentation.** The goal of segmentation analysis is the same as in the household consumer market: to take the heterogeneous business market and break it into segments that are

TABLE 5-2
Unique Features of the Business Market

Characteristics of Demand	**Characteristics of Market Transactions**
• Derived demand	• Diffused buying responsibilities
• Inelastic demand	• Interdependence of buyer and seller
• Fluctuating demand	• Leasing
	• Negotiation and bidding
	• Make or buy decision
Characteristics of Business Buyers	**Distribution Systems**
• Number and size of buyers	
• Knowledgeable buyers	
Geographic Concentration of Industries	

more homogeneous and manageable. "Effective industrial market segmentation helps capture a new business opportunity, protect market position, and avert competitive threats."[5] Motorola is a firm that takes the process of segmentation seriously. This highly successful global semiconductor and communications firm identifies six distinct segments in its annual report: the semiconductor products segment (semiconductors), general systems segment (cellular telephones), communications segment (wireless paging and data transmission), government and systems technology segment (global personal communications), information systems segment (data compression and networking), and the automotive and industrial electronics group (lighting and energy products). Firms like Motorola recognize the value of focusing their resources on well-defined products and customer segments in the business market.

There are six basic approaches to segmenting the business market for goods and services: type of organization, standard industrial classification (SIC), size of organization, geographic location, end-use segmentation, and horizontal versus vertical market segmentation.

TYPE OF ORGANIZATION SEGMENTATION

The broadest means of segmenting the business market is to recognize the types of organizations that constitute the realm of potential customers. In the most general sense, the market can be described as consisting of five basic **organizational types**:

- *Users.* These are organizations that purchase finished products for use in their businesses. The goods are not changed or incorporated in the manufacturing of other products. Machine tools, computers, vehicles, and office supplies are examples.
- *Manufacturers, Processors, Assemblers.* This type of organization purchases products to use in the production process or buys component parts of the finished product they sell. Raw materials, drive belts, and computer chips are examples of products sold to these buyers.
- *Resellers.* These are wholesalers, distributors, and retailers who buy finished products and resell them in the same form to all classes of business customers or to household consumers.
- *Corporate Service Organizations.* It is important to distinguish this class of customer—these organizations provide an intangible product to their customers. Service organizations typically purchase finished items like carpeting, office furniture, and operating supplies like stationery. These organizations are high potential customers for other services such as computer consulting. Examples would be the J. Walter Thompson advertising agency and the Coopers and Lybrand accounting firm.
- *Institutional Service Organizations.* These are not-for-profit organizations that by virtue of their unique status represent an entirely different customer class. All forms of government, educational institutions, research and teaching hospitals, and foundations are included here. This group represents enormous purchasing power.

STANDARD INDUSTRIAL CLASSIFICATION(SIC) SEGMENTATION

The **Standard Industrial Classification (SIC)** prepared by the U.S. Census Bureau, Bureau of the Budget, serves as an ideal tool for business segmentation. SIC codes are assigned in nine major groups with 48 total categories. The SIC provides uniformity in definitions and identifies the number of establishments engaged in each type of business. SIC category segmentation is one of the most common approaches to identifying business target markets.

SIC data can provide very specific information, however. Table 5-3 is taken from the *County Business Patterns* publication of the U.S. Bureau of the Census for Cuyahoga County, Ohio. Sample information is displayed for SIC codes in wholesale trade, retail trade, and services. Here a firm would be able to identify types of organizations, the number of establishments, and the number of employees in the relatively specific area of a single county within a state. While this type of information is somewhat superficial, it does alert a firm to the basic potential of the market area. For example, if NCR wanted to determine the market for its retail inventory tracking systems in Cuyahoga County, the firm could immediately identify that there are 8,773 retail operations in the area. This information would give NCR a general description of the business segment.

TABLE 5-3
Cuyahoga County, Ohio: Employees and Establishments by Industry in 1987

SIC Code	Establishment Description	Number of Establishments	Number of Employees
	Wholesale Trade	3,594	58,954
50	Wholesale trade—durable goods	2,633	37,923
501	Motor vehicles and auto equipment	239	5,581
5012	Automobile and other motor vehicles	38	598
5013	Auto parts and supplies	182	4,813
5014	Tires and tubes	18	170
508	Machinery, equipment, and supplies	1,044	15,213
5081	Commercial machines and equipment	239	5,286
5082	Construction and mining equipment	33	586
5083	Farm machinery and equipment	17	159
5084	Business machinery and equipment	355	3,531
5085	Business supplies	209	2,455
	Retail Trade	8,773	119,632
52	Building materials and garden supplies	288	3,167
521	Lumber and building materials	87	2,057
523	Paint, glass, wallpaper stores	72	330
525	Hardware stores	89	508
	Services	12,766	200,345
73	Business Services	2,433	41,335
737	Computer services	249	4,047
7372	Computer programming	105	1,416
7374	Data processing	89	2,311
7379	Computer-related services	50	346

Source: Adapted from U.S. Bureau of the Census, *County Business Patterns, 1987, Ohio* (Washington, D.C.: U.S. Government Printing Office, 1989), Table 2: 68, 70.

SIZE OF ORGANIZATION SEGMENTATION

Size of organization segmentation can be based on total sales volume of a potential customer or number of employees—both of which can be obtained from SIC code data. The data in Tables 5-4 and 5-5 demonstrate the value of SIC code analysis in this approach to segmentation. With these data, a firm can identify prospects based on size relative to the number of employees and the total payroll expenditures of the firms. One well-known firm has operationalized this type of segmentation in the insurance industry.[6] USF&G, a leading property and casualty insurer, has launched a program to provided increased building and general liability coverage to small business—competitors have ignored this segment. The firm expects to increase its small business premiums from $240 million to over $1 billion.

Another basis for size segmentation relates to large users and small users of a product category. This is similar to *volume of consumption* analysis used in household consumer market segmentation. A new competitor often finds a marketing opportunity among low volume users who are ignored by the large, established suppliers. This is precisely the strategy employed by Geneva Steel. This firm sells to steel service centers that buy, process, and then sell steel to mid-size and small users. Geneva avoids big, demanding buyers such as auto makers, and with this segmentation scheme based on customer size, it is one of the few profitable steel mills in the United States.[7] Conversely, many firms ignore small users because of the allure of large user potential. There are significant benefits of economies of scale in dealing only with large-volume buyers. The selling and distribution costs associated with a few large buyers are significantly less than dealing with many small customers. Firms compete vigorously for the favors of large-size customers. For example, it is not uncommon for a supplier to automobile manufacturers to have a sales office where the only customer is one automobile company.

TABLE 5-4
Business Establishments in the United States, 1988: Employees and Number of Establishments

Number of Employees	Percentage of Total Establishments	Percentage of Total Employment
1–4	54.9%	6.5%
5–9	20.1	9.0
10–19	12.2	11.3
20–49	7.9	16.4
50–99	2.8	13.1
100–249	1.5	15.4
250–499	.4	8.9
500–999	.1	6.9
>1000	.1	12.5
	Total Establishments = 6.02 million	Total Employment = 87.88 million

Source: Adapted from U.S. Bureau of the Census, *County Business Patterns, 1988, United States* (Washington, D.C.: U.S. Government Printing Office, 1990), Figure 2: x.

SIC Code	Industry	Number of Employees for Week Including March 12	Payroll ($1000) First Quarter	Annual	Number of Establishments, by Employment Size Class Total	1–4	5–9	10–19	20–49	50–99	100–249	250–499	500–999	1000+
	St Louis													
138	Oil and gas field services	146	495	2,263	7	4	—	1	—	2	—	—	—	—
1381	Drilling oil and gas wells	(C)	(D)	(D)	4	1	—	1	—	2	—	—	—	—
14	Nonmetallic minerals except fuels	230	1,343	6,079	15	5	2	5	2	1	—	—	—	—
142	Crushed and broken stone	132	760	3,257	5	—	1	2	1	1	—	—	—	—
1422	Crushed and broken limestone	132	760	3,257	5	—	1	2	1	1	—	—	—	—
144	Sand and gravel	93	555	2,706	7	2	1	3	1	—	—	—	—	—
1442	Construction sand and gravel	(B)	(D)	(D)	7	2	2	3	1	—	—	—	—	—
....	Contract construction	26,515	150,474	644,761	1,987	1,116	337	256	195	50	24	3	4	2
15	General contractors and operative builders	8,435	53,283,	213,519	554	353	89	62	32	9	4	1	2	2

(Excludes government employees, railroad employees, self-employed persons, etc.—see "General Explanation" for definitions and statement on reliability of data. Size class 1 to 4 includes establishments having payroll but no employees during mid-March pay period. "D" denotes figures withheld to avoid disclosure of operations of individual establishments, the other alphabetics indicate employment-size class—see footnote.)

Source: U.S. Department of Commerce, *Annual County Business Patterns* (Missouri), 111.

TABLE 5-5
Example of Data from County Business Patterns

GEOGRAPHIC LOCATION SEGMENTATION

Geographic location is a frequently used basis for segmentation in the business market because of the tendency for some industries to be geographically concentrated. Some business markets are regional in character due to the basic nature of the industry. Coal mining and other natural resource industries are examples. Some industries have become concentrated in certain areas of the country due to the emergence of one or more key competitors that ultimately attracted other competitors and suppliers. Textiles, automobile manufacturing, furniture, and pharmaceuticals are all examples of industries where firms have gravitated to the same region(s) of the country. Firms that serve industries based on a geographic segmentation scheme will often locate in or near the same geographic area in order to provide prompt and individualized service. Even without the predominance of an entire industry in an area, there are still tendencies within smaller market areas for concentration. Using the data in Table 5-5 once again, notice that in the St. Louis, Missouri, county area a large number of firms are in the general and contract construction industry. Several of these firms employ over 500 people. Such concentration makes this market attractive for construction equipment and materials suppliers as well as a variety of satellite firms that serve various needs of the construction industry, like equipment repair firms, for example.

END-USE SEGMENTATION

End-use segmentation refers to segmenting the market based on the final use or application of a product. If an electronic component is to be used in an inexpensive radio, the care exercised in product development and the manufacturing process and the scrutiny of the item by the buyer will be considerably different from that given to a similar component that is to be used in the control system of a passenger airplane. The use characteristics of different buyers can, therefore, form a basis for segmenting the business market. John Deere makes a wide range of agricultural machines and implements. When the firm identified the trend toward larger but fewer farms in the United States, it channeled its product development and production resources into larger and more powerful equipment to match the use characteristics of this group of large-farm potential buyers.[8]

Another aspect of end use as a basis for segmentation relates to original equipment manufacturers (OEM) versus after-market buyers. OEM customers buy products that are incorporated in the final product they manufacture. After-market customers are buying items to resell to their customers. An example is the automobile battery market. Ford Motor Company is an OEM that buys batteries to install in vehicles as they are assembled on the production line. Conversely, NAPA Auto Parts stocks batteries to sell to household consumers. These two business buying firms represent very different segments of the market and place different demands on their suppliers in all areas of the marketing mix. Ford Motor Company will want a relatively few number of different types of batteries. These batteries, however, may need to meet precise size specifications to fit particular vehicles. NAPA, on the other hand, will need a greater range of batteries to fit the broad range of household customer uses.

Closely related to end-use segmentation is benefit segmentation for business markets. Business marketers can demonstrate to potential customers that purchase of the firm's product will provide beneficial end results and enhance the buyer's operations. Xerox Corp. does just that for its buyers and expresses this benefit in the advertising theme, "The Document Company." Xerox marketing strategists point out that the firm isn't simply selling photo copy machines, but rather the benefits that come from *good* photo copy machines. The senior vice-president for worldwide marketing at Xerox said, "The kind of executives we're talking to aren't walking around thinking 'I've got document problems.' But they have business problems for which document solutions are the answer."[9] Thinking in terms of benefits to the buyer helps the selling firm identify product features and company service offerings that can be touted as advantages over competition.[10]

HORIZONTAL AND VERTICAL MARKET SEGMENTATION

Horizontal and vertical market segmentation is many times referred to as an overall marketing approach. You may have heard vertical market segmentation described as *niche marketing.* Actually, horizontal and vertical market analysis is merely another method of segmenting the business market. **Horizontal market segmentation** is the process of identifying potential customers *across* several industries. **Vertical market segmentation** is the process of segmenting the market based on identifying potential customers *within* a single organizational type or industry. An example will clarify the distinction. In the early days of Apple Computer's marketing strategy, Apple chose to segment the market vertically by concentrating all of its marketing efforts on educational institutions. These customers were *within* a single industry. In a very different fashion, IBM segmented the market horizontally by selling to a wide range of industries and organizational types including manufacturing firms, processing firms, resellers, *and* the university level of the educational market. Currently, small data processing firms, like Systems & Computer Technology Corp. are thriving by providing specialized services to vertical markets such as the banking industry, local government, and utilities.[11]

There are efficiencies and advantages to both of these strategies for segmentation. In horizontal market segmentation, a firm has the advantage of identifying a large number of potential customers, and risk can be spread across several industries and organizational types. If one industry suffers a downturn, the selling firm is buffered by having customers in other industries that may be prospering. The liabilities of horizontal segmentation can be formidable however. First, there is greater diversity among potential customers as applications for the product differ. This challenges the firm to try to understand all the different applications and adjust its marketing mix, including product design in many instances, for each different use situations. Second, the firm is likely to encounter a greater number of competitors. This again forces a more broad-based analysis and set of strategies.

Vertical market segmentation tends to avoid the primary liabilities of horizontal segmentation. It is easier to understand the needs and product applications of a more narrowly defined customer group and there is likely to be less competition within very specific market niches. However, a firm using a vertical segmentation plan runs the risk of suffering economic downturns along with the industry or organizational type it has targeted. Unless the firm is well diversified in a number of product areas, vertical segmentation can provide living proof of the liability of "putting all your eggs in one basket."

Overall, business market segmentation is more direct than household consumer market segmentation. The unique features of the business market discussed earlier in the chapter make the segmentation process somewhat more manageable. Similar to their household consumer market counterparts, business marketers can gain greater understanding of the marketing challenges associated with a product through a classification scheme. We will now turn our attention to such a scheme for business goods.

Classification of Business Products

Providing a classification of business products serves the same purpose as the classifications of household consumer products provided in the last chapter. The mere act of correctly classifying the type of product or service alerts marketers to basic requirements in the marketing mix strategy. The difference here is that the classification of business goods is based on *uses* for the product or service rather than *buying habits* upon which the consumer goods classification is based. Business goods are used in production, reselling, capital expansion, research and development, construction, and maintenance. The following is a list of the six categories of goods that make up the business classification scheme:

Raw materials
Component parts
Installations
Accessory equipment
Operating supplies
Services

The first two, raw materials and component parts are part of the construction of the final product. The last four, installations, accessory equipment, operating supplies, and services, facilitate the production and delivery of business goods.

Raw Materials

Raw materials are those goods that are sold in their original state before processing. The sources of supply of raw materials are the primary industries of agriculture, mining, forestry, and fisheries. Producer have few choices with regard to where the business is located since production must take place either where the resources are located or where conditions are favorable, as in the case of agricultural products. Simply, raw materials must be taken at the point where nature provides them. It is typical in this category that wholesale or cooperative organizations collect the products from numerous small producers, store them, and then resell the products to processors. In the case of wool and cotton, for example, intermediaries collect the crops from growers. They are often processed to the extent of ginning the cotton or combing the wool and then sold to manufacturers. In mining, lumbering, and petroleum production, however, direct sale to the first processor is the most common method of sale. The steel company USX Corp. owns iron mines, and Weyerhauser Lumber Company in the Pacific Northwest owns forests. Many large petroleum companies own their own oil fields. Copper and aluminum fabricating companies own their own sources of supply and ship directly to customers.

COMPONENT PARTS

Component parts are items that become part of the buyer's product without further processing. In purchasing component parts, the business buyer is delegating the manufacture of items that become part of the finished product to other organizations. Component parts are often custom-made according to buyer's specifications, although a component part may have several market applications and therefore can be sold to many buyers in different industries.

The best example of an industry where the purchase and sale of component parts is prevalent is the automobile industry. Custom-made plastic molded pieces, tires, fuel injector systems, brake systems, and drive belts are some of the component parts that become part of the final vehicle. Automobile manufacturers generally agree that they cannot duplicate the quality of component part manufacturers at a comparable cost. A high degree of emphasis is placed on component parts by manufacturers because these items can increase the appeal of the final product to the customer. When Ford Motor Company touts that its vehicles come factory equipped with Goodyear *Eagle GT* tires and ABS braking systems, the firm is using high-quality and widely recognized component parts as a basis for appealing to customers. Illustration 5-1 is an example of using a component part to appeal to customers. In this ad for Compaq Computers, Intel Corporations 486 microprocessor is the primary appeal in the advertising message. Intel microprocessors are the standard for performance in the PC industry and Compaq is using the component part as a basis for its end-product appeal.

INSTALLATIONS

Installations are capital goods—expensive, long-lived major equipment. Buildings, production machinery, material handling systems, aircraft, trucks, power generators, and mainframe computers are examples of installations. Perhaps more than any other category, installations typify the true meaning of a business good. No purchase decision of any type merits as much painstaking and careful consideration as that related to major installations. The cost of installations is high. Negotiations and planning run over long periods of time. Engineers or other personnel with highly specialized skills are involved in the purchase process on both the buyer and seller sides. Typically, the sale of installations is made directly from seller to ultimate user. All of the unique characteristics of business market transactions discussed earlier tend to be manifest in the purchase process related to installations.

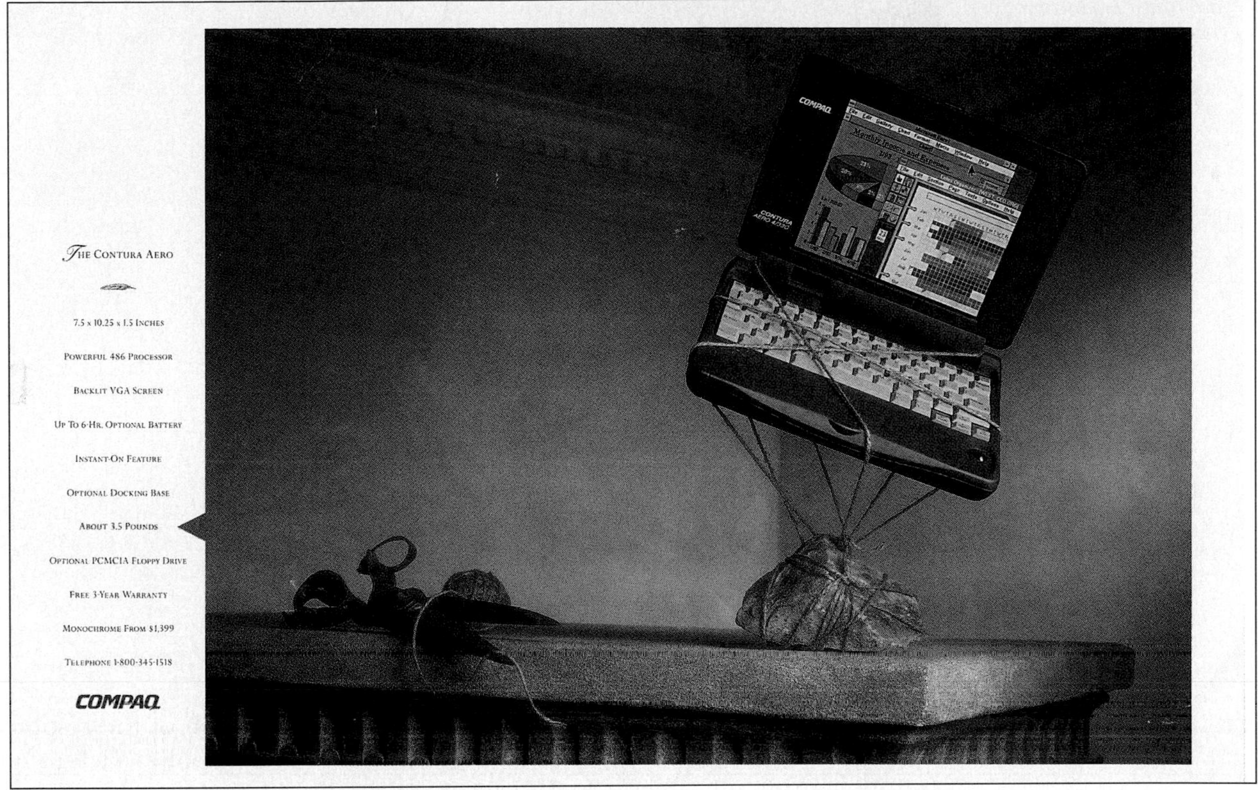

ILLUSTRATION 5-1
Compaq Uses Intel's 486 Microprocessor Component Part as the Basis for its Advertising Appeal

ACCESSORY EQUIPMENT

Accessory equipment is the term used to describe portable tools, small equipment, and office equipment. This class of goods does not become part of the buyer's finished product but rather facilitates the production process. Examples of accessory equipment are microcomputers, office furniture, photocopy machines, small power tools, quality-control devices, and calculators. The accessory equipment purchase decision is not as complex as that associated with installations, but the number of units purchased and, therefore, the dollar amount of a purchase can still be quite high. Buyers often require the technical assistance of production experts or other personnel with special knowledge in making product choices. Large manufacturers of equipment in this area usually have their own sales representatives who maintain contact with large users. Conversely, since this sort of equipment has applications across several industries and user types, distributors and selling agents are also used to achieve broad coverage of the market.

OPERATING SUPPLIES

Operating supplies, like accessory equipment, do not become part of the buyer's finished product. They are items necessary for the operation and maintenance of the buyer's business. Lubricants, fuel, office supplies, paint, janitorial supplies, and repair items are all operating supplies. Operating sup-

Installations, like this automated production system, represents one of the six classifications of business products.

plies seldom take a great deal of decision-making time. Much of the responsibility for buying is left to the purchasing agent. However, supplies such as fuel and lubricating oil, which can directly affect the production process, must be purchased with care. Where operating supplies are purchased in large quantities, contracts between buyers and sellers can run for several years. Although the unit cost of an individual supply item may be small, their widespread and constant use within organizations makes the total cost large and a significant factor when the cost efficiency of an organization is considered.

Many purchases of operating supplies are made directly from producers due to large quantity purchases and the related high-dollar amount of a purchase. Business supply houses and wholesalers also exist in this market to serve smaller quantity requests. Recently, a new form of distribution in the office supplies area has emerged, with firms like Office Max and Office Depot providing a retail-like purchase option for businesses.

SERVICES

Firms are heavily dependent on three types of **business services**: repair and maintenance services; transportation, storage, and logistical services; and professional services. The sophistication and complexity of installations and accessory equipment has become such that firms simply cannot afford to maintain personnel on staff with all the specialized skill needed to repair and maintain such equipment. Firms will now either purchase repair and maintenance contracts from the original supplier of the items or enter into annual contracts with local service providers.

Transportation, storage, and logistical services are crucial to a firm's ability to serve its customers in a timely fashion. Transportation services ranging from trucking companies and railroad carriers to overnight package delivery services like Federal Express are essential to the timely delivery of goods and the facilitation of transactions. Storage services and logistical services allow firms to locate inventory near customers and respond to customers' restocking requests quickly.

Professional services extend over a wide range. Interior design consultants, CPA firms, advertising agencies, research firms, temporary-help providers, and software consultants all provide services that contribute significantly to the overall performance of organizations. Again, most firms simply cannot afford to hire full-time staff with expertise in all these areas. Professional service providers have very specific training and tools with which they can make meaningful contributions to an organization's operations. Firms do not only buy the services related to internal operations, however. Hotel chains, car rental agencies, and airlines are examples of service organizations that compete vigorously for billions of dollars of corporate spending. The key element for sellers in these product categories is to engender loyalty within buying organizations.[12] That is why so many business service providers have "frequent user" programs (pioneered by the airlines) for their business customers.

The customization of services to suit the unique needs of each buyer is a key strategic feature of the business service area. This requires that service providers have direct, frequent, and intimate contact with buyers. The services of an advertising agency exemplify this feature of business services. Ad agencies must completely understand the full range of a client's corporate strategy in order to effectively develop promotional materials. Account supervisors and creative directors work directly with clients in order to understand the firm's product values and target markets upon which effective advertising is based. In most service areas, the provider must work closely with the buying firm to tailor the service to the firm's unique needs. Bids and contracts are common in the business service area, but some highly specialized services, such as management consulting, are often billed on an hourly basis.

Marketing Mix Strategy Implications of Business Product Classifications

Just as in the case of household consumer products, the proper classification of a business product does much to specify the nature of marketing mix decision making. Table 5-6 highlights the marketing mix strategy implications within each category of business goods. Across all categories, a high degree of buyer knowledge is assumed so this factor is not indicated explicitly.

The first column in this table gives common examples of each type of business product. The center column, "Unique Features of the Market," illustrates the variability in market features depending on the business product considered. The degree to which demand is considered to be derived, elastic, or fluctuating varies. Raw materials, component parts, and operating supplies are considered to be product categories in which the degree of inelasticity is high. Raw materials and component parts become part of the final product and contribute a relatively small amount to the end-user price. In the case of operating

	Product Examples	Unique Features of Market	Marketing Mix Strategy Implications
Raw Materials	Lumber Cotton Petroleum Copper	Derived demand Inelastic demand Fluctuating demand Few, large buyers Geographic concentration Variable distribution	Commodity product Nonprice emphasis Direct/indirect distribution Some sales force emphasis
Component Parts	Tires Computer chips Custom-made parts	Derived demand Inelastic demand Fluctuating demand Large order quantity Supply emphasis Geographic concentration Direct distribution	Detailed product specifications Nonprice emphasis Direct distribution Sales force emphasis
Installations	Production machinery Vehicles Mainframe computers	Derived demand Elastic demand Fluctuating demand High unit value Leasing Diffused buying responsibility Buyer/seller interdependence Direct distribution	Complex product Price negotiations Direct distribution Sales force emphasis
Accessory Equipment	Micro computers Portable tools Office furniture	Elastic demand Buyer/seller interdependence Variable distribution Leasing Diffused buying responsibility	Moderate product complex Price negotiations Direct/indirect distribution Sales force emphasis
Operating Supplies	Fuel Lubricants Office supplies	Inelastic demand Derived demand Centralized, routing buying Variable distribution Contract sales	Low product complexity Nonprice emphasis Direct/indirect distribution Delivery emphasis Low sales force emphasis
Services	Advertising Research Consulting Repair Hotels Transportation	Elastic demand Buyer/seller interdependence Customized to buyer needs Direct distribution	Customized product Nonprice emphasis Simultaneous production and distribution Multiple decision makers "Executive" sales force

TABLE 5-6
Marketing Mix Implications of Business Products Classification

supplies, buyers must ensure the smooth operation of the facility so price sensitivity is low. Installations, accessory equipment, and services show greater elasticity in the sense that organizations may delay the purchase of these items until either market conditions improve or price concessions can be negotiated with sellers. The other descriptions in this column follow the same sort of variability depending on the product considered.

The marketing mix strategy implications in Table 5-6 emphasize how strategic decision making is affected by the category of business good itself. Note that the four Ps—product, price, promotion, and distribution—differ depending on the category within which a product is classified and the unique features of demand associated with the class. *Product* decision making is driven by the complexity or standardization of the product class. *Pricing* is affected by the degree of elasticity evidenced in the market. *Distribution* relies on either direct delivery to the customer or the use of intermediaries, depending upon product complexity and the degree of customization of the product. Finally, in all but one of the business product categories, *promotion* is heavily dependent upon sales force contact with the buyer. Since there are fewer and more knowledgeable buyers who are buying products that are either high in unit value or are buying in large quantity, the sales force becomes an integral element in the marketing mix. Also, notice that in the case of services the sales force is made up of the executive core of the selling organization since business services tend to be negotiated at the highest levels of management.

Overall, the marketing mix decisions related to business products are clarified considerably by properly classifying the product in question. Strategists learn much about the nature of demand, the buying process, and the types of buyers by recognizing the product category. This categorization combined with a thorough environmental analysis sets the extent and requirements for marketing mix decisions.

The Business Market: A Global Perspective

As discussed earlier, one of the key dimensions that distinguishes business marketing from household consumer marketing is the close adherence to more formal buying procedures and more rational economic behavior that underlies the decision-making process. A focus on criteria such as performance capabilities, reliable delivery records, consistent quality, and pricing is perhaps no more clearly demonstrated than in business marketing activities. In general, business marketing practices are more globally oriented than household consumer marketing activities. Global strategies are based on business operations that take advantage of economies of scale, efficiencies of scope, and standardization of elements of the marketing mix. For example, manufacturers in Japan, the United States, and Europe often have their products produced and assembled in the same low-labor-cost countries (i.e., Mexico, Indonesia, and Malaysia), and then compete fiercely with one another in their own business markets and third-world markets. At the global level, large multinational companies seek to integrate R&D, marketing, production, and finance decisions in order to maximize worldwide market position and profitability, while medium- and small-size companies typically seek to niche their products in business markets via the strategies of exporting, joint ventures, and licensing. Finally, the relative ease of transferring technology, capital, and skills, coupled with the easing of tariff and trade barriers are trends that continue to have an influence on the competitive structure and dynamic nature of global business marketing activities.

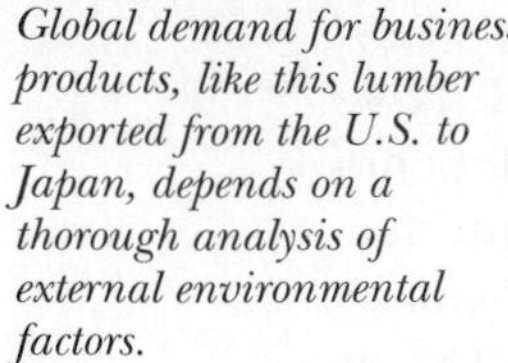

Global demand for business products, like this lumber exported from the U.S. to Japan, depends on a thorough analysis of external environmental factors.

Once again, many of the principles discussed earlier in this chapter will apply to business marketing at the global level. The characteristics of demand, the characteristics of business buyers, and their interactions with sellers; the nature of market transactions; and segmentation approaches remain crucial concepts in understanding business marketing. However, analysis of these same features will lead to different strategic and tactical approaches when operating at the integrated global level. The following sections of this chapter will identify the unique features of business marketing in the global context.

CHARACTERISTICS OF DEMAND IN GLOBAL BUSINESS MARKETS

Developing estimates of global demand for business goods and services involves the thorough sort of environmental analyses discussed in Chapters 2, 3, and 4. **Demand in global business markets** tends to be influenced by the stability and predictability of the markets involved and the stage of the product's life cycle in different global markets. Not surprisingly, firms with long-term experience in relatively stable markets are better able to make accurate predictions of global demand than firms that operate in more dynamic and less-predictable markets.

First, let's consider an example of why estimating global demand is so important to the international marketer. South-Western Publishing Company, the publisher of this textbook, operates primarily in the American market, although the company is owned by a British firm with global publishing and information technology interests. When the editorial staff makes decisions regarding the publication of a new edition of an established textbook, their decisions relating to the size of the initial print run will be based not only on past sales information and a competitive analysis of the American market but also on estimates of international demand. Input from the international division, which can offer insights regarding the stable and predictable demand for English-language texts in various markets (such as Scandinavia, the Benelux, and the U.K., or Canada, New Zealand, and Australia), is critical to the decision-making process because printing a book is a key production cost. Alternatively, carrying too many books in inventory adversely affects the profit contribution due to higher inventory costs. If domestic demand estimates are near the break-even point in terms of production costs, then knowing that there is potential to export an additional several thousand copies of the text will heavily influence the editorial team's decisions, since units produced after the break-even point greatly contribute to profit margins.

This provides an example of how a global company can use in-house information for business market analysis and for estimating global demand at the *firm level.* There are also other less controllable and predictable forces that will influence the global demand of a company's product or services. Large lending institutions, such as the Agency for International Development, the International Monetary Fund, the World Bank, or a consortium of commercial banks, strongly influence the derived demand in business markets, particularly in developing economies. Derived demand for earth-moving machinery, concrete, asphalt, travel agencies, and the wholesale market for swimming pool supplies, alcohol, and suntan lotion in Aruba (an island in the Caribbean with a developing tourist industry) will all be dependent on the successful securing of loans from large lending institutions.

Even trends in consumer markets can have a significant effect on business market demand. For example, one characteristic of economic growth is that the population experiencing the increase in prosperity tends to shift its protein source from vegetable to animal—a shift that dramatically increases grain consumption (you've got to run seven times as much grain through a cow to produce the same protein you would get from eating the grain itself). Should China increase its caloric intake by just 15 percent, the country would have to produce or import 150 million tons of grain. To trading companies such as Cargill, this number is very significant, since it represents the entire worldwide traded grain market[13]. Finally, long-term market stability and predictability will also influence the decision-making processes of business buyers for capital investments. Sales of German and Japanese industrial robots (the world leaders in this business market) will depend heavily on forecasts for long-term automobile sales in the United States. If the "big three" U.S. auto makers (Ford, GM, and Chrysler) all forecast long-term increases in the demand for small, fuel-efficient passenger cars, then they will make commitments of resources, including the purchase of robotic hardware and software, to produce for that market.

Now consider the case of firms operating in highly competitive and innovative business markets. Firms in these markets often find themselves introducing newer and more sophisticated products *before* they have fully recovered R&D and market-launch costs on the original product. Apart from the effects of competition, other market influences such as stricter environmental regulations or shifting customer preferences may force companies to investigate new markets and stimulate primary demand in those markets. None of this necessarily means that the original product is obsolete but rather is less competitive in a particular market. Thus, falling demand in one global market may cause

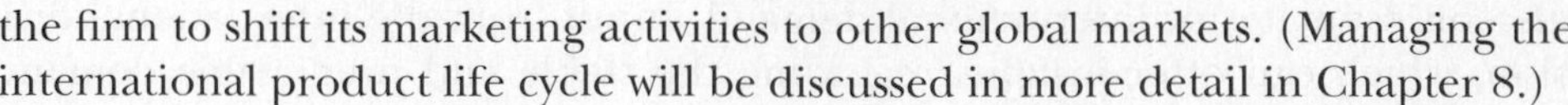

the firm to shift its marketing activities to other global markets. (Managing the international product life cycle will be discussed in more detail in Chapter 8.)

CHARACTERISTICS OF GLOBAL BUSINESS BUYERS

When dealing with the diversities of global markets, it's always easy to find exceptions to the rule, but generally speaking business demand is characterized by the concentration of a relatively small number of purchasers in each sector who have enormous purchasing power. The oligopoly market structure of the aircraft and airline industries or the monopoly structure of the health care, transportation, and telecommunications industries of many countries create a system with limited buyers. While companies in eastern European countries are moving slowly away from their cumbersome Foreign Trade Associations structure of central buying, there are still only limited numbers of knowledgeable buyers in these growing business markets. Generally speaking, markets characterized by oligopoly or monopoly structures or by Foreign Trade Associations tend to create situations where buyers exert strong influence over their suppliers.

While global business marketing remains a highly competitive activity, the number of global strategic partnerships and technological alliances among companies has increased. In the early 1990s, mergers and acquisition activities amounted to between $40 and $60 billion dollars per year.[14] These strategic moves influence business purchasing patterns as well, primarily through the practice of reciprocal buying. For example, the Dutch consumer electronics giant Philips and Japan's Sony not only compete directly against each other in world markets, they also buy and sell components from each other and have technology licensing arrangements worth millions of dollars. To take the example one step further, formal alliances and partnerships aren't even necessary for having a pattern of reciprocal buying: A U.S. company buying steel from a South Korean producer may expect that the Korean seller will purchase computer chips from an affiliate of the U.S. company based in Taiwan.

An important new development in global business-to-business marketing is the *Keiretsu* structure of Japanese corporations and the *Chaebol* structure of South Korean corporations. ***Keiretsu*** and ***Chaebol*** are groups of corporations that link powerful financial companies, such as banks and insurance firms, with industrial giants who manufacture and market products across a variety of industries. These stable, powerful alliances trade extensively within their own group of companies, as well as between *Keiretsu* (or *Chaebol*) groups. Manufacturers maintain very close links with their suppliers and distributors within these groups, and these stable alliances allow for long-term strategies of market conquest. To give an indication of just how interrelated the business activities of these companies can be, it is estimated that between 60 and 70 percent of the stock of publicly traded companies is held by these "stable shareholders."

THE STRUCTURE OF MARKET TRANSACTIONS IN GLOBAL BUSINESS ACTIVITIES

Two useful dimensions for understanding the structure of market transactions in global business marketing have to do with the *complexity of the transaction*

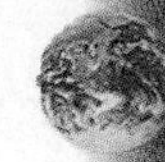

itself and the *complexity of the business environment* in which the transaction takes place. These dimensions can range from simple structures, such as straightforward rebuy situations via exporting to foreign markets with little or no regulatory restrictions, to highly complex transactions involving the participation and approval from a number of government parties, complex lending schedules from a consortium of financial institutions, legal commitments, and the exchange of personnel as well as products and services.

Complexity of the Transaction

As in all marketing exchange relationships, understanding which factors are necessary to develop and to sustain long-term mutually beneficial relationships is the key to a successful strategy. Having experienced global business partners who are well established in the markets in which they compete presents a totally different level of complexity in the process of developing and maintaining a relationship. This differs from the efforts required to enter new markets and to establish contacts with new suppliers and distributors. Many western European companies are discovering that the proper approach to developing business markets in eastern Europe has to go beyond simply getting the order, arranging financing in hard currency, and shipping the goods or providing the services. While relatively low risk, this simple export approach occasionally leads to a short-term relationship because their business counterparts may lack the resources and know-how to further market the product effectively in their home markets.

In many developing countries as well as in the emerging markets of eastern Europe, market entry requires production with extensive capital investment. This is especially true in business markets that affect the host nation's infrastructure—sectors such as transportation, health care, communication systems, or energy. In these business market situations, turnkey operations that feature training future managers and workers in the host country may be the essential ingredient to competing effectively and developing long-term relationships. With this technique, the host country gains an ongoing operation with up-to-date managerial know-how and technology that can be operated efficiently by host-country personnel (already a tremendous value-added component); the investing company receives a business opportunity with a known time horizon that enables it to calculate profit flows and return on investment. Often, the company will also receive a training and consulting contract that extends beyond the turnover date. These complex business transactions, in which marketing serves an integration role in production, human resources, finance, and R&D, are typical of the activities of globally oriented firms. Other entry strategies that are employed in global business operations will be discussed in Chapter 17.

Complexity of the Business Environment

Apart from the strategic and logistic obstacles already discussed, global business marketers are also faced with the additional challenge of understanding the varying rules of doing business in different markets and cultures in which they operate. Moving through the myriad of governmental agencies in order to gain permission to do business may be a simple and straightforward procedure or it could be as subtly complex as needing to know the right people in business or government in order to get the job done. The concept of relationship marketing discussed earlier in the chapter, is critically important to developing and sustaining working relationships in many cultures. Establishing reliable contacts with suppliers, distributors, and trading partners in the global market may occasionally be quickly and efficiently arranged by signing a contract, but relationships are more likely to evolve over a longer period of time wherein a mutual basis of trust is developed between individuals and companies.

There are many instances in which the rules for doing business are not fully agreed upon by all competitors in the global marketplace. For example, bribery has been proven to be an effective and extensively used form of promotion in several international marketing settings. For U.S. firms, bribery of foreign government officials or political parties is illegal under the 1977 Foreign Corrupt Practices Act. Given that bribery is illegal, that should make the decision-making process fairly simple: don't engage in illegal acts. However, bribery is not illegal in some countries where U.S. firms conduct business. In some cultures, it is an acceptable and common practice, and many non-U.S. firms that compete in global markets are not forbidden to use bribes and thus enjoy a competitive advantage over U.S. companies. If business products are seen as highly homogeneous in terms of quality, and cost structures in the industry lead to fairly even pricing strategies, then other aspects in the marketing mix may make the difference (bribes being an element of personal selling). Finally, the law itself is ambiguous. Bribery can take an endless variety of forms, so the firm may often be uncertain whether or not a particular payment could be construed as illegal. It would be much simpler if honesty were always the best, and most profitable, policy.

Another complicating factor of the business environment is that not all business transactions in global markets involve money. One of the largest markets in the world economy is the nonmonetary market of **barter and countertrade.** Many trading countries in the third world or in eastern Europe have no foreign exchange reserves, and their local currency is not seen as desired or easily convertible—characteristics of hard currency. Over 100 countries in the world use barter and countertrade, which accounts for roughly half of their total trade volume.[15] In most instances, this trading strategy is government mandated. In the United States, over half of the Fortune 500 companies are involved in some form of countertrade.

While various forms of this kind of activity exist, the basic principle underlying the exchange is that the exporter agrees to take products from the importer in full or partial payment for the exports. Instead of the liquidity and convenience of currency, the exporter accepts the more awkward form of payments in goods, with the intention of selling the goods in other markets for currency that the company can use. Countertrade opens up markets that would otherwise be closed to global marketers, and it permits governments that lack large amounts of foreign currencies to extend their trading activities and increase their exports. For the company playing the countertrade game, careful analysis needs to be done to ensure that the products received can be resold at a profit that covers not only the original profit potential in the exchange but also the costs of engaging in the countertrade agreement as well.

Exporters occasionally take products rather than money from importers as payment for services. Just such a "barter" arrangement is being used here as workers repack a shipment of herbs.

SEGMENTATION APPROACHES FOR THE GLOBAL BUSINESS MARKET

Given the tremendous costs and complexities of operating globally, a fundamental question in strategy development is: What is the appropriate basis for global business market segmentation? Broader corporate issues such as organizational structure, definitions of strategic business units (SBUs), resource allocation, and effective integration of corporate activities all have an influence on the answer to this question. The six basic approaches to segmenting the business market discussed earlier in the chapter provide a good framework for segmentation at the global level. Here the focus will be on the unique characteristics of global business markets that form a foundation for segmentation.

The most common approach to global segmentation of business markets is the **hierarchical segmentation approach**. This method first segments markets geographically and then along product lines or operating divisions within the firm. The reasons this method is so widely used are both historical and market-based. Traditionally, firms have expanded into international markets by treating each country as a separate market segment that was defined by geographic, economic, and political factors. Segmentation on the basis of national boundaries was often seen as practical due to import restrictions, duties, and government regulations. Figure 5-3 illustrates a business segmentation hierarchy for the firm SPSS International whose primary segmentation basis is geographic with the secondary dimension being operating divisions that service distinct business market segments.

The software company SPSS (Statistical Package for the Social Sciences) International is one of the dominant players in the market for analyzing data

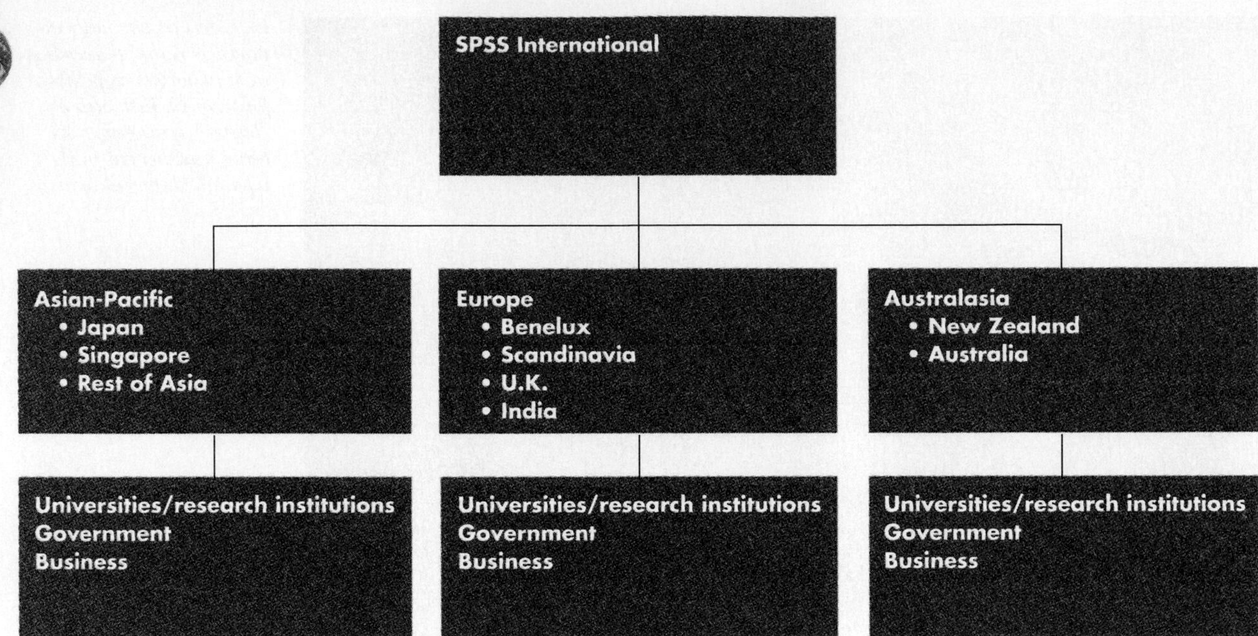

FIGURE 5-3
Hierarchical Segmentation of Global Business Markets

bases with statistical techniques. The traditional market of the Chicago-based company was universities and research institutions. The advent of powerful PCs, coupled with the increasing use of statistics as a tool to support business analyses, led to the expansion of the company into other business segments. Outside the United States, SPSS is organized into geographic regions (notice that for historical reasons India falls under SPSS's London office, instead of within the Asian-Pacific segment). Within regions, markets are divided into three segments: university/research institutions, government, and businesses. In most markets, SPSS delivers directly to the end user without using distributors or dealers. Most software dealers who service the same markets as SPSS also sell other less-powerful packages for data base analysis, such as Lotus or Excel, which are sold to a wide range of users. These dealers typically do not have the level of expertise or commitment to the product needed to provide training and after-sale service needed for the SPSS package. In markets where SPSS does not have sufficient revenues to support their own sales subsidiary (e.g., Spain, Italy, India, and parts of Asia), the firm has established partnerships with local dealers. SPSS helps these dealers develop business plans and marketing plans for the sale and service of the SPSS package.

Finally, in terms of global segmentation strategies, it should be noted that many of the trade restrictions that have characterized international marketing since the end of World War II will be relaxed throughout the 1990s. All business buyers view reliable, cost-efficient distribution as an important value-added dimension to the purchase. As Berlin, Prague, Budapest, and Warsaw develop more efficient distribution and communication infrastructures, these cities will become more important distribution centers for eastern Europe. In Asia, national boundaries are proving to be weak economic barriers as ethnic Chinese throughout the region form business networks based on family-ties and ethnic identity.[16] Standardizing SIC codes throughout the European community will greatly simplify the integration of business information for segmentation purposes. Technological improvements in communication such as videoconferencing and CD-ROM information storage will present new opportunities for reaching global business buyers. In summary, regulatory, political, technological, and economic changes will allow globally oriented firms to develop new competitive approaches to segmenting business markets.

Key Terms and Concepts

Business market
Derived demand
Inelastic demand
Fluctuating demand
Value added
Business buyers
Diffused buying responsibility
Interdependence of buyer and seller
Relationship marketing
Leasing
Negotiation and bidding
Make or buy decision
Business market segmentation
Organizational types
Standard Industrial Classification (SIC)
End-use segmentation
Horizontal and vertical market segmentation
Raw materials
Component parts
Installations
Accessory equipment
Operating supplies
Business services
Demand in global business markets
Keiretsu and Chaebol
Complexity of global business transactions
Complexity of global business environment
Barter and countertrade
Hierarchical segmentation approach

Questions and Exercises

1. Demand in business markets is described as derived, inelastic, and fluctuating. Discuss each of theses features of demand in the business market, and give an example of a business product in each area whose demand is affected by these factors.
2. Business buyers are said to be knowledgeable. Does this mean that business buyers use only functional criteria in their decision making? Do business buyers always choose the lowest-cost source of supply?
3. Define what is meant by diffused buying responsibility. Describe the role of the gatekeeper in a business transaction that has multiple decision makers.
4. Which characteristic of business market transactions often results in reciprocity between buyers and sellers.
5. Describe the advantages of leasing in the business market. Do these same advantages relate to purchases in the household consumer market?
6. Universities and large research institutions buy billions of dollars of high-technology equipment each year. How would you classify these organizations for purposes of business segmentation?
7. Give an example of a business product or service that would be most effectively marketed using horizontal market segmentation. Give an example of a product or service that should use vertical market segmentation.
8. Intel's 486 microprocessor was cited in the chapter as an example of a component part that helped sell the final product. Find another example of a manufacturer which uses a component part to appeal to potential customers.
9. One of the unique features of some global business markets is the prevalence of bribery as a business practice. How do you feel about U.S. firms being barred, in most instances, from engaging in bribery?

10. Describe why hierarchical segmentation has become prevalent in global business marketing from both a historical and market-driven basis.

References

1. Edmund Faltermayer. "A Long-Term Bet Pays off at Last." *Fortune* (August 23, 1993): 79; and Bill Richards "Makeover of Morrison Knudsen Comes Just in Time." *The Wall Street Journal* (March 26, 1993): B2.
2. Patricia Sellers. "How IBM Teaches Techies to Sell." *Fortune* (June 6, 1988): 141–146.
3. Gabriella Stern. "Chief Executives Are Increasingly Chief Salesmen." *The Wall Street Journal* (August 6, 1991): B1.
4. Bill Saporito, "PPG: Shiny, Not Dull." *Fortune* (July 17, 1989): 107.
5. Quote taken from James D. Hlavacek and B. C. Ames "Segmenting Business and High-Tech Markets." *Journal of Business Strategy* (Fall 1986): 39. See also, V. Kasturi Rangan, Rowland T. Moriarty, and Gordon S. Swartz. "Segmenting Customers in Mature Business Markets." *Journal of Marketing* (October 1992): 72–82.
6. Randy Meyers. "USF&G Launches Campaign to Woo Small Business." *The Wall Street Journal* (April 1, 1993): B2.
7. Clare Ansberry. "Utah's Geneva Steel Once Called Hopeless, Is Racking up Profits." *The Wall Street Journal* (November 20, 1991): A1 and A5.
8. James D. Hlavacek and B. C. Ames, op. cit., 39.
9. Thomas R. King, "'Document Company' Campaign By Xerox Is Starting Next Week." *The Wall Street Journal* (September 27, 1990): B6.
10. Cornelis A. de Kluyver and David B. Whitlark "Benefit Segmentation for Business Products" *Business Marketing Management* (November 1986): 273.
11. John W. Verity. "They Make a Killing Minding Other People's Business." *Business Week* (November 30, 1992): 96.
12. Michael Totty. "No-Frills Motels Upgrade to Grab Business Travelers." *The Wall Street Journal* (June 8, 1988): 31.
13. Bill Saporito. "Where the Global Action Is." *Fortune* (Autumn/Winter, 1993): 65.
14. "Business and Finance" in "The World This Week." *The Economist* (October 23, 1993): 33.
15. M. Luqmani, G. Habib, and S. Kassem. "Marketing to LDC Governments." *International Business Review* (Spring 1988): 56–67.
16. See "A Survey of Asia: A Billion Consumers." in *The Economist* (October 30, 1993); see also "China's Diaspora Turns Homeward." in *The Economist* (November 27, 1993): 65.

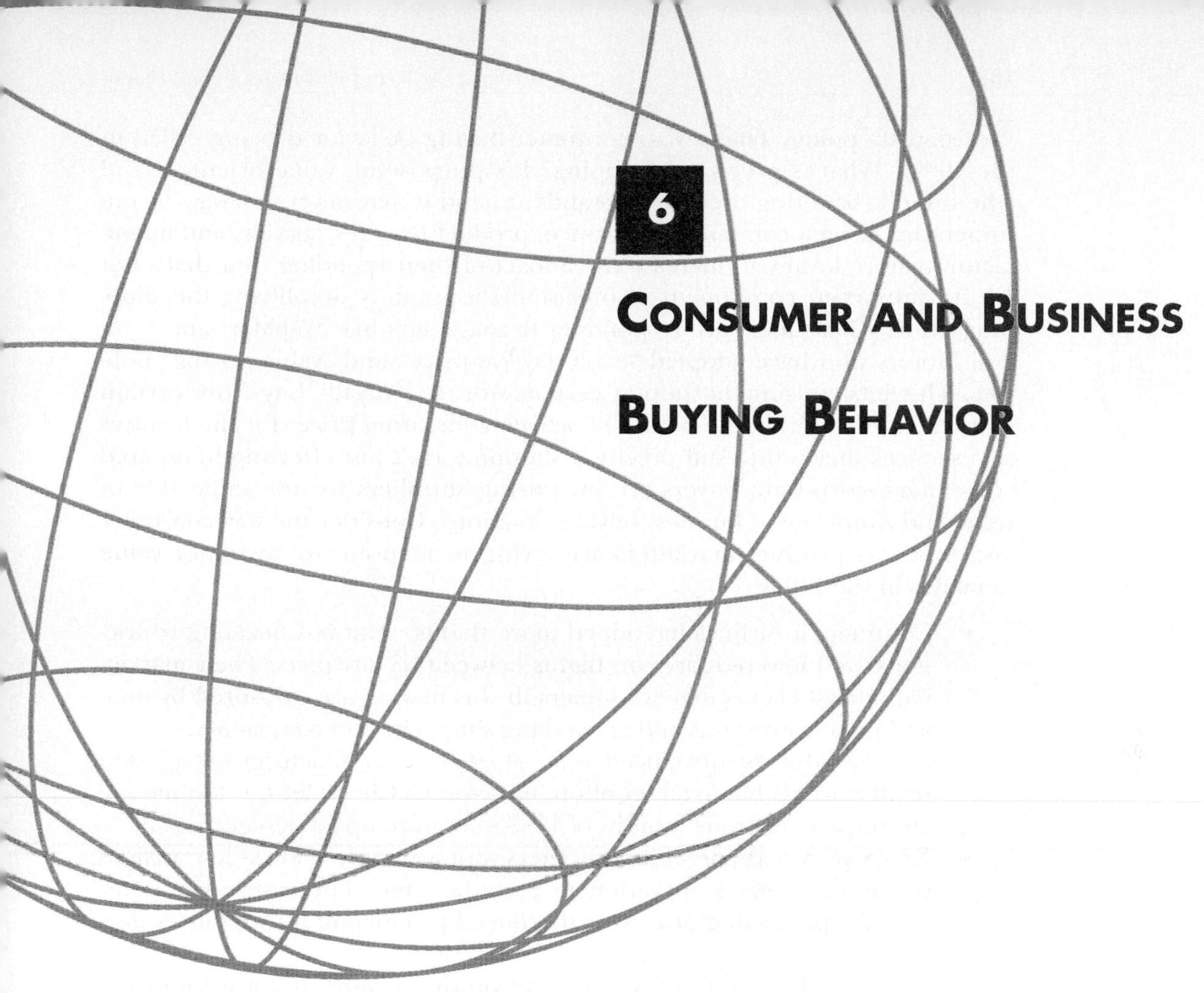

6

CONSUMER AND BUSINESS BUYING BEHAVIOR

AFTER STUDYING THIS CHAPTER, YOU WILL UNDERSTAND THAT:

1. While it might seem that consumers are disorganized and impulsive, they actually engage in a relatively structured process when making purchase decisions.
2. Household consumer behavior is influenced by a wide range of psychological and sociological factors.
3. Cultural influences affect what products and services consumers perceive to be relevant and appropriate.
4. Business buyers emphasize the economic aspects of purchase situations but are also subject to emotional influences in the decision-making process.
5. A global perspective on buying behavior reveals that cultural norms and traditions are powerful influences in both the consumer and business markets.

Precision shopping. That's what consumer buying behavior is being called in the 1990s. What is precision shopping? It's purposeful, value oriented, and "the trend is battering overpriced brands . . . and it may never go away."[1] Consumers are using a combination of price, product features, service, and manufacturer/store loyalty to increase the impact of their spending. But that's not all. An important component of precision shopping is simplifying the shopping effort. Consumers are responding to marketers like Wal-Mart and General Motors who have adopted "every-day-low-price" and "value-pricing" policies. This lets consumers shop at certain stores or loyally buy from certain manufacturers without the bother of *actually* comparing prices for the features and services they want. And precision shopping isn't just affecting household consumers, corporate buyers are pressuring suppliers for the same sort of value and simplicity in business buying situations. Consider the way consumer and business product marketers are trying to respond to customer value demands in the 1990s:

- Continental Airlines has added more flights, removed ticketing restrictions, and lowered fares on flights between 53 city pairs. Their marketing analyst claims that consumers in this market are pressured by time and price constraints and are seeking simplicity and consistency.
- General Motors introduced *value pricing*—a manufacturer's suggested retail price with a fixed set of options—on its Chevrolet *Cavalier* model. During the first nine months of 1993 sales were up 23 percent.
- Xerox provided one of its customers with a complete work-flow analysis of the customer's operation to provide value. The result was a customized publishing process that reduced production time from 45 days to 5 days.
- Herman Miller, the office furniture producer, now uses a team of ten different employees, including designers, engineers, and applications analysts to design furniture that is uniquely suited to technology works.[2]

While value may be a prominent motivation for buyers in the 1990s, consumer buying behavior is much more complex than the single perspective of value. Value is just one of many motivations and perceptions that consumers bring to a buying situation. One analyst put the challenge of trying to understand buying behavior succinctly by asking, "Do consumers buy things because the purchase makes them feel good? Or is it the product itself that interests them?"[3] Put another way, do consumers buy "image" or do they buy "reality"?

This chapter will discuss buyer behavior and underlying influences on both household consumer and business buyer decision making. Household consumer buying behavior is somewhat more elaborate than business buying behavior due to the greater number of purchase options and a broader range of influences on individuals. But, whether an organization is marketing to household or business buyers, knowledge of how a purchase decision takes place in these markets is imperative for a firm to develop a marketing mix strategy that delivers satisfaction and value. Because of the many important distinctions between consumer and business buyer behavior, we discuss them separately. The chapter concludes with a discussion of how culture and social structure affect buyer behavior in global markets.

CONSUMER BUYING BEHAVIOR

Can you explain why you buy the toothpaste you buy? Or the bread, cereal, or laundry detergent? What about your stereo system, watch, or shoes? If it's hard for each of *us* to describe why we buy what we do, just think how hard it is for *marketers* to understand (and try to predict) our behavior. The most astute marketers have come to the realization that the best way to try to understand household **consumer buying behavior** is to consider it as an instance of basic human behavior in a specialized context: consumption. In modern societies, consumption activities—deciding what to buy and the use and ownership of products—play a major role in people's lives. Because of the pervasiveness of consumption, marketers have turned to concepts from psychology, sociology, anthropology, and the newly established field of consumer behavior to better understand buying behavior.

In this section on consumer buying behavior, the process of consumer decision making will be highlighted. It is important to realize that while household consumers might seem disorganized and impulsive when they buy products, a fairly structured decision-making process has actually taken place. But, that process is subject to all sorts of influences both before and during decision making. By examining the types of decisions consumers make, the buying process, and the influences on that process, firms can more effectively develop and market products and services for the greatest satisfaction of those who buy and use them. The process and those influences are discussed in this chapter.

TYPES OF BUYING DECISIONS: THE ROLE OF INFORMATION SEARCH AND INVOLVEMENT

To describe the basic types of buying decisions household consumers make, it is first necessary to understand two underlying factors that are fundamental to consumer decision making: information search and involvement. These two factors affect the way individuals contemplate their purchases and the way in which they go about buying items. As such, they have a fundamental effect on behavior.

Information search relates to the amount of time and energy a consumer puts into the process of fact gathering before making a decision. All of us know people who tenaciously seek out information and agonize over decisions. Other consumers are quite nonchalant and put little effort into searching for information. The amount of information search varies between individuals and depends on the type of product being considered for purchase.

Involvement describes the intensity with which consumers approach a purchase decision. The degree of involvement consumers experience is related to several factors: the perceived pleasure that a product offers, its symbolic value, how important risk is to the consumer, and the probability and severity of a purchase error.[4] As each of these factors increase, so to does consumer involvement in the decision-making process. High-involvement purchases are often products and services that reflect an individual's social status, life-style, self-concept, or reference group affiliation. Low-involvement products are those that are less symbolic in nature and tend to serve rather mundane, utilitarian functions. The degree of involvement also depends on an individual's orientation to consumption and the nature of the product being considered. Some products, like automobiles, clothing, and other shopping goods, are high in symbolic value, risk, and purchase error severity and tend to elicit high involvement. Convenience goods, because of their utilitarian nature and low risk, are less involving for the typical consumer. But remember, any given consumer may be highly involved in the purchase of any item depending on his or her unique orientation to the decision. And the "new" consumer of the 1990s, with an emphasis on value and precision shopping, fits nicely into the general orientation of involvement. The consumer that firms are encountering in the 1990s is exhibiting a much higher degree of involvement than ever before. The value orientation, then, is not so much a unique consumption motive as it is a greater degree of involvement on the part of consumers than has traditionally been the case.

Information search and involvement establish a consumer's general orientation to purchase decision making. What is important is how these two factors combine to produce different types of buying decisions. When the involvement and information search factors are considered in combination, it is possible to portray these four types of buying decisions:

- *High-Involvement, Extensive Information Search.* This sort of decision making typically takes place in circumstances where a product is infrequently purchased and carries a high price, as do most shopping goods. Automobile purchases, furniture, financial services, or vacations would represent buying decisions where the high symbolic value, perceived pleasure or risk of the product may be a driving forces in the decision. Consequently, extensive fact gathering on different available alternatives is often undertaken.
- *High-Involvement, Little Information Search (Brand Loyalty).* Here, the consumer is highly ego-involved in the decision but does not spend much (if any) time seeking out information. Personal care products (like shampoo and deodorant), beer, soft drinks, and perfume typify purchase decisions in this category. Although the consumer may view these products as useful, little information search takes place because of the low risk and low severity of purchase error and the development of brand loyalty. That is, the consumer has discovered a brand that is consistently satisfying and feels comfortable purchasing the brand repeatedly.
- *Low-Involvement, Some Information Search.* In this category, products are not perceived by consumers to be particularly symbolic or important but there are enough differences among brands so that some comparison takes place (usually at the point of purchase). Many products and a substantial number of purchase decisions fit this category. Snack foods, cereals, window cleaner, and gasoline are products represented in this category. These are frequent, relatively low-risk purchases, and brand switching is prevalent.
- *Low-Involvement, Little Information Search (Habit).* Here, consumers see little consequence to the choice of one brand over another. This category

Some consumer purchase decisions are characterized by extensive information searching and high involvement.

is many times characterized by habit. That is, the consumer may habitually purchase the same brand not out of a sense of loyalty but rather out of a lack of desire to invest time in the decision-making process. Products like laundry detergent, paper towels, and dish soap are purchased on this basis by many consumers.

While differences among individuals and unique buying situations can provide exceptions to the involvement and information search combinations, these four categories provide a foundation for the different ways consumers approach buying decisions. But, the involvement/information search categories are merely descriptive of what consumers *do* rather than *how* they do it. To truly understand consumer buying behavior, we need to consider the way consumers make decisions.

THE CONSUMER DECISION-MAKING PROCESS

Years of developmental research regarding consumer behavior suggests that a fairly structured consumer decision-making process takes place when consumers seek out goods and services to satisfy needs. The process is characterized by a series of stages. Rarely are consumers fully aware that they are systematically working their way through a decision process. However, observing consumers suggests that, indeed, a process is taking place. The degree of involvement varies and each individual decides how much information search is needed in the process. The **consumer decision-making process** has six stages, as illustrated in Figure 6-1.

1. Need recognition
2. Information search
3. Evaluation of product alternatives

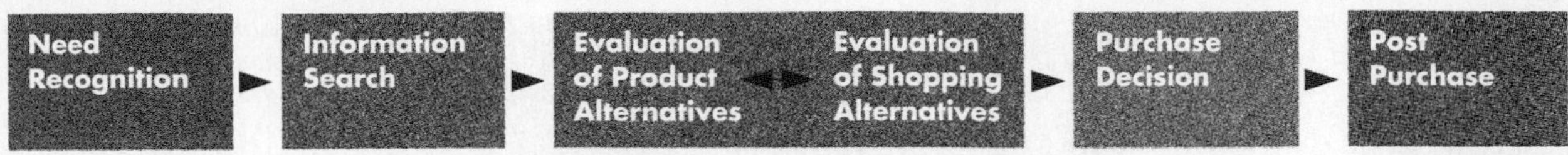

FIGURE 6-1
Stages in the Consumer Decision-making Process

4. Evaluation of shopping alternatives
5. The purchase decision
6. Postpurchase behavior

The elaborateness and duration of each stage varies depending on the degree of involvement and information search. For frequently purchased, low-cost, low-involvement type products (habitual buying), consumers may spend little time at each stage. There are few negative consequences to the purchase of an inappropriate product and a decision error can be quickly and easily corrected. In fact, there is evidence that in low-involvement situations like the one just described, the majority of consumers do not even check the prices on these low-cost items even to the point of not noticing that an item just purchased was "on special" and being sold at a reduced price![5] Even in a value-conscious era, low-involvement buying situations rarely result in significant effort on the part of consumers. However, if involvement is high and the product is expensive and has a long life (such as an automobile), then the decision-making process may be long and deliberate. Several weeks of search and extensive comparison of alternative brands is not uncommon in high-involvement situations.

Each stage in the consumer decision-making process has implications for the design of a proper marketing mix. It is important, therefore, to examine in detail the nature of each stage.

Need Recognition

Entry into the decision-making process is initiated by the consumer's recognition of a need. There are three types of **need recognition**: out-of-stock need, functional need, and emotional need.

Out-of-stock need is the most simple of the need states. This is the common situation where a frequently purchased, low-cost item is restocked on a regular basis. Toothpaste, laundry detergent, and food items are typical of products in the out-of-stock need category. The consumer feels little uneasiness during the decision-making process and is likely to spend little time fulfilling the subsequent stages.

Entering the decision-making process by virtue of **functional need** recognition is considerably more important to consumers. A functional need arises when the consumer is seeking a solution to a specific and generally more important need. The need for transportation (an automobile), a more comfortable living environment (furniture and appliances), or clothing are some examples. Functional needs can arise because of the breakdown or obsolescence of currently owned items or a significant change in the consumer's life (for example, buying a home). Functional needs are generally satisfied with products that are of higher cost and have longer life spans. As such, functional need recognition results in a more time-consuming and thoughtful progression through the decision-making stages.

The consumer decision-making process motivated by recognition of an **emotional need** is challenging for marketing decision makers. The difficulty stems from the fact that such needs can be manifest in the desire for a wide range of products. Consumers often seek satisfaction to such emotional needs as status, prestige, belonging, or achievement with shopping goods and expensive specialty goods. However, any product is capable of providing emotional satisfaction depending on the individual. For example, most consumers will enter the decision-making process for laundry detergent based on out-of-stock need recognition. But what about the consumer who purchases laundry detergent and is sincerely concerned that the family is satisfied with the result? An element of emotion is involved in this context.

Firms must understand that different need recognition can initiate the decision-making process. Depending on the need state, consumers place varying degrees of importance on the decision. Further, information desires vary between need states. By being aware of the out-of-stock, functional, and emotional need states, marketers can adjust product design, pricing, or promotional strategy to address the desires of potential customers.

Information Search

Once a need emerges, then **information search** begins. In low-involvement situations, information search may be brief or nonexistent. In high-involvement contexts, information search can be extensive. Low-involvement purchases are characterized by minimal information search. The consumer can rely on two basic types of information: internal and external.

Sources of *internal information* are the consumer's past experiences and stored information. Past experiences with brands provide the consumer with firsthand information regarding a particular item's ability to satisfy a need. Stored information also results from sources other than direct experience. Exposure to advertisements or friends' product use are the next most important contributors to stored information. Again, information from these encounters is retained in memory and contributes to a general predisposition (favorable or unfavorable feelings) toward different brands.

If reviewing internal information does not produce clear alternatives for need satisfaction, the consumer will then actively turn to *external information* sources: the media, friends or relatives, and objective product evaluations (such as buyers' guides or product tests). Current magazine, newspaper, and radio and television advertising will provide information about product alternatives available. Friends and relatives can offer insights based on their current and past product use. Conscientious buyers often turn to specialized publications that test products, and this information can be included in decision making. Once the potential buyer is comfortable with the amount of information obtained from both internal and external sources, the decision-making process continues.

Evaluation of Product Alternatives

In some cases, information search results in a clearly superior product choice for the consumer. In many instances, however, several items seem suitable, and the process continues to an evaluation of product alternatives. Consistent with the types of satisfaction sought by consumers discussed in Chapter 1, consumers can evaluate product alternatives using three general criteria: functional product features, the emotional satisfaction perceived to be provided by each product, and benefits that may accrue from ownership and use.

An evaluation by the consumer of **functional product features** includes factors such as price, performance characteristics, unique features, and any warranties or guarantees offered with the product. Evaluation of functional features relates most often to the economic and other "rational" aspects of a purchase. The shopping goods category of consumer goods is laden with functional features. In purchasing a shopping good like an automobile, consumers will evaluate miles-per-gallon, warranty, horsepower, trunk size, and a host of other functional features. It is critical for firms to properly assess the extent to which consumers are relying on functional features in their evaluation, however. Toyota experienced significant decreases in sales across the *Lexus* (-20.8 percent), *Camry* (-8 percent), and *Corolla* (-5.7 percent) product lines in 1993. Most analysts agree that Toyota "over-engineered" these cars and provided too many features and too much quality relative to consumers willingness to pay for these features. Even engineers from Toyota confessed, "We have to build a value-for-the-money car at a desirable price."[6]

The **emotional satisfaction** of each alternative is a perception. This perception may be stimulated by the manufacturer's portrayal and positioning of the brand as being related to important human values and emotions. Products may be evaluated for their potential to provide prestige or success with the opposite sex, for example.

The evaluation of products based on **benefits of use** and ownership is an area that fills a void between the functional and emotional evaluative criteria (see Illustration 6-1). For example, most people care little about the bits, bytes, RAM/ROM, and bus systems that make up the functional performance capability of personal computers. What consumers are interested in are the benefits of increased productivity and ease of word and data handling that such machines provide. Consumers often focus on benefits when they are either incapable of evaluating functional features or are simply not interested in taking the time to conduct a rigorous functional feature evaluation.

Different buyers approach product evaluation with varying degrees of emphasis on the criteria just discussed. It is *crucial* for marketing decision makers to accurately identify the criteria being used by consumers. Unless a firm accurately identifies which attributes are valued by the target segment (or segments), it cannot successfully convert these buyers to purchasers of the firm's brand or even effectively communicate the brand's values. Communicating functional features—like bits and bytes—to a buying segment that values benefits of use is futile. Consumers consider such a communication irrelevant to their needs and eliminate the firm's brand from consideration.

Evaluation of Shopping Alternatives

Once product evaluation is completed, the consumer will begin the **evaluation of shopping alternatives.** It is during this stage that the consumer decides which retail outlet to patronize. However, marketers should be careful not to overlook alternatives to retail shopping. Direct marketing sales has grown to be a $200 billion business as consumers have discovered the ease and conve-

You can't work any harder, but maybe your assets can.

You work as hard as you possibly can. Maybe even too hard to properly manage your assets.

At U.S. Trust, we've been successfully providing clients and their families with comprehensive asset management for over 140 years. Our investment strategy combines a disciplined search for value with appropriate asset diversification to limit risk and maximize returns. What's more, we create highly individualized plans to help each client meet their specific financial objectives.

If you're interested in having your assets work harder, please contact Richard E. Foley, Senior Vice President, at 1-800-U.S. TRUST.

U.S. TRUST
A TRADITION OF GROWING ASSETS
NEW YORK STAMFORD PRINCETON PALM BEACH BOCA RATON NAPLES DALLAS LOS ANGELES PORTLAND GRAND CAYMAN

ILLUSTRATION 6-1
Firms often stress "benefits of use" in advertising because consumers evaluate products and services on this dimension.

nience of shopping by phone and mail. Several firms, like Avon, Amway, L. L. Bean, and Eddie Bauer, have successfully initiated in-home and catalog selling programs. After evaluating product alternatives, a consumer may discover that the product is available by mail or telephone order and prefer this easy and convenient alternative.

Most consumer spending still takes place in retail outlets and consumers often rely on a trip to the store as a final opportunity for product information and evaluation. Especially for higher-cost, shopping good-type items, the in-store experience can be critical. The purchase of many products requires judgment and evaluation at the point of purchase, forcing consumers into making a shopping trip. Sales personnel in a store can be an important source of information and advice. Be aware that most consumers develop a set of favorite retail outlets that they regularly patronize and therefore don't go through a re-evaluation every time a purchase decision is made. This stage is most prominent when new product area purchases are encountered.

From a strategic standpoint, we should be aware that the product evaluation stage and the shopping alternative stage may actually take place simultaneously in many consumer decision-making situations. Consumers may use a trip to a retail outlet as the basis for making comparisons among all the alternatives available. In this case, the product/shopping alternative evaluation is collapsed into a single effort on the part of a consumer. This possibility is reflected in the relationship between these stages, as illustrated in Figure 6-1.

The evaluation stages in the consumer decision-making process also highlight several factors that are important in the strategic design of a marketing program. In order to properly design the distribution phase of the marketing mix, the marketing planner must be fully aware of consumer preferences and trends related to acquiring products (retail store versus mail-order) and the nature of the retail outlet from which a product may be acquired.

The Purchase Decision

In this stage the consumer incorporates the knowledge gained from information search, product evaluation, and shopping evaluation and makes a choice. A final decision is made to satisfy a need and it includes selecting a product type, a brand within the product type, a retail outlet (or other source), and a method of payment for the product. The process is not completed at this stage, however. A critical step for the consumer and marketer follows.

Postpurchase Behavior

Many firms overlook or are unaware of the fact that the consumer may engage in various types of behavior *after* a decision has been made. These behaviors have important implications for strategic marketing decision making. **Postpurchase behaviors** are of two types: additional information search and the acquisition of related products.

Additional Information Search

The motivation for seeking additional information after making a purchase is the result of either high involvement or a consumer's attempt to relieve cognitive dissonance. **Cognitive dissonance** is anxiety that results from having made a decision and a purchase commitment. The amount of postpurchase anxiety depends on several prepurchase conditions: the unit value of the item, the number of close alternatives identified before the purchase, the longevity of the product, and the importance of the decision to the buyer. As the level of each of these factors increases, more cognitive dissonance results. Additionally, dissonance is more likely in high-involvement purchase decisions. The uncomfortable mental state created by anxiety causes consumers to seek additional information to reaffirm that a correct purchase decision was made. A recent buyer will scrutinize media advertising in search of reinforcement. Friends and relatives are also bombarded with requests to view the new item and offer their praise to the consumer for making a good decision.

Astute marketers recognize situations where cognitive dissonance is likely to affect buyers and develop strategies that help relieve buyer anxiety. Many firms include a congratulatory note in the product package to immediately provide the buyer with reinforcement. For example,

Dear New Yamaha Owner:

It is our pleasure to welcome you into the family of satisfied Yamaha customers. Over a period of many years, Yamaha electronic products have earned a reputation for quality, dependability, and performance, and it is our desire to maintain this reputation with you.

Sincerely,

It is in the best interest of a firm to recognize the potential for postpurchase anxiety and to develop tactics that help the consumer relieve the discomfort of cognitive dissonance. Consumers will repeat behavior that is rewarding and enjoyable. Postpurchase anxiety threatens the level of satisfaction associated with product acquisition. The cost factors discussed in Chapter 1 highlighted anxiety as one of the costs consumers may incur in the acquisition of a product. Therefore, if a firm hopes to promote brand loyalty and repeat purchase behavior, then tactics that help relieve consumer anxiety as a type of cost must be initiated.

Acquiring Complementary Goods

The second crucial element of postpurchase behavior is the tendency of consumers to acquire goods that complement the original product purchased. This means that consumers, either out of a sense of necessity or enthusiasm, often purchase several other items related to an initial purchase. Buyers of automatic coffee makers become purchasers of coffee filters. Similarly, buyers of new cars frequently buy related items like CD players, floor mats, seat covers, or an extended service contract. This common behavior of acquiring complementary goods presents firms with an opportunity to extend their product lines and accommodate consumers' desires while serving the revenue generation objectives of the firm.

The decision-making process discussed here points out that consumers are not as capricious or unsystematic as one might intuitively believe. The underpinnings of human behavior are not always obvious, and the stages of consumer decision making are intended to show that consumption behavior can, in fact, be quite methodical. But this description of the consumer buying process should not lead to the conclusion that consumers are systematic, calculating, and totally rational. This is hardly the case. A variety of psychological and sociological influences affect the decision-making process and ultimately the final purchase decision.

PSYCHOLOGICAL INFLUENCES

As consumers contemplate a purchase, several psychological influences shape the nature of the decision. Marketing has progressed rapidly in its understanding of the relationship between psychological factors and consumption behavior. Although all aspects of psychological influence on the consumer are not completely understood, the following areas provide important insights: needs, learning, attitudes, perception, personality, and experiential-hedonic influences.

Needs

Basic human **needs** set a foundation for the consumer to seek satisfaction in the marketplace. A useful, well-organized description of how needs motivate behavior is provided by Abraham Maslow.[7] Maslow, a pioneer in the study of human motivation, conceived that human behavior progresses through the following hierarchy of need states:

- *Physiological Needs.* Biological needs that require the satisfaction of hunger, thirst, and basic bodily functions.
- *Safety Needs.* The need to provide shelter and protection for the body and to maintain a comfortable existence.
- *Love and Belonging Needs.* The need for affiliation and affection. A person will strive for both the giving and receiving of love.
- *Esteem Needs.* The need for recognition, status, and prestige. In addition to seeking the respect of others, there is a need and desire for self-respect.
- *Self-Actualization.* This is the highest of all the need states and achieved by only a small percentage of people according to Maslow. The individual strives for maximum fulfillment of individual capabilities.

It must be clearly understood that Maslow was describing *basic* human needs and motivations not *consumer* needs and motivations. But, in the context of a high mass-consumption society, the attempt by individuals to satisfy their basic human needs partly manifests itself in the acquisition of goods and services. Many products directly address the requirements of one or more of these need states. Home security systems and smoke detectors help address safety needs. Many personal care products, such as cosmetics, promote a feeling of greater acceptance by the opposite sex. In the pursuit of esteem, many consumers buy products they perceive to have status and prestige—expensive jewelry, automobiles, and residences are examples. Though it is difficult to *buy* self-actualization, there is evidence that product perception is affected by this need state.[8] And some products may be positioned to appeal to multiple need states such as designer clothing that is often portrayed as increasing both acceptance and prestige. Figure 6-2 graphically depicts Maslow's hierarchy.

Learning

In discussing the consumer decision-making process, we noted that consumers rely on past experiences and various sources of information in making a purchasing decision. The result of information and experience, over the long run, is **learning**. Much of the process of consumption is learned behavior and consumers behave differently based on what they learn from the process. There are several comprehensive learning theories. These theories identify the behavioral and cognitive aspects of human learning. The critical elements of learning, for marketing purposes, are *stimuli* and *reinforcement*.[9]

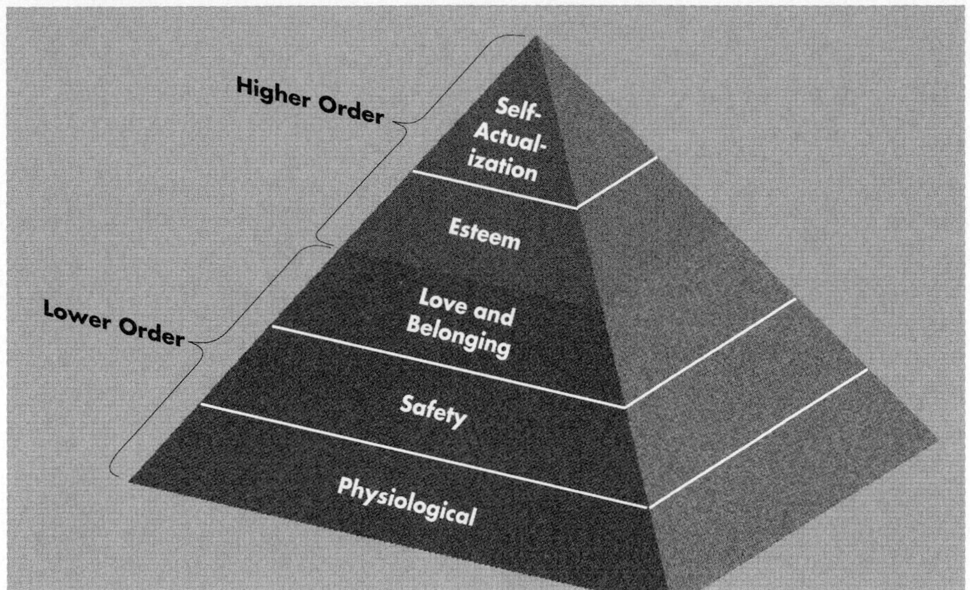

FIGURE 6-2
Maslow's Hierarchy of Needs

Stimuli are the many bits of information to which consumers may voluntarily or involuntarily be exposed. Much information is marketer controlled. Advertising, salespeople, the product package and label, coupons, and even the product itself stimulate a consumer. The marketing strategist attempts to design these stimuli so that they are meaningful and memorable to a consumer. Many other sources of information that consumers find relevant are beyond the control of the marketing process, though. The consumer's exposure to friends' recommendations or publicity about the product are also stimuli that promote learning. The end result of encountering various stimuli is that consumer behavior will be altered based on the newly learned information.

Reinforcement, the second basic element of learning, can have a powerful effect on consumers' subsequent decisions and activities. The most direct source of reinforcement in a marketing context is use of the product itself. A consumer can be positively or negatively reinforced depending on the level of satisfaction obtained from product use. If the product fails to meet a consumer's expectations, negative reinforcement results. This represents a barrier to the subsequent purchase and use of the product. On the other hand, a rewarding experience will motivate a buyer to engage in the same behavior again (that is, to repurchase the brand). Several marketing efforts can facilitate a positive reinforcement. The most powerful of these is that the product is properly designed and meets consumers' needs as closely as possible. Beyond this requirement, prompt and proper servicing of the product is important. Also, as pointed out earlier, postpurchase communications that support the buyer's decision can relieve cognitive dissonance and serve as positive reinforcement.

Attitudes

Over the last 15 to 20 years, a substantial body of research evidence has identified relationships between attitudes and consumer behavior. It is believed that attitudes are an extremely useful factor in understanding consumer decision making and in predicting behavior. The usefulness of attitudes in understanding behavior is based on the fundamental nature of an attitude.

An **attitude** is "a learned predisposition to respond in a consistently favorable or unfavorable manner with respect to a given object."[10] What *learned predisposition to respond* means in the language of consumer buying behavior is that when products are encountered in the marketplace, a favorable (positive) attitude will create approach behavior (that is, purchase and use). When an unfavorable (negative) attitude has formed, the consumer will be predisposed to avoid a particular product and seek alternatives.

An important influence of attitudes on product evaluation and choice is the affective or "feeling" orientation that attitudes can create in consumers. Often, we find ourselves saying that we simply like one brand more than another. When asked to explain why we like a particular brand better, we are hard pressed to articulate precisely the reasons. The influence of attitudes on consumer behavior is the basis for marketing and advertising strategies like the one used by Wal-Mart in its "Buy American" campaign and Mazda advertising that its cars "Just Feel Right."[11] Both of these campaigns rely on attitudes as the basis for consumer predisposition toward the firms and their products.

Perception

Perception is the manner in which an individual interprets stimuli from the environment. Each of us use perception to create our own reality. Because the human mind has limits on the amount of stimulation it can handle, we screen information from the environment in a way that is consistent with what each of us believes to be important and relevant. Perception creates an orientation to the world that is the result of past experiences, attitudes, cultural norms, and learned behavior. Perceptions are actually the combined influence of many of the psychological influences discussed so far.

The implication of perceptual processes is that consumers will ignore stimuli they deem irrelevant and interpret all stimuli in a way that is consistent with their personal version of reality. As such, information about products, their use, and benefits must be consistent with the consumer's definition of what is relevant. For example, health issues have created a heightened awareness among consumers of the fat and cholesterol content of foods. Firms have altered products to reduce fat and cholesterol and prominently display these reductions in advertising and on product packages.

Personality

Personality exerts a psychological influence on decision making similar to perception. While perception is an active and spontaneous process, personality tends to evolve over time and results in individual traits that create a general orientation to situations. There is some controversy in the marketing literature as to the effects of personality on consumer behavior.[12] Despite any controversy, it is reasonable to suggest that personality traits that describe characteristics of individuals like sociability and self-confidence will be manifest across a broad range of situations including product evaluation and choice. There is, for example, evidence of personality differences between consumers who buy so-called signature goods where brand names are emblazoned on the item and those who do not.[13] Buyers of signature goods have been found to be more outgoing and gregarious compared to nonbuyers. The use of personality as a predictor of consumer behavior has met with varying degrees of success.

Experiential-Hedonic Influences

A relatively new concept suggests that an important and heretofore underemphasized set of influences on consumption behavior has to do with the experiential and pleasure (hedonic) aspects of consuming products.[14] The influences discussed so far in the chapter suggest the human mind is working overtime to separate, evaluate, and direct consumption decisions. **Experiential-hedonic influences** emphasize the pleasure and personal enhancement that result from a consumption activity. That is, consumers buy and consume things because they derive pleasure from doing so, period. The thinking and research in this area is new and the influence of these factors has yet to be completely identified. But, a trend appears to be emerging in the United States toward greater pleasure seeking. Americans are exercising less, eating more pork, and not trying nearly as hard to avoid cholesterol. As one woman put it, "I would rather be a few pounds heavier and that much happier."[15]

The effects of psychological influences on the consumer decision-making process must be considered in the context of several environmental factors that also affect the consumer. We now turn our attention to these environmental factors.

SOCIOLOGICAL INFLUENCES

The psychological influences on consumer buying behavior provide useful insights. Consumers, however, do not make decisions in isolation. Rather, individuals live, work, and consume goods and services in a social setting. Sociological influences that provide additional insights into consumer behavior are culture, lifestyle, subculture, social class, reference groups, family, and situational factors.

Culture

Culture evolves through the behaviors, artifacts, and symbols that are passed from one generation to another in a society. Cultural influences have unavoidable effects on individuals as they carry out their consumption desires. The cultural values people learn are transferred, in part, to the evaluation of products. To appreciate the effect of culture on the American consumer, several existing and emerging cultural influences must be examined.

Existing Cultural Values

Convenience is a key variable in the culture of the United States, and its effects are pervasive and conspicuous in marketing. Products that are easy to open, easy to use, and disposable have made inroads in the marketplace as marketers recognize the national desire for convenience. Frozen foods were the first response to the influence. They were followed by products that were pre-prepared or came in plastic bags—ready for preparation and serving. We can now use and dispose of lighters, shavers, cameras, and literally every product package we buy. Entire industries have been spawned by the desire for convenience. The fast-food industry and convenience food stores are examples. Similarly, traditional consumer-oriented operations—such as banks and supermarkets—have responded to the desire for convenience by providing 24-hour banking machines and extended hours.

Closely related to convenience is the value placed on *time* itself. American consumers are tenacious about saving time and using time effectively. Busy schedules have spawned products that allow us to use time wisely and effectively, such as the timed recording options on most VCRs and the ever present "day timer" calendars that help us squeeze every last useable minute out of a day. Dramatic evidence of the value placed on time is contained in the results of a recent study in which participants indicated that the microwave oven was the second most important household product in their lives second only to the smoke alarm.[16]

Despite the earlier reference to hedonic consumption, *nutrition and health,* are still major influences on consumption behavior in the United States. This value in contemporary society has spawned multibillion dollar industries. As consumers have become sensitized to and educated about healthful living, the health club and fitness center industry has grown from a few facilities know as spas to thousands of modern, heavily patronized workout centers. The word "aerobic," which most people couldn't define ten years ago, is now a part of the life-style of millions of Americans. Over 50 percent of American consumers report that they try to avoid products that are high in sodium and cholesterol.[17] "Light" and nonalcoholic beers and products low in fat, sodium, and cholesterol are gaining market share as modern consumers try to live more healthful lives.[18] Sun screens, tartar control toothpastes, and high-fiber foods are other current examples of consumers' greater concern for health being.

Emerging Cultural Values

The discussion of the consumer market in Chapter 4 posed the proposition that American consumers are beginning to change their orientation to life. Such a change signals the emergence of new and different cultural values. These cultural values will in turn alter marketplace behavior. The challenge facing marketing decision makers is that the aging baby boom generation is experiencing dramatic life and attitude changes. There is evidence that this largest of population cohorts in the United States is rejecting materialism and conspicuous consumption, which fueled much of the economic growth of the 1980s, for more practical and pressing needs. This group now faces the reality of saving simultaneously for *both* their children's college education and their own retirements.[19]

While there is some controversy over the extensiveness and speed of change, there is little doubt that consumer values are in a state of transition. Brands that emerged as symbols of success and indulgence, such as *Hagen-Dazs,* BMW, and *Filofax* have suffered substantial declines in revenues and profits. By the end of 1991, sales of BMW automobiles in the United States had tumbled 32 percent from their peak in 1986. The stock market "crash" of 1987 and the extensive employment cutbacks in the early 1990s in so-called glamour industries like financial services, advertising, and computer technology would seem to have shocked this generation into a reassessment of their values.

Several new and different consumption values could likely emerge from such a change in cultural values. With a more conservative outlook on life and less of a desire to spend lavishly, *value* is now emerging as a significant product evaluation criterion. As the opening scenario to this chapter pointed out, consumers are now much more conscious and conscientious in their spending. They are willing and able to judge price and features and will demand more service. Consumers are also willing to spend more for quality indicating in a recent survey that they would pay from 10 percent to a whopping 72 percent more for higher quality in a variety of different product categories.[20]

Concern for the natural environment is a value motivating consumers to purchase and use products that are packaged in recyclable materials or are biodegradable. This value is finding its way into product features as well. Products that are more pure and natural are in greater demand. A concern about chemical additives, dyes, and gaseous fumes is motivating consumers to seek out products that are free of these hazards. Consumers are trying to eliminate unnecessary chemicals from their existence by purchasing convenience goods like fluoride-free toothpaste and mouthwashes without artificial coloring or preservatives. This concern for the internal as well as the external environment is fueling a host of new products and consumer buying behavior.[21]

The emerging cultural values raised here produce a very different profile of consumers from the "spend-and-get" consumers of the 1980s. Whether this orientation will persist remains to be seen. Its current momentum, however, is undeniable as many favored brands of prior decades are struggling to adjust to the shift in consumer orientation. The main issue is that marketers must carefully monitor these emerging values and determine the extent to which consumer behavior is being altered. For example, will the value placed on the environment overwhelm the existing value placed on convenience? In many instances, these two values are in conflict. The organization that does not respond quickly and accurately to values in the culture will find its products being assessed as obsolete and irrelevant.

Life-style

Life-style influences on consumer behavior are often referred to as *psychographics,* or that combination of values and activities that produce a way of life for an individual. And, a way of life will carry with it a wide array of product and service needs. The nonfamily household with a single individual is very different from a household with three children under 14 and a husband and wife who work outside the home. Marketers try to match life-style activities like hobbies, club memberships, and entertainment preferences with interests like career orientation, media use, and family values. These factors are then combined with the opinions people hold about important political, social, and self-perception issues. Combining these values with demographics produces a life-style profile that marketers must understand in order to devise an effective marketing mix.

Chapter 4 discussed the use of the VALS-2 system developed by SRI International as a way to track life-styles in the United States, Canada, Germany, Japan, and the United Kingdom. The VALS system helps firms target particular life-styles by establishing life-style groups with detailed activities, interests, and opinions.

Firms are using fewer chemicals in food production in response to consumers' desire for more pure and natural products.

Subcultures

Subcultures also exert an influence on behavioral norms. Ethnic background, age, and geography create subcultures that influence individual behavior. Subcultures are distinctive by virtue of their wanting or being forced to maintain a separate identity. These groups transmit values and establish norms of behavior. Unique value systems and behavioral tendencies are produced by subcultural influences.

Ethnic subcultures must be recognized by marketers as a formidable force in the United States in the years to come. Four of six Americans added to the population between 1980 and 1990 were non-white. Specifically, as of 1990, the ethnic subculture population of the United States was made up of 29.8 million African-Americans (up 13.2 percent from 1980); 22.3 million Hispanics (up 53 percent from 1980); 7.3 million Asian-Americans (up 108 percent from 1980); and 2 million Native Americans (up 37.9 percent from 1980). In total, ethnic subculture groups represent 61.5 percent of the U.S. population, up 33.8 percent from 1980 compared to the 3.7 percent growth rate of the rest of the population.[22]

Hispanics represent one of the most important subculture groups to marketers in the United States today. Spanish-speaking Americans make up 15 percent of the population and have over $130 billion in purchasing power. As a group they are more brand loyal and spend a disproportionate amount of their income on packaged goods.[23] The sheer size of this market and the unique purchase behaviors exhibited by its members have prompted firms like Procter & Gamble and Frito-Lay to specifically target this subcultural group for specialized products and marketing programs. In response to the large number of Hispanics immigrating to the United States, Procter & Gamble introduced a laundry detergent, *Ariel,* in the United States that it previously sold only in the Latin American market.

African-American consumers also display distinctive consumption-related behaviors. They are active shoppers who rely on advertising and personal selling for product information. They are more willing to switch brands than other consumer groups, and are also more willing to shop many stores for clothing bargains.[24] The African-American population is important to U.S. marketers because they represent a large population (31 million in 1992) with purchasing power in the range of $220 billion annually.

Social Class

An additional broad-based influence on the consumer is social class membership. Although a fundamental precept of society in the United States is its lack of class structure, social classes tend to evolve naturally as a sociological phenomenon for a wide variety of reasons. The importance of social class as a basis for analyzing consumer behavior lies with the fact that social classes are divisions within a society whose members adopt similar attitudes, values, and life-styles. The emphasis in this description highlights key influences on consumption behavior. As such, an analysis of the nature of social class provides an enriched view of the nature of influences on consumers. At the outset, it is useful to describe the factors used to identify **social class** membership:

- Education
- Occupation
- Area of residence
- Type of residence
- Source of wealth

Obvious by its absence is the income variable, per se. Quite simply, income has not proved to clearly delineate the social classes. A plumber and a middle-level executive can earn the same income, but their social class membership is different, primarily because their value systems as members of different social classes are also different. Therefore, source of wealth is used as a reflection of the income factor.

The most important distinctions in consumption behavior are recognizable between the higher classes and the lower classes. The higher social classes value the image they can portray with their product collection. Products that exude prestige, status, or even class membership are valued. The higher social classes are simply more conspicuous in their consumption. Again, this aspect of behavior must be analyzed in the context of emerging cultural values discussed earlier. Further, they own their own homes and invest heavily in products to complement the dwelling. On the other hand, the lower social classes place a greater value and emphasis on the family. Products that make life more comfortable and enhance the family's existence are more important. As marketers are able to find consistencies in behavior and consumption values with social class, then the ability to providing satisfying products to these segments is greatly enhanced.

Reference Groups

One of the strongest sources of persuasive pressure and influence on behavior is exerted by the reference group or groups to which an individual belongs. **Reference groups** can be large and diverse, such as college graduates, ethnic groups, or members of a political party. Groups can also be small and intimate, such as the family unit, work peers, or a social club. There is a strong tendency for individuals to conform to the norms of the groups with which they identify and to engage in behaviors the group deems to be appropriate. There is little mystery to this relationship since the person values group membership and joined the group because of its similar attitudes or interests. The group becomes a reference for judging behavior and determining future courses of behavior.

In the marketing context, knowledge of reference group theory proves useful in several ways. First, consumers can substitute reference group information for objective product information. If members of the group are using a product and gaining satisfaction from it, the consumer can then defer to this information in the decision-making process. Second, a marketer's portrayal of a product in use by a reference group member can serve as an added form of relevant purchasing information. When consumers see a person in an advertisement with whom they can identify, this adds another dimension to the image and meaning of a product. Third, the concept of aspiring group membership is meaningful. Beyond the groups to which individuals actually belong, many people aspire to affiliate with certain groups or to be identified with a particularly revered group. The use of sports heroes in advertising for many product categories is based on this sort of reference group influence. Consider the advertising theme used by Keds for its tennis shoes: "Keds—for those times in your life when you feel like a Pro." Experts can exert a reference group influence over consumers also. An expert referent is someone who consumers perceive to have special, reliable knowledge about a product and its performance. Nike uses Michael Jordan (the basketball player) to serve as a spokesperson for its shoe line.

One of the most important reference groups currently exerting an influence on marketing strategy is *you*. That's right, you, the one reading this book and the members of your class! If you were born between 1961 and 1981 you are part of what demographers have called the baby busters (the group following the baby boomers). That label, aside from being offensive, is absolutely wrong. For one thing, there are 61 million baby boomers and now over 80 million in your generation. Other labels applied to this group are Twentysomethings, **Generation X,** and Thirteeners (the thirteenth generation after the signing of the Constitution). Whatever the label, this is a very important reference group that is exhibiting distinctive values and behavior. Generation X is not interested in the simplification of life being touted by the baby boomers. In fact, Xers were asked if they would ever like to be like baby boomers, and four out five said no. Furthermore, Xers basically reject most of the boomer-conceived new priorities like family values and the New Age Movement. One author described Xers as a "carnival of culture featuring the tangible bottom lines of life—money, bodies, and brains."[25] Other recent research has found that the values in the group, while not like boomers, are not particularly radical either in that most are satisfied with their employment situations and show a strong loyalty to the firms for which they work.[26] Precisely how Xers will make their unique brand of culture known in the marketplace is still emerging, but the NEC ad in Illustration 6-2 suggests one company's perception.

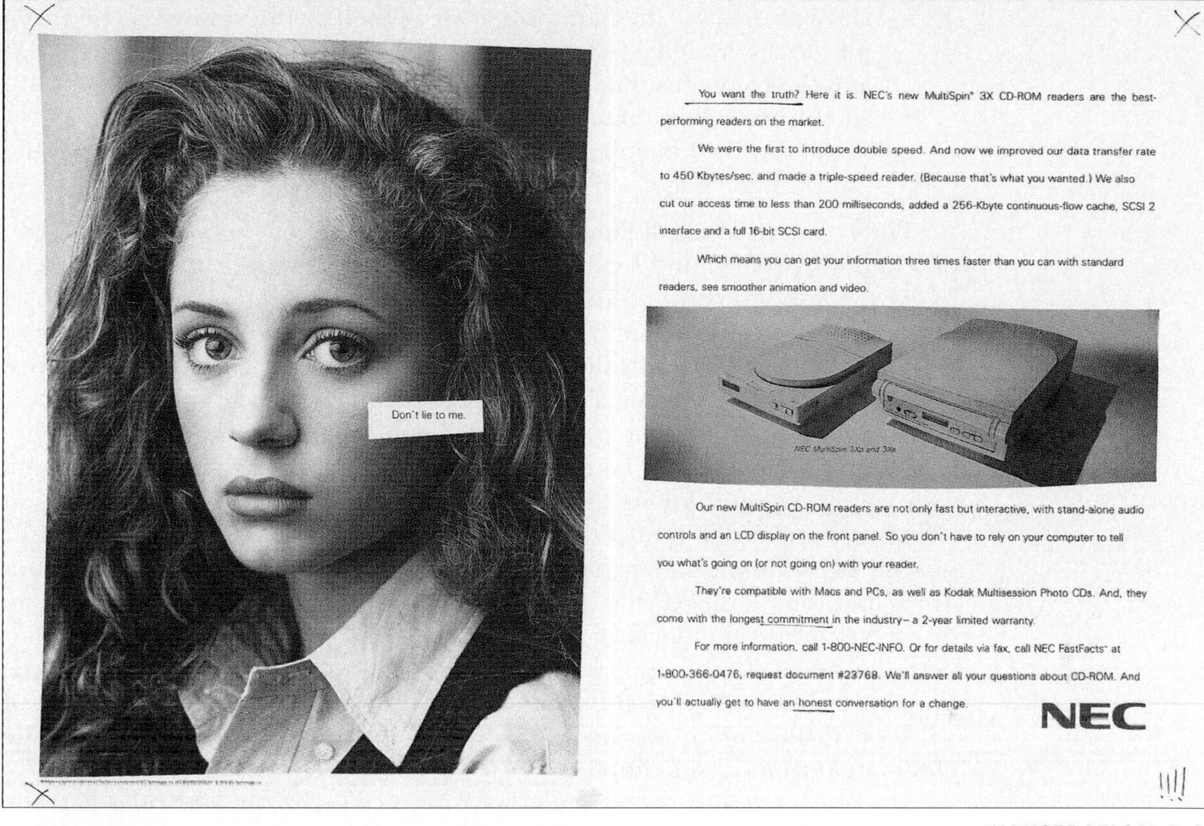

ILLUSTRATION 6-2
NEC Corporation Advertistment Aimed at Members of Generation X

Family

The family is such an important reference group in terms of its effect on consumption behavior that it warrants separate discussion. Think of your own consumption values and conventions. How many of them are the result of the way your family used to do things? How often do you change the oil in your car? What time do you prefer to eat dinner? Do you send your clothes to the dry cleaner or do you wash and iron them yourself? Your behaviors in these areas were probably shaped by family socialization. One means to gaining insight into the effect of family is by looking at the family life cycle. The **family life cycle** is a series of stages related to the way a family is formed, grows, evolves, and changes consumption patterns.

- A young single or young married couple who are just establishing a household have a broad range of product needs like appliances, furniture, and housewares. This group can be quite price conscious although willing to try new brands.
- The arrival of a child causes more product and service needs: life insurance, baby furniture, a minivan. The purchase of a home at this stage creates a wave of new purchases like a lawn mower, gardening equipment, security systems, and the like.
- As children grow, enter school, learn to ride a bike or drive a car, the need for another set of product needs evolve. Families with teenagers, for example, exhibit disproportionately high expenditures for food compared to families in other life-cycle stages.

- Divorce disrupts the family life cycle. Whether the young married couple or the middle-aged married couple divorces, separate households and the commensurate needs emerge.
- The process continues until a household returns to a two-member (or single divorced member) unit without children often referred to as the "empty nest" stage.

These various levels of family development influence the nature and scope of a family's product and service needs. Marketers monitor the trends in family size, age composition, and household formation to take advantage of opportunities related to family life-cycle effects on consumption behavior.

The **family decision-making process** is another aspect of family influence on decision making and must be understood if marketers are to direct their efforts properly. Within the context of the family, various aspects of consumption decision making may be controlled by different family members. Anyone with young children knows that they are a veritable fountain of information about toys and snack foods. And, the decision maker, actual buyer, and user may all be different members of the family. For example, in the multibillion dollar pet food industry, the actual consumer (the family dog or cat) has no direct input into the decision-making process. Because of this, pet food marketers must make the appearance and smell of pet foods appealing to the owner/buyer as well as to the animal. If the buyer finds a particular brand of pet food visually offensive (no matter how Fido responds), that brand will be eliminated from consideration.

Marketers are also becoming aware of the changing **gender roles** and the expanded influence of the female member of the household in making and influencing family purchase decisions. One estimate identifies that women now buy about 45 percent of all the automobiles sold and men account for about 40 percent of the spending on food products.[27]

Situational Factors

A recent and important addition to the recognized influences on consumer decision making and behavior are the situation factors associated with consumption. The originator of the concept of **situational factors** as a basis for understanding previously unexplained variations in consumer behavior defined these influences as:

All those factors particular to a time and place of observation which do not follow from a knowledge of personal (intra-individual) and stimulus (choice alternative) attributes and which have a demonstrable and systematic effect on current behavior.[28]

What this definition says is that both the fundamental psychological and sociological influences discussed thus far can exert a different influence, depending upon the *situation* surrounding the consumption act. To demonstrate the effect this factor can have on decision making, consider a woman's decision to buy a new dress. A new dress for the company New Year's Eve party will likely be vastly different from the clothing purchased to travel abroad or to wear to the office. The situation associated with the decision will have an effect on the decision criteria and the ultimate choice. Or consider your own decision-making process to choose a restaurant for dinner. You would likely choose different restaurants in each of these situations: a date, a quick meal before class, your aunt Elizabeth's upcoming visit. Another aspect of situational factors has an effect on communicating with consumers. It has been discovered that consumers who are intensely involved in a particular television program (such as the Super Bowl or the Olympics) show lower recall of advertising within the programming. A similar situational effect on communication is realized based on mood-inducing aspects of television programming. Programs that were deemed to be "happy" created better ad effectiveness and recall.[29] Marketing decision makers must be aware of situational influences if they are to fully understand the nature and variation of consumption acts.

Business Buying Behavior

In Chapter 5, we saw that the business market has demand and transaction features that create unique challenges for firms. The derived nature of demand, a small number of large buyers, and diffused buying responsibilities are factors that make the business market unique. However, just as in household consumer buying behavior, the buying process in business markets can be portrayed as taking place in a series of stages, as illustrated in Figure 6-3. The six stages of **business buying behavior** are:

1. Need recognition
2. Product and scheduling specifications
3. Evaluation of products and services
4. Evaluation of suppliers
5. Product and supplier choice
6. Product and supplier performance evaluation

These stages reflect similarities and differences between the household consumer buying process and the business buying process. Business buyers initiate a decision based on need recognition as do their household consumer counterparts, but this need recognition is more narrowly defined. First, due to production schedule demands and the nature of business products, the business buyer typically enters the **business decision-making process** based on *out-of-stock* or *functional need states.* By virtue of the diffused buying responsibilities (as discussed in Chapter 5), the business buyer is often influenced or directed by other members of the organization (such as engineers or the users of the product) in seeking out products to purchase. Next, *product evaluation* is predominately based on functional and benefits-of-use criteria rather than on emotional criteria. This is not to say that business buyers are not subject to risk anxiety and the desire for security in the decision-making process, which are emotional factors. Further, business buyers may also rely on reference groups for input on the usefulness of products, as the advertisement in Illustration 6-3 suggests. But, emotions tend to give way to the more rational bases for decision making in this highly structured and professional decision-making context. Finding the *supplier* who carries the product that meets the designated product and service specifications becomes an overriding consideration. Because of the importance of working relationships in the business market, the product and supplier evaluation stages often take place simultaneously. This aspect of product/supplier evaluation is depicted in Figure 6-3.

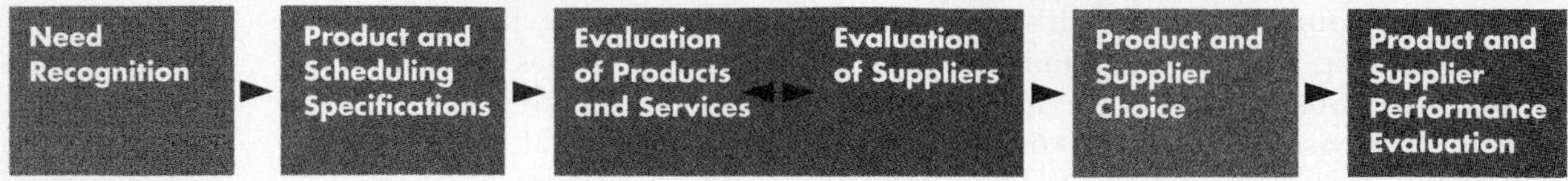

FIGURE 6-3
Stages in the Business Buying Process

A notable distinction between consumer and business buyers is the emphasis placed on *choosing the supplier* and scheduling the ordering of products. The source of supply carries greater importance to the business buyer since a variety of benefits (to be discussed later in this section) can result from choosing the right business suppliers. Similarly, the pressures of keeping an organization running smoothly with the needed production supplies and equipment place greater emphasis on scheduling.

In the business market, a *product and supplier performance evaluation* are much more formalized after a purchase than in the household consumer market. While household consumers often evaluate their decisions in the postpurchase stage, business buyers tend to have a more formalized procedure for generating direct feedback on product and supplier performance. This feature of business buying behavior has heightened the awareness of relationship marketing as we have discussed before. Buying and selling organizations now understand that nurturing long-term partnerships reaps tremendous rewards for both organizations. This feature of business buying has prompted suppliers like Great Plains Software, which creates accounting programs for small businesses, to meet regularly with customers to ensure that all aspects of the company's service are meeting expectations.[30]

THE NATURE OF DECISION MAKING IN THE BUSINESS MARKET

Psychological and sociological factors mediate consumer decision making. In business decision making, the nature of the process is affected by the decision styles used by business buyers and the type of decision that is being made. **Decision styles** refers to the observation that business buyers have been found to typically use one of two very different styles in going about the decision-making process. These two approaches are referred to as the rational decision style and the conservative decision style. The *rational decision style* is characterized by an effort on the part of the buyer to maximize the expected monetary value of the purchase. The buyer using this style will scrutinize price, product features, delivery schedule, and in general will be very deliberate in progressing through the stages of the decision-making process. Conversely, the buyer using a conservative decision style will not place primary emphasis on the monetary or economic aspects of the purchase, but rather places greater emphasis on reducing risk. The *conservative style decision* maker will rely on past experience with vendors and loyalty as primary factors in decision making. Some estimates suggest that as many as 70 percent of all business decision makers are using this conservative decision-making style thus placing risk aversion above economic considerations in the purchase process.

Rational and conservative decision makers will place different value on factors in the marketing mix of the firms with which they are doing business.

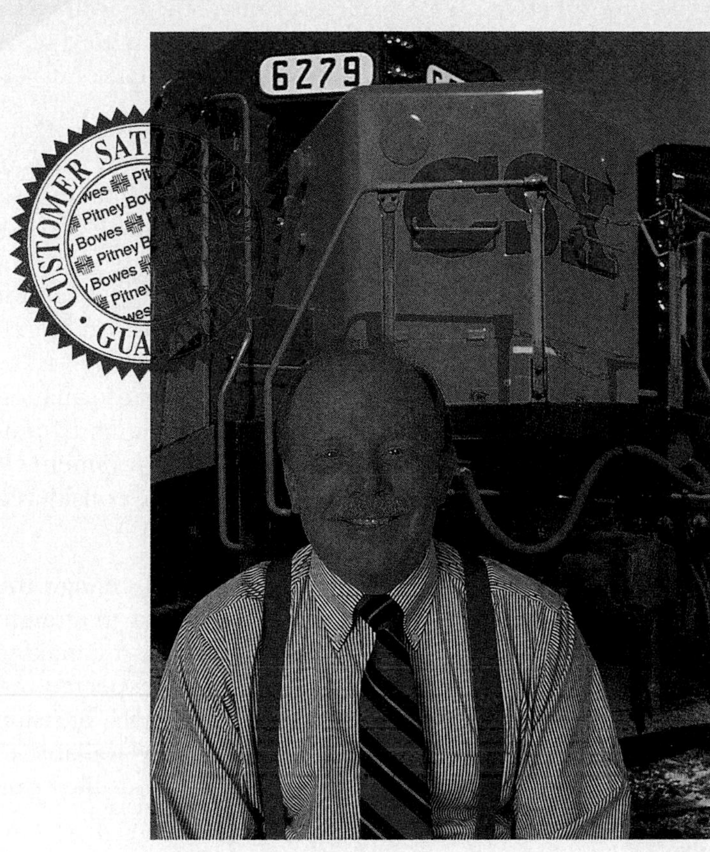

6279
CSX
CUSTOMER SAT
GUA
"CSX Transportation is spread all up and down the eastern seaboard. So we rely on fax machines for sending everything from bills of lading to employee time cards."
"Right now we've installed over 1200 Pitney Bowes fax machines...and we are updating our older equipment as fast as we can. Because for every existing fax machine we replace with a Pitney Bowes machine, we're saving money."
"Pitney Bowes fax machines give us the cost, service, and reliability we're looking for."
"We don't have any problems with service, there's very little upkeep, and anytime I have a question about the sale of a new machine or billing, one call gets me through to my rep and he takes care of it."
"Pitney Bowes makes you feel like you're the customer."
At Pitney Bowes, customer satisfaction is a commitment that's at the very fiber of our business. It shapes the attitudes and actions of our people. And it's reflected in the quality and reliability of our products. What's more, we back it up with our Customer Satisfaction Guarantee.SM For more information, call 1-800-MR BOWES ext. 1055.
"Pitney Bowes has replaced over 1200 fax machines for us...and we're ordering more. Every one we add saves us money."
Steve McCann
Manager, Office Equipment
CSX Transportation
Pitney Bowes
Facsimile Systems
Stamford, CT 06926-0700
Telephone: 1-800-MR BOWES
Postage Meters•Mailing, Shipping, Copying, Dictation, Facsimile and
ID Systems•Facilities Management•Equipment Leasing

ILLUSTRATION 6-3
Business buyers are also influenced by reference groups.

Rational decision makers will emphasize the product and pricing variables while the conservative decision makers will be more sensitive to distribution (i.e., availability and delivery of stock) and will respond to a different type of promotional appeal. Properly appealing to rational and conservative decision makers will require completely different marketing mixes.

The other aspect of importance in the nature of business buying is the type of decision buyers are engaging in. The **type of business decision** factor includes three possibilities: straight rebuy, modified rebuy, or new task.

- The *straight rebuy* is a common situation where a buyer is purchasing an item on a recurring basis and engages in little information search. Vendors are usually chosen from a pre-approved list. This type of decision is many times routine and typical for operating supplies and small component parts.
- The *modified rebuy* is also a recurring purchase, but product and vendor specifications can change over time requiring that information search be initiated.
- The *new task* type of decision is characterized by extensive information search. It is a new purchase decision and is typical for infrequently purchased business goods like installations and accessory equipment. It can also occur when major changes in sources of supply are considered for raw materials and operating supplies.

Recognition of the type of decision the buyer is making will change the emphasis within the marketing mix. Firms that are serving buyers in straight rebuy situations do all they can to retain preferred vendor status by making sure all aspects of product provision and service meet buyers' expectations. When a firm has the opportunity to compete for sales in a new task decision context, then large amounts of information must be made readily available to the buyer(s) including a fully prepared personal presentation about the firm, its products, and the value it has to offer.

EVALUATION CRITERIA USED IN BUSINESS DECISION MAKING

In analyzing household consumer behavior, we have discovered that a variety of factors, both psychological and sociological, influence consumers enroute to a purchase decision. Business buyers are also subject to a variety of influences, both economic and emotional, as we discussed in the decision styles section. These influences translate into a variety of evaluation criteria used in the decision-making process. The following are criteria used by business buyers to evaluate products, services, and the vendors who supply them.

Efficiency of Product Supplied

This can be based on such qualities as speed of performance, wear and repair aspects of an item, and ease of use or installation. For example, a product might have features that result in the possibility of using low-cost, semiskilled workers. This is often the case when antiquated production processes are enhanced with robotic assembly mechanisms. Or, in the case of microcomputers, clerical productivity can be increased to such a degree that fewer clerical staff may be needed to achieve the same level of output. One of the most powerful selling appeals a business seller can make to a business buyer is that the product will enhance the efficiency of the buyer's operations.

Certainty of Supply

A supplier may entice the buyer with lower prices but may not have the capability to guarantee a dependable, long-term supply of an item. In this case, business buyers will balk at entering a purchase agreement. No matter how attractive a price is, if the buyer fears that a supplier will be unable to provide the quantities desired over the long term, that buyer will likely shy away from a purchase. This circumstance is particularly prevalent in chemical, mineral, and raw-material supplies.

Dependability in Meeting Schedules

Business customers must meet their own schedules in production and sales and hence must assure themselves of supplies in the specified quantities and on the dates promised. Consider the disastrous circumstance of an automobile production line being held up because a 59-cent plastic-molded piece for the dashboard did not arrive on schedule!

Technical Assistance

This includes information on qualities and use of products or processes as well as advice on maximizing the customer's efficiency in their use. Problems of installing and incorporating equipment into existing production methods are also important to the customer in this area. Lanier, the supplier of office equipment, offers service contracts to buyers where the firm will respond within two hours to a request for technical assistance or repair.

Product Features and Vendor Patronage Motives

Business buyers base their purchase decisions on criteria related to both the product and the vendor that will supply the product as the factors discussed so far suggest. To establish the full range of evaluation criteria used in these two areas, the following listings will be helpful. Some typical product features emphasized by business buyers are:

- Efficiency
- Economy
- Quality
- Speed
- Strength
- Durability or endurance
- Protection from loss (warranty or guarantee)
- Dependability or reliability
- Accuracy
- Uniformity and stability
- Low maintenance cost
- Simplicity

Note that this list includes items that relate to all areas of product evaluation: function, emotion (risk aversion), and benefits of use. Each item on the list suggests appeals that the business buyer should respond to in a sales presentation.

The factor that determines choice in the business market is often the buyer's image of the selling institution. This is especially important when the decision relates to goods that are so nearly alike that it is difficult to provide clear differentiation from competitive products. Products such as operating supplies and raw materials fall into this category. When the product itself does not represent a significant basis for differentiation, then the vendor choice criteria carry the greatest weight in the choice process. Typical of the criteria used to evaluate vendors are:

- Completeness of line
- Completeness of stock
- Offer of free service
- Reputation in trade
- Reciprocal patronage
- Price and discount policies
- Monopoly position
- Financial or managerial connection
- Friendship
- Past services
- Research and pioneering

Overall, business marketers need to recognize that buyers, both rational and conservative, will consider a full range of factors in attempting to achieve the greatest value with purchases. Notice in this list of choice motives that the selling firm must respond to price and distribution factors that are important to the buyer. Suppliers must fulfill the fundamental requirement of putting together a marketing mix that provides satisfaction to buyers based on both product and vendor criteria.

Analyzing buyer behavior is a critical component in developing an effective marketing mix. The issues raised here provide a firm with the foundation for specifying product, price, promotion, and distribution features of its strategic approach to the market. The next section will consider decision making in the global context.

Analyzing Consumer and Business Buying Behavior: A Global Perspective

While the previous chapters' global sections have focused on broad-based issues such as stages of economic development and market analyses, the purpose of this section is to focus on the individual level and on the factors that influence the decision-making processes of consumers around the world—a formidable task! From a global perspective, this necessarily requires understanding the subtle complexities that the influences of *culture* have on marketing activities. Cultural factors explain the greatest amount of market variability in global markets. Many marketing failures at the global level can be traced to strategies and tactics that failed to take into account the complexities of cultural influences on the behavior of individuals and social systems within a specific cultural context.

A simple starting point for discussion of consumer and business buying behavior is to *always* keep in mind that both consumer behavior and business practices are determined to a large extent by the culture within which they take place. As individual consumers (and as students of business) we accumulate cultural values that influence our understanding of how the world works: how we perceive and organize information, develop sets of alternatives for evaluation, make choices, and evaluate those outcomes are all culturally influenced. Once cultural borders are crossed, we are confronted with other rules about how the world works. Consequently, our training and knowledge of how to behave as individuals, how other people behave, and how other social systems operate must be reexamined when the challenge of marketing goods and services is undertaken. Consuming McDonald's hamburgers, buying a Bic pen, or having access to Coca-Cola and a Mars candy bar dispensed from a vending machine may strike many consumers in open and affluent markets as relatively low-involvement consumption activities in which convenience is the common denominator. These products are also known to millions of consumers in dozens of countries around the world. However, you can be certain that convenience of acquisition and low-involvement are not the best descriptors of the decision-making process for consumers all around the world! In global marketing, what is important to consider is not what the products seem to mean to consumers in the home market, but what the product offerings mean within the cultural context of consumers in the target culture. Any tendency to rely on a *self-reference criteria,* which is the unconscious application of one's own cultural values to a market in another culture, must be kept in check. Complicating matters, the unconscious application of our own cultural values often gets expressed as **ethnocentric behavior**, which is the belief that one's own culture is superior to another: an offensive and erroneous perspective on the world.

Recall from earlier in the chapter that culture is the human-made part of the human (and business!) environment, expressed as the sum total of knowledge, beliefs, art, morals, laws, customs, and any other capabilities and habits acquired by humans as members of society.[31] In order to be successful, global marketing managers must be students of culture. Otherwise, the marketing concepts of satisfying wants and needs and delivering satisfaction and value to customer groups will not be efficiently or effectively realized. Global marketers need to develop a sensitivity to their own culture, know how it differs from other cultures, and understand the reasons for those differences. This is not to say that global managers must *personally* take on the cultural values of the markets in which they operate. Japanese managers operating outside of their own country retain their distinctive Japanese cultural character—to replace those values with other cultural norms would jeopardize their career path at home. However, what the Japanese do better than almost all other national groups is *learn* about other cultures—paying close attention to local customs, wants, and needs. In other words, they are conscientious and astute students of culture. This is a trait that contributes to their ability to establish valuable exchange relationships and ultimately a competitive advantage.

THE INTERACTIONS OF MARKETING AND CULTURE

Culture not only profoundly influences the types of marketing activities that are acceptable and effective in a given environment, marketers themselves also act as *agents of change* within a culture. Marketers can have an influence on

This McDonald's outlet in Moscow is affected by different cultures and in turn influences the culture of Russia.

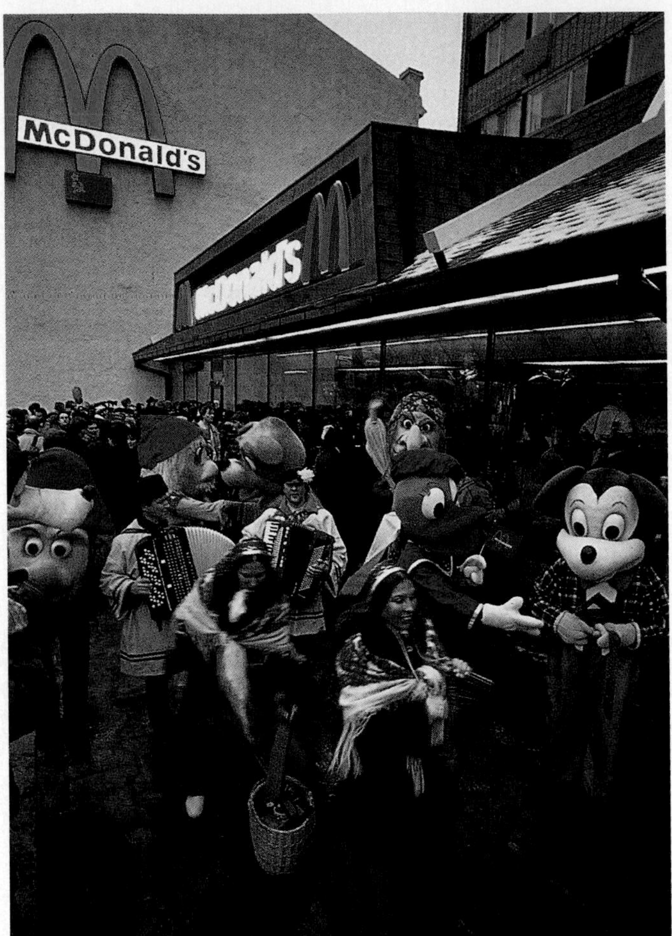

both the rate and type of change that takes place within a particular cultural setting. The stability of cultural norms and values, social roles, and social relationships are related to technological and economic development as well as to the degree of openness that characterizes a culture. McDonald's hamburgers, Visa Cards, Sony televisions, Revlon cosmetics, CNN, MTV, and countless brands of Japanese fax machines have penetrated markets the world over and have subsequently influenced the behavior and values of consumers exposed to these products and services.

The global success of these and many other offerings suggests that the world's needs and desires have become irrevocably homogenized and raises the question as to whether or not accounting for cultural differences is really critical to the success of global marketers. In a key article on this issue, Theodore Levitt suggests that companies must learn to operate as if the world were one large market and ignore superficial regional and national differences.[32] He argues that a global marketing infrastructure (e.g., global advertising agencies and marketing research firms) coupled with activities of increasing global travel and communication and advances in technology are forces that are homogenizing tastes across national boundaries. This in turn leads to a global standardization of marketing strategy. The strategy of treating the world as one homogeneous opportunity assumes that the price or product quality advantages emanating from standardization will outweigh specific customer preferences in enough cases to make it the appropriate strategic orientation.

Levitt's critics argue that the differences between countries are so great that even lower prices will not induce customers to buy standardized products; that a competitive product customized to local tastes can defeat a low-cost standardized global product even though its price is higher; and that advances in flexible manufacturing (short production runs in small quantity) are counteracting the cost advantages of standardized products. More importantly, the critics argue that cultural differences often require marketing programs uniquely designed for a country or, at a minimum, heavily modified to meet local needs. Examples supporting Levitt's side of the debate are typically luxury or mass-appeal products such as those mentioned above or highly standardized industrial products that have clearly defined benefits for industrial uses. In terms of actual practice, the majority of firms operating in global markets do tend to customize their activities for local market conditions. The conventional wisdom is to standardize elements of the marketing mix whenever possible and to localize the elements when necessary. As more markets become global and standardization of marketing mixes increase, however, the rate of cultural change will increase as well. Because of this, it is reasonable to suggest that the processes of cultural change and globally standardized strategies reinforce each other. The remaining portions of this chapter continue to explore this theme, identifying cultural similarities and differences that have effects on the decision-making processes of household consumers and business buyers. This involves a discussion of global life-styles as well as briefly reviewing how the concepts of social structure, societal orientation, and social class offer different implications for marketing in the global setting.

GLOBAL LIFE-STYLES?

While life-style has already been discussed in this chapter as a common basis for segmenting the consumer market, it deserves extra attention in this section since life-style has proven to be such a useful tool in segmenting consumer markets globally. Combined with geographic and demographic segmentation approaches, life-style variables add considerably to the marketing manager's understanding of how to best develop marketing mix strategies that can effectively cut across cultural borders. Following the *etic approach* to gathering information in cross cultural settings (review the discussion in Chapter 3), marketers group consumers in homogeneous life-style segments and develop standard marketing mixes that effectively reach those life-styles, regardless of nationality.

Table 6-1 presents data from the **Cross-Cultural Consumer Characterizations** (4Cs) study, which is a method for segmenting global markets developed by Young and Rubicam, a worldwide advertising agency. Using an algorithm that combines the consumer's socioeconomic profile with responses to 22 life-style statements, the 4Cs study gathers data from large national samples in

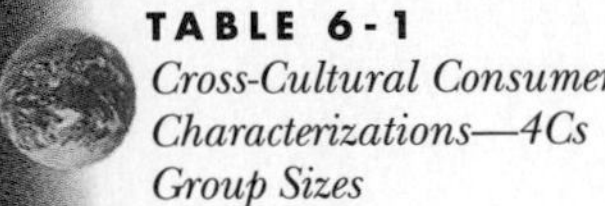

TABLE 6-1
Cross-Cultural Consumer Characterizations—4Cs Group Sizes

Lifestyle Group	COUNTRY United States	U.K.	Australia	France	Norway	Brazil
Constrained	11%	24%	23%	23%	14%	30%
Resigned	4	11	12	14	10	18
Struggling	7	13	11	9	4	12
Middle Majority	68	61	59	57	56	46
Mainstreamer	37	40	31	40	36	34
Aspirer	10	9	14	18	2	11
Succeeder	21	12	14	7	18	1
Innovators	21	15	18	20	30	13
Transitional	9	7	11	10	13	4
Reformer	12	8	7	10	17	9

The poorest 35% of the population was excluded from the Brazilian sample.

Key Descriptive Traits within Life-style Groups

Life-style Group	Dominant Traits
Resigned	Apathetic Complacent Passive
Struggling	Complaining Hopeful Doubtful
Mainstreamer	Conforming Satisfied Settled
Aspirer	Energetic Competitive Outward appearance important
Succeeder	Self-assured Arrogant Ambitious
Transitional	Seekers Self-expressive Individuality
Reformer	Deliberate Self-realization Moral conviction

countries throughout the world. Each country in the study weights the algorithm according to their own country's categories for socio-economic classification, and the resulting seven groups that are formed have highly similar life-style profiles, regardless of nationality. The dominant traits of each life-style group are briefly described in the table. It should be noted that while individuals never fit neatly into one life-style group or another, they are assigned as belonging *predominantly* to one life-style group for purposes of segmentation. In addition to the life-style grouping, a multitude of information is gathered concerning product usage, brand preferences, media habits, attitudes towards the environment, and politics as well as activities, interests, and opinions. This broad base of information allows for the analysis of similar life-style groups across countries and it serves as the basis for developing future plans.

For example, Volkswagen is currently preparing to launch a new compact electric car, due out in the mid-1990s. Using geographic and demographic segmentation approaches, they have already identified the target market for this car as economy-minded young urbanites who use cars for running errands in crowded urban environments. Economy, environmental friendliness, maneuverability, and compactness for parking are the car's key attributes rather than high-speed and comfort for long-distance touring. By using a tool to segment the market along life-style dimensions, VW can more clearly identify the proper positioning of the new product, develop effective promotional messages that work well across borders and within countries, and make the best advertising media selections. An important contribution of an approach like the 4Cs is the identification of similar norms and values across countries. Even more importantly, by matching the life-style groups to product usage and brand preference information, marketers discover that on occasion these similar norms and values get expressed in different forms of consumption behavior.

SOCIAL STRUCTURE

Imagine a situation where the marketing team responsible for the ice cream division of Nestlé, the Swiss food conglomerate, is meeting with the concessions division of EuroDisney Park (located just outside Paris). In addition to the EuroDisney staff, the amusement park's advertising agency, comprised of account managers from London, Los Angeles, and Paris are also present. Furthermore, two of the key managers from EuroDisney and one of the advertising account executives are female, and all three of them are American. While the formal negotiations would undoubtedly be conducted in the English language, English is the mother tongue to only a small portion of the managers present. Throughout the two days of meetings, there are numerous cross–conversations in French, English, and German. Sometimes using a multitude of languages aids the understanding of what is really meant by each party, and sometimes it cultivates suspicion between the parties. The Americans make powerful and dynamic presentations using color overheads. Later, in an attempt to join in a conversation between two of the Germans, one of the American women executives uses the informal form of "you" in addressing a man who is 20 years her senior. The German is taken aback by the informality in such a formal business setting. The rich diversity of the managers' cultural backgrounds, combined with the contrasting corporate cultures of three different industrial sectors result in a complex matrix of roles and objectives with a high probability for miscommunication regardless of the good intentions of all present.

The above example highlights that the nature and meaning of **social relationships** differs greatly among the world's cultures. As the degree of diversity among cultures increases, the need to drop your own assumptions about the structure of relationships is even greater. This is true for both household consumer market and business market situations. Generally, in more economically advanced countries, social relationships tend to be more ambiguous and dynamic, and in more traditional or less economically advanced countries, the social relationships are more clearly defined and stable. Even between cultures with fairly similar social norms, such as in the EuroDisney example, subtle differences can be critical to the success of negotiations and planning activities. This will ultimately influence the ways in which plans are perceived and executed and influence the manner in which consumers receive communications and product offerings that flow from the company's marketing mix. For example, portraying children as active participants in the decision-making process in the selection of breakfast cereals may be well-received in television ads in the United States, but would be viewed as highly incorrect and offensive to mothers in the U.K. and Europe where nuclear family ties and social roles within the family are more clearly defined. In terms of business marketing activities, the same general warning applies: drop the assumptions of what is the best way to do business, and *develop the ability to learn to understand* the nature and meaning of social relationships in the markets where you operate. Decisions for selecting a distributor in an Asian or Arab market can *legitimately* be made on the basis of kinship and trust and not on such criteria as shipping time, reliability, margins, or coverage in the market.

SOCIAL ORIENTATION

Kay Belk, a business woman with her own art studio and the wife of an American Fulbright Scholar who is spending a year in the coal mining and university town of Criova, Rumania, waits patiently in line for her chance to buy bread from the bakery. After waiting 90 minutes in line, an act that severely tests her American cultural values regarding the concepts of *time* and *convenience,* it is finally her turn. The bakery offers little assortment but is otherwise amply stocked with fresh bread. The one elderly woman behind the counter waits on customers one at a time and is absolutely unconcerned with the speed or efficiency of the service she offers. When Kay asks her Rumanian friends why the bakery doesn't improve service by employing more help during the morning hours when customers buy bread, they shrug their shoulders and are either unable or not interested in trying to provide an explanation.

In Holland, Germany, and most of northern Europe, customers take numbered slips of paper and wait their turn at the butcher or baker. Extra help is put behind the counters when demand is high, and each customer completes all transactions before the next customer has the opportunity to place his or her order. In southern Italy, the housewife at the front of the crowd in the butcher store asks for 200 grams of Parmesan ham, and the butcher casually shouts back to the crowd, "Does anyone else want Parmesan ham?"

In each of the three preceding examples, the concepts of *orderliness* and *efficiency* as well as the values related to *time* and *convenience* are culturally expressed through different forms of behavior. In Rumania and northern Europe, the cultures share a **monochronic orientation,** which is a linear process where each person receives full service and then the next person in the line is served. In Italy, the orientation is **polychronic**, with several people being served simultaneously. This approach appears chaotic to shoppers who do not share this cultural value, but to Italians, this approach has its own rhythm, orderliness, and sense of efficiency. In contrast to the linear, sequential time perception that is typical of American culture, many cultures view time as moving in a circle, wherein the past and present are together, with future possibilities. These different time perceptions have implications for decision-making processes—one manager may see negotiations leading to a final deal, while a manager with another cultural perspective on time may see the entire exercise as a continuum, wherein the deal may depend on the evolution of the relation. Figure 6-4 depicts the relationships in culture.

An additional dimension that is less obvious in the preceding examples deals with a culture's orientation towards initiative. In **individualistic societies,** typified by countries such as the United States, the United Kingdom, and Germany, effort and responsibility are assigned to the individual. In fact, showing initiative, and taking on responsibilities are behaviors that are viewed as positive. These behaviors are taught to us at home, in school (especially business schools), and in employment training programs. Further, these are behaviors that tend to be rewarded. In **collective societies,** such as Rumania, Sweden, China, and Japan, more responsibility is assigned to society and more collective efforts are required. Individuals operate more in group settings, accepting support from others and providing support. Social services and other forms of public support tend to be more comprehensive and are financed by relatively high corporate and individual tax structures. A culture's position along this continuum will influence a firm's marketing tactics. For example, in societies with a collective orientation, a marketing program promoting water conservation might be most successfully promoted on the basis of social benefits for all citizens, while in individualistic societies the most effective appeal may be to promote water conservation as a money-saving behavior that directly affects the individual. Figure 6-5 demonstrates this collective-individualistic continuum with a graph reporting on attitudes towards the environment. The percentage of people who agree or strongly agree with the statement "environmental protection begins with the individual citizen" is represented by the core group, while the extended group is the group that agrees or strongly agrees that "environmental protection should begin with the government." Note that the highly collective-oriented society of Sweden strongly favors government-supported initiatives for protecting the environment, while the highly individualistic societies of Germany and German-speaking Switzerland place the responsibility more on the individual.

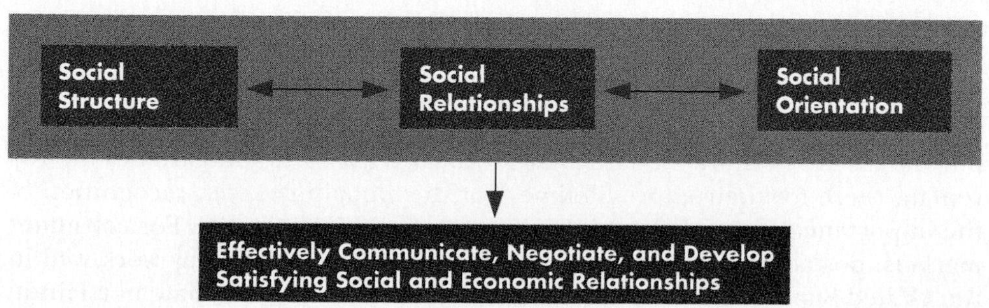

FIGURE 6-4
Culture and Social Relationships

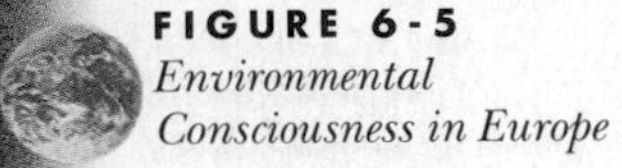
FIGURE 6-5
Environmental Consciousness in Europe

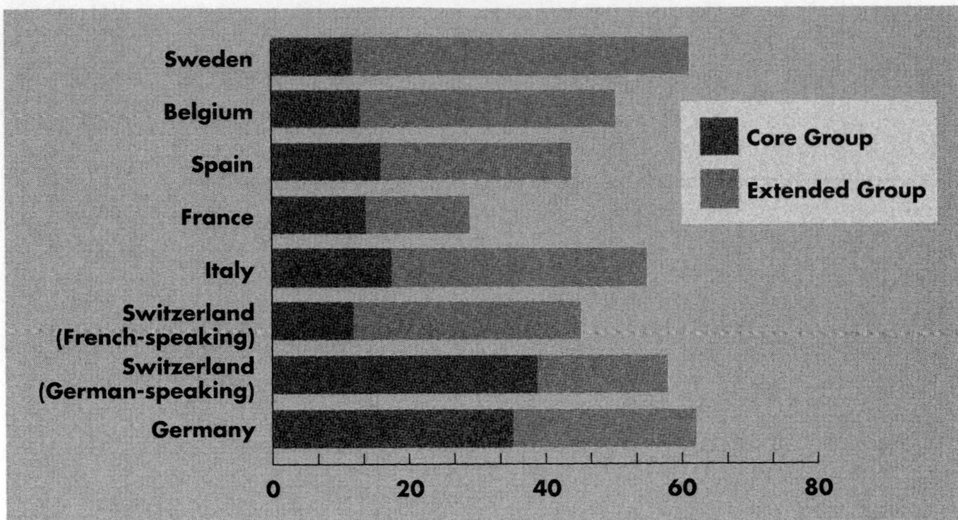

Note: Core group percentage indicates agreement with the statement "Environment protection begins with the individual citizen."
Extended group percentage indicates agreement with the statement "Environment protection should begin with the government."

SOCIAL CLASS

While social class was discussed earlier in this chapter, it is important to also put this social construct in a global perspective, since how one is viewed socially and the normative value of social class is so important around the world. Social orientation and structure are concepts that also relate to one's position within a society. In many societies, the assignment of one's position is *ascribed*—that is, status is attributed to you by birth, kinship, gender, age, and by your connections (who you know). In other societies, one's position is *achieved* and is based on recent accomplishments as well as on your achievements over time. In the U.S. market, the key components of operationalizing or measuring social class are educational level and occupational status. The cultural value of striving for upward mobility in social class is viewed as a legitimate personal goal, and the lines separating one social class category from another are not rigidly drawn. In many other markets, the component of *income* is the best surrogate measure of social class, with income and social class being highly correlative. While *all* societies follow some pattern of social ranking, it is the distribution of people among classes and their ability to move from one class to another (social mobility) that varies from one culture to another.

In many cultures, including societies in the economically advanced countries of western Europe, upward movement in social class is difficult, if not impossible. In India, and some Asian cultures (particularly in rural areas), individuals are born into a particular social class (or caste) and are destined to remain there for their entire lifetime. For the global marketer, recognition of the importance of social class and social class mobility is crucial. For consumer markets, positioning a product as a sign of upward mobility may work well in the United States, but would be entirely irrelevant or inappropriate in a Hindu or Buddhist market. For business marketers, recognizing the social position of ones' business partners and showing the proper respect for their station will be critical to the negotiation process and to establishing long-term relationships. For much of the world, *who* you are socially is as important, if not more important, than your recent achievements.

The beginning of this global section put forth the proposition that global marketers need to be students of culture in order to effectively operate in foreign markets. Hiring local nationals is one common approach to dealing with this need to understand, and the booming number of seminars to train managers to be culturally sensitive is further evidence of efforts being made to become more aware of the cultural challenge. In the final analysis, the purpose of all marketing activities is to create and manage mutually satisfying economic and social exchanges between parties. In the global context, it is the visitor and not the host who typically must adapt and understand.

Key Terms and Concepts

Consumer buying behavior
Information search
Involvement
Consumer decision-making process
Need recognition
Out-of-stock need
Functional need
Emotional need
Information search
Functional product features
Emotional satisfaction
Benefits of use
Evaluation of shopping alternatives
Postpurchase behavior
Cognitive dissonance
Needs
Learning
Stimuli
Reinforcement
Attitudes
Perception
Personality
Experiential-hedonic influences
Culture
Life-style
Subculture
Social class
Reference groups
Generation X
Family life cycle
Family decision process
Gender roles
Situational factors
Business buying behavior
Business decision-making process
Decision styles
Type of business decision
Cross Cultural Consumer Characterizations
Social relationships
Ethnocentric behavior
Monochronic orientation
Polychronic orientation
Individualistic society
Collective society

Questions and Exercises

1. Consider your own decision-making process as a consumer. Do you tend to evaluate products based on functional features, the emotional satisfaction a product may provide, or the benefits of use in owning a particular product?
2. Why is household consumer behavior consider actually basic human behavior in the context of consumption?
3. What role do information search and involvement play in the consumer decision-making process?
4. Describe a situation where one consumer buys toothpaste based on an out-of-stock need recognition and another consumer buys the same toothpaste with emotional need recognition.
5. Your friend Fred has just purchased a new car. He arrives at your apartment and begins showing you the features of the new auto. He pops the hood to display the fuel-injected V-6 engine, tells you to climb in and cranks up the stereo, and demonstrates the adjustable seats and power sun roof. Then Fred asks, Guess how much I paid? What do you think of the color? Didn't I get a great deal? What sort of behavior is Fred exhibiting? Why did he come over to show you his new car?

6. What criteria do you use in choosing where to shop for groceries on a regular basis? Is there one particular supermarket that you prefer? Describe why you find it a better place to shop than other stores you could shop at.
7. How does culture manifest itself in the way products are evaluated for purchase?
8. How are business buyers different from household consumers in terms of the decision-making process they use? Interview a business person about his/her decisions. How do they differ from your own?
9. Cultural setting affects marketing decision making. How do marketers act as agents of change with global marketing practices?
10. Global markets are characterized by different social orientations. Does the United States have a monochronic or polychronic orientation to market activities?

References

1. Rahul Jacob. "Beyond Quality and Value." *Fortune* (Autumn/Winter 1993): 8–11.
2. Examples taken from Rahul Jacob. *Fortune,* op. cit., 10–11.
3. Edward F. Cone. "Image and Reality." *Forbes* (December 14, 1987): 226.
4. Gilles Laurent and Jean-Noel Kapferer. "Measuring Consumer Involvement Profiles." *Journal of Marketing Research* (February 1985): 41–53.
5. Peter R. Dickson and Alan G. Sawyer. "The Price Knowledge and Search of Supermarket Shoppers." *Journal of Marketing* 54, no. 3 (July 1990): 42–53.
6. Larry Armstrong and Karen Lowry Miller. "While Toyota Loses Its Hold." *Business Week* (April 26, 1993): 28–29.
7. A. H. Maslow. *Motivation and Personality* 2d ed. (New York: Harper & Row Publishers, Inc., 1970).
8. Curtis Hamm and Edward W. Cundiff. "Self-Actualization and Product Perception," *Journal of Marketing Research* (November 1969): 470–472.
9. See for example, Gordon H. Bower and Ernest J. Hilgard. *Theories of Learning,* 5th ed. (Englewood Cliffs, NJ: Prentice-Hall, Inc., 1981): Section I, 21–298. For an example of the use of learning concepts in consumer behavior analysis, see Stephen J. Hoch and John Deighton. "Managing What Consumers Learn from Experience." *Journal of Marketing* 53, no. 2 (April 1989): 1–20.
10. Martin Fishbein and Icek Ajzen. *Belief, Attitude, Intention, and Behavior: An Introduction to Theory and Research* (Reading, MA: Addison-Wesley Publishing, 1975): 6.
11. See Karen Blumenthal. "Marketing with Emotion: Wal-Mart Shows the Way." *The Wall Street Journal* (November 13, 1989): B1, B4; and Edward F. Cone. "Image and Reality." *Forbes* (December 14, 1987): 226–228. Academics have written extensively on the roll of affective (feeling) responses in consumer behavior. For an interesting treatment see Robert Zojonc and Helen Markus. "Affective and Cognitive Factors in Preferences." *Journal of Consumer Research* 9, no. 2 (September 1982): 123–131.
12. For a good discussion of the issues see Harold Kassarjian and Mary Jane Sheffet. "Personality and Consumer Behavior: An Update." in *Perspectives in Consumer Behavior.* eds., Harold Kassarjian and Thomas Robertson (Glenview, IL: Scott Foresman, 1981): 160–180.
13. Marvin Jolson, Rolfe Anderson, and Neil Leber. "Profiles of Signature Goods Consumers and Avoiders." *Journal of Retailing* (Winter 1981): 19–25.
14. See for example, Elizabeth C. Hirschman and Morris B. Holbrook. "Hedonic Consumption: Emerging Concepts, Methods and Propositions." *Journal of Marketing* 46, no. 3 (Summer 1982): 92–101; and Morris B. Holbrook and Elizabeth C. Hirschman. "The Experiential Aspects of Consumption: Consumer Fantasies, Feelings, and Fun." *Journal of Consumer Research* 9, no. 2 (September 1982): 132–140.
15. Sandra D. Atchison. "Move over Jane Fonda, Here Comes Pudgeball Nation." *Business Week* (April 19, 1993): 29.
16. Alix M. Freedman. "The Microwave Cooks up a New Way of Life." *The Wall Street Journal* (September 19, 1989): B1.
17. Sandra D. Atchinson. *Business Week,* op. cit., 29.
18. See Michael Rogers. "A Sales Kick from Beer without the Buzz." *Fortune* (June 23, 1986): 89; and Christopher Power and Mark Landler. "And Now, Finger Lickin' Good for Ya?" *Business Week* (February 18, 1991): 60.
19. Good discussions of these changes in life orientation appear in Anne B. Fisher, "A Brewing Revolt Against the Rich." *Fortune* (December 17, 1990): 89–94; and Janice Castro. "The Simple Life," *Time,* (April 8, 1991): 58–63. With a more narrow focus, see Francine Schwadel. "Turning Conservative, Baby Boomers Reduce Their Frivolous Spending." *The Wall Street Journal* (June 19, 1991): A1, A8.
20. Survey results were cited in Faye Rice. "How to Deal with Tougher Customers." *Fortune* (December 3, 1990): 40.
21. Kathleen Deveny. "Putting It Mildly, More Consumers Prefer Products That Are 'Pure,' 'Natural.'" *The Wall Street Journal* (May 11, 1993): B1.
22. Statistics cited in Jon Berry. "An Empire of Niches." *Superbrands 1991,* Supplement to *Adweek,* 20.
23. Jon Berry. "Special Report: Hispanic Marketing." *Adweek* (July 9, 1990): 28.

24. Laura Bird. "Most Marketers Missing Out on Black Buyers. *The Wall Street Journal* (April 9, 1993): B1, B3.
25. Neil Howe and William Strauss. "The New Generation Gap." *The Atlantic Monthly* (December 1992): 68.
26. James Aley. "Slacker Myths." *Fortune* (February 21, 1994): 24.
27. Nancy Kate. "Who Buys the Pants in the Family." *American Demographics* (January 1992): 12.
28. Russell Belk. "Situational Variables and Consumer Behavior." *Journal of Consumer Research* 2, no. 3 (March 1976): 158.
29. See Marvin E. Goldberg and Gerald Gorn. "Happy and Sad TV Programs: How They Affect Reactions to Commercials." *Journal of Consumer Research* 14, no. 3 (December 1987): 387–404; and Mark A. Pavelchak, John H. Antel, James M. Much. "The Super Bowl: An Investigation into the Relationship among Program Context, Emotional Experience, and Ad Recall." *Journal of Consumer Research* 15, no. 3 (December 1988): 360–368; and Kenneth R. Lord and Robert E. Burnkrant. "Attention versus Distraction: The Interactive Effect of Program Involvement and Attentional Devices on Commercial Processing." *Journal of Advertising* (March 1993): 47–60.
30. Patricia Sellers. "Keeping the Buyers You Already Have." *Fortune* (Autumn/Winter 1993): 56.
31. Clifford Geertz. *The Interpretation of Cultures* (New York: Basic Books, 1973). For a discussion of the influence of culture and ethnicity on marketing and consumption, see: Janeen Costa and Gary Bamossy, eds. *Marketing in a Multicultural World: Ethnicity, Nationalism, and Cultural Identity* (Newberry Park, CA: Sage Publications, 1994).
32. Theodore Levitt. "The Globalization of Markets." *Harvard Business Review* (May–June 1983): 92–101.

SECTION THREE

Operationalizing the Marketing Process: The Marketing Mix

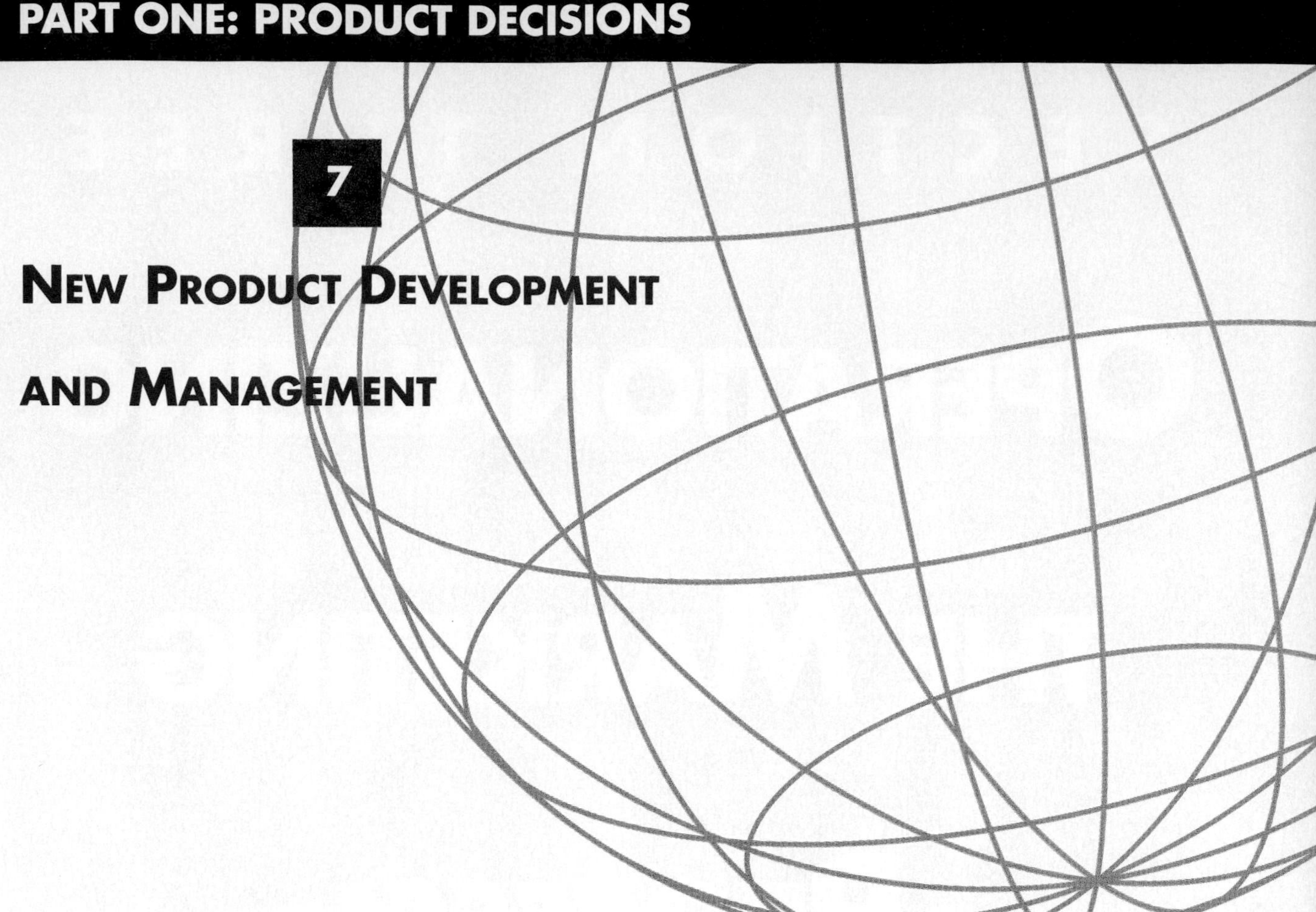

7

NEW PRODUCT DEVELOPMENT AND MANAGEMENT

AFTER STUDYING THIS CHAPTER, YOU WILL UNDERSTAND THAT:

1. The product variable in the marketing mix needs to be broadly defined in order to develop effective product strategies.
2. Developing new products is critically important to the long-term success of a firm.
3. New product development is undertaken either through external acquisitions or internal new product development processes.
4. The diffusion of innovations and product life cycle concepts are valuable tools for managing new products.
5. A global perspective on new product development and management requires a recognition of the cultural influences that often dictate new product features and the market's perception of newness as an influence on new product acceptance.

Talk about a turnaround! In 1982, Rayovac Corporation was in trouble. The Madison, Wisconsin, battery and flashlight maker had seen total revenues decline to $175 million, losses climb to $20 million, and market share dwindle from 35 percent in the 1950s to about 6 percent in 1982. What had happened to Rayovac? The firm failed to read the market properly and develop new products. It failed to introduce an alkaline battery, which had become the industry standard. The firm invested $12 million in an ill-conceived production facility that ended up never producing a single battery. But new owners have revived the failing firm. A combination of new product introductions, new packaging, new technology, and tightly focused market segmentation strategies have turned the firm around.

But Rayovac has not just been turned around—this firm is prospering! By 1993, sales had reached $500 million and the firm had captured nearly 11 percent of the $3 billion U.S. retail battery market. The essential strategies that helped turn this firm around were new product introductions. First, Rayovac introduced a new designer-styled flashlight with a lithium-powered backup system that will work for ten years. Then, the company started selling batteries in packages of six and eight instead of the traditional one, two, or four packs favored by their competition Duracell and Eveready. In 1993, Rayovac made its boldest move. The firm was granted one of two licensing agreements to produce a rechargeable alkaline battery. Up to this point, the only batteries that could be recharged were cadmium batteries. The new Rayovac *Renewal Rechargeable Battery* was introduced with a $20 million television advertising campaign during the 1993 holiday season and into the first quarter of 1994.[1]

In this Rayovac example, the new product and packaging strategies credited with salvaging the firm are new product development and management decisions. Of the four marketing mix variables, the product is generally considered to be the most critical element in the marketing decision-making process. It is from product decisions that the related pricing, distribution, and promotion strategies and tactics flow. Because the ultimate success of a product depends on satisfying consumer needs, the management challenge is to design and market products that satisfy those needs. This chapter and the next will explore the strategy issues associated with managing the firm's product offerings and the process of developing new products. Further, decisions related to branding, packaging, and image building for products are discussed in detail.

It is important to note that this chapter signals a significant shift in orientation in our study of marketing. The first six chapters covered the *macro* aspects of marketing that cut across all areas of strategic decision making and planning: the role and purpose of marketing, analyzing the environment, generating and using information, analyzing markets, and consumer behavior. These topics provide a foundation for all areas of strategic planning. This chapter marks our entry into the *micro* aspects of marketing. That is, the specific strategic planning areas of the marketing mix: product, pricing, promotion, and distribution. The first step in this microanalysis is to understand the process of new product development and management.

DEFINITION OF THE PRODUCT

Every product can be described by the firm that produces it, right? A product is merely a compilation of raw materials, component parts, production procedures, and costs, right? Not quite. That kind of description is useful for technical manuals but not for strategic marketing planning. For strategic planning, the *definition of the product* must take a broader, more market-oriented perspective. Before decision making and strategy planning in the product area can begin, a firm must recognize and appreciate all the *potential* meanings a product can have, especially from the perspective of the consumer.

To consumers, a product can be much more than a tangible object that performs specific functions and requires raw materials and production activities to manufacture. To be sure, a product is designed to serve users and provide conspicuous and identifiable results. But, the success of most products is related not to tangible features, per se, but rather to the *perception of value* held by consumers. As we have found in other chapters, consumers look to products to serve their needs in such a way that they perceive greater satisfaction than the cost they incur to acquire a product. They must see a product as a deal. They must see a product providing value.

Enlightened marketers have come to the realization that household consumers and business buyers alike seek more than functional features in a product. They often look well beyond simple function to benefits of use or emotional satisfactions that products can provide. The classic article in the area emphasizes that marketers must recognize that the products people consume include a wide range of expectations and perceived benefits that go well beyond functional features.[2] The firm that believes it is producing and marketing simply a tangible product is short-sighted and will find itself quickly at a competitive disadvantage.

For example, when a consumer buys a car, the consumer's choice criteria could include a long list of functional and performance features such as engine size, tires, seats, gas milage estimates, trunk size, price, and warranty. However, a buyer may also be seeking values in the car that are not directly related to functional features such as style, comfort, and prestige. For a product to be developed and marketed in a way that truly reflects an appreciation for consumers' expectations and desires, all the potential values being sought by consumers—tangible and intangible, functional and emotional, real and perceived—must be considered by the marketing strategist in the design and marketing of the product.

When customer expectations and desires form the basis for the definition of a product, then the marketing concept is the guiding framework in product development and management. With this perspective in mind, the definition of the product that is most useful for strategy planning is:

A product is a set of tangible and intangible attributes that provide real or perceived benefits in order to satisfy consumer needs and desires.

One aspect of clarification is needed at this point. The term *product* as it is used here and in most treatments of marketing includes the full range of possible market offerings including service products (e.g., banking or repair services), ideas (e.g., recycling programs), or people marketing (e.g., political candidates or celebrities). Our definition of the product provides for all these different types of market offerings even though you might not naturally refer to people or ideas as products. So, whenever the term *product* is used, it will refer to this very broad set of meanings, which includes all forms of market offerings: products, services, ideas, and people.

NEW PRODUCT DEVELOPMENT

The product area is the driving force for marketing mix decision making and the driving force of the product area itself is **new product development.** A primary management task is to continually search for ways to increase the revenue generating capability of the firm. One way is to sell more of the same products and services to existing customers—this is a market share battle. The other way is to develop new products that take advantage of opportunities in the market and appeal to specific segments in the market. For a firm to generate ever-growing revenues, it must be organized for new product development and must generate a flow of new product ideas.

Recognizing the importance of new product development is the first step a firm needs to take to successfully initiate a new product development process. Furthermore, the types of new products to consider, procedures for new product development, and the concepts of diffusion of innovations and product life cycle are critical areas of strategic decision making in new product development.

THE IMPORTANCE OF NEW PRODUCT DEVELOPMENT

Through marketing and geographic information systems, firms are much better at identifying consumer desires and recognizing competitive opportunities. Firms must be prepared to respond quickly to these changing consumer needs and competitive maneuvers. Technology has accelerated the pace of change and dramatically cut the effective lifetime of products. Because of the rapid pace of change, firms must accept as reality that new product development is essential to the future growth of a firm.

The importance of new product development and management to the ongoing success of a firm cannot be overstated. A variety of estimates suggest that 30 percent of corporate revenues in the next five years across all industries will come from products that don't even exist today.[3] 3M Corporation, recognized as a world leader in product innovation, generates more than 25 percent of its total $13.8 billion in revenues from products that are new to the firm during the last five years.[4] Or consider the fact that Amgen (a biotechnology firm) expects that two new products, one designed to treat anemia and the other to reduce the side effects of chemotherapy, will *each* generate $1 billion annually in revenue for the firm within three years after their approval by the Food and Drug Administration.[5]

Increased revenue generation is one signal of the importance of new products. Another is the extreme cost and, therefore, risk of new product development. How would you like to pay $6 billion for your next new car? Well, that's what Ford is spending on the development of its new "world car," called the *Mondeo* (although it is rumored to be marketed under the name *Contour*). This new mid-size, front-wheel-drive car is designed to be made and marketed around the world—one car for all markets to achieve economies of scale. GM spent $7 billion during the 1980s developing its mid-size line of passenger cars, and the new *Saturn* automobile introduced by General Motors in 1990 was estimated to cost nearly $5 billion to develop.[6] Introducing a new consumer snack food costs about $150 million and a new photo copier costs about $300 million.

But aside from sheer dollar cost as an indication of risk, the success rate of new products is not high. Consider the following uninspiring results of a recent assessment of new product success and failure. Only 8 percent of new product projects initiated in major corporations survived to full market entry. Of those that did survive to market entry, only 17 percent met the major objectives for revenue, profit, or market share for an overall failure rate of 83 percent or a 99 percent failure rate for new product projects initiated![7] The stakes are indeed high in new product development. As these examples indicate, spending to develop and introduce a new product can be formidable, but the payoff in future revenues can be enormous. Given the level of risk and potential reward, several aspects related to new product development must be considered in detail. These are types of new products, the new product development process, strategic factors in new product development, and why new

Ford Motor Company's new "world car" called the Mondeo is estimated to have cost $6 billion to develop.

products fail. Figure 7-1 shows the historic rate of success for new product ideas.

TYPES OF NEW PRODUCTS

A firm does not need to discover and introduce a world phenomenon to legitimately call a product new. Many new products are simply improvements of existing products or, more significantly, superficially changed existing products. Below is a categorization of the types of new products a firm may be dealing with in the new product development process.

- **True Innovation.** This type of product is new to the market. Historically, the telephone, radio, and television were true innovations. More recently, the VCR and CD player are revolutionary innovations made available to the mass market.
- **Adaptive Replacement.** This type of new product represents a significant adaptation and improvement of an existing product in the market. The color TV was an adaptive replacement for the black and white TV. Instant coffee was a significant adaptation of ground coffee.
- **Me, Too, Product.** This product is new to the firm that is marketing the item but not new to the market. When firms extend their product lines and enter new product areas they many times do so by simply introducing their own brand of an item that is already being sold by several other competitors—for example, P & G's introduction of *Ivory Shampoo and Conditioner* (known as "extension" brands) into the shampoo market, which already had a full complement of competitive brands.

Different types of new products have different development costs and require different marketing mix strategies. A true innovation may require

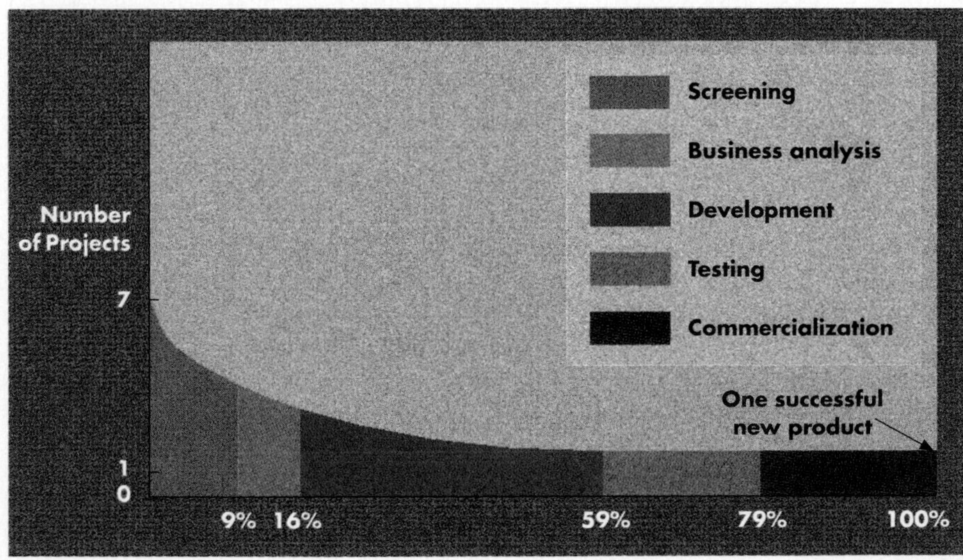

FIGURE 7-1
Decay Curve of New Product Ideas

years of development time and enormous cost to bring the product to commercialization. Conversely, a me, too (or extension), brand may be brought to market in a few months at relatively low cost to the firm. Further, true innovations may have formidable market barriers to overcome. The most significant challenge for marketers in successfully commercializing true innovations is to identify the extent to which primary demand needs to be stimulated. **Primary demand** is the process of stimulating demand for the *entire product category* not just a brand within the product category. True innovations tend to address needs in the market that were going unfilled until the time the product was introduced. For example, though it's hard to imagine this now, before the 1970s the ability to tape a program from the television for later viewing was a benefit unknown to the consumer market. In this instance, the task of primary demand stimulation was to *educate* consumers to the benefits of taping with a VCR. RCA and Sony, who first introduced the VCR (in VHS and Beta formats, respectively), to the mass market in the 1970s, had to stimulate primary demand for the innovation, which was a slow and costly process. Primary demand stimulation is not an issue with adaptive replacements and me, too, products. Consumers already understand the use and benefits of the product category and merely have another brand of the product type from which to choose.

Stimulating primary demand is the most critical difference in marketing mix decision making between the new product categories, but all the elements in the marketing mix are managed differently depending upon the type of new product being developed and ultimately marketed. Specific marketing mix adaptations will be discussed in greater detail later in the chapter when product life cycle management is considered.

THE NEW PRODUCT DEVELOPMENT PROCESS

The new product development process can be initiated either through the acquisition of products already on the market (being marketed by some other firm) or by internally developing new products through in-house research and development. Each of these approaches to new product development has advantages. Each approach also requires a commitment of different resources by the firm.

New Product Development through Acquisition

Many firms have successfully added new products to their overall set of market offerings by acquiring existing products produced by other firms. Some of the more notable recent acquisitions are listed in Table 7-1. Notice the large amount of money firms like AT&T, Merck, and General Motors are willing to spend to acquire products that enhance their current line of product offerings. New product development through **acquisition** is designed to provide firms with either improved market position or to establish a market presence for the firm in a totally new product category. It must be noted, however, that the motive for acquiring existing products can go well beyond the product itself. Some firms hope to achieve greater distribution efficiencies or perhaps an enhanced image in the market by acquiring existing brands. Merck's acqui-

Company	Acquisition	Reason for Acquisition	Cost
General Motors	50 percent stake in Saab	Increased presence in European market	$600 million
Monsanto	G.D. Searle Company	Rights to Nutra-Sweet sweetener	2.8 billion
Procter & Gamble	Noxell Corporation	Cover Girl Cosmetics line	1.3 billion
AT&T	McCaw Cellular	New cellular phone technology	12.6 billion
Merck	Medco Containment	Mail order prescriptions	6.0 billion
Tyson Foods	Arctic Alaska Fisheries	Diversify into fish products	202 million
Maytag Corp.	Magic Chef appliances	Diversify to low-cost products	736 million
Philip Morris	Freia Marabou	Global diversification (candy)	1.48 billion

TABLE 7-1
Recent Acquisitions of New Products

sition of Medco Containment Services, a mail-order prescription drug distributor, provided Merck not with new products but with an alternative distribution method for cultivating the market.

Advantages of Acquisition

New product development through acquisition has several advantages over internally developing new products:

- The failure rate of acquisitions is somewhat lower than for internally developed new products.
- A firm may not have to invest in costly capital equipment (like research laboratory facilities) or keep specialized personnel necessary for internal development efforts.
- A firm making the acquisition often buys the necessary marketing and managerial skills within the acquired firm. This is particularly important if the acquired product (or product line) represents a new competitive market for the firm.
- The acquired product or product line comes with established production procedures and sources of supply and distribution.
- A firm acquires an established market position and brand name recognition thus avoiding the lengthy and costly process of developing these market strengths.
- A firm usually realizes immediate cash flow and revenue from ongoing sales of the product.

Disadvantages of Acquisition

This list of the advantages of acquisition is not meant to suggest that the acquisition route to new product development is not without its difficulties. The acquisition approach has problems and risks as well:

- A firm making an acquisition is required to make substantial financial remuneration for the product, as the examples cited in Table 7-1 indicate. This may mean substantial debt, which can compromise the overall performance of the firm.

- Acquired products have an existing competitive position that has both strengths *and* weaknesses. A firm must be prepared to deal with the competitive liabilities it inherits.
- In many cases, a product or entire company that is ripe for acquisition is in such a position because of financial or market difficulties. This means the firm may have to initiate massive strategic alterations quickly.
- Finally, the trauma associated with assimilating new facilities, personnel, and operations is unavoidable.

The risks associated with acquisition are exemplified by the experiences of Maytag Corporation. In 1986, Maytag acquired Magic Chef, Inc., to enter the middle- to bottom-line appliance market. In 1989, it acquired the Hoover Division of Chicago Pacific Corp. in order to enter the vacuum cleaner market. With these acquisitions, Maytag's long-term debt soared from $24 million to $845 million, which by 1991 was threatening the firm's dividend that had been paid quarterly to stockholders since 1946. Perhaps worse was the risk that the lower-end products would do damage to the hard-earned reputation of Maytag's flagship brands. The newly acquired brands often appeared at the bottom of *Consumer Report's* appliance ratings and did, indeed, have performance and reliability problems after the acquisition.[8] The experience of Maytag highlights some of the potential problems and risks associated with assimilating acquired products. Newly acquired products need to match or be adaptable to a firm's current operations and market image. As new products depart from existing product lines and operations, difficulty in assimilation and distribution can occur.

Procedures for Acquisition[9]

A well-planned and systematic approach to the acquisition process is necessary for acquisitions to have a high potential for success. The following elements are essential for a well-planned acquisition:

1. Objectives for the acquisition should be stated with great specificity to ensure consistency with overall corporate and marketing objectives.
2. Management should be aware that financial considerations are not the only basis for acquisition nor should products alone be the focus of the acquisition. When Dow Chemical acquired Marion Laboratories and combined the new firm with its Merrill drug division, the combined companies gave the newly formulated Marion-Merrill Dow Company a much greater international distribution network.
3. The firm should evaluate acquisition candidates on a variety of criteria including not only potential profitability but also market position and strength, future market potential, compatibility with existing products and marketing activities (as in the case of Maytag), and compatibility with existing managerial skills.

Internal New Product Development

The other major option for developing new products is to internally maintain an organizational structure and facilities for new product development. Firms that choose to develop new products in-house, like General Electric and Johnson & Johnson, need to maintain and manage procedures, personnel, and facilities for this purpose.

The risks and expense of **internal new product development** can be greater than those associated with acquisition. Table 7-2 shows top firms in research and development (R&D) spending. Across all industries in the United States in 1992, R&D spending was $79.4 billion and represented about 3.7 percent of sales. Because of this large money outlay and the human resource commitment that is required for internal new product development, most firms will have highly structured procedures associated with the process.

Procedures for Internal New Product Development

The goals of the firm and the external environmental forces shaping the consumption environment (as discussed in Chapter 2) will be driving forces that motivate new product development. One way to ensure that new product development proceeds carefully and intelligently is to impose a well-conceived structure on the process. The following six-step procedure (illustrated in Figure 7-2) represents a systematic approach to new product development.

Step 1. Market Analysis and Identification of Market Opportunities

In keeping with the marketing concept approach to planning, new product development begins with market analysis and an identification of opportunities in the market. Firms use several methods to uncover significant market opportunities.

The most direct source is the firm's own Marketing Information System, the MkIS, as discussed in Chapter 3. Recall that through the MkIS (and the newer Geographic Information Systems), firms rely on input from internal and external sources of information. Company sales records, suppliers, wholesalers/retailers, and information directly from consumers alert firms to oppor-

TABLE 7-2
Top Ten U.S. Companies in R&D Spending in 1992

Company	R&D Expenses (in millions)
General Motors	$5,917
IBM	5,083
Ford Motor Company	4,332
AT&T	2,911
Boeing	1,846
Digital Equipment	1,754
Hewlett-Packard	1,620
Eastman Kodak	1,587
General Electric	1,353
Motorola	1,306

Source: Data cited in Peter Coy, et. al., "In the Labs, the Fight to Spend Less, Get More," *Business Week* (June 28, 1993): 103.

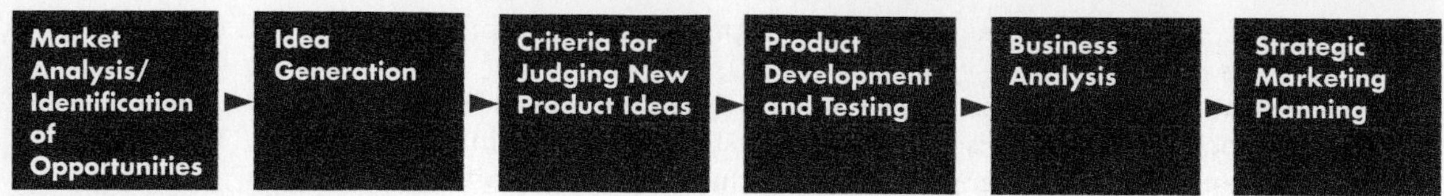

FIGURE 7-2
Procedures for Internal New Product Development

tunities for new product development. An assessment of competitive products in the market often signals an opportunity as well. Finally, the scientists and engineers working in R&D facilities can make discoveries that address important needs in the market.

What firms hope to discover at this stage is that consumers (or businesses) are not fully satisfied with either the existing products on the market or the way in which certain tasks are performed. For example, the high cost of the *Mercedes* line of luxury cars and the lack of performance of American luxury cars left a huge gap in this market. Toyota introduced the *Lexus LS400* and Nissan introduced the *Infiniti Q45* to fill the gap. These were luxury sedans that satisfied the market's desire for comfort and high performance at a lower cost.

Step 2. Idea Generation

Once a market opportunity is identified, a firm then tries to generate ideas for new products that are consistent with the opportunity identified. In some cases, product ideas may be very similar to existing brands on the market and a me, too, or extension brand product will take advantage of the opportunity. Or, radical new products may be the only way consumer desires can be fulfilled.

Firms use various techniques to generate new product ideas. The following are some of the most commonly relied on methods and sources:

- The R&D group within the firm.
- Consumers themselves may be the source of new ideas by proposing solutions in focus groups or perhaps through direct and unsolicited contact with the firm.
- Salespeople who have direct contact with customers.
- Retailers and wholesalers are good sources of ideas as are suppliers to the firm who bring a totally different perspective to new product ideas.
- Many firms turn to brainstorming among their management, marketing, and even production personnel.

The first two methods to generate new product ideas are referred to as *technology push* and *demand pull* factors, respectively. **Technology push** describes discoveries in laboratories and research and development facilities that have created valuable new products. Technology push is most prominent in technical areas such as information technology, communications, medical devices, and pharmaceuticals. A **demand pull** approach to product development follows the marketing concept and results in consumer demand "pulling" a new product through the development process and ultimately on to the market.

Step 3. Criteria for Judging New Product Ideas

Once reasonable new product ideas are identified, general criteria can be used to judge each idea for feasibility and potential. The following criteria are used to evaluate the potential for success of a new product and whether a new product proposal is consistent with existing corporate operations:

1. *Market Segment.* Does the new product have a well-defined, obtainable, and sufficiently large market segment? Competitive activities should be carefully considered here. This is the point at which revenue and profit projections are made for the product. Also, the possibility of securing protective patents is investigated at this point.
2. *Production Facilities.* Can the firm use existing production facilities to produce the product? The financial burden of new capital investment may reduce the feasibility of some new product ideas.
3. *Suppliers.* Can existing sources of supply be used to manufacture the product? Locating and establishing relationships with new suppliers is a costly procedure.
4. *Distribution.* Can existing distribution channels be used for the new product? Venturing into new relationships with distributors and retailers is expensive and sometimes difficult to accomplish. In the packaged goods product categories, retail grocery chains are now charging "slotting fees" to provide shelf space for new products. Such fees can cost manufacturers millions of dollars.
5. *Sales Staff.* Is the firm's sales staff qualified and large enough to handle a new product? Retraining or adding staff is an expense that must be considered.
6. *Management.* Are current management skills suited to marketing the new product? Products that reach beyond the expertise and experience of current management have a higher probability of failure.
7. *Image.* Does the new product fit the image of other products marketed by the firm? Products that differ substantially from the current company image may need to be marketed under a different brand name to ensure a consistent public image.
8. *Market Position.* Will the product have a distinctive market position relative to both competitors' brands and the firm's other brands? Careful internal and external positioning is essential for a new brand to be viewed as a distinctive choice by consumers. Additionally, if the new brand is not perceived as different from other brands the firm already markets, the danger of "cannibalism" of sales from the company's other brands is a real threat.
9. *Legal.* What are the legal ramifications, if any, of the new product?

There are numerous examples of new product introductions that have violated these criteria and created problems for firms. The Maytag example used earlier in the chapter was a direct violation of criterion 7, which deals with image and consistency with other brands in the line. Analysts suggest that the Cadillac *Allante* violated the criteria dealing with the sales force, 5, management expertise, 6, and company image, 7. With regard to criterion 8, a lack of precise positioning can have dramatic effects on the firm. Consider Figure 7-3,

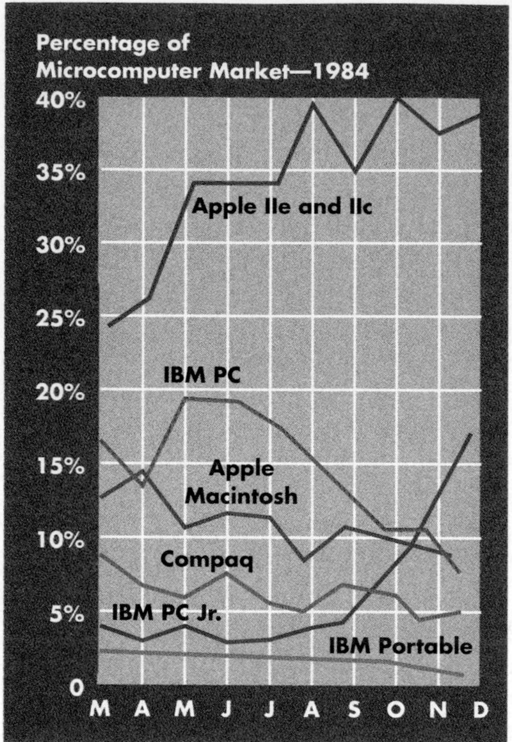

FIGURE 7-3
Graph of Microcomputer Sales. The IBM PCjr apparently cannabalized sales from the main IBM PC line.

which demonstrates what happened to IBM's PC sales when IBM introduced (and then corrected early design problems with) the PCjr. It was clear that the PCjr failed to represent significant competition for the Apple IIe against which it was externally positioned, but rather merely cannibalized sales of the primary IBM PC line. Kodak learned a $400 million lesson when it introduced an instant print film and camera that was ultimately deemed to have infringed on one of Polaroid's patents thus violating criterion 9.

An important point to remember regarding these criteria, however, is that a firm may answer "no" to criteria 2 through 7 and *still* proceed with product development. The reason is that criterion 1, the potential for revenue and profit, may hold such outstanding potential that the firm is willing to accept the challenges and liabilities of the other factors to pursue the opportunity.

In this regard, an interesting example of a firm that appears to have stuck closely to these criteria for most of its new product introductions and then ventured quite far from the criteria for other new products is Bic Corporation—these ventures are outlined in Table 7-3. Notice that Bic's first several product introductions followed the criteria quite closely. Then, two successive product introductions apparently did not fit any of the criteria. We can speculate that decision makers at Bic perceived great revenue (and perhaps risk diversification) with the sail-board and auto-rack products. Notice, however, that Bic's most recent new product, a disposable perfume, reverts back to following the criteria closely.

New Product Criteria	Products					
	Ballpoint Pen	Disposable Lighter	Disposable Razor	Sail-Board	Auto Rack	Disposable Perfume
Current production	yes	yes	yes	no	no	yes
Current suppliers	most	most	most	none	none	most
Current distribution	yes	yes	yes	no	no	yes
Salesforce expertise	yes	yes	yes	no	no	yes
Management expertise	yes	yes	yes	no	no	yes
Corporate image	yes	yes	yes	no	no	yes
Positioning	yes	yes	yes	likely	likely	yes

TABLE 7-3
Evaluation of Bic's New Product Introductions

Step 4. Product Development and Testing

If the firm decides that a new product idea meets enough criteria to represent an attractive opportunity, then it will invest in development. Here, the research and development department (or an outside contractor) begin with technical specifications and produce a prototype. Consumers may be recruited at this stage to test the product in a laboratory setting. Based on consumer reactions, the product may be redesigned. On occasion, distributors and retailers may be used as sources of feedback on product design. Some new products are put through full test markets, but the expense and complications of test markets have reduced the use of this method.

Step 5. Business Analysis

Of equal importance to new product development and testing is the development of the business analysis. While technicians are busily producing prototypes, marketing strategists are developing sales forecasts and revenue and cost projections. Projections must also include an estimate of the number of units to be sold over specified periods of time. Cost projections depend on development costs, raw materials costs, production costs, and marketing expenses associated with bringing the product to market.

The product development and testing stage and the business analysis stage often result in the abandonment of a new product idea. If consumer reaction to the product is poor or sales and profit projections are not favorable, the whole project can be scrapped.

Step 6. Strategic Marketing Planning

If the new product passes both the testing and business analysis stages, it is then poised for market introduction. The project is turned over to the marketing group at this point for strategic marketing planning. Market segmentation analysis is completed and target market identification is refined. Next, the marketing mix strategies and tactics are specified, including product differentiation and positioning, pricing, distribution channels, and promotional techniques. The product is now ready for commercial production and market entry.

Strategy Factors in Internal New Product Development

Two key strategic factors have recently come to light as crucial to the success of developing and introducing new products through internal methods. They are *semantic product design* and *speed of introduction*. These two factors are important enough that we will give them special treatment here.

Semantic Product Design

Beyond the engineering design of a product, which specifies its functional performance features, firms are recognizing that other design features can be critical to the market acceptance and success of a new product. These other design features relate to the semantics of a product. **Semantic product design** refers to the idea that the physical design of both household consumer and business products should communicate visually the purpose and benefits of the product. Firms are discovering that products must be designed to not only function according to consumer desires but must also look and feel as though they are designed to function properly. When Black & Decker redesigned its *Dustbuster* hand-held vacuum, consumers used the word "friendly" to describe the product and said the vacuum looked "powerful."[10] To achieve that look and feel, the designer reworked the design 30 times until the visual and physical balance was just right. When the new vacuum is held, it tilts slightly forward like it "wants" to pick up dirt. This input to product design is more than just metaphor and style, however. Xerox Corporation has been using semantics in the design of its copiers and claims this factor in product development results in less training for users and fewer service calls to remedy simple problems.[11]

The semantic design factor is believed to be so important as a strategic tool that one analyst claims, "Fifteen years ago companies competed on price. Today it's quality. Tomorrow it will be design."[12] More support for the importance of design comes from a recent poll conducted by the Gallup organization in which senior executives in U.S. firms rated industrial design to be 60 percent responsible for a product's success. These executives cited cost containment and consumer satisfaction as the primary rewards of effective design.[13]

Speed of Development

Speed of development as a strategic tool spans all phases of product management. A recent survey of 50 major U.S. firms found that nearly all the companies put time-based strategy at the top of their priority list. The reason is that speed kills the competition. There are very specific benefits to speedy development of new products. In an economic model developed by McKinsey & Co., a management consulting firm, high-tech products that come to market six months late but on budget will earn 33 percent less profit over five years. Conversely, getting the product out on time and 50 percent over budget cuts profits by only 4 percent.[14]

Table 7-4 shows that several prominent and highly competitive firms have taken to heart the concept of speed in new product development. Note that in

TABLE 7-4
Increased Speed in New Product Development

Company	Product Category	Old	New
		Development Time	
Honda	Cars	5 years	3 years
AT&T	Phones	2 years	1 year
Navistar	Trucks	5 years	2.5 years
Hewlett-Packard	Computer printers	4.5 years	22 months

Source: Brian Dumaine, "How Managers Can Succeed through Speed," *Fortune* (February 13, 1989): 54.

most cases these firms have cut the development time for new products in half. Such speed of development and product introduction catches competitors off guard. Also, think about the effort required on the part of competitors to respond. Developing an entirely new product is a formidable competitive task as compared to simply changing the price or running a new advertising campaign as a competitive counter move. One company that has suffered from bureaucratic entanglements, which caused it to reach the market more than a year behind its rivals with a new microprocessing chip, is Motorola. In 1985, 79 percent of the microprocessors on the market used a Motorola chip. By 1991, that market share had dwindled to 10 percent due to delays in introducing new versions of the microprocessor.[15] Now, those delays have been corrected.

To incorporate speed into the new product development process requires not so much a new procedure but rather valuing speed *within* the procedure. In order to make speed a priority in the new product development process, analysts suggest the following:

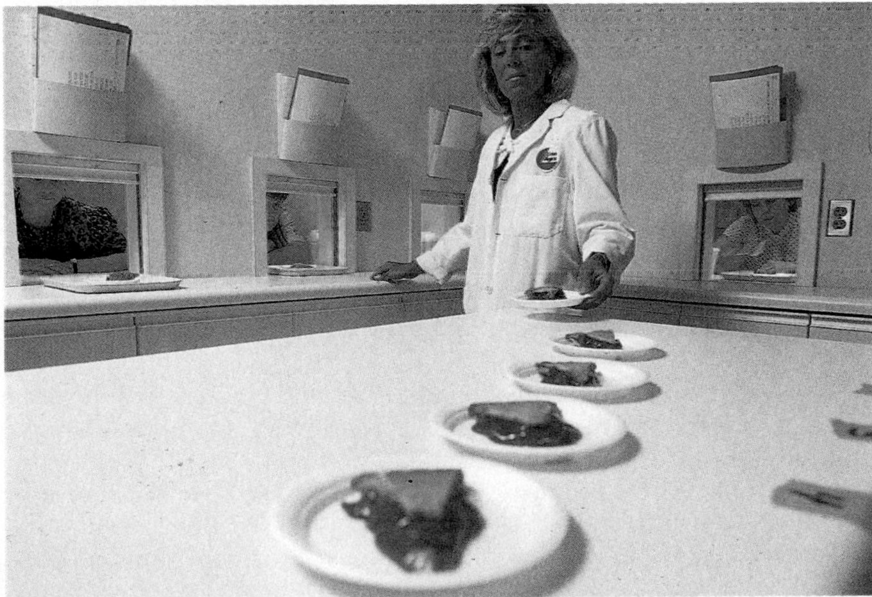

Firms use testing laboratories to develop and perfect new products.

- Reduce the number of times a product needs internal approval before final development.
- Develop new product teams that represent various parts of the organization and include engineers, designers, manufacturing experts, and marketers so that work and approvals can be simultaneous.
- Establish the schedule as the driving force in the development process. Speed and discipline in meeting deadlines must be the highest priority.
- Make speed pervasive in the corporate culture.

Speed in product development results in a variety of benefits for a firm. Being first in the market allows greater price flexibility until competitors catch up. Greater price flexibility normally means higher margins and profits as well. Early entry in the market increases the probability of acquiring large market share. This market share issue relates to the fact that it is much less costly to retain a customer as opposed to cultivating a new customer. Finally, speed can reduce the overall cost of product development in that resources are focused for shorter periods of time.

WHY NEW PRODUCTS FAIL

Earlier in the chapter, it was pointed out that only 17 percent of new products introduced to the market met the target objectives. Generally, new products fail because a firm has improperly assessed market potential or designed the product in a way that is either not appealing or does not serve the needs of a target segment. More specifically, new products fail for one or more of the following reasons:

1. *Lack of Primary Demand.* In many cases, truly innovative products enter a market environment where a conscious need (i.e., primary demand) among consumers does not exist. In the absence of primary demand, most new products will fail unless the firm has the financial resources to educate the market on the values of the product category.
2. *Diffusion Barriers.* Many innovative products violate one or more of the factors that facilitate diffusion and acceptance of products in the market (discussed in the next section).
3. *Lack of Differentiation.* The new product is not perceived to provide satisfactions in ways that are superior to or different enough from existing market alternatives.
4. *Improper Pricing.* The price is either too low or too high relative to consumer perceptions of value and existing alternatives. This factor also relates to the ability of a firm to realize profit and return on investment objectives.
5. *Poor Strategic Planning.* Failures stemming from this factor include poor product positioning, incorrect market segmentation, and inadequate understanding of consumer needs and desires.
6. *Competitive Reaction.* In some cases, competitors can react so vigorously that the product does not survive the competitive reaction.
7. *Product Performance Failures.* Due to technical or design problems, the product does not function properly.

8. *Poor Timing.* The product was introduced to the market too late to establish a sufficient competitive position.

Despite the fact that firms take the new product development process seriously and devote considerable resources to the process, there have been some classic product failures. Some recent successes and classic product failures are listed in Table 7-5.

PRODUCT MANAGEMENT

To this point, we have focused on new product development. Now, we will shift our attention to the process of product management. The remainder of this chapter and the next chapter will examine aspects of managing the product variable of the marketing mix. We will begin this discussion of product management by following up on the issues related to new product development. **Product management** begins in earnest when a product is introduced to the market for the first time. As a product establishes a market position and matures, new management challenges arise.

Two concepts are extremely valuable to bear in mind when managing products from market introduction through maturity. These concepts are *diffusion of innovations* and the *product life cycle.* Each provides managers with a tool to track product progress in the market and to anticipate changes that may need to be implemented in marketing mix strategies. The diffusion of innovations concept provides a particularly valuable perspective for managers because it bridges the tasks of new product and existing product management.

DIFFUSION OF INNOVATIONS

The relationship between consumer behavior and the way in which new products gain acceptance in the market is embodied in a concept known as the **diffusion of innovations.** The fundamental premise of this concept is that as an innovation is introduced into society, there will be a relatively patterned and predictable way in which the product is accepted or rejected.

TABLE 7-5
New Products That Have Succeeded and Those That Have Not

What's Hot . . .	What's Not
Motorola *MircoTac Cellular Phone*	Cadillac *Allante*
Gillette *Sensor Razors*	NeXT Computer
Chrysler LH "Cab-Forward" cars	Campbell's *Souper-Combo* (frozen soup and sandwich)
My First Sony (children's cassette player)	*Pepsi AM* (morning cola)
Apple *PowerBook*	*Fab 1 Shot* (washer to dryer packet)
IBM *ThinkPad*	Budweiser *Dry Beer*
Reebok *Pump Sneaker*	*Premier* Cigarettes (smokeless cigarette)

The key elements of this diffusion process relate to the characteristics of the product and the characteristics of consumer adopters who buy and use the product.

The *characteristics of the product* that will either speed or deter its acceptance by consumers are:[16]

1. *Perceived Complexity of Use.* If consumers perceive a product to be complex to use (not complex in design) then a product will have difficulty being accepted. CD players were readily accepted because the machines were perceived as (and actually are) easy to use.
2. *Compatibility with Consumption Values.* A product must be consistent with consumers' consumption values and use expectations. Microwave ovens (aside from some early safety hazards) were incompatible with the concept of a hardworking homemaker. Low-suds laundry detergents were and still are viewed as ineffective because the amount of suds in the washer is how the average consumer judges whether a detergent is working or not.
3. *Relative Advantage.* This is the product's perceived capability relative to alternative products. Relative advantage can be gained through functional superiority, lower price, unique design, or emotional appeal. Again, the CD is a good example. Compared to albums or cassette tapes, CDs have longer life, more durability, and higher quality sound reproduction—all relative advantages in the mind of the consumer.
4. *Observability of Value.* How observable (or tangible) the value of an innovation is does much to speed or slow the acceptance rate. It was clear to consumers that the color television had something different and better to offer over black-and-white models.
5. *Trialability.* If a new product can be tried on a limited, low-cost basis, the adoption rate is accelerated. Products that are high in price and/or require a long-term commitment, like microcomputers, suffer from poor trialability. Many firms will use demonstrations, free samples, or in-home free trials as a way to deal with this element.

Alert marketing strategists recognize the features of a new product that relate to the speed with which a product will be adopted and diffused through society. If a new product has features that violate one or more of the factors, then specialized marketing mix strategies must be developed to overcome these **barriers to diffusion**.

Another key element related to the diffusion of innovations is *characteristics of consumer adopters.* Some people like to try new products as soon as they are introduced. Others like to wait until the product has proven itself. These different types of people have been verified to exist en masse and can be discussed as distinct **consumer adopter categories**. The adopter categories, graphically represented in Figure 7-4, are described as follows:

- *Innovators.* These are people who are the first to try a new product. They are higher income, higher social class consumers who display great confidence in their buying skills. They tend to learn of new prod-

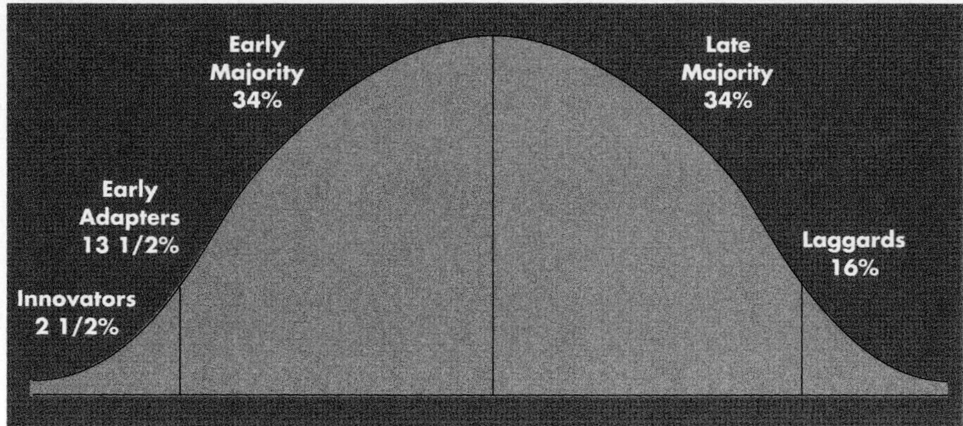

FIGURE 7-4
Diffusion of Innovations Adopter Categories

ucts through the mass media. Their higher education and secure financial status make them liberal in their buying behavior.

- *Early Adopters.* Still a high income, high social class group, the early adopters differ significantly from the innovators. Most notably, they rely on personal sources of information and act as vocal opinion leaders once they own a product.
- *Early Majority.* This group represents the opening of the mass market. Once a product has diffused to this point, it is purchased by people who are slightly above average in income, education, and social class. Members of this group use a broad range of information sources for product awareness including contact with the early adopter group.
- *Late Majority.* Once a product reaches this adopter category, it is firmly established in the market. At this stage in the adoption process, buyers are now lower in education, social class, and income. This group has been waiting for price reductions or product improvements before adoption.
- *Laggards.* This group of consumers is the most skeptical of innovation and the last to adopt a product. They can be from any social class or income group. Their membership here is based strictly on the fact that they are last in the adoption process.

These adopter categories are useful as a product management tool because they provide a description of the type of person most likely to consider purchasing a product at different points in time. It should be noted, however, that many products are developed, designed, and targeted for consumers who are really somewhere in the middle of the adopter categories rather than targeted solely at innovators. In this situation, the consumer adopter category feature of the diffusion of innovations is less important than the targeted segment. This concept is applicable to the consumer market and has only been narrowly applied to business products.[17]

THE PRODUCT LIFE CYCLE

The second broad concept in strategic product management is the **product life cycle** concept. Marketing experts have observed over time the tendency for new products to gain market acceptance, mature, grow old, and ultimately die. This tendency is apparent across many product classes and is of obvious interest to marketing decision makers.

Figure 7-5 shows how the product life cycle divides a product's commercial life into four stages as a way to track sales across an industry. The first is the **development stage**. Here a product is introduced to the market with limited distribution and perhaps only one or a few producers. It is at this stage in the life cycle that firms that introduce true innovations must be sensitive to the need for primary demand stimulation. Recall that this is the process of *educating* consumers to the value of the *product category* in general rather than concentrating on the promotion of specific brand features. The vast majority of product failures occur in the introductory stage.

Products that survive the introductory stage progress to the **market growth stage**. The beginning of the growth stage is marked by a rapid increase in the sales curve, as Figure 7-5 demonstrates. Sales in the industry are growing at an increasing rate and this stage is often referred to as the "take-off" period. Success in the growth stage is also characterized by competitors trying to copy the features of a successful product and win part of the market. This is another signal that the growth stage has begun—an increase in the number of competitors. Price competition may enter the picture and firms begin to make minor product alterations to achieve differentiation. This is also the stage where firms marketing true innovations begin selective demand stimulation—communicating to consumers the features of their *brand* and its superiority over competitors' offerings.

At the point when the mass market has adopted the product, the **maturity stage** begins. Industry sales are increasing at a slower rate since inventories are well stocked and the number of new users or adopters decreases. Because of these market conditions, firms concentrate their marketing strategy on achieving and holding brand loyalty. Strategy planning further emphasizes additional

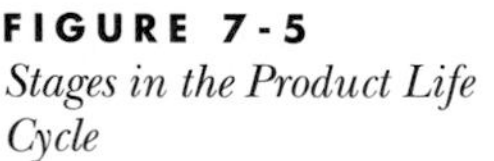

FIGURE 7-5
Stages in the Product Life Cycle

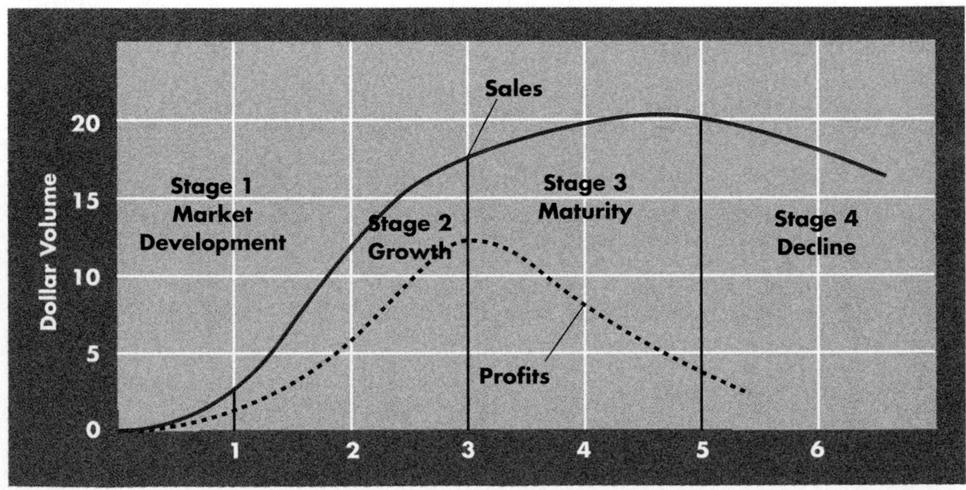

product changes many of which can be quite minor or cosmetic. Much of the emphasis in the marketing mix for any particular brand is on promotional efforts to maintain the market momentum of a brand. In contrast to the development stage where distributors and dealers were being relied upon to push the product, the maturity stage requires manufacturers themselves to stimulate demand among consumers. Distributors and dealers are typically stocking and selling the brands of many manufacturers in the product category and simply cannot afford to single out any one brand for special attention. Each manufacturer, therefore, must try to court dealers and distributors with discounts, price concessions, and special premiums. Price wars between competitors often erupt in the maturity stage as firms struggle to hold market share and retain the benefits of economies of scale in production and distribution.

The **decline stage** begins when, for one or more somewhat elusive reasons, the sales of the product level off or begin to decline. Such an eventuality often means that the weaker competitors are forced from the market. The remaining firms are those that have been most successful at anticipating changes in the market and have retained sufficient market share through their marketing mix strategy adjustments.

Profits in the Life Cycle

A common profit curve during the life cycle is shown by the dashed line in Figure 7-5. During the development stage, there may be no profits, but instead the typical firm incurs losses due to the large expense associated with market entry strategies. Profits tend to peak near the end of the growth stage and then fall off dramatically during the maturity stage. Recall that the maturity stage is characterized by the intensification of competition, product changes, and price concessions to dealers, all of which tend to erode profit margins. In the decline stage, many firms may begin to experience negative profits and withdraw from the market.

Managing and Extending the Life Cycle for a Brand

The product life cycle concept can be a valuable product management tool because it signals periods when changes in marketing mix strategy may be required. Be aware that the product life cycle is most accurate and useful for tracking the *industry sales* of a product. For the individual firm, however, the following industry signals of life cycle evolution provide important guideposts for marketing mix changes for the firm's brand as well. First, the trajectory of the sales curve signals to decision makers the progression of a product from the growth stage to the maturity stage and finally to the decline stage. Second, the number of competitors in the market is another signal that maturity is imminent or has arrived for a product. Third, total industry sales will signal the adoption of the product by the mass market and, again, maturity can be anticipated by this cue. Finally, as total industry sales begin to decline and competitors fall out of the market, the decline stage has arrived. All of these signals allow marketers to anticipate changes that will be required in the marketing mix for the firm's brand.

Firms that survive the shakeout in the decline stage can invoke a number of very specific strategies to extend the life cycle for their brand. Strategies for **extending the product life cycle** are:

- *Cultivate New Users.* Stimulating demand for the brand in new segments is a common extension strategy. Different age groups, social classes, or reference groups might be brought into the circle of the company's target even though the segment may have been outside the company's original market segmentation scheme. Johnson & Johnson is the classic example of a company that successfully used this extension strategy when it stimulated demand for its *Baby Shampoo* in many different age groups. More recently, Kellogg used precisely the same strategy for its *Frosted Flakes* cereal.
- *Develop New Uses.* Firms will often discover and develop new uses for the product and promote these new uses to consumers. Arm & Hammer's revival of baking soda was accomplished by promoting that product as a deodorizer for refrigerators. Dupont successively developed new uses for nylon in clothing, carpeting, and automobile tires.
- *Stimulate More Frequent Use.* This strategy concentrates on promoting more frequent use of the product by present users. Greater revenues are achieved by convincing current users to increase their consumption. Very successful campaigns of this type have been undertaken by the Florida Citrus Commission with its "Orange Juice Isn't Just for Breakfast Anymore" campaign and by P&G for its *Head and Shoulders* shampoo using the theme "Gentle Enough to Use Everyday." One of the most innovative strategies in this area is the campaign by McIhenny Co. to increase the frequency of use of its *Avery Island Tabasco Sauce.* An ad from this campaign is depicted in Illustration 7-1. Notice the firm is trying to increase the frequency of use by suggesting different foods on which tabasco can be used.

Timing is of the utmost importance in the use of any of these techniques. A firm must anticipate what is likely to happen in the marketplace with a minimum of 6 to 12 months of lead time so that a plan can be ready to execute well before a complete market decline. Some products, of course, simply cannot be saved. Technological or fashion obsolescence render many products useless or unappealing to consumers. The rotary dial telephone, slide rule, and Nehru jacket have all become part of history as will the record album and record turntable before too long. More products will follow them into oblivion with continued advances in technology and changes in consumer tastes.

This chapter has discussed the importance of new products and procedures for developing and then managing new products. In a very real sense, a new product has to be conceived and developed with a conscious recognition of its global potential. Because new product development is so important, a global perspective on this element of the marketing mix takes on added meaning.

New Product Development and Management: A Global Perspective

In a classic article published in the 1960s, Louis Wells refined the explanations of comparative advantage as a basis for explaining trading patterns among nations by adding the dimension of product life cycle to the discussion.[18] According to this version of the concept, many prod-

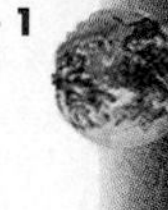

ILLUSTRATION 7-1
An Example of a Life Cycle Extension Strategy: Stimulate More Frequent Use.

The age-old question.

Most of the people who use Tabasco® brand pepper sauce prefer to think that the bottle is half-full. That there's still plenty of Tabasco® pepper sauce to drop into ground beef and make a batch of burgers that would bring the toughest crowd to its feet. Still enough to splash a teaspoon or two into a huge pot of homemade spaghetti for Monday

night football. And enough for baked potatoes, cold roast beef, scrambled eggs, and a hot dog or two. But whether the bottle of Avery Island's magical pepper sauce is half-full or half-empty isn't really of consequence to the real Tabasco® sauce aficionado. Because a true Tabasco® sauce user knows there's plenty more where that came from.

The lively taste of Tabasco® sauce.
Don't keep it bottled up.

For the recipes of Walter McIlhenny in "A Gentleman's Guide to Memorable Hospitality," send $3.25 to McIlhenny Co., Dept. GG, Avery Island, Louisiana 70513.

ucts move through a **trade cycle** wherein a nation initially begins as an exporter, then loses its export markets, and finally becomes an importer of the product. This process involves four phases, and Wells uses the United States as an illustration.

In phase one, new product development activities are likely to be related to the needs of the home market. New products will be produced in the home market because of such market conditions as the need to communicate with suppliers and customers and the relative price insensitivity by consumers for new, innovative products. In the second phase, local competition increases in the domestic market, and product familiarity in other countries increases via export activities of the originating country. Eventually, manufacturers in these second countries begin production for their own local markets, and U.S. exports fall. Wells cites the declining exports of home dishwashers as an example of a product in phase two.

In phase three, foreign producers gain production experience, and, coupled with their lower labor costs, their products become highly competitive with American exports in third country markets. Here, the example given is European exports of ranges and refrigerators to Latin America. In the fourth phase, price competition intensifies and production technology becomes so standardized and diffused that foreign production finally takes place in the lowest cost country, allowing it to export to the country where the product originated. At the time, Wells' refinement of the theory of comparative advantage was considerable, providing further insights into patterns of international trade and production and helping companies plan logistics and manage new product development.

While these trading patterns still hold true for some capital intensive industrial equipment or cutting-edge technology products, the global economy of the 1990s has dramatically shortened the trading patterns described in phases two and three or has eliminated them altogether. Basic research and new product development may still originate in the innovative home market, but this is far from being a hard and fast rule. Large global companies quickly move to production facilities that are often worldwide, take advantage of strategic alliances with business partners, and utilize worldwide distribution networks to bring new or modified products to current or new markets or to distribute established products in new markets. For example, Glaxo Holdings p.l.c., a British firm and one of the world's largest pharmaceutical companies, has an R&D staff of over 7,500 personnel located primarily in Europe and North America. In addition, they are active participants in a number of international research consortiums spread throughout the developed and developing world. Each of these different consortiums focuses on developing medicines that address health problems that are dominant in particular areas of the world. In addition to a global R&D network, the company constantly is scanning their markets for environmental changes that might provide them new opportunities. Glaxo Holdings' core business is the development and marketing of prescription medicines, and they believe that their corporate success comes from remaining focused on that business. Their recent joint venture with Warner-Lambert, a company with extensive experience in drug retailing in the United States, allows them to penetrate the growing over-the-counter market for drugs in North America with a modified version of *Zantac,* the world's best-selling prescription medicine (for ulcers).[19]

Related to Wells' conceptualization of comparative advantage is the issue of standardizing products and strategies across global market opportunities. Recall from Chapter 6 the brief discussion of Theodore Levitt's article on the globalization of markets.[20] The basic premise was that global communication and travel are worldwide socializing forces that lead to a homogenization of tastes, needs, and values in populations across all countries. This trend allows for global strategies of standardization, where reasonably priced products and services of good quality and reliability will be accepted. This standardization of products and services allows for rationalization of production and economies of scale, which permit profits at prices that are attractive to global markets. Advocates of standardization believe that price, quality, and reliability will offset any differential advantage of a culturally adapted product, while critics of this view stress the importance of cultural variation and the need to differentiate products in order to accommodate the unique social and cultural norms of different markets. Truly standardized global products are actually quite rare. American denim jeans, men's neckties, beer, wine, and cigarettes are some examples. With the Wells and Levitt conceptualizations as a foundation, the global perspective section of this chapter discusses two separate but related issues in new product development and management: (1) global management issues in the new product development process, and (2) issues related to the marketing of new products that are introduced globally.

GLOBAL MANAGEMENT OF THE NEW PRODUCT DEVELOPMENT PROCESS

If rationalization of production to gain economies of scale and efficiencies of scope are necessary conditions for global business activities, then a basic question facing management is "Where should we conduct our product development activities?" Before going into a detailed answer to this question, it is useful to clarify the meaning of the phrase *research and development,* since it is often rather freely used to describe a number of activities inherent to product development. The *research* aspect of R&D refers to basic research involving purely technical activities in which programming, engineering, physics, and/or chemistry predominate. This activity is complex, expensive, and usually highly centralized and closely guarded because of its potential commercial value. As basic research activities progress toward more applied research and the subsequent development of products, the need for decentralizing the activity increases. The research part of R&D then is a centralized, often scientific activity. The development part of R&D is the decentralized transfer of research to market applications and product development.

The upper portion of Table 7-6 shows R&D expenditures for the top ten U.S. and foreign companies in the world. Research and development are critically important and expensive activities. Reliable information on the exact breakdown of basic research costs and subsequent product development costs is difficult or impossible to acquire.

Domestic New Product Development for Global Markets

From both an organizational as well as a marketing standpoint, there are good arguments for following a strategy of **domestic new product development** for global markets. To begin with, the level of a company's current involvement in international markets will strongly influence this decision. Firms with only export and/or licensing strategies cannot realistically consider development abroad, unless they are willing to make a direct foreign investment or acquire an existing facility. Often, the domestic home office has the greatest experi-

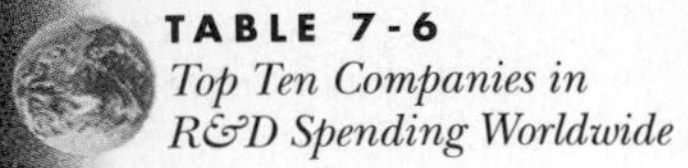
TABLE 7-6
Top Ten Companies in R&D Spending Worldwide

Top Ten Companies in R&D Spending in U.S. Dollars			
Foreign Companies	**Millions of Dollars**	**U.S. Companies**	**Millions of Dollars**
Siemens	$4132	General Motors	$5342
Hitachi	$3011	IBM	$4914
Matsushita Electric	$2432	Ford Motors	$3558
Philips Electronics	$2411	AT&T	$2433
Alcatel Alsthom	$2237	Digital Equipment	$1614
Fujitsu	$2097	General Electric	$1479
Toshiba	$1864	Du Pont	$1428
Nippon Tel. & Tel.	$1739	Hewlett-Packard	$1367
NEC	$1728	Eastman Kodak	$1329
Bayer	$1699	Dow Chemical	$1136

Top Ten Companies in R&D Spending as a Percentage of Sales			
Foreign Companies	**Percentage of Sales**	**U.S. Companies**	**Percentage of Sales**
Sextant Avionique	25.9%	Genetics Institute	12.4%
Synthelabo	18.2%	Centocor	71.0%
Astra	16.7%	Chiron	40.7%
Chugai Pharmaceutical	16.3%	Continuum	37.3%
Standard Elec. Lorenz	16.0%	Genentech	36.0%
CAE Industries	15.8%	Telematics International	31.0%
Finanziaria E. Breda	15.7%	On-Line Software Int'l	26.7%
Philips Kommunikations	15.4%	Int'l Microelectronic	26.4%
Wellcome	15.1%	Integrated Device Tech.	25.6%
Roche Holding	14.9%	Cypress Semiconductor	24.7%

Source: Standard & Poor's Compustat Services, in *Business Week* (December 2, 1991): 81.

ence and expertise in the new product development process as well as access to staff and the best facilities. Having new product development close to home provides the benefit of greater control, particularly if secrecy is an issue. Further, centralizing activities gives greater management focus and control over issues leading to economies of scale and reduces duplication of efforts.

To reduce some of the risks of domestic development of new products, foreign market needs can often be identified with proper screening or close communication with foreign subsidiaries. For example, Microsoft Corporation, the global giant in multi-industry software applications, brings university students from around the world to their home office. These students, who are fluent in the language as well as the basic computer uses of customers in *their* home markets, work in Microsoft's "localization programs." Their tasks involve working closely with programmers, translating on-line menus into foreign languages, and modifying features to accommodate local requirements such as accent marks.

Decentralized New Product Development

It is not at all unusual for well-established subsidiaries of multinational firms to make demands for local autonomy. Particularly if the subsidiary operates as a profit center, nationalistic pride and the desire to run the show motivate these kinds of initiatives. Other factors that promote **decentralized new product development** arise from environmental forces. The host government may require local production, or past tariff regulations may make for difficult market access. Then firms will necessarily institute local production and, eventually, local product development for not only their home market but for export markets as well.

Although the major arguments for centralized new product development are efficiency and economy of scale, sometimes efficiency may be greater with international division of labor. The traditional approach is to set up production facilities in low-cost centers and then transfer assembled products to export markets. For example, both Sony and Philips Electronics have large color TV production plants in Mexico. The output is used for the fast growing market in Mexico and is also exported to the United States. Technology also makes it possible to transfer value-added components from low-cost subsidiaries back to the parent company for further assembly. Texas Instruments uses highly skilled but relatively low-cost computer programmers in India to write sophisticated programming code for its specialized vertical market software systems. Each day, the program code is transmitted via satellite to TI's facilities in Texas.

Other environmental forces also influence decisions to decentralize, and certain industries and product lines can only compete well on a global basis when decentralization and local adaption is possible. When product development is slow and costly, involving a mix of expertise and talent, or when domestic R&D facilities are saturated, then companies are forced to decentralize in order to be efficient. Research and development in the industries of bioengineering and pharmaceuticals requires highly skilled, scientifically trained labor and tremendous capital investments. The low supply of trained personnel for these positions in the United States coupled with less-stringent research and drug registration regulations abroad encourages these high-technology firms to set up and operate R&D facilities around the world. The lower portion of Table 7-6 illustrates the considerable commitment that these cutting-edge technology firms must make to R&D. In all cases, the firms in the table have operations abroad as well as in the home market.

Market forces also play a key role in decisions relating to new product development. Generally speaking, there will be more decentralized new product development activities for household consumer goods than for business goods. A label that proclaims the item is "locally produced" usually enhances the image of a product destined for the household consumer market. Products that are sensitive to local market conditions, usage patterns or tastes, and products where the symbolic value is high, such as food or household furnishings, require careful adaption in order to be successfully developed. Campbell Soup, the New Jersey–based soup company that has historically had a very eth-

Campbell Soup operates taste kitchens in foreign markets to develop products that appeal to local tastes.

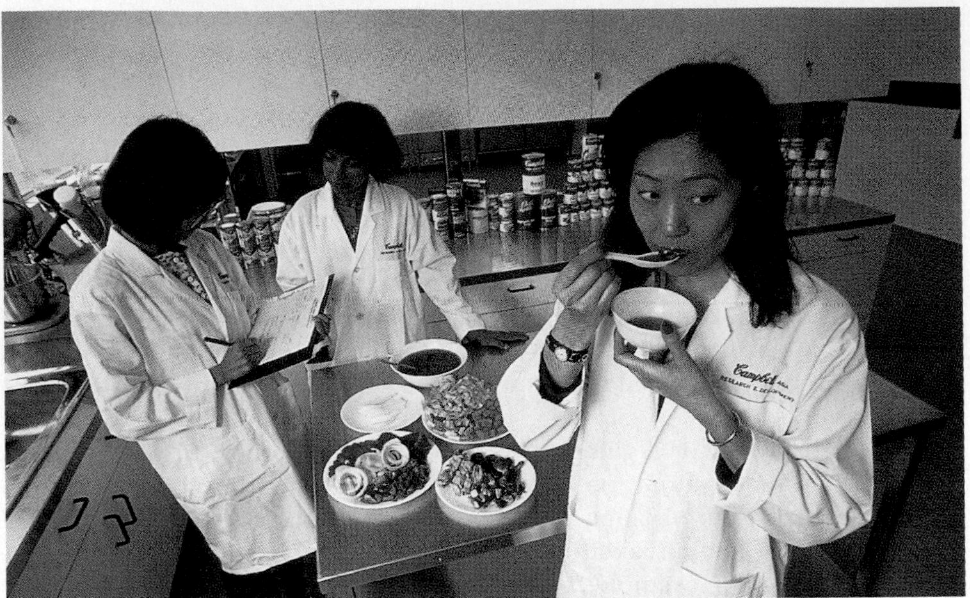

nocentric corporate view of the world, is finding that new product development is closely tied to local tastes. Operating local taste kitchens for new product development has been the key approach to satisfying local tastes. The success of their *Duck-Gizzard Soup* for China was developed in Hong Kong, not in Camden, New Jersey, and underscores the importance of a decentralized development approach.[21]

GLOBAL ISSUES IN PRODUCT MANAGEMENT

Earlier in this chapter, product was defined as "a set of tangible and intangible attributes that provide real or perceived benefits in order to satisfy consumer needs and desires." In the global context, the marketing challenge becomes one of understanding how cultural influences are interwoven with the perceived attributes and benefits of the product and the importance that the market places on the product. Keep in mind that both the perception of attributes and the importance of benefits are strongly influenced by the values and customs within a culture. Quite often both the acquisition of a new product and its bundle of features have complex symbolic meanings, even within one culture. But the *variation* of these meanings and the perceptions of the product's potential ability to satisfy are greatest when the product is marketed across cultures. To maximize the bundle of satisfactions received, adaptation of the physical as well as the psychological attributes of the product may well be necessary.

At the physical level, screening of physical changes in the product will be necessary as a first step in reducing the risk of failure. Choosing the correct color (or more importantly, avoiding the incorrect color!), having the correct voltage regulator, or supplying compatible component parts for products are simple examples. When analyzing a product for introduction to additional markets, the extent of adaptation will depend not only on cultural differences in product use but on differences in perceptions between the market the product was originally developed for and the new market. Unilever discovered that product modification was simpler than the subsequent consumer education that was needed when it tried to introduce its laundry detergent, *OMO*, in a concentrated form in rural South Africa. Acceptance of the concentrated version of *OMO* went smoothly in Europe. European retailers place a high premium on shelf space and preferred the smaller package. The use of extensive print and TV ads coupled with new usage instructions were sufficient to communicate the value of the new product to consumers. In rural South Africa, brand loyalty to *OMO* was already extremely high, but the reception of the new (and smaller!) package took extensive efforts with videos shown on monitors at country stores and personal demonstrations by sales women who could explain the concept of "less is more" to local housewives.[22]

Degree of Newness

A useful perspective in determining whether to adapt a product for a foreign market is to understand the **degree of newness** perceived in the offering by the intended target market. In understanding how a foreign market (a social system with cultural norms) reacts to a new product, the global marketer must remember to drop his or her self-reference criterion! How people *react to newness* and *how new* a product is to a market must be understood in terms of the target market's perceptions. Successful products in the United States and other highly developed economies may be in the maturity or decline stage of the product life cycle but may be new and innovative in another country or culture. Thus, marketing tactics in one market that stress price competition, intensive distribution, and advertising messages intended to remind and persuade may be totally inappropriate in another market, where developing product or brand awareness, selective distribution, and higher prices may be the optimal marketing mix.

This understanding of newness to a market is useful to a global marketer since marketing strategies can influence the rate of new product diffusion. It is the degree of a product's newness that has the greatest potential impact on patterns of consumption and behavior in global markets. A concept of newness portrayed along a continuum provides a useful set of categories for evaluating potential behavioral responses toward a product.[23]

1. A **continuous innovation** is a product that has the least disruptive influence on established consumption patterns. This is typically the alteration of an existing product rather than the creation of a new one. The alterations are designed to offer increased satisfaction derived from its use. Examples include menthol cigarettes, tartar-control toothpaste, or annual model changes in the stereo industry. Sometimes, a new product feature that was planned as a continuous innovation turns out to have a surprisingly significant impact on the satisfaction and use of the product. The introduction of simple-to-use laser beams to simplify the programming of VCRs by reading bar codes published in television guides has turned out to be a major improvement to this product class in Europe, stimulating both VCR sales among laggards and causing TV guide publishers to quickly add this feature to their magazines.
2. A **dynamically continuous innovation** has more disruptive effects on behavior than a continuous innovation, although it generally does not

involve new consumption patterns. It may stem from the creation of a new product or from considerable alteration of an existing product. It is generally disruptive and therefore resisted since old patterns of behavior must change if consumers are to accept and perceive the value of the innovation. A clear example would be the CD, which was a tremendous technological innovation, but only slightly altered consumers' behavior towards listening to music. Early resistance was due more to the limited availability of software (CDs) than to the hardware.

3. A **discontinuous innovation** involves the establishment of new consumption patterns and the creation of previously unknown products. It introduces new ideas or behavior patterns. Examples here include the television, the personal computer, the automobile, commercial jet travel, and microwave ovens.

The majority of consumer innovations in the United States tend to be of the continuous type. For the global marketer, the trick is to understand that while a product might be described as a continuous innovation in one market, it may be called a dynamically continuous innovation, if not a discontinuous innovation, in another market, even in other highly industrialized markets. Consider the diffusion process of the microwave oven as an example. Introduced in the late 1960s in the United States, microwave ovens spent a decade or more in the introduction and early growth stages of the product life cycle. Consumers did not see the immediate benefits of microwave cooking, and there was a large amount of distrust towards the product. This distrust stemmed from the ominous signs posted in public places where microwave ovens were in use warning people with heart pacemakers to avoid the area and from rumors of disastrous outcomes resulting from misusing microwaves. Real diffusion and acceptance occurred throughout the 1980s, brought about by technical and functional improvements in the product, changes in consumer life-styles, increased importance attached to time and convenience, changes in the composition of the work force, and the development of more tasty, nutritious foods that could be prepared in the microwave.

While microwave ovens are in the mature phase of their product life cycle in the United States, they are still in the growth stage in the Netherlands, the country with the highest per capita expenditures for household improvements of any country in Europe. Preparation of hot foods in the kitchen has special cultural value in Holland, where hearty winter dishes of meat and potato stews (*stampot*) combat the cold and damp climate. While the concepts of time and convenience are growing in importance, home cooking still occupies an important role in Holland. This eliminates or reduces the benefits associated with the microwave for the mass market. Similar obstacles for the microwave were encountered in high-income segments in Latin America where affluent consumers typically have cooks to prepare meals. Saving time for the cook is simply not perceived as an important benefit in those markets. Generally speaking, the more disruptive the innovation is in terms of the behavior associated with its use, the longer the diffusion process takes.

In summary, the extent of a product's diffusion and its rate of acceptance into the social system are dependent partly on the innovation's attributes. Each new product has both tangible and intangible characteristics, which are often interpreted differently in different markets. Adjustments in the product's attributes or in the marketing mix variables associated with the product's introduction will influence its ultimate rate of acceptance. The following chapter discusses a number of product line and product mix strategies that relate to marketing in different segments in domestic markets as well as product strategies for global markets.

Key Terms and Concepts

Definition of the product
New product development
True innovation
Adaptive replacement
Me, too, product
Primary demand
Acquisition
Internal new product development
Demand pull
Technology push
Criteria for judging new product ideas
Semantic product design
Speed of development
Product management
Diffusion of innovations
Barriers to diffusion
Consumer adopter categories
Product life cycle
Development stage
Market growth stage
Maturity stage
Decline stage
Extending the product life cycle
Domestic new product development
Decentralized new product development
Degree of newness
Continuous innovation
Dynamically continuous innovation
Discontinuous innovation

Questions and Exercises

1. Describe an automobile in terms of its tangible features. Now describe the same automobile using a perspective that emphasizes the *value* an automobile provides.
2. What are the advantages of new product development through acquisition as opposed to internal development? What are the risks of the acquisition method?
3. Rebook expanded its product line by acquiring Avia Sport Shoes and Frye Boots. How would you rate these new product acquisitions based on the criteria for judging new products presented in the chapter?
4. Identify a me, too, product you have recently seen introduced in the market? Do you think this product is going to be successful?
5. McCaw Celluar wants to start marketing celluar phones to household consumers. Explain to managers at McCaw the concept of *primary demand stimulation* and how it relates to their plan.
6. What is *semantic product design* and how is it argued to be significant to the success of a new product? Discuss a product you own that has elements of semantic design.
7. The microcomputer has never penetrated the household consumer market to nearly the degree that analysts thought it would. What barriers to diffusion have prevented the microcomputer from widespread adoption by household consumers?
8. Give an example of a brand that is currently being promoted in a way that suggests a product life cycle extension strategy is being attempted? Refer to the Tabasco advertisement in the chapter as an example of an extension strategy.
9. What factors promote centralized (domestic) versus decentralized new product development for global markets?
10. Discuss the categories of behavior response toward a product in foreign markets based on the concept of newness along a continuum.

REFERENCES

1. Adapted from Stuart Elliot, "The Big Three in Batteries Start New Campaigns," *New York Times* (September 29, 1993): 19; Sara Hebel, "Rayovac Taps into Reusable Batteries." *Advertising Age* (July 26, 1993): 10; Jeffery A. Trachtenberg. "Electrifying." *Forbes* (November 30, 1987): 196, 198.
2. Theodore Levitt. "Marketing Myopia." *Harvard Business Review* 38 (July–August 1960): 45.
3. Gabriella Stern. "To Outpace Rivals, More Firms Step up Spending on New-Product Development." *Fortune* (October 28, 1992): B1, B15.
4. *3M Corporation 1992 Annual Report* (St. Paul, MN: 3M Corporation): 3.
5. Louis S. Richman. "What America Makes Best." *Fortune* (Spring/Summer 1991): 79.
6. Data on costs for Ford cited in Alex Taylor III, "Ford's $6 Billion Baby." *Fortune* (June 28, 1993): 76–81; other development costs cited in David Woodruff and Karen Lowry Miller. *Business Week* (May 3, 1993): 116–126.
7. Statistics on failure rates cited in Cyndee Miller, "Little Relief Seen for New Product Failure Rate." *Marketing News* (June 21, 1993): 1, 10–11.
8. Robert L. Rose, "Maytag's Acquisitions Don't Wear as Well as Washers and Dryers." *The Wall Street Journal* (January 1, 1991): A1, A6.
9. This discussion is based in part on Yorum Wind, "A Research Program for a Marketing Guided Approach to Mergers and Acquisitions," in *1979 AMA Educators' Conference Proceedings,* ed. Neil E. Beckwith (Chicago, IL: American Marketing Association, 1979): 24–28.
10. Brian Dumaine. "Design That Sells and Sells and . . ." *Fortune* (March 11, 1991): 90.
11. Alix M. Freedman. "Forsaking the Black Box: Designers Wrap Products in Visual Metaphors." *The Wall Street Journal* (March 26, 1987): 41.
12. Dumaine. *Fortune* (March 11, 1991) op. cit., 86.
13. Gallup poll results cited in Paul Kunkel, "Competing by Design." *Business Week* (March 25, 1991): 52.
14. Brian Dumaine. "How Managers Can Succeed through Speed." *Fortune* (February 13, 1989): 54.
15. Stephen Kreider Yoder. "Motorola Loses Edge in Microprocessors by Delaying New Chips." *The Wall Street Journal* (March 4, 1991): A1.
16. This discussion is based in part on Everett M. Rogers and F. Floyd Shoemaker. *Communication of Innovations,* 2d ed. (New York: The Free Press, 1971), Chapters 4 and 5.
17. See for example, R. G. Cooper. "The Demand Characteristics of Industrial New Product Success and Failure." *Journal of Marketing* 43, no. 3 (Summer 1979): 93–103; and Hubert Gatignon and Thomas S. Robertson. "Technology Diffusion: An Empirical Test of Competitive Effects." *Journal of Marketing* 53, no. 1 (January 1989): 35–49.
18. Louis T. Wells, Jr. "A Product Life Cycle for International Trade?" *Journal of Marketing* (July 1968): 1–6.
19. Adapted from Glaxo Holding p.l.c. *Annual Report and Accounts,* 1993, and "The Boom in Depression," *The Economist* (August 8, 1992): 73–74.
20. Theodore Levitt. "The Globalization of Markets." *Harvard Business Review* (May–June, 1983): 92–101.
21. Joseph Weber. "Campbell: Now It's M-M Global." *Business Week* (March 15, 1993): 34–36.
22. Susan Poot, Clifford Shultz, and Gary Bamossy. "Ethnicity and Consumption in an Age of Urbanization and Global Marketing: The Case of Black South Africa." *23rd European Marketing Academy Proceedings,* ed. H. Kasper, 1994, (forthcoming).
23. Thomas S. Robertson. "The New Product Diffusion Process," in *Proceedings,* ed. B. A. Marvin (Chicago: American Marketing Association, June 1969): 81.

8

PRODUCT STRATEGIES

AFTER STUDYING THIS CHAPTER, YOU WILL UNDERSTAND THAT:

1. Firms use product line and mix strategies to alter the breadth and depth of their market offerings in order to compete more effectively.
2. Product differentiation is a strategy designed to create a perception among consumers that a firm's brand is different from brands being marketed by competitors.
3. Product positioning is the attempt to establish a unique niche in the market for a firm's brand.
4. A widely recognized brand name is valuable not only to the manufacturer but also to consumers.
5. Product strategy decisions in the global marketplace often involve broader-based business decisions relating to mergers and acquisitions, joint ventures, licensing agreements, and other forms of cooperative alliances.

Procter & Gamble, Philip Morris, Frito-Lay, and Gerber Products were all taken by surprise. These champions of packaged goods own many of the most widely recognized brand names in the world—*Crest, Marlboro, Fritos,* and *Gerber Baby Food.* But, as experienced and successful as these firms are, they simply weren't prepared for the rapid and dramatic rise in sales of "private label," low-priced brands over the last two years. The big, national name-brand firms used to enjoy the luxury of fierce brand loyalty in their various markets: 71 percent of cigarette smokers were brand loyal, 61 percent of toothpaste buyers, 48 percent of beer drinkers, and 53 percent of bath soap buyers.[1] However, in the early 1990s value-oriented consumers emerged and private label brands took off. By mid-1992, private label brands, which are lower-priced brands introduced by distributors, retailers, or minor competitors, were showing increases in sales of 20 to 90 percent in a single 12-month period and now constitute about 14 percent of total grocery sales in the United States. In European markets, private label brands equal 20 to 30 percent of all grocery sales.[2]

But, these big national competitors didn't roll over and die. They fought back with a variety of product strategies. Kraft and Gerber responded with lower prices on the highly visible *Kraft Singles* cheese and *Gerber Baby Food.* Both saw sales volumes increase by more than 5 percent. Frito-Lay improved product quality and introduced new varieties of its *Fritos* snack. Procter & Gamble combined weak brands with stronger ones, such as eliminating *Puritan* cooking oil and introducing *Crisco/Puritan.* Both firms have started to recoup market share.[3]

These well-known firms are using good, strategic product maneuvers to regain sales and market share: brand extensions, product line extensions, product line contraction, and differentiation. Chapter 7 dealt with the issues of new product development and managing products from market introduction through obsolescence and decline. This chapter covers the kinds of product strategies big packaged goods firms are implementing. Many of the issues and

Firms like Frito-Lay are combating private-label brands by developing and introducing new versions of popular brands.

concepts raised here are specific to existing products and entire product lines. Some of the strategies covered in this chapter also deal with new products but from a market strategy orientation rather than a development perspective.

Few organizations survive and prosper over the long term with only one product. Most firms work hard to proliferate the number of products and brands they market. The benefits of economies of size and scale are too valuable and profitable for firms to concentrate all their resources on one product or a very small product line. The topics raised in this chapter deal with product strategies that allow firms to compete effectively and manage a number of products simultaneously. Four essential product strategies form the framework for effective competition: product line and mix strategy, product differentiation, product positioning, and branding. Strategies and tactics associated with packaging and labeling are also considered. The chapter concludes with the key issues that shape product strategy in global markets.

PRODUCT LINE AND MIX STRATEGIES

The first product strategy decision a firm must make has to do with how extensive its product line and mix will be. Or, for a well-established firm, whether to maintain or change its existing line and mix. A **product line** is a group of similar products marketed by a firm that serve a similar purpose for users. A line of soap products marketed by Colgate-Palmolive and a line of cosmetic products offered by Revlon are examples of product lines. Examples of business product lines are photocopy machines sold by Xerox and the line of long-haul trucks sold by Navistar. A firm's **product mix** is the sum total of the different product lines that are manufactured or marketed by the organization. AT&T has a line of computers, telephones, and communications services, which make up part of the extensive mix of products it offers to both household consumer and business markets.

The challenge facing an organization is to strategically manage its product line and mix for maximum revenue generating potential. The product line and mix strategy decisions are the most far reaching and important of the product strategies undertaken by a firm.

PRODUCT LINE STRATEGIES

Two basic strategies are employed in managing a firm's product lines. Decisions must be made regarding (1) the breadth and depth of the product line, and (2) expansion and contraction of the product line. Product line breadth and depth refers to how many different products and how many variations of those products a firm attempts to market simultaneously. As an example, consider tennis products. A firm could achieve great **product line breadth** by marketing a large range of different types of products associated with tennis: rackets, balls, shoes, apparel, ball machines. Firms will often achieve breadth in their product lines designing products for different demographic target markets. A common strategy in this regard is to market products for men, women, and children as Penn does in the tennis apparel and equipment market and The Gap does in its retail clothing stores. As a firm attempts to supply consumers with many types of related products across the line, the line achieves great breadth.

The strategy of **product line depth** is pursued when a firm offers a wide variety of choices of the *same* product type. Procter & Gamble offers the consumer a choice of six different bar soaps: *Ivory, Lava, Camay, Zest, Safeguard,* and *Coast.* Even further depth in a line is achieved when different sizes of each brand are offered. *Ivory* soap, for example, comes in three different sizes as a solid bar soap and also comes as a liquid soap in a pump dispenser.

Breadth and depth in a product line allow a firm to penetrate different market segments with similar products. Products in the line are designed with slight differences to satisfy varying consumer needs and desires. But satisfying consumer needs and desires is not the only reason firms will increase the breadth and depth of product lines, however. Broad and deep product lines allow firms to occupy greater amounts of retail shelf space and therefore achieve a competitive advantage through greater presence at the retail level. Further, larger product lines can result in economies of scale across a variety of marketing activities. When sales people have a broad product line to sell, then the fixed and variable costs of sales calls are spread over a greater number of items thus increasing the contribution to profit margin of each item in the line. Similarly, advertising can highlight several items in a line, which again spreads costs over a greater number of units sold and economies of scale are again realized.

The second major product line strategy has to do with **product line expansion** and **product line contraction.** Expansion and contraction of the product line involves the addition or deletion of a product from the company's line of offerings. The decision to cease the production and marketing of an item from the line is influenced by profitability, cost of production, changes in consumer tastes and demand, and competitive pressures. General Motors has several product line contractions in the works. First, the *Cadillac Allante* was eliminated from production in 1992. High costs and minimal demand killed the product. A much more far reaching product line change will take place at GM at the end of the 1996 model year. GM will eliminate the Oldsmobile *Cutlass Ciera* and *Buick Century* because the two lines have become badly outdated compared to their competition the Chrysler *LH* models introduced in 1993.[4] GM eliminated particular items within its lines as a product line contraction. Nissan, on the other hand, has expanded its product line in recent years with the addition of two new lines of vehicles: the *Infiniti* and the *Altima.*

Product lines are expanded to provide firms with greater market coverage in the product group, to attract a different segment, use excess production capacity or take advantage of existing distribution opportunities. In 1988, American Express successfully introduced the *Optima* card to its line of credit card options available to consumers. The *Optima* card was the first card issued by American Express that offered consumers revolving credit unlike the *Green, Gold,* and *Platinum* American Express cards, which require payment of the full balance at the time of billing. While the *Optima* card has had some growing pains, it achieved great success very quickly and grabbed a 3 percent market share after only 18 months on the market.

Two important tactics in product line expansion are trading up and trading down. **Trading up** occurs when a firm introduces a new product that is priced high in the range of products available on the market. **Trading down** results when a product is targeted at the low end of the competitive price structure. The best historical example of a firm successfully using a trading up strategy is Honda Motors. Beginning with a very small and inexpensive two-seater *CVCC* automobile in the early 1970s, Honda has continually traded up within the product line and introduced larger and more expensive models. First the *Accord* was introduced as a larger four-door model. Then, the *Prelude* was added as a two-door, sporty model and again carried a higher price. Then, Honda extended its line and traded up to the luxury market with the Acura Division where the *Legend* model commands a price of over $30,000.

There are definite risks associated with both trading up and trading down. Since both strategies require a deviation from the firm's basic and traditional price level, consumers may not perceive the new product to be consistent with the image they have of the firm and its products. Recall from Chapter 7 that one of the criteria for screening new product ideas is that the newly proposed product is consistent with the current image of the firm in the market. Aside from consumer perception, another risk is that trading up and trading down may challenge management to compete in a level of the market in which they have little experience. This often results in a competitive disadvantage.

PRODUCT MIX STRATEGIES

The issues associated with product mix strategies are similar to those related to the product line. The major difference is that product mix decisions are much more dramatic. They may involve changing the very nature of the firm's business. The fundamental strategic decisions associated with the product mix have to do with expanding and contracting the mix. That means adding or deleting a *full line of products or services* from a firm's business. **Product mix expansion** is achieved by adding an entire product line to the firm's market offerings. Expansion can occur by adding product lines that are relatively close to the firm's primary business, or expansion of the mix may result in a firm venturing well beyond its traditional product areas. Circuit City, the nation's largest chain of electronics and appliance stores, is proposing one of the oddest product expansions in history. The firm has begun to open used car lots![5] Management feels that the service, warranty, and trained staff that make the appliance stores successful will carry over to selling cars. In a more traditional move, Blockbuster Video has expanded its mix by adding a line of record stores, Sound Warehouse, which markets items similar to videos.[6] The motivations for a firm to expand the product mix are the same as for product line expansion: to increase revenue generation by appealing to a new segment or to take better advantage of opportunities for increased economies of scale and scope with a new product. Additionally, expanding the product mix can diversify a firm's market risks. As a company expands into new areas (usually those with projected high growth rates) and begins to market products somewhat different from those in its current mix, the risks of falling prey to a decline in overall corporate performance are lessened. If consumer tastes shift, technology changes, or increased competition damages a firm's profitability in one product or market area, a broad product mix will help ensure that total corporate performance is still good.

Several significant challenges are associated with product mix expansion. When a firm expands its product mix, it generally ventures beyond the competitive and customer markets with which it is familiar. In this case, a firm's existing resources may be insufficient to manage a new decision-making environment. A new product line many times requires new production facilities, new sources of supply, and different channels of distribution. Additional staff and facilities may be required to successfully market the product. All of these potential changes can dilute corporate resources to the point that effectiveness and efficiency suffer. Such would seem to have been the case when Coleman, the camping products company, expanded aggressively into several new lines of business. From its base of highly profitable camping gear, Coleman expanded into sailboards (*Hobie Cat*), ski boats (*MasterCraft*), air guns (*Crossman*), and riding lawn mowers (*Dixon*). These product lines were far from Coleman's core expertise and required specialty distribution with which Coleman had no experience. Coleman also found that its good name in camping equipment did little to sell products like sailboards. The company ultimately sold off many of the product lines with which it tried to expand its mix.[7]

Product mix contraction means that a firm has decided to delete an entire product line from its product mix. Contraction of a product mix is typically a difficult decision. The firm generally increases its market risk because after the contraction it will be competing in at least one less area. The impact of such a decision can affect capital equipment utilization rates, employees, and the firm's other product lines. The decision to contract the mix and drop an entire product line focuses on products with declining demand or products that the firm finds itself incapable of handling. AT&T and GE both dropped significant product lines recently. AT&T divested itself of its insurance and investment banking businesses. Once major contributors to profits for AT&T, these product lines contributed less than 4 percent to corporate profits in 1992. For different reasons, GE sold its aerospace division to Martin Marietta. GE felt that in light of cuts in defense spending the division held less promise.[8] Once a firm realizes that a product line does not fulfill either market objectives or revenue objectives, then the product strategy of mix contraction should be seriously considered.

PRODUCT DIFFERENTIATION

The next level of product strategy decision making deals with product differentiation. **Product differentiation** is creating in the minds of consumers a perceived difference between the firm's product or service and that of the competition. Notice that this definition emphasizes that product differentiation is based on *consumer perception* with respect to differences between competitor's products and those that a firm markets. Whether there are real differences between brands is not the issue. The issue is whether consumers *perceive* a difference. If consumers do not perceive a difference, then whether actual differences exist or not does not matter—in the mind of the consumer, there are no differences and that perception is the reality.

Product differentiation is considered one of the most critical marketing strategies. If a firm's product is not perceived as distinctive and attractive by

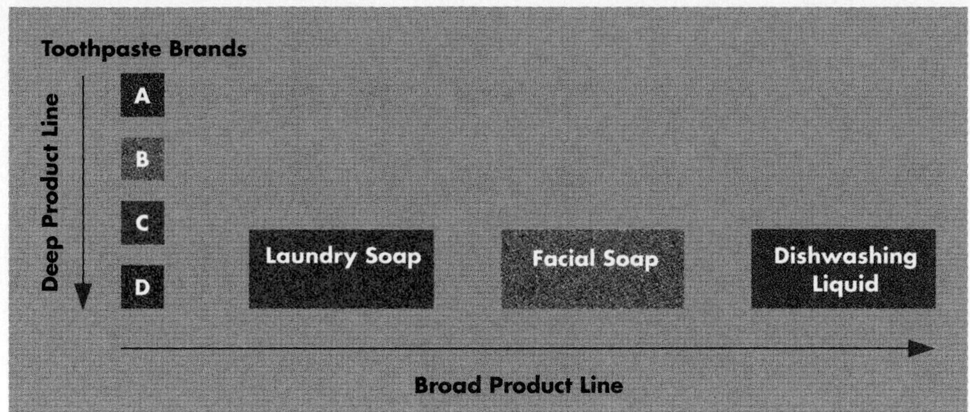

ILLUSTRATION 8-1
Product Lines Can Be Deep and Broad

consumers, then consumers will have no reason to choose that firm's brand over the competition. And, without distinctiveness, consumers will have difficulty identifying and remembering a firm's brand when making their decisions. The best way a firm can differentiate its product is to focus on the different types of satisfaction sought by consumers. These categories of satisfaction were discussed in Chapter 1 and again in Chapter 3 as motivations for consumer product evaluation and choice. The categories of functional, emotional, and benefits of use satisfaction provide a logical basis for structuring the options available for strategic product differentiation.

FUNCTIONAL DIFFERENTIATION

Functional differentiation is based on the physical, tangible features of a product. Such features are standardized, measurable criteria that can be used by consumers to make direct comparisons with competitors' products. Measures of performance, product size, ingredients, durability, reliability, warranty, and price are examples of product features that can form a basis for functional differentiation. The shopping goods consumer product category is particularly well suited to functional feature differentiation because products in this category are heavily feature laden. In addition, consumers are more highly involved in the shopping goods search process and compare features among brands. The ad in Illustration 8-2 is a good example of providing consumers with functional feature information and attempting to differentiate a brand based on these features. The Buick *Roadmaster* has several functional features, including price, with which it can differentiate itself from the Lincoln *Town Car.*

A firm attempting functional differentiation can go about the process in several different ways. One choice is to develop a product so that it has more features than competitors. With this strategy, each additional feature provides a basis for differentiation. The new Sony mini-component stereo systems have built-in graphic equalizers as a feature to differentiate them from the competition. Alternatively, a firm can develop a product with fewer but superior features. The Nissan *Infiniti Q45* has fewer luxury features than its primary competitor, the Toyota *Lexus LS 400,* but Nissan touts the *Infiniti*'s superior

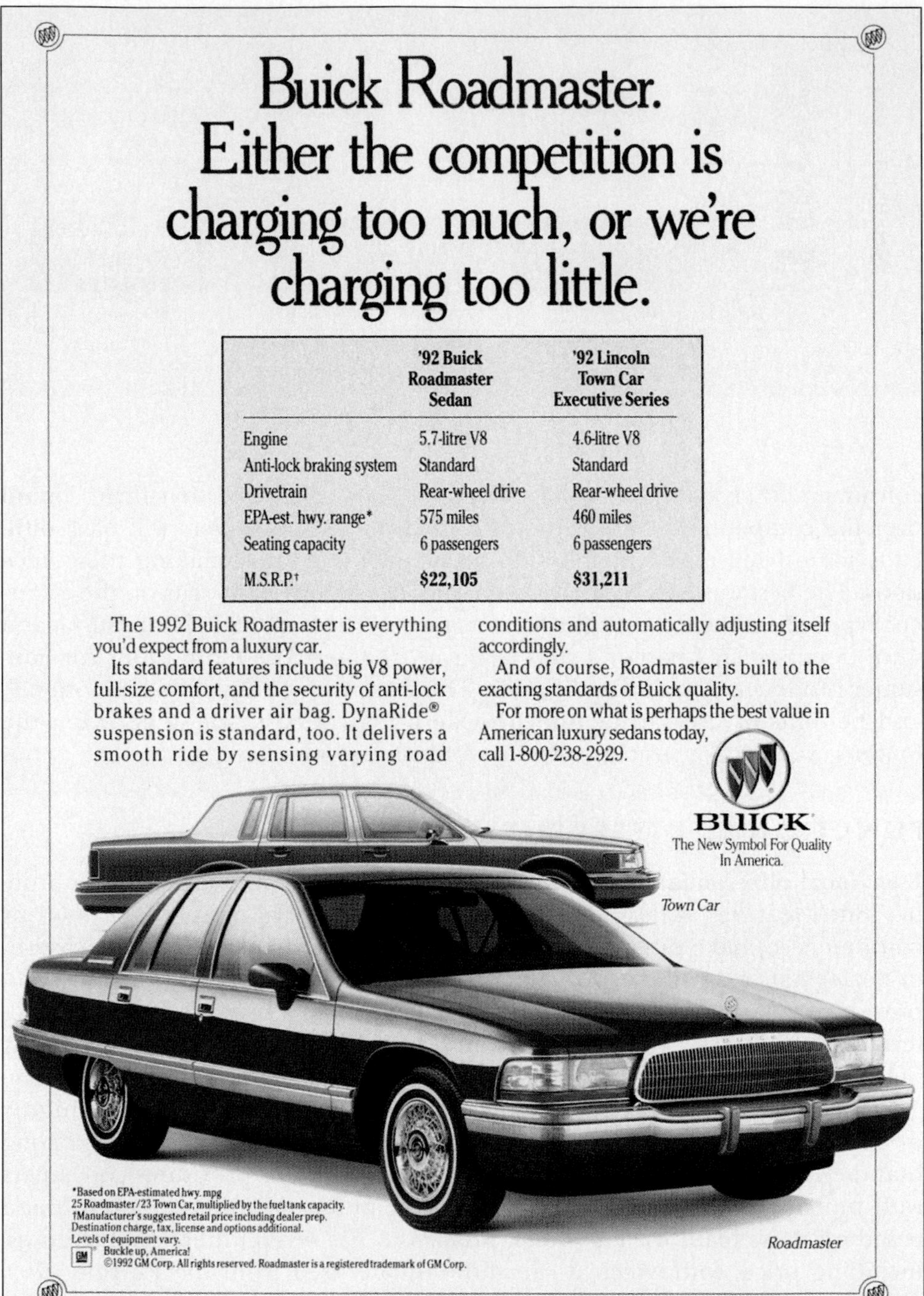

Buick Roadmaster.
Either the competition is charging too much, or we're charging too little.
'92 Buick Roadmaster Sedan
'92 Lincoln Town Car Executive Series
Engine 5.7-litre V8 4.6-litre V8
Anti-lock braking system Standard Standard
Drivetrain Rear-wheel drive Rear-wheel drive
EPA-est. hwy. range* 575 miles 460 miles
Seating capacity 6 passengers 6 passengers
M.S.R.P.† $22,105 $31,211
The 1992 Buick Roadmaster is everything you'd expect from a luxury car.
Its standard features include big V8 power, full-size comfort, and the security of anti-lock brakes and a driver air bag. DynaRide® suspension is standard, too. It delivers a smooth ride by sensing varying road conditions and automatically adjusting itself accordingly.
And of course, Roadmaster is built to the exacting standards of Buick quality.
For more on what is perhaps the best value in American luxury sedans today, call 1-800-238-2929.
BUICK
The New Symbol For Quality In America.
Town Car
*Based on EPA-estimated hwy. mpg
25 Roadmaster/23 Town Car, multiplied by the fuel tank capacity.
†Manufacturer's suggested retail price including dealer prep.
Destination charge, tax, license and options additional.
Levels of equipment vary.
GM
Buckle up, America!
©1992 GM Corp. All rights reserved. Roadmaster is a registered trademark of GM Corp.
Roadmaster

ILLUSTRATION 8-2
Firms often use functional features as a basis for differentiation.

acceleration (0–60 mph in 6.7 seconds) and handling (computerized suspension) as the basis for differentiation. Finally, a firm's brand may have neither a greater number of features nor particularly distinguished functional features, but it can differentiate itself on quality dimensions like durability and reliability. This is how Eveready tries to differentiate itself in the battery market with the Bunny that "keeps going and going and going. . . . "

EMOTIONAL DIFFERENTIATION

In many product categories, and especially in consumer convenience goods, ingredients are standardized and there simply are not significant functional feature differences between brands. This being the case, many firms rely on an emotional basis for differentiation. In cases where real differences do not exist or the differences between brands are trivial, emotions provide a basis for differentiation. Developing a unique *image* for the brand is the umbrella strategy associated with **emotional differentiation.** Status, prestige, and exclusivity are also common grounds on which firms like BMW, Rolex, and Polo attempt to differentiate their brands. The use of reference group appeal is another way to emotionally differentiate a brand based on consumers' desire for affiliation and acceptance. Style in the physical design or promotion of a product are nonfunctional, emotional bases for distinguishing a brand from all the competitive brands on the market. Vidal Sassoon shows stylish people in stylish places using the brand and tries to establish this element as the distinguishing feature of its shampoo and conditioner line.

Critics of marketing often point to the trivial differences in products that come about through attempts at emotional differentiation. The critics argue that few *real* differences between brands exist and this creates social costs from too many products with too few features being on the market. The charge is also leveled here that firms plot to create *style obsolescence* through emotional differentiation and, again, create waste in the market.

BENEFITS OF USE DIFFERENTIATION

In cases where consumers are unable or unwilling to spend the time to identify functional differences between products, then **benefits of use differentiation** becomes a basis for comparison. Firms with superior service capability use this approach as the basis for differentiation. Wal-Mart does not claim to be superior to or different from Kmart in the products its stores carry, or in its store hours, price discounts, or any other functional feature. *But,* Wal-Mart will claim to be superior and different from Kmart in the area of friendly, courteous service: a benefit of using Wal-Mart stores as a place to shop. Financial services organizations have little latitude in the actual services they can offer. Because of this restriction and consumers' general lack of knowledge of investment options, firms like Merrill Lynch and Dean Witter portray the *benefits* of using their organizations. Advertisements for these firms often show couples in happy and secure retirement or families that have successfully financed their children's education by using the services of the brokerage firm.

Whether a firm has a functional, emotional, or benefits of use basis for differentiation, every firm *must* differentiate its product in the minds of consumers. In the absence of successful differentiation, a firm will have no identity in the market. In the absence of an identity, consumers will have no reason to choose that company's products over those of the competition. Here, we have identified that the three bases for consumer satisfaction form a logical basis for the differentiation strategy. Next, every firm must decide on a strategic market position for its product.

Product Positioning

Product positioning was identified as an area of decision making in Chapter 7. There, the concept was introduced as one of the criteria used in screening new product ideas. Points were raised regarding the challenge of positioning the product both internally, that is, with respect to other products offered by the firm, and externally, by establishing a market position relative to competitive products. Here we will concentrate on the strategy issues regarding external positioning.

Successful external, competitive positioning depends directly on the differentiation strategy decided upon by a firm. After a firm decides on functional, emotional, or benefits of use differentiation, it must then execute that strategy by positioning the product in the market.

In a very real sense, a firm can position its product in the market in an infinite number of ways. The fundamental goal of **product positioning** is to identify a unique niche that a brand can occupy relative to its competition. You may have heard the process of positioning referred to as *niche marketing*. While there are any number of ways to execute a position strategy, the basic categories of positioning are as follows:

- **Direct competitive positioning** Here the primary focus of the positioning strategy relates to identifying a position for the company's product strictly based on an assessment of competitors' products. Ideally, a firm will be able to find a unique position within the competitive realm where the product is distinctive and clearly different from competitive brands. If not, then direct head-to-head competition may be required. The beer brewers in the United States accept the fact that head-to-head positioning is a necessary strategy. The beer drinking market is so narrowly defined that the only sufficiently profitable segment is the same segment every competitor is after. Recent attempts by brewers to create a distinctive position have resulted in the introduction of "dry" and "ice" versions of beers.
- **Target market positioning** Competition is not the main criterion in this strategy, but rather the target market and its preferences drive the decision making. Demographics, life-style factors, or product use characteristics can all serve as a basis for a target market positioning strategy. The Pontiac *Gran Prix* is a sedan targeted to young, male professionals. The Chevrolet *Lumina* is a sedan positioned to appeal to families with young children and older couples with no children.
- **Benefits positioning** With this strategy, products are positioned based on the benefits provided. In the chewing gum market, *Big Red* freshens your breath, *Wrigley's Spearmint Gum* can be chewed instead of smoking cigarettes, and *Dentine* helps clean your teeth.

One method firms use to help determine positioning strategy is known as perceptual mapping. **Perceptual mapping** is a method that uses consumer perceptions of competitive brands currently available in the product category and creates a visual representation of the relative position of the brands. Through an assessment of consumer choice criteria, consumer perceptions of brand features, and preference for brands currently marketed based on these features firms can identify "gaps" in the market. These gaps represent areas of opportunity for new brands. Figure 8-1 represents a hypothetical perceptual map for the luxury automobile market. Notice a gap in the central right-hand sector where a firm might find the opportunity for introducing a new brand.

Once a firm has decided on a strategic position to pursue, that position must be reassessed periodically to ensure that it is not becoming outdated or obsolete. General Mills has redesigned the image of the *Betty Crocker* character several times over the last 30 years to help keep the *Betty Crocker* brand relevant through target market positioning for evolving demographics and life-styles. Conversely, VF Corp., the maker of *Lee Jeans,* failed to react to the environment and reposition its products in line with target customer choice criteria. As the population of young people aged 12 to 24 began to decrease and body shapes of the baby boom generation began to change, *Lee Jeans* found itself occupying an obsolete position in the market. Competitors' had introduced redesigned, more stylish jeans, while Lee neglected to keep up with market preferences and marketed old-style, blue denim. The result was a 23 percent decline in jeans sales over the 3-year period 1987–1990.[9] VF Corp. has now redesigned its line of both men's and women's jeans and revamped the advertising to achieve a more contemporary look and feel for the *Lee* brand. The experience of VF Corp. highlights another important aspect of positioning strategy: positioning

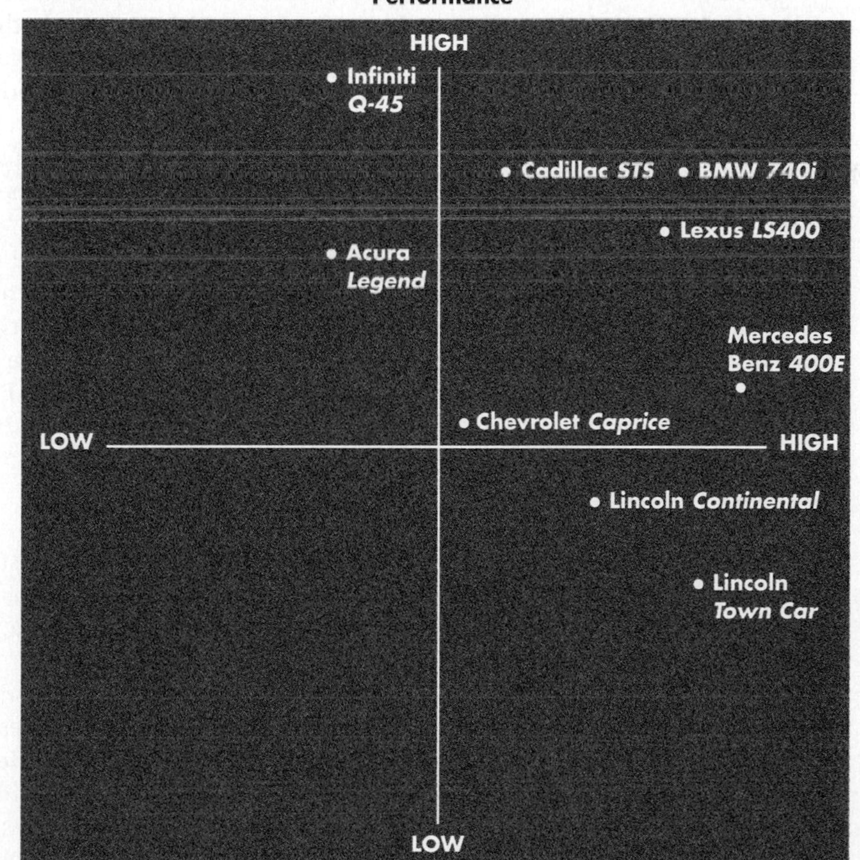

FIGURE 8-1
Perceptual Map of Luxury Automobile Market

is not just for new products—the repositioning of existing brands can be crucial to survival in the market.

Along with the broad-based line, mix, differentiation, and positioning strategies, more specific product decisions must be made regarding branding, packaging, and labeling. These issues can be essential to the success of a product in that the brand name and package follow through on the more broad-based product strategies just discussed. We will consider each of these important elements in strategic product management now.

BRANDING

This chapter began with a description of how large and very successful firms, like Procter & Gamble and Philip Morris, have seen some erosion of market share in their highly visible brands. But, these powerhouse marketers are not about to let private label brands like Presidents Choice and Western Family take over the market. They are battling to regain market share with more tightly focused products and lower prices. This battle highlights one important fact: consumers are, indeed, brand oriented. The reason is that branding gives consumers the ability to evaluate alternatives in the market. For this reason, marketers need to recognize the power and value of branding.

Branding is establishing a name, term, symbol, or design that identifies a product with a particular seller and clearly distinguishes that product from products offered by competitors. A distinctive brand name or mark can help a company crystallize for a consumer the positive goodwill of a product. The brand can become a representation of satisfaction that influences a consumer to repeatedly choose a particular company's product over a competitor's products. The more favorable and powerful the positive associations are, the greater the sales potential for the product.

Positive brand associations in the minds of consumers are the result of many factors. The design and function of the product itself are, of course, the most basic and straightforward way in which satisfaction and therefore positive brand associations can be achieved. The brand name may also have come to represent status and prestige (as do Mercedes for automobiles or Piaget for watches), thus providing a positive association in a less tangible fashion. Just such a prestige brand image for the Visa *Gold* card is being pursued with the advertising in Illustration 8-3.

A firm's *logo* is related to branding in that it is a visual symbol for a brand. Logos appear on the brand package, in advertising, on corporate stationery, and on business cards. The logo can be a symbolic reminder for consumers of the brand name. Because of its ability to call to mind the brand name, the logo plays an important role in branding.

Branding is considered critically important to a firm's overall product strategy because consumers need to relate their consumption experiences to some tangible, visible markings. A brand name or symbol (along with the logo) provides a visible, tangible representation for consumers of their experience with a particular product from a particular manufacturer. Whether the experience was satisfying or dissatisfying, the consumer has an easily identifiable piece of

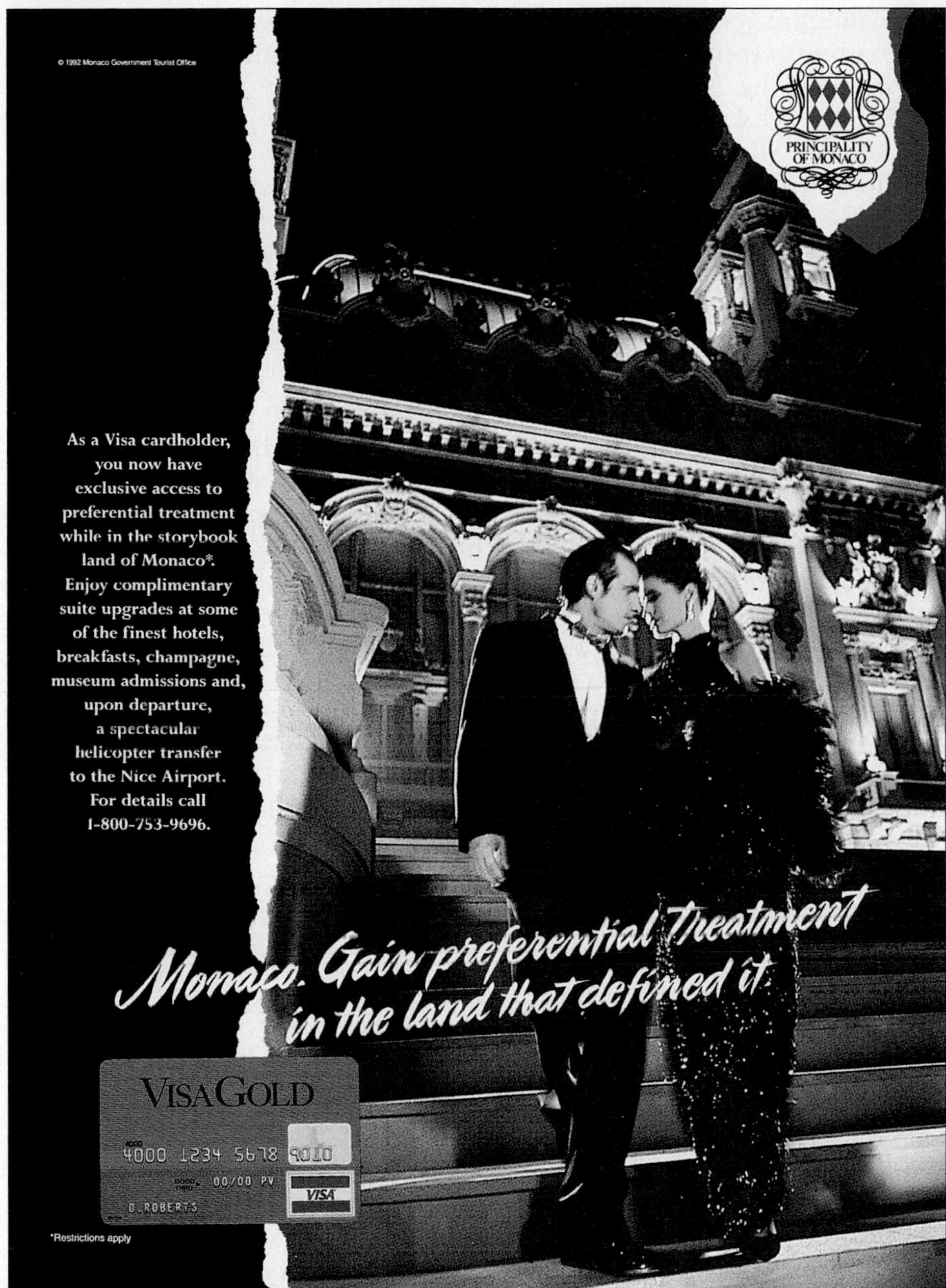

© 1992 Monaco Government Tourist Office
PRINCIPALITY OF MONACO
As a Visa cardholder, you now have exclusive access to preferential treatment while in the storybook land of Monaco*. Enjoy complimentary suite upgrades at some of the finest hotels, breakfasts, champagne, museum admissions and, upon departure, a spectacular helicopter transfer to the Nice Airport. For details call 1-800-753-9696.
Monaco. Gain preferential Treatment in the land that defined it.
VISA GOLD
4000 1234 5678 9010
00/00 PV
D.ROBERTS
VISA
*Restrictions apply

ILLUSTRATION 8-3
"Imagery" advertising can stimulate a positive association with a brand.

information upon which to rely during the next buying decision process. If there were no name or symbol with which to associate the experience of, for instance, drinking a soft drink, the consumer would find it difficult to repeat or to avoid the experience. Consider the unusual (or, perhaps, silly) circumstance of encountering a soft drink vending machine where none of the buttons are labeled with brand names. You would have no basis, in the absence of the visible markings, to choose the item you personally find most satisfying. Because manufacturers produce different products for different consumer tastes and preferences, brand names and symbols allow consumers to identify differences between those products and to choose those they find most appealing and satisfying.

The market share of leading brands in various product categories is listed in Table 8-1. No doubt, many of those listed are products you use. Maybe your favorite brand is even listed. Notice that in all the product categories listed except for cereals the top two brands dominate the market: 37 percent in automobiles, 54 percent in toothpastes, 47 percent in dog foods, 54 percent in athletic shoes.

STRATEGIC BENEFITS OF BRANDING TO MANUFACTURERS

Branding, as we have discussed, has overall value in the market because it allows for a shorthand communication between manufacturers and consumers. Individual consumers are able to identify and distinguish the offering of one seller from another with brand names and symbols. Effective branding, however, accrues several very specific strategic market benefits to manufacturers.

Brand Equity

Because of the consumer recognition brands create, one of the strategic **benefits of branding to manufacturers** is referred to as brand equity. **Brand equity** is the market recognition and monetary value a brand name itself acquires when the name creates a positive and recognizable identity in the market. When R. J. Reynolds purchased Nabisco, the purchase price of over $20 billion was far greater than the true asset value of the firm. The additional value was the equity embodied in brand names like *Shredded Wheat, Honey Maid Honey Graham Crackers,* and *Ritz Crackers.* Brand equity is gained through years of careful development of brand image and identity. As a product line is extended using the same brand name, the equity will grow as well. Finally, the monetary value of the equity of any particular brand is greater if the items carrying the brand name can be licensed. The equity of professional sports team "brands" is high because the items carrying, for example, the Chicago Bulls' or the Oakland Raiders' logos can be licensed for sale on a variety of items from coffee mugs to easy chairs.

Greater Product Differentiation

As one of the cornerstones of competitive market strategy, every opportunity to enhance product differentiation must be seized. Branding is integral to the product differentiation process. The only way a firm can distinguish its market offering from competitors is to create a unique and valuable product. Once that valuable product is created, however, consumers must have a way to identify it within the myriad of products available. Branding is the method through which a firm can provide that needed identity for consumers and thus achieve the product differentiation effect. This is why firms with established brand names like *Q-Tip, Xerox, Jell-O,* and *Kleenex* struggle against their brand names becoming a generic representation of an entire product class. If "Q-tip" starts to be used by consumers as a designation for *any* cotton swab on the market,

TABLE 8-1
Leading Brands in Various Product Categories for 1992

Product Category	Leading Brands	U.S. Market Share (percentage)
Automobiles	Ford	20.3%
	Chevrolet & Geo	16.7
	Toyota	7.2
	Dodge/Chrysler	6.5
	Honda	5.0
	Total Market	**12.8 million units**
Cereals	Cheerios	4.5%
	Kellogg's Frosted Flakes	4.0
	Honey Nut Cheerios	3.2
	Rice Krispies	3.0
	Kellogg's Corn Flakes	2.9
	Total Market	**$7.5 billion**
Toothpastes	Crest	32.4%
	Colgate	21.6
	Arm & Hammer	9.4
	Aqua Fresh	8.5
	Close-Up	5.3
	Private label	1.6
	Total Market	**$1.4 billion**
Laundry detergent	Tide	29.7%
	Wisk	9.4
	Cheer	7.5
	Surf	6.3
	All	4.5
	Private label	3.1
	Total Market	**$4.5 billion**
Dog food	Purina	29.0%
	Ken-L Ration	18.0
	Kal Kan	13.3
	Alpo	8.6
	Friskies	7.1
	Total Market	**$2.9 billion**
Soft drinks	Coca-Cola Classic	20.0%
	Pepsi	18.0
	Diet Coke	9.1
	Diet Pepsi	6.1
	Dr. Pepper	5.9
	Total Market	**$47.4 billion**
Athletic shoes	Nike	30.1%
	Reebok	24.4
	Keds	6.1
	L.A. Gear	5.2
	ASICS	3.7
	Total Market	**$12.0 billion (approx)**

Source: Data cited from various industry statistics and trade association in *Advertising Age* (September 29, 1993): 4, 6, 12, 17, 24, 30.

then a consumer who asks for "Q-tips" in a drugstore doesn't really mean the *Q-Tip* brand of cotton swab. What's more, if such common usage were to occur, the shopkeeper wouldn't think the shopper really wanted *Q-Tip* brand, either. In such a case, *Q-Tip* has lost all its meaning and identity to consumers as a representation of a particular *brand* of cotton swab with unique, identifiable qualities. The ultimate threat of such an evolution in the marketplace is that if a brand name ever does achieve such generic representation in the minds of consumers (and shopkeepers), the firm can lose its legal rights to the name as well. This actually happened to "formica" which used to be a registered trade name and now simply represents a type of construction material. When such a legal designation is made, the firm has lost the time, money, and effort that went into developing all the positive associations that can be identified with and by the brand name. Firms threatened with their names becoming generic representations many times engage in advertising campaigns that point out that the brand name represents a unique product produced by a particular firm. Both *Jell-O* and *Xerox* have conducted such campaigns. The *Xerox* campaign was memorable for the oft-repeated phrase during the ad, "It's just as good as a Xerox."

More Precise Market Segmentation

Branding can provide strategic value to firms by making the market segmentation process more precise. Especially in situations where a firm has several products in a single product category, such as toothpaste, soft drinks, or laundry detergents, brand names allow the firm to effectively segment the market by attaching a different brand name to each version of the product directed to a different segment. This effect is closely related, of course, to product differentiation. The difference between the two effects is that branding for product differentiation is primarily designed to distinguish a firm's brand from competitors'. In the case of the market segmentation effect, the attempt is to distinguish brands *within* a firm's product line to attract and serve several different segments.

Enhanced New Product Introduction

New product introduction is also enhanced by strong marketplace recognition of a brand name. By satisfying customers with products carrying the General Electric brand name, GE can rely on the goodwill (closely related to brand equity) created by the name to ease the process of introducing new products. The new product is aided by the existing image and reputation created by branding.

Several firms have successfully marketed new products by "hitchhiking" on existing brand names on products marketed by the firm. *Mr. Coffee* coffee was a logical product line extension for the coffee maker firm. Due to the success and recognition of the *Mr. Coffee* name not a single retailer refused to carry the new coffee brand when it was introduced. Procter & Gamble's highly successful *Ivory Dishwashing Liquid* allowed P & G to capture 8 percent of the profitable shampoo and conditioner market in less than a year by borrowing the name and introducing *Ivory Shampoo and Conditioner.*[10]

Pricing Flexibility

The successful establishment of a brand name can result in a pricing advantage to a firm. As consumers are satisfied with a particular brand, they are also less likely to be sensitive to price changes. A firm may be able, therefore, to raise the price on a successful brand without suffering a commensurate decrease in demand. This effect of branding is referred to as decreasing the "elasticity" (sensitivity) of demand to price changes. It is also an element in the phenomenon of *brand loyalty*, which will be discussed shortly.

More Efficient Promotion

Branding can greatly increase the efficiency of communications efforts. As consumers begin to relate the unique features and values of a product to a specific brand name, it is easier and less costly for a firm to use various forms of promotion. Once a brand name is established and recognized, a firm is able to communicate information to consumers simply by displaying the brand name or symbol. Mere exposure to the names BMW, Whirlpool, Crest, and McDonalds brings an image and meaning to the mind of consumers.

Broader Distribution

A well-established, successful brand will prompt wholesalers and retailers to carry and stock the item. When consumers demand a brand at the store level, retailers are compelled to keep the item in stock to satisfy their customers. Further, successful brands will generally command more retail shelf space thereby aiding in-store identification of the brand within the clutter of all the other brands displayed.

Once retailers stock the brand because of consumer demand, then wholesalers are also required to carry the item to serve the demands of retailers. The distribution effect of branding, in general, is that it gives the manufacturer greater control over the channel of distribution. In the absence of strong brand demand, retailers and wholesalers would have little motivation to carry the item and the manufacturer would have to try to put forth much greater effort to get the brand through the channel. With strong brand identity and preference among consumers, retailers find it in their best interest to stock the brand thus relieving the manufacturer of the need to push the item.

Brand Loyalty

The strategic value of achieving brand loyalty among consumers cannot be overstated. Brand loyal customers provide a firm with steady and predictable levels of revenue. They are more prone to try and then become brand loyal to new products introduced by the firm. They are a source of positive word-of-mouth advertising about the brand and are likely to accept price increases with little complaint. Promotion aimed at brand loyal customers can be done inexpensively and retailers want to carry brands that please their customers. In general, brand loyalty represents the ultimate achievement on the part of a firm.

The point has been raised before that it costs about five times more to attract a new customer than to retain an old one. In a related sense, one analyst estimates that the probability of converting a non-user to your brand is about 3 in 1000![11] These are not the kind of odds that make for successful marketing programs. Brand loyalty means that the majority of a consumer's purchases in a product category over a year are of one brand. It is unrealistic to expect that consumers would be 100 percent brand loyal. In the face of competitive strategies like new product introductions and couponing, few consumers can resist the allure of something new or less expensive. Some estimates of levels of brand loyalty in different product categories are provided in Figure 8-2. Even at the lower end of brand loyalty, 23 percent brand loyal customers for garbage bags is considered quite good. Also illustrated in Figure 8-2, in many product categories where consumers might be expected to display relative indifference, there is actually fairly high brand loyalty. Apparently the euphemism "an aspirin is just an aspirin" doesn't really hold in the marketplace as headache remedies show a 56 percent brand loyalty rate.

Legal Protection

Finally, two aspects of the branding process can provide marketers with legal protection for their brands. A *brand mark* includes the visual and symbolic parts of a brand that have come to represent to consumers the offering of a particular manufacturer. Distinctive coloring, lettering, symbols, or designs as well as a firm's logo can all be part of a distinctive brand mark. The Chevrolet brand symbol and the script lettering used in the Coca-Cola brand mark are examples. A *trademark* provides legal protection for a seller to exclusively use a brand name or brand mark. Having legal protection for brand names and brand marks is valuable because it protects the goodwill marketers have earned with their brands and gives consumers a way to seek out the products of particular marketers without confusion.

REASONS NOT TO BRAND

In the face of all the values of branding just presented, why would any firm choose to produce but *not* brand an item? There are many **reasons not to brand**—many manufacturers are content to simply produce items and allow other firms to brand and market them. It is also true that many wholesalers, distributors, and retailers never develop their own brand name items even though the practice is relatively common among members of the distribution trade. There are several good reasons why manufacturing and trade organiza-

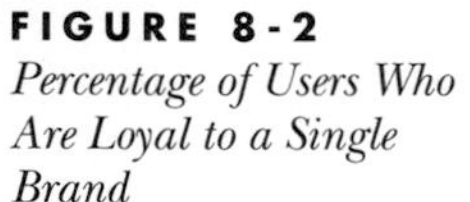

FIGURE 8-2
Percentage of Users Who Are Loyal to a Single Brand

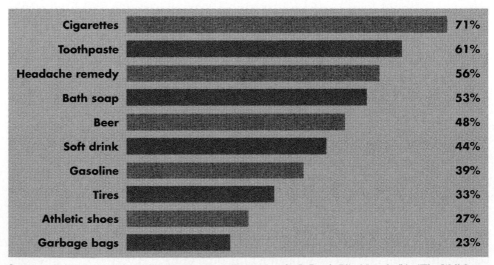

Source: Adapted from data cited in Ronald Alsop, "Brand Loyalty Is Rarely Blind Loyalty," in "The Wall Street Journal Centennial Survey," *The Wall Street Journal*, October 19, 1989, B1.

tions, despite the many values of branding, avoid getting involved in branding and then marketing their own brands.

First, the firm marketing a brand is responsible to the consumer for the maintenance of quality of each item sold. As consumers begin to rely on a brand for certain satisfactions, it is the responsibility of the branding organization, whether it is the firm that manufactures the item or not, to maintain quality.

Second, the firm that brands the item is responsible for stimulating demand for that item. This requires planning and investing in promotional activities to keep the brand viable in the marketplace. The branding firm must also maintain personnel capable of making decisions regarding distribution, pricing, packaging, and all the other aspects associated with putting together a sound marketing plan for the brand. If L.L. Bean, the outdoor outfitters, experiences delays in getting merchandise from firms with which they have contracted for manufacturing, then it is L.L. Bean, the branding agent, that has to deal with customer complaints. These factors create responsibilities to consumers and overhead costs that many manufacturing firms simply cannot or will not accept.

Finally, any liability stemming from injury by virtue of use of the product falls primarily with the branding organization. In general, many firms, both manufacturers and resellers in the trade channel, do not want to assume the primary liability for an item.

VALUES OF BRANDING TO SOCIETY

There is some controversy over whether branding products is a help or a hinderance to consumers in a society. The following are some of the **values of branding to society**:

- Branding makes shopping more efficient because it allows for rapid comparison between products.
- Branding increases competition because firms attempt to develop new brands to remain competitive.
- Product quality is higher because firms are directly responsible for the items they brand.
- Consumers are given greater variety and choice in the marketplace because branding allows firms to distinguish products from one another.

Overall, proponents of branding suggest that in a free enterprise system, branding is a way for competitors to attract and retain customers. Further, consumers are better off in the presence of branding because it contributes to greater efficiency in the product acquisition process.

Critics of branding, however, point out the ill effects of the process:

- Branding leads to insignificant and trivial product differences.
- Branding places more emphasis on status and class distinctions.
- Due to the need to promote the differences between brands, branding increases the cost of products to consumers.
- Developing new and different packaging for each brand is costly and wasteful.

Essentially, critics are pointing out that branding contributes to environmental problems and promotes a materialistic orientation within a society.

BRANDING STRATEGIES

The most basic breakdown of brands is the distinction between manufacturer brands and private-label brands. **Manufacturer brands** are brands developed and marketed by firms that actually produce the items. These are the big national and multinational brands that are most familiar to us: Coca-Cola, Hitachi, IBM, Del Monte, and Colgate for example. **Private-label brands** are brands marketed by firms that contract out the manufacturing of the item. These are the types of brands that were highlighted in the chapter introduction. There are two types of private-label brands. One type are the branded items marketed by wholesalers, distributors, and retailers. Examples are *IGA* brands in grocery products and The Gap's private-label clothes. The other type are broadly distributed private-label brands marketed by firms that contract out the production of the items. An example in this category is the *President's Choice* line of food items marketed by the Canadian firm Loblaw Cos., which now has over 500 different items and $750 million in total sales. Within each class of brands, there are basic strategies to be considered.

The strategic decisions facing manufacturers and private-label marketers of branded items have to do with using either a family branding, separate branding, brand extension, or co-branding strategy. A **family branding** strategy means that all brands produced by the firm will carry the manufacturer's name. Campbell, Del Monte, Heinz, and BMW all use the family branding policy. A variation on the basic family branding strategy is to use the family brand name combined with a separate brand name for each different item in a line such as *Kellogg's Corn Flakes* and *Miller Lite.* The **separate branding** strategy simply means that every product in the manufacturer's line carries its own exclusive brand name. General Motors has *Chevrolet, Geo, Cadillac,* and other names as separate brands. Procter & Gamble follows the same strategy with 14 separate brands of laundry detergent.

The strategic choice between family or separate branding is dependent upon several factors. A separate branding strategy is most appropriate when there are clear price and quality differences between items. In this way, the firm can both avoid confusion between brands and also target different segments with different brands. Separate branding can also be important to distribution strategy when a firm has a proliferation of brands in a single product category. For instance, the firm that brands five different hair shampoos can, with a separate branding strategy, achieve dominance of shelf space at the retail level. But a separate branding strategy requires greater financial resources in that each brand must have its own unique promotional campaign and marketing program. Also, the branding strategy that results in excessive proliferation of brands can target segments that are too narrow to be profitable.

Family branding is most effective when all the products in the company line are of similar quality and similar price relative to competitive offerings in the same product class. The family brand approach provides an umbrella for marketing the entire product line. A good example of a successful and consistent line of family branded items is the Del Monte food products line. One argument for family branding is that the marketing process is more efficient. Advertising for one item in the line constitutes promotion for all the items in the line. Similarly, new product introductions are aided more by a family branding strategy than by a separate branding strategy.

The third manufacturer branding strategy is referred to as *brand extension* (also known as *flanker branding*). **Brand extension** relies on the use of an established brand name in one product category to introduce a new brand in a different product category—it exemplifies the "equity" embodied in a good brand name. Examples cited earlier in the chapter are *Mr. Coffee* coffee and *Ivory Shampoo and Conditioner.* Other brand extensions recently introduced to the market are *Minute Maid Orange Soda, Easy-Off Window Cleaner, Levi* shoes, and *Mars Ice Cream Bars.* Compared to the time, expense, and risk associated with developing a new brand name, these extended brands are relatively inexpensive and safe bets. Firms are counting on the goodwill carryover effect when brand extension is used. Brand extension is not a guarantee of successful line extension, however. Research evidence suggests that if consumers perceive the extension to be too far from the original brand, such as McDonald's photo processing, consumers will develop a negative attitude toward the extension.[12]

A relatively new strategic approach to brand is called *co-branding* (also referred to as *double branding*). **Co-branding** is when different companies combine separate brand names on the same product. An example is *Betty Crocker Supreme M & M's Cookie Bars. Betty Crocker* is a General Mills brand name and *M & M's* is a Mars Candy brand name. Other co-branded products are listed in Table 8-2. The reasoning behind the co-branding strategy is simple. If a good, well-managed brand name can attract and retain the loyalty of consumers, then two good, well-managed brand names will amplify the effect. An additional effect claimed for the food products area is that co-branding "helps consumers differentiate between what otherwise may seem to be commodity products."[13] Co-branding has increased dramatically in recent years as noncompeting marketers look for market advantage using this branding strategy. But co-branding has two distinct risks. If the new combined brand fails, then each of the separate brand names may be damaged. The other risk is

TABLE 8-2
Co-branded Products: Combining Two Brand Names from Separate Companies

Co-branded Product	Companies
Pop-Tarts with Smuckers Fruit Filling	Kellogg and Smuckers
Fat-Free Cranberry Newtons with Ocean Spray Cranberries	RJR Nabisco and Ocean Spray
Betty Crocker Sunkist Lemon Bars	General Mills and Sunkist Growers
Pillsbury's Chocolate Deluxe Brownies with Nestlé Syrup	Pillsbury and Nestlé
GM Visa Credit Card	General Motors and Visa

over-exposure for a brand name, which can potentially confuse the image of the brand in the minds of consumers.

BRANDING BUSINESS PRODUCTS

Up to this point, the discussion of branding issues has focused on household consumer goods. Business manufacturers can realize the same values from branding as household consumer goods manufacturers. This is true whether the business product is an inexpensive, frequently purchased operating supply or a specially engineered installation. Business sellers can establish a better competitive position and greater buyer loyalty by **branding business products** and developing a strong brand image.

IBM, Xerox, AT&T, 3M, and GE benefit from the widespread recognition of their corporate names. Buyers have come to perceive a difference in products manufactured by these giants in computer products, office equipment, communications services, office products, and aircraft engines. The most successful business branding effort in history was initiated by Intel in 1990. Intel has successfully branded its microprocessors for PCs by attaching the 286, 386, 486, and Pentium brand name designations to its microprocessor. Now, consumers search machines for the "Intel Inside" logo when evaluating PCs.

All of the values of branding are achievable in the business market setting. The focus of the branding process, however, is somewhat different than for consumer goods brands. Rather than being image oriented as the brand emphasis often is in the consumer market, business brands have to focus on the business buyer choice criteria listed in Chapter 6. Factors such as superior technical performance, certainty of supply, dependability in meeting delivery schedules, and technical assistance may be the values of the brand that attract and retain customers.

Branding is not just a phenomenon in the household consumer market. Astute business marketers recognize that product differentiation, product positioning, market segmentation, and other aspects of the marketing effort are enhanced by the establishment of strong brand-name recognition in the market.

SELECTING A BRAND NAME

Choosing a brand name is a blend of art, science, and luck. One study identifies that more and more firms are adopting an orderly, research-based approach to selecting brand names rather than relying solely on judgment or intuition.[14] The actual brand name chosen can be critical to the success of a product because it can affect consumers' image of the brand. It can also serve as a memory-aid to consumers in the purchase decision-making process. Two important phases in the brand name selection process are generating a list of potential brand names and then evaluating the names generated.

Generating Potential Brand Names

The process for generating brand names is similar to the process for generating new product ideas. Consumers are an obvious source of brand name ideas

Business products benefit from branding as much as consumer products.

because the ultimate purpose of a brand name is to effectively communicate to a group of consumers. Using consumers as a source of brand name ideas requires the use of interviews or focus groups with consumers who represent the segment to which the product will be marketed. Free association or sentence completion tasks can be used to obtain suggestions. The problem with this approach is that it is time consuming and costly. Also, no single name may emerge from the many that consumers suggest. At some point in the process of name generation, however, consumers should always be used as a source of evaluation.

Experts can also be used in the name generation process. Personnel in the organization who were involved in the product development process are experts who may have ideas regarding a name—the *Z28 Camaro* was actually the corporate code name for the vehicle during its development at Chevrolet.

Or a firm can turn to consulting firms who are experts in naming brands. Name consultants Lippincott & Margulies, Inc., generate an average of 500 potential names for every brand name chosen.[15]

Evaluating Potential Brand Names

Regardless of how potential names are generated, it is necessary to establish criteria upon which to base the final choice. Since the intended effect of a brand name is to be memorable and attract consumer attention, a good brand name should:

1. *Be easy to pronounce and spell.* Short, easily identifiable brand names help the consumer recall and recognize the product. Names like *Bold, Brim, Geo,* and *Dawn* are examples.
2. *Specify product use or benefit.* If a brand name can relate to the product's primary use, it will be more memorable and communicate valuable information to the buyer. Names like *Easy-Off, Gleem,* and *Sof-Scrub* all suggest the products use and uniqueness.
3. *Suggest an image.* A brand name will be more meaningful to consumers if it enhances the image of the firm or the product. *Craftsman* tools and *Die Hard* batteries are names that fulfill an image objective.
4. *Clearly distinguish the brand name from competition.* A brand name should be different enough from competition that consumers can easily recognize it as being associated with a single source. Also, a distinctive brand name can avoid legal problems. *Xerox* and *Coca-Cola* are distinctive in highly competitive markets.
5. *Be timely and adaptable.* A good brand name will avoid the pitfall of being bound to a unique period of time or single application. It should also be adaptable to a variety of packaging and advertising applications. Apple Computer discovered that its *Apple* brand name was well suited to the primary and secondary school market but not well received by the business market.

Only a few brand names will be so well conceived that they fit every criterion. *Minute Rice* and *Liquid Plumr* are brand names that would seem to fit all the criteria. There are numerous examples, though, of successful brand names that don't seem to meet any of the criteria, such as *Exxon, Xerox,* and *Kodak.* The ultimate test of whether a brand name is good is if it serves to help both the buyer and the seller in the marketplace.

GENERIC BRANDS

The concept of **generic** or *no-name* products originated in France in the 1970s. The attractiveness of generics is their lower price. Such products come in plain-looking black and white packages. They are marketed with the claim that they offer similar quality to national brands at lower cost due to simple packaging and the elimination of advertising expense. Some evidence suggests that in the early days of generics in the United States, the generics were making inroads in the market share of national brands in the grocery products area.[16] By 1980, generics were being carried by 25 percent of all grocery stores and the market shares of both national brands and intermediary brands had decreased noticeably. However, more recent studies suggest that generics are losing their market appeal. Sales of generic grocery products have slid from 16.8 percent in 1982 to only 12.9 percent in 1987.[17] This slide will likely continue as the private-label brands discussed earlier offer the values of branding but at lower cost as well. Stores that once allocated full aisles to generics now relegate the products to a small section of the store.

The appeal of generics is actually restricted to price-conscious consumers who value a "deal." This group has traditionally represented a relatively small and well-defined type of consumer. This fact coupled with the values of branding to consumers would have predicted a modest market share for the generics from the outset. However, under ever-changing economic conditions and the emergence of the private-label brands, the future of generics is still unknown.

PACKAGING

In the words of one consultant, "packaging is the last five seconds of marketing."[18] While the basic purpose of packaging seems fairly obvious, it can also be a highly potent product strategy. When the candy company Just Born, Inc., changed its old-fashioned looking black and white packages to colorful new packaging featuring animated grapes and cherries, sales soared 25 percent in one year. A company marketing official said, "Kids say we went from dull to definitely awesome without a single product or advertising change."[19] Additionally, the Point-of-Purchase Advertising Institute claims that more than 80 percent of supermarket purchases now result from in-store decisions, up from 65 percent a decade ago.[20] This again highlights the need for effective packaging.

In the simplest terms, **packaging** involves decisions regarding the container or wrapping for a product. The package for a brand adds another strategic dimension and can serve an important role in differentiation. It can also affect consumer behavior relating to brand evaluations and the level of use. The package provides strategic benefits to manufacturers and values to resellers and consumers.

STRATEGIC BENEFITS OF PACKAGING TO THE MANUFACTURER

Packaging provides several strategic benefits to the manufacturer. First, packaging has an effect on promotional strategy. The package carries the brand name and communicates the name to a consumer. In the myriad of products displayed at the retail level, a well-designed package can attract a buyer's attention and induce the shopper to more carefully examine the product. Several firms attribute renewed success of their brands to package design changes. Kraft Dairy Group believes that significant package changes helped its *Breyer's Ice Cream* brand make in-roads in markets west of the Mississippi. A package consulting firm came up with a black background package, which was a radically different look for an ice cream product. The westward expansion was a huge success and Kraft believes that the prominence of the new package on the shelf was a major contributing factor.

A second value to manufacturers is the role packaging plays in differentiation. The successful market entry of *L'eggs* panty hose was aided by a unique package that required special in-store display. The package distinguished *L'eggs* from competitive brands. Aside from mere appearance, a package that provides added convenience to consumers can be a feature that gives consumers reason to choose one brand over another. Procter & Gamble's Neat Squeeze package dispenser for *Crest Toothpaste* now accounts for 5 percent of all toothpaste sales and had a sales increase of 55 percent in a single year.[21]

Third, packaging can be used strategically to bring about consumption effects. By providing packages of different sizes, firms are better able to serve the needs of different segments. "Family size" packages serve the needs of households with many members. "Individual serving" packages serve the needs of the growing number of single-person households. Multiple packaging, such as six or twelve packs, reduces the number of out-of-stock conditions experienced by consumers and tends to increase consumption.

An additional value of packaging has to do with creating a perception of value for the product with the package. The formidable packaging surrounding computer software is made more substantial simply to add tangibility to an intangible product. Similarly, when consumers are buying image, the package must reflect the appropriate image. *Perrier,* one of the most expensive bottled waters on the market, has an aesthetically pleasing bottle compared to the rigid plastic packages of it competitors. Perfume manufacturers often have greater packaging costs than product costs to ensure that the product projects the desired image.

Finally, packaging serves the basic purpose of protection for the product, thus reducing the firm's liability for damaged goods. The well-designed package can also spare the firm the expense and customer dissatisfaction that comes from damaged or spoiled products.

VALUES OF PACKAGING TO THE RESELLER

The distribution process is considerably aided by a well-designed package. Distributors and retailers are required to perform several functions that are facilitated by easy-to-store, easy-to-handle, and easy-to-display packages. Packages that are not designed for easy storage and handling result in increased expenses for resellers. Further, a package that does not adequately protect the product creates losses for members in the channel of distribution. Resellers are more prone to carry a firm's brand if its package serves their needs for handling, display, and protection.

VALUES OF PACKAGING TO THE CONSUMER

Several aspects of the package benefit the consumer. One of the primary benefits is convenience. Products that have pump applicators, pour spouts, and are easy to open are all more convenient for consumers and, therefore, more satisfying. Related to convenience is economy. Resealable and no-spill packages prevent waste. Reusable packages are also appealing.

An additional value a package can provide is safety. A child-proof cap or unbreakable container decrease the hazard of having certain products in the home. Tamper-proof packages give consumers a sense of security especially when using over-the-counter drug products. Finally, product packaging can increase the aesthetic appearance of products. Facial tissues and room deodorizers come in decorative packages for added attractiveness when the product is on display in the home.

The environmental impact of packages and package design will be covered in detail in Chapter 19 when social, ethical, and environmental issues are discussed. Solid-waste disposal, pollution created during package manufacturing, and resource waste are all environmental issues related to packaging. More firms and even entire industries are developing strategies to cope with the waste and pollution created by excessive and nonfunctional packaging.

LABELING

Closely related to both branding and packaging is **labeling.** The label is the wrapping on the product container that carries the brand name and important product use information. The Federal Fair Packaging and Labeling Act (1966) contains several requirements for manufacturers' compliance regarding labeling information for products sold in the United States. One of the more commonly recognized regulations in this act requires that labels on food packages must list all the ingredients in descending order of weight or volume. More recently, the Nutrition Labeling and Education Act (1990) now requires uniformity in the nutrition labeling of food products and establishes strict rules for health claims.

The information contained on labels can also serve some important strategic purposes. The label can contain very specific information regarding instructions for using the product. Firms have discovered that consumer dissatisfaction is often the result of improper product use. If a product is designed to function through a particular, precise application, the firm must ensure through label instructions that the consumer is made aware of use procedures. Many firms have added toll-free 800 numbers to help concerned or confused consumers with product use. Clairol, the cosmetics marketer, estimates customer inquiries regarding product use handled through their 800 number cost 50 percent less than inquiries handled by mail and that customer satisfaction is greatly enhanced by an immediate response.[22]

The label also provides a manufacturer with a method of communicating warranties. If the product is backed by a warranty, then the label can explain its terms and conditions. Use hazards and warnings are also contained on the label. Products that are flammable or otherwise hazardous to user under certain conditions have warnings on the label. Over-the-counter medicines, for example, have historically stated that use is not suggested by certain individuals or in combination with other medicines.

Labels may be acquiring a new level of importance in the overall scheme of product strategies. As consumers are becoming more health and value conscious, they are scrutinizing product labels more. They are looking at nutritional information and scrutinizing labels for chemical additives. This consumer trend will motivate manufacturers to make label information more precise and readable as consumers adopt the label as a source of information in the choice process.

Product Strategies: A Global Perspective

The managerial issues discussed earlier in the chapter for developing product line and mix strategies remain fundamentally the same for global decision making. However, the level of complexity in dealing with these issues rises dramatically as a function of the number and diversity of countries and markets. Further, product decisions in global markets take on significant strategic importance since the ability to offer products on a competitive basis globally often involves broader-based decisions about business activities. Decisions relating to mergers and acquisitions, joint ventures, licensing agreements, or other forms of cooperative alliances are more prevalent in the global context and affect product decisions relating to (1) acquiring or developing new products and technology, (2) gaining market access with an established partner, or (3) acquiring a well-known brand name. Figure 8-3 identifies the strategic management issues and product line and branding issues that underlie the complex tasks of developing and managing a truly global product line.

Keep in mind that the ability to create, develop, and service the demand for products on a global basis is a tremendous undertaking. Activities necessary to carry out these tasks include many negotiations and ultimately securing the cooperation of resellers, wholesalers, sales agents, warehousers, transportation companies, creditors, and the media in each region or country where the product is marketed. Many firms are simply too small to directly manage and sell their own product lines in each country where they do business. As an example, Richard D. Irwin, Inc., the textbook publisher who specializes in business and economics texts, has a well-established niche in the U.S. market and also operates a Canadian subsidiary. Similar market conditions between these two countries means that Irwin can generate sufficient revenues to support a Canadian sales force and even localize some of the texts for the larger markets. However, Irwin's relatively narrow product line (primarily books sold in business schools) limits sales internationally, where markets are more diverse than between the United States and Canada. In these markets, revenues can't support an in-house sales force or large-scale subsidiary operation. So the company uses independent sales representatives and book distributors in each foreign market outside the home markets of the United States and Canada.

No single product line can reasonably be expected to play the lead role in all markets where a firm does business. As examples, Matsushita Electric and JVC manufacture and market hundreds of different consumer electronic products under their own brand names in Japan and in a number of countries

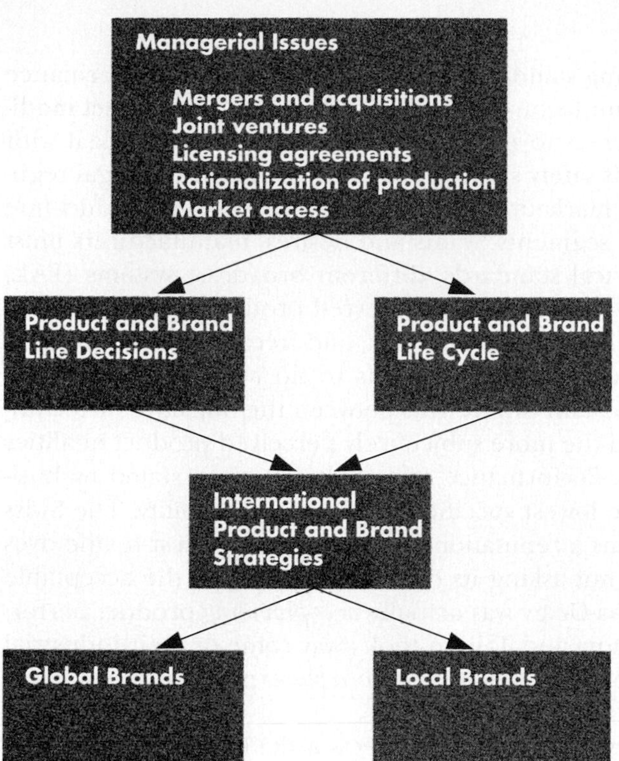

FIGURE 8-3
Managerial Issues in Global Product Strategies

around the world. Yet, in Europe, these same firms choose to develop new markets using a low-cost, low-risk strategy of entering into OEM (Original Equipment Manufacturer) agreements with Saba, Telefunken, Blaupunkt, and Thorn—all European firms with established names and distribution systems.

These examples point out that when product strategies are considered in the global context, a variety of factors not particularly significant in the domestic market become driving forces in international product strategy decisions. We will focus our discussion of global product strategy on issues related to product modification, level of local market development, and the product life cycle as they apply to global markets.

PRODUCT STRATEGY ISSUES

Underlying the decision to introduce products into any market is the basic premise that the good or service offered will satisfy the wants and needs of the consumers in that market. While Chapters 3, 4, and 5 discussed in detail the management processes of gathering information for assessing and analyzing the potential for consumer and business markets, the focus here is on the issue of how to introduce products in promising global markets. Introducing products into global markets requires:

1. Product modification
2. Assessing the level of local market development
3. Application of the product life cycle concept

Product Modification

Tariff regulations and differing standards for manufacturing and performance create situations wherein manufacturers need to make required **product modifications** in order to gain access to markets. These regulations can deal with such diverse product issues as safety standards, quality standards, or legal regulations. Consider the case of marketing VCRs globally. Apart from product-line decisions based on different segments' wants and desires, manufacturers must comply with differing electrical standards, different broadcast systems (PAL, Mescam, Secam, and NTSC), *and* different preferred product features such as timed recording, hi-fi stereo record and playback, and freeze-frame features.

Another factor in product modification has to do with level of performance. There are often important differences between the objective or technical qualities of a product and the more subjectively perceived product qualities that are held by consumers. Performance standards are often stated by business buyers in terms of some lowest specified level for acceptability. The Swiss chemical giant Ciba-Geigy has a reputation for making the purest textile dyes in its industry. However, by not asking its customers to specify the acceptable level of product needed, Ciba-Geigy was actually *over-providing* product performance. Competitors from India and Taiwan took away some of their industrial accounts by offering modified dyes of lower but *acceptable* purity at much lower prices.[23]

Making optional product modifications reflects a deliberate move on the part of a producer to build stable foreign markets by aligning the product with local market needs. While these moves are optional in the legal sense, they are often required in order to effectively compete in the market. For example, American textbook publishers often sell "International Student Editions" of textbooks in price sensitive European markets. Student committees often suggest a price ceiling for textbooks used in courses in many Scandinavian and Dutch universities, where English is commonly read at the university level. While these suggestions are not legally binding, they do strongly influence the final selection. By publishing in paperback, extending the print run beyond domestic requirements, and using a variable-cost approach to accounting, American publishers can compete very effectively on price with local books that often have smaller print runs due to the production constraints imposed by local language markets. In other market situations, price is not the issue, but quality is. Golden Axis, a Thai company that makes casual shirts, has discovered that buyers for Japanese retail chains do not just look to see if seams are straight. They count the number of stitches per centimeter! Golden Axis has set up two separate factories to make the same type of shirts. One supplies Europe and America, the other exclusively supplies Japan.[24]

Decisions to make product modifications will depend on a number of factors. As a general rule, nondurable consumer goods that appeal to individual tastes, habits, and customs are more likely to require modification. This is less often the case for business products that have common functional characteristics across markets. Being able to sell products without modification offers many advantages: offering the same product across borders eliminates duplication of costs for such activities as research and development, product design, setting up differing production runs, and separate packaging. Apart from costs, having a standard offering increases marketing efficiency. Firms can deal with customers in a consistent fashion with respect to product style, brand name, and recognizable packages and can establish a common image for the brand worldwide. Further, the sales force does not have to be trained on different standards for different markets. However, if product acceptance, market growth, and profitability can only be attained through modifications such as alterations in design, features, styling, or packaging, then these options must be carefully considered. Ultimately, the decision to modify products can be best analyzed by trying to quantify the cost/benefit aspects of the decision: if the benefit of modification exceeds the costs of doing so, then product modification, coupled with consistent changes in the other elements of the marketing mix is a reasonable course of action.[25]

Assessing the Level of Local Market Development

In Caracas, Venezuela, clerks are paid to hold phones to their ears for hours, waiting for a dial tone. Local phone service is so unreliable that business executives often route crosstown calls via the United States, using AT&T's international network. Estimates of global market growth from AT&T are that during the next decade, more money will be spent on phone gear worldwide than has been spent since the invention of the telephone in 1876. Sales should nearly double to about $192 billion by the year 2000, from $101.6 billion in 1991.[26] U.S. phone companies see tremendous growth opportunities in Latin America and eastern Europe for local switching networks, a product market where the technology is standardized and the growth opportunity in the U.S. market is limited. There are also new growth markets for cutting edge technologies that make use of hypermodern, long-distance switching stations. The government of the new Republic of Ukraine, a country the size of France and with a population of 52 million, has made the commitment "to move straight into the twenty-first century" by signing a $1 billion joint venture contract with AT&T and the Dutch PPT to build a cutting-edge telephone system for their new country.[27]

These developments are not only good news for the manufacturers and service providers of high-end switching equipment but also for low-end manufacturers of phone gear in Taiwan, Hong Kong, and Singapore. Markets for these products in the past decade have also become mature and highly price competitive. The new global growth in consumer segments of the telecommunications business presents them with new market opportunities in which they have a competitive advantage.

Application of the Product Life Cycle

The above examples illustrate the importance of being able to accurately assess the stage of market development in different countries as an approach to product line management in global marketing. The product life cycle introduced in Chapter 7 is not just a useful framework for managers to develop and prune product lines in domestic markets. Using the concept of the product life cycle to understand the unique challenges and opportunities of marketing products in the varying stages of introduction, growth, maturity, and decline is a useful tool in global marketing as well. It can help managers understand what types of adjustments need to be made in the total marketing mix in order to best serve global markets. If a product's foreign market is in a different stage of the product life cycle, then this situation needs to be recognized. For example, when Polaroid introduced the *Polaroid Swinger* instant camera in France, the firm failed to recognize that the concept of instant photography and its benefits were unknown to French consumers. While the product was in its mature phase in the United States, it needed to be treated as though it were in the introductory phase in France. Recall that this would require a promotional campaign designed to stimulate primary demand that clearly demonstrated the concepts of the technology and the benefits of use.

Product modification, level of market development, and the product life cycle all serve as frameworks for marketing managers to assess the potential of and the challenges associated with marketing the firm's product in every different foreign market. The next decision facing the decision maker is to determine what sort of branding strategy is appropriate across global markets.

GLOBAL BRANDS OR LOCAL BRANDS?

Since the end of World War II, the organizational structure of many multinational firms has encouraged marketers to research local consumer differences rather than transnational commonalities. While the admonishment to "think globally, act locally" has been popular in marketing for the past decade, most firms act otherwise. Many would-be global brands were developed in multinational regimes where the approach was "think locally, act globally *if* circumstances permit." Since the 1980s, the strategic importance of branding as a competitive tool in global marketing has vastly increased due to two important and interrelated factors. The emergence of global media is one important factor. Television networks, newspapers, and weekly magazines with global broadcasts and circulation have enabled companies to reach global markets. The second factor has been the tendency for large, multinational firms to develop strategies focused on becoming world leaders in a few markets rather than minor players in many markets. These two broad developments are highly interdependent. Global media need advertising revenues to flourish, just as global marketers need global media to carry out their promotional strategies. Many consumer goods markets are now dominated by a few world manufacturers. The competitive advantages that these firms enjoy are based largely on their marketing efforts to building tremendous goodwill with a specific corporate name or brand name—that is, owning and continuing to develop brand equity on a worldwide basis.

While global brands attract a lot of attention, the problems regarding consumers' shifting value of brands, discussed at the beginning of this chapter, extend beyond the United States. In much of the developed market economies, the economic turndown of the 1990s is affecting market share of well-known global brands. Apart from the more value-oriented consumer already mentioned, increasingly many consumers perceive that *product parity exists,* and that there are little or no relevant or discernible differences between many products and brands. In many instances, these perceptions are largely accurate—technological advances in manufacturing have raised the quality of most goods and made it easier for competitors around the world to copy one another's innovations. As goods become less unique (or differentiated), they have become bewilderingly abundant. For example, there are now over 200 brands of breakfast cereal in America, 220 types of cigarettes in Holland, and over 100 perfumes available in Argentina.[28] For many products, this torrent of brands and the advertising avalanche that comes with it has only bolstered the belief that brands are largely the same.

Product proliferation has also led to severe competition in terms of retailer promotion. Faced with so many brands, retailers (especially in the United States, and later, in Europe) bargained for greater discounts and even forced manufacturers to pay fees to supermarkets to stock their products—a trend that caused many major brand manufacturers to push through price increases for their products. As more of manufacturers' advertising budget was shifted to retailer promotions, retailers gained more strength in competitively pricing their own products. Together, these trends have produced the *own-label threat,* wherein store-label products are growing in shelf space and market share in many product categories that were once dominated by well-known brand names during the 1980s. Figure 8-4 summarizes this trend for a number of developed country markets.

Fortunately for global branders, these negative trends are not true for all regions of the world in which they operate. Across Asia and in much of Latin America global U.S. and European brands are still in high demand and command premium prices over what are perceived to be inferior products produced locally. Countries, like companies, have positions in the minds of consumers, and the United States, Japan, and selected other nations are seen as

FIGURE 8-4
Supermarket Power

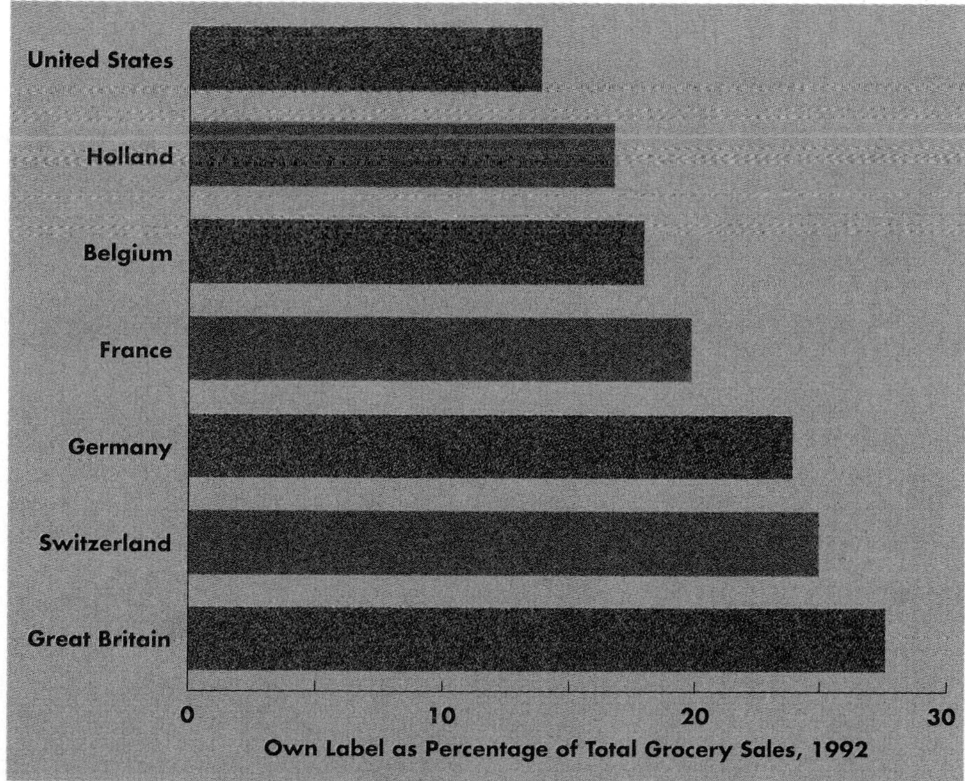

Source: Neilsen Europe; Information Resources.

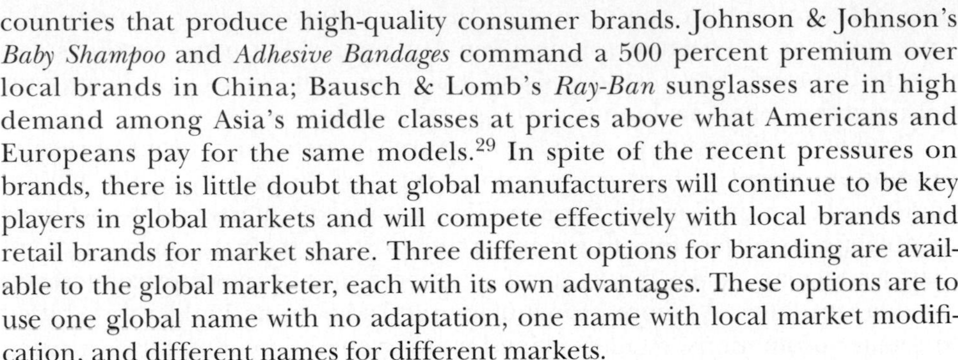

countries that produce high-quality consumer brands. Johnson & Johnson's *Baby Shampoo* and *Adhesive Bandages* command a 500 percent premium over local brands in China; Bausch & Lomb's *Ray-Ban* sunglasses are in high demand among Asia's middle classes at prices above what Americans and Europeans pay for the same models.[29] In spite of the recent pressures on brands, there is little doubt that global manufacturers will continue to be key players in global markets and will compete effectively with local brands and retail brands for market share. Three different options for branding are available to the global marketer, each with its own advantages. These options are to use one global name with no adaptation, one name with local market modification, and different names for different markets.

One Global Name with No Adaptation

This branding strategy is most effective when a company has only one or a few products to market and the products are widely distributed. Coca-Cola and Mars (with the extended brands *Coca-Cola Light,* and *Mars Ice Cream Bar*), or Levi Strauss and Company with its product line of denim blue jeans are examples that use this corporate branding approach. The worldwide use of one brand name gives greater identification with the company and allows for greater consistency and coordination of the promotional mix, particularly global advertising. Perhaps the greatest single benefit of this branding approach is the clearer sense of consumer familiarity that develops from only having one name, symbol, logo, or trademark.

There are times when using the corporate name, rather than the individual brand's name is the approach that is strategically appropriate. Many large and diversified multinationals often operate in several consumer and business markets making a single *product* brand name simply not feasible. The 3M company, for example, has hundreds of products for industrial, commercial business, and household consumer markets. Their *corporate* logo offers a consistent symbol of recognition and is particularly important in international markets where identity and packaging problems have become difficult due to multiple sources of supply, different languages, and multiple channels of distribution. Here, the corporate name rather than the individual brand's name serves an important purpose for recognition and identity.

One Name with Local Market Modifications

Many companies use standard trademarks for all their products but are flexible in the use of brand names, which take into account local consumer norms and values, translation problems, and other market factors. One straightforward benefit of this approach is to establish the presence of the product locally and to remove any doubts about "foreignness" in the market with respect to the company's operation. Having the officially registered name of "Apple Computer Nederland, B.V." clearly establishes this American computer company as a locally operated firm in Holland. This boosts the firm's credibility with local customers regarding delivery, after-sales service, and support. The use of *corporate surnames* as in *Ford Escort,* and *Schweppes' Tonic Water,* or always attaching the corporate logo to local brand names as VW does with its *Golf* and *Passat* models are also ways to develop a family identity for global product lines.

Different Names for Different Markets

One of the underlying motivations for companies to get involved in merger, acquisition, or joint venture activities is to gain access to markets and to well-known brand names in those markets. Often, one of the major costs in acquisition is the value of *brand equity* on the balance sheet. When a product is manufactured and sold locally and is one of the leading brands in the market, then retaining the local brand name is a significant advantage, and this equity will show up in the price of the acquisition. Sara Lee Corporation, perhaps best known for cheesecake and chocolate brownies, has over the years acquired *L'eggs* panty hose, *Hanes* men's underwear, *Bali* bras, and *Playtex* apparel, which are all well-known brand names in the United States and in Europe. The company's strategy for global growth has been similar. It targets markets that are dominated by private-label goods, snaps up huge market share and capacity through acquisitions, and uses the resulting economies of scale to keep costs and prices low. In Europe, Sara Lee has quietly grown to be the fourth largest U.S.-based consumer products company (trailing only Philip Morris, Coca-Cola, and Procter & Gamble) with revenues of $3.2 billion. Much of that success is due to the strategy of acquiring local brands, such as *Dim* (France's leading hosiery maker and the label that Sara Lee sews on men's underwear and T-shirts there) and *Douwe Egberts* coffee and *Van Nelle* (cakes and desserts manufacturers).[30]

Aside from the market strengths provided by local brand names, there is some value in keeping the corporation somewhat anonymous. When the French holding company Source Perrier had to take *Perrier* mineral water off the market in 1990 due to the discovery of benzene contaminants in the water, the decline in revenues was not as dramatic as it could have been because the firm had several other brands on the market with which the corporate name was not associated. For Source Perrier, the main problem was one of containing the damage and then reestablishing the integrity and image of their flagship brand. While the *Perrier* brand is a major contributor to profits, it makes up only 10 percent of the company's mineral water sales. When the brand was removed from the shelves in the United States, sales of Source Perrier's other brands of water increased by 9% (*Arrowhead, Great Bear,* and *Poland Spring* are not family branded with the Perrier group).[31]

DEVELOPING BRAND NAMES FOR GLOBAL MARKETS

As you discovered earlier in this chapter, selecting a good brand name for a product can be an arduous and complex undertaking. The process gets even more complicated as firms attempt to develop names for global markets. Companies go to great expense to test new brand names with language firms who deal exclusively with these problems. Apart from the legal issue of the availability of a name in different markets, some names take on entirely different meanings when used in a market where the written and spoken language differ from the home market's language. Examples of mistakes are abundant and often humorous. A major U.S. manufacturer of soap was considering a name for a new soap powder and wisely ran a translation check on the proposed name in 50 major languages. In English and most major European languages the name meant "dainty." Not an unreasonable association for a soap product.

Levis enjoy the benefits of using one global brand name in all markets worldwide.

But in Persia the name meant "dimwitted"; in Korea the name sounded like the word for a person out of his mind; and in all the Slavic languages the name was considered obscene and offensive[32]—not exactly the images a company wants to conjure up when asking customers to wash their clothes in the product! Can you identify the problems with the following brand names that are acceptable in their home markets, but had considerable drawbacks for global use? Chevrolet *Nova,* AMC *Matador,* Ford *Pinto,* Rolls Royce *Silver Mist,* and Sunbeam Corporation's *Mist-Stick* mixer (hint: the problems were in Spain, Puerto Rico, Brazil, and Germany).*

PACKAGING, SERVICE, AND WARRANTIES

In global marketing, packaging tends to be the one element most likely to undergo modification. These modifications may be for no other reasons than to accommodate the local market's language and legal requirements for content labeling. Packaging has two roles: physical containment and psychological appeal. The physical construction of the package is important because the product must be able to withstand the rigors of shipping in order to arrive at the international destination undamaged and unspoiled. Packaging is critical for shippers and distributors who often take legal title as well as possession of the product during this stage of marketing. In markets with essentially undifferentiated products and a high degree of price sensitivity, economical and effective methods of physical distribution may well be a key selling point to channel members. At the consumer level, psychological packaging features,

*__Answers to International Brand Names:__[34] In Spanish, *Nova* can easily be seen as two separate words: "no va" meaning "it doesn't go." *Matador* means "killer" in Puerto Rico, a country with a high rate of traffic mortality. *Pinto* is a slang expression for "a small male appendage" in Portuguese-speaking Brazil. *Mist,* spelled and pronounced exactly the same in German, means "manure. The Sunbeam mixer translates roughly as a "manure wand."

such as the shape of the package, the use of colors, logos, symbols, and figures, will vary from one market to another based on socioeconomic and cultural factors. Visual aesthetics and government regulations are key factors influencing packaging in developed countries. In many developing countries, the physical qualities of the package may take on more significance since the package may be kept and used as a container. When this occurs, the package not only takes on the value-added function as a container but may also project a sense of status as well as serving as a constant reminder of the company's brand name.

As globally minded household consumers and businesses come to expect more from products and suppliers, managing the product line with a "total product offering" view becomes more important and commonplace. Beyond the basic product offering, effective global management of the product line now often means offering services such as installation, delivery, warranties, and repair service. Free or quick delivery may make the product much more attractive to consumers or business clients, especially in markets where customers have limited transportation resources.

Warranties and after-sale service are also key marketing tools for differentiating products from competitors and positioning the product as having superior quality. In Europe, Japanese manufacturers of consumer electronics and automobiles have invested heavily in full-service dealerships that service what they sell, recognizing that this is essential to the consumer who must decide about major purchases. In Japan, BMW has built a warehouse near its distributor in Tokyo to guarantee delivery of spare parts within 24 hours, a move that helped them gain a 25 percent share of the imported car market.[33]

Deciding on the level of warranties and services to provide is an important element of product line management, since the investments necessary to carry out these activities are considerable. The perceived level of need to offer the services to customers, the company's experience in the market, and the amount of service offered by the competition are key factors in developing these plans in global applications. Viewing service as an investment for future volume rather than as a recurring cost is often the best perspective for developing and sustaining competitive advantage.

Key Terms and Concepts

Product line
Product mix
Product line breadth
Product line depth
Product line expansion
Product line contraction
Trading up
Trading down
Product mix expansion
Product mix contraction
Product differentiation
Functional differentiation
Emotional differentiation
Benefits of use differentiation
Product positioning
Direct competitive positioning
Target market positioning
Benefits positioning
Perceptual mapping
Branding
Importance of branding
Benefits of branding to manufacturers
Brand equity
Reasons not to brand
Values of branding to society
Manufacturer brands
Private-label brands
Branding strategies
Family branding
Separate branding
Brand extensions
Co-branding
Branding business products
Generic brands
Packaging
Labeling
Product modification

Questions and Exercises

1. Procter & Gamble sells *Cover Girl Lip Advance, Cover Girl Clarifying Make-up, Oil of Olay Face Wash,* and *Vidal Sassoon AirSpray.* P & G also sells paper products, beverages, soap products, and health care products. Which of these describes a *product line* and which describes the *product mix.*
2. Identify the market advantages a firm enjoys when its product line has breadth and depth. What problems do firms have with limited product lines face in trying to compete effectively?
3. What role does consumer perception play in a firm's attempt to successfully achieve product differentiation?
4. Give an example of products currently being marketed using functional differentiation, emotional differentiation, and benefits of use differentiation.
5. How are the strategies of product positioning and product differentiation related?
6. Why do commodity-type products like table salt, rice, fruits, and vegetables benefit from an effective brand name?
7. What are the values of branding to consumers? What arguments do critics offer for the drawbacks of branding? What are your personal feelings about the values of branding?
8. Packaging plays both a functional and a strategic role. Explain these roles. Identify a product you buy and use because of the package.
9. How does the level of local market development affect global product strategies?
10. When can a firm use one global brand name for all the international markets within which it markets a brand. Is this the most common approach to global branding, or is this the exception?

References

1. Ronald Alsop. "Brand Loyalty Is Rarely Blind Loyalty." *The Wall Street Journal* (October 19, 1989): B1.
2. See Kathleen Deveny. "More Shoppers Bypass Big-Name Brands and Steer Carts to Private-Label Products." *The Wall Street Journal* (October 20, 1992): B1; and Eleena deLisser and Kevin Helliker. "Private Labels Reign in British Groceries." *The Wall Street Journal* (March 3, 1994): B1, B5.
3. See Lois Therrien, et al. "Brands on the Run." *Business Week* (April 19, 1993): 26–29; Zachary Schiller. "Procter & Gamble Hits Back." *Business Week* (July 19, 1993): 20–22.
4. See Deidre A. Depke. "Allante Goes to the Big Garage in the Sky." *Business Week* (November 30, 1992): 46; Joseph White and Neal Templin. "GM Ends Plans to Revise Key Midsize Line." *The Wall Street Journal* (November 11, 1992): A3.
5. Ellen Neuborne. "Need a car? Try Circuit City." *USA Today* (April 7, 1993): B1.
6. Michael J. McCarthy. "Blockbuster Moves to Enter Record Business." *The Wall Street Journal* (October 20, 1992): B1.
7. Michael Selz. "Coleman's Familiar Name Is Both Help and Hindrance." *The Wall Street Journal* (May 17, 1990): B2.
8. Tim Smart. "So Much for Diversification." *Business Week* (February 1, 1993): 31; Sarah Lubman and Amal Kumar Naj. "Martin Marietta to Buy GE Aerospace for $1.8 Billion in Cash and Preferred." *The Wall Street Journal* (November 24, 1992): A3.
9. Teri Agins. "Once Hot Lee Jeans Lost Their Sex Appeal in a Hipper Market." *The Wall Street Journal* (March 7, 1991): A1, A8.
10. Ronald Alsop. "Firms Unveil More Products Associated with Brand Names." *The Wall Street Journal* (December 13, 1984): 29.
11. Ronald Alsop. "Brand Loyalty Is Rarely Blind Loyalty." *The Wall Street Journal* (October 19, 1989): B1, B9.
12. David A. Aaker and Kevin Lane Keller. "Consumer Evaluations of Line Extensions." *Journal of Marketing* 54, no. 1 (January 1990): 27–41.
13. Richard Gibson. "Co-branding Aims to Double the Appeal." *The Wall Street Journal* (August 3, 1993): B1.
14. James McNeal and Linda Zeren. "Brand Name Selections for Consumer Products." *MSU Business Topics* (Spring 1981): 35–39.
15. Suien L. Hwang. "Picking Pithy Names Is Getting Trickier as Trademark Applications Proliferate." *The Wall Street Journal* (January 14, 1992): B1, B5.
16. Joanne Kirch. "National Brands vs. Generics." *Marketing Communications* (March 1981): 21.

17. Ronald Alsop. "What's in a Name? Ask Supermarket Shoppers." *The Wall Street Journal* (May 9, 1988): 21.
18. Alecia Swasy. "Sales Lost Their Vim? Try Repackaging." *The Wall Street Journal* (October 11, 1989): B1.
19. Ibid., B1.
20. Figures cited in Bernie Ward, "Wrap It Up!" *Sky Magazine* (November 1987): 100.
21. Kathleen Deveny. "Toothpaste Makers Tout New Packaging." *The Wall Street Journal* (November 11, 1992): B1.
22. "Clairol Succeeds with the Customer." *Telemarketing,* The Bell System (June 1981).
23. Jonathan Levine. "It's an Old World in More Ways Than One." *Business Week International* (December 2, 1991): 30.
24. "Slaves of Fashion." *The Economist* (December 7, 1991): 84.
25. Ralph Z. Sorenson and Ulrich E. Wiechmann. "How Multinationals View Marketing Standardization." *Harvard Business Review* (May–June 1975): 38–56.
26. Peter Coy. "Dialing for Dollars, Far from Home." *Business Week International* (January 13, 1992): 55.
27. "Telefoonorder van Oekraïne voor PTT." *De Telegraaf,* Amsterdam (January 10, 1992): T7.
28. "Shootout at the Check-out." *The Economist* (June 5, 1993): 65–66.
29. Adapted from "Proctor & Gamble Hits Back." *Business Week* (July 19, 1993); and "Asia, Where the Big Brands Are Blooming." *Fortune* (August 23, 1993): 55.
30. Lois Therrien. "This Marketing Effort Has L'eggs." *Business Week International* (December 23, 1991): 72–73.
31. Perrier Groupe, Annual Report, 1990.
32. David A. Ricks. *Big Business Blunders: Mistakes in Multinational Marketing* (Homewood, IL: Dow-Jones Irwin, 1983).
33. "Foreign Car Firms Make Inroads in Japan." *The Wall Street Journal* (August 19, 1986): 32.
34. Ricks, op. cit

9

PRICING OBJECTIVES AND METHODS

AFTER STUDYING THIS CHAPTER, YOU WILL UNDERSTAND THAT:

1. Price has a broad meaning to household consumers and business buyers that goes beyond the mere dollars and cents of the price of a product.
2. The key parties who affect a firm's pricing decision are customers, members of the channel of distribution, competitors, the government, and the firm itself.
3. Pricing has important but restricted strategic power in an organization's overall marketing mix.
4. Several strategic considerations influence and often change the basic price of a product determined through standard pricing methods.
5. Pricing in the global context requires a knowledge and understanding of factors that go beyond the basic cost and market demand influences used in typical price-setting methods.

One of the most surprising entries into the U.S. auto market was the introduction of the Hyundai *Excel* in 1988. With an aggressive pricing strategy, this Korean car was selling at an annual rate of more than 400,000 units. This was the most spectacular sales growth for a new automobile in any market any where in the world. But, by 1990, sales of Excel were so *low* that Hyundai seriously considered closing its dealerships and pulling the product from the U.S. market.[1]

Faced with severe price competition from private-label brands and a keen awareness of the value-seeking consumer of the 1990s, Procter & Gamble slashed the price of *Luvs* disposable diapers by 16 percent in May 1993. The result: by September 1993, dollar volume sales of *Luvs* were *down* 10.9 percent, and, what's worse, the lower-priced *Luvs* cannibalized sales from P & G's premium brand *Pampers*. Furthermore, two of P & G's biggest retailers, Safeway supermarkets and Toys "R" Us, stopped carrying *Luvs*.[2] The net result of Procter & Gamble's pricing strategy for *Luvs*: total sales declined $57.2 for *Luvs* and *Pampers* combined, unit sales for the two brands combined were essentially flat, and the firm lost two key retailers.

The Meaning of Price

Why weren't Hyundai and Procter & Gamble more successful with their pricing strategies? The reasons illustrate the **broad meaning of price** to consumers: the ticket price placed on a product is just *one* of *many* cost factors considered by consumers when they make a purchase decision. Just the customer satisfaction > cost inequality discussed in Chapter 1 emphasized that the dollar and cents price of a product is weighed by consumers against other costs of acquisition and against the satisfaction each brand in the market offers. In the P & G example, while P & G was busy cutting prices, Kimberly Clark was rolling out two new products: extra-thin diapers and training pants. Kimberly Clark gained important market share during that period with unit sales up 13.1 percent. And even though Kimberly Clark was caught in the same price pressure environment, their dollar sales remained the same during the period due to the sales growth of new products.

In the Hyundai example, the automaker underpriced the car to gain a foothold in the U.S. market. Over time, the low price left little margin with which to provide services, expand the dealer network, or improve the car. These are all factors related to the satisfaction consumers seek in a product choice. The lesson in these two examples is best expressed by Peter Drucker who said, "Of the two marketing lessons for the highly competitive 1990s, the most crucial one may well be that buying customers doesn't work."[3]

What Drucker is saying and what firms must realize is that price must be viewed as multidimensional and only *one* of the strategic tools used to attract and retain customers. First, and most basically, price sets a basis for culminating an exchange between parties. As the discussion in Chapter 1 pointed out, the broad economic role of marketing is to facilitate exchange. The price placed on a product sets the exchange value for parties to either negotiate or agree upon. That is, a buyer is willing to exchange dollars-and-cents value for some other kind of values a firm has built into a product. We have learned that the price of a product is but one of many costs consumers incur in the acquisition of an item. The monetary cost represented by the price of a product is weighed by the consumer against other costs of acquisition like time, convenience, opportunity, and risk. Hyundai lost customers because the service and dealer network fell behind competitors' values offered in these areas. Finally, price is a significant concern for a firm itself because it is the price received for products that determines the level of revenue generated by the firm.

These many meanings of price represent perspectives of both buyers and sellers. Buyers use price as a yardstick against which to *judge the value* and potential for satisfaction they perceive a product to hold. If the price exceeds buyers' perceptions of value and satisfaction, then they will not buy the product and no exchange occurs. Sellers use price to *express value* to potential customers and generate revenues for the firm. It is critically important for sellers to recognize these internal bases for establishing a price as well as several external influences on the price level. The next section identifies the many parties who influence a firm's decision regarding prices for its products and how the judged value and expressed value get translated into actual market prices and pricing strategies.

Key Parties Affecting Pricing Decisions

The most serious error managers can make in setting a price for a product is to consider only the cost of production and marketing as the basis for a price. While such internal cost considerations are undeniably important to price determination, a successful market price may be based entirely are demand and competitive factors that are external to a firm. To be sure, a manager cannot price a product below the level at which it can cover costs and ultimately earn a profit. However, a price that is set based on cost and profit requirements alone may be too high or too low for market conditions.

Properly pricing a product depends on recognition of a firm's cost and profit needs as well as the desires and motivations of the key parties in the market who will evaluate the price. These key parties are:

- Customers
- Members of the channel of distribution
- Competitors
- Government
- The firm itself

Each of these key parties and their influence on the firm's pricing decision will be discussed.

Customers

Current and potential customers represent the most important group affecting the pricing decision. Firms need to understand the way customers will judge a product for value and satisfaction and the role price plays in this judgment process. Every firm that markets a product must assess the price customers perceive to be appropriate. This assessment relies heavily on market research data and the firm's experience with pricing the particular item.

Understanding the concept of *elasticity of demand* is key to understanding customer perceptions of prices. That is, managers must understand how sensitive consumer demand is to changes in prices. **Elasticity of demand** is defined as a measure of the change in units purchased and revenue generated relative to a change in price. In other words, when a price cut increases the number of units purchased and a price increase decreases the number of units purchased, demand is *elastic*—consumers are sensitive to price changes and will buy more units of a product if the price goes down and fewer units of a product if the price goes up. If a change in price results in very small changes in units demand, then demand is *inelastic*

Figure 9-1 is a graphic representation of the effect price changes have on consumer demand under conditions of elastic and inelastic demand. With an elastic demand curve (D_1), quantity demanded (from Q_1 to Q_2) decreases dramatically with a change in price. When demand is inelastic as in demand curve D_2, then the same change in price results in only a minor decrease in quantity demanded (from Q_1 to Q_3).

Elasticity of demand is a very real phenomenon in the marketplace. Some segments of the market respond vigorously to changes in prices. If a product has an elastic demand, consumers will either consume more of the product or stock-up on the item when the price goes down. Conversely, a product with inelastic demand will experience relatively little decline in demand when the price is raised. The so-called cola wars are an example of elastic demand at

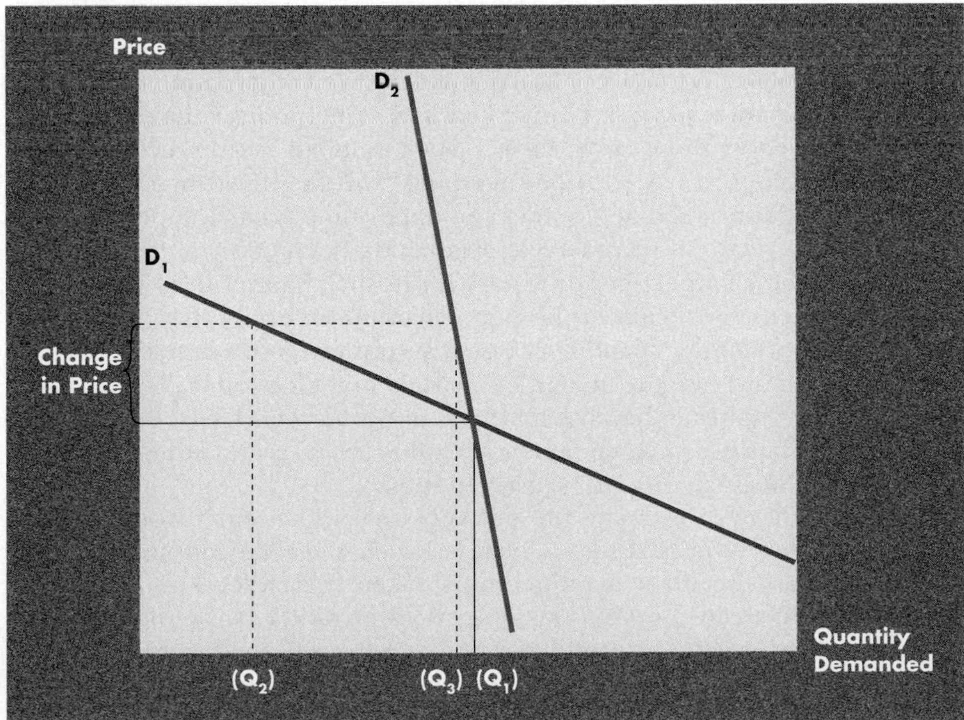

FIGURE 9-1
Elasticity Affects Quantity Demanded

work. Coca-Cola and PepsiCo regularly decrease the price on *Coke* and *Pepsi* to stimulate increased buying of the brands. When specials are run on each brand, consumers rush to stock up at the lower price. Further, each firm realizes that it can motivate brand switching by some consumers and take revenue away from the competitor. You might be wondering why Coca-Cola, PepsiCo, and other marketers bother to cut prices when all they seem to accomplish is getting consumers to stock-up at lower prices—this question is discussed later in the section entitled "The Strategic Power of Pricing."

The ultimate goal of every firm is to have its product so highly prized by consumers that demand is inelastic. Inelasticity is manifest in the market by **brand loyalty.** When consumers are fiercely loyal to a brand, they are less prone to curtail consumption or switch brands when the brand's price is increased or when competitors decrease their prices. Cultivating brand loyalty within a substantial number of consumers accords the firm a very strong position when price increases must be initiated. But, managers must realize that attracting buyers can never happen unless an effective price strategy for members of the channel of distribution is carefully developed.

MEMBERS OF THE CHANNEL OF DISTRIBUTION

Members of the channel of distribution are critically important to the successful pricing of a product. Wholesalers, distributors, and retailers perform various services for customers and manufacturers. Those services generate costs, and members of the channel must be adequately compensated for those costs as well as earn a profit on the items they handle. Wholesalers, distributors, and retailers put considerable effort into determining what their customers will pay for various items. Because of close contact with customers, the trade is sensitive to the nature of demand at various price levels. Additionally, the channel members are also careful to identify their cost of procurement, maintaining inventories, performing services, and administration of their businesses—all of which must be covered by the price charged. The amount they mark up a product must cover those costs, earn a profit, and still not exceed what customers are willing to pay. Channel members will buy from manufacturers, therefore, only at prices that give them an opportunity to mark up items a sufficient amount. There is considerable negotiation between manufacturers and members of the channel about the services in the channel they will provide and the compensation (earned through a markup on price) they will receive. This is an important negotiation because markups taken throughout the channel continue to increase the final price charged to the customer. These negotiations are also important because there is a fine ethical and legal line between good, honest business negotiations and collusion or price fixing. The legal constraints on negotiations will be covered shortly.

Managers have to estimate the markups that will occur throughout the channel in order to project the ultimate price charged the consumer or business buyer. The percentage markup on cost taken at each level in the channel varies by product category and by the services provided at each level. In the *most general* terms, manufacturers mark up items from 10 to 25 percent, distributors and wholesalers mark up in the 20 to 40 percent range, and retailers typically mark up items from 40 to 100 percent. Again, these are the most general levels of percentage markup on cost. Depending on the product category and the types of services provided as the product is passed from one level of the channel to the next, the boundaries of these ranges may be exceeded. For example, May Department Store may add a 40 percent markup to Sony televisions because of the many services the retailer accords its customers. The identical Sony television may be sold at only a 15 percent markup at a CostCo outlet because CostCo incurs fewer costs of operation by providing fewer services. Decision makers at Sony must understand that if multiple channels of distribution are to be used, then its products will be selling for different prices in different outlets. Some firms restrict distribution to avoid these price variations. It is more common, however, to allow a particular product to be priced differentially in order to reach different segments of buyers.

COMPETITORS

Managers have to recognize the effect of direct and indirect competition when establishing a price. Competitors' pricing practices on items directly comparable to a firm's own item—Ford against Chevrolet, Nike against Reebok shoes, Borland against Lotus computer software—represent direct competitive pricing influence. Another competitive influence on price comes from the pricing of substitute items—*Duncan Hines Cake Mixes* against a local bakery, plastic against steel, or teleconferencing against airline travel. This is the effect of indirect competition. Both of these factors need to be taken into consideration when the price is established. If price is out of line with either direct or indirect competitive alternatives, customers will have a reason to avoid the firm's product and choose a competitor's product.

A second basic competitive effect on pricing decisions is the reaction competitors have to specific pricing decisions a firm makes. If a firm raises its price, do competitors hold their price steady and hope to attract customers? If a firm lowers its price, do competitors immediately follow the reduction, move more aggressively, and retaliate with an even lower price or simply ignore the maneuver? Every firm is challenged to anticipate and plan for the reaction of competitors to specific price changes. Without advance planning a firm can be caught off guard and find itself at a disadvantage. This means that any contemplated price change should be preceded by an attempt to anticipate competitors' reactions.

THE GOVERNMENT

Various government bodies can have an influence on pricing decisions. No government entity can mandate what a firm charges for a product. However, constraints and prohibitions can be imposed by the governments, for example, firms are barred from engaging in price fixing. **Price fixing** is alleged to occur when competitors agree to raise or lower prices in concert or to charge the same price. Firms are also prohibited from **price discrimination** in the channel of distribution, which is charging different prices to different trade buyers unless there is evidence that selling to one trade buyer costs more than selling to another. The Clayton Act (1914) and Robinson-Patman Act (1936) directly prohibit price discrimination.

Competitors affect a firm's pricing decision. Southwest Airlines is one of the most aggressive price competitors in the Unites States.

Price advertising to household consumers must be truthful and is regulated under the Federal Trade Commission Act (1914). Advertised price reductions and claims of prices lower than competitors must be based on verifiable facts. A related and also prohibited practice is called **bait-and-switch** advertising. This is the deceptive tactic in which a product is advertised to consumers at an exceptionally low price (the "bait") and then when consumers arrive at the retail outlet seeking the product, they are "switched" to a higher-priced item by being told that the advertised item is out-of-stock or of inferior quality.

Several states have enacted **minimum price** unfair trade practice regulations. These regulations specify that no retailer can sell a product below cost if the intent is to harm competition. Cost is defined in these regulations as the invoice price plus a stated markup to cover the costs of preparing goods for sale. Increments of 5, 6, or 7 percent are the norm in most states. At present, however, few states are effectively policing these regulations.

THE FIRM

The pricing decision is affected by the firm itself in the form of corporate objectives, corporate resources, and decisions that are made in other areas of the marketing mix. The *corporation's objectives* can affect a variety of decisions at the corporate level that ultimately affect pricing. Procter & Gamble has several corporate objectives related to the environmental quality of its products, and the costs of making packaging materials and performing production procedures in an environmentally sound manner result in increased costs to P & G. In turn, these increased costs will translate into higher product prices in the market.

A very basic influence on pricing comes from the level of *corporate resources* available. The resources of the firm frequently influence price because they affect the amount of risk a firm can take. A firm that has strong financial resources, good production facilities, adequate funds for promotion, and some control in the distribution system can take risks that a resource-poor firm cannot take. A strong firm has many options available regarding pricing, whereas a weak firm may have no choice but to follow price leaders in the market.

Finally, other *marketing mix variables* affect pricing because the firm incurs costs to execute marketing strategies. Several features of the product, both real and perceived, affect the latitude of the pricing decision. These key product features are:

- *Quality and Image of a Brand.* High quality often means higher costs for materials and production. Maintaining a potent and distinct brand image may require a variety of efforts across the mix that generate costs. Volvo's commitment to making a safe automobile requires the firm to devise a product with structural features that are far more costly than the average car on the market.
- *Perishability.* The perishability of a product increases costs and risks to the producer, wholesalers, and distributors. Prices of perishable foods and fashion items have to cover risk associated with marketing these goods. Seasonality has a similar effect related to generating enough revenue during short selling seasons to cover the cost of doing business during the off-season.
- *Homogeniety.* The degree to which consumers perceive homogeneity in a product category is another product influence on pricing. If consumers believe that one brand can easily be substituted for another, as in the convenience goods category, then firms have little latitude in pricing because consumers will readily accept lower-priced substitutes. Conversely, sales of specialty goods are often not greatly affected by price because little homogeniety is perceived, and buying decisions are made on the basis of unique characteristics of brands.
- *Patent Protection.* A final product factor affecting pricing is whether a firm has patent protection for its product. Patents protect firms from direct competition and therefore allow a greater degree of price flexibility. Many firms have realized pricing benefits from patent protection. Intel, 3M, and Polaroid have all been granted patents that protect them from direct competition for many of their products. The result is that these firms have greater flexibility in pricing.

The promotion decisions made by a firm can greatly affect the final price of a product. The most obvious influence is that promotional expenditures represent an additional cost to the firm. These costs, as a percentage of the selling price, vary depending on the type of product and competitive situation facing the firm. Advertising, personal selling, and sales promotion costs can equal 2 to 20 percent of gross revenues. Also recall, however, that the demand stimulation effect of promotion can contribute to economies of scale in production and marketing and may actually lower total costs. Such a reduction may or may not be passed on to buyers in terms of a lower price, however.

The effect of distribution on prices was discussed in the trade section earlier in the chapter. One additional consideration is that as the channel of distribution gets longer—that is, as more intermediaries are used—each of the participants will add a percentage markup to the price. These markups are necessary to cover the costs incurred at each level of distribution and provide wholesalers and retailers with a profit.

Finally, services provided as part of marketing mix strategy can contribute significantly to the price of an item. Credit, delivery, installation, training, customization, and even extended store hours are costly services to provide. Warehouse outlets like CostCo and Home Depot are able to charge lower prices because they incur few service expenses. Nordstrom's and specialty boutiques like Henri Bendel pamper customers with a wide range of services and recoup those expenses by charging higher prices.

Each of the parties discussed here exerts an influence on price decisions. This relationship is depicted in Figure 9-2. No one entity consistently affects pricing more than another. Depending on the product, customer, and market conditions, any or all these parties can influence the price decision.

THE STRATEGIC POWER OF PRICING

To fully appreciate the strategic power of pricing, we have to remember that the price variable is only one of the four primary tools available to the marketing strategist in the marketing mix. As such, it will play an important role in the overall strategic approach to the market. However, it is often argued that the price variable is less strategically powerful than the other variables the marketing strategist has available in the marketing mix.

The position that pricing is less potent than the other marketing mix variables is certainly debatable. After all, don't firms frequently run price specials? Aren't 1990s consumers value oriented and searching for deals? The example at the beginning of the chapter in which Hyundai was unable to "buy" customers is reinforced even further by the low pricing experience of the Big Three U.S. automakers. During the last half of the 1980s, Ford, GM, and Chrysler offered round after round of special incentives: discounts, cash bonuses, low-interest rates, and no-interest financing. Peter Drucker again points out,

FIGURE 9-2
Key Parties Affecting Pricing Decisions

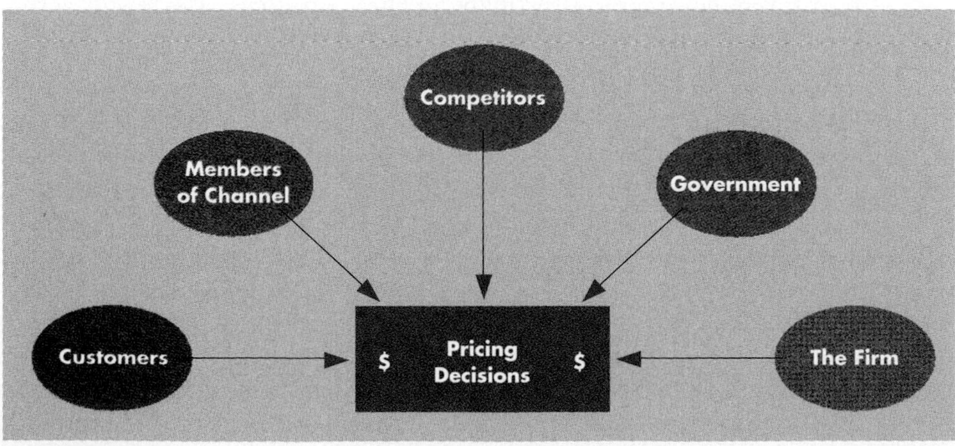

The offers attracted few if any new buyers; customers who had already decided to buy a domestic car simply waited for the next special offer to come along. Potential customers, however, were turned off. "If they can sell cars only by giving them away," was the reaction, "they can't be much good." Thus, the American public brushed aside the very real improvements the Big Three have made in the past five years in quality, service, and styling.[4]

When Ford, GM, and Chrysler made important and significant improvements in styling, safety, and performance, they regained market share beginning in 1993.

There are several factors expressed in Drucker's comments that relate to the weakness of pricing as a strategic tool. First, as we have discussed before, consumers will evaluate the features of a product as well as the price. If no features are highlighted, as the Big Three failed to do in the late 1980s, then consumers have no context within which to judge price. Price is used by consumers as a measure of *value*. This forces marketers to build value into the product with the marketing mix variables other than price: product features, distribution, and the image of the brand all contribute to the perceived value consumers hold of a product and therefore influence the price they are willing to pay. Once again, recall the discussion in Chapter 1 of the relationship between customer satisfaction and cost. Monetary cost (or price) is only one of the cost factors consumers use in judging the potential for satisfaction a product holds.

Second, and closely related to the first consideration, firms that use price as the primary market appeal for the product reduce the item to a commodity in the minds of consumers. That is, the product has nothing to offer except a low price. This leaves the consumer with very little basis upon which to choose the product as opposed to choosing a competitor's product. As consumers encounter competing brands that offer specific functional, emotional, or benefits of use values, they are more apt to see the potential for satisfaction in these competing brands. This **commodity phenomenon** created by a price emphasis also invaded the personal computer industry in the United States in the early 1990s. With literally hundreds of companies assembling PCs with identical Intel processors and Microsoft operating systems, price warring erupted and eroded profit margins.[5] None of the competitors was able to differentiate its offering on the basis of product features, promotion, distribution, or services, and as a consequence prices tumbled. Once prices hit rock bottom in late 1993, price competitors lost their advantage and power, and performance features lured buyers back to the big brand names.[6]

Finally, while pricing can create short-term spikes in demand and sales, it represents a weak long-term strategy for establishing a defendable market position. The reason is that a price strategy is the easiest one for a competitor to copy. Firms can match a competitor's price change literally overnight. Think of how many times you've seen the claims, "We match any competitor's price!" or "We honor competitors' coupons!" When Smith's Food and Drug, a western-region grocery store chain, vowed to offer the "lowest prices on grocery products," their primary competitor, Albertson's, readily admitted it had sent people into Smith's stores the next day to check prices and then match them. On the other hand, it is considerably more difficult for competitors to respond to changes in product features, effective promotional campaigns, or changes in distribution strategy that consumers find appealing and valuable.

Don't misinterpret these discussions. There is no doubt that price is important to consumers. No buyer, household or business, has unlimited financial resources, but consumers' emphasis on price and the role price plays strategically for a firm must be put in proper perspective. If price were the overwhelming factor in the consumer decision-making process, we would all be driving *Yugos*—the lowest-priced car ever sold in the United States. But the *Yugo* failed because it had *only* a low price to offer and not enough *value* as a product. The role of price as a strategic tool must be considered in the broad context of consumer decision making and effective competitive positioning. Management of the marketing mix in such a way that a firm's reliance on price as a market appeal is minimized is known as *nonprice competition.* That is, firms will shape the marketing mix to reduce consumer emphasis on price in the decision-making process. This allows firms to have greater stability and flexibility in pricing and protect revenue from the degenerating effects of price reductions—even in an era when consumers are insisting on value.

Pricing Objectives

Like every other variable in the marketing mix, pricing decisions must be guided by objectives. The process of setting pricing objectives is made more complex by the issues raised to this point. Decision makers have to recognize the influences on price—both external and internal—and the potency of price as a strategic tool.

Because of the need for setting pricing objectives, firms will carry out the process in a relatively structured manner. This is not to say that setting objectives for the price variable is mechanical. Quite to the contrary, pricing objectives must have a strategic orientation as well. The principal bases for setting pricing objectives are:

- Target return on investment
- Maintaining or increasing market share
- Maintaining status quo
- Maximizing profits

These objectives are not necessarily mutually exclusive. A firm may achieve a desired return on investment while increasing market share, for example. Pricing objectives have value only if they work toward achieving overall marketing and corporate objectives. Recall that objectives in each area of the marketing mix must be conceived within the context of overall corporate goals and objectives. The nature and value of each of the pricing objectives will now be discussed.

Target Return on Investment

In administering a **target return-on-investment (ROI) objective,** the price setter will establish a target goal for return on investment, for instance, of 12 percent. A return-on-investment approach to pricing requires information related to development and capital expenditures that are to be charged to the product. Additionally, some time frame must be established (usually five years) against which the return on investment can be judged. A target return-on-investment objective focuses a firm's pricing effort on recouping expenses associated with developing and producing a product rather than on market conditions—a decidedly internal focus with potentially disastrous results. A firm will also establish a realistic profit level for a product on an annual basis as well as estimate the variable costs associated with marketing. The ROI objective, profit, and costs will then be combined to establish market price.

This internal focus on ROI can result in over or under pricing the item because it does not recognize the consumer perspective raised earlier. The value of this approach lies in its recognition of the need to recover costs associated with product development and introduction and the need to maintain careful scrutiny over the contribution of every product to overall corporate profits.

MAINTAIN OR INCREASE MARKET SHARE

In contrast to the return-on-investment objective, **market share objectives** are completely outward looking and demand oriented in orientation. Market conditions, opportunities, and threats are the driving forces in adopting this objective. One advantage of pricing to maintain or increase market share is that market share is specifically measurable. Trade associations in most industries report total sales for an industry. With this information, the individual firm can measure quite accurately its market share against competitors. Another aspect of this objective that makes it popular is that market share is a widely accepted measure of how well a firm is doing. Market share is a better measure than total sales because it provides a *relative measure* of performance rather than an absolute measure. A rate-of-sales increase that is faster than the industry average is an indication of consumer acceptance and widespread brand recognition.

There are drawbacks to using this objective, however. First, caution needs to be exercised so that maintaining or increasing market share is not pursued simply with *lower prices*. Earlier discussions in this chapter have pointed out the problems that result in using price as the primary method of attracting customers. Second, increased sales resulting in larger market share does not necessarily mean increased profits. As the big national packaged goods firms have sought to gain market share back from private-label brands, price wars and heavy promotional expenses have resulted in heavy losses such as the $50 million revenue decrease P & G experienced in the diaper market. Finally, market share objectives must be established in concert with overall corporate objectives. For example, a firm that is intent on being the quality leader in an industry typically finds a market share objective is inappropriate. The firm will pursue high-margin, premium-pricing strategies instead and will be little concerned with the percentage of the market its high-end products capture.

MAINTAIN STATUS QUO

A **status quo pricing objective** is pursued by firms who do not want to risk upsetting present market conditions and prefer that competition be focused on factors other than price. Meeting competitors' prices, using follow-the-leader pricing, or pricing to achieve price stabilization are all status quo pricing objectives. Maintaining status quo is usually found in industries with a recognized price leader or several equally strong competitors with a standardized product where no one company can greatly influence market prices. The steel and chemical industries are examples where these conditions are found in business markets. Automobile tires and athletic shoes are household consumer product examples. Status quo pricing objectives do not mean that all firms set the same price, but rather a relationship exists between the industry leader's price and the prices set by competitors.

Status quo pricing is also prevalent in markets where price wars would prove to be devastating. Product markets characterized by high fixed costs of operation, homogeneity between brands, low-profit margins, and high distribution costs are vulnerable if prices wars break out. The retail gasoline industry and grocery products industry are examples. Ever since the energy crises of the 1970s, retail gasoline firms have conscientiously tried to avoid price wars and have ardently pursued status quo pricing. The cost of operations and low-profit margins leave competitors in this industry few options except status quo pricing.

MAXIMIZE PROFITS

The **maximizing profits objective** is an often-stated pricing strategy. It is also potentially the most dangerous unless everyone in the organization understands and wholeheartedly believes that *long-run profit* is the objective. When quarterly or annual profit is established as the criterion for measuring performance, the tendency is to increase profits by cutting costs. Too frequently, cost cutting results in diminishing the quality of marketing activities from customer service through the quality of a firm's advertising. Another cost-cutting measure is neglect of investment in capital equipment. All of these short-term and short-sighted measures to maximize profits are ill-conceived and signal disaster for the firm over the long term.

In economic theory, profit is maximized when marginal revenue equals marginal cost. In practice, the determination of where this point occurs is difficult due to the complexity and dynamic nature of business operations. In order to pursue a profit maximization objective, a firm must be able to estimate the marginal contribution to profit at various price levels and quantity demanded at those price levels. In addition, profit maximization can be implemented only with a very good understanding of the elasticity of demand characteristics of a product.

THE VALUE PRICING CHALLENGE

Before we turn our attention to the mechanical aspects of pricing methods, we need to consider the value pricing challenge. Much has been made throughout the text of the new value oriented consumer and the value era of the 1990s. It is worth considering how firms are dealing with the challenge that contemporary value emphasis represents to the price-setting process. Some feel the value emphasis will be a permanent part of how household consumers and business buyers judge products. Others are unsure how long such an orientation will persist. For the time being, the value orientation across many product categories and markets is changing the way firms approach the pricing decision.

Value pricing is currently being defined as offering buyers more for a lot less.[7] *More* in the value pricing context can mean more quantity, more features, more quality, more service—generally, more of everything that a product can be to contribute to customer satisfaction. The combined influence of buyers' increased understanding of product features, tougher economic conditions, and astute marketing strategies by private-label marketers have focused attention on value pricing. But firms have learned that value pricing doesn't just mean cutting price—it means balancing product values with lower prices.

Individual firms are taking a variety of approaches to dealing with customer demands for value pricing. McDonalds and Taco Bell are offering "Extra Value Meals" and a "Value Menu" respectively. Both fast-food chains are combining several food items in a package at a value price.[8] Oldsmobile Division of General Motors has its own version of value pricing. Marketing strategies there have simplified the pricing process by reducing the number of models offered from 22 to 15 and packaging two or three equipment combinations with each model. A standard value price is then set on each model/package combination.[9]

Business product marketers are also challenged to provide value pricing. Jack Welch, the chairman of General Electric, believes the expectations of industrial product buyers have fundamentally shifted and says, "The value decade is upon us. If you can't sell a top-quality product at the world's lowest price, you're going to be out of the game."[10] Welch has struck on the key dimension in value pricing for the business market: top-quality at low price. GE Medical Systems sells a $350,000 CAT scanner, but its best-selling CAT scanner is the more powerful $850,000 model. The new Boeing 777 jets will be priced around $100 million each, but the plane can be completely reconfigured—seating, galleys, and lavatories—in 72 hours. Siemans, Apple Computer, and Dow Chemical are other business products manufacturers who are pursuing the value challenge with product design and pricing.

VALUE PRICING STRATEGIES

Because of the pervasiveness of the value pricing orientation across both household consumer and business markets, several strategies are recommended for offering products and services that respond to this challenge. From manufacturers of children's clothing to industrial ball bearing producers, firms are adopting a pricing strategy that borrows an important philosophy from the marketing concept: work backwards from the consumer to establish a price. That is, identify the value price and product features most appealing to consumers and then design or redesign the way a product is produced and delivered to meet that price point. Specifically, a broad value pricing approach can employ the following strategies:[11]

- **Target Pricing.** This is the opposite of full-cost pricing (discussed in the next section) and a radical departure from traditional pricing methods. This strategy identifies a target market price and this price establishes the cost structure. Target pricing often means reengineering procedures within the firm to speed new product introductions, simplify design, and restructure work methods.

- **Value Pricing.** The namesake of the whole value pricing movement, this strategy avoids coupons and rebates and concentrates on stable, low prices. Both Sears and Wal-Mart have been using this sort of value pricing strategy in retailing.
- **Stripped-down Pricing.** Here, a firm will offer a version of a product with basic features and fewer options. General Electric's lowest price CAT scanner and Oldsmobile's most basic model reflect this strategy.
- **Value-added Pricing.** A variation on the value pricing strategy, a firm will introduce products with innovative features and price them at a slight premium over competitive products. Kimberly Clark's extra-thin diapers is an example of this strategy.

Value consciousness is currently so important in the market that recognition of how firms are responding is useful. More fundamentally, firms are relying on basic pricing methods to arrive at prices. The methods that follow are not inconsistent with the value pricing strategies just discussed.

PRICING METHODS

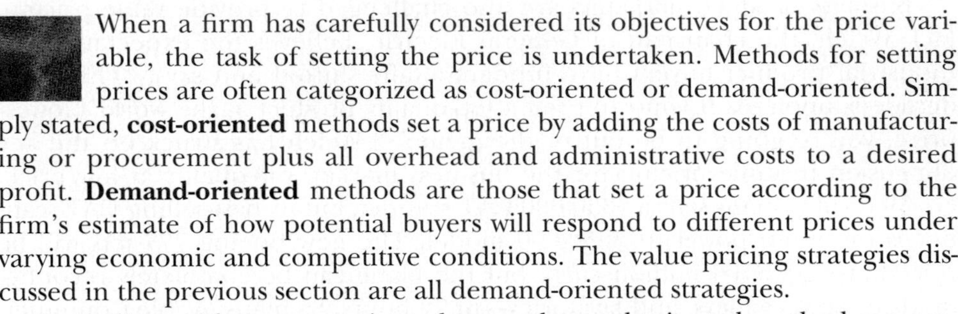

When a firm has carefully considered its objectives for the price variable, the task of setting the price is undertaken. Methods for setting prices are often categorized as cost-oriented or demand-oriented. Simply stated, **cost-oriented** methods set a price by adding the costs of manufacturing or procurement plus all overhead and administrative costs to a desired profit. **Demand-oriented** methods are those that set a price according to the firm's estimate of how potential buyers will respond to different prices under varying economic and competitive conditions. The value pricing strategies discussed in the previous section are all demand-oriented strategies.

In reality, neither a cost-oriented nor a demand-oriented method can produce an appropriate price without full recognition of the factors contained in the other. In the long run, all costs must be recognized and covered by the selling price. On the other hand, unless there is sufficient demand for the product, not enough revenue will be generated to cover costs and produce a reasonable profit. It is more appropriate, therefore, to say that some methods place more emphasis on cost and others on demand. The basic pricing methods available to a firm for setting the final price are:

- Full-cost pricing
- Markup pricing
- Incremental-cost pricing
- Break-even pricing
- Geographic pricing
- Lease pricing

FULL-COST PRICING

Full-cost pricing, which is often referred to as *cost plus* pricing, is expressed simply by the following equation:

Price = Production costs + Administrative costs + Distribution costs + Profit

Full-cost pricing has long been an appealing method for setting a selling price because it is relatively straightforward and relies on the fundamental premise that if all costs and a profit are accounted for, the firm will prosper. However, this approach assumes that the firm can precisely identify all costs associated with a product *and* that the product can be sold at that cost-covering price. It is a decidedly internal approach to the price determination process.

The different types of costs factored into a full-cost pricing method are explained in the following list and their changing relationships as levels of output change are shown in Tables 9-1 and 9-2.

- *Total Fixed Costs.* These are ongoing costs that are incurred whether or not any products are produced and sold. Costs for production facilities, administrative salaries and expenses, property taxes, insurance, and budgeted advertising are examples of fixed costs. They remain constant in the short run.
- *Total Variable Costs.* This is the sum of costs directly attributable to making and marketing the product. Costs for materials, sales force commissions, shipping expenses, and hourly production wages are examples of variable costs. At a production level of zero units, total variable costs are

TABLE 9-1
Costs for Company A with Fixed Costs of 20 Percent and Variable Costs of 80 Percent of Total Costs at Base Level of Production

Level of Production	Total Fixed Costs	Total Variable Costs	Total Costs	Average Fixed Costs	Average Variable Costs	Average Costs per Unit
0	$1,200	—	$ 1,200	—	—	—
100	1,200	$ 4,800	6,000	$12	$48	$60
200	1,200	9,600	10,800	6	48	54
300	1,200	14,000	15,600	4	48	52
400	1,200	19,200	20,400	3	48	51
500	1,200	24,000	25,200	2.40	48	50.40
600	1,200	30,000	31,200	2	50	52

TABLE 9-2
Costs for Company B with Fixed Costs of 80 Percent and Variable Costs of 20 Percent of Total Costs at Base Level of Production

Level of Production	Total Fixed Costs	Total Variable Costs	Total Costs	Average Fixed Costs	Average Variable Costs	Average Costs per Unit
0	$4,800	—	$ 4,800	—	—	—
100	4,800	$1,200	6,000	$48	$12	$60
200	4,800	2,400	7,200	24	12	36
300	4,800	3,600	8,400	16	12	28
400	4,800	4,800	9,600	12	12	24
500	4,800	6,000	10,800	9.60	12	21.60
600	4,800	8,400	13,200	8	14	22

zero. As more units of a product are produced, total variable costs increase.

- *Total Costs.* This is the sum of total fixed and total variable costs. Total costs increase as production increases because of the added variable costs.
- *Average Fixed Costs.* These are the costs *per unit produced.* They are the result of total fixed costs divided by the level of production. Notice for both Company A and Company B in Tables 9-1 and 9-2 that average fixed costs decrease as the level of units produced increases. This is the phenomenon of *economies of scale* at work. Total fixed costs are spread over ever-greater units of production thus reducing the average fixed cost per unit produced.
- *Average Variable Costs.* These are the variable costs *per unit produced.* In Tables 9-1 and 9-2, average variable costs are represented as constant through 500 units of production. It is possible, however, for average variable costs, like average fixed costs, to decline with unit volume increases. As workers gain experience or as machinery operates at full efficiency, average variable cost reductions can be realized. At some point in production, it is common for average variable costs per unit to increase. This is shown in the tables at 600 units of production. This increase represents the phenomenon of *diseconomies of scale.* Inefficiencies in the production process can show up due to worker fatigue, equipment breakdowns from overuse, or overtime hourly wages.
- *Average Cost per Unit.* This is the quotient obtained when total costs are divided by the number of units produced. Unit costs decline as production increases by virtue of economies of scale until a point of diminishing returns is reached. At this point, either fixed or variable costs or both increase thus affecting average cost per unit.

It is important to recognize how the ratio of fixed to variable costs affects the use of full-cost pricing. Tables 9-1 and 9-2 show data for two companies with very different cost structures. Company A has relatively low fixed costs compared to variable costs in production. Company A has a ratio of fixed costs to total costs of 20 percent ($1,200 ÷ $6,000) and a ratio of total variable costs to total costs of 80 percent ($4,800 ÷ $6,000) at a level of production of 100 units. Company B is a firm with high fixed costs relative to variable costs—80 percent fixed-cost ratio to total costs and a 20 percent variable cost ratio to total cost.

You can see that in order to use the full-cost pricing method a firm needs to be able to clearly identify all the costs associated with production and appreciate the relationship between fixed and variable costs. Further, the nature of elasticity of demand for the product is critical to successfully establishing a price level using this method that will produce profits for the firm. Full-cost pricing is a clear example of why pricing methods cannot be considered solely on the basis of cost or a demand orientation as discussed earlier.

MARKUP PRICING

Markup pricing is widely used by members of the channel of distribution, although manufacturers can use the method as well. In markup pricing, wholesalers and retailers add some amount, usually stated as a percentage of the *selling price,* to the cost of goods to arrive at a selling price. This tends to cause some confusion because the urge is to perceive a markup as a percentage applied to the cost wholesalers and retailers pay for an item. This markup on cost is an alternative approach that will be discussed shortly.

The percentage markup on selling price is roughly equal to the gross margin required by channel members to cover administrative and operating costs plus a profit. Markups vary among lines of merchandise and types of wholesalers and retailers. Supermarket markups average approximately 20 percent of retail sales prices. This average is derived, however, from markups on household cleansers (6 to 8 percent), fresh meat and produce (25 to 30 percent), and some nonfood items (40 percent). The national average in the United States of 40 to 45 percent markup in department stores also is an average of different lines of merchandise they sell. The percentage of markup depends on the amount of service provided by the channel member, the efficiency of the physical facilities, rate of inventory turnover, competitive influences, and the effort needed to complete a sale. These factors explain why warehouse stores like Pace have lower average markups (and therefore prices) than department stores, appliance stores, and hardware stores on identical items.

As stated earlier, markups may be expressed as a percentage of cost or of selling price. In comparing the markup used on different items, you must know whether the markup is based on cost or selling price. Markup on selling price is often expressed as *markup on retail.* Markup percentages are easily computed as follows:

$$\text{When markup is based on cost: Markup percentage} = \frac{\text{Dollar markup}}{\text{Cost}}$$

$$\text{When markup is based on selling price: Markup percentage} = \frac{\text{Dollar markup}}{\text{Selling price}}$$

To fully understand these alternative approaches to markup pricing, exercises are provided in Figure 9-3. In Exercise A, assume a cost of $100 for an item and a markup of 40 percent on selling price; the selling price is the base and therefore is 100 percent. Hence, the selling price is computed as follows:

Selling price = 100%
Cost = 60% of selling price (100% – markup of 40% = 60%)
Cost of $100.00 = 60% of selling price
Selling price = $100 ÷ 60% = $167.00

FIGURE 9-3
Markup Exercises

Exercise A Markup on Selling Price	**Dollars**	**Percentage**
Cost	$ 100	
Markup		40%
Selling Price		100% of cost

Exercise B Markup on Cost	**Dollars**	**Percentage**
Cost	$ 100	100%
Markup		40
Selling Price		140% of cost

Warehouse outlets like Pace can use a lower percentage mark-up in pricing because of lower costs of operation than other types of stores.

In Exercise B where the markup is 40 percent of cost, cost equals 100 percent because the cost is the basis for the markup calculation. Therefore, selling price is 140 percent of cost or $140.

Markups based on selling price are more commonly used in retail operations. The reasons retailers use selling price as a base are:

- Expenses and profits are computed as a percentages of sales so using selling price as the basis for markup aids in profit planning.
- Manufacturers' prices to wholesalers and retailers are usually based on suggested retail prices.
- Adequate, timely cost data for inventory and cost of operations are not always readily available, but retailers do know the dollar amount of sales in a period thus aiding in the calculation of profits for a period.

INCREMENTAL-COST PRICING

Incremental-cost pricing is a method in which price is set on the basis of variable costs only. When a firm has unused production capacity, pricing an item at a level that just covers direct labor and materials costs may be acceptable. Such pricing can be used to keep the labor force intact and avoid the cost of a production shutdown. Firms may encounter legal problems in using this method, however. First, if a firm deals in interstate commerce, which most do, incremental-cost pricing is prohibited as price discrimination under the Robinson-Patman Act under certain conditions. Second, if the sale is made outside the United States, it may be prohibited as *dumping* under provisions of the General Agreement on Tariffs and Trade (GATT), which regulates pricing practices in international trade.

These legal problems do not affect a retailer or other firm doing only local business. Price discounts used to dispose of off-season merchandise or to clear inventory often are calculated using an incremental-cost method. Firms that sell and install heating and air-conditioning equipment will offer low, incremental-cost prices in slow sales seasons because they want to keep their skilled people employed and generate cash flow. The risk of incremental-cost pricing is that discounted prices may lead customers to expect and anticipate price reductions. This leaves the firm vulnerable to generating sales only when such low prices are offered.

BREAK-EVEN PRICING

Break-even analysis is undertaken to determine the point at which a firm's revenues equal its total fixed and variable costs. This analysis can be used to establish **break-even pricing.** The firm can identify several price points and calculate the number of units that would have to be sold at a particular price to break-even. The break-even point can be calculated by using the following formula:

$$\text{Break-even point in units} = \frac{\text{Total fixed costs}}{\text{Selling price (average variable costs)}}$$

To illustrate this calculation, we can use the cost figures from the first production level in Table 9-1 and identify selling prices of \$50 and \$60.

At a selling price of \$50, break-even in units for Company A would be:

$$\text{Break-even point in units} = \frac{\text{Total fixed cost of \$1,200}}{\text{Price of \$50 (average variable cost of \$48)}} = \frac{\$1{,}200}{50-48}$$

$$= \frac{1200}{2} = 600 \text{ units}$$

At a selling price of \$60.00 break-even in units for Company A would be:

$$\text{Break-even point in units} = \frac{\text{Total fixed cost of \$1,200}}{\text{Price of \$60 (average variable cost of \$48)}} = \frac{\$1{,}200}{60-48}$$

$$= \frac{1200}{12} = 100 \text{ units}$$

Notice the dramatic drop in units that need to be sold at a \$60 selling price versus a \$50 selling price. Such information needs to be interpreted with caution, however. Raising the selling price on an item by \$10 (or 20 percent in this example) may call into play elasticity of demand effects and the firm may not be able to sell even 100 units at the higher price. Second, for illustration purposes, this is a relatively dramatic example of the affect on break-even an increase in price can have. Under most conditions, firms would not experience such radical changes in unit break-even points.

Using break-even analysis as a method for establishing price levels requires precise information on fixed and variable costs. Despite these information demands, however, break-even analysis is a useful tool for understanding the effect of the ratio of fixed to variable costs. With the break-even method of pricing, firms can quickly identify the influence on price that adding to fixed costs of operations will have. Similarly, any contemplated increases in variable costs can be quickly factored into the price needed to achieve profitability.

GEOGRAPHIC PRICING

Under certain circumstances, the price decision is affected by geographic factors related to shipping and delivering goods. Typically, geographic pricing practices are employed when transportation costs are high due to the heavy weight or large bulk of a product. There are a variety of **geographic pricing methods.** *Free on board (FOB)* pricing establishes a price at either the factory or the delivery destination. *FOB factory* means that the title to the product passes to the buyer at the manufacturer's point of shipment. The costs and risks of moving the product fall on the buyer at that geographical point. *FOB destination* means that the manufacturer assumes all risks and costs of shipping until the product reaches the buyer and title passes at that geographic point. The geographic proximity of competitors to buyers and the expense of shipping determine whether a manufacturer absorbs the shipping costs or tries to pass them on to the buyer.

Zone pricing also has two basic forms: uniformed delivered pricing and zone delivered pricing. *Uniformed delivered pricing* is the practice of charging the same price to all buyers regardless of their geographic location. This form of zone pricing is common in industries where shipping costs are small in relation to the value of the goods. The ability to compete in distant markets without shipping costs affecting prices too greatly is the primary reason for using such a pricing method. In *zone delivered pricing,* sellers specify two or more geographic areas and a uniform delivered price is established for each zone. The shipping costs are more evenly distributed than in uniform delivered pricing.

Freight absorption pricing is the final method of geographic pricing. To be competitive in a geographically distant market, a seller will quote a price that includes shipping and delivery costs equivalent to what a competitor close to the customer would charge. It is a way to offset the advantages of FOB pricing used by competitors located closer to customers. It is also used by firms trying to break into new geographic territories.

LEASE PRICING

Leasing was raised as an issue in Chapter 5 as it related to the nature of transactions in business markets. The increased prevalence of leasing in both the business and household consumer markets has made the practice an important pricing strategy. Recall that leasing presents a customer with an alternative to purchasing. **Lease pricing** is really a calculation of monthly payments over a specified time based on the residual value of the item at the end of the lease. Residual value is the market value of the now used item. Leases typically apply to higher priced, longer life products in both the business and household consumer markets. In the business market, machinery, office equipment, computer and communications equipment, and vehicles are commonly leased. In the consumer market, furniture and automobiles are the most common items leased. In fact, in 1993, fully 25 percent of all new cars and trucks sold were leased, which accounted for $43 billion in revenue. In the luxury car category, the percentage of leased vehicles can be 50 to 80 percent of unit volume.[12]

On goods of higher value, several benefits accrue to the customer who opts for a lease rather than an outright purchase. Sales taxes are often not charged on leased items. Buyers may have to come up with smaller down payments and monthly payments can be significantly lower on lease terms than on purchase terms. Finally, buyers reduce the risk of technological obsolescence in many product categories by leasing an item.

Beyond attracting a greater number of customers with lower monthly payments, leasing has several other advantages. One advantage is that leasing maintains the listed price of an item—unlike discounts and rebates, which reduce the base price. Another advantage is that in many product categories, new customers or younger customers may be attracted by the lower price. This allows for a more refined market segmentation strategy.

While lease pricing as a method can serve sellers well, the risks of leasing must be recognized. Over the lease period, sellers are subject to market conditions that can greatly affect the residual value (the value of an item at the end of the lease period) of the leased item. Rapid changes in technology or changes in consumer tastes and preferences represent great profit risks to lessors if the used items do not match the residual value established at the time of the lease. Such a miscalculation of residual value did affect the luxury car market in the United States when BMW, Mercedes-Benz, Toyota, and Cadillac discovered that cars being turned in on lease agreements were worth up to $8,000 *less* than the original residual price specified on the lease. Attempts to cover that risk either by lowering the residual value or building protection into the lease amount undermine the attractiveness of leasing to the buyer because these factors raise the monthly lease payment. It remains to be seen whether these market risks will ultimately cause a decline in the use of leasing as a pricing method.

Factors Affecting Basic Price Decisions

Setting objectives for the price variable and employing one of the pricing methods just discussed will establish a basic price for a firm's product. Beyond these basically cost-oriented foundations for price determination, however, decision makers will take into account a variety of demand-oriented factors that can affect the basic price decision. Market opportunities and certain price allowances made to the trade can dictate that the basic price be adjusted. The most common factors affecting the basic price decision are trade discounts and allowances, new product/new market introduction, psychological factors, and inventory management.

Price Discounts and Allowances

Manufacturers must carefully cultivate a relationship with their wholesalers and retailers. This is necessary because unless the wholesalers and retailers accept and sell the product, it will never effectively reach the end user. Similarly, wholesalers must maintain a good working relationship with retailers who buy from them. Since relationships along the channel of distribution are so important, a variety of adjustments to price are often used as ways to cultivate and maintain good relations between channel members. The **price discounts and allowances** most often used are as follows:

- *Quantity Discounts.* Quantity discounts are reductions in base price awarded on the basis of the size of an order. *Noncumulative* quantity discounts are based on the size of a single large order. *Cumulative* quantity discounts allow a buyer to accumulate order volume over a period of time and a discount is awarded at some specified volume level. Noncumulative discounts encourage large single orders, and cumulative quantity discounts encourage buyers to continue ordering from the same supplier over a long period of time.
- *Cash Discounts.* Cash discounts are prevalent whenever goods are sold on credit. They are used to encourage early payment. Common terms that offer a cash discount to a buyer are specified as "2/10 net 30 days." This means that a 2 percent discount will be given if full payment is received within 10 days and full payment is due in 30 days with no discount. Sellers offer cash discounts to increase cash flow.
- *Seasonal Discounts.* Manufacturers and distributors of goods that have seasonal demand, such as sporting goods and motorcycles, may offer discounts for purchases made during the off season. The discounts are offered to stimulate off-season buying, which can help to level out production schedules.
- *Interest Rate Discounts.* Offering very low interest rates on credit purchases may attract the attention of buyers. This form of discount is used in the trade but it is also common in the consumer market for large cost purchases such as automobiles.
- *Promotional Allowances.* Manufacturers commonly offer their trade buyers an advertising allowance. If a retailer features a particular manufacturer's brand in local advertising, the manufacturer will rebate some portion of the cost to the retailer. This practice is known as *co-op advertising.* Cents-off coupons, allowances for trade-ins, and product premiums given to consumers that are paid for in total or in part by the manufacturer are other forms of promotional allowances.

NEW PRODUCT/NEW MARKET INTRODUCTION

When a manufacturer plans to introduce a new product or introduce an existing product into a new market, specific introduction pricing strategies may be used that deviate from the basic price. The two primary product/market introduction pricing strategies are skim pricing and penetration pricing.

A **skim pricing strategy** sets the price high in the range of competitive prices. A skimming price strategy is feasible only under certain conditions:

- The product has strong relative advantage.
- The product has low elasticity of demand.
- The product is being marketed to a sufficiently large segment that is relatively insensitive to price.
- Competition is not anticipated in the short term because the product is difficult to copy, has strong patent protection, or production processes are hard to duplicate.
- The total market is not expected to be large. Even though margins and profits may be high due to a sustainable high price, total dollar profits in the market are not large enough to attract strong competitors.

The introduction by Hewlett-Packard of the original hand-held calculator in the late 1960s is a classic example of a successful skim pricing strategy. The product was targeted to engineering and scientific users who were not price sensitive. Hewlett-Packard knew it had at least an eighteen-month lead on the nearest competitor, and the product had tremendous relative advantage over existing calculating machinery, which was bulky and slow. Many firms that provide specialty products to niche markets are able to use a skim price strategy. The products tend to be developed for very specific applications, which makes them hard to copy, and limited demand discourages competitors from investing in the development of a similar product.

In **penetration pricing strategy** a very low price is set and other elements of the marketing mix are used to reach the mass market as fast as possible. Several conditions make the use of penetration strategy appropriate:

- The product does not offer significant relative advantage nor is it particularly distinctive.
- Significant economies of scale in production and marketing result from large-scale operations.
- The product has high elasticity of demand.
- Strong competition exists or is anticipated in the short run.

Penetration is common for "me, too," products brought to market relatively late by a competitor. Similarly, regional competitors will use a penetration strategy to break into new geographic markets. Firms can use a *temporary* penetration strategy by using cents-off introductory pricing with new products or when trying to crack new markets.

PSYCHOLOGICAL FACTORS

The basic methods for setting price may be affected by psychological factors that influence consumer price perceptions. Price lining, prestige pricing, and odd-even pricing are strategies that respond to these psychological influences on basic price.

Price lining is the practice of setting only a few price levels for many items in a product line. A men's clothing retailer may set prices for all suits in the store at $99, $199, and $299 with no suits at any prices in between. Price lining has been widely used in retailing for clothing, appliances, and more recently computers. The principal advantage claimed for price lining is that consumers with different price elasticities can be appealed to using differential price lines. A secondary advantage is that it reduces confusion. Consumers can more easily make comparisons and choices when there are three or four price levels than when there are many prices with smaller intervals of difference.

Prestige pricing refers to putting a high price on an item to suggest high quality or status. Most consumers would question the value of a diamond ring for $45 or a sports car priced at $6,000. And it is unlikely that they would buy a 99 cent bottle of perfume to give as a gift. Prestige pricing is a reaction to the tendency on the part of consumers to perceive a price-quality relationship. Consumers frequently use price as a guide to, or even surrogate for, quality. The extent to which potential buyers use price as an indicator of quality is related to several market and product factors:

- Large perceived quality differences exist between brands on the market.
- Product quality is difficult to judge without direct experience.
- High risk is perceived in choosing a poor-quality product.
- The product is highly visible to people whose opinions are important to the buyer.

A product and buying circumstance that fits these conditions perfectly is the choice of new automobile tires. The buyer is likely to assign high risk to choosing a poor-quality product. Family and friends may scrutinize the choice due to the safety issues related to product performance. Finally, the decision to buy auto tires is one that is very infrequent and the buyer may have direct experience with only one or two brands.

Odd versus even number pricing is a strategy in which prices are set either just under a round number (odd pricing), for example, $2.49 or $3,573 or exactly at an even number, like $60. Proponents of odd pricing say that odd pricing works because customers tend to believe that an odd price implies careful costing and the price is, therefore, set as low as possible. It is also argued that consumers perceive a price of $2.98 to be well-below $3 rather than simply a two-cent savings. The use of even-numbered prices is most common for prestige products in exclusive retail shops. Prices are set in round numbers, such as $80 or $1200. Even number pricing is alleged to connote status and puts distance between the product and other mass-marketed, bargain items that use odd-numbered pricing.

INVENTORY MANAGEMENT

Inventory management represents a relatively new and different effect on basic price decision making. When firms use a *just-in-time (JIT)* inventory management system, production levels are set to meet product demand as close as possible to the time buyers need items. In this way, inventory carrying and storage costs are minimized and products are provided through the channel just in time for customer purchase. While the process was conceived as a way to reduce the costs of carrying inventory, it has also produced the opportunity for manufacturers to engage in power pricing. **Power pricing** comes about when inventories are low and customers feel they are in no position to argue about prices nor do they anticipate price breaks. As one analyst put it, "No inventories means greater pricing power."[13]

While the strategic management of inventories may provide firms with the opportunity to maintain or even increase price levels, risks are involved. If demand is not precisely estimated, then inventory will not be just in time but may end up being late. In this case, customers may seek competitors' products. Under the same condition of underestimating demand, the firm may generate extraordinary expenses in running production facilities overtime or using costly modes of distribution to serve customers waiting for products. Under both circumstances, profit is eroded even if prices were maintained.

To this point in the chapter, we have seen that the pricing decision takes into account a wide range of cost and demand factors. Managers must under-

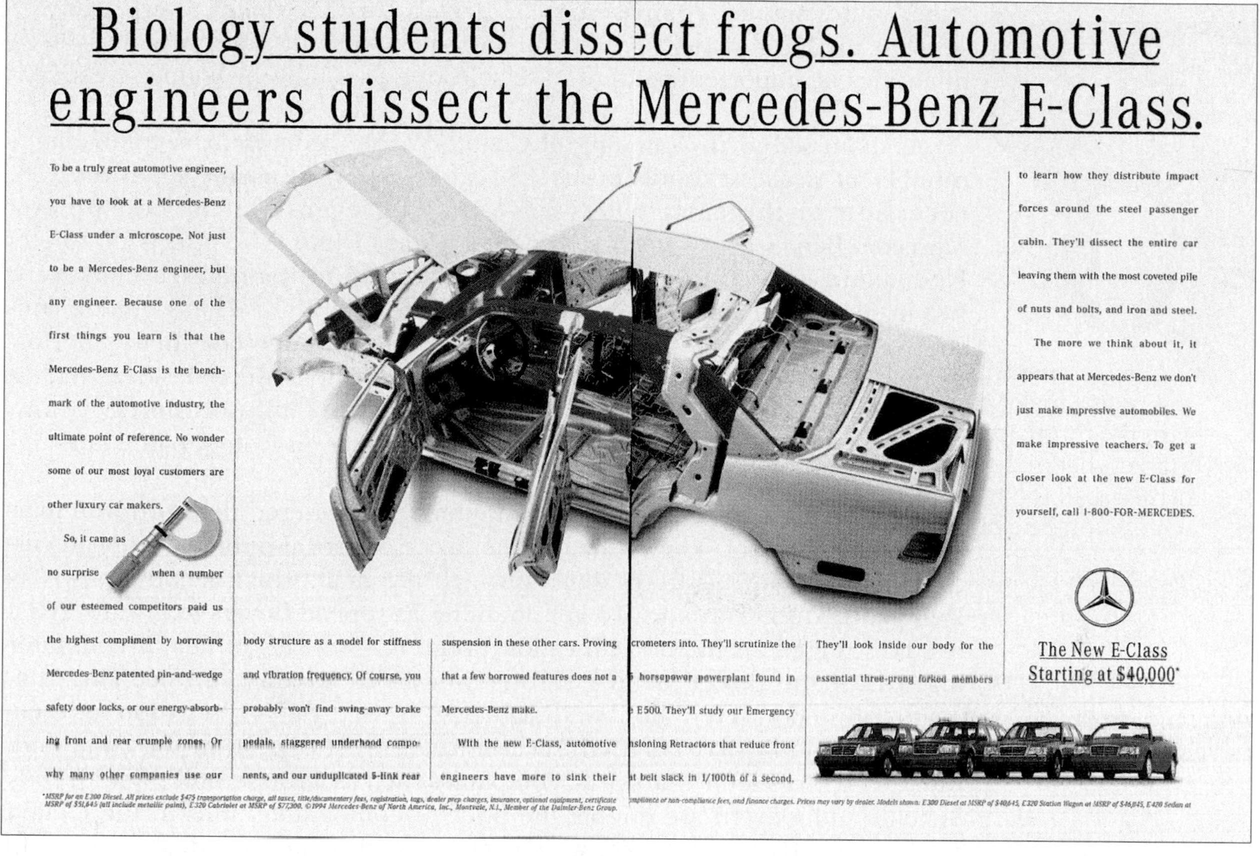

Biology students dissect frogs. Automotive engineers dissect the Mercedes-Benz E-Class.
To be a truly great automotive engineer, you have to look at a Mercedes-Benz E-Class under a microscope. Not just to be a Mercedes-Benz engineer, but any engineer. Because one of the first things you learn is that the Mercedes-Benz E-Class is the benchmark of the automotive industry, the ultimate point of reference. No wonder some of our most loyal customers are other luxury car makers.
So, it came as no surprise when a number of our esteemed competitors paid us the highest compliment by borrowing Mercedes-Benz patented pin-and-wedge safety door locks, or our energy-absorbing front and rear crumple zones. Or why many other companies use our
body structure as a model for stiffness and vibration frequency. Of course, you probably won't find swing-away brake pedals, staggered underhood components, and our unduplicated 5-link rear
suspension in these other cars. Proving that a few borrowed features does not a Mercedes-Benz make.
With the new E-Class, automotive engineers have more to sink their
crometers into. They'll scrutinize the horsepower powerplant found in E500. They'll study our Emergency nsioning Retractors that reduce front t belt slack in 1/100th of a second.
They'll look inside our body for the essential three-prong forked members
to learn how they distribute impact forces around the steel passenger cabin. They'll dissect the entire car leaving them with the most coveted pile of nuts and bolts, and iron and steel.
The more we think about it, it appears that at Mercedes-Benz we don't just make impressive automobiles. We make impressive teachers. To get a closer look at the new E-Class for yourself, call 1-800-FOR-MERCEDES.
The New E-Class
Starting at $40,000*
*MSRP for an E300 Diesel. All prices exclude $475 transportation charge, all taxes, title/documentary fees, registration, tags, dealer prep charges, insurance, optional equipment, certificate mpliance of non-compliance fees, and finance charges. Prices may vary by dealer. Models shown: E300 Diesel at MSRP of $40,645, E320 Station Wagon at MSRP of $46,845, E420 Sedan at
MSRP of $51,645 (all include metallic paint), E320 Cabriolet at MSRP of $77,300. ©1994 Mercedes-Benz of North America, Inc., Montvale, N.J., Member of the Daimler-Benz Group.

ILLUSTRATION 9-2
Even-number pricing, like the $40,000 price for Mercedes E-class cars, is often used for prestige and luxury products.

stand and accommodate the internal needs of the firm while at the same time recognizing and complying with the influences that customers, the trade, government, and competitors have on the price decision. Imagine the additional complexities faced by marketing managers when multinational pricing programs must be developed. It is this challenge we will now consider in pricing from the global perspective.

PRICING: A GLOBAL PERSPECTIVE

As an introduction to the variety of issues that directly and indirectly affect pricing in global markets, consider the following three brief examples. In 1991, bowing to heavy pressure from U.S. trade negotiators, the Thai government opened its $744 million cigarette market to imports. But not before they imposed high import duties, a cumbersome customs-clearance procedure, and a stiff ban on cigarette advertising. While sales of U.S. cigarettes are brisk in higher-income segments, (60 percent of

Asian males smoke, compared to 27 percent of U.S. males, down from 57 percent in the mid-1950s) much of the sales are unit sales, literally—large quantities of imported cigarettes are sold one at a time by young street vendors.[14]

As discussed in the opening of Chapter 2, Mercedes-Benz is combating a number of negative trends in its U.S. market sales. At a time when the U.S. recession of the early 1990s was pinching even wealthy consumers, Mercedes-Benz's prices seemed very much out of line. The effects of a hefty U.S. luxury tax and the dollar's weakness relative to the deutsch mark were two major reasons unit sales plunged 24 percent in 1991. That's quite a contrast to the recession of 1982, which barely affected Mercedes-Benz's performance. The big difference in the latest decline was that Mercedes-Benz had to try to convince U.S. consumers that a Mercedes was still worth every penny, even if its cost was a good deal more than the new rivals from Japan, *Lexus* and *Infiniti.*[15]

When the PC discounter Dell Computer Corp. entered the European market in 1987, the firm knew it had to win over a skeptical public. European customers didn't buy big-ticket items through the mail, which was the only way Dell planned to distribute. To get doubting European buyers to give its PCs a try, Dell waged an intense education program—a series of ads in computer magazines and direct mailing throughout the U.K. and Europe. The campaign, printed in seven different languages, stressed Dell's reputation for quality, service, and price. For Dell, success has been strongest on the continent, where PC prices set by European companies such as Groupe Bull's Zenith Data Systems and Olivetti are double the price of comparable units in the United States. Even IBM and Apple, which sell through expensive dealer networks that Dell doesn't use, were vulnerable. Ninety-five percent of Dell's sales are to business customers, and Dell has surprised the competition by going from zero sales in 1988 to $240 million in 1991.[16]

These three brief examples preview the complexity of issues in developing prices for global markets. Government duties and cumbersome customs procedures that increase the costs of doing business await U.S. tobacco companies in Thailand. Mercedes-Benz has had to cope with recession in the U.S. market, the effects of a strong deutsch mark, consumers' changing perceptions of value, and competition from Japanese luxury cars costing almost half as much. The American-based computer distributor Dell is currently on the other side of the coin, so to speak, using cost-effective distribution methods and a dollar that is weak relative to European currencies in order to take market share from higher-priced competitors.

Global pricing strategies can be influenced by a wide range of factors, and only a few are under the direct control of the firm. Figure 9-4 identifies the most common variables that can influence international pricing strategies. While company factors, market factors, and environmental factors are separated for discussion, you should keep in mind that they are in fact interrelated. Furthermore, market and environmental forces, which are more uncontrollable, are often the most disruptive elements that affect international pricing. Taken together, these two sets of factors are often the best explanation as to why an otherwise well-conceived marketing strategy ends up as unprofitable.

FIGURE 9-4
Factors Affecting International Pricing Strategies

COMPANY-BASED FACTORS

There should be little doubt that environmental and market factors have strong influences on a company's global pricing strategies. The increased emphasis by firms on global marketing, the increased pace of deregulation of the European market in 1993, the increased competition from newly industrialized countries, and the shift to offshore production all contribute to the development of pricing policy within global-oriented firms. Understanding the strategic emphasis on price in the marketing mix of a firm together with the amount of influence the parent company wants to exert in controlling global pricing strategies are useful starting points for assessing company-based influences on pricing policy.

The strategic emphasis put on price competition as the key element in the total marketing mix influences the parent company's policy on pricing globally. Historically, U.S. firms have relied on nonprice competition by attempting to develop competitive leverage in global markets via advertising, personal selling, and product differentiation. As mass markets developed in the 1960s through the 1980s in western Europe, and now in Asia, the use of price competition has increased dramatically. For global companies with active marketing programs in a number of countries, the strategic use of pricing becomes more important and more complex to manage. For example, in global markets where there is little or no competition, a skim pricing strategy may be used to contribute to overall corporate return on investment, to finance market penetration in growth markets where penetration pricing tactics are being used (dumping), or to finance capital investment and R&D efforts. Contrast these broader goals with companies who view foreign markets with a lower priority. These companies may be content to sell whatever they can via exporters, and price is only important to the extent that sales to the exporter contribute to overall profit margins. Whatever the strategy may be in any one country, the principal objective of the parent company is to set intrafirm prices that will maximize the long-term economic interests of the total company.

Regardless of whether a company is an active global marketer or merely an international marketer focusing on simple export strategies, the marketing manager will ultimately take a large portion of the responsibility for establishing price tactics for a company's international operations. Even for firms with clearly developed and explicitly defined pricing policies, the pricing tactics used are most often determined by expediency rather than design. Each market presents its own unique problems stemming from a variety of factors such as the nature of local competition, the length of the channel and the markup practices of the channel members, local inflation rates, tariffs, currency fluctuations, and government regulations, which are all at play in price setting. In spite of all these unpredictable and uncontrollable elements that ultimately affect price, firms still have a large degree of control over their pricing strategies. Most often, a deliberation over global pricing begins with an assessment of a company's relevant cost structures.

Cost Factors in Global Pricing

As discussed earlier in the chapter, the basis for any effective pricing policy is a clear understanding of the cost and profit factors involved. In global pricing, firms must decide between variable-cost and full-cost approaches to price setting. With *variable-cost pricing,* firms only consider the marginal costs of producing goods that will be sold in foreign markets. These firms tend to view export sales as a bonus and assume that any return over the variable costs is a contribution to profits. In contrast, companies using a *full-cost pricing* approach spread fixed costs over all units produced, regardless of where they are sold. Full costs don't have to be covered in every single market in which the company operates, as long as total company sales cover all costs of marketing globally. The variable-cost approach allows companies to more effectively compete on price and to treat foreign sales of subsidiaries as profit centers. The choice of approaches depends not only on local market conditions such as competition or the consumer's ability to pay, but also on the broader-based corporate issues mentioned earlier.

In addition to these primary cost factors, there are a number of other company cost issues are exaggerated in or unique to the global marketing context. These include tariffs and taxes, transportation and insurance, and transfer pricing policies.

Tariffs and Taxes

A **tariff** is a fee charged when goods are brought into a country from another country. A tariff can be expressed as a flat fee per unit (i.e., $6 per pair of imported ski boots), or *ad valorem,* which is a duty based on a percentage of the value of the goods imported. This latter method is particularly important for marketers, since the form in which a good enters a country may strongly influence the tariff rate assigned. Importing unassembled goods (i.e., the cab and bed of a pick-up truck as separate pieces) creates jobs in the host market and stimulates the local economy. When tariff rates on assembled goods exceed the cost of local assembly (they typically will!), then companies most often choose importing parts and contracting for local assembly, even if assembly costs would be lower at the original production site. Whatever the type of tariff, these import taxes serve to discriminate against all foreign goods, and it is ultimately the consumer who pays the price. One estimate on tariffs of Japanese autos sold in Europe came to $7 billion![17] In addition to tariffs, many

There are 3.785 liters in an American gallon. Taxes in the Netherlands make gasoline prices rather high. Using today's exchange rate, what is the price for a gallon of premium unleaded (Super Plus)?

countries also have purchase or excise taxes that apply to various categories of goods (recall the Mercedes-Benz example in the U.S. market).

Transportation and Insurance Costs

Generally speaking, transportation costs are higher in global marketing even when the actual distance traveled may be less than in the domestic market. Transporting Fords from Detroit to dealers in Los Angeles is a considerably longer haul than transporting Peugeots from Lyon, France, to Amsterdam, in the Netherlands, although the unit transportation costs will be higher for the Peugeots than for the Fords. This can be explained by the higher costs of fuel, road taxes, and the fees of insurance carriers who will write a policy valid in three countries (France, transit through Belgium, and the Netherlands).

Tariffs, taxes, transportation costs, and long-distribution channels can combine to escalate the final foreign market price of a good to a level considerably higher than in the domestic market. This process of price escalation could raise the price so much to the ultimate consumer that demand falls. Table 9-3 illustrates this price-escalation problem. Apart from investing in a regional or local production facility in order to eliminate many of the steps that lead to price escalation, companies try to combat the problem in a variety of ways. Lowering the export price at its origin will reduce the multiplier effect at all subsequent markup steps, although this also affects the firms' profit contribution. Lowering product quality or eliminating costly product features for export markets may help improve the bottom line, but it may also reduce the attractiveness of the item to the target market. Shipping modified or unassembled products may save shipment volume and considerably reduce transport costs as well as qualify the product for a lower tariff rating in the country of import.

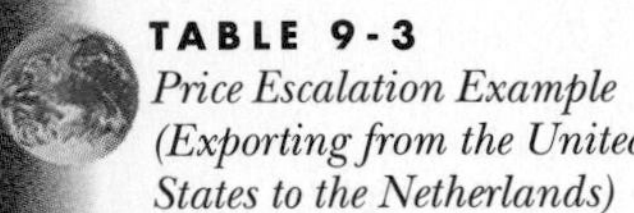

TABLE 9-3
Price Escalation Example (Exporting from the United States to the Netherlands)

	Domestic Market Transaction	Dutch Transaction
Manufacturing price in the U.S.	$ 66	$ 66
Unit transportation costs to U.S. Wholesaler or European exporter	4	6
	$ 70	$ 72
Export documents		3
Handling fees for overseas shipment		3
Overseas freight and insurance		11
		$ 89
Import tariff for luxury good: 22%		19.58
Handling fees in Rotterdam		2
Transportation fee from harbor to importer		5
U.S. transportation fees from wholesaler to retailer	5.50	
Importer markup: 15%		17.34
		$132.92
Wholesaler markup: 8% in U.S.; 14% in NL.	5.60	18.61
Retailer markup: 40% in U.S.; 50% in NL.	30.24	75.77
	$111.34	$227.30
Sales tax in U.S.: 6%	6.68	
Sales tax in NL: 17.5%		39.78
Final retail price	$118.02	$267.08

Transfer Pricing Policies

As global companies increase their number of subsidiaries, off-shore manufacturing plants, joint venture arrangements, and consolidate their operations through such vertical integration strategies as owning their own distribution companies, the price charged to all these separate affiliates is known as **transfer pricing.** In general, transfer pricing policies tend to be strictly under the control of the parent company.

Costs and ultimately the prices assigned to goods that are transferred from one corporate operation to another can be manipulated to enhance the profit to the overall corporation. For example, a toy manufacturer with production costs of $10 per unit transfers the items to its international division at a price of $12.50 per unit, with an additional cost for shipping and duty of $2 per unit. In the foreign market, which is price sensitive and has a high corporate tax structure, the selling price to consumers is limited to $17.50. For the subsidiary, the sale is not all that profitable, since the profit reflects only a 17.1 percent return on sales. The total profit is however, $6, or 34.3 percent, if all the profit in the corporate structure is taken into account.

Using a minimum transfer price, companies can lower duty costs when shipping goods into high tariff countries. By over-pricing goods, companies can eliminate profits in countries with high tax structures and shift profits to lower tax-rate countries. But, be certain that these various tax and financial manipulation possibilities used in transfer pricing are not lost on government authorities! While global companies may have pricing objectives of maximizing profits of the corporation as a whole, the objective of government authorities is to extract the full legal amount of tax liability from the company using fair standards of accounting. What is considered fair is most often defined as the amount that would be priced in quotes between independent companies—governments expect firms to use this as a guideline in establishing or evaluating their transfer pricing tactics for each country and subsidiary. A government that tries to force on multinational firms prices similar to those faced by unrelated firms misses the point of engaging in multinational business: to cut costs and maximize returns by locating business activities more efficiently around the world.

MARKET-BASED FACTORS

Although cost information is vital, it is only one aspect considered in developing global pricing strategies. In practice, prices need to reflect the realities of each market in which the company competes. As such, the marketing manager's decisions relating to price must take into account local market conditions such as local income levels and market segments. Additionally, the unique nature and the competitive structure in each market, the channel structure, and competition from other markets must be recognized as effects on price. Each of these market-based factors will be considered separately.

Local Market Conditions

As pointed out at the beginning of this chapter, the price for a particular product is only one of many considerations that go into the overall purchase decision. Demand analysis in the global setting involves estimating the relationship between price level and demand on a market-by-market basis. Attempting to estimate the effects that other variables will have on demand, such as ability and willingness to buy, the role of a particular product in the life-style of a consumer group, or unfulfilled demand is a complex task.

Elasticity of demand is particularly useful in assessing the effect of local market conditions on price. Generally, countries with high income levels will display lower price elasticities for basic necessities such as food, shelter, and health care. More specifically, elasticity of demand analyses are most accurate when applied to demand assessments in different market segments. For example, skewed income distributions create small and narrow segments in developing countries where prices for a variety of consumer goods (and especially luxury goods) are highly elastic. In a country like Turkey, import duties on new automobiles effectively triple the price to the consumer, making autos a product that is available only to the wealthy. Given this market situation, a change in the price of gas will not have much effect on the total demand for gas.

Another local market condition affecting global pricing has to do with unfulfilled consumer demand in some global markets. As eastern Europe and Russia open markets and as a growing middle class in many Asian countries

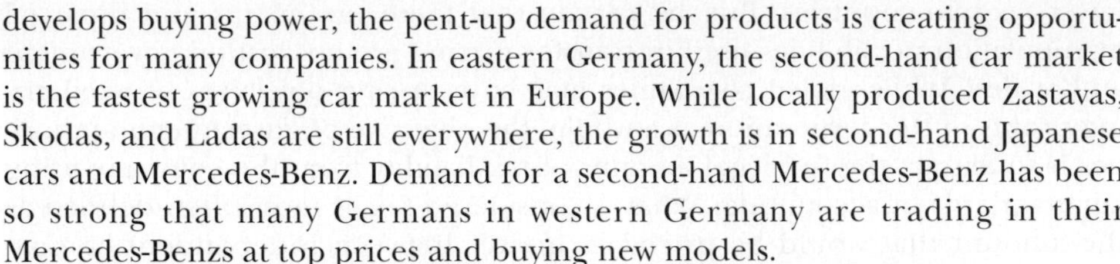

develops buying power, the pent-up demand for products is creating opportunities for many companies. In eastern Germany, the second-hand car market is the fastest growing car market in Europe. While locally produced Zastavas, Skodas, and Ladas are still everywhere, the growth is in second-hand Japanese cars and Mercedes-Benz. Demand for a second-hand Mercedes-Benz has been so strong that many Germans in western Germany are trading in their Mercedes-Benzs at top prices and buying new models.

For business markets where expensive capital goods and equipment are sold, a critical element in the manufacturer's pricing strategy is often that of helping secure financing for the buyer. In countries where there is a shortage of hard currency and/or an unwillingness to make a long-term purchase commitment, this local market condition then promotes leasing as an attractive pricing technique. Leasing transfers the burden of service and maintenance to the lessor and relieves the lessee of the risk of taking legal ownership of expensive equipment. Many countries offer investment incentives for leased equipment or plants thus creating an opportunity for a sale. For the lessor, the entire lease price or rental can be written off as an expense for income tax purposes and many leasing arrangements include an option to sell the equipment at a greatly reduced price to the lessee at the end of the contract. As you can see, the conditions in certain global markets create a situation where leasing as a pricing strategy has significant advantages similar to those discussed earlier in the chapter.

Competitive Structure

The competitive structure in each country in which a firm operates is another factor to consider in setting prices. The nature of the competition, the size and number of competitors, and low barriers to entry into a market will all influence the pricing strategy used. In situations in which a company is operating as sole supplier of a product or service, greater pricing flexibility exists. However, as markets open up and more companies view the world as their market, this monopolistic approach to pricing will become less prevalent. For example, many of the recently deregulated telephone service companies in Europe are being attacked with pricing strategies by foreign competitors such as MCI, Sprint, and AT&T.

In many markets, local competition forces foreign companies to price competitively in that market. German and Japanese car manufacturers carefully watch the price strategies of Ford, GM, and Chrysler, and within the same segments attempt to compete on nonprice elements. Often, cost structures will be different for local competitors relative to foreign competitors resulting in different prices. Dell Computer Corp.'s original success was based on buying PCs in large volume to meet demand for their U.S. market. As Dell developed this market, it also gained competitive advantages based on volume discounts from American and Asian suppliers which were then used to create a price advantage when entering European PC markets. European dealers have trouble competing with Dell on price because individually they don't generate the kind of volume necessary to command huge discounts from suppliers. Further, European sellers don't offer PCs via direct marketing methods because the structure of their local markets has never forced them to compete on price.

Channel Structure

The ultimate price to the consumer will be strongly influenced by channel structure including the length of the channel and the markup practices of local channel members. As a general rule, most foreign firms tend to operate with longer channels (that is, more levels within the channel) than do firms in the United States. This can significantly increase end-user prices, since each level of intermediary takes a markup, which accumulates as the product moves through the channel structure. The length and diversity of channels used and the lack of consistent or regulated markup methods often leaves many producers unaware of the ultimate price to the buyer.

The most difficult situation for managing price in global markets occurs when a manufacturer has little or no choice in the selection of intermediaries within the channel structure to reach the desired target market. If a market is dominated by one distributor, then accepting the terms of trade from that distributor may be the only feasible method for entering the market—no matter how unfavorable the markup terms may be. These kinds of market imperfections often lead to the development of parallel markets, or gray markets.

Competition from Gray Markets

Price differences can be large between markets due to a company's intrafirm pricing policies, different pricing strategies between countries, currency fluctuations, or the markup practices of channel members. When this occurs, enterprising distributors within an established channel or independent entrepreneurs will appear and buy products in low-price countries in order to re-export them to higher-price countries. These parallel imports take place outside of the regular trade channels that are controlled by company-owned subsidiaries or independent distributors and are referred to as **gray markets.** They can have a significant negative impact on the sales volume and profits of the established market players.

Several factors contribute to the emergence of competition from gray markets. Intrafirm pricing policies that create large price differentials between markets is one source of the development of gray markets. For example, U.S. publishers of leading-edge scientific and academic texts and journals are often small so they sign over the international distribution of their products to larger publishers, export agents, or international book distributors. Given the relatively high price elasticity for these products, coupled with the low volume of units sold, the firms involved in distributing and selling these books and journals take large markups. Faced with shrinking budgets, many university librarians in Europe have stopped ordering from these agents and now buy directly from wholesalers and booksellers in the United States because books are relatively inexpensive to ship, do not perish, and have very low import tariffs.

Large differences in the value of currencies between countries also lead to gray markets and parallel imports. In 1984, one U.S. dollar could be exchanged for 3.8 deutsch marks, making it worthwhile for Americans to flock to Germany and buy BMWs and Mercedes for half the price found in the United States. In the 1990s, with the exchange rate decreasing to the 1.6 to 1.8 range, a completely different situation has arisen in which German entrepreneurs are rushing to buy American PCs and peripheral equipment directly from U.S. distributors instead of via established German dealers.

Combating parallel imports is an endless battle for companies and most often a losing one at that. Using pricing policies that offer similar prices for standardized products across markets is one approach that takes some of the gray market incentive away. Getting distributors and wholesalers to sign contracts prohibiting them from re-exporting to higher priced markets is another safeguard, but this is difficult to control and enforce. In 1993, European countries began expediting the process of aligning taxes, tariffs, and price structures, and by 1999 at the latest they will all change over to a common currency. These structural changes will remove many of the market imperfections that currently encourage gray markets.

ENVIRONMENTAL FACTORS

Up to this point, cost and market factors of global pricing have been examined. In addition to these factors, there are other external factors that are also beyond the control of the company and affect global pricing strategies. These other factors are foreign exchange rate fluctuations, differing rates of inflation, and governmental price controls.

Exchange Rate Fluctuations

Currency swings, or **exchange rate fluctuations,** are considered by many global companies to be a major trade barrier. Consider the fluctuations of the U.S. dollar. Throughout the 1980s and into the 1990s, the dollar was first weak against European currencies and the Japanese Yen. Then it was extremely strong (from roughly 1983 to 1986), and then once again it was at a very low rate relative to its major trading partners. These movements in exchange rates, which can be 50 percent or more over a period of years, directly influence a firm's ability to compete on price and improves or weakens its competitive position in the world. When an American company's home currency is strong, its ability to purchase raw materials and labor abroad is improved, but its position as a seller of finished products abroad is weakened, since the good's selling price is based most often in the expensive currency. Likewise, a foreign competitor's offering, which is cost-based in less expensive currencies, is cheaper in the United States.

Exchange rate movements are especially critical in long-term strategies and contracts. The longer the time between the signing of an order and the actual delivery of goods and receiving of payment, the greater the exposure to **foreign exchange risk.** For subsidiaries of multinational companies, the course of the exchange rate over a period of 12 months can have an extremely favorable or unfavorable impact on the ability to show a profit at the home company, regardless of real market performance. If Unilever's subsidiaries in the United States increase their market share in the packaged foods markets in the United States by 1 to 2 percent, but the dollar falls 20 percent against the British pound and Dutch guilder (Unilever is an Anglo-Dutch firm), then corporate profits suffer in spite of the efforts of the subsidiaries.

Firms can try to manage foreign exchange fluctuations, but they cannot have any control over them. One common approach to coping with foreign exchange risk is simply doing nothing and hoping that there will be no dramatic movement in the values of the currencies involved. Many European cur-

A Russian comments on the exchange rate value of the Ruble to other currencies.

rencies are strongly linked to each other, and movements within a period of 90 days are seldom dramatic. Companies trading in the more stable currencies (the French franc, deutsch mark, Swiss franc, British pound, or Dutch guilder) run a risk, but it tends to be minimal. A second approach is called *hedging* in the forward market. Hedging involves agreeing to buy a currency at a fixed price 30 to 90 days in the future, regardless of the spot rate (the actual price) on the day of settlement. This allows the seller to incorporate a firm rate in price determination, and/or the buyer to have a firm rate in the purchase price. Some of the possible export strategies under varying currency conditions are summarized in Table 9-4.

Large multinationals that deal with literally dozens of currencies at a time will likely have currency management departments. Their function is to match the various subsidiaries' needs for different currencies internally rather than through the money markets. Finally, as Europe moves towards monetary union by the end of the 1990s, the ECU (European Currency Unit) may become the single currency in Europe, reducing and simplifying foreign exchange transactions among the three most important trading currencies of the next decade, the dollar, the yen, and the ECU.

Inflation Rates

When a company sells its products in a country that has a high rate of inflation, the risk is that once the constantly devaluing local currency is converted

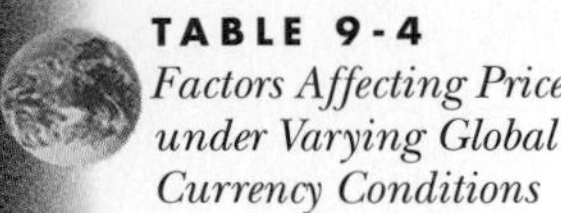
TABLE 9-4
Factors Affecting Price under Varying Global Currency Conditions

When Domestic Currency Is WEAK . . .	When Domestic Currency Is STRONG . . .
• Stress price benefits	• Engage in nonprice competition by improving quality, delivery, and after-sale service
• Expand product line and add more costly features	• Improve productivity and engage in vigorous cost reduction
• Shift sourcing and manufacturing to domestic market	• Shift sourcing and manufacturing overseas
• Exploit export opportunities in all markets	• Give priority to exports to relatively strong-currency countries
• Conduct conventional cash-for-goods trade	• Deal in countertrade with weak-currency countries
• Use full-costing approach, but use marginal-cost pricing to penetrate new/competitive markets	• Trim profit margins and use marginal-cost pricing
• Speed repatriation of foreign-earned income and collections	• Keep the foreign-earned income in host country, slow collections
• Minimize expenditures in local, host country currency	• Maximize expenditures in local, host country currency
• Buy needed services (advertising, insurance, transportation, etc.,) in domestic market	• Buy needed services abroad and pay for them in local currencies
• Minimize local borrowing	• Borrow money needed for expansion in local market
• Bill foreign customers in domestic currency	• Bill foreign customers in their own currency

Source: S. Tamur Cavusgil, "Unraveling the Mystique of Export Pricing." Reprinted from *Business Horizons* (May–June 1988). Copyright © 1988 by the Foundation for the School of Business at Indiana University. Used with permission.

to the sellers' currency, the resulting amount won't even cover product costs. Soaring inflation, particularly in Latin America and eastern Europe, makes widespread price controls a constant threat. Foreign aid in the form of monetary loans to the CIS countries (former republics of the Soviet Union) is essentially an attempt to allow the different republics to purchase goods and services for the purpose of developing their own economies. Purchasing goods and services needs to happen with something besides their highly inflationary (and highly undesirable) ruble. In countries with extremely high inflation rates, companies may price their products in a stable currency, such as the U.S. dollar, and translate prices into the local currency on a daily basis, or if possible, insist on payment in another currency. Illustration 9-3 shows an advertisement sponsored by InterContinental Hotels and American Express. The prices quoted for rooms in Cairo, Caracas, and Jakarta are in United States dollars, while all other prices are in the local currency.

Government Price Controls

In addition to channel member and local competition's activities, a company's pricing strategy in a particular market may also be directly or indirectly influ-

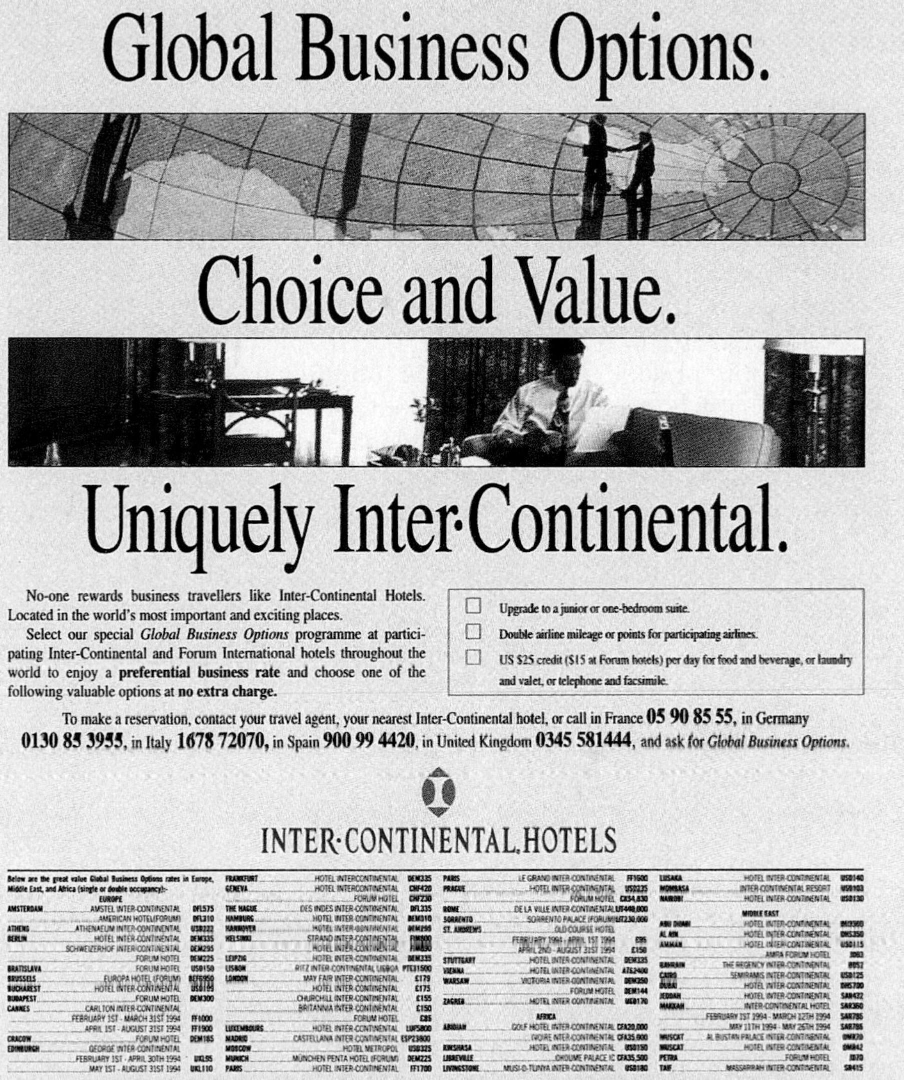

ILLUSTRATION 9-3
Use today's currency conversion rates to calculate the U.S. dollar price of rooms in different countries.

enced by the government. Various forms of price control via government regulation can be found in every country of the world. In an effort to control prices, governments have a number of measures open to them.

The most direct approach is to simply dictate the price that is to be used in the market. In many countries, the government sets the price of gasoline via a combination of directives to oil companies and imposing sales taxes, which are collected at the retail pumps. Indirectly, governments can also influence prices by dictating the margins allowed to intermediaries and not allowing deviation from those margins. By establishing upper and lower limits of markups, governments can create price floors and ceilings. In developing countries, food staples and medicines are often subject to price ceilings in order to make the products available at affordable prices, while price floors are used to discourage the consumption of luxury goods such as alcohol and jewelry. Government controls on pricing can also stem from industry regulations. For example, in Japan, the government requires any brewer who wants to commercially produce beer to be able to produce a minimum of 2,000 kiloliters per year. This effectively eliminates any entrepreneur who wants to start a microbrewery and protects the monopoly structure of Japan's four large beer makers. It also explains why Japanese beer drinkers pay an average of $13 per six-pack for domestic beer.[18]

Government subsidy is another technique that allows companies to compete globally with price. In some cases, the subsidies are direct, such as paying a producer a subsidy on each unit produced. The producer can then reduce the price of the product in the local or global market by the amount of the subsidy or can use the subsidy for capital investments to increase capacity and eventually economies of scale. Government subsidies can also be received indirectly. Operating under the belief that a well-educated population will ultimately lead to a long-term, sustainable, competitive advantage, the Dutch government subsidizes the costs of education. By offering all students beyond the high school level a scholarship and using centralized buying to negotiate with suppliers who sell to educational institutions, the Dutch government's commitment to education is an indirect subsidy that not only encourages foreign investment in the country but eventually delivers benefits to business and society as a whole.

Governments can also operate as monopoly players in a given market, eliminating competition and controlling prices offered in the market. Their monopolistic position gives them tremendous negotiating strength with suppliers and can be used to play suppliers against each other to secure the most advantageous price and terms.

As you now realize, a global perspective on pricing requires that marketing strategists understand and respond to a broad range of influences. Some influences, like competition and market conditions, present challenges that are commonly faced in the domestic market. Others, like currency exchange rates, transfer prices, and multiple rates of inflation, are new and different challenges in the price setting process. Overall, global pricing involves some of the

TABLE 9-5
The Cost of Consumer Goods in Various Asian Cities (in U.S. dollars)

Product	Tokyo	Beijing	Hong Kong	Jakarta	New Delhi
Pepsi-Cola, 355 ml can	1.03	.24	.35	.44	.16
Nescafe Classic Instant Coffee 100 g	5.69	2.64	2.39	1.77	1.58
Johnnie Walker Black Label, 750 ml	32.65	25.28	33.62	36.30	N/A
Kellogg's Corn Flakes, 350 g	5.40	3.42	2.05	3.76	N/A
Campbell's Vegetable Soup, 298 g	2.61	.80	.69	.96	N/A
Gillette Razor Plus Two Blades	6.44	4.42	2.95	4.09	4.20
Fuji Film for prints, 36 exp., 100 ASA	4.20	2.15	2.95	3.37	2.88

Source: Adapted from *Far Eastern Economic Review* (July 1, 1993): 56.

most complex decisions marketing strategists must make. To close this chapter and to once again illustrate the variability of prices, consider the data in Table 9-5, which documents the prices for a number of consumer goods sold in various Asian countries, one of the fastest growing consumer market regions in the world. Notice again that exchange rates clearly do not explain all the differences in prices.[19]

Key Terms and Concepts

The broad meaning of price
Elasticity of demand
Brand loyalty
Price fixing
Price discrimination
Price advertising
Bait-and-switch advertising
Commodity phenomenon
Target return on investment objective
Market share objective
Status quo objective
Maximize profit objective
Target Pricing
Value pricing
Stripped-down pricing
Value-added pricing
Cost-oriented vs. demand-oriented pricing
Full-cost pricing
Markup pricing
Incremental cost pricing
Break-even pricing
Geographic pricing
Lease pricing
Price discounts and allowances
Skim pricing strategy
Penetration pricing strategy
Price lining
Prestige pricing
Inventory management
Power pricing
Global pricing objectives
Tariffs
Transfer pricing
Gray markets
Exchange rate fluctuations
Foreign exchange risks

Questions and Exercises

1. What role does price play in the process of exchange?
2. Why is it the goal of every firm to have inelastic demand for its product? What is the relationship between brand loyalty and elasticity of demand?
3. Strategy decisions in the marketing mix affect pricing decisions. Describe three different factors related to the product area of the marketing mix that can influence the price decision.
4. Why is it claimed that the pricing variable is the *least potent strategic tool* marketing decision makers have available? Give three arguments to support the claim. What arguments can you offer against this claim?
5. What is value pricing? Why has value pricing emerged as such an important perspective on the pricing process in recent years.
6. Using the format provided in Figure 9-3, assume an item costs $100 and will carry a markup of 20 percent. Calculate what the selling price would be using a markup on selling price versus a markup on cost.
7. Using the data from Table 9-1, calculate the break-even point in units if a product is priced at $55 per unit.
8. Leasing is becoming more popular among firms as a pricing method. What uncontrollable factors in the environment represent a great risk to firms who use lease pricing?
9. Explain transfer pricing as an affect on pricing in the global marketing context.
10. How do currency exchange rates and rates of inflation across different countries further compound the complexity of pricing in global markets?

REFERENCES

1. Peter F. Drucker. "Marketing 101 for a Fast-Changing Decade." *The Wall Street Journal* (November 20, 1990): A16.
2. Gabriella Stern. "P & G Gains Little from Diaper Price Cuts." *The Wall Street Journal* (October 10, 1993): B7.
3. Drucker, op. cit.
4. Ibid.
5. William M. Bulkeley. "Computers Become a Kind of Commodity, to Dismay of Makers." *The Wall Street Journal* (September 5, 1991): A1, A6.
6. Jim Carlton. "Popularity of Some Computers Means Buyers Must Wait." *The Wall Street Journal,* (October 25, 1993): B1; Kyle Pope. "Computers: They're No Commodity." *The Wall Street Journal,* (October 15, 1993): B1.
7. Joseph B. White. "'Value Pricing' Is Hot as Shrewd Consumers Seek Low Cost Quality." *The Wall Street Journal* (March 12, 1991): B1.
8. See Patricia Sellers. "Look Who Learned about Value." *Fortune* (October 13, 1993): 75; and Joseph B. White. *Fortune,* op. cit.
9. Greg Gardner. "Olds Boosts Its Offense with Simpler Pricing, Models" *Detroit Free Press,* (August 24, 1993): C1.
10. Stratford Sherman. "How to Prosper in the Value Decade." *Fortune* (November 30, 1992): 91.
11. Adapted from discussions in Christopher Farrell, Zachary Schiller, et al. "Stuck." *Business Week* (November 15, 1993): 146–55.
12. David Woodruff, et al. "Leasing Fever." *Business Week,* (February 7, 1994): 92.
13. Craig Torres. "Pricing Power May Signal Strong Earnings." *The Wall Street Journal,* (October 31, 1991): C1.
14. Pete Engardio and Robert Neff. "Asia: A New Front in the War on Smoking." *International Business Week* (February 25, 1991): 68.
15. Mark Landler. "Mercedes Finds Out How Much Is Too Much" *International Business Week* (January 20, 1992): 57.
16. Patrick Oster, et.al. "Dell: Mail Order Was Supposed to Fail." *International Business Week,* (January 20, 1992): 56.
17. "Protectionist Free Trade." *The Economist* (October 9, 1993): 35.
18. Robert Neff. "Well, It's a Start." *International Business Week* (September 13, 1993): 18.
19. Adapted from "The Cost of Living the Good Life." *Far Eastern Economic Review* (July 1, 1993): 56.

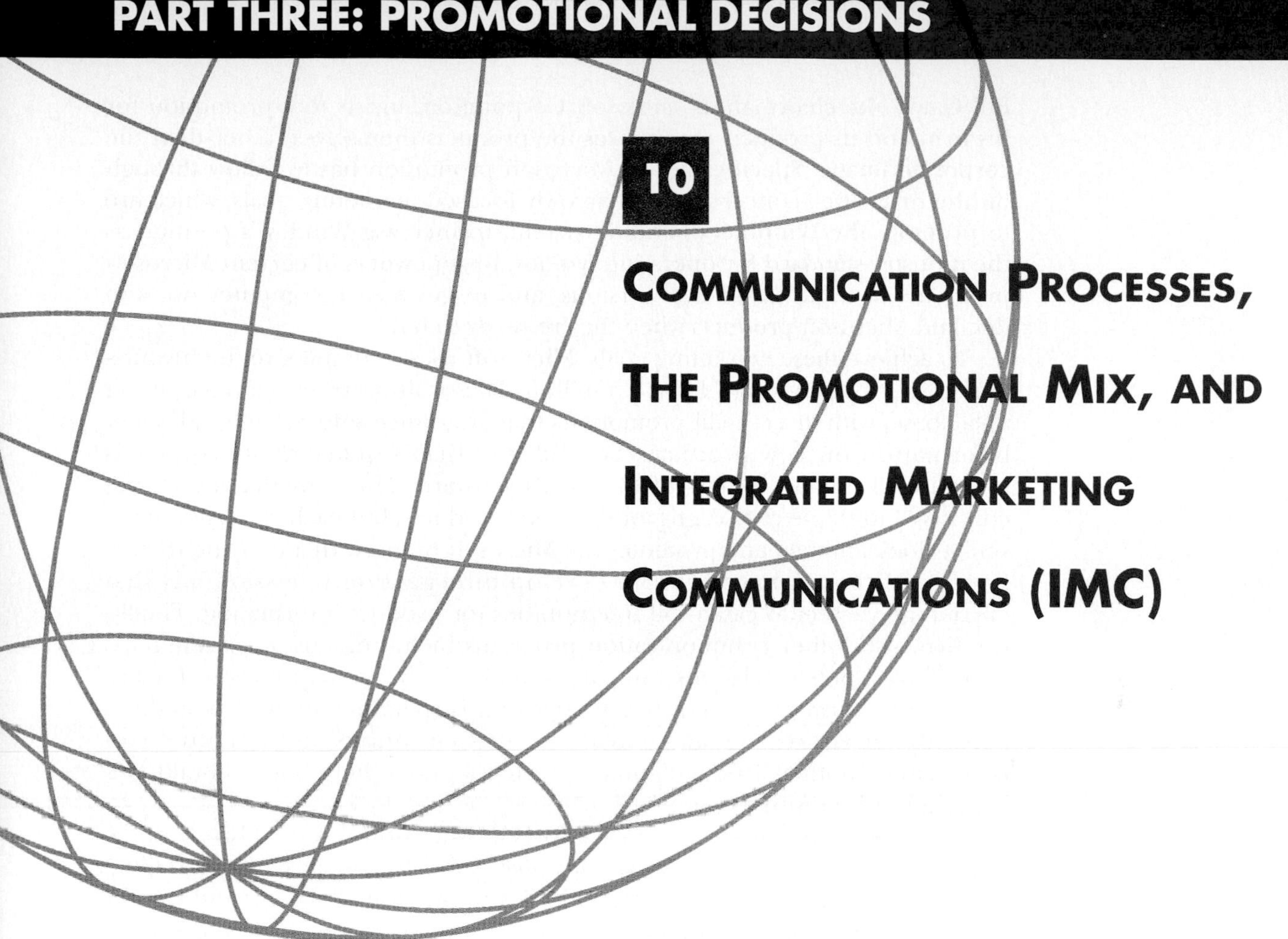

10

Communication Processes, The Promotional Mix, and Integrated Marketing Communications (IMC)

AFTER STUDYING THIS CHAPTER, YOU WILL UNDERSTAND THAT:

1. Mass communication and personal communication are the communication processes that firms use to inform and persuade consumers.
2. The promotional mix is a blend of communications methods used by firms to relay information to consumers; it includes advertising, personal selling, sales promotion, direct marketing, and public relations.
3. Integrated Marketing Communications (IMC) is a new concept that views customers as partners in the communication process and emphasizes the coordination of all available promotional tools for a synergistic communications effect.
4. Promotional objectives are an extension of a firm's overall marketing mix strategies and establish specific goals for communication.
5. Communication processes in global markets are often dictated by media development and by cultural norms from country to country.

Bill Gates, the chairman of Microsoft Corporation, insists that promotion for his firm and its products emphasizes the products themselves rather than the corporate image. Specifically, any Microsoft promotion has to follow through on the firm's well-conceived and narrowly focused marketing goals, which are to promote the Windows operating system, to increase Window's position as the industry standard for operating systems, to get owners of current Microsoft programs to trade up to new versions, and to get novice computer users to demand Microsoft products when they're ready to buy.

To achieve these marketing goals, Microsoft uses a complex yet highly integrated set of promotions. First, 8.5 million Microsoft users are targeted, using a database, with direct mail promotions that announce software upgrades and information on new products. Second, the firm's quarterly newsletter is mailed to 3 million owners of the firm's software. Third, media advertising consists of multiple campaigns for different products, but each campaign has a similar look and feel and promotes the Microsoft brand with a unifying theme. Fourth, Microsoft has begun to develop direct-action television ads that encourage viewers to call a toll free number for product information. Finally, the firm uses other communication programs including customer seminars, trade shows, public relations campaigns, and telephone help lines to further promote the firm's products. In all, Microsoft is spending about $160 million annually on efforts to communicate with its customers and potential customers and another $100 million a year on telephone help lines to build lasting relationships with its users.[1]

These multiple communications efforts by Microsoft rely on a broad range of promotional tools and *communication processes*—advertising, personal selling, direct marketing, public relations, and sales promotion. This new and rapidly expanding practice of coordinating and integrating diverse efforts to form a single unified impression is referred to as *integrated marketing communication.*

This chapter begins the discussion of the promotion area of marketing—the third of the Four Ps in the marketing mix. **Promotion** in marketing includes all the personal and mass media communications used to create a favorable predisposition in the mind of the receiver toward a product, service, idea, or person. Product and service promotions are the type that are most common. An example of the promotion of an idea would be a public service campaign against drunk driving. Promotion of a person is most prevalent in the political and entertainment areas. The discussions in this first chapter of the Promotion Section emphasize the scope and purpose of promotion. Basic issues related to communication processes and a discussion of promotional tools are covered as well as the new area of integrated marketing communications. Chapter 11 focuses specifically on mass communication promotion options—advertising, sales promotion, direct marketing, and publicity. Finally, Chapter 12 covers personal selling, which is the personal communication process in marketing.

A Communications Perspective

In order to fully understand all the strategic opportunities in the area of promotion, it is necessary to adopt a communications perspective and understand the component parts of communications in marketing. First, **communication processes** in marketing are of two types: mass communication and personal communication. Mass communication relies on mass media like television, radio, and newspapers to communicate with current and potential customers in both the business and household consumer markets. Personal communication in marketing is the personal selling effort firms use to sell their products and services. The goal in promotion is to use these communication processes to inform the market regarding features and availability of a firm's product/service and persuade buyers that the firm's products offer superior value and satisfaction. Second, the **promotional mix** is the blend of communications tools used by a firm to communicate directly with the target market (or audience, in the language of communications). These communications tools are advertising, personal selling, sales promotion, direct marketing, and public relations. Finally, the new concept of **integrated marketing communications (IMC)** is the process of creating a comprehensive communications plan using the promotional mix tools in a unified effort where synergistic effect between elements occurs.

As these definitions suggest, the promotion area of the marketing mix serves first and foremost a communications purpose and it is important to emphasize a communications perspective when thinking about this area of marketing. It is the *only* area of marketing where the firm can communicate to current and potential customers about products, services, and other values that make the brand appealing and capable of providing satisfaction.

The reason we emphasize a communications perspective is that some firms look to promotion as the sole solution to languishing sales and adopt a "sales" perspective rather than a communications perspective on promotion. The result is that the promotion area is unduly burdened with the responsibility for creating sales. Remember, though, that sales revenues result from a carefully planned and fully integrated marketing mix with no one variable in the mix capable of creating sales by itself. Sales will result only when a product is properly designed, priced distributed, *and* promoted. The tools of promotion are capable of having a powerful, persuasive impact on buyer decision making. The promotion area of the marketing mix cannot be burdened with more than its fair share of the responsibility for generating sales revenue. The apparel marketer Calvin Klein learned this lesson in grand style. In October 1991, the firm spent a reported $1 million to run a 166 page insert in *Vanity Fair* magazine. The insert carried suggestive ads (the trademark of Calvin Klein advertising) of leather jacketed bikers and couples embracing backstage at a rock concert. This extravagant advertising effort was supposed to revive Klein's troubled jeanswear division—it didn't. Six months after the insert appeared, retailers reported that the advertising (and the rush of publicity surrounding such a bold maneuver) failed to translate into increased sales. As one retailer put it, "Denim is a hot commodity right now, but Calvin jeanswear isn't doing so well."[2]

The experience at Calvin Klein highlights the importance of a communications rather than a sales perspective on promotion. Maintaining a communications perspective makes for more effective strategic use of this area of the marketing mix. First, by viewing promotion as primarily a communication effort, marketers can consider a broader range of promotional strategies. As an example, few of us as average consumers have considered purchasing high-speed photocopying equipment or large-capacity computers. Despite this fact, both Xerox and IBM regularly direct promotional messages at general consumer audiences through mass media. Neither of these highly sophisticated firms has any intention of selling their business products or services to household consumers. Generating a *sale* is not the objective of these communications efforts. Rather, establishing a broad-based image in the market is the goal. Many legitimate promotional efforts do not focus on sales, per se. Union Pacific Railroad ran a television advertising campaign with the theme, "We're Union Pacific—We Can Handle It." This campaign was not directed at Union Pacific's customers at all, but rather at the firm's own employees. The purpose of the campaign was to boost employee morale and reduce turnover. A second major benefit of emphasizing a communications perspective is to gain a greater appreciation for the complexity of the promotional process. Designing a promotional program with the idea that sales is the sole objective neglects aspects of message design, media choice, or sales force deployment, which can create synergy within the promotional mix. Advertising messages that reinforce the efforts of the sales force is one example of coordinating the entire communication process through the promotional mix.

This chapter discusses the basic aspects of the promotion area of the marketing mix. We begin by considering the nature of communication processes, both mass and personal communications. Then we will briefly examine each area of the promotional mix—advertising, personal selling, sales promotion, direct marketing, and public relations. Next, integrated marketing communications will be considered and how this new concept in the promotional area is making its mark in business practice. Then, the tasks related to setting objectives and budgeting for promotion are identified. Finally, application of promotional processes and promotional tools in a global context are considered.

Communication Processes

The fundamental process underlying each element in the promotional mix is communication. Communicating with current and potential customers is a firm's chance to tell them what it has to offer and why the offer has value. Each element in the promotional mix uses either a mass communication or a personal communication process to deliver a message to buyers. These two different communication processes have unique characteristics and are discussed separately.

MASS COMMUNICATION

Mass communication is the process of communicating an identical message to a large number of people at a particular point in time through the mass media. Mass communication is called an impersonal form of communication because the mass media, such as magazines, newspapers, radio, and television, are used to transmit messages. Figure 10-1 is a model of mass communication that represents how the process takes place in marketing.[3] Each component in

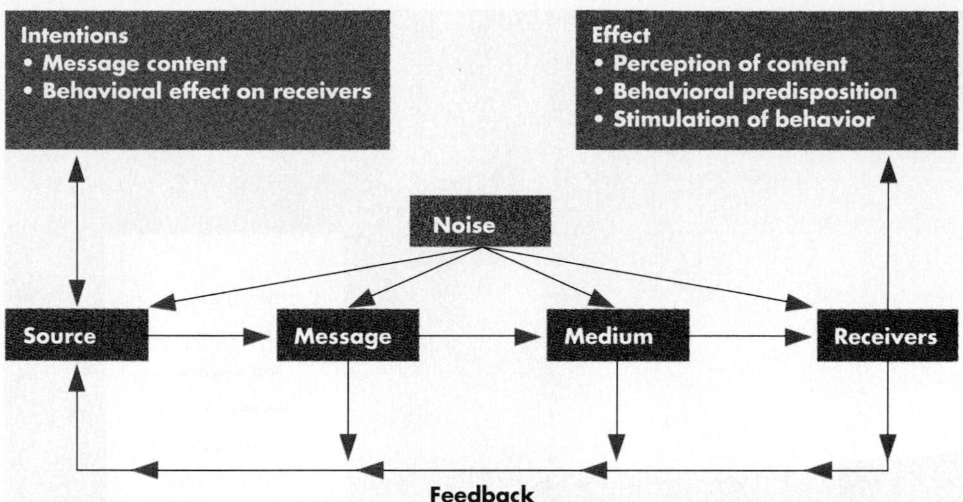

FIGURE 10-1
The Mass Communication Process

the model warrants some discussion to truly appreciate how this communication process works.

Intentions

A mass communication effort in marketing begins with **intentions** for message content and the behavioral effect the communication is expected to have on those who receive the message. *Intended message content* identifies the informational and persuasive language and visual content in a message. Developing a mass communication message relies on an analysis of the external environment (see Chapter 2) and the criteria being used by buyers in the market to judge products. As we saw in Chapter 6, household and business buyers will seek out information during the decision-making process. Intentions for message content will emphasize providing *relevant* information. What information is relevant to buyers? Relevance depends on buyers' perceiving that a product or service meets their needs, that is, the product or service has satisfaction to offer that is greater than the cost of acquisition. And, recall from the discussions of buyer behavior that specific information that is relevant to potential buyers can be functional, emotional, or benefits of use features of a product or service. When this sort of information is put in a context that is consistent with influences from the external environment—like social and cultural trends or economic influences—then a message is deemed relevant.

The *intended behavioral effect* on receivers is rarely immediate. In general, mass communications messages are designed to create a favorable *predisposition* toward a firm's product, and a delayed response is to be expected. In most cases this means a favorable image or attitude toward the brand. Then, at some future point in time, the goal is to have receivers recall the message and judge the product as one that can satisfy their current needs. Illustration 10-1 is typical of advertising designed to create a favorable impression. In some cases, mass communication messages implore consumers to take immediate action. Advertisements, for example, that urge consumers to call a toll free number to place an order are designed to illicit an immediate response. These are called direct response ads.

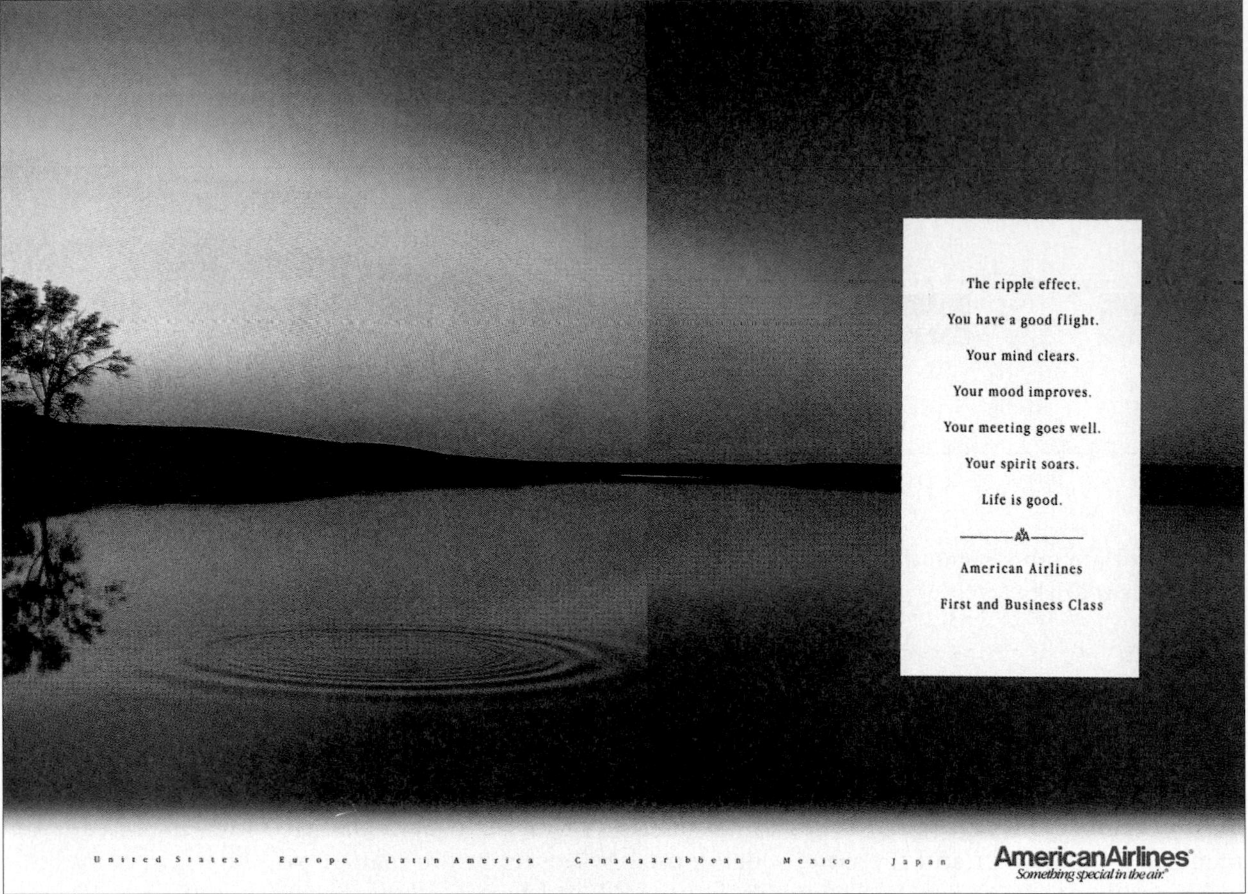
The ripple effect.
You have a good flight.
Your mind clears.
Your mood improves.
Your meeting goes well.
Your spirit soars.
Life is good.
American Airlines
First and Business Class
United States
Europe
Latin America
Canadaaribbean
Mexico
Japan
AmericanAirlines
Something special in the air.

ILLUSTRATION 10-1
Most mass communication messages, like this advertisement, are designed to create a favorable predisposition toward a firm's product or service over the long term.

Source

The **source** of a mass communication message is the organization marketing the brand and its advertising department or advertising agency. Those who are responsible for preparing the advertisement are guided by all the information the firm has gathered about the target market and all the influences on the target that affect their evaluation of products and services. When General Motors discovered that only 44 percent of prospective car buyers believed that it built quality cars, the company undertook a massive "Putting Quality on the Road" image campaign to change their minds. Within four months, among those who had seen the ads, 56 percent thought that GM built quality cars.[4] The campaign apparently was changing the predisposition of these receivers toward GM products.

Message

The **message** contains the information designed to inform or persuade consumers that the firm's product or service provides superior satisfaction. In mass communication, one difficulty is constructing a message that is suitable for a large number of receivers. The message must be a generalized representation of many different judgment criteria used by buyers. If the analysis of the external environment is done well, the message can contain reasonably specific information relating to buyers' judgment criteria. Remember, those criteria can relate to functional features, emotional factors, or benefits of use.

The overriding consideration for message content is, again, that it is deemed *relevant* by consumers. If consumers perceive a message to be irrelevant or contradictory to their beliefs, it will be ignored. The makers of Häagen-Dazs ice cream have taken the issue of relevant information to heart. The ice cream food category saw a 4 to 5 percent contraction in consumption in the United States each year during 1989 and 1990. Consumers concerned about fat and cholesterol began turning away from super-rich ice creams. Häagen-Dazs Co., in an effort to recruit new users, launched a $4 million ad campaign with the theme, "Enter the State of Häagen-Dazs" for consumers who wanted to indulge and reward themselves. The vice president of marketing said of the campaign, "We want to make the brand relevant to a broader group of people."[5]

Medium

The **medium** is the vehicle through which a message is transmitted to receivers. In marketing, newspapers, radio, television, magazines, billboards, and direct mail constitute standard media for transmitting mass communications messages. Each of these media has the capability of reaching a large number of receivers at low cost per contact and at frequent intervals.

The medium chosen has much to do with the effect of the communication. The broadcast media of radio and television have the advantage of audio and/or audiovisual presentation of the message. The print media can provide more detailed information but a product cannot be demonstrated. Firms often use a combination of media to achieve overall communications intentions. Acushnet, the makers of *Titleist* golf equipment, can use advertisements in *Golf Digest* to communicate the functional features of its golf balls and then use television ads during a major golf tournament to demonstrate the features of the ball in action.

Receivers

The **receivers** of a message are the household consumers or business buyers targeted by a firm in its market segmentation strategy. Reaching these consumers is accomplished by carefully choosing media. The media organizations—newspaper agencies, magazines, radio, and television stations—provide relatively accurate, up-to-date information on their readers, listeners, or viewers. In this phase of the mass communication process, the most important information is a firm's strategy regarding segmentation and positioning. The target segment constitutes the audience to whom the message is directed. The positioning strategy affects message content.

Effects

The **effects** in a mass communication process are determined by identifying receivers' perception of message content, behavioral predisposition toward the product, and the amount and type of behavior stimulated by the communication. Identifying what was *actually perceived* relative to the intentions can be a lengthy and costly process. Only through market surveys can such information be obtained. The critical issue about content perception is that intentions for the content match the perception of content. Behavioral predisposition as an effect of mass communication is measured by identifying the overall image of (or attitude toward) the product or service created by the communication and consumers' intention to buy after exposure to a message.

The amount and type of behavior stimulated is an important measure of communication effect. Unfortunately, it is the most difficult to measure. Because consumers may not draw on information obtained from a mass communication message for a long time, being able to attribute behavior to a particular message is nearly impossible. For direct response messages that implore immediate action, the task is a bit easier. This would simply entail monitoring calls received or orders obtained after the message was sent. In assessing the behavioral effect a message has had, perhaps the least informative measure is total sales. Again, any form of promotion, including those that use mass communication, can be only partly responsible for sales revenues. The consumer may have been stimulated to purchase from a different source of information altogether, such as a friend's recommendation. This type of sale, of course, has little to do with the effects of mass communication.

Noise and Feedback

In a mass communication effort, **noise** is any disturbance that inhibits message transmission to the intended receiver. As Figure 10-1 indicates, noise is pervasive in the system. Noise-affecting intentions come in the form of inaccurate or incomplete information about the environment that results in poor understanding of receivers. Noise emanating from the source of the message occurs when a product feature does not match what receivers deem to be relevant in the product category. The message itself contributes to noise if the language used or visualization is confusing to receivers. Clutter in the chosen medium produces noise as competing messages interfere with one another. Finally, noise is present at the receiver level if distractions occur during message reception. Overall, noise results in reducing the impact of a mass communication or it can result in total lack of reception.

Feedback in mass communication provides measures of the following:

- Who were the actual receivers of the message?
- What was the perceived content of the message?
- What behavioral predisposition toward the product resulted from receipt of the message?
- What type of behavior was stimulated by exposure to the message?

Once this valuable information is obtained, changes throughout the system can be made—message content can be changed, media placement can be adjusted, or new receivers can be targeted. The feedback process provides the opportunity to enhance future mass communications efforts.

PERSONAL COMMUNICATION

In a **personal communication** process, transmission of a message takes place in a face-to-face setting. In marketing, personal selling is the method of personal communication. Figure 10-2 depicts a model of personal communication. Note its similarity to the mass communication process just discussed in that there are similar intentions, development of message content, and effects. However, the communicator, delivery of the message, nature of the effect, and noise and feedback have unique characteristics and warrant specific description.

Communicator

Because the person speaking for the firm encounters receivers face-to-face, several aspects of the communicator's task change in a personal communication. Rather than simply relaying a generalized message prepared in advance, the communicator must physically approach receivers. This requires complete knowledge of product/service features and applications and preparation to answer any questions a receiver may have. In order to fully take advantage of the opportunity to deliver a message in person, the communicator must understand as completely as possible the specific needs and desires of each receiver. Also, in some personal selling situations, the salesperson/communicator is instrumental in the delivery, installation, or servicing of a product. By virtue of direct contract with receivers, the salesperson must realize that his or her manner of speaking, dress, and other nonverbal cues can convey different meanings to different receivers. The well-designed personal communications

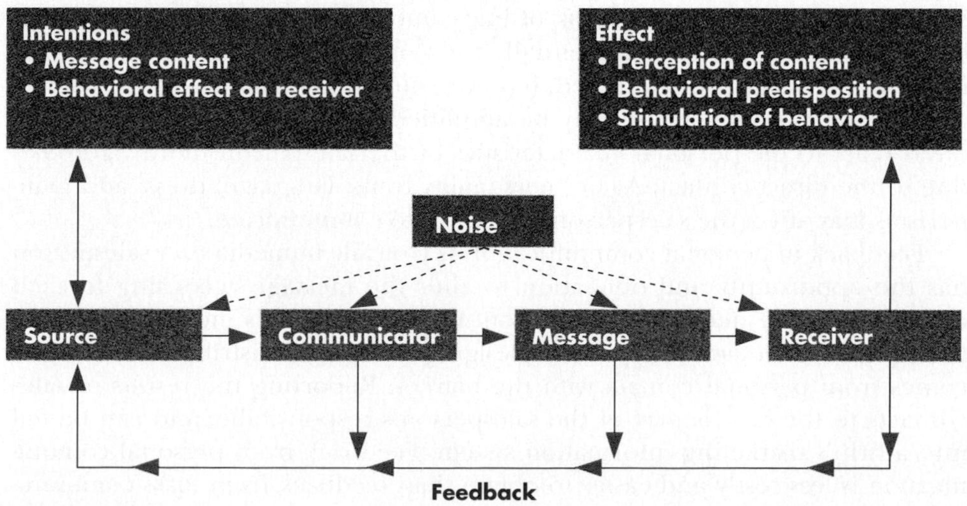

FIGURE 10-2
A Personal Communication Process

system, therefore, must prepare the communicator for several ancillary tasks and other contingencies.

Message Delivery

While the planning that goes into message content in personal communication is similar to mass communication, the delivery differs considerably. First, notice that the model of personal communication (Figure 10-2) has no medium as the mass communication model (Figure 10-1) did. The communicator acts as the medium. Second, a great advantage of a personal communication setting is the opportunity for the communicator to tailor the message for each receiver. The values of the product can be portrayed differently according to each receiver's unique perspective and judgment criteria. Further, the salesperson can respond to inquiries or objections raised by the receiver. The mass communication message must remain general in order to be relevant to as many receivers as possible. In personal communication, a different message can be constructed during each contact.

Effect

The effect in a personal communication process is somewhat easier to determine than in the mass communication process. Because the salesperson can alter the message and reply to questions from receivers immediately, the probability increases that the perceived content of the message will be the same as the intended content. Also, because part of the salesperson's job is to close a sale, the behavioral effect of the message is more closely linked to communications objectives from the outset. It should not be concluded, however, that the goal of *every* personal communication is to consummate a sale. As we will learn in Chapter 12, there are forms of personal selling where simply developing a favorable predisposition of potential buyers toward the product is the goal, just as in mass communication. Sales may, indeed, be realized well after an encounter and the effect can be delayed much as it is in mass communication.

Noise and Feedback

The nature of interference in personal communication differs from the noise in mass communication. The risk of inaccuracies in information and adverse receiver predisposition are essentially the same. The danger of relaying an inappropriate message is lessened, however, due to the communicator's ability to alter the message. Noise may be amplified when it does exist. Receivers often react to the personal characteristics of the salesperson more vigorously due to the direct contact. Again, personality traits, language, dress, and mannerisms may affect the salesperson's attempts to communicate.

Feedback in personal communication is typically immediate. A salesperson has the opportunity and obligation to alter the message according to each receiver's unique need for information. One of the firm's most useful monitoring systems for assessing product design, pricing, and distribution strategies comes from personal contact with the market. Reporting the results of sales contacts to the firm is part of the salesperson's responsibility and can be fed into a firm's marketing information system. Feedback from personal communication is less costly and easier to obtain than feedback from mass communication.

DIFFERENCES BETWEEN MASS AND PERSONAL COMMUNICATION PROCESSES

The preceding discussions have touched on the differences between mass and personal communication processes. It is useful to summarize these differences and highlight the advantages of one system of communication over the other. The differences relate to the overall effectiveness and efficiency of each system and, therefore, a manager's ability to properly use each type of system according to the communication needs facing the firm.

Cost

Mass communication offers a great cost advantage over personal communication with respect to the cost of communicating with each receiver. Through the mass media, a large number of receivers can be reached for pennies each or less. By contrast, the cost of a personal sales call could be $300, or more!

Setting

An obvious difference between the two processes is the setting in which communication takes place. In mass communication, the receiver may be comfortably situated at home or in an automobile. The communicator is a remote entity who is relatively anonymous. Distractions abound since the receiver's attention is diverted by competing stimuli: other advertisements, other tasks (like driving a car), or interruptions to viewing, reading, or listening.

Personal communication takes place in a more intimate and controlled setting. The receiver is face to face with the communicator. The setting may be either familiar, like the receiver's office, or unfamiliar, like a retail store. Since buyer and seller are coming together with the intention of information exchange, the chance that a message will be effectively communicated is greatly increased.

Nature of the Message

The mass communication message must be prepared in a way that fits the medium within which it is transmitted. It must also be generalized to accommodate a wide range of judgment criteria potentially being used by different receivers. Again, personal communication offers the tremendous advantage of being able to be tailored for each receiver.

Reach and Selectivity

Mass communications are designed to reach a large number of receivers. Further, these receivers can be reached in many different ways and places depending on the media used. Personal communications are restricted to one or a small group of receivers at a time. This, of course, greatly restricts the potential reach of the system.

Mass communications efforts can try to selectively reach targeted consumers by carefully choosing the media through which messages are transmitted. Even the most selective media, however, result in "wasted circulation" or reaching unintended receivers. Personal communications can be highly selective on the other hand. A salesforce can be deployed to call on only those potential customers that precisely match the firm's market segmentation and positioning strategies.

Noise and Feedback

The potential for noise interference is much greater in mass communication. The setting and impersonal nature of media create a reception environment that is potentially fraught with noise. A well-planned personal communication effort can control for noise and make the reception environment as conducive as possible to message transmission. The same sort of dichotomy exists with respect to feedback: mass communication feedback is slow and imprecise whereas personal communication feedback can be immediate and exact.

The value in summarizing the differences between the two processes is to clearly identify the efficiency and effectiveness aspects of each process. A communication process is *efficient* when the largest number of *specific receivers* is reached at low cost. A communication is *effective* when the intentions specified for the effort closely matched the effects realized. Mass communication is far more efficient because a large number of receivers is reached at low cost. However, due to the generalized nature of the message, a great number of distractions, and long delay in feedback the system suffers significant threats to effectiveness. Personal communication, on the other hand, is much more effective with its specialized message and more highly controlled reception environment. The extremely high cost of personal communication makes it far less efficient, however.

The Promotional Mix

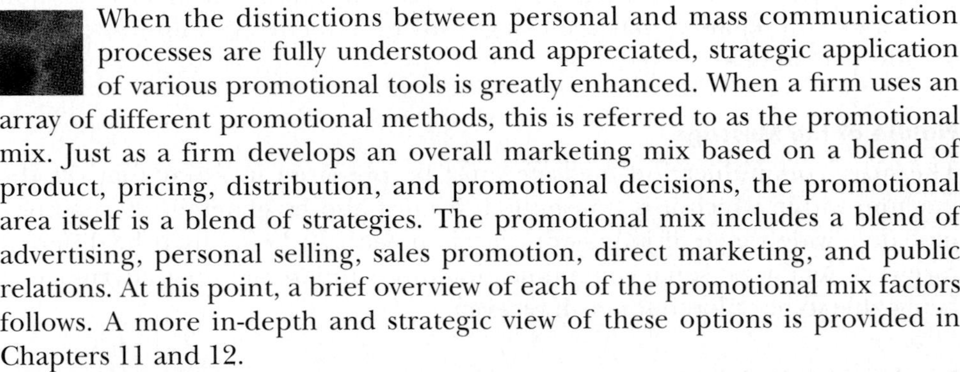

When the distinctions between personal and mass communication processes are fully understood and appreciated, strategic application of various promotional tools is greatly enhanced. When a firm uses an array of different promotional methods, this is referred to as the promotional mix. Just as a firm develops an overall marketing mix based on a blend of product, pricing, distribution, and promotional decisions, the promotional area itself is a blend of strategies. The promotional mix includes a blend of advertising, personal selling, sales promotion, direct marketing, and public relations. At this point, a brief overview of each of the promotional mix factors follows. A more in-depth and strategic view of these options is provided in Chapters 11 and 12.

ADVERTISING

Advertising is any paid form of nonpersonal presentation of information about a product or service through the mass media by an identified sponsor. To appreciate the nature of advertising, a good starting point is to recognize the importance and scope of the process in the United States. One measure of the importance of advertising is the large amount of money spent by firms in the United States. Table 10-1 shows that while the rate of increase in spending has slowed from 1983 to 1994, the absolute dollar amount is still enormous. Another indication is the amount of spending on advertising related to sales.

TABLE 10-1
Spending on Advertising in the United States, 1983 to 1994

Year	Billions of U.S. Dollars	Percentage Change
1983	$ 75.8	+13.9%
1984	87.8	+15.8
1985	94.8	+ 7.9
1986	102.1	+ 7.7
1987	109.7	+ 7.4
1988	118.1	+ 7.7
1989	124.8	+ 5.8
1990	128.6	+ 3.1
1991	126.7	- 1.4
1992	130.9	+ 3.3
1993	138.1	+ 5.5
1994*	146.8	+ 6.3

*Estimated.

Source: For 1983 through 1989 data, McCann-Erickson analysis, cited in Thomas R. King, "Spending on Ads Expected to Rise Only 4.6 Percent in 1991," *The Wall Street Journal,* December 11, 1990, B1. For 1990 through 1994 data estimate, statistics cited in Jerrold Ballinger, "Mail Volume, Spending Rose in 1993 and More Growth Is Seen, Says Coen," *Direct Marketing News* (December 13, 1993): 2.

Across all industries, U.S. firms spend about 7 percent of gross sales on advertising. This exceeds the average amount, across all industries, spent by firms on research and development!

But advertising is much more than simply large dollar expenditures. The process is complex and requires careful planning and execution to fulfill communications objectives. Advertising is, therefore, carried out in a relatively structured fashion. The major tasks involved in developing and carrying out effective advertising are:

- Determining the proper audience to target with the advertising.
- Developing a message based on an assessment of the environment and the judgment criteria used by the target audience to evaluate a product or service.
- Developing sensory stimuli such as visualizations, words, and special effects to creatively relay message information.
- Placing the advertising in media that reach the target market.
- Measuring the effectiveness of the advertising effort.

PERSONAL SELLING

Personal selling is the presentation of information about a firm's products or services by an individual to another person or small group of people. The factors discussed regarding the personal communication process are the basic activities of a personal selling effort. The major targets of personal selling differ greatly between the business market and the household consumer market. In the business market, professional buyers in organizations constitute the target market. In retail sales, household consumers are the target for the communication. In general, however, the *categories of activities* involved in the personal selling process are the same regardless of the target customer:

- Identify and research high-potential prospects.
- Prepare the message presentation.
- Approach the prospect.
- Deliver the sales presentation.
- Demonstrate the product or effects of the service.
- Negotiate the sale.
- Follow up on negotiations.

Personal selling dominates the promotional mix of many major corporations. It is the essential communication method in business-to-business promotion. This is because features of the business market such as product complexity, larger dollar expenditures, negotiated contracts, and more knowledgeable buyers all warrant more specific and tailored information. But, personal selling is relevant to household consumers because they often rely on the input of sales people when they embark on high-dollar purchases such as shopping and specialty goods.

SALES PROMOTION

Sales promotion is the use of incentive techniques to generate a specific and short-term response from a household consumer, trade buyer, or business buyer. Free samples, coupons, premiums, and point-of-purchase displays are the primary methods of sales promotion in the household consumer market. Illustration 10-2 shows an example of a sales promotion for a household consumer product. In this case, the firm is offering consumers a savings on the purchase of the product through the use of a coupon. The business market relies more on trade shows, demonstrations, premiums, and sales force or dealer contests as incentive techniques. Sales promotion is designed to stimulate short-term purchasing in the target market and enhance dealer effectiveness in promoting a firm's product. Firms must be judicious in the use of sales promotion techniques. It is often the case that a vicious cycle is created when sales promotions are overused—because of the frequent use of sales promotion, firms have a difficult time attracting customers without it.

DIRECT MARKETING

Direct marketing is defined as "an interactive system of marketing that uses one or more advertising media to effect a measurable response and/or transaction at any location."[6] Direct marketing includes all catalog and telephone selling. It also includes the use of toll free numbers to induce consumers to call immediately to place an order after seeing a television, magazine, or newspaper ad or hearing a radio ad. Direct marketing differs from the other tools of the promotional mix. First, the ability of the consumer to order directly is different from other forms of advertising in that traditional advertising is not designed to elicit immediate action. Second, personal selling does not use mass media as direct marketing does. Finally, the aspect of direct marketing that attempts to "effect a transaction at any location" is unique in the realm of

ILLUSTRATION 10-2
Sales promotions, like this two-for-one coupon, can stimulate a short-term surge in demand for a product.

promotional activities. This means that transactions may be culminated from the buyers home, by mail, or literally any place the consumer can communicate with the marketing organization.

Direct marketing has experienced spectacular growth in recent years. Historically, direct marketing has gone by different names such as *mail-order marketing* and *direct-mail.* Today, the widespread use and sophistication of direct marketing techniques by firms like L. L. Bean and Time/Warner suggests that the technique is indeed a major promotional mix tool. Direct marketing through catalogs alone generated $62 billion is sales revenues for catalog marketers in 1993. Another $2.5 billion in merchandise was ordered by consumers from home shopping networks.[7] One reason for the explosive growth of direct

Direct marketing through home shopping networks generates over $2 billion in sales annually. Here, order takers quickly and efficiently serve customers via computer terminals.

marketing is the increased ability to measure the effect of direct response appeals to consumers. When consumers are asked to make an order via a catalog or toll free number, their actions can be attributed to no other source of information.

PUBLIC RELATIONS

As part of being a good corporate and community citizen, a firm will use public relations as a way to establish a good image and reputation. **Public relations** is a management function that focuses on fostering communication and goodwill among a firm and its many constituent groups. These constituent groups include customers, stockholders, suppliers, employees, government entities, citizen action groups, and the general public. Public relations is used to highlight positive events in an organization like quarterly sales and profits or noteworthy community service programs established by the firm. Or, conversely, public relations is used strategically for "damage control" when adverse publicity strikes an organization. Johnson & Johnson relied heavily on public relations in 1982 when its *Extra-Strength Tylenol* product had been tampered with causing death to several people. Johnson & Johnson's public relations people handled literally thousands of inquiries from the public, distributors, the press, and police. The firm quickly and carefully issued coordinated statements to the general public, the press, and government authorities to provide clarification wherever possible. The result was that through conscientious and competent PR activities, Johnson & Johnson came through this disaster viewed as a credible and trustworthy organization.

Public relations is not viewed to be as strategically controllable as other areas in the promotional mix. The dissemination of public relations information is imprecise and not always fully controlled by the organization. Press releases are the best example of a public relations tool that is not totally within the control of the firm. Once a press release reaches the media, the firm is never sure if it will ever get printed or aired. Similarly, publicity about a firm is totally beyond the firm's control and may be positive or negative. Despite the lack of control, there are many circumstances that warrant a public relations effort.

FACTORS AFFECTING THE PROMOTIONAL MIX BLEND

When promotional strategy planning begins, decision makers must decided how much emphasis to put on each area of the promotional mix. Decision makers at Kellogg's know that the promotional mix for its cereal brands will be dominated by advertising. The convenience goods category, which includes packaged goods like cereal, is characterized by widespread distribution and broad market segments ideal for advertising. Bergan-Brunswick, a pharmaceutical wholesaler, will invest almost exclusively in personal selling to communicate with its customers. And 3M, which has both business and household consumer products, will use the complete array of promotional mix tools in its overall strategy. When specifying the amount of advertising, personal selling, sales promotion, and direct marketing to use, the firm must analyze in detail influences that dictate the reliance on each. Factors affecting promotional mix strategy are characteristics of the market, the product, the firm, and the distribution system.

CHARACTERISTICS OF THE MARKET

The characteristics of the market within which communication will take place are an important influencing factors on decision making. The effect of the external environment is unavoidable in all areas of marketing. With respect to promotional mix strategy decisions, three influences from the market must be considered: type of consumer, geographic considerations, and competition.

Type of Customer

Deciding which promotional mix tools to use depends on which of the three basic customer groups—household consumers, business buyers, the distribution trade—a firm needs to communicate with. Typically the business buyer and members of the distribution channel are more knowledgeable and more price and service oriented. The individualized communication provided by personal selling addresses the needs of these types of customers better. And, since there are fewer total customers in the business and trade markets (compared to the household consumer market), this makes personal selling more economically feasible.

The household consumer, on the other hand, often needs to be reached through a combination of advertising, personal selling, sales promotion, and direct marketing. The large number of potential buyers makes advertising a logical choice. Consumer tendencies for comparison shopping in some product categories calls personal selling into play. The growing demand for convenience in the consumer market, increased access to cable television, and a continued willingness to accumulate credit card debt makes direct marketing a legitimate choice. Much of the strategy planning for promotion to the household consumer market is driven by the nature of the product, which is discussed in the next section.

Many firms deal with more than one customer type for every product they market. Colgate-Palmolive, for example, has a broad line of consumer products. It spends nearly $450 million annually on media advertising to communicate with household consumers. Colgate must also stimulate demand within the distribution trade. It directs a considerable amount of money and effort in its promotional mix to wholesalers and retailers through personal selling and sales promotions. According to one marketing official, Colgate spends "a good deal more" on trade promotions than the $450 million spent on traditional advertising.[8]

Geographic Considerations

Two basic geographic considerations can influence the promotional mix: concentration of the market and breadth of the market. The more geographically concentrated a firm's market, the more personal selling will be a useful strategy tool. A widely dispersed market lends itself more to advertising. With regard to geographic breadth, emphasis in the promotional mix can vary greatly depending on the local, regional, or national scope of the firm's market. As the scope of the market broadens, more emphasis will be placed on advertising. Local retailers will rely heavily on advertising in local media that have limited geographic reach.

Competition

Competitors' strategies cannot be ignored as the promotional mix is being devised. This is not to say that firms copy each other's promotional strategies. But, in many industries, firms tend to come to the same conclusions with regard to the use of promotional mix options. Each competitor often recognizes the same influences on strategy. However, a strategic maneuver by one competitor may force all the others to follow suit. For example, one competitor may suddenly increase advertising in a business target market with heavy geographic concentration—a condition that would normally dictate heavy reliance on personal selling. To meet such a competitive thrust, the other firms in the industry are likely to do the same.

Competitors' strategies need to be tracked as a matter of good business practice as a part of the firm's environmental scanning. But, merely following competitors means that a firm is always (at least) second in the market with a strategy. It is better to simply be aware of competition and then determine promotional strategy based on market and product needs. By responding to the market, a firm may produce more effective and innovative promotion than would be created by merely following the competition.

CHARACTERISTICS OF THE PRODUCT

The product or service a firm is promoting is an overriding consideration in promotional mix decision making. The effect here comes from fundamental characteristics of the product rather than from specific differences between brands. These fundamental characteristics are the product category and stage in the product life cycle.

Product Category

One of the most informative considerations for determining the weight of each variable in the promotional mix is the product category of the item. Convenience goods, shopping goods, specialty goods, and services in the consumer market each require a different blend of variables in the promotional mix.

Convenience goods, which are simple, frequently purchased items characterized by brand switching, have broad demographic and geographic market segments. Promotion for convenience goods relies on advertising and sales promotion because of these factors. In contrast, shopping goods require greater emphasis on personal selling because of their higher price, complexity, and the fact that consumers comparison shop and judge the product at the point of purchase. The emphasis on brand name in the specialty goods category reduces the usefulness of sales promotion for products in this category. However, because of the exclusive nature of distribution, advertising is typically needed to identify for consumers outlets where the product can be obtained. Services often require the combined use of advertising and personal selling. Advertising is used to inform consumers of the availability of the service. Personal selling is used because most services are tailored to each consumer's specific needs. Sales promotions are often used because of the intense competition in service products and such discounts often allow customers to try a new service provider at reduced risk. Often you will see ads for service organizations such as carpet cleaning services where advertising is used to reach customers, a free estimate is offered (personal selling), and the ad also contains a coupon for a discount (sales promotion).

The promotional mix for business goods relies more heavily on personal selling for several reasons already mentioned. Higher unit cost, larger order size, fewer and more educated customers, customization, and ancillary services all warrant a greater reliance on personal selling. Sales promotions are also widely used. Trade show demonstrations, premiums, and dealer contests help attract the attention of business buyers.

Stage in the Product Life Cycle

The discussion of the product life cycle in Chapter 7 pointed out that every product passes through several stages of market development. During each stage, promotional requirements change. In the introductory stage, the need for personal selling is acute as the firm tries to gain acceptance for the product at the wholesale and retail trade level. Also, at this stage, advertising may be used to stimulate primary demand. Advertising will continue to be dominant through the growth stage as selective demand stimulation for a brand begins. The middle stages of the life cycle will see a decline in emphasis on personal selling as the members of the trade have already been cultivated. The middle stages will also see periodic heavy emphasis on sales promotion. In these stages, firms make minor alterations in differentiation and positioning strategy, and coupons and contests may be used to attract attention to the brand. During the maturity and, especially, the decline stage, sales promotions become prominent and advertising is usually eliminated. The goal here is to clear out inventories and eliminate advertising to reduce costs.

CHARACTERISTICS OF THE FIRM

The nature of the promotional mix is also influenced by a variety of factors internal to the firm. In many cases, firms will be using promotional mix strategies that seem totally inappropriate given the nature of the external environment and characteristics of the product. The explanation for these somewhat unusual promotional mix decisions usually lies with influences stemming from the characteristics of the firm itself.

Push versus Pull Strategy

Reliance on the tools in the promotional mix varies greatly depending on whether a firm decides to use a push or pull promotional strategy. The most common is a **push strategy** where a manufacturer promotes the product to wholesalers and distributors, who then promote the product to retailers, who in turn use promotional tools to communicate with consumers. When promotion is used within the channel of distribution in this fashion, it is said to be "pushed" through the channel to the end user. Manufacturers, wholesalers, and distributors primarily use only personal selling and sales promotion, whereas retailers use the full range of promotional tools. In a **pull strategy,** a manufacturer uses advertising to stimulate demand among consumers who then demand the product from retailers who in turn demand the product from wholesalers, who then order the product from the manufacturer. In this situation, consumers "pull" the product through the channel. Figure 10-3 graphically depicts the difference between push and pull strategies. In a push strategy, personal selling and trade sales promotions dominate the promotional mix. A pull strategy may rely on any form of promotion depending on other factors affecting the mix. We will reconsider this topic in Chapter 13 as an issue in distribution channel management.

Funds Available

The funds available for promotion can dictate a heavy reliance on personal selling. This may seem contradictory since personal selling was cited earlier to be less efficient than advertising. However, when a firm is strapped for funds, it is more feasible to maintain a sales force that works on commission than to undertake expensive advertising campaigns with up-front capital requirements. With limited funds, a firm can deploy a sales staff and try to cultivate wholesaler and retailer support. Also, the sales staff can be used to set up and service dealer displays and attend trade shows.

Size of the Sales Staff

When an organization has a relatively small sales staff, it may rely on other forms of promotion or on members of the trade for promotional support. A small sales staff severely constrains a firm's ability to effectively reach all customers. One common solution is to deploy a small sales staff to trade shows rather than calling on individual customers. Another is to use direct response advertising to generate sales leads. Sales promotion and direct marketing are used to bolster the weakness in the sales staff. The same is true when a firm

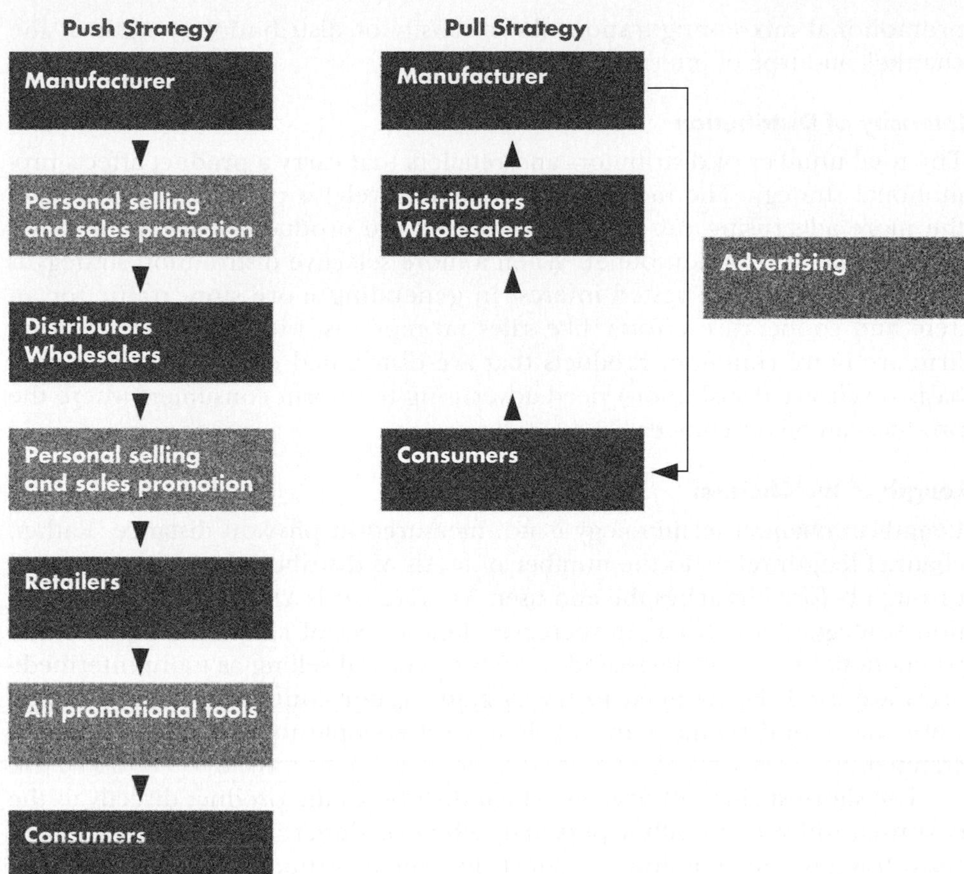

FIGURE 10-3
Push versus Pull Strategies Use Different Promotional Mix Tools

has a competitively inferior sales staff. Certainly, no organization wants to carry on for very long knowing its sales staff is inadequate. However, the talent available in some industries can be so limited that firms often have to accept the fact that areas other than personal selling will be emphasized until the sales force can be bolstered either in size or capability.

Extent of the Firm's Product Line

When a firm has a broad and deep product line, the nature of the promotional mix changes in several ways. Extensive product lines lighten the personal selling task at the wholesale and retail level because the efficiency of the firm's sales staff is greatly increased when each staff member has several items to sell. Also, depending on the branding strategy, advertising efficiency can be greatly enhanced. Using any of several "family" branding strategies means that communication about each brand in the line will automatically promote all the other brands in the line. Finally, joint brand efforts in couponing and in-store displays are feasible with an extensive product line.

CHARACTERISTICS OF THE DISTRIBUTION SYSTEM

Marketing mix strategies related to the distribution system have direct bearing on the promotional mix. Three types of distribution decisions will affect the promotional mix configuration: the intensity of distribution, length of the channel, and type of intermediary.

Intensity of Distribution

The total number of distributors and retailers that carry a product affects promotional strategy. The more intensely (extensively) a product is distributed, the more advertising can be used to presell the product before a consumer contacts the distribution outlet. When a more selective distribution strategy is used, retailers have a vested interest in generating more store traffic for an item and cooperative efforts, like sales promotions, with the manufacturing firm are more common. Products that are distributed on a highly restrictive basis (exclusive distribution) need advertising to inform consumers where the product can be purchased.

Length of the Channel

Length in channel terminology is not measured in physical distance. Rather, channel length refers to the number of levels of distribution a product passes through before it reaches the end user. As more levels are used in the distribution strategy, channel length increases. One effect of channel length on the promotional mix is an increased need for personal selling as more intermediaries are used. Firms need to try to gain tighter control over distributors, wholesalers, and retailers and to deploy salespeople to help manage a long channel.

The shortest channel strategy, which distributes the product directly to the end user, will rely on either personal selling or direct marketing techniques. Advertising is often employed in short channels as a supportive effort to create a favorable predisposition. Avon, Century 21 Real Estate, and Charles Schwab Discount Brokerage are examples of firms that use short channels and support the personal selling effort with mass communication.

Types of Intermediaries

The types of distributors, wholesalers, and retailers used in the channel change promotional strategy. Wholesalers with large sales staffs and complete delivery and installation services, relieve the producer of the responsibility for stimulating demand at the retail level. If a firm chooses lower cost wholesalers who do not provide promotion and service, then the firm itself will have to configure a promotional mix to cultivate retail support.

At the retail level, the type of retail outlet carrying the product has a pervasive affect on promotional strategy. In some cases, the retailer will be the dominant force in the promotional program. This is especially true in product categories where retailers are typically better known than the manufacturers such as in the furniture and plumbing fixtures product categories. Another important consideration at the retail level is the amount of in-store personal selling that retailers provide. Many self-service retailers, like Kmart, carry the same items as full-service department stores. Products like home entertainment items and hardware items are examples. The more a retailer is self-service oriented, the more the manufacturer must pre-sell items to consumers through advertising. As the retail outlet provides more demand stimulation at the point of purchase through personal selling, the manufacturer can rely on this communication to consumers and adjust the promotional mix strategy accordingly.

	Advertising	Personal Selling	Sales Promotion	Direct Marketing
1. Characteristics of the Market				
a. Type of Customer				
Intermediaries, business buyers		x	x	
Household consumers	x	x	x	x
b. Geographic Considerations				
Concentration		x		
Breadth				
c. Competition	x	x	x	x
2. Characteristics of the Product				
a. Product Category				
Convenience	x		x	
Shopping		x		
Specialty	x			
Services	x	x		x
Industrial		x	x	
b. Stage in the Life Cycle				
Early	x	x		
Late			x	
3. Characteristics of the Firm				
a. Push strategy		x		
Pull strategy	x		x	x
b. Limited funds available		x		
c. Small sales staff			x	x
d. Extensive product line	x		x	
4. Characteristics of Distribution				
a. Intensity of distribution	x			
b. Channel length	x	x		
c. Types of intermediaries				
Full service	x			
Limited service	x		x	

TABLE 10-2
Factors Affecting the Blend of Promotional Mix Tools

In this section on factors affecting promotional mix blend, none of the elements can be analyzed or interpreted in isolation. Quite the contrary, it is only through a comprehensive assessment of *all* the influencing factors that an appropriate mix of promotional options can be achieved. Table 10-2 provides a summary of the factors that affect the promotional mix. The final decision regarding emphasis within a promotional mix depends on an astute interpretation of the effect of each influence in the context of all others.

INTEGRATED MARKETING COMMUNICATIONS (IMC)

Some would argue that integrated marketing communications (IMC) is nothing more than the coordination and integration of the promotional mix variables and is a concept that has traditionally received attention in basic treatments of promotion.[9] But the concept of coordinating and integrating promotional efforts to achieve a synergistic effect—the whole of promotional efforts is greater than the sum of the parts—has gained much greater sophistication in recent years.[10] Four features of contemporary IMC programs distinguish the process from historic applications:[11]

1. *Outside-in Approach to Developing Communications.* In IMC, the firm starts with the customer or prospect and works backward toward the brand or organization. This helps ensure that customers get information when and how they want it rather than when and in what form the firm deems appropriate.
2. *Comprehensive and Detailed Knowledge about Customers and Prospects.* IMC programs are much more database driven than traditional integrated promotional programs. This feature was employed by Microsoft when it first compiled and then used a database of 8.5 million customers as the basis for its direct-marketing efforts.
3. *Brand Contact Perspective.* **Brand contacts** are all the ways in which customers or prospects come in contact with the firm. This aspect of IMC takes the communication process well beyond media or personal selling communication processes. Here, brand contacts identify *every* encounter customers or prospects have with the firm and product: packaging, employee contacts, in-store displays, sales literature, *and* sales and media exposure. Each contact must be evaluated for clarity and consistency with the overall IMC program.
4. *Centralized Coordination.* The effectiveness of an IMC program is greatly increased by appointing a single person or a group to control and evaluate all communications and contacts with customers and prospects.

Integrated marketing communication takes a much more comprehensive and systems oriented approach to the communication planning process. Its implementation shares database information with the overall marketing program. This database foundation is considered critical to the success of IMC programs by 9 out of 10 marketing and advertising agency people questioned in a recent survey.[12]

The overall implementation of an IMC program and its coordination with the overall marketing effort within a firm are depicted in Figure 10-4. Notice that the program begins with a database on customers and product category behavior, identifies distinct segments in the market, and progresses through the brand contacts discussed earlier. Ultimately, specific communication tools are considered for maximum impact in the given segment/brand contact situation. This is just the sort of IMC program Southwest Airlines used when it inaugurated service on the East Coast. Several months before service was initiated, the firm developed a comprehensive database on the area. Then, public relations announcements were made regarding the initiation of service. After these public announcements, special events, advertising, and promotions were used to increase awareness in the market. As the director of marketing and sales at Southwest described it, "We try to fire all the guns at once."[13]

Setting Promotional Objectives

With a full appreciation of the nature of the communication process and the tools available within the promotional mix, it is now possible to discuss setting objectives for the promotional process. Setting **promotional objectives** is essential in order to tightly focus limited resources of an

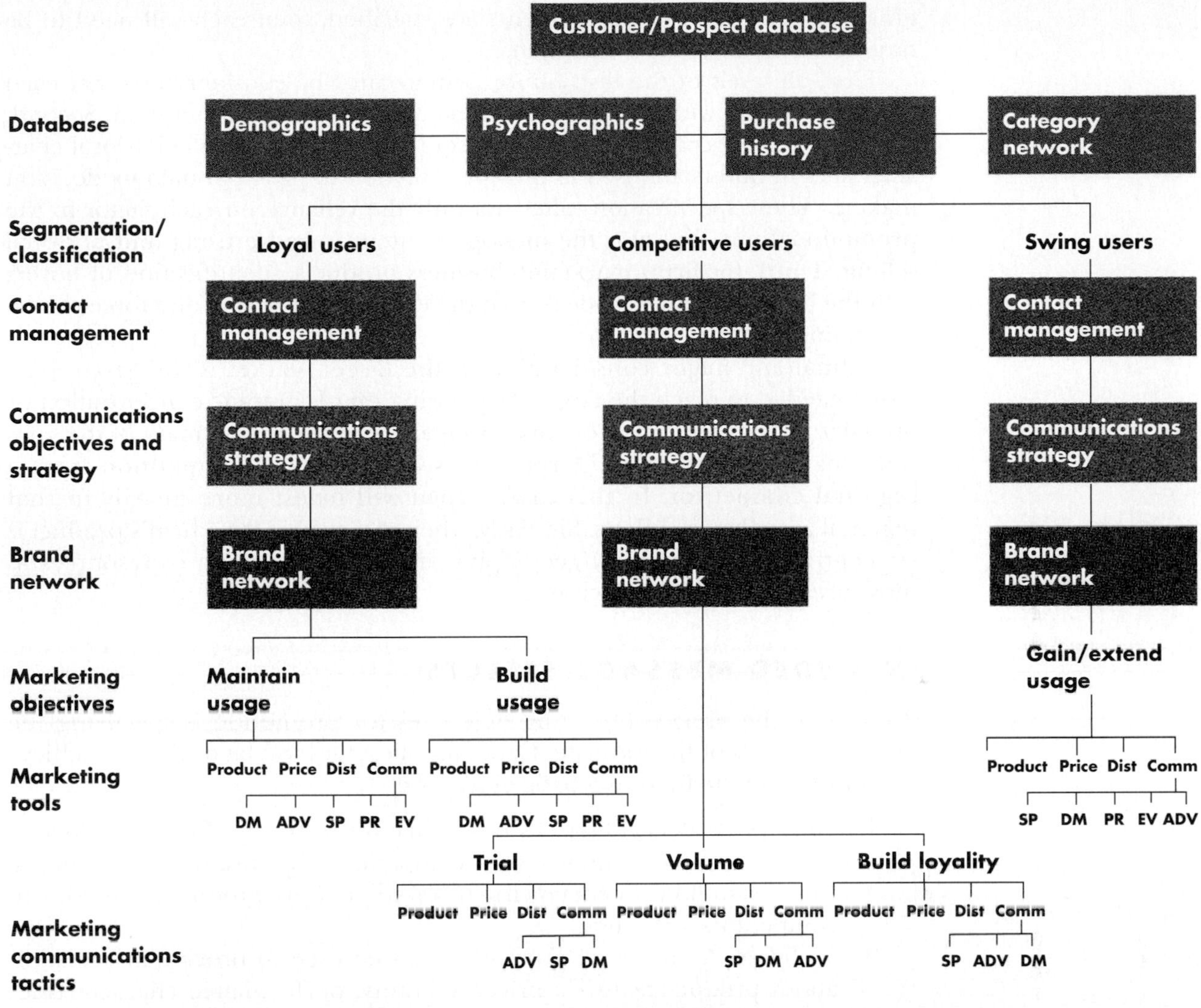

Source: Don E. Schultz, Stanley Tannenbaum, and Robert Lauterborn, *Integrated Marketing Communications,* (Lincolnwood, IL: NTC Business Books, 1993), 54. Used with permission.

FIGURE 10-4
The Integrated Marketing Communications (IMC) Process

organization. The primary role for promotion is to stimulate demand and communicate values offered by the firm. Promotional objectives are a combination of the firm's marketing mix objectives and the specific communication goals set for promotion. Specifically, objectives for the promotional effort will be set with respect to the target market and intended message and behavioral effects.

TARGET MARKET

Objectives relating to target markets for promotion are dictated by the market segmentation analysis conducted by a firm. Given that a product is designed to satisfy a particular group of consumers, the first stage in setting promotional objectives will be to design a promotion mix to reach this group effectively and efficiently. If several target segments are specified, then each will need to be targeted separately with promotion.

First, all levels of the distribution system must be considered so that each type of customer with the channel is targeted with proper promotion. Second, at the household consumer level, demographic, life-style, and behavioral characteristics of buyers are used to provide direction to promotional mix decision making. These specifications alter not only the reliance on each factor in the promotional mix, but also the message content for advertising and personal selling. Third, for firms marketing business products, identification of buyers with the best potential is made so that the deployment of the sales force can be determined.

A final and major consideration of the target market is the geographic scope needed to reach the target. Depending on geographic concentration or diversity, the concentration of advertising and size and deployment of the sales staff change considerably. A related issue is rigorous competition from a regional competitor. In this case, a firm will invest more heavily in that regional area than in others. Similarly, when the market for a firm's product is concentrated in several key geographic areas, the allocation of resources to those areas will be highly focused.

INTENDED MESSAGE EFFECTS

Primary to the process of setting objectives for promotion is specifying the intended effects of the message. Generally, messages will be devised to achieve one or more of the following basic objectives:

1. *To Persuade* Persuading the target market to try the firm's product or service is a fundamental goal. A competitive objective related to persuasion has to do with convincing receivers that the product is superior to competitors' offerings.
2. *To Inform* All forms of promotion can be used to provide information about product features: price, warranty, performance characteristics and other functional features.
3. *To Create Awareness* One of the most common promotional objectives is to create awareness of a firm or its product/service. A typical objective would be "to increase awareness of the brand name by 30 percent over the next twelve months among 25- to 34-year-old women." Illustration 10-3 is a magazine advertisement portraying this objective.
4. *To Establish, Reinforce, or Change an Attitude* This promotional objective is perhaps the most challenging one of the most powerful. Recall from the discussion of consumer behavior that attitudes exert a strong and persistent influence on purchasing behavior. Most objectives related to attitude effects are executed using messages that rely on imagery and emotional response.

The following example illustrates the fourth intended message effect. When General Electric entered a partnership with a Hungarian firm, it agreed to supply a variety of products to the country as part of Hungary's move toward a market economy. GE created a television advertisement that mentioned this agreement and promoted the partnership as evidence that GE is

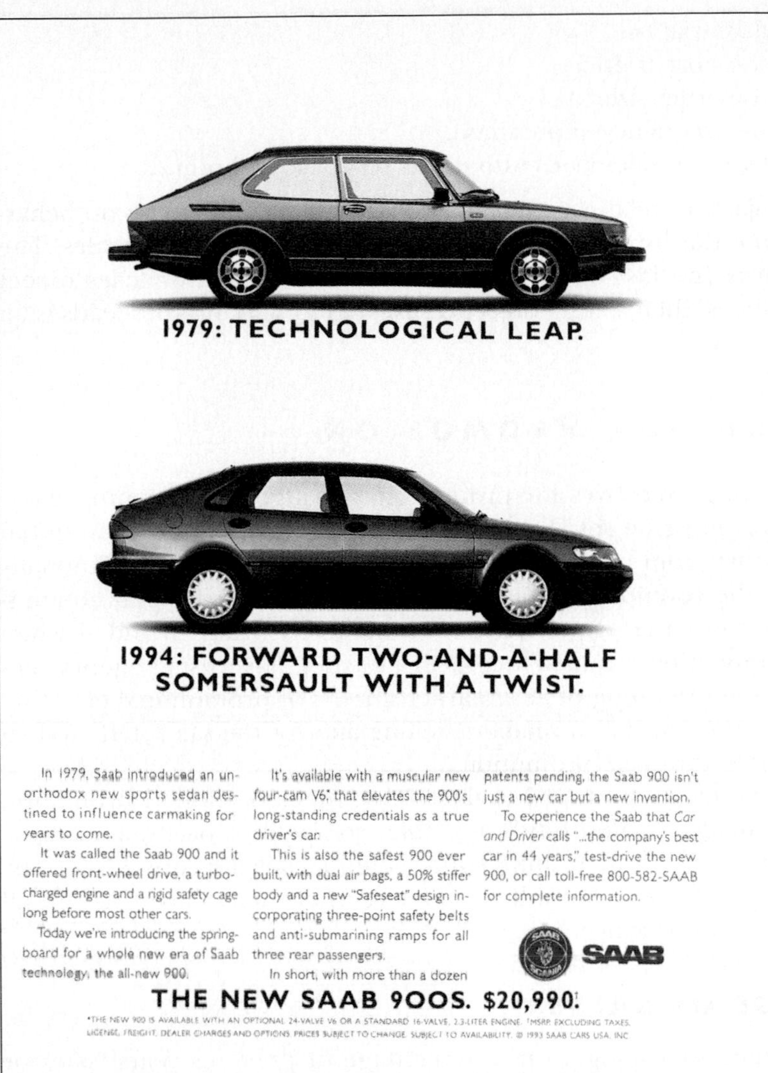

ILLUSTRATION 10-3
One of the basic objectives of promotion is to create awareness of a brand and its features.

forward looking, altruistic, and upholds the ideals of freedom. No specific mention of the firm's products was ever made. The imagery of the advertising was intended to positively affect the predisposition and attitude of viewers toward GE.

INTENDED BEHAVIORAL EFFECTS

Because of the demand stimulation purposes for promotion, objectives related to behavioral effects are appropriate. But, these objectives should be focused on behaviors that can legitimately be anticipated from the effect of promotion. Appropriate objectives for behavioral effects are:

- To stimulate trial use.
- To increase store traffic.
- To increase order size.
- To increase frequency of purchase.
- To affect sales or sales leads with direct response techniques.

Note that objectives relating to behavioral effects really do focus on behaviors *in the market* rather than on the singular purpose of generating sales. The only exception is the last objective listed. When promotion uses direct response techniques, then setting objectives related to sales or sales leads is an appropriate objective.

Budgeting for Promotion

After setting objectives for promotion, a budget for pursuing those objectives must be set. The items charged against the promotional budget vary from firm to firm. Two relatively large costs traditionally *not* included in the promotional budget are sales staff salaries and commissions and market research expenses. Items characteristically included when **budgeting for promotion** are media costs of all types, advertising agency fees for production and pretesting of ads, market surveys of promotional effectiveness, cooperative programs with retailers, selling aids for the sales staff, and all expenses associated with sales promotions.

The traditional techniques used to determine the allocation of promotion funds are: percentage of sales, funds available, competitive parity, and objective and task. Only one of these budgeting techniques is appropriate for any given promotional situation. We will consider each of them since they are all used in actual business practice.

Percentage of Sales

Basing the promotional budget on a percentage of previous years' sales or forecasted sales is a standard decision-making tool in many organizations. It is a favored approach because it is easy to calculate and defend. It also generally provides more dollars for promotion from year to year. Several problems can arise with this method, however. First, when a firm's sales are decreasing, the promotional budget will automatically contract. This is despite the fact that a possible aid to the declining sales problem might be increased awareness in the market, which would require *more* not less promotion. This, of course, is increasingly difficult as the budget shrinks. Second, this technique can easily result in *overspending* on promotion. Once funds have been earmarked for spending, they usually get spent whether there is justification or not. Third, and most problematic, this method implicitly suggests that promotion is a *result* of sales rather than a contributing factor. Overall, the speed of calculation and ease of implementation of this method are its only advantages.

Competitive Parity

The promotional budget can be determined by monitoring the amount spent by competitors. A firm will either try to match competitor spending on a dollar-by-dollar basis or spend an amount proportional to the market share the firm holds relative to competition. Whether this technique can ever really be implemented is questionable. First, even if the total dollar figure spent by the competition on promotion were obtainable, firms attempting to copy still wouldn't know the amount spent in any particular area of promotion. Second, competitors may be using a very different allocation procedure thereby deceiving the firm that attempts to copy the budget. Finally, this approach is totally reactive and violates the basic premise that promotion is a tool at the disposal of the firm to strategically position its product in the market.

FUNDS AVAILABLE

In some situations, an organization is so concerned with accountability that the promotional budget is the result of "leftovers." Only after all direct costs for manufacturing, administration, and marketing have been accounted for, plus a profit allocation, does the decision maker identify funds for promotion. The typical result is that insufficient funds are made available. Granted, there are times when firms are in a crisis situation regarding cash flow and financial liquidity. Notwithstanding these pressures, budgeting for promotion on this basis is simply inappropriate. It fails to draw on information relevant to the objectives for promotion or the nature of the environment within which promotion will be carried out.

OBJECTIVE AND TASK

By now it is obvious that none of the approaches to budgeting discussed thus far draw on the objectives established for promotion. The budgeting technique that is most appropriate and useful is **objective and task budgeting.** This technique is implemented as follows.

1. *Objectives.* The firm begins with the stated objectives for each area of the promotional mix. Goals for target market reach, message effects, behavioral effects, and geographic coverage are identified.
2. *Tasks.* The decision maker then determines what tasks will be needed to accomplish the stated objectives. Tasks such as production of advertising and sales promotion materials, media expenses, frequency of sales calls, cooperative retail advertising programs, coupon distribution, and the like are outlined.
3. *Costs.* Dollar amounts are assigned to the cost of each task thus producing a dollar amount for the promotional budget. In this fashion, the objectives for promotion are the basis for establishing the budget for promotion.

The objective and task approach may result in an *ideal* budget figure. The figure may need to be reconciled with the firm's ability to invest in promotion. But even if a reconciliation results in a reduced budget, at least the firm is aware of what *should* have been spent to accomplish promotional objectives. To implement the objective and task approach, firms need merely to attach costs to tasks and estimate these costs over the specified time frame of the mass communications or personal communications effort.

Marketing Communications: A Global Perspective

Regardless of whether the promotional mix element is advertising, personal selling, sales promotion, or public relations in a global context the underlying activity remains that of communication. The communications models presented at the beginning of this chapter provide a useful structure for conceptualizing communication processes *within* individual markets. However, when the task turns to developing effective promotional strategies *across* global markets, the communication effort takes on added complexities. The "Global Perspectives" sections in Chapters 11 and 12 will deal with specific issues and trends in global advertising, sales promotion, publicity, and personal selling. The remainder of this chapter will concentrate on the fundamental media and message issues that influence the development of marketing communications and the promotional mix globally. The media component of communications is singled out for treatment at this point because it represents a broad-based influence that can shape the nature of a firm's overall promotional program including the extent to which the firm will need to rely on mass communications instead of personal communications. That is, media issues such as availability and legal restrictions often become the determining factors in promotional strategy development in global market contexts. This is very different from the supportive role media plays in developing an integrated marketing communication program as discussed in this chapter. By virtue of this primary influence played by media, this chapter will focus on mass communications issues. Global perspectives on personal communications will be discussed in Chapter 12.

The first major challenge for global marketers is to identify all the potential constraints to effective global communications, prominent among which are media availability and potential legal barriers such as what can be said, to whom, and in what fashion. The next challenge, which may be even more formidable, is to develop a sense of **cultural empathy** for the process of communicating in markets that are distant in many ways from a firm's home market.

Most mass communication problems occur when the firm does not fully understand the subtle nuances of successful communication in markets around the world. Cultural empathy for both the message and the medium is needed in assessing the important similarities and differences among countries with respect to communication. In short, global marketers must not only cope with a variety of differing obstacles in attempting to physically reach their targets, they are also faced with the challenges of developing messages that can be understood and will elicit the desired response from the receivers of the communication. Figure 10-5 shows the mass communication model we've seen before and adds the important global dimension of communicating from one cultural context to another.

Media Issues in Global Communication

Many nations in the world have essentially the same kinds of media available. However, there are dramatic differences in the level of media development

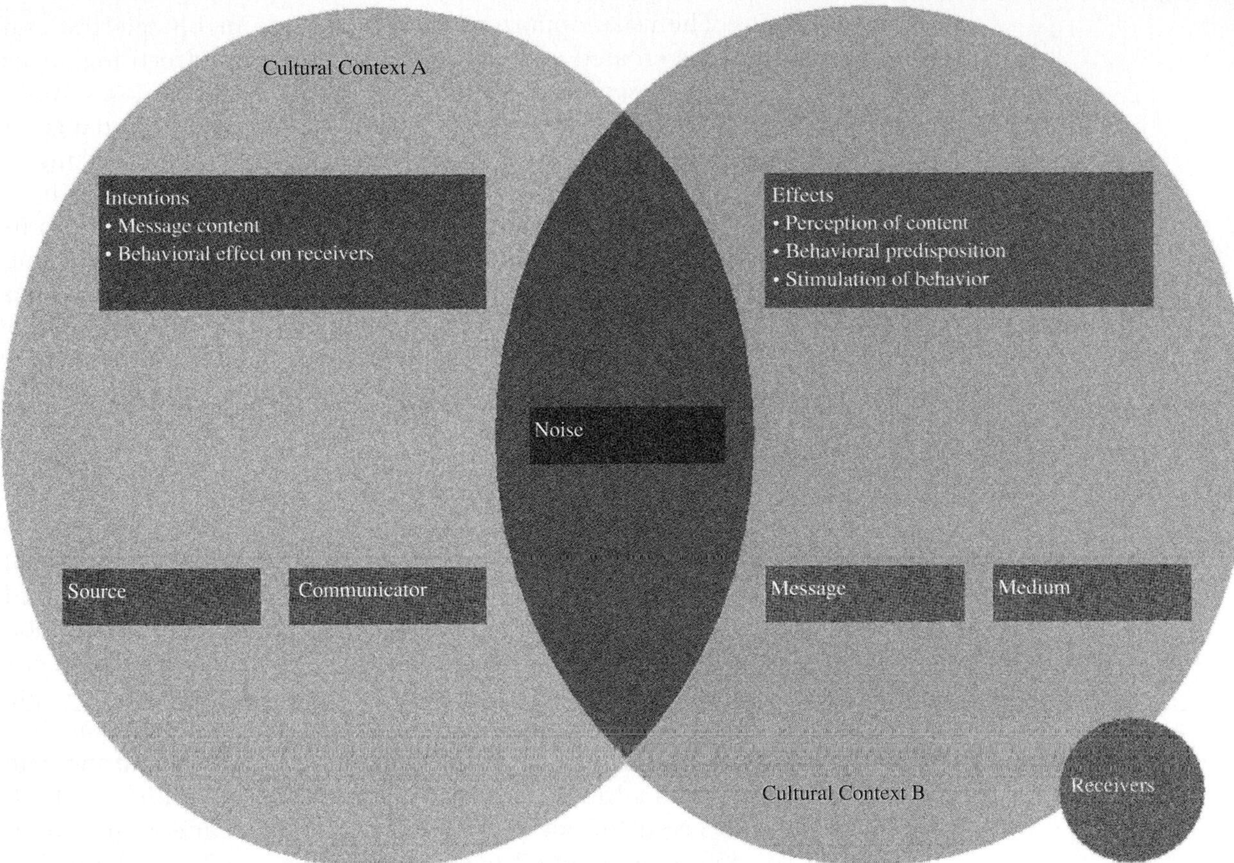

FIGURE 10-5
Model of Global Mass Communications

and effectiveness of media operations from one country to another, which greatly influences the development and execution of a firm's marketing communication strategy and promotional mix. In spite of the rapid development over the past two decades of global media in print, radio, and television, global marketers are more often confronted with differences from market to market rather than similarities when considering the use of media for promotional efforts. Mass media are most highly developed in North America, western Europe, Japan, and much of Asia. In eastern Europe and in less-developed countries (where approximately two-thirds of the world's population lives), the development of mass media is likely to be constrained by a combination of political, technological, and cultural factors. In practical terms, media constraints relating to availability, cost, and coverage all influence the promotional efforts of global companies.

Media Constraints

Media constraints in global markets can include a complete lack of media, a narrow selection of media choices, or a limited choice of appropriate media. These constraints create a market situation with limited media booking capacity for advertisers plus high cost for media space or time. For example, in Japan, a country with an extremely high level of media use among consumers, the leading daily newspaper *Asahi* is read by over 80 percent of business lead-

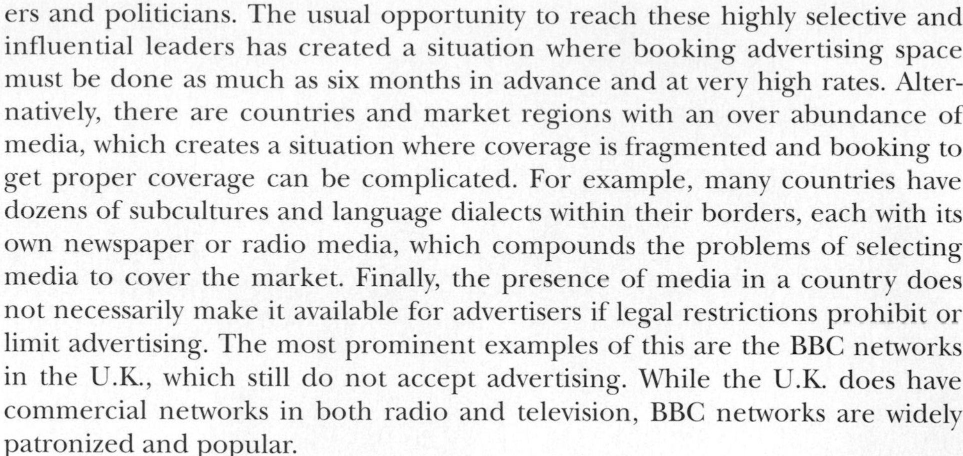

ers and politicians. The usual opportunity to reach these highly selective and influential leaders has created a situation where booking advertising space must be done as much as six months in advance and at very high rates. Alternatively, there are countries and market regions with an over abundance of media, which creates a situation where coverage is fragmented and booking to get proper coverage can be complicated. For example, many countries have dozens of subcultures and language dialects within their borders, each with its own newspaper or radio media, which compounds the problems of selecting media to cover the market. Finally, the presence of media in a country does not necessarily make it available for advertisers if legal restrictions prohibit or limit advertising. The most prominent examples of this are the BBC networks in the U.K., which still do not accept advertising. While the U.K. does have commercial networks in both radio and television, BBC networks are widely patronized and popular.

The types of media constraints encountered in trying to effectively construct a communications effort in global markets is highlighted when separate media are considered. In spite of the growth of strong global or regional papers, such as the *The Wall Street Journal, The International Herald Tribune,* and *USA Today,* newspapers are actually the most heterogeneous media worldwide and require the greatest amount of local knowledge in order to be correctly used as an advertising medium. For the most part, decisions need to be made on a country-by-country basis. Several examples will illustrate this. In Mexico, advertising can be sold as a news column, and there is no need to indicate that the "story" is a paid advertisement—a situation that can influence both the placement and layout of ads that compete for the readers' attention. Turkey has over 350 daily national newspapers while the Netherlands has only 3—situations that create different kinds of booking problems. Further, many newspapers, particularly regional papers, are positioned in the market with a particular political stance. Advertisers must be aware of this, making certain that their product's position with their target market is not in conflict with the position of the medium in which they have placed the advertisement.

In most economically advanced countries, magazines are an excellent medium for reaching clearly defined target markets. Further, global magazines such as *Time, Newsweek, National Geographic, Paris Match,* and *The Economist* have the ability to reach people with cosmopolitan life-styles as well as effectively reach narrowly defined market segments within different countries. Apart from a relatively small number of global or regional magazines, this medium is characterized as fragmented in that few magazines have large global circulation or dependable global circulation figures. Finally, in countries with low literacy rates, advertisers wishing to use any print media have the additional problem of simply not being able to communicate at all. In cases where illiteracy creates such a problem, the use of billboards with illustrations and trademarks or logos, cinema advertising, or the use of traveling sound trucks with powerful loudspeaker systems have proven to be effective alternatives to the print media.

No media reach a larger proportion of the world's population than the broadcast media. Most countries in the world have at least one broadcast chan-

Global broadcast media can reach billions of consumers. Here, a Hungarian woman enjoys MTV.

nel for television and several radio signals. Global brand names reach consumers even in the poorest of countries and in the most remote regions thanks to shortwave transmissions and transistor radios. Broadcasters such as the BBC World Service, CNN, and MTV can reach literally *billions* of consumers, especially when broadcasting world class sporting events such as the Olympics or the World Cup. The tremendous growth of satellite and cable television also cuts across borders and creates opportunities for global advertising messages. In a period of less than five years, cable and satellite broadcasters have built an audience of over 60 million households in Europe, and the growth potential in the new markets of eastern Europe will significantly increase the reach of these broadcast media. While European households don't receive the high number of channels that cable provides to most American households, they do offer a rich variety of international options in both programming and advertising. The standard cable offerings for television to households in Amsterdam include 24 stations and broadcasting in Dutch, German, French, Flemish, Italian, Turkish, Arabic, and English. Figure 10-6 highlights the growth of TV and radio availability throughout the world over the past three decades. In particular, note the dramatic increase in Asia and Latin America countries—regions of the world with the most promising growth forecasts for consumer markets in the 1990s.

The availability of advertising space and cost for advertising in the broadcast media varies greatly. Space may be made available on the basis of open

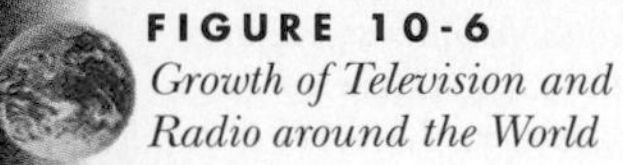
FIGURE 10-6
Growth of Television and Radio around the World

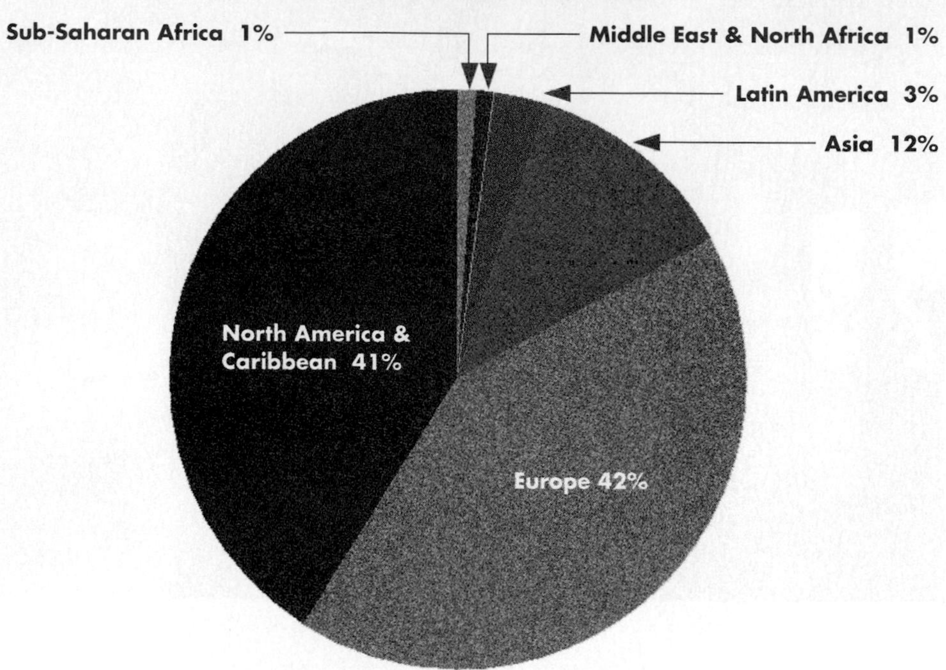

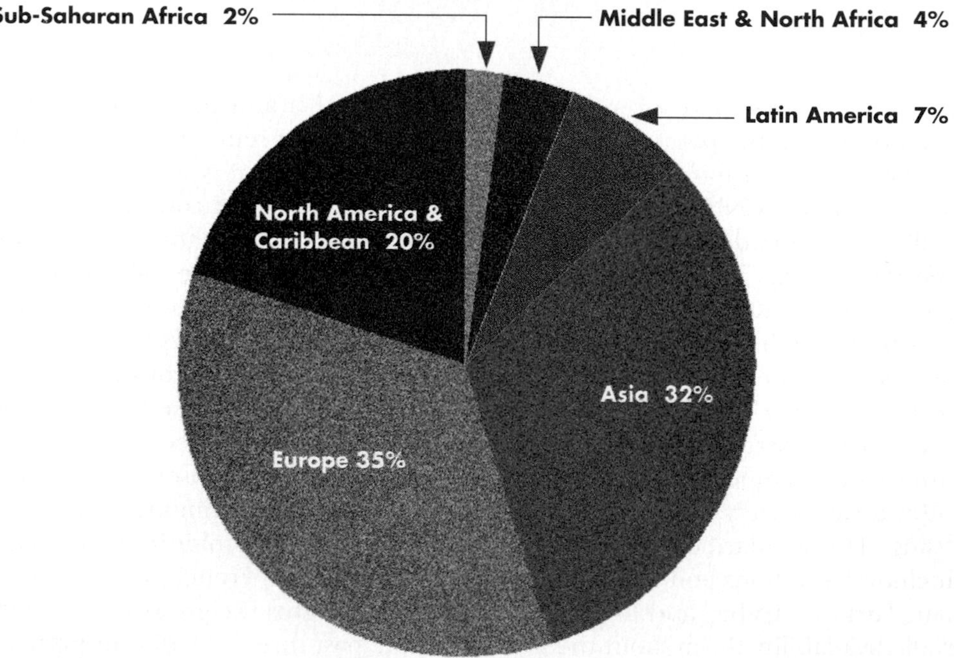

and free competition, and rates are thus set on a competitive basis by the broadcasters. Alternatively, in some markets access is controlled by a monopoly or prices and the number of advertising time slots are dictated by the government. In many European countries where radio and television have historically

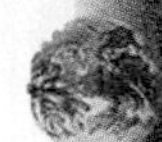

FIGURE 10-6
continued

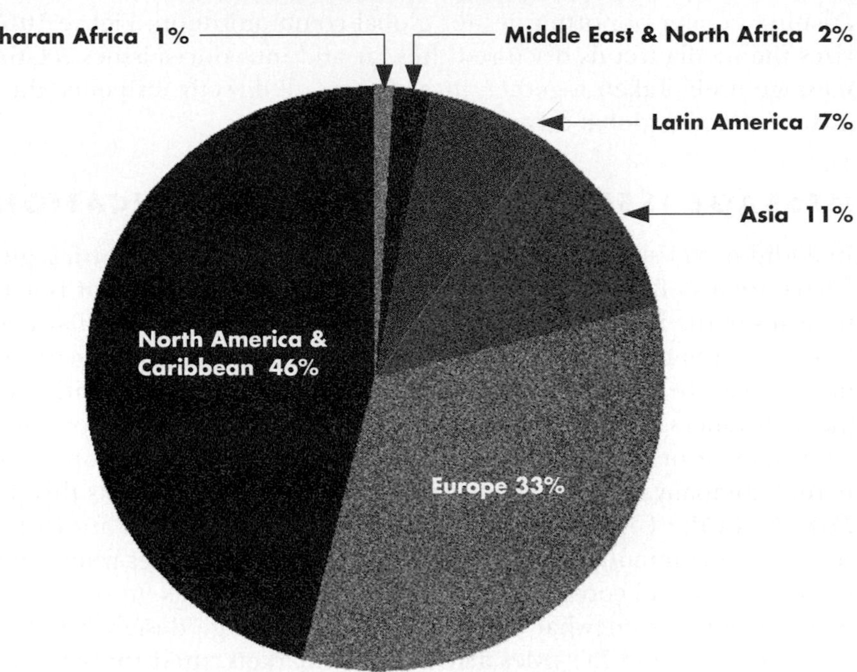

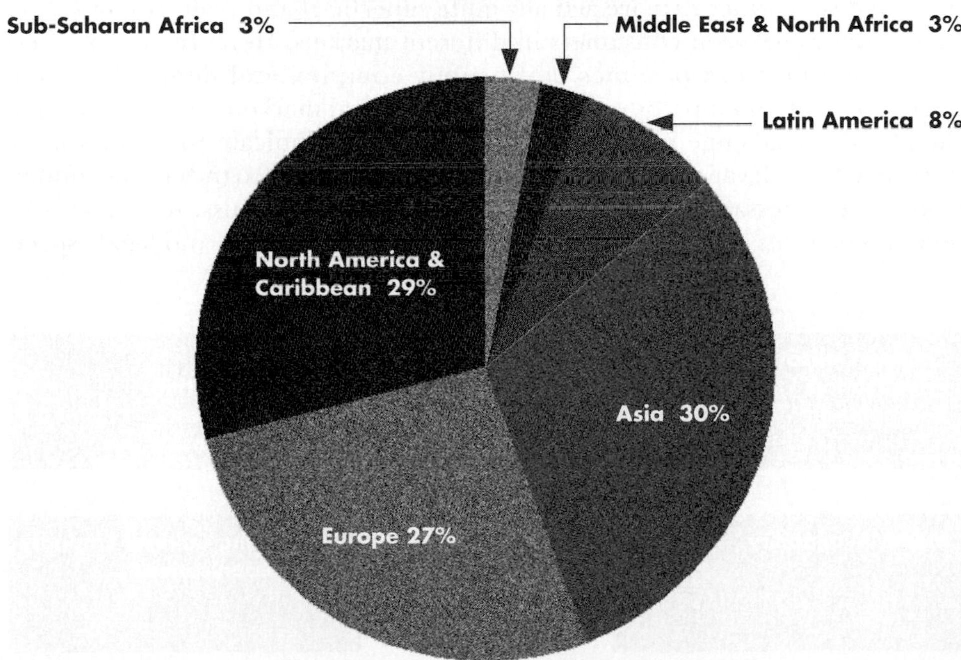

been government owned and controlled, advertising may be limited to a certain number of minutes per day or to specific time slots such as just before or just after the evening news. Generally, the trends of commercialization, privatization, and deregulation of media coupled with the growing worldwide

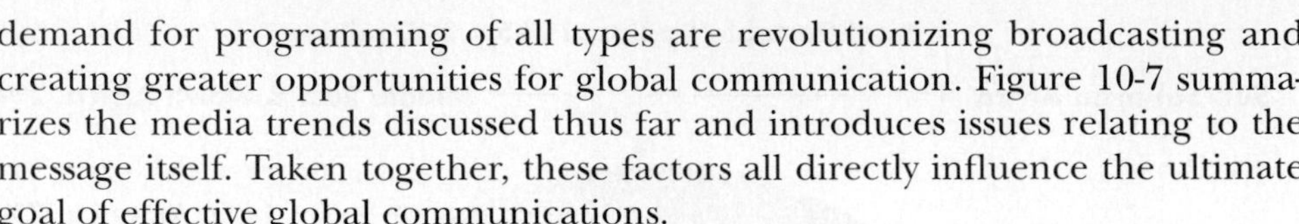

demand for programming of all types are revolutionizing broadcasting and creating greater opportunities for global communication. Figure 10-7 summarizes the media trends discussed thus far and introduces issues relating to the message itself. Taken together, these factors all directly influence the ultimate goal of effective global communications.

MESSAGE ISSUES IN GLOBAL COMMUNICATION

In addition to issues related to media access in different countries, global marketers are also faced with the challenge of understanding what is appropriate in terms of the intended message. Certainly, there are both similarities and differences among national markets, and global marketing practices in the past decade have been concentrating more and more on the similarities. For example, consumers with active life-styles tend to place a high value on the ease and convenience of Vidal Sassoon's *Wash & Go* shampoo and conditioner—the parent company of Vidal Sassoon, Procter & Gamble, markets this product as *Pert Plus* in the United States. The benefits of this product are easily demonstrated and communicated via TV in a number of countries where the cultural values of time and convenience are found across markets. In situations where a firm can find a somewhat universal basis for message design based on a similarity of values and life-styles across global markets, then the same basic message can be run in several markets at once.

Major problems occur, however, when promotional programs are based on perceived similarities that are actually quite superficial and really not based on shared values between consumers in different markets. Here, the art of effective communication becomes more subtly complex and demands a high degree of cultural empathy on the part of the global marketer. Remember that the ultimate challenge in message design is to communicate *relevant* information. What is relevant in each global market must be recognized and understood when messages are developed. Consider Levi Strauss, which sells its denim blue jeans in over 100 countries with different cultural and legal aspects

FIGURE 10-7
Media and Culture Effects on Global Communications

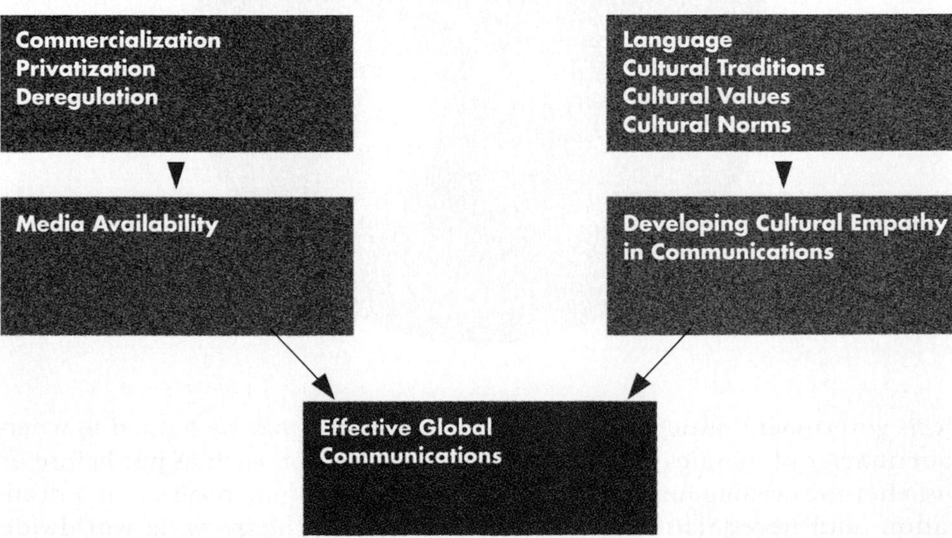

affecting the design of communications. In the U.K., the cowboy image and wild west setting is used to emphasize that Levi's are an American brand. Across the channel on the European continent, the tone of Levi's TV ads is much more sensual in its orientation than in either the U.K. or the United States. In Brazil, young consumers are much more likely to take their fashion leads from the European continent, so the ads there typically have a European backdrop, such as the nightlife of Paris. For this market, understanding the local issues relating to norms, values, and life-styles is the key to communicating.

The main point here is that while it is not always difficult to identify similar needs across cultures, it continues to be difficult to develop appropriate messages that effectively communicate across cultures. Marketers tend to approach a promotional problem from an ethnocentric perspective, believing that the way of doing things in the home market is best—especially if it has proven to be successful. What actually works best depends on the characteristics of the local target market, and the use of locally based agencies who are sensitive to local conditions is an advisable practice. Some of the important limitations on global promotion are discussed here. More specific discussions of the problems of developing global plans for advertising and personal selling will be discussed in the next two chapters.

A fundamental starting point in demonstrating cultural empathy in communication is showing respect for a country's traditions, values, and norms. Recognizing appropriate behavior can strongly influence the choice and execution of promotional messages. For example, using women as sales force representatives or depicting them as the decision maker in an advertisement is common practice and acceptable in many world markets. However, depicting women in these roles would be much less acceptable and less credible in Japan, the Middle East, or in much of Latin America. Similarly, individuality and competitiveness may be highly valued traits that underlie the reward system for sales personnel in the United States, while group effort, group recognition, and cooperation are more appropriate and normative behaviors for motivating and rewarding a sales force in Japan.

Finally, in terms of formulating basic message considerations, firms need to understand the consumption patterns and psychological characteristics that consumers in different countries hold. Insights into how consumers purchase and use products as well as understanding their basic attitudes toward products and brands are critical preconditions to developing communication that achieves the desired impact on the receiver of the firm's message. Examples are endless: advertisements depicting wine consumption in a wide variety of social situations are appropriate in France and Italy but not in the United States where wine consumption is typically restricted to adults in a relatively formal dinner setting. Advertising a special sales price on prime cuts of horse meat may be a way to get shoppers into a major supermarket chain in the Netherlands but not in the chain's stores in other countries. There's little sense in promoting a firm's products via direct mail in Italy where the postal system has a reputation for being inefficient and unreliable.

While many affluent consumer markets share similar attitudes toward products, the strength of those beliefs vary considerably. Prevailing attitudes regarding products directly influence the firm's ability to standardize messages in terms of information content or persuasive appeals. For example, as of 1994, advertising a can of tuna as "dolphin free" would be meaningless to most European housewives as would putting information regarding the cholesterol level of food products on packaging. The cultural values that make information like this relevant to American buyers are simply not relevant to European buyers.

Just as in developing a promotional mix for a firm's domestic market, selecting the appropriate media and developing effective messages must be done within the context of the firm's entire marketing mix. Global marketers need to keep in mind that promotion often is the first and most visible element in reaching their diverse target markets throughout the world and is therefore the one element that is most susceptible to misunderstanding by the target market. As such, even more care in the planning process needs to be exercised since a market's entire perception of the firm may be initiated by the promotion members of the market encounter.

Key Terms and Concepts

Communication processes
Promotion
Promotional mix
Integrated marketing communications (IMC)
Mass communication
Intentions
Source
Message
Medium
Receivers
Effects
Noise
Feedback
Personal communication
Communicator
Reach
Selectivity
Advertising
Personal selling
Sales promotion
Direct marketing
Public relations
Push strategy
Pull strategy
Brand contacts
Promotional objectives
Budgeting for promotion
Objective and task budgeting
Cultural empathy
Global media issues
Global message issues

Questions and Exercises

1. Why is it so important to maintain a communications perspective on the promotional area of the marketing mix?
2. Why is mass communication referred to as an impersonal form of communication?
3. How does a firm specify the intended message content for a promotional effort?
4. What is integrated marketing communications (IMC)? How is it distinguished as a separate concept in the promotion area of marketing.
5. Why are sales of a product the least useful measure of intended effects in mass communication? What are better measures of effect?
6. Identify and discuss three fundamental differences between mass communication and personal communication.
7. Discuss a sales promotion effort used by a firm that motivated you to try the product being promoted. Why did this sales promotion work on you?
8. If a firm is marketing a convenience good, what variable in the promotional mix is likely to be dominant? What influences dictate that this variable will be the one most heavily relied upon?
9. Why are media issues so critical to understanding the challenges of communication in global markets?

10. What does it mean to have cultural empathy in developing communication messages for global markets?

REFERENCES

1. Bradley Johnson, "In a Millisecond, Microsoft Boots up Marketing Database," *Advertising Age*, November 8, 1993, S-6.
2. Teri Agins, "Klein Jeans' Sexy Insert Didn't Spur Sales," *The Wall Street Journal*, May 5, 1992, B1 & B8.
3. The model displayed in Figure 10-1 is an adaptation of an excellent model that originally appeared in James F. Engle, Martin R. Warshaw, and Thomas C. Kinnear, *Promotional Strategy*, 4th ed. (Homewood, Il: Richard D. Irwin, Inc., 1979), 20.
4. Joseph B. White, "GM's New Ad Campaign Puts a Shine On Its Image—but Not Yet a Deep One," *The Wall Street Journal*, October 8, 1990, B1 & B12.
5. Thomas R. King, "Häagen-Dazs Goes Whole Hog To Keep Dessert Eaters Indulging," *The Wall Street Journal*, April 19, 1990, B4.
6. Statistic cited in *Direct Marketing*, May 1988, 35.
7. Catalog sales data cited in Laura Loro, "Catalogers Foresee Happy Holidays," *Advertising Age*, October 25, 1993, S4; Television shopping sales data cited in Scott Donaton, "Home Shopping Audience Widens," *Advertising Age*, November 22, 1993, 19.
8. Joann Lipman, "Spending Forecast Augurs Ho-Hum 1990," *The Wall Street Journal*, December 12, 1989, B6.
9. As an example of a basic and traditional treatment of promotion that suggested coordination and integration of the promotional mix variables see Roy T. Shaw, Richard J. Semenik, and Robert H. Williams, *Marketing: An Integrated-Analytical Approach*, 4th Ed., (Cincinnati, OH: South-Western Publishing, 1981), 237–238.
10. Tom Duncan, "Integrated Marketing? It's Synergy," *Advertising Age*, March 8, 1993, 1.
11. Don E. Schultz, "Maybe We Should Start All Over with an IMC Organization," *Advertising Age*, October 25, 1993, 8.
12. Adrienne Ward Fawcett, "Integrated Marketing Door Open for Experts," *Advertising Age*, November 8, 1993, S2.
13. Jennifer Lawrence, "Integrated Mix Makes Expansion Fly," *Advertising Age*, November 8, 1993, s10.

11

Advertising, Sales Promotion, Direct Marketing, and Public Relations

AFTER STUDYING THIS CHAPTER, YOU WILL UNDERSTAND THAT:

1. Firms use four basic mass communication tools—advertising, sales promotion, direct marketing, and public relations—to reach a large number of current and potential customers.
2. Advertising messages are based first on marketing mix strategies, and then on techniques of creative communication that inform and persuade potential buyers.
3. Sales promotion techniques must be used judiciously and only with clearly specified goals and objectives.
4. Direct marketing has grown dramatically in the United States due to several cultural and technological changes in the external environment.
5. Mass communications decisions for global markets are affected by the extent to which brand features and the message for the brand can be standardized across markets versus the need to customize features and messages for different global markets.

"It's trench warfare," says the advertising manager at Saab-Scania, the makers of *Saab* automobiles.[1] With 602 car models, minivans, trucks, and off-road vehicles all going after the U.S. auto market, auto firms have increased the intensity of advertising, sales promotion, and direct marketing in an attempt to gain the attention of buyers besieged with choices. Nissan Motors is one of the fiercest competitors. Nissan relies primarily on television and magazine advertising to increase awareness of its *Stanza* compact car. But, in a recent direct challenge to Honda's dominance in the compact car market, Nissan initiated a unique sales promotion campaign by offering to pay $100 to prospective buyers who test drove a *Stanza* but decided to buy a Honda *Accord* instead. The firm was demonstrating to consumers how confident they were that the *Stanza* would be more appealing than a Honda *Accord*. Through direct marketing, thousands of letters were mailed to current compact car owners announcing the program. Nissan's national advertising manager said that before the promotional campaign, "the world at large wasn't sure where the *Stanza* fit in the marketplace."[2]

In order to respond to the highly competitive environment in the auto market, Nissan marshalled all the mass communications tools available to promote the *Stanza* and to communicate to consumers where the car fit in the market. First, *advertising* was used to broadly disseminate information and reach as many potential auto buyers as possible. Then, a $100 *sales promotion* was used to draw attention to the *Stanza* and give buyers another reason to consider it. Finally, a *direct marketing* promotion was tightly focused on those buyers who had previously shown an affinity for cars like the *Stanza*. Overall, Nissan used the tools of mass communication to stimulate demand for its product.

Advertising, sales promotion, direct marketing, and public relations represent the mass communication vehicles a firm can use to reach large numbers of potential buyers. Each of these methods is considered highly efficient because current and potential customers can be reached at relatively low cost—typically a few cents for each contact. Advertising, sales promotion, direct marketing, and public relations all use the mass media, but they are quite different in nature, purpose, and effect. This chapter discusses the features of these four promotional options and their applications. In addition, issues are raised regarding the managerial decisions related to their use.

ADVERTISING

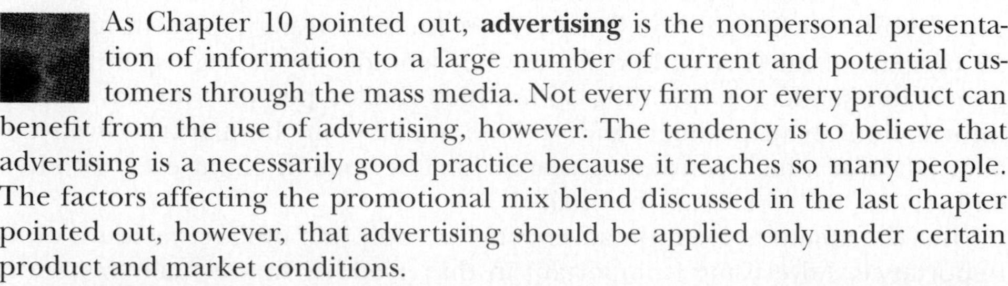

As Chapter 10 pointed out, **advertising** is the nonpersonal presentation of information to a large number of current and potential customers through the mass media. Not every firm nor every product can benefit from the use of advertising, however. The tendency is to believe that advertising is a necessarily good practice because it reaches so many people. The factors affecting the promotional mix blend discussed in the last chapter pointed out, however, that advertising should be applied only under certain product and market conditions.

To fully appreciate the nature of advertising, we will examine advertising from several perspectives. First, the importance of advertising will be discussed in the context of its economic role. Firms in the United States make an enormous monetary investment in advertising and its effects are realized throughout the economic system. Second, the different types of advertising will be identified and discussed. Third, the creative effort in advertising is highlighted because this factor often means the difference between effective and ineffective advertising. Fourth, the critical stage of sending the message to receivers is discussed. Finally, the role of the advertising agency in the process is considered.

THE IMPORTANCE OF ADVERTISING

Advertising is fundamentally important to economies that operate according to the principles of capitalism and free enterprise. An economy based on these principles requires that firms have methods for stimulating demand for their goods and services. Advertising is a basic tool used by firms to achieve **demand stimulation**—attracting revenues from customers for the firm's products and services. And, as more firms around the world establish economic systems with features resembling capitalism and free enterprise, advertising will continue to grow in importance as a worldwide force in stimulating demand.

In the United States, one of the premiere capitalistic economies in the world, firms invest heavily in advertising to communicate with consumers and stimulate demand. Table 11-1 shows that over $130 billion was spent by U.S. firms on advertising during 1992. Table 11-2 lists those firms that were the biggest spenders. Notice that all of the top ten firms in Table 11-2 are engaged in marketing household consumer products and the top two spenders, Procter & Gamble and Philip Morris, market products in the convenience goods category. These products require heavy advertising since personal selling can play no role in persuading consumers to try packaged goods. Also, notice that in 1992, Chrysler Corp. had a huge increase (38.3 percent) in advertising spending. Recall that this was the year that Chrysler introduced its new line of "cab forward" autos and spent heavily on advertising to introduce the new products to the market.

The amount spent on advertising in the United States is truly enormous in absolute dollar terms. But this spending needs to be put in perspective. The $2.16 billion spent by Procter & Gamble represents only about 8 percent of their sales. Viewed from another perspective, if you buy *Crest* toothpaste made by P & G, you're spending about 15 cents for information about the product. General Motors, expenditure of $1.3 billion is certainly a lot of money, but it is only about 1 percent of GM's total sales revenue. Across all product categories, expenditures by firms in the United States for advertising represent only 6 to 12 percent of sales. A middle-income household with average spending on goods and services is spending about $600 dollars per year for advertising information about products and services available in the market. Given the alternative of a time consuming search for information about every product and service, the cost seems reasonable!

But the amounts spent on advertising are only one indirect measure of its importance. Advertising is important in that products may actually *cost less to produce* partly *because of* the effects of advertising. As firms are able to stimulate demand for large quantities of their products, economies of scale in produc-

TABLE 11-1
All U.S. Advertising Expenditures in Major Media, 1991–1992 (in millions of dollars)

Medium	Advertising Expenditures 1992	1991	Percentage change
Magazines	$7,105.1	$6,515.2	9.05%
Sunday magazine	941.9	794.0	18.63
Local newspaper	9,920.1	6,837.3	45.09
National newspaper	963.7	862.9	11.71
Outdoor	655.0	684.0	(4.23)
Network TV	10,752.5	10,101.9	6.44
Spot TV	9,399.7	8,751.2	7.40
Syndicated TV	1,286.6	1,204.7	6.81
Cable TV networks	1,590.5	1,211.6	31.29
Network radio	549.1	578.7	(5.01)
Spot radio	1,092.4	1,141.6	(4.29)
Media totals	$ 44,256.7	$ 38,683.0	14.5
All other advertising	85,843.3	88,017.0	(2.46)
Total of all advertising	$130,100.0	$126,700.0	2.68%

Source: Data for media spending adapted from *Advertising Age Fact Book* (January 3, 1994): 24. (Crain News Service/*Advertising Age*, Copyright Crain Communications, Inc. All rights reserved.) Data for total of all advertising obtained from Jerrold Ballinger, "Mail Volume, Spending Rose in '93 and More Growth Is Seen, says Coen," *Direct Marketing News* (December 13, 1993): 2.

tion, distribution, and administration may be realized. These economies of scale will spread fixed costs of operations over a larger number of units produced and sold, thus lowering the unit cost of each item. In the absence of large expenditures on advertising, the average household might actually spend far more on increased product costs than the $600 cost now spent for information.

Finally, two other factors suggest that advertising is important in an economic sense. First, firms use advertising to contribute to building brand loyalty among customers. Brand loyal customers are much less expensive to serve than attracting new customers. So again, advertising can contribute to lowering the cost of operations. In a very different measure of importance, the billions of dollars spent on advertising in the mass media support the very existence of those media. As such, the television shows, magazines, and newspapers that inform and entertain us are fostered by advertising.

TYPES OF ADVERTISING

It is important to recognize that the term *advertising* does not describe a single effort in mass communication. There are various types of advertising each of which has different characteristics. By recognizing these different types of advertising, more opportunities for effective communication and fulfillment of corporate communications objectives present themselves.

TABLE 11-2
Leading National Advertisers in the United States, 1991 and 1992

Top Ten Companies	Expenditures (in millions of dollars) 1992	1991	Percentage Change	Rank
Procter & Gamble	$2,165.6	$2,150.0	0.7%	1
Philip Morris	2,024.1	2,071.3	(2.3)	2
General Motors	1,333.6	1,476.8	(9.7)	3
Sears, Roebuck & Co.	1,204.6	1,195.6	0.8	4
PepsiCo	928.6	903.9	2.7	5
Ford Motor Company	794.5	689.7	15.2	6
Warner-Lambert Co.	757.5	657.0	15.3	7
Chrysler Corp.	756.6	547.1	38.3	8
McDonald's Corp.	743.6	695.7	6.9	9
Nestle SA	733.4	643.4	14.0	10
Other Leading Companies				
Kellogg Co.	630.3	578.0	9.1	17
Walt Disney Co.	524.6	495.0	6.0	24
Honda Motor Co.	349.1	339.9	2.7	33
U.S. Government	331.0	262.5	26.1	34
Nike	230.8	224.4	2.9	48
Wal-Mart	222.4	190.3	16.9	50
Levi Strauss & Co.	211.9	129.5	63.6	53
MCI Communications Corp.	156.2	141.4	10.5	77
Wendy's International	142.6	124.1	14.9	82
Nynex Corp.	112.6	97.1	15.9	100

Source: Adapted from *Advertising Age Fact Book* (January 3, 1994): 14.

Type of Customer

Advertising and its execution will differ depending on the type of customer the advertising is trying to reach. Different customer audiences, such as household consumers, business users, members of the channel of distribution, or professionals (like doctors, lawyers, or engineers) tend to seek different information and respond to different advertising appeals. Other unique audiences, such as the firm's own employees or government officials, occasionally constitute the target audience. The message theme and information emphasis vary in advertisements aimed at these different types of customers.

Product/Service or Institutional

All advertising is either product/service or institutional. Product/service advertising focuses on the attributes and benefits of a specific product/service or brand. The majority of advertisements in the mass media are of this type.

When Prudential Insurance and Lennox Home Heating and Air Conditioning run ads during prime time, these firms are touting the specific benefits of the services and products they market. Additionally, retailers that feature a particular item in their advertising are also using product advertising.

Institutional advertising is broader in scope and doesn't single out a product or brand for promotion, but rather promotes an entire organization or corporation. One of several purposes can be served with this type of advertising. Corporations often employ this type of advertising to build goodwill and create a generally favorable predisposition toward the entire firm. Dow Chemical, in an attempt to shed the image it acquired during the Vietnam War, has run ads showing what a great place Dow is to work for bright college graduates.[3] In these ads, proud parents watch their sons and daughters receive diplomas during graduation exercises. The voice in the background describes Dow's commitment to providing quality career opportunities for young people. Several firms regularly run institutional advertising that feature the firm rather than its products specifically. Such corporate image campaigns have been run by Waste Management, Sara Lee, and Phillips Petroleum. Illustration 11-1 is an example of an ad run by IBM that typifies institutional advertisement.

Trade and industry associations also employ institutional advertising to stimulate demand for the product or service of an entire industry. The National Dairy Association runs advertising that promotes the nutritional

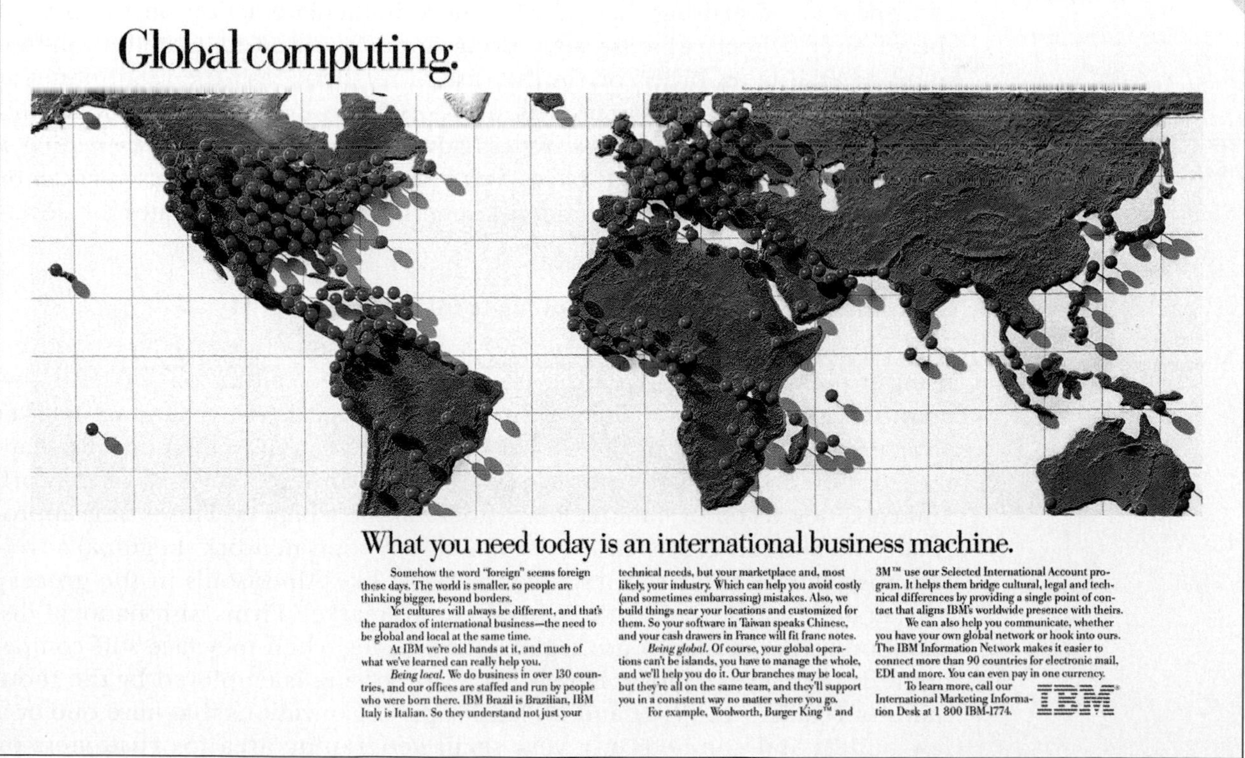

ILLUSTRATION 11-1
IBM is using institutional advertising to promote the entire firm, not an individual product.

value of milk. In fact, U.S. dairy farmers ranked 61st in the list of leading national advertisers in 1992 with $189.6 million in spending. Finally, when retailers like Dillards and The Gap do not single out a particular brand in their advertising but rather promote the store and their name, they are using an institutional approach to persuade consumers to shop at their store for product needs rather than at competitors' outlets.

Primary versus Selective Demand Stimulation

The distinction between primary and selective demand stimulation was defined in Chapter 7. It is crucial that an advertiser recognizes those situations where primary demand advertising (i.e., educating the audience to the values of the product category) is required as opposed to the more common situation where selective demand stimulation is needed (i.e., touting the features of an individual brand). Recall that early in the product life cycle of true innovations, advertising that stimulates primary demand is needed. But this is not the only time primary demand stimulation may be called for, however. Facing declining attendance, the National Association of Theater Owners decided to invest in advertising to reach infrequent moviegoers. The ads were designed to show the values of going to the theater rather than staying home to watch a movie on tape or television. The ads did not feature any particular movie, which would have been selective demand stimulation. Rather, the entertainment value and pleasures of attending the theater were highlighted in classic primary demand stimulation fashion.[4]

Direct Response versus Awareness

A firm must decide whether to use advertising designed to create image and awareness or advertising that calls for more immediate action on the part of the receiver. **Direct response advertising** implores receivers to call a toll-free number, mail in an order, or (in the case of retailers) visit the retail outlet at some specified time. This approach draws on direct marketing techniques discussed later in the chapter. **Awareness advertising** has the goal of creating a favorable image in the minds of receivers toward an organization's product or service over a long period of time. Awareness advertising dominates the advertising efforts of most firms.

International, National, Regional, or Local

The geographic scope of the advertiser's market also defines the type of advertising it uses. International advertising is carried out either on a country-by-country basis or ads are prepared with global appeal. (International market advertising is discussed in the Global Perspective section at the end this chapter.) National advertising can be accomplished through the use of network and cable television or national magazines and newspapers. This is only appropriate when an advertiser has a national distribution network. Regional advertising is used by firms with regional markets, like Albertson's in the grocery market and Nordstroms in the specialty store market. Firms with national distribution will occasionally use regional advertising when they face stiff competition in particular regions. Finally, local advertising is employed by the thousands of retailers and civic and philanthropic organizations that have one or a few outlets and compete in a very small geographic area for customers or patrons.

THE CREATIVE EFFORT

The factor that often distinguishes advertising from other forms of promotion is the creative effort. Because advertising must use a generalized message transmitted through an impersonal medium, creative execution can make the difference between effectively communicating and not communicating at all. Using creativity to highlight uniqueness and to break down the perceptual defense mechanisms of consumers requires tremendous imagination and talent. The creative skills needed to develop effective advertising are so specialized that most firms enlist the services of an advertising agency.

It might be surprising to learn that the creative effort is relatively structured. Marketing strategists will work with advertising people in the firm or with an ad agency to determine methods for attracting and holding attention and to identify the message strategy to be used for the ad. Through these decisions, priority is given to making the advertising fulfill various objective like providing product information or developing a corporate image.

Attracting and Holding Attention

The use of action, color, sound, and creative headlines and copy can break through barriers to communication. In developing features of an advertisement that will attract and hold attention, care must be taken not to overemphasize these features. When attention-getting techniques overwhelm the message content, the communication is rendered useless. In the ongoing cola wars, Coke and Pepsi have both resorted to the use of celebrities as a way to attract attention to various brands. At one point, Art Carney, Vanna White, Madonna, and Billy Crystal were featured in *Diet Pepsi, Diet Coke, Coke Classic,* and *Pepsi* ads. What's more, in the prior year *Coke* and *Diet Coke* commercials featured 27 different celebrities plus 31 NFL football players![5] Celebrities can do much to attract attention to a brand and hold the viewer's attention. But, that sort of blizzard of celebrities will ultimately overwhelm any clear and meaningful communication. The goal for attracting and holding attention is to identify a feature of the product that is a relevant choice criterion to receivers and highlight it as the attention device. In this way, meaningful product information is integral to attracting and holding the attention of the audience.

Message Appeals

Several different message appeals can be used in advertising. The goal of creative message development is to make the communication about a product/service as appealing and memorable as possible. The message appeal is brought to life by the copy—the words in the message and the headline—prepared for an ad and the visualizations that accompany the copy. The following are the broad categories of message appeals and the distinctive features of each.

INFORMATION ONLY

The **information-only appeal** which often employs a "reason why" sort of logic, provides straightforward, factual information about the product. Consumers who emphasize functional feature information in their decision making find this approach appealing. It is also prevalent in highly technical products advertised to business, trade, and professional types of customers.

EMOTIONAL

Emotional appeals take several forms. Ads that tout products as providing prestige, status, or sex appeal are using an emotional appeal. A category of emotional appeals is the "heart sell." This sort of ad creates warm, emotional settings that are touching. Kodak and AT&T have used the heart sell to show how their products promote the warmth and love that come from close contact with family and friends. Illustration 11-2 shows a mild emotional appeal being used for Michelin tires.

HUMOR

The **humor appeal** in advertising is often favored by both advertisers and receivers. But the effects of this appeal are mixed at best. Little Caesars Pizza advertising featuring the "pizza-pizza" humor was rated the most outstanding advertising campaign by consumers in 1992, but in 1993 the campaign had dropped to fifth with other humor ads slipping as well.[6] Humor ads tend to be entertaining, but they don't always achieve effective communication. One problem is that the humor may overwhelm the informational and persuasive content of the advertisement. Also, humor ads tend to wear-out quickly and simply aren't funny the second time around. There is also the risk that humor may create an unintended and unfavorable image for the brand or the firm.

ILLUSTRATION 11-2
Emotion can be a highly effective creative technique.

A LOT OF TIRES COST LESS THAN A MICHELIN.
THAT'S BECAUSE THEY SHOULD.
To everyone out there looking to save a few dollars on a set of tires, let's not mince words. You buy cheap, you get cheap.
There may be a lot of tires out there that cost less than a Michelin.
The only question is, what do you have to give up if you buy one?
Do they handle like a Michelin?
Do they last like a Michelin?
Are they as reliable as a Michelin?
Then ask yourself this: Do you really want to find out?
At Michelin, we make only one kind of tire. The very best we know how.
Because the way we see it, the last place a compromise belongs is on your car.
As a matter of fact, we're so obsessed with quality we make the steel cables that go into our steel-belted radials.
We even make many of the machines that make and test Michelin tires.
And our quality control checks are so exhaustive that they even include x-rays.
These and hundreds of other details, big and small (details that may seem inconsequential to others), make sure that when you put a set of Michelin tires on your car, you get all the mileage Michelin is famous for.
True, there may be cheaper tires. But if they don't last like a Michelin, are they really less expensive?
So the next time someone tries to save you a few dollars on a tire, tell him this: It's not how much you pay that counts. It's what you get for your money.
And then *he'll* know that *you* know that there's only one reason a tire costs less than a Michelin.
It deserves to.
MICHELIN
BECAUSE SO MUCH IS RIDING ON YOUR TIRES.

Fear

Fear appeals in advertising show the harmful consequences of not using the firm's brand. Receivers are shown scenes of either actual or impending physical harm or social embarrassment from not using the brand. Products ranging from life insurance to dishwashing liquid have used fear appeals. Fear is much like humor as a message technique. The effects of fear appeals are variable and somewhat unpredictable. Marketing researchers have advocated the use of fear as a potentially effective creative technique. Social scientists, on the other hand, cite adverse effects on communication from this form of appeal. The risk is that the information content of the ad is short-circuited by anxiety created in the receiver by the fear appeal. Fear appeals tend to be most effective when an ad is delivered by a credible source. The *American Express Traveler's Cheque* ads featuring Karl Malden as spokesperson used this technique. Another circumstance where research indicates fear may be effective is when an ad threatens social embarrassment or physical harm to the receiver's loved ones.

Comparison

The **comparison appeal** uses the tactic of comparing features of the advertiser's brand with one or more competitors' brands, either explicitly or implicitly (e.g., "compared to the leading brand"). This technique has never been illegal, but for years advertisers feared that the mere mention of competitors' brands would benefit the competitors. However, research suggests that comparison advertising is more effective than harmful as a technique when the comparison is done properly.[7] Comparison ads are most effective when the firm is relatively unknown, its brand has small market share, and comparison is made explicitly to leading brands in the market. Brands with leading market share should not use this technique. Comparison to lesser brands only serves to reduce the stature of the leading brand in the minds of consumers. Illustration 11-3 is an example of a comparison ad that follows all the rules for effectively using this technique.

Slice of Life

The basis for the **slice-of-life appeal** is reference-group theory. Slice of life ads present a scene in which a product is being used and providing satisfaction to a user who represents the target market. Scenes of the housewife who has cleaner clothes or the harried business executive who gets headache relief from a pain reliever are examples of reference-group theory in action. Slice-of-life ads are popular in the convenience good category where consumers believe all the brands are nearly identical. Consumers substitute reference-group information for actual product information in this situation.

Testimonials

Despite the prior discussion of the overuse of celebrities, **testimonials** can be an effective creative technique. Having a spokesperson champion a brand is a popular appeal among advertisers. Several different types of spokespersons can deliver testimonials. A firm can create an "expert" like "Mr. Goodwrench" (the GM auto mechanic) who appeals to the receiver's need for professional advice. The "average person" makes an ideal brand champion when consumers respond to information from a person similar to themselves. The most

ILLUSTRATION 11-3
Effective use of comparison as a creative technique.

widely used version of the testimonial is to use a celebrity. Bill Cosby (Kodak film), Michael Jordan (Nike and McDonalds), and Arnold Palmer (Pennzoil) all serve to attract attention to a brand. It is interesting to note that empirical research and consumer opinion polls show that messages delivered by celebrities are no more persuasive than noncelebrity ads.[8]

Animation

Perhaps because of the success of films like and *Beauty and the Beast* and *Aladdin* or the fact that baby boomers are sitting around watching cartoons with their kids explains the growing popularity and success of **animation** in ads. Some brands have used animation for years, like Keebler with its elves and Metropolitan Life Insurance with Snoopy. The California Raisins, McDonalds' "Little Mermaid," and the Energizer battery bunny are highly successful ads that use animated characters. Animation does allow greater breadth in the creative execution. The risk is that animation does not match the image and stature of the brand.

Advertorial

An **advertorial** is a special advertising section designed to look like the print publication in which it appears. Advertorials are so named because they have the look of editorial content of the magazine or newspaper but really represent a long and involved advertisement for a firm and its product/service. *The Wall Street Journal, Redbook,* and *New York Magazine* have all carried advertorials.

Sports Illustrated has inserted advertorials for the Kentucky Derby and the National Basketball Association. The potential effectiveness of this technique lies with the increased credibility that comes from the look and length of the advertisement. These features have, however, raised controversy. Some critics believe that most readers aren't even aware they're reading an advertisement because of the similarity in appearance to the publication.[9] This raises the question of misrepresentation.

INFOMERCIAL

An **infomercial** is the television equivalent of an advertorial. With this technique an advertiser buys from 5 to 60 minutes of television time and runs a documentary like program that is really an extended advertisement. Real estate investment programs, weight loss products, and cookware have dominate the infomercial format. A 30-minute infomercial can cost from $50,000 to $1.2 million to put on the air. The program usually has a host who is providing "information" about a program and typically brings on guests to give testimonials about how successful they have been using the featured product. Most infomercials run on cable stations, although networks have sold early morning and late night time as well. Recently, big firms have turned to infomercials. Philips Electronics has had great success with a 30-minute adventure-like infomercial for its Compact Disc Interactive (CD-i) player. Philips spent nearly $20 million to produce and buy prime time for their infomercial. Philips contends it is much more effective than the print advertising it replaced.[10]

In deciding among the many message appeals available, one important rule should be followed: the appeal that will be most effective is the one that relays *relevant information* to receivers. Regardless of the specific message technique used, the message must emphasize recipients' criteria for judging products. That's what receivers will deem relevant. To devise an appeal that is attention getting *and* relevant, marketing strategists working with creative professionals must rely on information about the market segment and the environment.

Much confusion surrounds the issue of subliminal advertising. **Subliminal advertising** is a form of stimulation that attempts to communicate to a receiver below the threshold of conscious awareness. Subliminal advertising is not a legitimate creative communication technique in commercial applications. Aside from its illegality, research evidence strongly suggests that subliminal stimulation does not work in an advertising context anyway. It is important to realize that communicating subliminally is, indeed, possible. Information can be processed by the mind below the level of conscious awareness. However, the vast majority of evidence indicates that subliminal messages are *ineffective* for influencing motives and actions.[11] This means that a person may be processing information subliminally, but the information is unlikely to affect product choice decisions or actions. If the rumors are true that some advertisers are actually using subliminal messages in their ads, the conclusion is that they're wasting their money.

MEDIA SELECTION AND STRATEGY

Once the creative effort has been carried out, then decisions regarding how to reach the target market with the advertising must be made. That is, media must be selected and strategically managed for greatest impact. An advertising effort can be completely undermined if mistakes are made in choosing and managing the media.

Media Selection

Proper media choice requires an understanding of the inherent characteristics of the media available for advertising. Inherent characteristics relate to the technical capabilities of a medium and consumer reactions to the medium. Table 11-3 rates each of the major mass media on different inherent characteristics and capabilities.

Coverage, as used in Table 11-3, is a rating of a medium's ability to reach a target market within a specified geographic area. Coverage is indicated at both the local and national level. **Selectivity** indicates the ability to reach a specific type of receiver based on demographic, life-style, socioeconomic, or some other segmentation descriptor. Magazines and direct mail are the most highly selective media. Magazines, because of their appeal to specific interests, and direct mail, because of the technical ability to put together a tightly targeted mailing list, are the most selective of the mass media. **Consumer acceptance** of a medium refers to how credible consumers perceive the medium to be as a source of product information. Because newspapers are considered a factual information source, their credibility has a positive effect on advertisements.

The way in which consumers listen to or view a medium is an indication of **consumer attentiveness**. Some media, like magazines, are carefully examined. Others, like television and billboards, are viewed passively. The degree to which consumers are attentive to a medium has implications for creative execution. The less attentive consumers are, the more an ad has to successfully attract and hold attention. **Reproduction quality** rates a medium on audio and visual reproduction capability. Many products require high-quality reproduc-

TABLE 11-3
Evaluation of Major Media

Characteristics	TV	CA-TV	Radio	Newspaper	Magazine	Direct Mail	Billboards
Coverage							
Local	H	M	H	H	L	H	H
National	H	H	L	L	H	M	L
Selectivity							
Demographic	M	H	M	L	H	H	L
Geographical	M	M	M	H	H	H	H
Consumer acceptance	M	M	M	H	H	L	M
Consumer attentiveness	L	L–M	L	M	H	L	L
Reproduction quality	M	H	M	L	H	H	M
Flexibility	L	M	H	H	L	H	M
Use by retailers	M–H	L	M	H	M	M	M
Cost							
Per contact	L	L	L	L	M	H	L
For national coverage	H	M–H	H	H	M	H	H

Note: L = low, M = medium, H = high capability.

tion so that the values of the product can be fully appreciated. **Flexibility** pertains to two characteristics of a medium: the length of time an ad must be submitted before it can appear and the ability of the advertiser to acquire space. Some media are characterized by long lead times and chaotic buying.

Use by retailers is an indication of the medium's compatibility with a retailer's advertising needs. Finally, **cost** is a consideration in two ways. On a per-contact basis, cost is figured on the dollar amount it costs to reach each receiver. The cost for national coverage is an indication of how costly it will be to use a medium to cover a large geographic area.

Two important changes have occurred over the last several years related to media. First, the growth of cable television has made many advertisers reassess their traditional investments in network television. By 1994, over 65 percent of all U.S. households were receiving basic cable service. With this sort of reach and with the greater specificity of programming on cable, some big advertisers like Anheuser-Busch and General Mills have diverted as much as 15 percent of their media advertising budgets to cable.[12] Channels like ESPN, with its heavy emphasis on sports, and Nickelodeon, with its emphasis on children's programs, allow advertisers to reach highly selective audiences at lower cost than do the less-focused networks. Second, a shift in consumer media habits has forced some advertisers to realign their promotional budget allocations. Direct marketing, sales promotions, and public relations campaigns are proving to be effective ways of reaching target segments and avoiding the clutter of conventional mass media. This means that more funding is being diverted to these promotional mix variables and being taken away from expenditures for mass media. These changes have created upheaval in the media and advertising industries. Some major media organizations are less profitable than in prior decades. Similarly, ad agencies that depend on media expenditures for the bulk of their revenue have had to branch out their services to include sales promotion, direct marketing, and public relations services for their clients.

Media Strategy

As the prior section on media selection showed, each medium is inherently capable of performing in certain ways. Strategic management of the media means decisions must be made with respect to reach and frequency, pulsing, and audience duplication techniques. Media strategy helps ensure that messages placed within the chosen media have as much impact as possible.

Reach refers to the number of different homes that will be exposed to an advertisement during a given time period, usually four weeks. Television and national magazines have the largest and broadest reach of any of the media due to their national coverage. **Frequency** is the number of times a home within an area is reached by an advertisement. Related to reach and frequency is **gross rating points (GRP)**, which is a measure of reach × frequency. An important aspect of GRP is that it can now be calculated with the elimination of duplicated audience. That is, reaching the same homes or viewers more than once can now be removed from the calculation. This is important because if reach rather than frequency is an important advertising objective, then GRP ratings that reflect unduplicated audience are needed.

Pulsing is a media-scheduling technique that has both financial and effectiveness implications. Pulsing, also referred to as *flighting* or *wave theory,* is achieved by scheduling heavy advertising for a period of time, usually two weeks, then stopping advertising altogether for a period, only to come back with another heavy schedule. Pulsing is used to support special merchandising efforts or new product introductions. The financial advantages of pulsing are that better prices for space or discounts might be gained by concentrating media buys in larger blocks. Communication effectiveness may be enhanced because a heavy schedule can achieve repeat exposures necessary to achieve consumer awareness.

Audience duplication is another media-scheduling strategy that can have a strong impact on communication effectiveness. The objective of audience duplication is to reach the same group of receivers through different media with an essentially identical ad. One preferred tactic is to run the sound track from a television ad as a radio spot. The visualization stimulated in the receiver results in a high level of recognition of the brand. Another version is to send a direct mail piece that duplicates a magazine ad. In the Nissan example used earlier, much of the television and direct mail advertising for the $100 sales promotion achieved audience duplication.

ROLE OF THE ADVERTISING AGENCY

For all firms, the appropriate use of an advertising agency can be of tremendous benefit and result in greater efficiency and effectiveness in the advertising process. Ad agencies have highly talented people with experience in all phases of advertising. No firm could afford to hire and maintain the same level of expertise as can an agency. Ad agencies are of four types:

- **Full-Service Agency.** Large full-service agencies provide a complete range of services to their clients. These services include creative development, media scheduling, and technical production. Some of the largest agencies will provide even more services like market research, package design, and evaluation of advertising effectiveness.
- **Creative Boutiques.** These agencies specialize in preparing only the creative execution of the ad. The firm would need to enlist the services of a production company and media buying service to supplement the effort of the creative boutique.
- **Media Buying Service.** This type of agency is really a clearinghouse for media time and space. It merely buys time for the client in specified media without suggesting placement or strategy.
- **Media Agencies.** Several members of the broadcast media have developed what are essentially their own in-house agencies. What used to be production facilities in radio and television stations now have creative personnel and directors to assistance clients in the preparation of their advertising.

Methods of compensation to an outside agency vary. The majority of full-service agencies operate on a compensation schedule that is based on 15 percent of total media expenditures (16 2/3 percent on outdoor ads) on ads prepared by the agency. If large-scale production is involved, then additional negotiated fees may be charged. Media buying services typically charge a fee ranging from 3 to 5 percent of media billings. The creative boutiques are compensated on a negotiated fee basis. The media agencies many times provide their services at no charge if the firm buys media time with the radio or television station.

Sales Promotion

Sales promotion is a very conspicuous form of promotion. Coupons, contests, free samples, premiums, and special events attract attention and motivate consumers to try a product. Used properly, it is capable of having important effects on demand stimulation. As a promotional tool, **sales promotion** is defined as the use of incentive techniques to generate a specific response within a consumer, trade, or business market.

Sales promotion affects demand quite differently than does advertising. Whereas advertising is designed to have long-term image and preference affects on a brand, sales promotions are designed to elicit a more immediate reaction from consumers. Coupons, samples, rebates, and sweepstakes associated with a brand offer the consumer an advantage, such as cost savings or the chance to win a prize, over competitors' brands. Sales promotions tend to be more effective in the convenience goods category where brand switching and perceived homogeneity between brands characterize the market. But sales promotions are used across all consumer goods categories and in the trade market as well.

The importance of sales promotion to commerce in the United States should not be underestimated. Sales promotion may not seem as glamorous and sophisticated as media advertising, but its application in marketing practice in the United States is impressive. During the 1980s, sales promotion expenditures grew at an annual rate of 12 percent compared to a 9 percent rate for advertising.[13] In 1991, expenditures on sales promotions exceeded $140 billion.[14] The development and management of an effective sales promotion program requires a major commitment by a firm. Procter & Gamble estimates that during any given year, 25 percent of sales force time and 30 percent of brand management time is spent on designing, implementing, and overseeing sales promotions.[15] The rise in use of sales promotions and the enormous amount of money being spent on the technique makes it one of the most prominent forms of promotion. It must be undertaken only under certain conditions and carefully executed for specific reasons.

SALES PROMOTION OBJECTIVES

Sales promotion in its many forms should be implemented only after setting very specific objectives for its use. Casual and frequent use of sales promotions can trap the firm into a price competition cycle. Further, regular and ill-conceived use of sales promotion can affect consumer perceptions of a brand. If a brand is always discounted through a sales promotion, consumers will begin to see the brand as worth buying *only* when it is discounted. The following basic objectives can be pursued with sales promotion:

1. *To Attract New Users.* When a firm introduces a brand to a new segment or attempts to convert nonusers of a product category to users, sales promotion tools can reduce consumer risk of trying something new.

2. *To Stimulate Repeat Purchases.* In-package coupons good for the next purchase or the accumulation of "points" with repeated purchases can keep consumers loyal to a particular brand. Hyatt Hotels successfully launched a "Frequent Stay" program much like the airlines' frequent flyer programs. The program rewards business travelers with free luggage tags and other premiums if they continue to stay at Hyatt Hotels.[16]
3. *To Stimulate Larger Purchases.* Price reductions or two-for-one sales can motivate consumers to stock up on a brand thus allowing firms to reduce inventory or increase cash flow. Shampoo is often "double-packaged" to offer a value to consumers.
4. *To Increase Store Traffic.* Retailers can increase store traffic through special promotions or events. Door prize drawings, parking lot sales, or live radio broadcasts from the store are common sales promotion traffic builders.
5. *To Introduce a New Product.* Because sales promotion can attract attention and reduces consumer risk of purchase, it is a commonly used technique for new product introduction. Gillette used several different sales promotion techniques to introduce the *Sensor* razor. Free samples, rebates, and in-store displays not only launched the brand successfully but vaulted the new razor to a leading market share.

CONSUMER MARKET SALES PROMOTION TECHNIQUES

Several sales promotion techniques stimulate demand and attract attention in the consumer market and help implement a pull strategy (discussed in Chapter 10) for a manufacturer. They are coupons, premiums, contests, trial offers and samples, rebates, and event sponsorship. Sales promotions in the consumer market are predominantly used with convenience goods. But, marketers of consumer shopping goods like automobiles and camping gear can also make effective use of sales promotion.

Coupons

The use of **coupons** is well advised when price sensitivity is verified for a product category. The other appropriate application of coupons is when there is evidence of brand switching by consumers. Cents-off coupons placed either in the media or in the product package provide a catalyst for consumers to choose one brand over another when homogeneity between brands is perceived. There is some evidence that coupons in the package stimulate greater brand loyalty than media-distributed coupons.[17] Also, it seems that particular groups of consumers are more prone to be affected by such product deals.[18] The use of coupons is an effective way to gain new users for a brand and to stimulate repeat purchases. Annually, nearly 300 billion coupons are distributed to American consumers with redemption rates ranging from 2 to 20 percent. In 1990, consumers in the United States saved more than $4 billion through coupon use.[19]

Premiums

Premiums are items offered free with the purchase of another item, or they may be offered at a greatly reduced price. Many firms will offer a related product free, such as a free granola bar packed inside a box of cereal. Service firms, like a car wash or optical shop, may offer a two-for-one deal to get consumers to try the service. These types of premium tactics must be considered carefully. First, the cost of the premium must be measured against the amount of demand it will stimulate. Second, the appropriate premium must be chosen so that it is an attractive inducement for the consumer. Illustration 11-4 is an example of the use of a premium.

Contests and Sweepstakes

Games and contests of all sorts can draw attention to a product or service. Many times this tactic is implemented on a cooperative basis between manufacturers and local retail outlets. The airline companies regularly give away

ILLUSTRATION 11-4
Premiums are items offered for free or at a discount with the purchase of another product.

free trips in cosponsorship with a local travel agent. Contests can have a great effect on generating traffic in retail outlets. Another benefit of contests is increased name recognition for local retailers. **Contests and sweepstakes** can be national and international as well. British Airways ran a contest with the theme, "The World's Greatest Offer" in which it gave away thousands of free airline tickets to London and other European destinations. While the contest served to increase awareness for the airline, a spokesman said there was definitely another benefit of the contest: "We're creating a database with all these names. All those people who didn't win will be getting mail from us with information on other premium offers."[20]

Trial Offers and Samples

Getting consumers to actually try a product can have a powerful effect on future decision making. This being the case, **trial offers and free samples** are sales promotion devices designed to do just that. Free samples of detergents, shampoos, cereals, and the like are distributed through the mail or in a Sunday newspaper to achieve this trial use with consumers. Sampling is particularly useful for new products, but it can also be used successfully for brands with weak market share in specific geographic areas. Some firms have experienced immediate sales volume increases as great as five to ten times normal with lasting effects on volume in the 10- to 15-percent range by using sampling.[21] Trial offers have essentially the same intent but are used for more expensive items. Appliances, watches, hand tools, and consumer electronics are items often offered on a ten-day free trial to reduce consumer risk. The expense to the firm, of course, can be formidable. Segments chosen for this promotional device must have high potential.

Rebates

Giving rebates to consumers was started in the mid-1970s when auto dealers feared price freezes would be imposed by the government as a means to curb inflation. Auto dealers discovered that a **rebate** on the purchase price of a car was a way around the impending price freeze. Well, the price freeze never materialized, but rebates have been a fixture in sales promotions ever since. The rebate technique has been refined over the years. Now marketers of appliances to home and garden equipment and motor oil use the rebate technique. Rebates are also particularly well suited to increasing the quantity purchased by consumers. Firms can offer a rebate for "every two" of an item purchased.

Event Sponsorship

Event sponsorship, where a firm contributes funds to support an event, has become increasingly popular as firms try to reach well-defined audiences. Sporting events, auto racing, golf and tennis tournaments, and art events are heavily sponsored by corporations. It is estimated that in 1992, 4,500 companies spent approximately $3.3 billion sponsoring events.[22] Figure 11-1 shows the different types of events firms have invested in with sponsorship promotions. One problem with event sponsorship is that it is very hard to track the impact of the promotion. Unlike other sales promotion tools where short-term sales effects are anticipated, event sponsorship is far less direct and predictable.

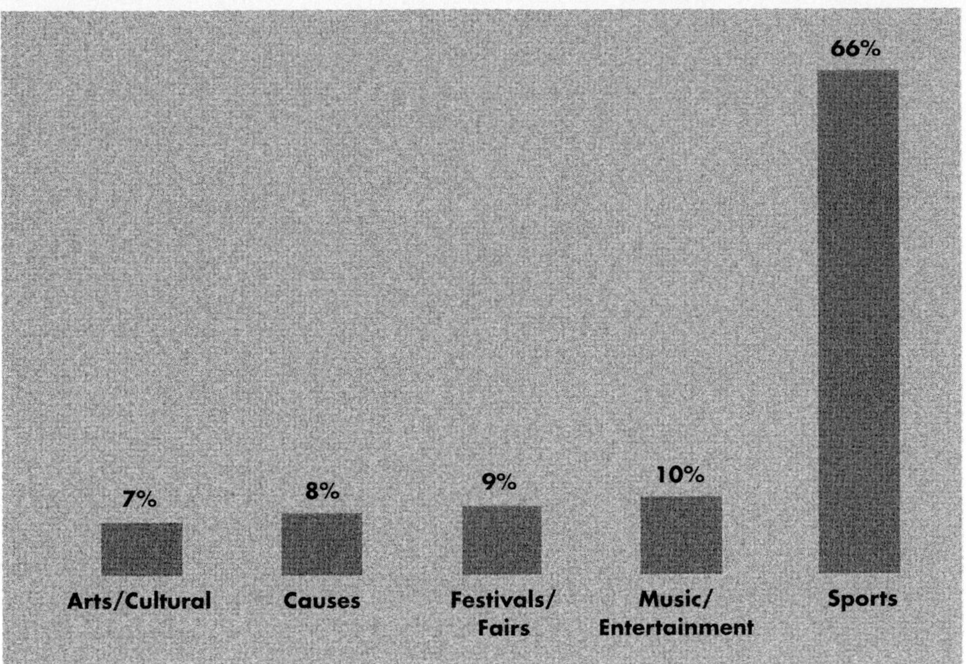

FIGURE 11-1
Types of Events Firms Sponsor

Source: Estimates provided in Scott Hume, "Sponsorship up 18 Percent," *Advertising Age* (March 23, 1992): 4.

TRADE MARKET SALES PROMOTION TECHNIQUES

Sales promotions directed to members of the trade—wholesalers, distributors, and retailers—are also designed to stimulate demand in the short term and help push the product through the distribution system. Within this very important market group, effective sales promotion efforts can generate enthusiasm for a product and contribute positively to the loyalty trade members exhibit toward a manufacturer.

Point-of-Purchase Displays

Product displays and information sheets, so-called **point-of-purchase materials,** are useful in reaching the consumer at the point of purchase and often encourage retailers to provide special displays for a firm's brand. Many times the product display is designed to draw attention to the product. Equally as often, it is a technique for gaining precious shelf space and exposure in the retail setting. Handout materials at the point of purchase can be an important complement to the personal selling process for shopping goods. In situations where consumers are comparing brands on features and actually engaging in rather complete judgment of the brands at the point of purchase, additional information at this stage in the decision-making process can make an important difference in brand choice.

Incentives

Incentives to members of the trade include a variety of tactics not unlike the types of promotions used in the household consumer market. Awards in the form of travel, gifts, or cash bonuses can induce retailers and wholesalers to give a firm's product added attention. The incentive does not have to be large or expensive to be effective. Weiser Lock offered its dealers a *Swiss Army Knife* with every dozen cases of locks ordered. The program was a huge success. One risk with incentive programs at the retail level is that salespeople can be so motivated to win an award that they may try to sell the product to every customer whether it is appropriate for that customer or not. Another risk with incentives is the firm must carefully manage such programs to ensure that ethics are not violated. The incentive method can look a lot like a bribe unless it is carried out in a highly structured and visible fashion.

Allowances

Various forms of *allowances* are given to retailers and wholesalers with the purpose of increasing the attention they give to a firm's products. *Co-op advertising allowances* let a retailer run advertising in local media featuring a brand and have the cost subsidized by the manufacturer. *Merchandise allowances* are payments to the trade for setting up and maintaining displays. The payments are typically far less than manufacturers would have to spend to maintain the displays themselves. *Slotting fees* are a phenomenon of the 1980s and describe a process where manufacturers make direct cash payments to grocery retailers to stock items, especially new items. Such fees are most commonly charged for the more favored shelf locations like eye level and end-of-aisle displays. Soft drink competitors are now paying as much as $25,000 per package type—six packs, quarts, etc.—which can push fees into the hundreds of thousands of dollars per year.[23] *Case allowance* is a somewhat dated term that refers simply to a discount for an order that exceeds a certain number of cases of an item. The reason this factor is listed as a sales promotion technique is because many times the allowance is paid in the form of product rather than cash payments.

BUSINESS MARKET SALES PROMOTION TECHNIQUES

The range of possibilities for effectively using sales promotion in the business market are far more restrictive than those discussed for the household consumer and trade markets. It would appear that games, incentives, and rebates are considered too unprofessional to be viewed as appropriate for business selling situations. Also, as Chapter 6 emphasized, business buyers are paid to behave rationally. They use a list of criteria to judge products and vendors. This being the case, rebates, contests and premiums are generally less effective on business buyers than on household consumer or trade customers. As such, a primary method of sales promotion for business products is the trade show. **Trade shows** are events where several related products are displayed and demonstrated to members of the industry that constitutes the potential market. In conjunction with trade show booth displays, company representatives are on hand to explain the product and perhaps make an important contact for the personal selling effort. The use of trade shows can be carefully planned and can be an important part of the business promotional program. The trade show can be critically important to small firms that cannot afford advertising and have a sales staff that is too small to reach very many potential customers. Through the trade show route, sales people can make far more contacts than would be possible with direct sales calls.

To a lesser extent, other sales promotion techniques used in the trade and household consumer markets are used in the business market. Business market customers occasionally offer incentives such as premiums or gifts for purchasing. Rebates are sometimes offered to business customers as are premiums. For example, a computer hardware manufacturer may offer a significant price reduction on or even give away a printer if a firm buys a certain number of computers. Business firms are also prominent sponsors of events such as golf tournaments or marathon runs and often give away premiums (caps, t-shirts) that carry the corporate name and logo.

RISKS OF SALES PROMOTION

Sales promotion is a valuable promotional tool and can achieve some very specific objectives for the firm. There are, however, some very significant risks associated with its use. First, since sales promotions rely on some sort of price break or give away, a firm runs the risk of having its brand perceived as price-oriented with no real value or features other than a low price. Second, management must realize that sales promotions are short-term strategies designed to reduce inventories, increase cash flow, or show periodic boosts in market share. The liability of this effect is that the firm may be borrowing from future sales. Consumers and business buyers who may have purchased from a firm anyway, may be motivated to buy sooner or buy more at lower prices. This would result in the firm witnessing a reduction in sales over the next time period of measurement. Third, sales promotions are costly and time consuming. Funds allocated to sales promotions may be taking funds away from advertising. Advertising is a long-term, market share building process that should not be compromised for short-term goals.

Sales promotion has an allure that must be kept in perspective. Sales promotions make things happen—quickly. While this is valuable and exciting in the short term, sales promotions will not form the foundation for a successful market share strategy. All forms of promotion must be incorporated into this phase of the marketing mix in order for the long-term goals of a firm to be accomplished.

DIRECT MARKETING

Direct marketing has evolved from its humble beginning in direct mail to a highly sophisticated, data-base driven, fully integrated mass communication technique. Currently, this form of promotion is best viewed as a method of selling and distributing products that relies on various media to elicit a direct response from a customer. Most direct marketing efforts are targeted to the household consumer market but can be applied in certain trade or business situations as well.

Direct marketing has the advantage of more tightly focusing a firm's media expenditures by reaching highly selected markets. The ability of direct marketing techniques to reach narrowly defined target markets led Warner Bros. studios to use Hollywood's first direct-mail campaign to promote the film *Memphis*

Belle.[24] Executives at Warner Bros. felt that the film lacked the broad box office appeal that would make traditional television and print ads effective. Instead, they devised an elaborate direct marketing campaign that involved "sneak previews" in 500 theaters and additional screenings in the top 65 markets for high school students. Aside from the heavier than normal "sneaks" schedule, thousands of direct-mail pieces promoting the film were mailed in selected markets. This aspect of selected targeting has contributed significantly to the broad and rapid growth of direct-marketing techniques.

THE GROWTH OF DIRECT MARKETING

On any number of measures, the direct marketing industry is huge. The most recent data suggest that consumers purchase over $200 billion annually through various forms of direct marketing. The Direct Marketing Association estimates that the number of catalogs alone mailed in 1990 reached 13.6 billion.[25] Direct marketing can claim 70 percent of all magazine subscription sales, more than 50 percent of all book sales, and nearly 20 percent of all the film processing in the United States.[26] The major techniques of direct marketing include direct-mail promotions, catalogs, direct response advertising in both print and broadcast media, and telemarketing sales. The rapid and expansive growth of the use of direct marketing can be traced to several technological and cultural factors.

- *Computer Technology*. The advancement of computer technology has allowed firms to better target customer groups with computerized mailing lists and computer prepared mailings.
- *Communications Technology*. The proliferation of toll free numbers has given firms a way to access consumers while keeping consumer cost and risk low. Catalogers like L.L. Bean and Orvis receive most of their orders by phone.
- *Life-style*. Dual breadwinner households and the importance of convenience have fostered more "non-site" purchase decisions. Access to a wide range of products through direct marketing saves these types of households precious time.
- *Gaps in Retailing*. Many products successfully direct marketed were products simply not available through traditional retail outlets. One survey of direct buyers found that 37 percent of their purchases were motivated by these gaps in retailing.[27]
- *Growth in Consumer Credit*. The acceptance and use of credit by consumers has greatly affected the evolution of direct marketing. Because credit cards are the primary means of payment in direct marketing, consumers' willingness to use credit cards and accumulate credit card debt has been fundamental to the growth of direct marketing.
- *Interactive Media*. While interactive media may only now be emerging, marketers are preparing for widespread use of the technology. JCPenney plans to test an interactive version of its catalog in 150 households in Texas. Macy's has announced it will launch its own 24-hour shopping channel and Nordstroms believes it can offer its "personal shopper" service through interactive access by 1998.[28]

Nordstrom is experimenting with interactive media as a method of direct marketing.

Direct marketing should be recognized as a major force in mass communications. Not only are firms investing billions of dollars in this method, but the application of direct marketing techniques is proliferating to include all product categories and forms of services. Direct response is no longer the mainstay of late-night, off-price television promotions. Firms like Time-Life Publications and Fidelity Investments have joined the growing list of firms that rely on this promotional tool.

But the future for direct marketing needs to be contemplated. Environmental concerns may ultimately restrict the mailing of catalogs and other promotions to consumers. Rising costs for paper and mailing may infringe on direct marketers' ability to successfully cultivate markets. Finally, consumers' desire for privacy may cause them to request that their names be removed from mailing and telemarketing phone lists—the lifelines of direct marketing techniques. All of this is pure speculation, but the movements already exist with regard to the environment and may ultimately infringe on the application of direct marketing techniques.

Public Relations

In 1993, Pepsi had a public relations nightmare on its hands. Complaints were coming in from all over the United States that cans of *Pepsi, Diet Pepsi,* and *Caffeine Free Diet Pepsi* contained syringes. Other callers claimed their cans of *Pepsi* had a screw, a crack vial, a sewing needle, and one with brown "goo" in the bottom. The management team at Pepsi that was mobilized to handle the crisis immediately considered a national recall of all Pepsi products. But, the Food and Drug Administration told Pepsi there was no need since no one had been injured and there was no health risk. The Pepsi team was also sure that this was not a case of tampering in the production facility. A can of *Pepsi* is filled with cola and then sealed in nine tenths of a second—making it virtually impossible for anyone to get anything in a can during production.[29]

The president of Pepsi appeared on national television to explain the situation and to defend his firm and its products. The Commissioner of the FDA said publicly that many of the tampering claims could not be substantiated or verified. A video camera in Aurora, Colorado, caught a woman trying to insert a syringe into a *Pepsi* can. Pepsi was exonerated in the press, but huge public relations problem remained for the firm to retain its global stature and credibility.

What happened to Pepsi highlights why **public relations** is such a difficult form of promotion to manage. In many cases, a firm's public relations program is called into action for "damage control" just as Pepsi had to do. The firm had to be completely reactive to the situation rather than strategically controlling it as with the other tools of mass communication. But, while many episodes of public relations must be reactive, a firm can be prepared with public relations materials to conduct an orderly and positive goodwill and image building campaign among its many constituents.

TOOLS OF PUBLIC RELATIONS

A firm can make positive use of publicity through several vehicles. The goal is to gain as much control over the process as possible with these methods.

Press Releases

Maintaining a file of corporate activities and information that can be used for **press releases** puts the firm in a position to take advantage of free press opportunities. Information and activities that can be conveyed through a press release are:

- New products
- New personnel
- New corporate facilities
- Innovative corporate practices, like energy saving programs or employee benefit programs
- Charitable and community service activities

The only drawback to press releases is that a firm often doesn't know if or when the item might appear in the media. Also, the news media are free to edit or interpret a news release, which may alter its meaning.

Company Newsletter

In-house publications can disseminate positive information about the firm through employees. As members of the community, employees are proud of achievements by their firm. Newsletters can also be distributed to important constituents in the community like government officials, the Chamber of Commerce, or the Tourist Bureau. And, newsletters can be mailed to supplier, who often enjoy reading about an important customer.

Interviews and Press Conferences

As in the Pepsi tampering crisis, interviews and press conferences can be a highly effective public relations tool. Often an interview and press conference is warranted in a crisis management situation. Firms have successfully called press conferences to announce important scientific breakthroughs or to explain the details of a corporate expansion. The press conference has an air of importance and credibility because it uses a news format to announce important corporate information.

Sponsored Events

A firm can become involved in local community events through sponsorships. Fundraisers of all sorts for not-for-profit organizations give positive visibility to corporations. Chevrolet has been sponsoring college scholarships through the NCAA by choosing the best offensive and defensive player of a game. The scholarships are announced at the conclusion of weekly televised games. This sort of publicity for Chevrolet creates a favorable image in the minds of an important future market segment.

Publicity

Publicity is unpaid media exposure about a firm or its products and services. Publicity is handled by the public relations function but cannot be strategically controlled like other public relations activities. It can, however, prove to be an image builder and heighten consumer awareness for products and organizations. An organization needs to be prepared to take advantage of events that make for good publicity and to counter events that are potentially damaging to the firm's reputation. One advantage of publicity is that it has credibility. Publicity items are carried as news stories in the media and therefore assume an air of believability. And, not-for-profit organizations have been able to use publicity such as news stories, interviews, and press releases in such a way that wide visibility is gained for the organization.

Mass communications is an expansive and challenging area for managers. The tools of mass communication are diverse and complex. The process is involved and costly. But, as complex and costly as mass communication is in a domestic setting, it becomes even more so when decision making moves to the global context.

Mass Communication: A Global Perspective

What do Procter & Gamble's *Oil of Olay, Oil of Ulay,* and *Oil of Ulan* have in common? Well, for one thing, they're all the same product. Although the names vary across international markets, they all share a common theme of promoting youthful looking, beautiful skin. Repositioning the skin moisturizer, which was originally aimed at the fifty-something female market, all the ads now prepared for this brand are aimed at a newly defined target market of younger women. In the United States, *Oil of Olay* is aimed at active women who are independent, drive sports cars, and hope to defy old age. In the U.K., *Oil of Ulay* takes the credit when a young woman and her mother are mistaken as sisters. In Asia, P&G takes a soft-sell approach, targeting *Oil of Ulan* to women as they go through major life changes such as marriage and childbirth. The one major change in the global repositioning of this product was primarily achieved by the new advertising campaign. Other elements of the marketing mix relating to the product, price, and channels of distribution remained essentially the same. *Oil of Olay* and other P&G nonfood products such as cold remedies, detergents, and disposable diapers are products that deliver nearly identical end benefits to consumers around the world, creating an opportunity for highly standardized and global advertising strategies.[30]

Advertising, sales promotion, direct marketing, and public relations are the mass communications tools used in global markets. Advertising often plays the leading role in promotional mixes used in affluent consumer markets around the world. To a certain extent, powerful environmental trends such as the global homogenization of life-styles, more women working outside the household, and smaller households lend support to an advertising emphasis in the promotional mix. For global companies selling fast-moving consumer goods, advertising remains the key promotional variable in persuading consumers to try the product. Table 11-4 identifies the top ten global advertising agencies and lists their global revenues. Figure 11-2 identifies the change in advertising spending for the top five and bottom five global markets. Notice that the countries with the strongest growth in advertising are all developing economies with rapidly expanding consumer markets.

While the broadcast media continue to grow globally, it is important to remember that advertising seldom, if ever, operates as the single tool in a firm's promotional efforts. Consider Mattel Corporation, whose overseas sales now comprise 50 percent of total revenues—up from 20 percent in 1980. Mattel has been able to double sales revenues for the *Barbie Doll* line of toys in the past four years, mostly due to a combination of increased advertising expenditures, setting up their own marketing operations, and a sales staff who have called on retailers in Europe and Latin America. [31]

TABLE 11-4
Top Ten Advertising Agencies by Worldwide Revenues

Agency	**Worldwide Revenues (in millions)**
Dentsu	$1.36 billion
McCann Erickson Worldwide	920 million
Euro RSCG	880 million
Young & Rubicam	820 million
J. Walter Thompson	770 million
Saatchi & Saatchi Advertising	690 million
BBDO Worldwide	680 million
Hakuhodo	660 million
Leo Burnett	640 million
Ogilvy & Mather Worldwide	640 million

Source: "The World in 1994," *The Economist Publications* (The Economist Newspaper Group, Inc. 1994): 93.

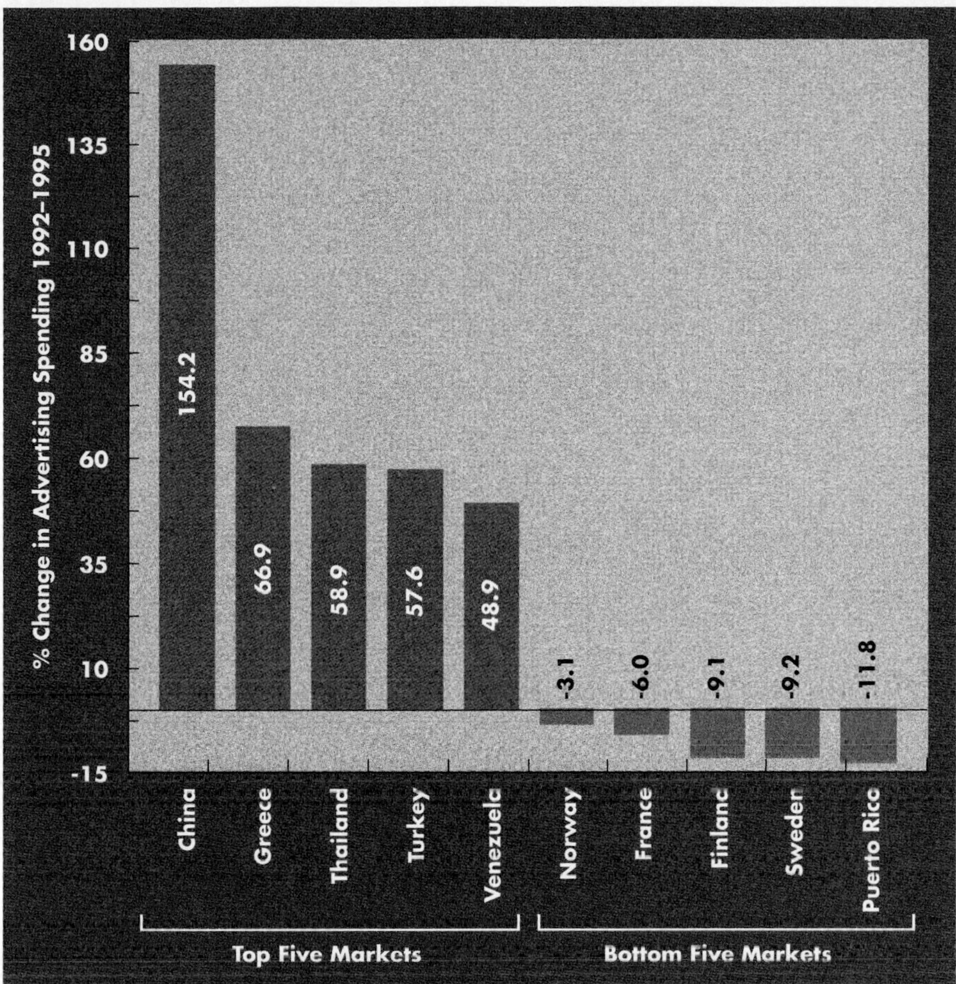

FIGURE 11-2
Change in Advertising Spending for the Top Five and Bottom Five Global Markets 1992–1995

Advertising is also often used as a strategic tool in combination with other elements of the marketing mix. Without a broader distribution network, Japan's Kao Company lost it's chance to dominate market share in the concentrated detergent market. In the United States, Procter & Gamble copied the product concept that was developed by Kao and then used a heavy advertising campaign coupled with their strong channels of distribution network to capture top share in the United States with its own concentrated detergent, *ERA*. Unilever used a similar combination of resources to capture top share in the European market with *Omo*.[32]

USING MASS COMMUNICATIONS IN GLOBAL MARKETS

Reconciling an international advertising and sales promotional effort with both the local market structure and the cultural uniqueness of individual markets is the challenge confronting the global marketer. This section of the chapter identifies and discusses the issues that influence decisions relating to advertising, sales promotion, direct mail, and publicity in the global arena.

Global Advertising

One of the most widely debated issues in global marketing focuses on the degree to which advertising can be standardized or must be customized in global marketing strategy. Those who favor the global, standardized approach assume that similarities as well as differences between markets should be taken into account, arguing that standardization of messages and advertising themes should occur whenever possible, adapting the message only when it is culturally necessary to do so. For example, Mars Inc.'s U.S. advertisements for their *Pedigree* dog food use golden retrievers, while the use of poodles is more effective for their positioning and image in Asia. Otherwise, the advertising campaigns are identical in terms of media strategy and basic message appeals.[33] Those who favor the customized approach see each country or region as a unique communication context arguing that the only way to achieve adequate and relevant advertising is to develop separate campaigns for each market. These different viewpoints reflect the "multidomestic" or "global" philosophy that a company finds appropriate, and both positions have merit. The advantages and disadvantages of these two perspectives and the four basic approaches for dealing with worldwide advertising are discussed below.

Issues in Standardization of Global Advertising

The two fundamental arguments *for* **standardized advertising** are based on potential cost advantages and creative advantages. Just as companies seek to gain economies of scale in production, they also look for opportunities to streamline the communication process. By using just one or two multinational advertising agencies to represent them worldwide, global companies have more centralized control over their corporate promotional budgets and more quality control over the production of the message. Similar to full-service agencies, the multinational ad agency offers the full services of a major agency, coupled with the sophistication that comes from having local representation in key markets throughout the world. Having one standard theme to communicate allows the company to focus on a uniform brand or corporate image worldwide, develop plans more quickly, and make maximum use of good ideas. This fundamental global theme strategy should not be confused with the company's advertising of individual products in separate markets. For example, the Gillette Company sells over 800 different products in more than 200 countries around the world, often using local adaptations of messages and different brand names for their products. Their corporate philosophy of globalization is expressed in their "Gillette, the Best a Man Can Get" theme, which is used in all ads for its men's toiletries products.

Arguments *against* standardization tend to center on issues relating to local market conditions and on cultural constraints both within the company as well as within the marketplace. If products are clearly in different competitive situations or different phases of the product life cycle, then standardized messages are likely to be ineffective across markets. Within the target market of each country, the product or brand's benefits must be clearly understood and must be similarly viewed in terms of importance and interest in order for a standardized message to have meaning. Within the various divisions of the company itself there can also be reluctance to participate in global campaigns. Strong local brand managers with their own sense of autonomy may resent global campaigns and greet them with a negative attitude, particularly when a portion of their local promotional budget is assigned to the global campaign by the home office. Finally, if the standardized campaign defies local customs, regulations, or ignores the efforts of local competition, then the strategy is not likely to be successful.

Approaches to Global Advertising

The issue of standardization is also the determining factor in specifying the type of advertising that will be used in global markets. However, standardization in this context is applied to both the product/brand description as well as to the nature of the advertising to be prepared. The degree to which standardization or customization is desired or needed in both the brand/product decisions and communications decisions provides the full range of strategic options available for global advertising.

Brand/Product Standardized and Advertising Standardized. Developing a truly standardized global brand with a standardized global advertising message can only be successful when one can find similar needs, feelings, or emotions to communicate across cultures. Finding "culture-free" appeals for products or services is not an easy task for the global marketer. For example, appealing to "the desire to be beautiful" or "brotherhood" are the fundamental themes that underlie the global communication strategies of P&G's *Oil of Olay* and *Coca-Cola,* respectively. Appealing to basic needs, emotions, or basic frames of mind and life-style are often easier to execute within homogeneous segments. Within consumer markets, relatively culture-free products such as credit cards, perfumes, and other luxury products can be targeted to upscale consumers who can be reached through global print and broadcast media. The trend in the 1990s of increased popularity of American pop culture and American heritage also provides opportunities for global appeals. Ray Charles and the Marlboro Man both have positive, worldwide appeal for Pepsi-Cola and Philip Morris, while advertising the unique American images of Tennessee whiskey and Kentucky bourbon have played a key role in increasing export sales for Jim Beam Brands Co. and United Distillers.[34]

Within business-to-business markets or capital goods markets, the opportunities for global appeals are more easily identifiable since the buying motives and purchase decisions are often similar across business markets and made explicit by established industry purchasing procedures. Many business products, including raw materials and technologically sophisticated products, are being marketed to an increasingly concentrated set of business buyers. Within these markets, standardized advertising in carefully selected trade media is more likely to play an information role, supplementing the efforts of a company's personal sales force.

Finally, global marketers need to distinguish between strategy and execution when using a global approach to advertising. The basic emotion or need that is identified may well be universal, but communication about the product or service that offers satisfaction of the need may be strongly influenced by cultural values in different markets and thus not well suited to standardization.

Recall the example in Chapter 2 of AT&T's "Reach Out and Touch Someone" campaign. The campaign was highly successful in the United States in communicating the universal need to keep in touch with loved ones but was viewed by European audiences as too sentimental in style and execution.

Brand/Product Standardized and Advertising Customized. This approach calls for different communication strategies for a standardized product or brand. In countries where products are in different stages of the product life cycle, where the product serves a different function in different countries, or when the market's basic buying behavior differs, firms will need to adapt the message for each market. For example, by advertising year round and emphasizing their standard store formula of low prices and "no quibble" return policy, Toys 'R' Us was able to enlist Germans to buy toys for children throughout the year rather than just during the concentrated sales period at the end of the year. In fact, having Toys 'R' Us advertise year round forced other traditional toy resellers in Germany to do the same, a move that helped increase the total industry's revenues by 50 percent to $4 billion since 1987. Toys 'R' Us realized roughly 25 percent of that increase. The company currently has 234 stores outside the United States, and its greatest expansion plans are in international markets where aggressive toy advertising has not been a common competitive strategy.[35]

Brand/Product Customized and Advertising Standardized. In this situation, the same communication strategy is used worldwide, and the product is adapted for different markets. Exxon Corp. is probably the best example of a global firm following this strategy with a consistent corporate communications program worldwide and different combinations of leaded/unleaded and octane solutions for their gas products in different markets. However, some communication adaptation may be necessary—for example, in Thailand the tiger used in Exxon's advertising is not a symbol for strength. Branded fashion clothing companies such as T.J. Maxx, Benetton, and Levi Strauss also follow this strategy. Each company offers slightly different models or versions within their product lines to accommodate local fashion tastes. However, since what gets communicated is the life-style around the product rather than the product itself some of their advertising campaigns can be aired worldwide.

Brand/Product Customized and Advertising Customized. These are local product situations with strong local brand names and a need for local and customized communication strategy. When the American firm Sara Lee acquires a strong local brand such as *Douwe Egberts Coffee* in Holland, one of the key costs of acquisition is buying the goodwill associated with that brand. For the local markets where the brand is well known, no changes would likely take place. However, the coffee company's production for export markets would likely be adapted to local tastes, using advertising campaigns with local emphasis. In another example, CPC International sells 15 different versions of minestrone soup in Europe under different brand names and with separate, local advertising efforts.

The argument that standardization of global advertising will increase is based on the assumption that consumer markets are becoming more homogenized, especially in highly industrialized countries. In part, this trend toward similarities is fueled by the broadcast media, many of which are heavily

For many brands, both the product and its advertising must be customized for each different global market.

financed by global advertisers. Clearly, the identification and targeting of highly similar life-styles across cultures is well underway. However, cultural differences and differences in rates of market development will always prevent complete standardization of advertising strategies from taking place. In spite of the deregulation of the airways in Europe and the growing, pervasive influence of broadcast media throughout the world, there will always be legal and cultural limitations to a firm's mass communication advertising efforts.

GLOBAL SALES PROMOTION

The basic purposes of gaining attention, interest, and motivating a behavioral response within a target market remain the same for **global sales promotion** as for domestic sales promotion. The challenge for global managers is to assess the promotional effectiveness of sales promotion efforts across different cultures and markets. This assessment of effectiveness needs to take place at both the channels level as well as at the consumer level and must take into account the varying cultural, economic, social, and legal aspects of different markets.

Coupons and the other promotional tools discussed earlier in the chapter essentially are designed to either reduce price or add value (or perceived value) to the product offering. As a general rule, in underdeveloped market economies, sales promotional activities emphasize the economic benefits of the offering. In markets with higher levels of development, sales promotion offers typically require a basic level of literacy and some level of consumer sophistication in order to be evaluated and acted upon. Retailers in particular must have the capacity as well as the motivation to process the redemption of coupons or rebates in cooperation with wholesalers, import agents, or manufacturers. In markets where retailers are small, scattered all around the country, and highly disorganized, the logistics of sales promotions become difficult and expensive. At the other extreme, in markets with highly organized retail structures where one dominant player controls most of the market, sales promotions may be seen as a nuisance and cooperation may be difficult to achieve between the manufacturer and retailer.

The use of trade allowances to induce retailers to increase orders or provide more shelf space is a common practice in much of the world. However, the typical retail store format is much smaller in Europe and Asia than in the United States, making this kind of trade sales promotion a very difficult strategy to implement. The notions of "channel captain" and "channel power" will be more fully discussed in Chapter 13 and relate directly to manufacturers' abilities to use sales promotional efforts in global channels.

Apart from economic conditions and channel structures in various countries, the norms of behavior inherent in a sales promotion offer may also vary. Point-of-purchase displays may work well in situations where self-service behavior is typical and acceptable. However, in less-developed economies where labor costs are low or in small shops where the shop keeper provides individual attention to customers, point-of-purchase offerings may violate behavioral sensibilities of both customers and shop owners. Finally, there are seemingly unlimited legal requirements that allow, strictly prohibit, or limit sales promotional offers. Ultimately, the cost and legal aspects coupled with the market structure of each country will influence the decision whether or not to run promotions.

GLOBAL PUBLIC RELATIONS

While the Pepsi-Cola example on page 383 illustrates just how difficult managing public relations can be, the positive note to that example is that the negative publicity was confined to the domestic market! Exxon's Valdez oil spill or Union Carbide's tragic accident at its plant in Bhopal, India, were situations that affected the companys' image worldwide. Negative publicity is not just limited to companies. The Sicilian Wine Growers Association produces some excellent red and white wines, yet has problems in distributing the wines or gaining consumer acceptance because of the negative publicity stemming from the mafia's presence on the island. Usually, companies have less control over global publicity relative to domestic situations, and no corporations are powerful enough to control a host country's media. At best, attempts are made to provide positive information about the company directed at influential targets such as members of the broadcasting media, editors, or journalists. For example, to reduce the trend of "Japan bashing" in the early 1990s in the United States, Japanese corporations have made use of public relations firms who assist in developing positive publicity regarding the companies' philanthropic activities in America. These are all examples of **global public relations.**

TRENDS IN GLOBAL DIRECT MARKETING

The world's most advanced, competitive, and innovative market for direct marketing activities is in the United States. The five technological and cultural factors discussed earlier in the chapter combine to create a market environment for direct marketing that is unmatched in any other country in the world. Japan has the technological and cultural prerequisites to evolve into a key market for direct marketing, but their long tradition of distribution via multilayered channels still dominates the market. Acceptance of direct marketing in Japan is coming about slowly, via young consumers who are less loyal to the traditional department store retail structure in Japan and are interested in purchasing high-involvement products such as casual wear clothing.[36] Estimates are that Europe, the other leading region in the world for direct marketing activities is running behind developments in the United States, although this gap is rapidly closing. The world's second largest direct marketing market is the United Kingdom, where 90 percent of the industry's annual sales of $6.1 billion are generated by just five companies. These companies, which started after World War I to sell to the working class on credit, still cater to lower-income households. This has left a market opportunity for upscale consumers, and the current global trend is to target affluent consumers.[37] Within many developed country markets there is a trend for fast moving consumer goods companies to move more of the mass communications budget out of mass advertising to activities such as public relations and direct marketing. In France, Nestle has successfully launched *Le Relais Bébé,* which are rest-stop structures along the highways where French families on vacation can stop to feed their babies and change their baby's diapers. Each summer, 64 hostesses welcome 120,000 baby visits, and dispense 600,000 samples of baby food and free disposable diapers. Creating a data base from the visitors that notes the date of the baby's birth, Nestle sends messages over time that track the development and growth of the baby and offer information and product advice to parents. They even send a Mother's Day mailing, "signed" from Baby to Mama. As a result, Nestle's share of the market has increased by 24 percent over the past years in spite of being out spent 7-to-1 in advertising by the market leader Bledina. [38] Apart from these below-the-line shifts in certain markets, television's share of the global advertising market will continue to grow as well, as the number of TV stations multiplies globally and as consumer markets in Asia and Latin America continue to expand.[39]

Postal regulations, unreliable postal service, and a lack of telecommunication and credit services (i.e., 800 numbers and credit card purchases via the phone) have somewhat restricted direct marketing opportunities for U.S. and other global firms. In response to these conditions, AT&T has launched its

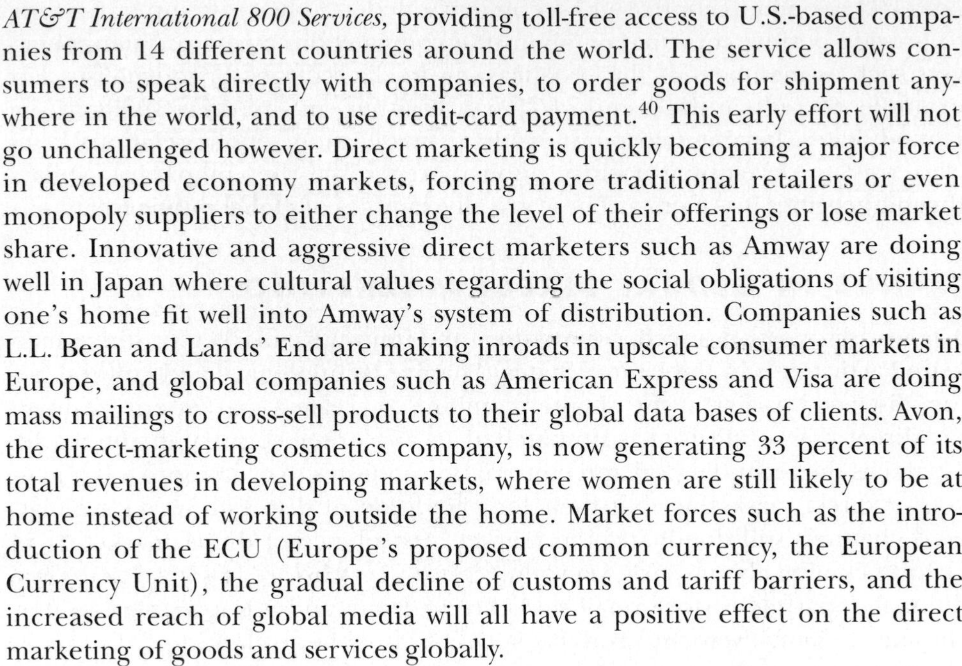

AT&T International 800 Services, providing toll-free access to U.S.-based companies from 14 different countries around the world. The service allows consumers to speak directly with companies, to order goods for shipment anywhere in the world, and to use credit-card payment.[40] This early effort will not go unchallenged however. Direct marketing is quickly becoming a major force in developed economy markets, forcing more traditional retailers or even monopoly suppliers to either change the level of their offerings or lose market share. Innovative and aggressive direct marketers such as Amway are doing well in Japan where cultural values regarding the social obligations of visiting one's home fit well into Amway's system of distribution. Companies such as L.L. Bean and Lands' End are making inroads in upscale consumer markets in Europe, and global companies such as American Express and Visa are doing mass mailings to cross-sell products to their global data bases of clients. Avon, the direct-marketing cosmetics company, is now generating 33 percent of its total revenues in developing markets, where women are still likely to be at home instead of working outside the home. Market forces such as the introduction of the ECU (Europe's proposed common currency, the European Currency Unit), the gradual decline of customs and tariff barriers, and the increased reach of global media will all have a positive effect on the direct marketing of goods and services globally.

Key Terms and Concepts

Advertising
Demand stimulation
Direct response advertising
Awareness advertising
Information-only appeals
Emotional appeals
Humor appeals
Fear appeals
Comparison appeals
Slice-of-life appeals
Testimonials
Animation
Advertorial
Infomercial
Subliminal advertising
Coverage
Selectivity
Consumer acceptance
Consumer attentiveness
Reproduction quality
Flexibility
Reach
Frequency
Gross rating points (GRP)
Pulsing
Audience duplication
Full-service agency
Creative boutique
Media buying service
Media agencies
Sales promotion
Coupons
Premiums
Contests and Sweepstakes
Trial offers and free samples
Rebates
Event sponsorship
Point-of-purchase materials
Incentives
Allowances
Trade shows
Direct marketing
Public relations
Brand/product standardization
Brand/product customization
Advertising standardization
Advertising customization
Global sales promotion

Questions and Exercises

1. What is your reaction to the billions of dollars spent on advertising as displayed in Table 11-1? Do you think consumers are paying too much for advertising information?
2. Why is it argued that products may actually cost less because they are advertised?
3. Distinguish between primary and selective demand stimulation. Which type of demand stimulation is used in the typical ad you see on television or in a magazine?

4. What role does (should) a firm play in developing the creative execution of an advertisement?
5. What strategies can a firm use in sales promotion? What are the risks of using sales promotion?
6. What factors have given rise to the increased use of direct marketing? Do you feel direct marketing will continue to grow as a promotional/marketing method? What environmental forces are working against its continued growth?
7. Why will public relations never be the leading strategic tool in a firm's promotional mix?
8. What are arguments for and against the standardization of advertising for global markets?
9. Under what global product/market conditions can a firm market a standardized product but must use customized advertising?
10. Why is direct marketing less prevalent in global markets than it is in the United States? Use the concepts discussed in Chapters 4 and 6 to identify global opportunities for growth in direct marketing activities.

REFERENCES

1. Jacqueline Mitchell, "More Car Ads Challenge Rivals Head-On," *The Wall Street Journal* (June 25, 1990): B1.
2. Ibid.
3. Ann B. Fisher, "Spiffing up the Corporate Image," *Fortune* (July 21, 1986) 68–72.
4. Richard Turner, "Video Retailers, Cinemas Plan Generic Ads," *The Wall Street Journal* (March 12, 1991): B1, B5.
5. Thomas R. King, "For Colas, the Fault Is in Too Many Stars," *The Wall Street Journal* (January 24, 1990): B1.
6. Kevin Goldman, "Pizza Ads with Dash of Humor Top Pops," *The Wall Street Journal* (March 9, 1993): B1; and Kevin Goldman, "Year's Top Commercials Propelled by Star Power," *The Wall Street Journal* (March 16, 1994): B1.
7. See William L. Wilkie and Paul W. Farris, "Comparison Advertising: Problems and Potential," *Journal of Marketing* 39 (October 1975): 7; and Debra Scammon, "Comparison Advertising: A Reexamination of the Issue," *Journal of Consumer Affairs* 12, no. 2 (Winter 1978): 381; Cornelia Pechmann and David W. Stewart, "The Effects of Comparative Advertising on Attention, Memory, and Purchase Intentions," *Journal of Marketing* 17 (September 1990): 180.
8. Ronald Alsop, "Jaded TV Viewers Tune out Celebrity Commercials," *The Wall Street Journal* (February 7, 1985): 37.
9. Cynthia Crossen, "Proliferation of 'Advertorials' Blurs Distinction between News and Ads," *The Wall Street Journal* (April 21, 1988): 33.
10. Kevin Goldman, "Philips Infomercial Does Its Thing in Popular TV-Watching Hours," *The Wall Street Journal* (September 23, 1993): B6.
11. Timothy E. Moore, "Subliminal Advertising: What You See Is What You Get," *Journal of Marketing* 46, no. 2 (Spring 1982): 38–47.
12. Ronald Alsop, "Cable TV Attracts More Ads But It Still Needs Fine Tuning," *The Wall Street Journal* (February 13, 1986): 39.
13. Russ Brown, "Sales Promotion," *Marketing and Media Decisions* (February 1990): 74.
14. Joe Mandese and Scott Donaton, "Media, Promotion Gap to Narrow," *Advertising Age* (June 29, 1992): 16.
15. Robert D. Buzzell, John A. Quelch, and Walter J. Salmon, "The Costly Bargain of Sales Promotion," *Harvard Business Review* (March/April 1990): 141–149.
16. Constanza Montana, "Hotels Offer 'Frequent Stay' Plans to Lure Repeat Business," *The Wall Street Journal* (January 6, 1987): 31.
17. Joe A. Dodson, Alice M. Tybout, and Brian Sternthal, "The Impact of Deals and Deal Retraction on Brand Switching," *Journal of Marketing Research* 15 (February 1978): 72.
18. Robert Blattberg, et al., "Identifying the Deal Prone Segment," *Journal of Marketing Research* 15, (August 1978): 369.
19. Joanne Lipman, "Amid Recession, Firms Clip Coupon Value," *The Wall Street Journal* (May 9, 1991): B5.
20. Thomas R. King, "Marketers Bet Big with Contests to Trigger Consumer Spending," *The Wall Street Journal* (April 4, 1991): B8.
21. Alix M. Freedman, "Use of Free Product Samples Wins New Favor as Sales Tool," *The Wall Street Journal* (August 28, 1986): 19.
22. Scott Hume, "Sponsorships Up 18 Percent," *Advertising Age* (March 23, 1992): 4.
23. Marj Charlier, "Beer Makers Frothing over Plan to Charge for Retail Shelf Space," *The Wall Street Journal* (April 22, 1994): B1.
24. Laura Landro, "Warner Tries Target Marketing to Sell Film Lacking Typical Box-Office Appeal," *The Wall Street Journal* (October 3, 1990): B1.

25. John B. Hinge, "Catalog Companies Retrench as Recession and Spiraling Mailing Costs Slow Growth," *The Wall Street Journal* (April 4, 1991): B1.
26. Herbert Katzenstein and William S. Sachs, *Direct Marketing,* (Columbus, OH: Merrill Publishing, 1986): 15.
27. Ibid., 18.
28. "Penney Plans to Test Interactive Sales of Its Catalog Merchandise," *Marketing News* (January 3, 1994: 13; and Laura Zinn, et al., "Retailing Will Never Be the Same," *Business Week* (July 26, 1993): 54.
29. Annette Miller, Daniel Glick, and Sherry Keen-Osborn, "The Great Pepsi Panic," *Newsweek* (June 28, 1993): 32.
30. Gabriella Stern, "P&G Cutting Number of Ad Agencies Assigned to Vicks Line, Spic and Span," *The Wall Street Journal* (June 1, 1993): B8; Zachary Schiller and Rischar A. Melcher, "Marketing Globally, Thinking Locally," *International Business Week* (May 13, 1991): 23.
31. Robert Neff, "Mattel: Looking for a Few Good Boy Toys," *International Business Week* (December 9, 1991): 76.
32. Ted Holden and Zachary Schiller, "Kao: The Global Challenger in P&G's Backyard," *International Business Week* (May 13, 1991): 22.
33. Zachary Schiller and Rischar A. Melcher, op. cit.
34. Christopher Power and Robert Neff, "Sweet Sales for Sour Mash—Abroad," *International Business Week* (July 1, 1991): 54.
35. Joseph Pereira, "Toys 'R' Us to Buy Stock for $1 Billion," *The Wall Street Journal* (January 12, 1994): A3, A5; Patrick Oster and Igor Reichlin, "Breaking into European Markets by Breaking the Rules," *International Business Week* (January 20, 1992): 56.
36. Karen Miller, "You Just Can't Talk to These Kids," *Business Week* (April 19, 1993): 104–6.
37. Mark Maremont, "Look Who's Storming Britain's Shores Now," *International Business Week* (November 18, 1991): 24.
38. "Nestle Banks on Databases," *Advertising Age* (October 25, 1993): 16, S7, S10.
39. "The World in 1994," *The Economists Publications* (The Economist Newspaper Group, Inc., 1994): 93.
40. *AT&T U.S. Directory* (Basking Ridge, N.J.: AT&T, 1993).

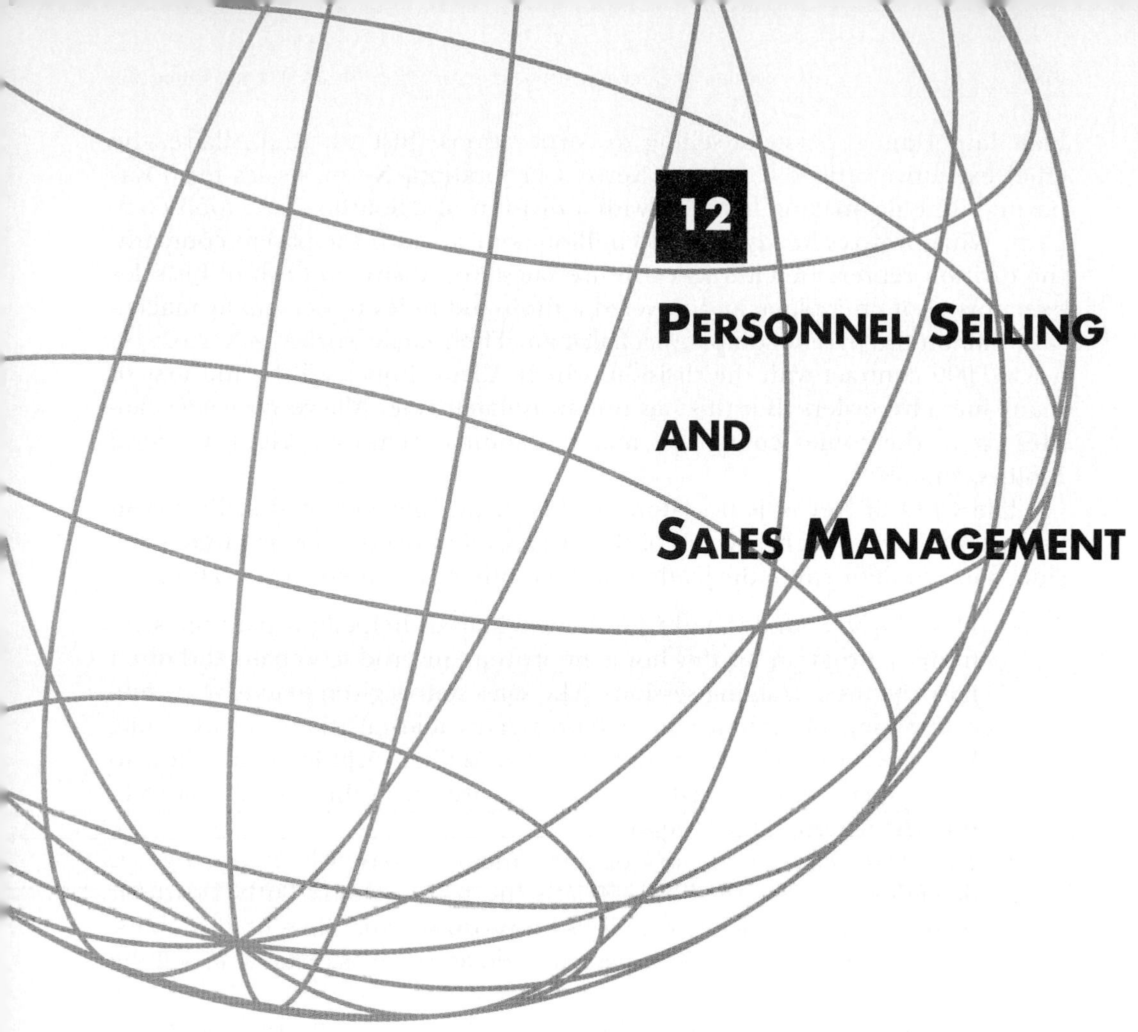

12

PERSONNEL SELLING AND SALES MANAGEMENT

AFTER STUDYING THIS CHAPTER, YOU WILL UNDERSTAND THAT:

1. Personal selling is the most important promotional tool in many corporations.
2. Professional salespeople perform a variety of activities beyond selling that include market analysis, sales forecasting, and customer service.
3. Setting objectives for personal selling must go beyond simply setting sales objectives and should include the identification of important customer-oriented objectives.
4. Sales force management encompasses a wide range of responsibilities to ensure the effective and efficient operation of the sales force.
5. Personal selling and sales management in the global context require a renewed commitment to avoiding self-reference criteria in both the selling process and the sales management effort.

How important is personal selling to corporations? Just ask Paul Allaire, the chief executive officer (CEO) of Xerox Corporation. Xerox's sales team was having difficulty making headway with a division of a Southeastern food company. While Xerox already had a $3 million contract with the parent company, the division represented attractive future sales. So, Allaire and two of his sales executives got on a plane and traveled a thousand miles to personally make a sales call on the parent company's chairman. Their tactic worked—Xerox won a $300,000 contract with the division, which Allaire hopes will be the first of many lucrative orders. But this was not an isolated case. Allaire *personally* handles six of the copier company's major accounts including AT&T, General Motors, and 3M.[1]

The CEO of Xerox is not alone in his belief that personal selling is so important that the highest levels of the organization need to be involved. Consider the commitment of the leaders at these other prominent corporations:

- *Home Depot.* Founder and CEO Bernie Marcus helped prepare the sales training program for this home improvement products chain and often participates in training sessions. The sales staff is given extensive technical training—how to lay tile and do electrical installations, for example. But, the staff is also trained in effective selling techniques like how to listen to customers' needs and walking customers through the store to find the materials they require.[2]
- *Fifth Third Bank.* The CEO of this Cincinnati-based bank, George A. Schaefer, Jr., likes to "blitz." That's the term used at Fifth Third for bank executives making sales calls on prospects and current customers. All the bank's officers are expected to do as much as possible to sell the bank's services.[3]
- *Dell Computer.* The manager of network communications for Banyan Systems, Inc., got a surprise recently—a sales call from Michael Dell, founder and CEO of Dell Computers. After meeting with Dell, the manager said, "He asked me what I'd like to see in the machines; he actually took notes."[4]

The leaders of these highly successful organizations don't just support the personal selling process. They get directly involved in the training and in some cases deliver a sales pitch to customers. The reason they've made such a commitment to personal selling is to help ensure that this phase of the promotional mix follows through on the implementation of critical marketing strategies.

The Importance and Role of Personal Selling

Despite the conspicuousness of advertising and sales promotion, personal selling is truly the most important force for revenue generation in many corporations. For firms like IBM, Xerox, State Farm Insurance, and a variety of retailing organizations, the personal selling effort is primarily responsible for customer contact and culminating sales. The expense for personal selling can equal as much as 15 percent of gross revenue. And the average cost of a single sales call is about $292. Combine that cost with the fact that it takes an average of 3.7 calls to close a sale, and an organization is spending a whopping $1,080 on average to get an order![5]

Aside from the sheer expense of the process, though, another measure of the importance of personal selling is the number of people employed in the profession. The most recent statistics from the U.S. Department of Labor put the number of people employed in sales jobs at about 14 million or nearly 12 percent of the civilian labor force in the United States![6] Another view of the value of personal selling to employment in the United States is provided in Table 12-1. Here you can see certain industries employ an enormous number of people in the personal selling process. Also, it is estimated that there will be tremendous growth in sales employment in industries like financial services and retail sales through the year 2005

Personal selling dominates the promotional mix for many firms for a number of good reasons. The discussion of personal communication in Chapter 10 highlights the potency of face-to-face communication. Products that are higher priced, complicated to use, require demonstration, are tailored to users needs, involve a trade-in, or are judged at the point of purchase are heavily dependent on personal selling. Household consumers and business buyers are frequently confronted with purchase decisions that are facilitated by interaction with a salesperson. In many decision contexts, only a qualified and well-trained salesperson can address the questions and concerns of a potential buyer.

All measures of the importance of personal selling, however, pale in comparison to the **role of personal selling** in an organization. Two aspects of personal selling are critical to a firm. First, salespeople are responsible for implementing marketing strategy. In a very real sense, the sales force is the embodiment of the entire marketing program for a firm. The responsibilities of salespeople have expanded to include a variety of activities associated with not just selling but with marketing as well. The role of the modern salesperson typically includes the following marketing strategy activities:

TABLE 12-1
Personal Selling Employment in Selected Industries

Sales Occupations	Estimated Employment 1990	Percentage Change in Employment 1990–2005	Numerical Change in Employment Expected 1990–2005
Insurance sales	439,000	20%	88,000
Manufacturers' and wholesale sales reps	1,944,000	15	284,000
Real estate agents, brokers	413,000	19	79,000
Retail sales	4,754,000	29	1,381,000
Securities and financial services sales reps	191,000	40	76,000
Services sales	588,000	55	325,000
Travel agents	132,000	62	82,000

Source: U.S. Department of Labor, Bureau of Labor Statistics, *Occupation Outlook Quarterly* (Washington, D.C.: U.S. Government Printing Office, Spring 1992): 25.

- *Market Analysis.* Contact with customers allows salespeople to provide the firm with several different types of information related to market analysis. Feedback to the firm on trends in overall demand can be provided. Competitors' activities are detectable through regular contact with buyers who are also buying competitors' products. This information can be fed directly into the MkIS used for overall market planning.
- *Sales Forecasting.* Related to the market analysis role is sales forecasting. Salespeople can give their estimates to marketing planners in the firm regarding sales potential for both the short and long term. Such estimates are based on the competitiveness of the firm's products as well as overall conditions in customers' industries.
- *New Product Ideas.* Chapter 7 pointed out that salespeople are a direct source of new product ideas. Close contact with customers allows the sales force to detect unmet needs in the market and relay this information to the new product development function in the firm.
- *Buyer Behavior Analysis.* The salesperson is in the best position to analyze buyer behavior tendencies. In negotiating sales with customers, the salesperson learns the criteria upon which different buyers are basing their decisions. Again, this information is fed back to the marketing strategists who continuously adjust the marketing mix.
- *Communications.* To effectively inform and persuade customers, salespeople must be expert in communications methods. No matter how well the marketing mix is conceived, it is up to the sales force to effectively deliver the message to customers regarding the satisfaction to be gained from buying from the firm.
- *Sales Coordination.* The salesperson must act as the coordinator between the firm's many marketing and sales activities and the buyer. The salesperson is often the leader of team selling efforts. At Dupont, groups of sales representatives, technicians, and factory managers work together to solve customer problems, create, and sell new products.[7]
- *Customer Service.* Customers are looking to the salesperson to provide a wide range of post-purchase service support. Salespeople can coordinate product delivery, installation, training, and financing.
- *Relationship Building.* As part of the whole "relationship marketing" movement, salespeople play an important role in building long-term relationships with customers—this has come to be referred to as *relationship selling.* As an example, Merck spends 12 months training its sales representatives not just in knowledge of pharmaceuticals, but also in trust-building techniques. And, reps are required to take regular refresher courses. Similarly, General Electric has stationed its own engineers full time at Praxair, Inc., a user of GE electrical equipment, to help the firm boost productivity. As a GE manager put it, "Customers demand a new intimacy."[8]

The second major role played by salespeople relates to implementing the marketing concept to ensure total customer satisfaction. Since salespeople play a marketing strategy role, they no longer simply approach customers with the intention of making a sale. Rather, they are problem solvers who work in partnership with customers. The salesperson is in the best position in the firm to analyze customer needs and propose solutions. By accepting this role, the sales force helps determine ways in which a firm can provide total customer satisfaction not just through the personal selling process but with the entire marketing mix.

TYPES OF PERSONAL SELLING

A variety of different **types of personal selling** are used to implement marketing strategy and following through on the marketing concept. Basically, every salesperson is engaged in personal communication, as we discovered in Chapter 10. But, there are types of selling that are quite different from one another. A salesperson can be engaged in order taking, creative selling, or supportive communication. The discussion that follows demonstrates that the communication task for each type of selling is vastly different.

ORDER TAKING

The least complex type of personal selling is order taking. Its importance, however, should not be underestimated. **Order taking** involves accepting orders for merchandise or scheduling services either in written form or over the telephone. Order takers deal with existing customers who, as we have learned, are lucrative to the firm due to the low cost of generating revenue from this group. Order takers are responsible for communicating with buyers in such a way that a quality relationship is maintained. This type of selling rarely involves communicating large amounts of information. Nor does order taking typically warrant in-depth analysis of the customer.

The retail clerk who simply takes payment for products or services is considered an **inside order taker.** In this situation the buyer has already chosen the product/service and merely uses the salesperson to make payment. The person who runs the cash register at a Safeway supermarket and the people manning the phones at an L.L. Bean catalog center are examples of inside order takers. The other type of order taking task is performed by an outside order taker. **Outside order takers** typically call on business buyers or members of the trade channel and perform relatively routine tasks related to orders for inventory replenishment or catalog orders. The customer accounts have been established and the salesperson merely services them on a regular basis. Order takers act as an interface between a firm and customers but do not engage in many of the marketing strategy activities discussed earlier. They are an important link for the firm to the market, however, in that they still help bring about the marketing concept: courteous, timely, and attentive service by order takers helps increase the satisfaction a firm provides to its customers.

CREATIVE SELLING

Creative selling requires considerable effort and expertise. Situations where creative selling takes place range from retail stores through the selling of services to business and the sale of large industrial installations and component

Creative selling often requires that the salesperson provide complex technical product information to potential buyers.

parts. **Creative selling** is the type of selling in which a customer relies heavily on the salesperson for technical information, advice, and service. At the retail level, stores that sell shopping and specialty goods have a fully trained sales staff and emphasize customer and product knowledge. The services of an insurance agent, stockbroker, or real estate agent represent another type of creative selling. These salespeople provide services customized to the unique needs and circumstances of each buyer.

The most complex and demanding of the creative selling positions is in the business market. Many times, these salespeople have advanced degrees in technical areas like chemical or mechanical engineering and computer science. Business salespeople who deal in large dollar purchases and complex corporate decisions for capital equipment, specialized component parts, or raw materials have tremendous demands placed on them. They are often called on to analyze the customer's product and production needs and carry this information back to the firm so that product design and supply schedules can be tailored for each customer. At MCI, sales representatives can spend weeks inside a customer's organization determining the precise mix of hardware and communications services needed to solve customer problems.

Two particular types of creative selling in the business market are worth particular attention: team selling and systems selling. In **team selling,** a group of people within the organization from different functional areas are assembled as a team to call on a particular customer. Sales teams are prevalent in the areas of communications equipment, computer installations, and manufacturing equipment. This is how a sales team might work. A sales engineer is called on to analyze the customer's operations and design a product; a financial expert works out a purchase or lease agreement that fits the customer's financial situation; and a service representative participates with the team to ensure that delivery, installation, and any training that may be necessary are carried out properly. When IBM reoriented its personal selling effort in the late 1980s, it created selling teams deployed to implement the firm's new Information System Investment Strategies (ISIS) program. A marketing strategist, salespeople, and financial experts operated as a team that consulted with customers such as G. Heilemann Brewing and Gulfstream Aerospace. The team spent several months interviewing customer management, touring facilities, analyzing operations, and looking at the customer's information systems. The team then built financial models of the customer's company six years out, with and without new investments in IBM computer software. The president of G. Heilemann Brewing reacted to IBM's team selling approach by saying the system turned complicated decisions about investing in computer systems "into terms that senior management can understand."[9]

The other noteworthy form of creative selling that has emerged in the last few years is system selling. **System selling** entails selling a set of interrelated components that fulfill all or a majority of a customer's needs in a product or service area. System selling has emerged as a form of selling because of the desire on the part of customers for "system buying." Large industrial and government buyers, in particular, have come to demand working with one or a small number of suppliers that can provide a full range of product and service needs in an area. Rather than dealing with multiple suppliers, these buyers can deal with one or a few. This "systems" trend in both buying and selling emphasizes even more the relationship aspects of selling process discussed earlier. Large government purchases in China and eastern Europe demand a relationship selling approach. Huge infrastructure projects like sea ports, airports, and communication systems demand that huge project engineering firms like Bechtel employ a system selling approach..

Creative selling tasks call for high levels of preparation, expertise, and close contact with the customer, which are primary to the process of relationship building. It is this sort of personal selling that assumes a comprehensive marketing strategy role within an organization. Table 12-2 identifies the types of creative selling positions that are found in organizations.

SUPPORTIVE COMMUNICATIONS

When a sales force is deployed with the purpose of **supportive communication,** it is not charged directly with the responsibility of generating revenues for an organization. Rather, it is the objective of people in this sales area to provide information to customers, provide services, and generally to create goodwill. Salespeople involved in supportive communication try to ensure that buyers are satisfied with the firm's product and services. Supportive communication takes place with salespeople in different roles. The **missionary salesperson** calls on accounts with the express purpose of monitoring the satisfaction of buyers and updating buyers' needs. Product information may be provided after a purchase. Many firms have turned to telemarketing techniques that use telephone, fax, and computer (e-mail and voice mail) communications as part of the supportive activities of missionary sales. The **detail salesperson** introduces new products and provides detailed product information to potential

TABLE 12-2
Creative Selling Positions

Account Representative	This type of salesperson calls on large established accounts. Account representatives are used in industries like consumer packaged goods, textiles, clothing, bulk chemicals, and after-market auto parts. Account representatives sell to retailers, wholesalers, and distributors primarily but may also sell to large manufacturing customers.
Detail Salesperson	The primary tasks undertaken by this type of salesperson are providing product information and introducing new products to potential customers. The pharmaceutical drug industry and textbook publishing industry are the heaviest users of detail salespeople. Their tasks can be described generally as missionary selling and emphasize relationship building with customers.
Nontechnical Industrial Products Salesperson	This group sells all categories of nontechnical industrial products to end users. Examples of products this type of salesperson would handle are paper products, cleaning agents, lubricants, and office furniture.
Sales Engineers	These are industrial salespeople with specialized training in engineering or science. Products and services in the areas of communication, production, and computer applications (hardware and software) are handled by this type of salesperson.
Service Salesperson	Two types of salespeople actually fall into this category. First, there are the service sales reps who handle the post-purchase services associated with the sale of tangible products. They will handle delivery, installation, training, and product information needs of customers. The other type of service salesperson sells pure services such as a financial planner, real estate agent, or consultant.
System Salesperson	One of the most demanding of creative selling positions, the system salesperson must understand the needs and demands of large industrial and government buyers. System salespeople attempt to design an entire "system" of interrelated products and services for largescale projects. Examples are integrated manufacturing facilities or government public works projects like airports and water treatment plants.
Team Salesperson	The distinguishing feature of this creative selling position is that the person is part of a team selling effort perhaps only as a small part of his or her primary job. A team salesperson may be a financial analyst, an engineer, an accountant, or a salesperson, per se. The important issue here is that this person performs an important role on a selling team that is assembled to deal with a customer's product and service needs.

buyers without attempting to make a sale, per se. Detail salespeople are widely used by large pharmaceutical firms to introduce new prescription drugs to physicians and to provide information about the drug's application and efficacy.

Setting Objectives for Personal Selling[10]

The appropriate overall objective for any element of the promotional mix, including personal selling, is to communicate.[10] What is communicated is the value contained in a firm's product or service and the satisfaction buyers will receive by purchasing these products and services. Because several of the types of personal selling just discussed involve culminating a sale, a sales objective is also primary. Because a salesperson is typically present when a contract is signed or an order is placed, the direct effect of personal selling on sales is more identifiable than the effect of other elements of the promotional mix.

It is possible to identify a set of **objectives for personal selling** in specific terms. Every encounter with a potential buyer can be approached with a clear set of objectives in mind. These objectives must be operational and lead to the general purpose of simply making a sale, however. The objectives a salesperson can pursue during a sales call, which include making a sale but also focus on the customer, are:

- To create a profitable differential competitive advantage.
- To accord uniqueness to each potential buyer.
- To manage a set of buying-selling relationships for mutual profit.
- To control the communication without seeming to do so.

CREATING A PROFITABLE DIFFERENTIAL COMPETITIVE ADVANTAGE

Buyers will ultimately choose the product they perceive to be best suited to their needs. Stated in the context of the marketing concept, buyers are looking for satisfaction that is greater than the costs they will incur. In a personal selling situation, it is up to the salesperson to quickly understand what is "best" from the buyer's perspective. As discussed in Chapter 6, different buyers value different attributes of a product—functional, emotional, or benefits of use. Further, the services offered by an organization will also be factored into an assessment of satisfaction and value—delivery, installation, and repair services, for example. The salesperson must identify what is valued and then pursue the objective of demonstrating to the buyer that the firm's products and services match the buyer's needs more closely than competitors. In this way, a **profitable differential competitive advantage can be created** as the buyer learns how the firm's products and services are superior to those of the competition.

ACCORDING UNIQUENESS TO EACH POTENTIAL BUYER

A second objective is to **accord uniqueness to each potential buyer**. This is accomplished by managing the communication process in such a way that a buyer does not feel like he or she is being "sold." Rather, a potential buyer must come away from the contact feeling like a decision to buy has been made. The salesperson who treats each buyer as unique will exert a powerful impact during the communication process. An important part of accomplishing this objective is for the salesperson to *listen attentively.* Good listening skills allow the salesperson to truly grant a buyer unique status by actually learning the buyer's individual needs and desires. This also allows a salesperson to shape the communication specifically to each buyer's unique desire for information thus taking full advantage of one of the primary distinctions of personal communications over mass communication: tailoring the message to each receiver.

MANAGING BUYING-SELLING RELATIONSHIPS FOR MUTUAL PROFIT

One of the greatest challenges facing a salesperson is determining how her or his firm is uniquely capable of satisfying customer needs. By matching what the firm is capable of doing with what a buyer desires allows both parties to enter a buying-selling relationship that is mutually profitable—this is called **managing buying-selling relationships**. The salesperson must determine which of the following criteria form the basis for providing satisfaction to individual buyers:

- Product superiority
- Service superiority
- Price superiority
- Source (company) superiority
- People superiority

Depending on the expression of needs by a buyer, a salesperson can determine what is most highly valued in the purchase decision from the list above. Through such a determination, the salesperson can then emphasize the firm's unique capabilities in satisfying the customer. A sale can be negotiated emphasizing the ability of the firm to provide superior satisfaction on the desired factors.

CONTROLLING THE COMMUNICATION

On the surface, this objective may seem contrary to the spirit of the marketing concept. However, it is to the mutual benefit of both buyer and seller if the communication process is managed efficiently. The salesperson is in the best position to bring about effective and efficient information exchange by **controlling the communication.** If a salesperson can control the content and direction of the encounter, the potential buyer will be able to learn quickly and accurately what the firm has to offer.

It is important to note that the preceding objectives for personal selling are external in their orientation. Each focuses on *the buyer.* The emphasis of each objective is to understand buyer's needs, and with that understanding provide information on how the firm is capable of satisfying those needs. If these objectives are accomplished, the probability of a sale resulting from the contact increases greatly.

The Personal Selling Process

Objectives for personal selling are only achievable in the context of a well-conceived and well-executed sales effort. In other words, time and care must be devoted to the *process* of personal selling itself. It is unreasonable and unrealistic to view personal selling as an isolated contact or series of contacts with buyers. As a means of operationalizing the marketing concept, it is essential to recognize the *buyer's state of mind* during a selling encounter. The **personal selling process** requires that salespeople attend to the need states of buyers individually (that is, accord them uniqueness) rather than treating all buyers as though they were the same. This orientation also takes advantage of the ability of personal communication to tailor a message specifically to an individual customer.

In order to fully adopt a process approach, the selling effort must be organized into a sequence of well-defined activities. The sales force must be able to understand characteristics of existing and potential customers, make a persuasive presentation, close a sale, and follow-up on the entire effort. Every organization has its own unique perspective on the steps associated with an effective personal selling process. Generally, a well-conceived personal selling process will entail seven distinct activities: preparation, prospecting, initial contact, presentation, handling objections, closing the sale, and follow-up. The activities in the personal selling process are graphically depicted in Figure 12-1. We will discuss each of these activities separately.

PREPARATION

Preparation for a personal selling contact is really a very focused environmental analysis not unlike one that a firm would conduct to develop overall marketing strategy. Preparation involves gathering relevant information about current customers, potential customers, product characteristics and applications, product choice criteria, corporate support activities (such as advertising

FIGURE 12-1
Activities in the Personal Selling Process

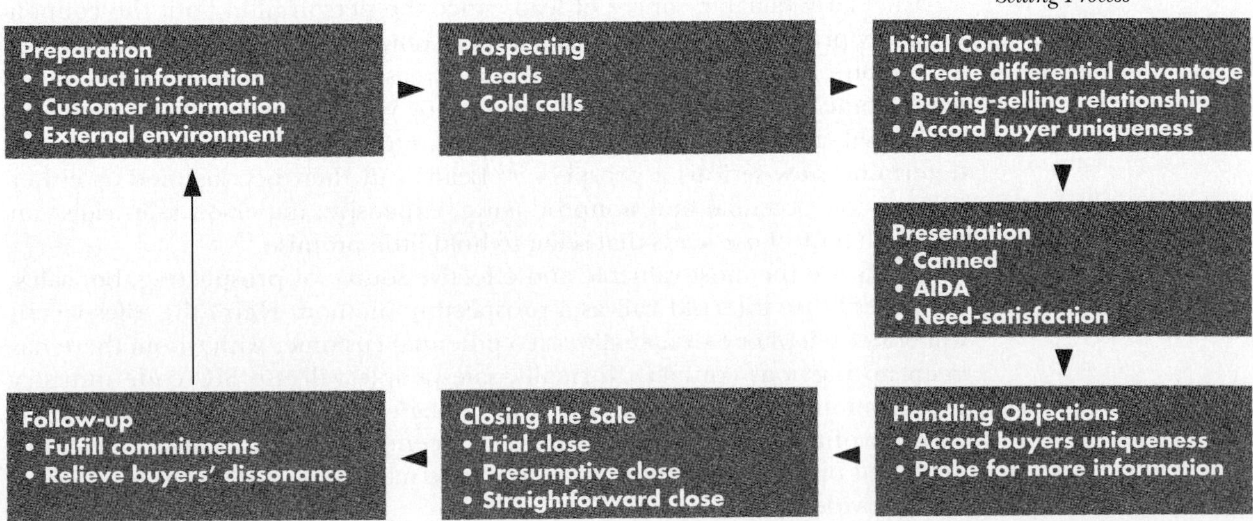

and trade channel support), and competitors' products and activities. Further, economic and demographic trends that affect customers will also be analyzed. The firm that maintains an effective marketing information system greatly aids its salespeople in preparing for sales calls. An MkIS will contain data about purchasing behavior in the market as well as records relating to past behavior of current customers. Without comprehensive information in the areas just described, a salesperson cannot hope to accomplish sales objectives.

For example, a well-prepared salesperson may recognize that potential business buyers of drilling equipment have a general dissatisfaction with suppliers' ability to deliver on a dependable schedule. Recall from Chapter 6 that this criterion—dependable delivery—is a primary motive in business buyer behavior. Armed with such knowledge, the salesperson can approach a prospect with a sales presentation that highlights the reliability and dependability of the firm's distribution and delivery program.

Overall, preparation involves knowing the firm's capabilities in all areas of the marketing mix, competitors' strengths and weaknesses, effects of the external environment, and customer choice criteria. With this information, the salesperson is prepared to deliver a selling message that is relevant and persuasive to buyers.

PROSPECTING

Much of the growth in total revenues for a firm depends on the sales force cultivating new customers. Therefore, primary in the selling process is for salespeople to engage in **prospecting** for new accounts. A variety of traditional methods are used to carry out this activity. Successful prospecting is greatly enhanced by generating leads—that is, generating names of new potential buyers. Several sources can be tapped for generating leads. Current customers are an excellent source of leads since the salesperson benefits from a personal introduction to a potential customer. Advertising can create leads for the sales force with mail-in coupons placed in trade magazines. Mail-in coupons can be a particularly valuable source of leads since the person filling out the coupon normally provides the name of the proper contact including a current address and phone number. Telemarketing has increased the efficiency of the use of leads. Some firms maintain a staff and employ WATS lines to qualify sales leads generated through the methods described. Qualifying a sales lead means to determine how serious a prospect is. Leads can then be classified as either high or low potential and nonproductive, expensive, in-person sales calls can be avoided for those leads that seem to hold little promise.[11]

Leads are the most valuable and effective source of prospecting, but salespeople still use the cold call as a prospecting method. Here, the salesperson will either telephone or actually visit a potential customer with whom there has been no previous contact. Normally, salespeople will use SIC code industry classifications to narrow down the cold calling effort. This is an inefficient and rarely profitable approach, however. A recent survey indicates 8 sales were made out of 100 cold calls, but 28 sales were made out of 100 calls when leads were provided.[12]

INITIAL CONTACT

The **initial contact** with a potential customer is a critical step in the process. It is at this point that the salesperson must begin to address the objectives of creating a profitable differential advantage, according each buyer uniqueness, and developing the buying-selling relationship. Merely stopping by to call on a potential customer with only vague notions of what might be accomplished during an initial contact is not a good idea. Such a call is likely to be viewed by a potential customer as an intrusion and a waste of time. A professional, well-planned, purposeful, and brief initial contact can establish the salesperson as a new and important source in the mind of the buyer. Reasonable activities in an initial contact can include leaving comprehensive information about the firm and its products, introducing the buyer to corporate selling programs, and gathering information about the buyer's organization and product needs.

PRESENTATION

The **presentation** is an important focal point of the personal selling process. On rare occasions, it will occur during the initial contact. Normally, it is a separately scheduled phase of the process. A presentation can be carried out in several ways. Only one is consistent with a well-conceived, market-concept-oriented approach to the market, however.

Some firms will require a **canned presentation.** This method has a salesperson recite, nearly verbatim, a prepared sales pitch. The reason some firms use a canned presentation approach is that it ensures important selling points are covered. It can also enhance the performance of marginally skilled salespeople. The drawback of the canned presentation is severe in that it undermines fundamental advantages of personal communication: tailoring the message to the unique buyer's needs and responding to buyer feedback. Further, such an approach downplays the need to engage in comprehensive preparation as part of the selling process in that it presumes every buyer faces a similar buying situation.

An often implemented but obsolete approach is **AIDA** (Attention, Interest, Desire, Action). In this form of presentation, the salesperson carefully structures the selling contact so that the first part of the presentation gains the buyer's *attention.* Then, *interest* in the firm's offering is stimulated by touting product and service attributes. Next, the salesperson will try to stimulate a *desire* on the part of the buyer by demonstrating how the firm's offering fulfills the buyer's needs. Finally, an attempt is made to close the sale thus creating an *action* on the part of the buyer. The reason this approach is considered obsolete is that it grants the buyer very little participation in the process. The salesperson dominates the communication, leading the buyer through various stages. The experienced buyer, after years of being subjected to this technique, will find it tiresome and obvious. It does have the advantage of controlling the communication, but goes too far in this regard to the detriment of the process.

A far more sophisticated and informed approach to the presentation is referred to as **need satisfaction.**[13] This is a customer-oriented approach that relies strictly on the marketing concept for its execution. With this technique, the salesperson recognizes that during every sales encounter, each buyer's need state must be assessed and the selling effort adjusted to that need state. First, there are buyers who are in the *need development* stage. These are potential customers who are beginning to form a recognition of the types of problems that exist in their organizations. With a buyer in this need state, the salesperson does very little talking and is monitoring feedback almost exclusively during the presentation. It is at this stage that the salesperson concentrates on according uniqueness to the buyer. Next, there are those buyers who are at the *need awareness* level. This type of buyer is able to articulate specific needs in his or her organization. The salesperson who encounters this type of buyer can help define the buyer's needs relative to products and services that address those needs. Finally, there is the buyer who is in the *need fulfillment* stage. Here the buyer is fully aware of what products and services are needed and the salesperson assumes a dominate communication role by demonstrating how the firm and its products can fulfill the needs. It is with this sort of buyer that the salesperson must concentrate on creating differential competitive advantage.

The superiority of the need-satisfaction orientation is that it explicitly recognizes that a sales presentation will emphasize different information depending on how developed the buyer's need recognition is. Buyers in the need awareness stage must be allowed to express themselves in relatively general terms. Buyers who have progressed to need awareness are ready to entertain propositions related to product solutions to their needs. The buyer who is at the need fulfillment stage is aware of product solutions and is prepared to listen to detailed information about the selling firm's unique ability to satisfy those needs. It is possible that a salesperson can lead a buyer through all the need stages in a single presentation. More than likely, buyers will be encountered who are already at different levels and the salesperson will be required to adjust the presentation accordingly. The need-satisfaction approach emphasizes the buyer and the buyer's state of mind. It also takes full advantage of direct feedback and tailoring the message according to that feedback.

HANDLING OBJECTIONS

During a presentation, objections on the part of the buyer will surface, especially with buyers in the need fulfillment stage. The most serious objections relate to the buyer's perception that the firm's product is not well suited to the need being discussed. The salesperson must be prepared to deal with objections, which is a highly sensitive endeavor that requires great skill. The salesperson must counter objections without seeming argumentative. Objections cannot be met with defensiveness or brushed aside as insignificant or irrational. Again, the buyer must be accorded uniqueness, which means *every* objection is legitimate and reasonable. The best method for **handling objections** is to probe for the exact nature of the obstacle and then try to lead the buyer to proposing a solution. In this way, the salesperson has created an alliance with the buyer and they can work in partnership to solve the customer's problem.

CLOSING THE SALE

After the presentation or perhaps several separate presentations, the time arrives when a salesperson must attempt to close the sale. **Closing the sale** is generally regarded as the most difficult part of the personal selling process—for good reason. This is the stage at which a salesperson is asking a buyer to incur costs—monetary, time, risk, opportunity, and, potentially, anxiety costs. The salesperson must ensure during closing that the buyer perceives that satisfaction can be obtained that will be greater than the costs being incurred. This is another reason why the need-satisfaction approach to the presentation can be so effective.

Effectively closing a sale involves a variety of techniques. Critical to the process is the salesperson actually asking for the order. Amazingly, some surveys indicate that about 60 percent of the time salespeople never ask for the order! They seem to rely on the customer to close the sale.[14] The first rule in closing a sale is to ask for an order. One technique in asking for the order is the *trial close.* Here the salesperson poses a question like, "Would you like gray or oak finish?" or, "Would you like this gift wrapped?" Another closing technique is the *presumptive close* in which the salesperson, presuming a sale has been agreed upon will ask something like, "What address should appear on the invoice?" These techniques run the risk of being offensive and are, frankly, not very skillful.

The best approach to closing is for the salesperson to use a *straightforward close.* With this method, a salesperson must sense when to ask for an order in a straightforward, courteous manner—no tricks, no presumptions, no innuendo. If a salesperson has successfully achieved the objective of developing a buying-selling relationship for mutual profit, then a buyer will find this method most acceptable.

FOLLOW-UP

Two distinct and very important activities occur after a sale has been made. First, a salesperson must ensure that all commitments of the negotiated sale are fulfilled. Shipping dates, installation, financing, and any training required can be monitored by the salesperson. Second, dealing with buyer post-purchase behavior is a critical **follow-up** activity. Relieving any cognitive dissonance experienced by a buyer will make the purchase more satisfying and lay the foundation for future sales. Salespeople can address dissonance through direct communication either written or oral. Salespeople at Nordstrom's send a handwritten and personalized note to customers within three days of a purchase. The note expresses appreciation for the purchase and encourages a recent buyer to contact the salesperson for any future clothing needs. Another important aspect of dealing with post-purchase behavior is for a salesperson to inquire about needs for related items. As the discussion of consumer behavior in Chapter 6 highlighted, many consumers will purchase items that complement an initial purchase either out of enthusiasm or newly recognized needs. For firms with broad product lines, a salesperson has an ideal opportunity to approach recent buyers with opportunities for additional purchases.

Viewing personal selling as a process that includes a series of related and integrated stages greatly enhances the performance of sales personnel. The process itself, however, must not become the overall goal. Rather, the potential impact of each stage in the process must be recognized and nurtured. Related to carrying out the process of personal selling is the environment within which salespeople operate. The contemporary selling environment has evolved and changed over the last several years.

THE NEW ENVIRONMENT FOR PERSONAL SELLING

Three changes in the broad business environment have created a significantly **new environment for personal selling.** First, the increased *sophistication of marketing planning* has greatly altered activities of salespeople. With more precise means of segmenting markets, efforts of the sales force are more tightly focused on very specific types of customers. Also, new marketing planning efforts are relying more on telemarketing techniques. This affects salespeople in two ways. As mentioned earlier, telemarketing helps qualify leads. It can also relieve the sales force of repeated calls on existing customers who now are serviced by phone rather than in person. Finally, greater efficiency is being achieved throughout the marketing process by virtue of enhanced marketing planning efforts. Salespeople are able to respond more quickly to customer requests because the market effort is more narrowly defined on a customer-by-customer basis. The effect of this greater efficiency has meant a reduction in the size of the sales force in several industries. As marketing efforts are better coordinated, the activities of salespeople can be made more efficient as well.

A second major change in the environment affecting salespeople has to do with *information technologies.* In a very real sense, the personal selling process is now data base driven. Salespeople have come to rely on in-house MkIS to store knowledge about customers, markets, and company products. General advances in computers and communications technology have changed the way salespeople carry out their activities. Hewlett-Packard's introduction of the *HP 95LX* palm-top computer is an example. The device weighs 11 ounces and is the size of two personal checkbooks. It has enough power and memory to operate Lotus 1-2-3 and carry large amounts of customer data. A salesperson can get ready for a sales call by entering pricing and sales forecast data. As orders are booked, the forecasts can be updated and upon returning to the office downloaded to a desktop computer that is tied to the firm's MkIS.[15]

Communications technology provides salespeople with an arsenal of tools to communicate both to customers and to the firm. Fax machines, cellular phones, video-conferencing, electronic data exchange, and voice mail all increase the efficiency and effectiveness of the sales force. The ability to manage data and information is greatly enhanced with these electronic wonders. Judicious use of such devices is paramount, however. If the only contact a customer has with a sales representative is voice mail messages or fax transmissions, the lack of personal attention can strain an otherwise healthy relationship. These are *tools* through which the sales force can conduct its affairs more

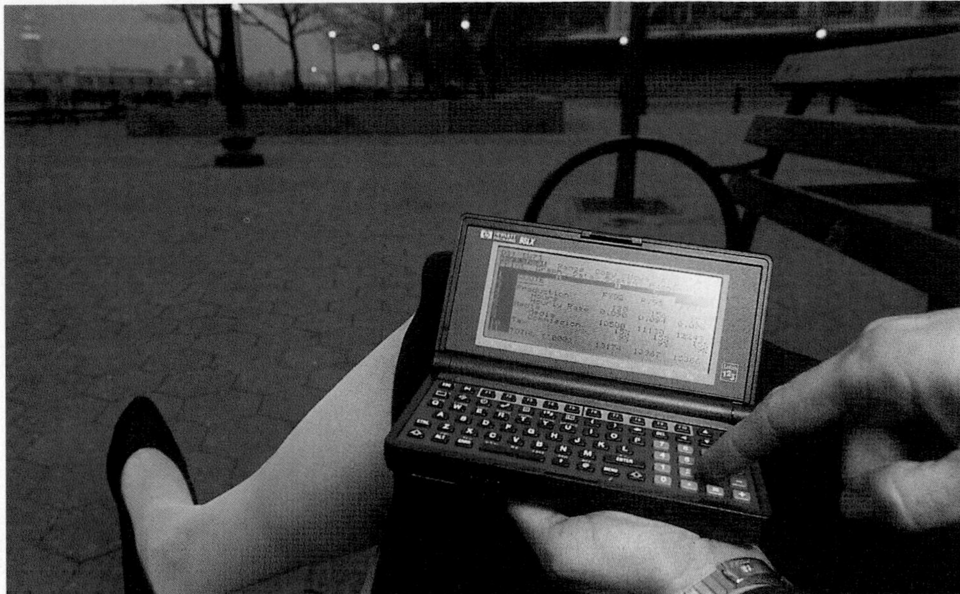

Advances in information technologies, like this palmtop computer, have created a new environment for personal selling.

efficiently. They are not substitutes for the personal selling process and customer service.

Finally, salespeople now deal with *more demanding buyers*. Buyers in both the trade channel and business sectors have become more sophisticated and demanding. While salespeople have benefitted from readily available and larger amounts of information, so have buyers. Wolverine World Wide, a $314 million footwear marketer, had to respond to demands from JC Penney Co. Penney's wanted 24-hour inventory replenishment, direct computer hook-up to Wolverine for reordering, and sophisticated financial analysis of each footwear category. Wolverine World Wide responded with just-in-time inventory procedures and a computer link to the firm.[16] The household consumer is also more knowledgeable by virtue of being exposed to more advertising about products. This point was raised in Chapter 6 when we discussed the new value-oriented customer of the 1990s. Another aspect of the demanding nature of buyers in the current environment is the increase in expectations buyers have both of products and of the firms that provide them. Competitive pressures to satisfy customers have escalated the average level of product performance and service. As such, sellers have to perform to higher standards than in years past. Salespeople are unavoidably affected by this increase in expectations. Both household and business consumers will expect the salesperson to provide timely and high-quality service and to respond to specific requests.

Sales Management

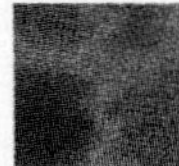

The process aspects of personal selling are critically important to the efficacy of the sales effort. Equally important, however, are the activities associated with managing the process. Salespeople are responsible for managing their own individual efforts. It is the sales management team, however, that is responsible for the overall performance of the entire sales force. The discussions that follow identify all phases of **sales management** from establishing objectives for the selling effort to creation of a sales staff through performance evaluation. Figure 12-2 identifies the areas of responsibility for sales management, which are conceived to ensure that the sales force is effectively designed and efficiently deployed to carry out its role in the organization. Notice in Figure 12-2 that areas of responsibility are depicted in a circular fashion. This is because sales managers are constantly working on all phases of the management process simultaneously rather than in a hierarchical manner.

SITUATION ANALYSIS

Managers of the sales process must engage in a comprehensive situation analysis. This **situation analysis** is very much like an environmental analysis conducted for overall marketing planning. Here, however, the analysis is much more narrowly defined in that the selling effort is the focus. Both internal and external aspects of the situation facing the sales effort are analyzed. An *external situation analysis* identifies trends in the industry, technological advances in product categories, economic conditions that may be affecting the firm's customers, competitors' activities, and choice criteria being emphasized by buyers. The external situation analysis will also rely on an evaluation of the markets within which the firm has a significant competitive advantage. New product and market potentials are also estimated here.

Apple Computer provides an example of the impact of an external analysis. The new CEO at Apple Computer was interested in combatting inroads made by competitor IBM into Apple's traditional school and college markets. As part of an external situation analysis, Apple sent its sales force into the market to survey these customers to see what they wanted in new software and

FIGURE 12-2
Areas of Responsibility for Sales Management

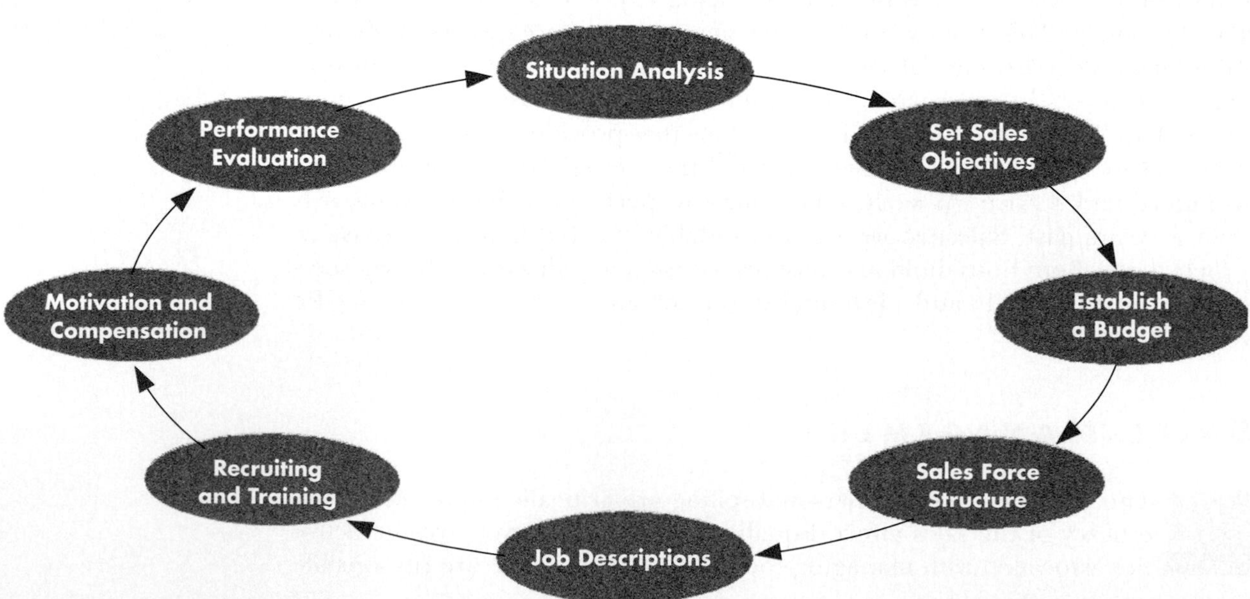

hardware. To better understand the higher-education market, teams of employees were sent to universities on "'camping trips' to pick the brains of students and faculty."[17] The teams then relayed information back to sales management personnel in the organization to be incorporated into future product development and planning for the sales effort.

An *internal situation analysis* entails assessing the strengths and weaknesses of the sales force and corporate support for the selling effort. Strengths and weaknesses of the sales effort are determined by using evaluation components, the last factor in the sales management process, which will be discussed shortly. Note from Figure 12-2 that performance evaluation feeds directing to this situation analysis. In addition, sales force knowledge and training, and its strengths and weaknesses, can be examined relative to competition. Corporate support for the sales force is evaluated by examining the nature of the marketing mix. Corporate activities regarding product development and positioning provide the sales force with its primary basis for competing in the market. The pricing component of the mix relates to the ability of the sales force to offer competitive prices on products as well as price incentives and financing options to customers. The distribution variable directly affects the sales force in that inventory levels and delivery schedules will impact the ability to serve customer demand quickly (time and place utility). Finally, the promotional mix lends support to the sales force by stimulating demand in the market through advertising, sales promotions, and publicity. As an example, when General Mills offered free *Polaroid* film with the purchase of *Kix* children's cereal, the firm was giving parents another reason to purchase *Kix* over competitive brands with the sales promotion. This sales promotion provided the sales force with a reason to encourage grocery store retailers to increase their order size for *Kix* in anticipation of greater demand for the cereal.

SETTING SALES OBJECTIVES

In the discussion of the personal selling process, it was emphasized that the objectives for personal selling must relate to communication: create profitable differential competitive advantage, accord each buyer uniqueness, manage the buying-selling relationship, and control the communication. **Sales objectives,** however, focus on sales and are set at various levels. At the broadest level, estimated *total sales* is a statement of sales objectives. This figure is determined by sales forecasts that draw on projections of total industry sales and the firm's estimate of its share of those sales. The next level of specificity is to estimate *sales by territory or product category.* Here different geographic territories or product groups are evaluated for conditions that may affect the firm's ability to generate sales over a given time period. Different areas of the geographic market may have unique economic or competitive conditions as will different product categories. These conditions may represent either significant challenges or opportunities to generating sales. Quarterly and annual sales objectives are set for territories and product categories.

The most specific level of setting objectives is by *individual salesperson.* The most common method for setting objectives here is to use sales quotas. A sales quota can be specified for each salesperson in several ways, but a percentage of prior years' sales (usually greater than 100 percent) is the most prevalent method. Factored into the quota determination are the effects of new products brought to the market, competitor's activities, economic conditions in the salesperson's territory, and nonselling tasks such as post-purchase customer service demanded of the salesperson. Recall that a variety of other objectives are related to the efforts of the salesperson aside from sales.

ESTABLISHING A BUDGET

A task that requires painstaking effort is **establishing a budget** for the overall personal selling effort. Normally, factors charged to the personal selling budget include:

- Recruiting costs
- Training costs
- Travel expenses
- Promotional materials—samples, catalogs, product brochures
- Salaries and benefits
- Incentive programs—bonuses, awards

Recruiting, training, travel, salary, and benefit expenses are cost factors that are self explanatory. Promotional materials relate to those materials provided to salespeople to support their selling effort. For example, an auto parts sales representative may have a catalog of several thousand items, which is provided to customers to facilitate the ordering process. In selling college textbooks, literally hundreds of samples of a new text will be mailed to prospective adopters at colleges and universities. College professors need a sample copy of the textbook to make an informed decision. The cost of sending samples to these professors can be tens of thousands of dollars. Normally, such costs are charged to the overall selling effort.

The methods employed in establishing a budget for the personal selling effort are identical to several techniques discussed in Chapter 10 for setting the overall promotional budget. A *percentage of sales* approach can be used but suffers from a lack of recognition of unique challenges facing the sales force such as introducing a new product or expanding into a new geographic territory. A *competitive parity* approach can be used whereby a firm sets its personal selling budget (particularly salary, benefit, and bonus programs) relative to what other firms in the industry are doing. Again, this technique is inappropriate because the objectives of competitors and therefore the activities of their salespeople may be very different. Use of the competitive parity approach can easily result in over- or underpaying salespeople. The *objective and task* method for budget determination is the most effective. Management assesses the objectives that are established for the overall selling effort. Based on those objectives, tasks for the sales force are specified as are compensation and incentive programs. All costs associated with the tasks are determined and the budget is then projected. This method relates activities to costs and is the only rational and reasonable basis for establishing a budget.

SALES FORCE STRUCTURE

A critically important strategic decision for sales management is how the sales force will be structured to achieve the goals of market coverage and cultivation. A **sales force structure** can be based on product lines, type of customer, or geographic territory.

When a sales force is structured by *product lines,* sales people are assigned to handle only specific products. The most common reason for structuring the sales force around product lines has to do with the nature of the product. For products that are technologically complex, individual salespeople will need specialized training and experience to successfully sell the product. Conversely, nontechnical or standardized items require less expertise and can be handled by a different sales force. Pharmaceutical firms that manufacture both prescription and over-the-counter drug items often have a separate sales force for each product line based on the complexity of the product.

An alternative structure is to organize the sales effort around the *type of customer.* Customer groups can be segmented based on order size, position in the channel, or product use characteristics. Some firms employ a "key account" system where a separate sales staff will call on large buyers like Kmart and Wal-Mart. Similarly, one sales staff can be deployed to call on wholesalers while another calls directly on retailers. Finally, pharmaceutical firms might use this structure rather that the product line structure described earlier by having separate sales staffs call on physicians, pharmacists, and grocery store buyers.

Finally, the sales force can be structured by *geographic territory.* In this arrangement, each salesperson is assigned a designated geographical territory. This structure requires that each salesperson call on all types of customers in the area and is prepared to sell the firm's entire product line. This deployment of the sales force is most appropriate for standardized items that are sold to a variety of different customers. Stanley Tools, for example, can have its sales force call on hardware stores, home improvement centers, and discount retailers with the firms' entire line of standardized items—hammers, screwdrivers, wrenches, and the like. These are simple, relatively standardized products that are packaged and distributed similarly to all different types of customers. The decision regarding sales force structure is driven by two factors: the nature of the product and the nature of the market. If products in the line are highly sophisticated or the line contains a wide range of different items, the product-line structure is most appropriate. These conditions will require special expertise and extensive product knowledge on the part of the sales staff so product-line emphasis is called for. Knowledgeable buyers and easily segmented customer groups facilitate a type of customer structure. This structure evolves quite naturally from the nature of the market. Product lines with standardized items that are sold without alteration to a variety of different customers suggest a geographic structure for the sales force. No specialized expertise is needed in the selling process based on the nature of the product nor does the market itself suggest any natural basis for separate segments.

JOB DESCRIPTIONS AND QUALIFICATIONS

The sales management task also includes hiring salespeople. Before recruiting can be undertaken, however, complete job descriptions and the qualifications an individual must have are prepared. The **job description** will identify all the tasks to be performed by salespeople. The components of a job description cite both selling and nonselling tasks. The types of selling tasks that will be required depend on the type of product, the types of customers being called on, and the anticipated dollar volume a salesperson is expected to produce. Nonselling tasks involve the amount of paperwork required—invoice preparation, activity reports, expense reports—and service activities expected of the salespeople. Service activities may include product display maintenance, coordination and monitoring of delivery, and arranging financing or training for the customer. Depending on the mix of selling and nonselling tasks, very different job descriptions will be produced.

The tasks included in a job description translate directly into the **qualifications** of the individuals needed to fill positions—the combination of skills and training that relate to effective performance. Very different types of people will need to be recruited depending on the job requirements. Highly technical selling jobs will require people with relevant technical training. Job descriptions that include significant nonselling tasks mean the firm will have to find people with training or experience to carry out the nonselling activities effectively. In technical product categories, firms often recruit people with engineering degrees. Conversely, in nontechnical product areas, people with backgrounds in marketing or communications are highly sought after. For jobs with both technical selling requirements and significant nonselling tasks, a technical background with an advanced business degree is a common qualification.

Firms also draw on their experience with current sales personnel in determining what qualifications are most directly related to success. State Farm, the insurance giant, has learned over the years that people who have an "entrepreneurial spirit" prosper in the State Farm system. Most of the people in State Farm's sales force are college graduates and many are ex-teachers. This profile of the successful agent has worked well for the firm. Of every 100 agents that State Farm hires, 80 are still working for the firm four years later. This retention rate is far greater than the insurance industry as a whole where fewer than 30 out of 100 agents are with the same firm after four years.[18]

Personal characteristics of individuals can also be included in a statement of qualifications. While legislation bars firms from including criteria in a job description related to age, sex, or race of an individual, there is research that suggests that compared with unsuccessful sales people, a successful salesperson will be a good listener, enjoy social events, feel socially satisfied, and be more individualistic. They also tend to be more disciplined, aggressive, and creative than unsuccessful sales people.[19] Today, recruiters say over and over that they are looking for people with good written and oral communication skills and people who are comfortable around other people and can be effective in a team setting.

RECRUITING

Well-written job descriptions and statements of qualifications provide management with guidelines for both the type and number of salespeople that will be needed. At this point, the firm can begin to recruit people to meet staffing needs. An important aspect of **recruiting** is that it should be a continuous process. A firm must seek out qualified people on a regular schedule so that a file of qualified applicants is available. The firm that begins to recruit only when a need arises may be tempted to accept unqualified or inappropriate people.

Successful recruiting procedures depend on identifying sources of qualified applicants and using effective screening and evaluation techniques. Several sources can be used to generate a pool of qualified applicants. College and university campuses offer a highly structured environment for recruiting. Firms can schedule recruiting visits and indicate what background, experience, and degree the firm requires for the job. Employment agencies represent another useful source of recruits. Professional employment agencies charge individuals or firms or both parties a fee to match individuals with jobs. Classified advertisements in the employment section of local newspapers can also be a source. Normally, applicants for selling jobs that require very little skill can be generated in this way. However, firms occasionally advertise much more highly skilled positions in local newspapers to fulfill equal employment opportunity requirements. Other outlets for advertising that have proven successful for some firms are trade publications. Trade publications subscribed to by members of a specific industry many times carry employment ads. Finally, intra-firm recruiting has become more popular of late. Procter & Gamble regularly moves salespeople between its Noxell, Revlon, and Richardson-Vicks divisions. When IBM initiated a corporate restructuring program, the firm redeployed 21,500 employees. Of that total, 11,800 were shifted to the field sales force.[20]

To effectively and efficiently recruit the proper individuals, a firm can rely on several *screening and evaluation* techniques. A resume is valuable in assessing an individual's qualifications. Information on educational background, work experience, and references is useful in evaluating potential applicants. A variety of psychological tests can also be used to screen applicants. These tests are designed to identify personality and motivation characteristics that may be related to job success. Some firms will administer standardized psychological tests to their most successful salespeople and use those results as a benchmark for evaluating applicants' scores on the same tests. The logic is that similar scores should be an indicator of success for an applicant. Finally, a personal interview can be invaluable as an evaluation technique for discovering attributes of an individual that a resume or tests cannot identify. Traits such as personal appearance and verbal skills are discovered only through personal contact.

TRAINING

Whether a sales staff is being assembled or a new salesperson is being added to the existing staff, **training** individuals for the sales task is a critical sales management responsibility. The personal selling process is complex. Further, the personal selling effort is integral to achieving corporate revenue objectives. Because the selling effort is so important, the firm must have a well-planned sales training program. A number of decisions need to be made about training.

1. *Content of the Program.* Depending on the sales force structure, type of product, selling/nonselling tasks involved, and the objectives set for the selling effort, the content of the training program will vary. Product knowledge and choice criteria used by customers are required content in any program. Beyond these basics, industry trends and economic conditions affecting the firm's market may also be included. Another decision here relates to the training techniques to be used. Role play-

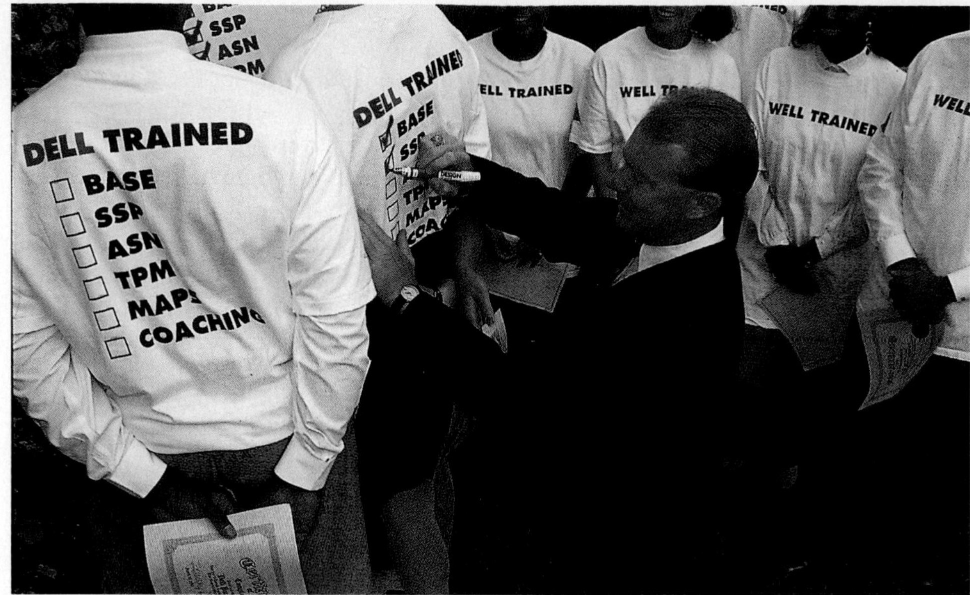

Trainees at Dell Computer receive their certifications at the end of the firm's extensive training program.

ing, classroom lectures, videotaping of presentations, computer simulations, and tours of corporate facilities are some of the techniques used by firms to train sales personnel. The new environment for personal selling requires that team selling techniques be part of an effective program. These include team building, team managing, and team membership skills.

2. *Duration of the Training.* Firms must decide how long it will take to properly train individuals. At Procter & Gamble the training period lasts 12 to 18 months; at State Farm training is a two-year stint; Dow Chemical requires 30 weeks; and Merck puts marketing reps through an initial training period of 12 months with frequent refresher courses. The duration of training depends on several factors. The complexity of the selling task and the company's product line is the over-riding influence. The individual trainee's background and experience also dictate how long it will take for training to be completed.
3. *Training Personnel.* Many firms rely on experts outside the firm to conduct some or all of their training programs. Professional organizations like Learning International provide complete sales force training. Universities and colleges of business often have corporate training programs many of which concentrate on selling tasks. Alternatively, sales managers and highly successful members of the current sales staff can act as trainers.
4. *Location of the Training.* The issue here is whether training is conducted in a laboratory/classroom setting or whether the trainees go out into the field for the learning experience. The laboratory/classroom has the advantage of being a low-pressure environment where there are few consequences of the trainees' activities. Training in the field has the advantage of allowing the salesperson to encounter actual selling situations under the tutelage of an experienced salesperson. The drawbacks

of the field are the mistakes a trainee might make with customers and the time drain on the salespeople who must supervise the field training.

Sales training should not be reserved for new salespeople. As the external environment changes, the firm develops new products and customer knowledge, and new selling techniques are discovered, members of the existing sales staff can benefit greatly from regular training sessions. These sessions would differ greatly from those conducted for new hires, but it is a mistake to presume that current sales people do not need regular retooling.

COMPENSATION AND MOTIVATION

Compensation and motivation efforts may be the most challenging responsibilities of sales management. Three basic compensation alternatives are available for monetary remuneration of the sales staff: straight salary, straight commission, and some combination of salary and commission. Figure 12-3 indicates the factors influencing the use of salary and commission alternatives.

If the sales staff is highly skilled, the selling effort is drawn out over a long period of time, there are time consuming nonselling tasks, or a team selling approach is being used, then the most appropriate compensation method is straight salary. As the selling task becomes less complex and requires few service activities on the part of the sales force, then the commission approach is more feasible. Many firms use a combination plan since many selling efforts include features of both ends of the spectrum. An unfortunate circumstance arises when a firm relies on a commission compensation program but the selling task strongly warrants a salary arrangement. What tends to happen is that in their effort to generate sales and, therefore, income for themselves, the salespeople do not attend to important nonselling tasks like customer needs for extensive product information or service. Such a conflict of interest on the part of salespeople usually spells disaster for the firm. Customers are dissatisfied and seek satisfaction of their product needs elsewhere. Because customer satisfaction is so important to long-term success and profitability, firms like General Electric and AT&T are tying sales force compensation to customer satisfaction surveys.[21]

Compensation is itself motivational, but the issue of motivation is far more complicated than simple dollar-and-cents rewards. The amount of satisfaction and sense of personal achievement individuals feel from performing tasks are also important to motivation. Several techniques can be used to increase the motivation of the sales staff that are not directly tied to the basic compensation program:[22]

FIGURE 12-3
Influences on Sales Force Compensation Alternatives

Straight Salary

- High-cost items
- Long planning intervals
- Highly technical sales efforts
- Well-structured sales task
- Numerous service functions

Compensation

$

Straight Commission

- Lower cost, high-volume items
- Few nonselling tasks
- Need for motivation
- Little management supervision
- Financially weak firm

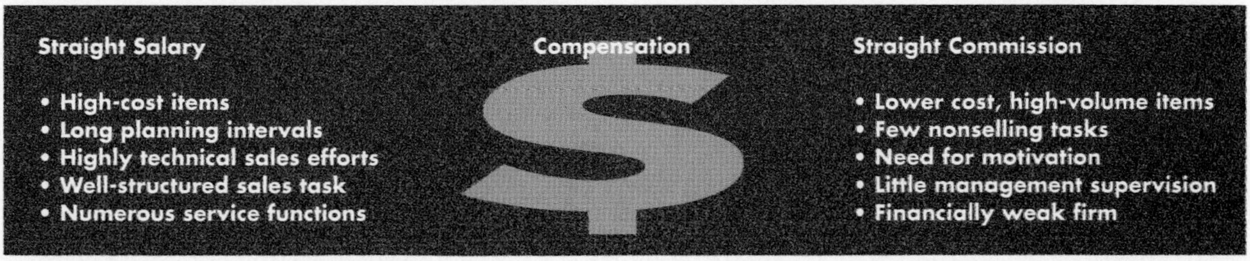

1. *Task Clarity.* Sales people will be more motivated when their realm of responsibility is well defined. Further, clarification of the criteria upon which they will be evaluated will produce goal-oriented behavior. This is motivational in that the salesperson will feel that there are attainable goals to be pursued.
2. *Recognition of Goal Attainment.* It is important for the organization to recognize the attainment of both short and longer term goals by salespeople. Short-term goal attainment, such as exceeding sales quotas, should be rewarded with incentive pay such as bonuses or stock options. Longer term goal attainment, such as market or customer development, should be rewarded with status-enhancing recognition. Such recognition can come in the form of promotions or job titles.
3. *Job Enrichment.* There are several ways to motivate salespeople with job enriching experiences. Many firms send sales people to professional conferences. Paid attendance at sales training programs is a similar reward. The firm can also consider allowing salespeople to participate in corporate planning sessions with management personnel. This can give the sales force a sense of ownership in the corporate strategies they will be asked to support.
4. *Perquisites.* In addition to compensation or bonuses, sales positions provide the firm an ideal opportunity to reward employees with "perks." A new car every year or so, membership at a health club, dinner at fine restaurants, or season tickets to sporting events are all legitimate business expenses for cultivating sales. In turn, salespeople can enjoy these activities while doing business.

The motivational impact of the above factors is derived from both monetary incentives and public recognition of achievement and hard work. The rewards of motivation accrue not just to the salespeople. Well-conceived motivational programs should result in greater productivity from the sales force as well as lower turnover. Both of these factors translate directly to increased profitability for the firm.

EVALUATION

Evaluation of the performance of salespeople draws directly on the objectives set for the personal selling process and sales objectives. Sales staff members can be judged on several objective and subjective criteria. Table 12-3 outlines these criteria.

The objective criteria need to be carefully applied. For example, the total dollar volume of sales must be judged against the order size and expenses generated. A salesperson might be rated highly on total dollar volume at the expense of many, repeated small orders at great cost to the firm. Also, depending on the specific objectives of the sales effort and the selling tasks involved, it may be that the nonselling tasks are critical to long-range plans even though current dollar volume sales are compromised. An important criterion in contemporary evaluation of salespeople identifies customer satisfaction. As part of the whole process of relationship building, quantifiable customer satisfaction criteria can be of value to both management and the salesperson. Astute interpretation and application of the objective criteria is key to a useful evaluation.

TABLE 12-3
Criteria for Evaluating Sales Staff Performance

Objective	Subjective
1. Sales	1. Appearance
Total dollar volume	2. Preparedness
Total unit volume	3. Customer relations
Percent of quota	4. Attitude
Dollars or units by product line	5. Product knowledge
Dollars or units by territory	6. Team relationships
Dollars or units by customer type	
2. Profit (margin) generated	
Total profit in dollars	
Average margin in percent	
Dollars or percent by product line	
Dollars or percent by territory	
Dollars or percent by customer type	
3. Orders	
Number	
Size	
Returns	
4. Sales calls executed	
5. Expenses generated	
6. Nonselling activities	
Number and type of services rendered	
Display maintenance	
Follow-up	
7. Customer satisfaction ratings	

The subjective criteria can be very difficult to operationalize. Being judgmental by nature, management must be willing to be flexible and allow individual styles to manifest themselves. The strength of any particular salesperson may lie in his or her unique style. Suppression of individual differences may be inefficient and demoralizing. The criteria related to team relationships is a difficult one as well. Teams often function in high-energy and high-stress situations. When people fail to cope with that stress, less-than-ideal performance results.

The evaluation of sales personnel is important for two reasons. First, salespeople need feedback upon which they can base future efforts. An evaluation exercise can itself be motivational to the sales staff. The evaluation is also the basis upon which management will make annual salary and bonus decisions. Second, and referring to Figure 12-2 again, evaluation of the staff is a primary source of information for an internal situation analysis. From the evaluation effort, managers can determine strengths and weaknesses in the sales staff, changes that need to be made in the nature of the selling task as it is currently conceived, and the level of corporate support needed for the sales staff.

We are so accustomed to encountering salespeople in our daily lives that there is the tendency to believe that personal selling is a process that is universal in character. Quite to the contrary. Perhaps more than any other topic presented thus far in the text, activities of salespeople must be carefully adapted to the context within which the process takes place. We will consider this global challenge now.

Personal Selling and Sales Management: A Global Perspective

Throughout this text, the need to drop one's self-reference criteria and consider local cultural and market conditions has been stressed over and over. As the world becomes more interdependent, and as companies become more dependent on foreign earnings, there is a growing concern within many companies for developing cultural awareness in all aspects of their operations. More and more, annual reports from multinational corporations are mentioning their firm's cultural diversity as a resource that they intend to develop and use as a strategic weapon to create long-term and sustainable competitive advantages. While this new sense of awareness should take place at all levels within the organization, it is perhaps most critically needed during the ongoing processes of interaction between a company and its clients—that is, during the personal selling process.

As mentioned at the outset of this chapter, personal selling is truly the most important force for revenue generation within many corporations. While the need-satisfaction orientation to personal selling provides a sophisticated and informed approach to the selling situation, the perspective needed in selling across cultures involves recognizing that there can (and will!) be subtle and important differences in the elements that determine needs as well as satisfaction! Early in this chapter, we discussed the importance of personal selling with respect to product characteristics such as price, product complexity, need to demonstrate, and tailoring product use to the customer. In this section, we stress that knowing your customer in international sales means more than knowing your customer's product needs; it includes knowing your customer's culture. The activities involved in developing and then managing a global sales force bring a new set of complex challenges to international marketing managers. The remaining sections of this chapter identify and discuss these issues.

DEVELOPING A GLOBAL SALES FORCE

Two fundamental approaches are used in **developing a global sales force.** The first approach involves the use of other intermediaries' sales representatives such as import firms or wholesalers operating in a region or country to service a new market. For many small and medium-sized companies with a limited product line, this arrangement is the most economically feasible. The producing firm gets personal representation but does not directly employ or control these indirect sales personnel. Firms with expansion plans and an interest in becoming more involved in foreign markets will eventually take control of implementing their own marketing strategies and establishing and managing their own direct sales forces.

An alternative strategy that is more common among larger multinationals is to service foreign markets with sales personnel they already have in place from other export bases. For example, many British textbook publishers send sales representatives to the European continent for sales calls that last from one to three weeks. Once sales reach a certain volume in a new market, the decision may be made to set up a sales office in a particular country for serving that market. Whether the new unit is strictly a marketing/sales arm or also involves a production facility will depend on the company's overall strategies and objectives. In any event, the firm makes a commitment of resources to develop their own direct sales force that will sell the firm's offerings and serve the firms' clients in that market. Regardless of which approach the company uses to establish their own sales force, they will have to make some decisions regarding the selection of personnel. Personnel for sales forces in global markets can be comprised of expatriates, local nationals, or third-country nationals. Each nationality type brings its own set of potential advantages and problems to international selling.

Expatriate Personnel

Expatriate personnel are employees working in a country other than their home country, such as a Dutchman working for Unilever in Chile. A firm might make use of an expatriate with proven managerial talents to establish a new local operation and to hire and train a local sales force. For some types of projects, technical expertise may be critical to the sales effort, and an expatriate may be the best suited person for the project. For example, when the German computer company Siemens Nixdorf sold a computerized system to run all aspects of Singapore's new Dragon World Park theme park, the sales effort involved German technically trained sales personnel working closely with Chinese construction workers and technicians.[23] Finally, the firm may be involved in a large market expansion effort or a complex purchasing situation that involves extended negotiations and/or a significant commitment of the company's resources. In this case, a team of home office managers including a marketing or sales manager will typically be on site for a number of years to manage the expansion program, oversee the terms of the sales contracts, and set up after-sales service support.

For American companies in particular, the use of expatriates has been a traditional practice. Expatriates with years of proven sales talent may be especially useful in the start-up phase of establishing and training local sales personnel, but they typically do not have the deep understanding of local culture that is required for effectively establishing long-term relationships and selling in the local market.

The trend over the past 20 years has been away from using expatriates, particularly in sales situations. For one thing, the costs for transferring and establishing an expatriate in a new country are roughly 200 to 300 percent more than hiring a domestic sales person. Apart from the financial costs to the company, relocation often brings additional personal costs to many managers and their families. A typical overseas assignment runs from two to five years, and the most common reasons for returning from an overseas assignment before the scheduled return date have to do with the managers' or the family's inability to cope with the challenges of working and living in a new cultural environment. Finally, while many globally oriented firms make it clear in their personnel policy statements that an important aspect of cultivating their managers for promotion requires overseas experience, many managers never shake the suspicion that once they are away from the home office, their chances for career advancement are limited.

Local Nationals

Local nationals are sales employees based in their home country. A Thai who sells Honda automobiles in Thailand is a local national sales person. The trend recently has been toward using local nationals in global business and in particular for personal selling. Understanding the cultural and social norms of a country with respect to selling is key to the process of selecting effective sales people in global markets. In countries with rich ethnic compositions like Brazil, Malaysia, or Indonesia, or in regions with highly proscribed social norms of behavior like the Middle East, the hiring of local nationals to manage the sales operation is more likely to be necessary than in countries where selling practices share a highly similar cultural context with the home country. Large differences in languages (and acceptable dialects!), social customs, and the scope of personal influence as well as government regulations will sometimes dictate the wisdom of local hiring. Simply put, local nationals bring a superior understanding of the local market conditions. Their ability to work within its cultural and social norms while pursuing the company's sales objectives very often make them the most effective and economically efficient choice.

Third-Country Nationals

Third-country nationals are usually employees who are citizens of one country, employed by a corporation from a second country, and working for that corporation in a third country. A German manager who supervises the retail sales operations of the Anglo-Dutch Shell Oil Company in South Africa is a third country national. The distinct features of these managers has more to do with their ability to operate easily and effectively in a variety of situations than with the combination of nationality, employer, and work location that go into the definition of a third country national. The increase in global trade has led to an increase in the demand for cosmopolitan-minded managers with a broad world view. Typically, managers of this type are at the upper-middle management level or higher. They are managers with a highly developed sense of cultural empathy for both their company's clients as well as their company's employees. They are managers who are often fluent or comfortable with three or four languages and who have advanced training in either technical or management studies. This relatively new breed of global manager almost always spends time in a sales management function as part of their cultivation for higher-level corporate positions. Managers of this caliber are in low supply and high demand. Their number is slowing growing, however, as a function of the increased level of experiences that are gained from operating in an increasingly global market and from training programs that emphasize increased need for cross-cultural skills in managers of global business.

MANAGING THE GLOBAL SALES FORCE

The tasks involved in **managing a sales force in the global context** are not fundamentally different in scope from the management tasks in the domestic setting. What does change from managing a sales force domestically is the nature of the activities within a task area. The following are discussions of two areas where significant differences in sales force management exist: training and motivation/compensation programs.

Training salespeople for assignments in foreign markets focuses on the culture and customs of the country.

Training

The process and nature of a training program for global sales personnel will depend in large part on whether the training is intended for expatriates or foreign personnel. Expatriate training will mostly focus on the customs and special conditions of acculturation and selling that will be encountered in their new assignment. Foreign national personnel training will place more emphasis on the company and its products, selling methods, and procedures. In short, training for expatriates is intended to familiarize personnel with the country culture in which they will be working. This orientation may involve video lectures and language classes, having the employee and his or her family visit the country for a few weeks, or receiving training to enhance one's awareness of self-reference criteria and increase sensitivities to the culture where they will be working. For example, recall the discussion in Chapter 6 regarding individualistic versus collective orientations. In individualistic orientation, effort and responsibilities are assigned to the individual, and taking individual initiative and making decisions are viewed as normal behaviors. In collective orientation, responsibility, negotiations, and decision making are much more likely to be group activities and require more time. Being aware of each culture's perspective will be an important first step in developing a relationship. Table 12-4 summarizes both perspectives and offers tips to keep in mind when dealing with another culture's perspective in a sales situation. The perspectives offered in this table are typical of the content of training global personnel. Finally, in global companies with a well-organized expatriate program, meeting with expatriate groups who have returned from assignment in the country in question has proven to be an effective tool in preparing new personnel for their assignment.

Training for foreign personnel tends to focus on the corporate culture within which the salesperson will interact on a regular basis. Apart from the basics relating to selling the company's products and teaching them company procedures, the real value in training programs for foreign personnel is to cultivate within that group a sense of identification with the company. Just as expatriates are captives of their own habits and patterns of behavior when

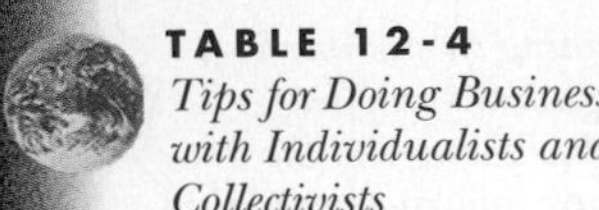

TABLE 12-4
Tips for Doing Business with Individualists and Collectivists

Dealing with Individualists	Dealing with Collectivists
1. Prepare for quick decisions and sudden offers not referred to headquarters.	1. Show patience for time taken to consent and to consult with the home office.
2. Negotiator can commit those who sent him or her and is very reluctant to retreat from an undertaking	2. Negotiator can only agree tentatively and may withdraw an undertaking after consulting with superiors.
3. The toughest negotiations were probably already done within the organization while preparing for the meeting. You have a tough job of selling them the solution to your meeting.	3. The toughest negotiations are with the collectivist you face. You must somehow persuade them to grant to you points which the multiple interests in your company demand.
4. Conducting business alone means that this person is respected by his or her company and has its esteem.	4. Conducting business when surrounded by helpers means that this person has high status in his or her company.
5. The aim is to make a deal quickly.	5. The aim is to build a lasting relationship. Deals evolve over time.

Source: Fons Trompenaars, *Riding the Waves of Culture: Understanding Cultural Diversity in Business* (London: The Economists Books, 1993): 61.

moving abroad, foreign personnel live and work in their own local environment where their local habits and customs are continually reinforced. Regular training and social contacts between foreign markets and the home office may be important simply because of the lack of routine contact with the parent company and its marketing personnel. Likewise, astute companies in global marketing make a point of training their home personnel staff to make them responsive to the needs of the foreign sales personnel. Sending home-office personnel abroad periodically to increase their awareness of the problems encountered in foreign operations tends to be effective and good for the morale of both working groups.

Motivation and Compensation

Just as sales personnel need to take their clients' norms and cultural values into account in the design and execution of sales efforts, companies must likewise consider culture in the design and execution of programs for compensating and motivating their global sales force. Developing an equitable and functional compensation plan that motivates a sales force is difficult enough in a domestic market situation. It becomes even more of a challenge when the company operates in a number of countries, when individuals work in a number of countries, and when the sales force is comprised of expatriate and foreign national personnel who have regular contact with each other.

A common guideline in developing a package of compensation is to ask the question, "What are people of this level paid in this market?" Real differences in the basic salary scales between countries for performing what is essentially the same work can lead to perceived feelings of inequality between sales personnel and can have a devastating effect on morale. Notice that the key word in the discussion is *package* of compensation. In high tax countries, sales personnel press for packages that include more liberal expense accounts and fringe benefits that are nontaxable, instead of direct income and financial bonuses tied to performance that are subject to high taxes. Cost-of-living allowances, private-school tuition for school-age dependents, home-leave travel for a manager and his or her family, and contributions to domestic benefits plans or retirement programs can all be part of the expatriate's compensation package, which can increase total expenses 200 to 300 percent of the base salary. These costs, coupled with the strong belief that local nationals can more effectively operate in a local sales environment largely explains the trend for hiring locals.

Personal selling is hard, competitive work regardless of the cultural setting in which it takes place. International sales managers work hard, travel extensively, and deal with a wide variety of day-to-day challenges. All of these activities require support from the home office and a constant flow of inspiration in order for salespeople and managers to keep functioning at an optimal level. Salary, expense accounts, and fringe benefits are an important part of the motivational process in any sales management effort. However, in the global context motivational programs need to be examined for their local cultural compatibility. Economic incentives such as bonuses and company recognition for outstanding individual performance can be effective motivators for the sales force in North America and Northern Europe. In Japan and other Asian cultures, the emphasis on paternalism, collectivism, and a system of lifetime commitment between the company and the employee will likely lead to other forms of rewards and motivational offers.[24]

GENDER BIAS IN GLOBAL PERSONAL SELLING

This section of the chapter began with a plea to drop one's self-reference criteria and argues that behavior that demonstrates empathy and respect for the cultural norms of the market is a fundamental prerequisite to the success of personal selling efforts. This being the case, firms need to recognize that there are many traditional, male-dominated societies in the world, which brings up the issue of **gender bias in global personal selling.** In many of the world's cultures—Asian, Arab, Latin, and in southern and well as northern Europe—women are not typically hired for management-level sales positions (or for any management-level position). If the prevalent norm is that women are not accepted in managerial roles within a culture, then a foreign woman may not be any more acceptable. This argument is often used by multinational firms to deny international positions to women.[25]

This cultural bias raises the question in global selling contexts of whether a woman can be effective in establishing and maintaining a successful business relationship with host country clients. In Japan, for example, business relationships are typically cemented over dinner. Drinking and dining events are a significant part of doing business and more work may actually get done after hours than during the day. The professional problem a woman might encounter at a business dinner is that the Japanese might be reluctant to include her in conversations simply because they aren't, culturally, used to women participating in these types of business negotiations. Further, little social stigma is attached to being intoxicated in Japan. Drunkenness is an accepted way to relieve personal and professional tensions, break down the protective walls, and establish a basis for trust. In these situations, many Western women would naturally feel awkward as would their Japanese hosts.[26]

Should a company choose to send a woman to a country with a norm for gender bias (as many companies do), then they can improve the chances for success by forewarning their clients that a woman will represent them. A woman representative should be introduced on the basis of her qualifications, her authority to act on behalf of the company, and with a clear message of the company's confidence in her role and competence. Under such circumstances, status and social roles are predefined and established and more clearly understood. Initial respect may stem from showing respect for the firm that the woman represents, but professional behavior on the part of all parties often reduces resistance or makes it less severe than anticipated.

In closing, it should be noted that one of the trends of the 1990s is the clear commitment that many global companies are making to training programs that enhance the quality of sales personnel and management generally. Increasing numbers of foreign nationals are being sent by their companies to American and European Business schools for full-time or part-time studies ("executive" programs that have concentrated blocks of time in the classroom). Many of these programs have a strong global marketing emphasis and a large number of different nationalities in the class. Combining students from different nationalities into teams for experiential exercises and group projects provides one of the most valuable learning experiences. Global companies regularly hire outside consultants and firms to run cultural sensitivity seminars for their sales teams and other management groups who regularly come into contact with clients and co-workers from other cultures. International project teams that are comprised of managers from a variety of countries are also growing in popularity. These teams are designed to increase cultural understanding of management issues within the company. They meet periodically to exchange ideas and experiences and work on regional or global projects that require coordination.

Key Terms and Concepts

Role of personal selling
Types of personal selling
Order taking
Inside order taker
Outside order taker
Creative selling
Team selling
System selling
Supportive communications
Missionary salesperson
Detail salesperson
Objectives for personal selling
Creating profitable differential competitive advantage
Accord each buyer uniqueness
Manage buying-selling relationship
Control the communication
Personal-selling process
Preparation
Prospecting
Initial contact
Presentation
Canned presentation
AIDA
Need satisfaction
Handling objections
Closing the sale
Follow-up
New environment for personal selling
Sales management
Situation analysis
Setting sales objectives
Establishing a budget
Sales force structure
Job descriptions and qualifications
Recruiting
Training
Compensation and motivation
Evaluation
Developing a global sales force

Expatriate personnel
Local nationals
Third-country nationals
Managing a global sales force
Gender bias in global personal selling

QUESTIONS AND EXERCISES

1. The modern view of the role of personal selling recognizes that salespeople are essential to implementing marketing strategy. What types of activities do sales people engage in, beyond selling, that are related to this view?
2. If support communications as a type of personal selling does not specifically identify sales as an objective, what purpose does such selling serve? Do you think it is worth deploying salespeople to engage in supportive communication?
3. Discussions in this chapter argue that both the buyer and the seller benefit if the salesperson controls the communication in a sales encounter. Do you agree or disagree with this position?
4. What are the areas of information that constitute proper preparation for the personal selling process?
5. Why is the AIDA approach considered outdated as a presentation technique. What approach is considered far superior and why?
6. In following up a successful sales effort, what two factors should a salesperson concentrate on to take advantage of opportunities at this stage of the selling process?
7. What has changed in the last several years to create a new environment for personal selling?
8. In sales force management, what are the three alternatives for sales force structure? What conditions suggest the use of each alternative?
9. Discuss the three options a firm has in hiring personnel when developing a global sales force. Frame the discussion in terms of markets that display highly similar cultural values versus markets with highly diverse cultures. Which type of option would best apply in each situation?
10. Gender bias in global personal selling is a fact of business life. How do you feel about such a circumstance? How would you advise a female colleague to cope with this factor in the selling process?

REFERENCES

1. Gabriella Stern, "Chief Executives Are Increasingly Chief Salesmen," *The Wall Street Journal* (August 6, 1991): B1, B5.
2. Walecia Konrad, "Cheerleading, and Clerks Who Know Awls from Augers," *Business Week* (August 3, 1992): 51.
3. Laura Zinn, "A Bank That's Puttin' on the Blitz," *Business Week* (August 3, 1992): 50.
4. Stephanie Anderson, "Customers Must Be Pleased, Not Just Satisfied," *Business Week* (August 3, 1992): 52.
5. Statistics from Cahners Reports cited by Richard Van Baasbeck in "Marketers Can't Afford to Invest More in Personal Sales Calls," *Marketing News* (September 13, 1993): 22.
6. U.S. Department of Labor, *Handbook of Labor Statistics,* (Washington, D.C.: U.S. Government Printing Office, 1989), Table 1: p.7, Table 18: p. 91.
7. Christopher Power, Lisa Driscoll, and Earl Bohn, "Smart Selling," *Business Week* (August, 3, 1992): 48.
8. Ibid., 48.
9. Patricia Sellers, "How IBM Teaches Techies to Sell," *Fortune* (June 6, 1988): 146.
10. This section is based on an excellent discussion of setting objectives for personal selling that appears in Gary M. Grikscheit, Harold C. Cash, and Cliff E. Young, *Handbook of Personal Selling* (New York: John Wiley & Sons, 1993), Chapter 1.
11. "Telemarketing: Marketing System for the 1980s," (The Bell System, 1981).
12. "Numbers Game," *The Competitive Advantage,* 1989, 6.
13. Grikscheit, Cash, and Young, op. cit., 15.
14. Joseph P. Vaccaro, "Best Salespeople Know Their ABCs (Always Be Closing)," *Marketing News* (March 28, 1988): 10.

15. Alan Farnham, "The PC You Put in Your Pocket," *Fortune* (May 20, 1991): 113–114.
16. Power, Driscoll, and Bohn, op. cit., 48.
17. Barbara Buell, et al., "Apple: New Team, New Strategy," *Business Week* (October 15, 1991): 93.
18. Carol Loomis, "State Farm Is Off the Charts, *Fortune* (April 8, 1991): 80.
19. Bradley D. Lockman and John H. Hallaq, "Who Are Your Successful Salespeople?" *Journal of the Academy of Marketing Science* (Fall 1982): 463–468, and Timothy J. Trow, "The Secret of a Good Hire: Profiling," *Sales & Marketing Management* (May 1990): 44.
20. Sellers, op. cit., 141.
21. Powers, Driscoll, and Bohn, op. cit., 48.
22. This section is based in part on Leon Winer, "Motivating Industrial Sales Reps: A Six-Point Plan," *Marketing News* (February 19, 1982): 7.
23. Siemens Nixdorf I.T. World News, *The Economist* (February 22, 1992): 58.
24. See Bob Hagerty "Companies in Europe Seeking Executives Who Can Cross Borders in a Single Bound," *The Wall Street Journal* (January 25, 1991): B1, B3; and Charles Siler, "Recruiting Overseas Executives," *Overseas Business* (Winter 1990): 30–33.
25. Julie Solomon, "Women, Minorities, and Foreign Postings," *The Wall Street Journal* (June 2, 1989): B1.
26. Deidre Sullivan, "An American Businesswoman's Guide to Japan," *Overseas Business* (Winter 1990): 50–55.

13

CHANNELS OF DISTRIBUTION

AFTER STUDYING THIS CHAPTER, YOU WILL UNDERSTAND THAT:

1. The channel of distribution plays an important role in creating value and affects overall customer satisfaction.
2. Participants in the channel of distribution, called intermediaries, perform specialized functions that increase the efficiency of channel activities.
3. There are conventional, multiple, and integrated channel systems for both consumer and business goods.
4. Characteristics of the market, the product, and the firm affect channel design and operation.
5. Channel design for global markets requires a well-conceived and well-articulated global distribution strategy.

Ernest & Julio Gallo's image in the vaunted wine market is middle-of-the-road at best. Gallo's wines, despite winning numerous and prestigious awards, are considered "adequate" and would *never* be served for special occasions. While Gallo's image at the retail level may only be moderate, the firm's success as a competitor is first-rate. Most wineries completely entrust their marketing activities to independent distributors. Gallo, on the other hand, uses a blend of its own distribution in large markets and carefully selected independent distributors in other markets. To make more effective use of the independent distributors, the firm has produced a 300-page manual covering all aspects of wine marketing that highlights Gallo wines. The firm owns its own trucking company with 200 semi-tractors and 500 trailers to haul in raw materials and then haul out the finished product. Gallo makes the two million bottles a day it needs to contain the wine produced, and one of its subsidiaries, MidCal Aluminum Company, makes the screw caps for the bottles.[1] The firm invests more heavily in advertising than any other wine producer to help retailers successfully sell Gallo wines. The result of all these activities is that Gallo holds nearly 30 percent of the domestic wine market in the United States while the nearest competitor holds barely an 8 percent share. Ernest & Julio Gallo has risen to the top of the wine market by carefully managing the channel of distribution. The firm has devised a system that blends vertical integration (owning and operating different levels in the channel) with independent distributors and a dose of control strategy to crush the competition.

The topics covered in this chapter will illustrate why the distribution variable in the marketing mix holds tremendous potential for firms to achieve competitive advantage while at the same time providing increased satisfaction to customers. Many analysts believe that the distribution factor is underappreciated for its potential to contribute to the efficiency and effectiveness of a firm's overall marketing operation. And, as firms attempt to cultivate global markets, channel design and strategy are critical to success in taking advantage of global market opportunities. The essential issues in the development of channels of distribution in global markets are discussed in the global perspectives section at the end of the chapter.

The Nature of Distribution

In Chapter 1, the distribution variable of the marketing mix was described as the "place" component of the Four Ps. In terms of strategic impact, though, distribution activities go well beyond the mere effects of the location where products and services are available. The channel of distribution, as the Gallo example suggests, is diverse and complex. It is best conceptualized as a channel because it represents a flow of goods, services, information, and funds between manufacturers, market intermediaries, and the end user of the product. **Channel of distribution** is defined as:

Sets of interdependent organizations involved in the process of making a product or service available for use or consumption.[2]

The reason it is important to understand the concept of a channel in the distribution area of marketing is that a channel concept highlights the efficiency and effectiveness aspects of distributing goods and services. When attention is focused only on the participants in the channel—wholesalers, distributors, agents, brokers, and retailers—the most important reasons for analyzing distribution are lost. The concern should not be with the participants, per se, but rather with the added value that results when certain activities take place in the channel.

VALUE-ADDED IN THE CHANNEL OF DISTRIBUTION: UTILITIES

At various points throughout our discussion of marketing, the concept of value has been discussed. Recall that consumers perceive value in products and services that seem to give "more satisfaction for less cost." Value-oriented customers will be looking for satisfaction from those firms that provide more added value than others. The channel of distribution is an excellent vehicle for value-added activities.

Participants in the distribution channel engage in very basic activities that provide time, place, and possession utilities to customers. Recall from Chapter 1, that these utilities are economic values that translate directly into customer satisfaction. They are essential to the overall economic role of marketing. **Time utility** refers to the satisfaction gained by consumers from having a product available at the time at which it is desired. Examples of providing time utility are convenience stores like 7-11, which are open 24 hours a day, seven days a week, and shopping malls, which generally open their doors daily from 10 a.m. to 9 p.m.

Place utility provides satisfaction by having products located where consumers can conveniently acquire them. In a consumer study by Sanford C. Bernstein & Co., most shoppers surveyed indicated that location was the most important feature in choosing a discount store.[3] In the fast-food market, McDonalds has nearly 10,000 outlets in the United States to provide place utility. Kmart has installed a checkout scanning system that feeds data instantaneously into a computerized inventory network at wholesale distribution centers to ensure that products are on the shelf when consumers want them. The ultimate translation of place utility is the convenience of catalog shopping through retailers like L.L. Bean and Land's End and the home shopping television networks where consumers simply order by phone from the comfort of their homes. Or consider the emerging trend of ordering by fax or using a computer with a modem to order products from direct-marketing merchants.

Possession utility occurs when intermediaries in the channel provide services so that consumers can acquire and use products with as few deterrents as possible. Activities designed to create possession utility occur throughout the channel but are most visible at the retail level. Credit, delivery, and installation are crucial to bringing about possession utility at the retail level. In Michigan, the 3,000 stores who are members of Associated Food Dealers have begun accepting credit cards for grocery purchases.[4] Wal-Mart has taken the interpretation of possession utility to an extreme. Not only are store managers instructed to keep extra check-out lanes open for customers, but the firm has installed a $20 million satellite network that links all stores to the headquarters. This system cuts approval time on credit-card purchases to 6 seconds![5] The system gets shoppers on their way with as little delay as possible thus making the acquisition and possession process as quick and easy as possible. In the business market, financing large equipment purchases and providing training to employees to use business machines are examples of providing possession utility to business users.

Why Are Intermediaries Used?

There is little question that time, place, and possession utility are valuable ramifications of the activities that take place in the channel. But why are intermediaries like wholesalers and retailers used? Why does Black & Decker rely on retailers like Kmart and Sears to distribute its products? Why not deal directly with the end user? The reason producers use intermediaries has to do with the *efficiency* provided by intermediaries in the distribution process and the *functions* they perform for producers in getting the product to the end user.

EFFICIENCY PROVIDED BY INTERMEDIARIES

Intermediaries exist and persist because their use results in lower prices to customers and greater net returns to producers. How can that be since intermediaries must be paid for their services? The answer lies with the fact that intermediaries greatly increase the efficiency in the channel. And, the reason intermediaries increase efficiency is because of economies of scale and specialization. **Efficiency** means achieving a desired result with the least possible cost and effort. Efficiencies in the channel result from **economies of scale** when fixed costs of channel operations can be spread over more units handled. It costs less per unit for consumers to buy from a retailer where many items are available rather than for each consumer to travel to every factory where goods are produced. For example, Pioneer Wholesale, a wholesaler of hardware items, can make a sales call to Home Depot to present all 1,000 items in its catalog from many manufacturers. On the other hand, Stanley Products, which produces hardware items, would have to send a separate sales representative to present the firm's single product line to that same retailer. Similarly, it costs about the same to haul a truck full of several dozen different items from many manufacturers as it does to haul one or two from a single manufacturer. These examples illustrate how the cost of distributing an item is reduced when an intermediary—wholesaler, distributor, agent, broker, or retailer—is in a channel and handles a large volume of items, which creates economies of scale.

Another aspect of efficiency is **specialization** in that intermediaries concentrate their efforts on just a few highly valued activities in the channel and develop a high level of expertise in performing those activities. The result of this is that the total number of transactions associated with exchange is reduced when intermediaries are used. This aspect of efficiency is depicted in Figure 13-1. Note on the left side of the figure, if every producer called on every customer, the number of contacts needed would be much greater than if intermediaries were used. When producers sell to intermediaries, as depicted

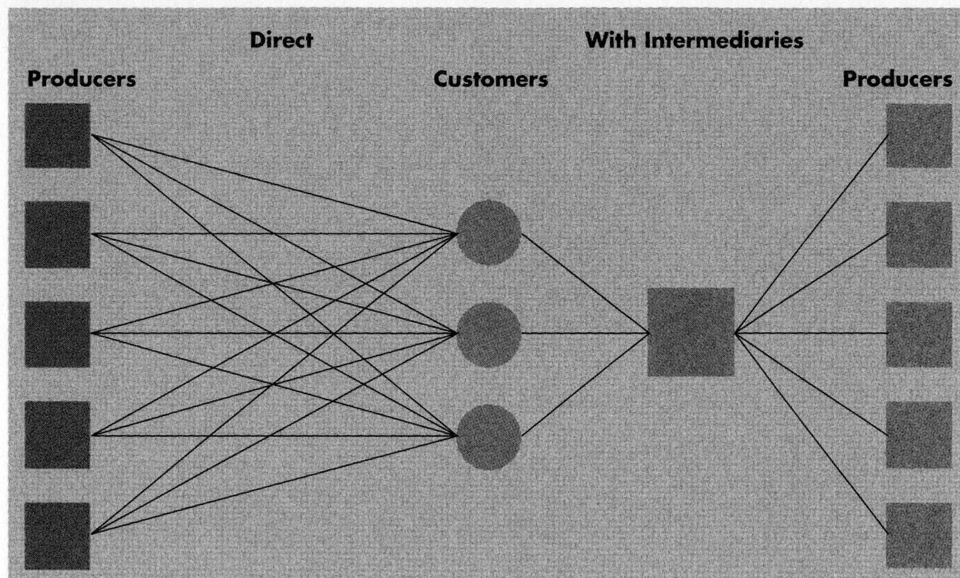

FIGURE 13-1
Intermediaries Increase Efficiency in the Channel through Specialization, Which Reduces the Number of Transactions Needed to Serve Customers

on the right side of Figure 13-1, the same number of customers can be reached with far less effort and consequently less cost. When the producers in Figure 13-1 contact each of three customers separately, the result is 15 total contacts. When an intermediary is used, a total of only eight contacts is needed for all the customers to be reached. Placing an intermediary in the system has reduced the number of contacts by nearly one-half and greatly increased the efficiency of the system.

FUNCTIONS PERFORMED BY INTERMEDIARIES

In order to bring about efficiencies and utilities in the exchange process as we've discussed, a variety of functions must be performed in the channel of distribution. Specifically, functions in the marketing channel include:

- Functions of exchange
    - Buying
    - Bulk breaking
    - Negotiation
    - Promotion
- Functions of physical supply
    - Storage
    - Materials handling
    - Transportation
- Facilitating functions
    - Financing
    - Risk taking
    - Standardizing and grading
    - Market information

In performing **functions of exchange,** intermediaries buy goods in large quantities. Then, bulk breaking occurs, which is breaking down a large quantity into smaller quantities for distribution to the next level in the channel. For example, wholesalers may take shipments in car load lots, then bulk break the quantity to case lots for shipment to retailers. Retailers then break the case lots into single units for purchase by household consumers. Negotiation in the channel is the process whereby the details of price and terms of transfer are established. Finally, promotion consists of the activities necessary to attract customers. Wholesalers and agents typically use personal selling and trade show displays while retailers engage in advertising in local and regional media.

The **functions of physical supply** have largely to do with materials handling activities, shipping, and the need to keep inventory at various levels in the channel. As wholesalers, distributors, and retailers accumulate goods for sale to their customers, these goods need to be stored in inventory and then effectively moved from inventory for acquisition by the customer. Wholesalers transport products to retailers' receiving docks. Retailers then move the inventory from "back room" storage to the store shelf for consumers to buy. The functions of physical supply will be covered in detail in Chapter 15 when physical distribution is discussed.

Facilitating functions, as the term implies, are activities that contribute to the smooth operation of the exchange and physical supply functions. One of the most important facilitating functions is providing financing to members in the channel. Short-term lines of credit can be essential to ensuring the movement of goods through the channel. Risk taking is a function that every member in the channel of distribution must be willing to accept to earn a profit.

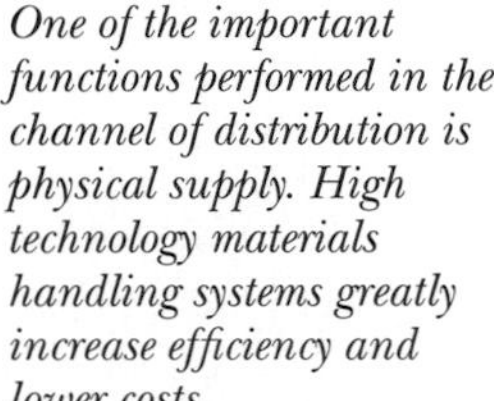

One of the important functions performed in the channel of distribution is physical supply. High technology materials handling systems greatly increase efficiency and lower costs.

Any time goods are purchased for the purpose of resale with the intention of making a profit, risk is involved. This acceptance of risk is particularly prevalent for manufacturers and wholesalers in the current environment where retailers are trying to keep a tight control on inventory. Children's Palace/Child World Toys, Inc., asked its suppliers to hold merchandise but would not promise an order. This forced manufacturers and wholesalers to hold larger inventories in case they were needed.[6] Standardizing and grading are additional facilitating functions that assist the exchange process because the need for close physical inspection at the next level in the channel can be greatly reduced or even eliminated. Machine parts, fuels, and cereal grains, for example, are purchased to standardization and grading standards. Because of activities in the channel, buyers are ensured that a coupling will fit, a fuel has a specific Btu capacity, and a particular grain contains only the allowable impurities. Finally, because channel members deal with customers at various levels in the channel, they can provide market information to the prior level in the channel. Recall from Chapter 3 that wholesalers, retailers, and manufacturers' representatives were cited as valuable sources of market information because of their contact with customers and knowledge of competitors' activities.

An important point needs to be made with regard to functions within the channel of distribution. Producers can, at their discretion, choose to eliminate an intermediary at any level in the channel. For example, producers can (and sometimes do) ship large quantities directly to retailers thereby eliminating wholesalers; wholesalers can sell in case lots directly to end users. *But,* while an intermediary can be eliminated, *the functions performed cannot be eliminated.* In other words, if a producer makes the choice to eliminate a wholesaler from the channel, the producer will either have to pick up the financing, storage, transportation, and bulk-breaking functions or try to shift those functions to the next level in the channel. The wholesaler can be eliminated but the functions cannot. Bed, Bath, and Beyond is a household goods chain of stores that offers consumers a wide range of high-quality, bargain-priced merchandise. Outlets in this chain deal directly with manufacturers to re-order items, but to do so, each store is enormous and has merchandise stacked floor to ceiling.[7] In other words, the retail outlets of Bed, Bath, and Beyond have eliminated the wholesale participant in the channel but have to perform the functions a wholesaler would have performed—inventory and storage. As stated earlier, intermediaries exist and persist because they provide values and efficiencies in the system. Rarely does eliminating an intermediary result in cost savings. Other benefits may be gained by eliminating a participant in the channel, but due to specialization and economies of scale, cost reduction is usually not accomplished.

Types of Intermediaries

In the previous sections, reference was made to several different types of intermediaries: wholesalers, distributors, agents, brokers, and retailers. The specific types of intermediaries involved in channel transactions need specific definitions, however, since each type plays a unique role in bringing about transactions in the channel. **Retailers** buy goods and resell them to household consumers. Retail operations vary by size of product lines carried and market strategy. Most retailers operate stores like JC Penney and Dillards, but catalog retailers, direct response advertising, and vending machine sales account for a considerable dollar volume of retail sales.

Wholesalers and distributors buy goods and resell them to retailers, business users, other wholesalers, exporters, institutions, or the government. The primary advantage of including wholesalers and distributors in the channel is that when they buy goods producers are relieved of the cost and risk of holding inventory near the point of sale. Most wholesalers and distributors handle many different items and frequently carry competing brands within a product category. Wholesalers and distributors perform a variety of functions including maintaining a sales force, providing inventory and storage, financing, and delivery. Some even offer maintenance and repair services to their customers.

Agents provide the facilitating functions of exchange but normally do not take title or possession of goods. Manufacturers' agents' principal service is to provide aggressive selling on a commission basis. They commonly handle only a few complementary but noncompeting lines and specialize in one or two industries. Producers must bear the cost and risk of carrying inventory when the agents are used.

Finally, **brokers** function solely to bring buyers and sellers together in markets where contact might otherwise be difficult to accomplish. Brokers do not take title or possession to goods and are often used for seasonal products. Brokers work on a fee or commission basis.

Channels for Consumer Goods

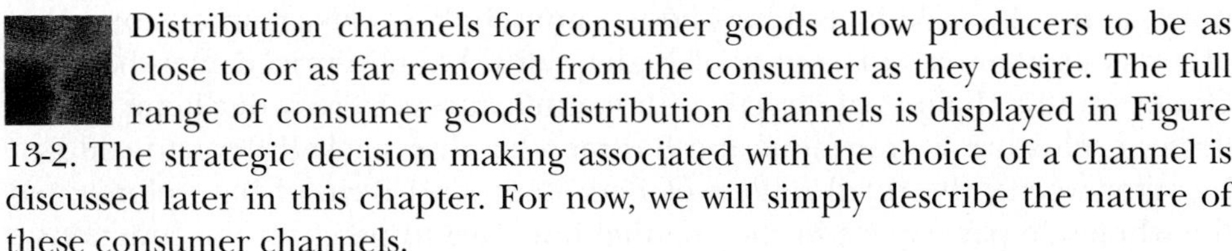

Distribution channels for consumer goods allow producers to be as close to or as far removed from the consumer as they desire. The full range of consumer goods distribution channels is displayed in Figure 13-2. The strategic decision making associated with the choice of a channel is discussed later in this chapter. For now, we will simply describe the nature of these consumer channels.

CHANNEL 1: PRODUCER DIRECT TO CONSUMER

In a channel where a product is distributed directly to the consumer, a producer assumes the responsibility for performing all the exchange, physical supply, and facilitating functions needed to complete a transaction. Because a producer accepts responsibility for these functions for a large number of consumers who typically buy in small quantity, it is easy to see why this channel design generally has the highest marketing costs. Activities that must be provided but which also contribute to the costly nature of this channel are:

- Building and maintaining a large and well-supervised sales staff.
- Building and maintaining extensive systems for storage and inventory control to make prompt delivery to many different customers.
- Assuming the risk of financing.

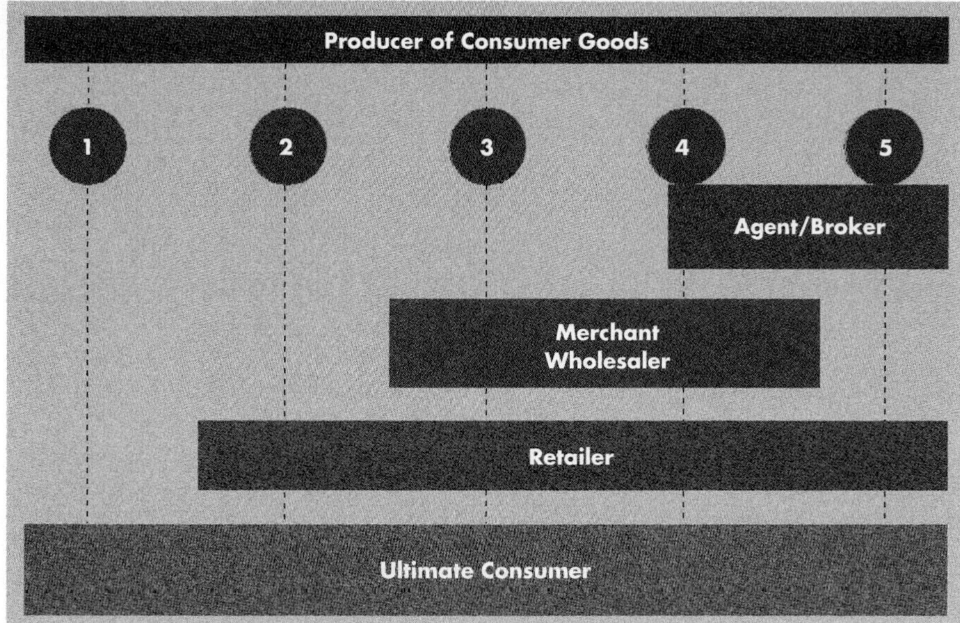

FIGURE 13-2
Conventional Channels of Distribution for Consumer Goods

Producers may decide that increased effectiveness of dealing directly with the consumer is worth the increases in cost that are incurred with this channel design. In directly selling to end users, producers can realize the following advantages:

- More aggressive, concentrated, and controlled selling effort.
- Closer contact with the customer making it easier to determine the needs of the customer.
- The opportunity to control the provision of technical information, proper installation, and service after the sale.
- Elimination of the margins that normally accrue to intermediaries in the channel.

One of the best examples of a firm that has successfully used this channel design to sell to consumers is Dell Computer. While Dell sells to business buyers as well, a substantial portion of the firm's gross revenues comes from consumers who directly contact the firm through a toll-free phone line. Dell has had to carefully develop this channel option in order to make it work. First, Dell keeps manufacturing costs low so it can sell at a price low enough for consumers to feel the risk of buying a computer by phone is offset by the low price. Second, the firm maintains almost no inventory because assembly of a computer begins after an order is received. Third, Dell has built a highly sophisticated shipping facility to deal with the thousands of orders that must be expedited on a monthly basis. Finally, a large staff is maintained to deal with customers' technical problems after the purchase. The firm's technical support hotline claims to solve 90 percent of reported problems within six minutes. If customers need detailed system information, Dell operates a toll-free "TechFax" line, which provides responses 24 hours a day, seven days a week. With all these mechanisms carefully designed to provide the functions normally provided by intermediaries, Dell can successfully use a channel that sells directly to the household consumer.

CHANNEL 2: PRODUCER TO RETAILER TO CONSUMER

Some producers find it desirable and feasible to bypass the wholesale level in the channel and deal directly with retailers. This channel is especially preferred when producers want greater control over the handling of their products. The need for closer control usually occurs if the product is perishable, has seasonal demand, or is a fashion item. A producer may also prefer direct contact with retailers for strategic reasons as well. With products of high unit value, such as pianos, fine jewelry, or industrial machinery, the profit margin in each unit is usually large enough to easily cover the overhead costs of selling directly to the retailer. Aside from the control issue and the ability to finance such a relatively direct approach to distribution, the factors that encourage direct selling to retailers are:

- The products of a single manufacturer constitute a substantial part of the retailers' stock, and economies of scale in selling and shipping can be realized.
- The retailers are large enough to take over the functions normally performed by wholesalers in the channel.
- Products that require installation and/or replacement parts that need to be stocked often incur unique demands from each buyer thus necessitating closer contact.
- The product is large, bulky, or heavy and more direct distribution may reduce shipping costs.

By relying on their own sales forces rather than using wholesalers to represent them, producers know they will receive the concentrated effort desired. A producer will not have to compete with other products in a wholesaler's line including, perhaps, the wholesalers own private label items. Additionally, when a producer's sales representative visits a retail outlet, an opportunity arises to build goodwill. The sales force can also pass on important sales information and help maintain point-of-purchase displays. This channel design facilitates cooperative advertising and promotional campaigns between the producer and the retailer without wholesaler intervention. The close contact can be used as a means to resolve difficulties and promote better cooperation.

The motivation for bypassing wholesalers in the channel comes not only from producers, however. Often, large retailers can assume a power position in the channel and dictate the channel structure. Large retailers like Sears, Kmart, Wal-Mart, and Home Depot may be able to perform the buying and bulk breaking functions more efficiently than most wholesalers because of their large volume purchase capability. As such, these large retailers may be able to increase profit margins by dealing directly with manufacturers in selected product areas.

The disadvantages and risks of this channel design should be fully recognized. Typically, producers must be willing to accept that dealing directly with retailers entails:

Producers will often distribute directly to retailers in the channel of distribution.

- Higher selling costs and order processing costs in dealing with a large number of individual retail accounts rather than a small number of wholesale accounts (see Figure 13-1).
- Bearing the risks of credit extension and financing.
- Accepting the responsibility for physical distribution of goods in small lots to many locations.
- Maintaining storage facilities and inventories.

The foregoing conditions simply reflect that if a producer chooses to eliminate wholesalers from the channel, then many of the functions performed by wholesalers must be performed by the producer. The attempt can be made to push some of the responsibilities down to the retail level, like storage and inventory, but retailers may be ill-equipped or unwilling to assume more channel responsibilities.

CHANNEL 3: PRODUCER TO WHOLESALER TO RETAILER TO CONSUMER

This is by far the most widely used channel of distribution for consumer goods. In fact, it is commonly referred to as the traditional or customary channel. Despite its popularity, it rarely represents the sole channel used by producers to reach their household consumers. Most manufacturers exercise the right to sell directly to large chains or large individual retailers. The reason the channel is the predominant choice, however, is that such a structure takes full advantage of specialization and the benefits of economies of scale that often result from specialization. As discussed earlier, when wholesalers and retailers develop specialized facilities and business practices at their level in the channel, each can perform distribution functions more efficiently than any participant trying to perform those same functions from a different level in the channel. Customer satisfaction is greatly enhanced when a specialist performs the needed functions at the wholesale and retail level.

CHANNEL 4: PRODUCER TO AGENT/BROKER TO WHOLESALER TO RETAILER TO CONSUMER

This is the longest of the consumer channels in that it enlists the services of the most participants. In this channel structure, agents or brokers are used to contact wholesalers. The primary function of the agents or brokers is selling. Agents and brokers have been most useful to producers who are not large enough to support their own sales representatives. Additionally, some producers use agents and brokers because they prefer to concentrate the firm's resources on production and give the marketing responsibility to external facilitators.

CHANNEL 5: PRODUCER TO AGENT TO RETAILER TO CONSUMER

This channel is frequently used in the clothing industry and in other industries characterized by a large number of small manufacturers who use agents to call on large retail chains. Many items in supermarkets are sold through food brokers, which is a special type of channel agent. Many nonfood items that require more promotional efforts than are typically provided by food wholesalers are handled by these agents. For manufacturers whose product lines are too limited to support a corporate sales force, they can enlist the services of agents who serve several manufacturers.

CHANNELS FOR BUSINESS GOODS

The channel alternatives for business goods are depicted in Figure 13-3. Notice that the channels available parallel those used for household consumer goods. The major difference is that business producers do not use retailers to reach business customers. It should be recognized that there is a trend in some product categories, most notably office supplies, for business buyers to purchase items from an outlet that is very much like a retail outlet. Stores like Biz-Mart and Avery Office Products serve both household consumers and business buyers out of warehouse-like distribution facilities. In channel concepts, however, any purchase made by a business buyer, even if it is made through a traditional retail outlet, is considered a wholesale purchase. As such, a retail level is not indicated in the channels for business goods.

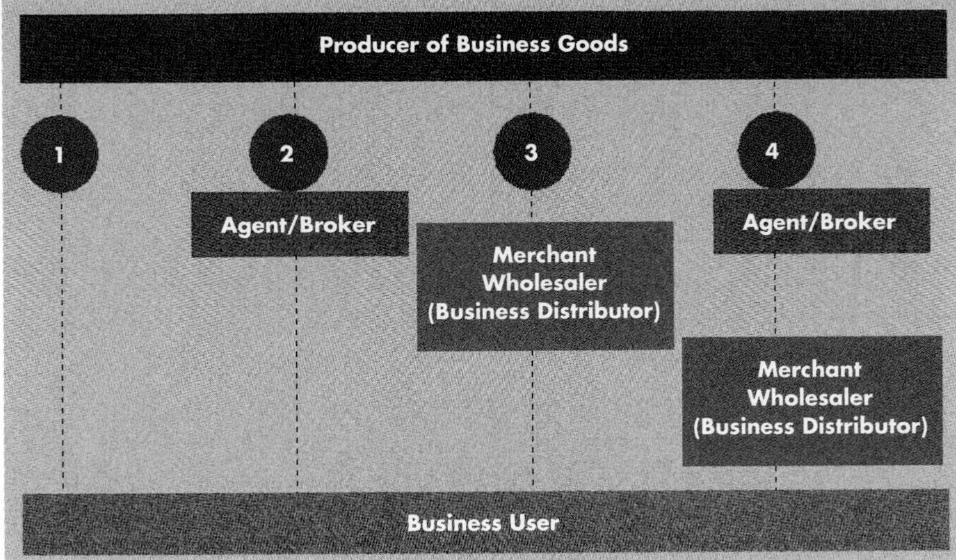

FIGURE 13-3
Conventional Channels of Distribution for Business Goods

CHANNEL 1: PRODUCER TO BUSINESS BUYER

This channel is much more common in the business market than in the consumer market. For all categories of business goods, producers often deal directly with their buyers. This channel is more common in the business market for a variety of reasons:

- Business buyers often buy low-cost items in large quantities. The economies of scale in shipping large quantities makes direct distribution feasible.
- High-cost business products, like major installations, provide enough margin for producers to cover the increased costs of direct distribution.
- Complex business products that require installation or training for proper use need direct distribution so the producer can better control the process and help ensure customer satisfaction.

In order to effectively use a direct channel structure like this, producers often maintain their own sales force. For the reasons cited above, the time and expense of managing an in-house sales staff is feasible and often necessary for the proper distribution of certain business goods under certain circumstances. Other alternatives are available for direct distribution, however. Many industrial supply houses for electronic component parts, for example, sell directly to business buyers using catalogs. Other producers have turned to telemarketing for direct contact, sales, and ultimately direct distribution to business buyers.

CHANNEL 2: PRODUCER TO AGENT/BROKER TO BUSINESS BUYER

This channel is common for business products that are standardized, low unit cost items. Raw materials, accessory equipment, and operating supplies can be effectively distributed using agents and brokers. Since agents and brokers often represent several producers in a product category, they cannot be expected to have intimate knowledge of every producer's product line. For standardized and relatively low-cost items, an external agent can effectively handle the selling function but little else. Since agents and brokers do not take title to or physical possession of the products they sell, the producer bears responsibility for storage and inventory and often must provide financing to buyers.

CHANNEL 3: PRODUCER TO DISTRIBUTOR TO BUSINESS BUYER

Distributors are used in the business market when a producer is trying to reach a large number of small users. Normally, these small users are also geographically dispersed and a network of distributors (or a large national distributor) can be used to achieve adequate geographic coverage. Such a channel structure will work effectively for producers if little control is needed over how the product is handled. Like the agent/broker channel, low-priced standardized items are more appropriate for distribution through distributors.

CHANNEL 4: PRODUCER TO AGENT/BROKER TO DISTRIBUTOR TO BUSINESS BUYER

This longest of all business channels is used only under specific circumstances. A producer using this channel structure is usually a small producer of a single product or perhaps a limited product line. The producer does not have the market clout nor a sales staff to effectively sell to distributors (much less directly to buyers). As such, the services of an agent or broker are required to facilitate contact with distributors. Like other circumstances where distributors provide efficiency and effectiveness in the channel, the type of product that moves through this channel design is small, standardized, low-cost, widely distributed, and frequently purchased.

MULTIPLE CHANNEL DESIGNS

Under a variety of conditions, producers may choose to use multiple channels from the consumer and business channels just discussed. Weiser Lock sells both residential and commercial grade door locks and accessories. The firm is required to use a **multiple channels design** to serve both household consumer and business markets for, in several circumstances, an identical product. But even within the consumer lock line, Weiser uses a multiple channel design. The home office sells directly to large retail accounts like CostCo and Price Savers and ships in large quantities to these retailers. In addition to this channel, Weiser sales representatives are assigned geographic territories and sell the Weiser line to smaller retail accounts and regional distributors.

Another example of the use of multiple channel design is Compaq Computer. For years Compaq sold only through computer dealers who had highly trained sales personnel and often had on-site repair facilities. Recently, Compaq has added two different routes to the end-user in its channel structure. First, superstores like Office Depot and Circuit City have been added to its distribution network. These superstores sell a wide range of products and have a much more self-service orientation to the sale of computers. Next, Compaq has started its own mail-order system not unlike the channel Dell Computer uses.[8] Multiple channel systems like these allow producers to reach different customer groups or achieve greater geographic coverage than a single channel structure would allow.

INTEGRATED CHANNEL SYSTEMS

The channel systems discussed so far are very individualistic in nature. Each participant in the channel operates somewhat independently from the other channel members. In these channels, the welfare of one channel member is related to the welfare of other channel members. However, strategic planning tends to take place at *each level* of the channel rather than in a coordinated or integrated fashion. There are, however, two types of integrated channel systems. An **integrated channel system** is one where planning is coordinated and activities are carried out in such a way that the *interdependence* of channel participants is recognized and taken advantage of. These integrated channels are known as vertical marketing systems and horizontal marketing systems.

VERTICAL MARKETING SYSTEMS

Vertical marketing systems are defined as "professionally managed and centrally programmed networks, pre-engineered to achieve operating economies and maximum marketing impact."[9] Vertically integrated marketing systems emerge when producers, wholesalers, brokers, and retailers in a channel coordinate and integrate their activities to achieve maximum impact and efficiency of the entire channel operation. There are three types of vertical marketing systems: corporate-owned, contractual, and administrative.

Corporate-owned Vertical Marketing System

A **corporate-owned vertical marketing system** exists when a participant at one level in the channel owns and operates facilities at another level (or other levels) in the channel. Producers can use **forward vertical integration** by owning and operating their own wholesale or retail operations. Singer, Sherwin-Williams, and Kuppenheimer Clothiers are examples of manufacturers that have used forward integration to form a vertical marketing system. A retailer or wholesaler may establish **backward vertical integration** by purchasing a manufacturing operation or by owning a wholesale supply facility. The Limited in the apparel industry and American Stores in the grocery industry have their own wholesale distribution operations.

Corporate-owned vertical marketing systems have several advantages. Operating economies are often achieved because absolute control of at least two levels in the channel is maintained. The division of labor in the channel is designed to realize as much efficiency as possible. The elimination of duplicate effort is ensured and most channel members maintain a commitment to the entire channel, not just one level in the channel. Well-run, corporate-owned vertical marketing systems represent one of the best methods of bringing economies of scale to the channel of distribution and, in turn, profits are often increased.

Contractual Vertical Marketing System

A **contractual vertical marketing system** is one in which channel relationships between participants at different levels in the channel are formalized by legally binding contracts. These contracts specify the role that each channel participant plays in moving the product from producer to end user. Specifically,

> *Contractual integration occurs where the various stages of production and distribution are independently owned but the relationships between vertically adjacent firms are covered in contractual agreements.*[10]

Contractual vertical marketing systems, like corporate-owned systems, achieve economies through the coordination of channel functions and the elimination of duplicate tasks. Contractual systems are somewhat unique in that they combine the strong features of both big and small business. The dedication and profit concerns of the small business owner can be combined with the marketing impact and scale economies of large business organizations.

The three most common types of contractual vertical marketing systems are wholesale-sponsored voluntary chains, retail-sponsored cooperatives, and franchise organizations. The **wholesale-sponsored voluntary chain** develops when a wholesaler bonds together a group of independent retailers. When such a bonding takes place willingly, advantages accrue to both the wholesaler sponsoring the arrangement and the retailers who participate. The most prominent wholesale-sponsored voluntary chain is the Independent Grocers Alliance: IGA Food Stores. By cooperating with a regional wholesaler, numerous small, independent grocery retailers have been able to compete with large food chains. The IGA affiliation allows them to order in large quantities and to share advertising expenses and certain administrative costs like accounting systems. Other examples of wholesale-sponsored voluntary chains are Ace Hardware and Trustworthy Hardware.

Retail-sponsored cooperatives operate in a similar manner to the wholesale-sponsored group, but the organization differs in some important ways. The usual procedure in this system is for a group of retailers to organize themselves and manage their own wholesale operation. Through such a cooperative effort, the retailers are able to take advantage of economies of scale as well as achieve some of the market impact of large organizations. Retail cooperatives have emerged mainly in the food industry with Associated Grocers (AG) being the most notable example.

Franchise organizations account for the majority of corporate revenues generated through contractual channel arrangements. Franchising is a form of marketing and distribution in which a parent company grants an individual or small company the right to do business in a prescribed manner over a

Franchises are a form of a vertical marketing system that is either corporate owned or a contractual channel arrangement with independent ownership.

certain period of time in a specified place.[11] The franchise agreement usually takes the form of a legal contract stating what the franchisor and the franchisee will and will not do in the relationship. The average franchise fee is about $150,000 for the right to open an outlet, but some franchises can cost as much as $10 million. Franchising has shown tremendous growth in recent years. The number of franchise business establishments stood at 430,000 in 1992 with combined sales of nearly $250 billion in the United States.[12]

Numerous franchise arrangements exist, but four types are the most common. First, manufacturers often franchise retail operations for the marketing and selling of specific products. Examples include automobile dealerships and gasoline service stations. Second, manufacturers also sponsor wholesale franchises. Coca-Cola franchises local bottling companies to bottle *Coke* products and distribute them to retailers in a limited geographic area. Third, wholesalers will establish franchises for retailers. Rexall Drug franchises independent drugstores to market the firm's private label products. Fourth are service firms that franchise retailers. The service franchisor authorizes an independent businessperson to offer the firm's service. Hertz Car Rental and Holiday Inns are traditional service franchisors. New service organizations offering franchises are Subway Sandwiches, Little Caesar's Pizza, and TCBY Yogurt. In all of these franchise arrangements, the parent company will establish strict operating procedures including facility design as a way to both assist the franchisee and control the distribution process. The parent firm in return will support its franchisors with product development and national advertising and marketing campaigns.

Administrative Vertical Marketing System

An **administrative vertical marketing system** exists when one or more of the channel members achieves channel-wide economies of scale, coordination of operations, and control through size and power rather than by contract or ownership. Administrative vertical marketing systems develop not by virtue of legal agreements, but because one channel participant emerges as powerful within the channel and can exert control over the other channel members. Because of the power of one member, other channel members are motivated to participate in the programs because the firm developing the program maintains some control over their ability to generate revenue. One of the most important control elements that promotes channel power and control is strong consumer demand for a producer's product. If a producer markets a product with strong consumer preference, retailers may be forced to stock the product simply to satisfy their customers expectations. For example, grocery stores need to carry the products from Kraft, Borden, Frito-Lay, and Lever Bros. and are willing to cooperate with these and other packaged goods companies that have developed strong consumer preferences for their brands. Increasingly, retailers are achieving power in the channel and are beginning to exert the same sort of control that traditionally only producers could exert. With sophisticated new inventory tracking systems, retailers know which items have profitable turnovers, can dictate the merchandise mix themselves, and are no long dependent on suppliers' records. Further, regional and national retail chains know what products are profitable in different geographic areas. This information coupled with large purchasing power allows some retailers to tell producers what they want in terms of product mix and promotional programs.

HORIZONTAL MARKETING SYSTEMS

The vertical marketing systems just discussed can be conceptualized as a set of relationships that develop as the product flows "down" the channel (vertically) from producer to consumer or business buyer. **Horizontal marketing systems** emerge at a *single level in the channel* rather than between levels in the channel. A horizontal system results when operations at the same level in the channel operate under one management. In some cases, firms establish horizontal systems with operations that are very similar. The Limited operates its flagship store, The Limited, as well as The Limited Express, Structure, and Victoria's Secret among others. All of these stores carry merchandise of similar quality although each appeals to a different segment of the market. Other firms use horizontal systems to sell very different merchandise. Dayton-Hudson also operates Target Discount stores, Kmart owns and operates Walden Books, and Nordstrom owns and operates the Nordstrom Rack to sell lower-priced clothing. In fact, The Limited is an excellent example of an organization that employs both vertical and horizontal systems in its channel design. The channel system used by The Limited is depicted in Figure 13-4.

Horizontal systems provide several opportunities for increased efficiency in the channel. Retailers often use one form of retailing to dispose of slow moving inventory from another form. This was the logic in Nordstrom's initiation of the Rack stores. Firms can make better use of specialized personnel such as in-house market analysts and advertising specialists. The economies of scale that result from more units of operation create overhead cost savings. It must be realized, however, that most attempts at horizontal integration are conceived as market strategies whereby the organization can cultivate a new target market and/or compete more effectively for revenues in current markets.

Channel Management Decisions

To this point, we have established the importance of the distribution factor, described the nature of channels of distribution, and considered alternative channel designs. The focus now will turn to managerial decision making with regard to channels. Channel management decisions must be made in three areas: channel length, the intensity of distribution, and choosing intermediaries to perform functions within the channel.

Channel Length

The length of a channel has nothing to with physical distance between participants. Rather, **channel length** describes the number of levels in a channel design. A short channel would be producer directly to end user. A long

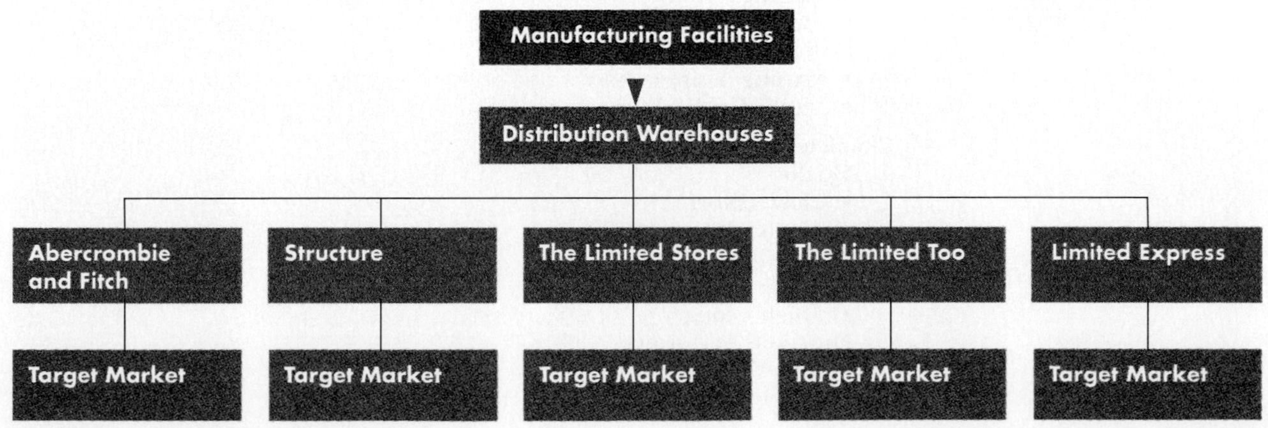

FIGURE 13-4
The Limited Stores Employs Both Vertical and Horizontal Systems in Its Channel Design

channel would employ wholesalers, agents, and retailers. The decision as to how long or how short a channel can be or needs to be is affected by several factors. These influences are summarized in Table 13-1. Note that these factors fall into four major categories: characteristics of the market, characteristics of the product, the nature of the firm, and the quality and availability of intermediaries. A channel will get longer as the total number of customers increases, customers are geographically dispersed, and orders are made in small quantities. If the product is standardized, does not need installation, and is lightweight, the channel also tends to be long. However, if the firm is well financed, desires control over the manner in which the product is handled, and feels that existing intermediaries are inadequate, then the channel will be short.

TABLE 13-1
Factors Affecting Channel Length

1. Characteristics of the Market
   a. Number of potential customers
      - small number = short channel
      - large number = longer channel
   b. Geographic concentration
      - highly concentrated = short channel
      - widely dispersed = longer channel
2. Characteristics of the Product
   a. Complexity
      - complex, needing technical assistance and training = short channel
      - simple = longer channel
   b. Standardization
      - customized = short channel
      - standardized = longer channel
   c. Order size per transaction
      - large = short
      - small = longer
3. Characteristics of the Firm
   a. Financial resources
      - strong = short
      - weak = longer
   b. Sales force
      - strong = short
      - weak = longer
   c. Desire for control
      - strong desire = short
      - little desire = longer
4. Characteristics of Intermediaries
   a. Quality
      - low = short
      - high = longer
   b. Availability
      - low = short
      - high = longer
   c. Functions performed
      - few = short
      - many = longer

INTENSITY OF DISTRIBUTION

The **intensity of distribution** describes the degree of market coverage a producer deems necessary to successfully serve the target market(s) for a product. There are three levels of intensity of distribution: intensive, selective, and exclusive. **Intensive distribution** means widespread coverage. For many products, especially those in the convenience goods category of household consumer goods, maximum exposure to the market is essential to capture a significant market share. *Wrigley's Chewing Gum, Gillette Razors, Coca-Cola, Scotch Tape,* and *Kleenex Tissues* are examples of products that are found in a variety of distribution outlets—drug stores, supermarkets, variety stores, convenience stores, not to mention vending machines, magazine stands, and candy counters. Because brand switching is so prevalent with products like these, producers must either arrange their channels to provide widespread availability or must be content to serve only the most profitable accounts. Achieving intensive distribution usually requires the use of multiple channels. Large and powerful producers like those given as examples often sell directly to large retail accounts and use wholesalers and brokers to service smaller accounts. The primary disadvantage of intensive distribution is that the producer has very little control over the way brands are priced and displayed.

Selective distribution employs a limited number of intermediaries who meet the producer's need for personal selling, promotion, and service for a product. Selective distribution is used for shopping goods in the household consumer market and a wide variety of business goods that are standardized items and sold nationally through distributors. Beyond the personal selling and service requirements, producers use selective distribution to achieve greater control over the marketing of their products. Producers also often want their brands to be sold only through outlets that have an image that is consistent with the image of the brand. To effectively use selective distribution, producers need to establish a well-planned network of intermediaries that share the same goals and objectives with the producer and reach the desired target market.

Exclusive distribution means that a producer will select only one retailer or wholesaler to handle a product in each market. In very large markets, a limited number of outlets may be used but far fewer than in a selective distribution plan. Exclusive distribution extends the advantages of selective distribution. By carefully selecting qualified intermediaries, producers can expect close cooperation and enthusiastic promotion of their products. They can also select outlets that will provide a maximum of prestige and status for their brands. Specialty goods and complex, expensive business goods rely on exclusive distribution to achieve product and market objectives. Producers run the risk, however, of not having the product distributed widely enough to achieve adequate market coverage. They may also provoke the ill-will of prominent dealers in a market who were not offered the opportunity to sell the product.

In summary, the channel management decision related to intensity of distribution is affected by three factors. First, the nature of the product itself will dictate how much coverage is needed. Second, the degree of control desired by the producer will influence how widespread the distribution network is. Finally, the image the firm hopes to achieve for a brand will affect how many and what type of intermediaries are used.

CHOOSING INTERMEDIARIES

In addition to deciding how many intermediaries to use, managers must also **choose intermediaries** through which the product will be distributed. First and foremost, the intermediaries to be used must *achieve target market selectivity*. That is, the intermediaries must provide the geographic coverage needed and otherwise appeal to the segment targeted for the product. For example, since Guess ?, the clothing manufacturer, wants to reach young women from 15 to 25 years old, it will seek retail outlets that target this group, like Contempo Casuals stores rather than Talbots or Jacobsen's, which target older women.

Second, intermediaries throughout the channel must *perform functions and create utilities* that match the specifications of the producer. As the discussion earlier in the chapter indicated, intermediaries are critical to bringing about time, place, and possession utilities with their policies and operating procedures. Further, intermediaries may be expected to perform a variety of functions related to exchange, physical supply, and facilitating the purchasing process. If intermediaries are chosen that do not perform a wide range of functions, then producers must accept the responsibility and expense of those functions.

Finally, intermediaries, particularly at the retail level, must *match the image of the producer* and the producer's products. Producers often grant exclusive distribution rights to certain retailers in an attempt to control distribution and maintain a high quality image. Some analysts argue that both the *Calvin Klein* and *Liz Claiborne* lines suffered image dilution by allowing their brands to be distributed through self-service discount chains. Conversely, Raytheon Corp. refuses to permit its *Amana* brand of appliances to be sold through discount stores in an effort to maintain the high quality image of this line.

ISSUES IN CHANNEL MANAGEMENT

Managers must be prepared to deal with several challenging issues in managing the channel of distribution. No matter how much care has been exerted analyzing the factors that affect channel design, issues will arise related to promotion in the channel, cooperation and conflict in the channel, and power in the channel.

PUSH VERSUS PULL PROMOTION IN THE CHANNEL

Recall the discussion in Chapter 10 regarding the effects on the promotional mix of a firm's decision to use a push versus a pull strategy. This strategy figures prominently once again as an issue in channel management. The issue is the extent to which a producer will use promotion to pull a product through the channel versus pushing the product at each level of distribution. A **pull promotion strategy** is implemented by producers by promoting a product extensively and creating so much demand at the end-user level that wholesalers and retailers are essentially forced to carry the item in inventory. Pulling a product effectively requires a heavy advertising effort and often includes the use of sales promotion. Conversely, a **push promotion strategy** relies primarily on personal selling and the sales force to sell the product at each successive level in the channel: the producer's sales representatives sell to wholesalers, wholesalers sell to retailers, and retailers sell to consumers.

For a firm that is financially capable of implementing a pull strategy, there are two distinct benefits. First, a pull strategy provides greater control over intermediaries. Wholesalers and retailers realize it is in their best interest to fill the demand created at the end-user level. Second, if a producer can successfully pull a product through the channel with promotion, then less pressure is put on personal selling at the wholesale and retail levels, which do not always function to the producer's complete satisfaction anyway.

COOPERATION AND CONFLICT IN THE CHANNEL

Cooperation and conflict in the channel can occur between levels (vertically) or at the same level (horizontally) between competitors. Horizontal channel conflict is a normal part of the competitive nature of business and is to be expected. *Coke* battling *Pepsi* at the producer level and Auto Zone competing with Checker Auto Parts at the retail level are horizontal channel conflicts that are normal. Conflict between channel participants *vertically*, however, is more problematic. Members of the channel *should* be cooperating with each other and coordinating their activities for mutual benefit.

Conflicts between manufacturers and wholesalers and agent/brokers and conflicts between manufacturers and retailers are relatively common, unfortunately. The reason is that each of these entities has a different perspective on the market and has unique goals and objectives that may not be completely compatible with each other. As an example, consider manufacturers' strategies associated with brand extensions, in other words, introducing new flavors, sizes, or varieties of existing brands to appeal to different segments in the market. In 1991, brand extensions in consumer products included 64 spaghetti sauces, 103 snack chips, 54 laundry detergents, 91 cold remedies, and 69 disposable diaper varieties![13] While such brand proliferation by producers may serve their product development and segmentation needs well, it creates havoc for retailers who are trying to deal with the shelf space problems they cause. Further, such a landslide of new products can be confusing to consumers who tend to blame the retailer rather than the producer for the confusion. The conflict between manufacturers and retailers escalates over this issue when retailers have to eliminate their highly profitable and newly popular private brands from the shelves to make room for heavily promoted, new national brands.

Another form of conflict in the channel comes when producers bypass wholesalers and agents to deal directly with large retailers. Producers claim that wholesalers do not sell aggressively enough and do not give their product lines the special attention they need. Wholesalers counter with the argument that they are unable to sell aggressively when all the high profit, large accounts are taken by the producers and only the high cost, small volume accounts are left for wholesalers to handle. This point of contention also causes conflict between retailers and wholesalers when retailers press producers for direct distribution. When Wal-Mart announced that it would no longer deal with brokers but only with the "principals," or key decision makers, of major producers, brokers charged that Wal-Mart was coercing manufacturers to fire brokers to increase profit margins.[14] Wal-Mart countered by saying that it desired to deal direct because of a need for improved communication and increased reaction time.

POWER IN THE CHANNEL

Power in the channel was discussed earlier as one of the bases for the development of an administrative channel. **Power in the channel** is an issue when one channel participant emerges as a channel leader (or "channel captain" as it is often referred to) and influences the behavior of other channel participants. Power in the channel can be exerted at any level of distribution. Typically, producers such as P & G, Honda Motors, and Novell hold power because their products are in such great demand by end users that all participants in the channel benefit by complying with these powerful producers. However, retailers and wholesalers can also hold power and emerge as channel leaders. Sears, Kmart, and Wal-Mart are so prominent in the market and order in such large quantities that producers and wholesalers comply with the policies and desires of these retailers. A similar circumstance arises at the wholesale level by the Independent Grocers' Alliance (IGA), which orders in large quantity for its many member grocery stores. Due to its financial strength, IGA can exert power both over producers from which it buys and retail grocers to which it sells.

Holding power in the channel and emerging as a channel leader is desirable because channel leaders seize control over channel activities. With control, the leader can influence performance of channel participants to serve the leader's own best interest. Power in the channel typically results from one participant having superior financial and market strength. But power can also come in the form of procedures and operations. Rubbermaid, Inc., has gained power and control over retailers not with superior financial strength or even extraordinary market strength but rather with operating procedures that serve the interest of retailers so well that they have given control over to this producer. What Rubbermaid has done is devised a system that keeps track of its customers' inventories via a computer installed at the retailers' point of sale. Through this system, Rubbermaid can replenish retailers' stock quickly and relieve the retailers of carrying large amounts of Rubbermaid inventory.[15] Retailers simply accept Rubbermaid shipments knowing that the producer has a superior inventory system that is operating in their (the retailers') best interest.

The issues discussed so far establish that the channel of distribution provides many opportunities and challenges. From the standpoint of opportunities, channel activities can create added value and utilities and increase customer satisfaction. However, the challenges of channel design and management are formidable, indeed. At this point, we will focus our attention on the issues of channel development and management in the global context.

CHANNELS OF DISTRIBUTION: A GLOBAL PERSPECTIVE

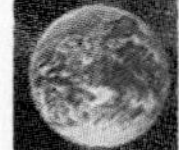

Over the past 20 years, Toys "R" Us has revolutionized the children's market in the United States by dealing directly with manufacturers as well as opening suburban stores with more than 5,000 square meters of selling space surrounded by plenty of parking. These tactics have allowed the firm to cut prices by 20 to 30 percent and have given the company over 20 percent of the U.S. toy market. Anticipating the day when it would saturate its domestic market, America's largest toy retailer went international in 1984, first in Canada then in Europe, Hong Kong, and Singapore. Profits from the sales generated in U.S. stores of the New Jersey–based Toys "R" Us are used to finance global expansion, and the company now has 581 stores in the United States and 234 outlets overseas. Toys "R" Us has announced plans to open 10 stores per year from 1993 to the end of the decade, with the Middle East countries of Qatar, Bahrain, Oman, Kuwait, and the UAE scheduled as the key targets beginning in 1995.

Japan, with more than $4.7 billion in annual sales in 1990, is the world's number two toy market and has always been a tempting target for Toys "R" Us. However, Japan's Large Retail Store Law, aimed at protecting the country's politically powerful small shopkeepers, seemed an unbreachable barrier. The law was enacted in the decade following World War II and was in line with developments in other countries such as the United States, Britain, and West Germany, which were also using legal measures to protect weaker industries while the war recovery progressed. But, whereas other countries had outlawed most anti-competitive retail practices by the 1970s, Japan left its Resale Price Maintenance Act and Large Retail Store Law on the books.

Apart from the unfavorable legal environment for starting up operations in Japan, a review of demographic trends in the country would also seem discouraging for a toy retailer. Birthrates in Japan are down 20 percent from just one decade ago and 38 percent below levels of 15 years ago. In the early 1990s, the average birthrate was 1.5 children per family compared to an average of 4 children per family in 1945. However, this demographic profile only tells part of the story. In terms of spending on children, the trend in Japan is that fewer kids are surrounded by more wealthy adults (parents and grandparents!), and that means that the money spent on each child increases. Money is being lavished on children as never before, and companies are crowding into the business of providing kids with expensive goods and services.

When Toys "R" Us opened its first store in Japan on December 20, 1991, in Ami, a suburb 40 miles north of Tokyo, it was not simply a celebration of opening a new store in a potentially lucrative international market. It was also an event to celebrate the culmination of three years of coping with tedious, costly, and time-consuming Japanese bureaucracy; negotiating with local vested interests; working through complicated and expensive real estate practices; and responding to heavy, hostile Japanese press coverage.

The opening was also the culmination of longer term efforts by government officials to open the Japanese retail market to large retailers. Pressure to do so had been mounting from the U.S. Department of Commerce, from large Japanese retailers, and from Japanese consumers who have been calling for more efficient retail outlets and lower prices for both domestic as well as imported goods. A survey done in 1990 by the U.S. Federal Trade Commission of a range of internationally traded goods in stores in Tokyo, New York, London, Paris, and Frankfurt found the prices of imported goods to be 80 percent higher on average in Japanese stores than in their country of origin. But foreigners paid an average of only 20 percent more for imported Japanese goods in their own stores. In the Spring of 1989, Japan's Ministry of

International Trade and Industry (MITI) unveiled its new retail industry revision, which included the eventual relaxation of the Large Retail Store Law.

In an effort to speed up the process of gaining access to the Japanese market, Toys "R" Us entered into a joint venture with McDonald Co. Japan. More important than providing Toys "R" Us with a new financial partner, the deal gave the toy company access to McDonald's president, Den Fujita, who had in 20 years built McDonald's into Japan's largest fast-food company with $1.3 billion in sales. In addition to being bicultural and having 20 years experience in doing business in Japan, Mr. Fujita is an expert in retail property in Japan and a graduate of the elite University of Tokyo Law School. His real estate knowledge was invaluable in selecting retail locations and his business and social contacts helped speed up the lobbying efforts at the many government agencies involved in the process.

Throughout the years in gaining permissions to enter the Japanese market, Toys "R" Us met with a great deal of hostile publicity from Japanese toy makers and retailers. Not surprisingly, the American retailer was seen as a real competitive threat to the established toy industry. Each of the new stores scheduled to open until the end of the century is expected to generate sales of at least $1.5 million in its first year. This translates into annual sales of $1.5 billion by the year 2000, roughly half of which would be from toys made outside Japan. The typical small Japanese toy store stocks between 1,000 and 2,000 different items, while Toys "R" Us will start out with about 8,000 items, rising to 15,000 over time. If it can offer toys for 10 to 15 percent less than competitors, as it has done in other world markets, then the company will have a huge impact on Japanese toy retailing.

Thus far, the company is still meeting obstacles to its price-cutting strategy. The required shift in the balance of power between retailer and manufacturer has been difficult for Toys "R" Us to replicate in Japan. The company has managed to sign contracts with 50 Japanese toy manufacturers but as yet has not been able to persuade many other Japanese manufacturers to sell to it directly, cutting out the layers of distributors that make prices so high in Japan. Many Japanese toy companies are tempted to do such deals, but they remain nervous about upsetting their old customers among distributors and other retailers. Nintendo, the world's largest video game maker, has agreed to sell directly to Toys "R" Us (the retailer is an important major client for Nintendo in the U.S. market) but at prices that will not offend other long-term Japanese retailers. Bandai, Japan's leading toy maker, is absorbing three levels of its own wholesale affiliates in a bid to reduce its own distribution costs so it can retain margins on toys it will eventually sell to the American retailer. In addition to the problems in establishing low-cost, direct-supply relationships with local suppliers, the high price of real estate in Japan and the high distribution costs prohibits the price discounting strategy beyond 15 percent . Nonetheless, the company remains optimistic about their expansion plans in Japan. Future plans involve new sites with mini-malls surrounded by huge car parks along main roads in Japan. The malls will contain an outlet of Blockbuster Entertainment (the U.S. video rental chain) as well as a McDonald's restaurant and a Toys "R" Us store.[16]

THE DEVELOPMENT OF GLOBAL DISTRIBUTION

While the issues of channel efficiency, channel length, power, and channel cooperation and conflict have already been discussed earlier in the chapter, the story of the attempt by Toys "R" Us to enter the Japanese market illustrates that these are issues in the global distribution context as well. More generally, the example points out the tremendous commitment of time, money, and managerial energy that typifies the development of global distribution systems.

At the level of channel development and strategy, only a small number of companies have the kind of resources, supplier relations, store formats, and managerial expertise that allow them to be successful globally. Sears and the United Kingdom's Marks & Spencer are successful international department stores, although their global operations are relatively close to home. Sears operates in Canada and Mexico and Marks & Spencer on the European continent. Specialty retailers such as Toys "R" Us, Timberland, and Sweden's IKEA have been more successful in developing niches throughout the world, and fast-food chains with successful formats have also been leaders in global retailing. Retail outlets with a highly successful and standardized formula that are expanded via a franchising strategy have done very well in global distribution. Given all the joint ventures, investment, and licensing arrangements that were continually being announced in the press during the early 1990s, specialty stores with successful retail strategies seem to have a particularly bright future in the emerging markets of Eastern Europe.[17]

In the past 15 years, joint ventures, mergers, and acquisitions have increased dramatically as approaches to global market development and as means of expanding channels to gain access to markets. Often, these ventures are related to the company's core business focus. As an example, when France's Perrier Holding purchased the American company Arrowhead, they gained not only a new product to complement their existing line of bottled waters, but they also gained Arrowhead's vast fleet of trucks and access to Arrowhead's established distribution channels in the U.S. market. The joint venture of Coca-Cola and Nestle is another arrangement with market access as one of the key components. Coca-Cola gains the product expertise and brand awareness that Nestle has developed over the years and the Swiss giant gains Coca-Colas' worldwide distribution network, which is the overwhelming leader in the global distribution of beverages.

As a general rule, companies tend to develop a global distribution system that reflects their domestic strategy, and in many cases this makes the most sense. Manufacturers of luxury items such as *Rolex* watches desire control over their products' positioning in the luxury market and seek out selective and exclusive distributors to maintain their image on a consistent basis worldwide. Likewise, business products and services are often sold through professional sales staffs throughout the world since specialized knowledge and service may be requirements which remain constant across markets.

Given the cost and effort of establishing channels in any market, companies need to have a well-conceived and articulated global distribution strategy. In particular, small and medium-sized companies tend to be overwhelmed by the abstraction and complexity of global distribution issues. This often leads to a policy of following the strategy used in the domestic market, or even worse,

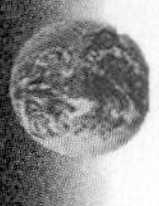

Coca-Cola is the leader in global distribution of beverages. Here, Coke products are being delivered in Guangdong, China.

no policy at all. Developing a distribution policy for global marketing and making the decision to invest in channels or to select independent channel partners depends on the company's resources and objectives and ultimately requires an understanding of what is appropriate in terms of meeting the needs of the company's target markets. This is exactly the type of situation that Coca-Cola and PepsiCo find themselves in with respect to gaining a foothold in China. Currently, approximately 2,800 local soft-drink bottlers are located in China and cover 75 percent of the market. Many of these bottlers are small, inefficient state-owned operations, and of these, some are operating in remote areas where they have a virtual monopoly. China's high transportation and distribution costs mean that plants need to be situated close to their markets. Otherwise, in spite of the country's increasing wealth, a *Coke* or *Pepsi* risks being priced as a luxury. Rather than striking out on their own, both Coca-Cola and PepsiCo intend to develop distribution by taking the politically correct route and expanding through joint ventures with these local bottlers. Currently, Chinese consumption of soft drinks is still only 13 bottles per person per year, compared with 750 bottles per person per year in the United States. As the market expands, both companies calculate a return on investment of about 20 percent per year on their newly acquired and modernized plants.[18]

SELECTING CHANNEL MEMBERS FOR GLOBAL MARKETS

The fundamental criteria for selecting channel members holds for global markets as well: the chosen channel members should reach the target segment and be consistent with the image of the product. But, earlier sections of this chapter also discussed selection criteria for channel members that dealt with the managerial issues of cooperation and control. An understanding of these issues becomes even more critical in global distribution decisions because of the varying economic, social, cultural, and competitive environments that influence the nature of the channel relationship in different countries. Inherent in the process of developing a sound basis of cooperation and control in global channel relations are five dimensions: geographic, temporal, social, cultural, and technological distances.[19]

The **geographic distance** is the physical distance that separates two channel partners. Typically, the greater the distance between the two, the less opportunity for control and the greater the need for establishing an efficient system of communication. Telecommunications, fax, and global e-mail have done much in the past decade to shrink the geographic distance between parties and improve their ability to provide support to each other in their common distribution efforts.

Temporal distance is the length of time between the placement of an order and the actual delivery of the product or service. In practical terms, this distance is related to geographic distance, although the choice of transportation methods can obviously influence temporal distance. If quick and reliable delivery are part of the differentiating features of the company's product, then guidelines and norms can be established between producer and channel members regarding delivery times, especially for unusual situations such as out-of-stocks or special orders.

Social distance results from a lack of understanding of a business partner's operating methods. French construction workers and most of the local companies who supply this industry go on vacation during the month of August—*all of them.* Non-French manufacturers who supply this industry should not expect to use August as a month to make on-site visits, renew contracts, or ask for special processing of an order. In Spain, many wholesalers and retailers who sell specialized technical and medical books only send out billings to their clients on a quarterly basis. Consequently, it is not unusual to have accounts receivable that average over 120 to 180 days, a condition that upsets many of the publishing companies that supply them.

Cultural distance reflects differences in the values, norms, and ranges of acceptable behavior between the parties. The greater this distance, the greater the opportunity for misunderstanding and conflict instead of cooperation and control. For example, in order to reduce this distance, North American and Latin American partners may need to establish what kinds of delivery circumstances constitute an "urgent" situation and develop explicit norms of the acceptable speed of reaction time to a situation that is deemed urgent. In the Toys "R" Us example, the cultural value of loyalty is highly regarded among Japanese business partners, and the economic incentives offered by the toy retailer are seen as conflicting with this value.

Technological distance can be described in terms of the competitiveness, compatibility, and quality of product lines currently carried by potential intermediaries and includes differences in product experience and process technologies. This distance has largely to do with an assessment of the competencies of the channel member to market a manufacturer's product in the desired fashion. To continue with the technical and medical book example, consider that booksellers of these highly specialized books often must do their own mailings to professionals and actively promote the books at trade shows and conventions. Personal selling to universities and research institutions, which are often under budgetary constraints and make limited purchases, requires specialized knowledge of the market. As a result, these booksellers often carry the books in their own inventories for many months to try to accommodate these institutions. All of these additional functions plus the added financial risk for carrying stock for extended periods of time require careful analysis and selection for both the publisher and bookseller.

Every year during the second weekend in October the French Wine Growers Association brings the year's Nouveau Beaujolais to market. The wine arrives with great fanfare in supermarkets, wine boutiques, liquor stores, and restaurants throughout the world on exactly the same day. This creates a great deal of publicity. The fanfare along with paid promotions for the wine result in the year's entire stock typically being sold out within three months of introduction. All this activity requires great planning and logistical effort. Careful selection of intermediaries throughout the world who are both interested and capable of providing an intense amount of attention to the handling, promotion, and selling of the wine within a short time period are critical to the product's introduction and short life cycle.

USING EXPORT MANAGEMENT COMPANIES

Large multinationals are most likely to have an investment approach that integrates global distribution activities into their own business portfolio, although they may also use independent agents to reach their global markets. Investing in the development of their own global channels is beyond the resources and expertise of most small and middle-sized companies. For these firms, selecting a channel member for global distribution most often means choosing an independent company, such as an **export management company** (EMC). Because of the critical importance of the EMC to so many firms, we will discuss this global distribution resource separately.

There are over 1,200 EMCs in the United States, most of them concentrated in cities with major ports. EMCs tend to carry a number of related but noncompetitive product lines. They typically handle the entire export function for a manufacturer, and in all their contacts with overseas clients they operate under the manufacturer's name, using the company's stationery and promotional materials. EMCs see the exporters as their clients and not as employers. They receive compensation in the form of commission on goods sold. They typically do not take title or possession of goods, although many provide financial services to their clients. Benefits provided by EMCs to their clients include these activities:

- *Credit Assistance.* EMCs often do their own financing, paying manufacturers in dollars before the export order leaves the United States and thus relieving the client of foreign exchange risk.
- *Licensing.* When local competition, import barriers, or transportation charges make the effective distribution of the exporters' products impractical or impossible, the EMC can help arrange for local production via joint ventures or via a royalty license arrangement. Because of their knowledge of the market through continuing activities in it, the EMC can advise their client if this is a feasible approach.

Export Management Companies (EMC) consolidate shipments from several clients and lower shipping costs for each client.

- *Shipping Expenses.* By consolidating shipments from several clients to one overseas destination and shipping under one bill of lading, the EMC can provide savings to all their clients.
- *Demonstrations.* EMCs arrange overseas demonstrations and technical support training to foreign users or foreign sales representatives; this can be done either by the EMC or the manufacturer's technical staff.
- *Specialization.* Because the EMC specializes in related but noncompetitive product lines, it helps the sales of each individual line.

To explain how a typical EMC provides the needed global distribution services, suppose that an EMC handles electrical components and small machinery for construction. An overseas contractor asks for a price quote on compressors but also needs other equipment for field operations. The EMC is in a position to offer related product and price information from its various clients for the project benefiting all concerned, including the overseas customer who has the opportunity to deal with a single source of supply.

THE CHALLENGE AND IMPACT OF GLOBAL DISTRIBUTION

Companies can either choose to develop their own channels as part of their global investment and marketing objectives, they can choose to work with independent channel specialists who distribute and represent their goods and services globally, or they can choose some combination of both approaches. Whatever the approach, the global marketing manager has the challenge and responsibility of integrating the global distribution system into the firm's marketing mix and managing the relationships within the distribution systems of different countries and market conditions.

Very few goods and services are sold in the world today as undifferentiated commodities. This only serves to increase the importance of selecting appropriate channel members to distribute and represent a company's products to end users. For small and medium-sized companies, the efficient delivery and effective representation by channel members provides the key, and often, only, opportunity that the company has to deliver satisfaction to its users and to establish a longer term relationship. For multinational corporations such as Toys "R" Us, PepsiCo, and Coca-Cola with global strategies and marketing plans, decisions relating to channel investment and the global management of channel members' activities are strategic issues and need to be integrated into the company's overall objectives. In all cases, global distribution is a critical aspect in successful international marketing. As the world continues to get smaller and as global markets continue to open up and become more competitive, the utilities created by efficient distribution and effective representation will become even more important as a competitive tool for delivering satisfaction to global markets.

Key Terms and Concepts

Channel of distribution
Time utility
Place utility
Possession utility
Efficiency
Economies of scale
Specialization
Functions of exchange
Functions of physical supply
Facilitating functions
Retailers
Wholesalers and distributors
Agents
Brokers
Channels for consumer goods
Channels for business goods
Multiple channel designs
Integrated channel system
Vertical marketing system
Corporate-owned vertical marketing system
Forward vertical integration
Backward vertical integration
Contractual vertical marketing system
Wholesale-sponsored voluntary chain
Retail-sponsored cooperative
Franchise organization
Administrative vertical marketing systems
Horizontal marketing systems
Channel length
Intensive distribution
Selective distribution
Exclusive distribution
Choosing intermediaries
Pull promotion strategy
Push promotion strategy
Cooperation and conflict in the channel
Power in the channel
Development of global distribution
Geographic distance
Temporal distance
Social distance
Cultural distance
Technological distance
Export management company (EMC)

Questions and Exercises

1. Think about your own recent shopping experiences. Give an example of how distribution either did or did not provide you with time, place, and possession utility. How much were these factors related to your personal satisfaction with the entire purchase decision and acquisition process?
2. If producers can gain greater control over the handling of their products and can eliminate wholesaler and/or retailer margins by dealing directly with end users, why don't more producers eliminate these intermediaries and sell direct?
3. From the example of Dell Computer provided in the chapter, identify the functions of exchange, functions of physical supply, and facilitating functions Dell engages in to deal directly with end users.

4. Why is a producer to end user (or buyer) channel more prevalent for business goods than for household consumer goods?
5. How does an administrative system evolve in distribution? What is the relationship between an administrative system and a pull promotional strategy?
6. Why is the channel for convenience goods typically a long channel of distribution?
7. Describe what is meant by vertical conflict in the channel. Identify a recent practice by producers that has created vertical channel conflict.
8. Over the last 15 years, what methods have firms used as a means of expanding distribution into global markets?
9. Identify and briefly describe the five factors that affect cooperation and control in global channel relations. How do your country's norms and values on these dimensions compare with its important trading partners around the world?
10. What is an EMC? How does this type of organization facilitate distribution in global markets?

REFERENCES

1. Jaclyn Fierman, "How Gallo Crushes the Competition," *Fortune* (September 1, 1986): 24–31.
2. This definition is adapted from Louis W. Stern and Adel I. El-Ansary, *Marketing Channels,* 3d. ed. (Englewood Cliffs, NJ: Prentice-Hall, 1988), 3. Stern and El-Ansary use this phraseology to define marketing channels. The definition applies equally well to channels of distribution and is preferred for the treatment presented here.
3. Bill Saporito, "Is Wal-Mart Unstoppable?" *Fortune* (May 6, 1991): 54.
4. Cynthia Crossen, "Putting Plastic on the Checkout Lanes: More Supermarkets Accept Credit Cards," *The Wall Street Journal* (February 5, 1990): B1.
5. Amy Dunkin, et al., "Power Retailers," *Business Week* (December 21, 1987): 88.
6. Dana Milbank, "As Stores Scrimp More and Order Less, Suppliers Take on Greater Risks, Costs," *The Wall Street Journal* (December 10, 1991): B1, B6.
7. Richard S. Teitelbaum, "Companies to Watch: Bed, Bath, and Beyond," *Fortune* (December 14, 1992): 101.
8. Kyle Pope, "Dealers Accuse Compaq of Jilting Them," *The Wall Street Journal* (April 7, 1993): B1.
9. Bert C. McCammon, Jr., "Perspectives for Distribution Programming," in *Vertical Marketing Systems,* ed. Louis P. Bucklin (Glenview, IL: Scott, Foresman, 1979), 43.
10. Donald N. Thompson, "Contractual Marketing Systems: An Overview," in *Contractual Marketing Systems* ed., Donald N. Thompson (Lexington, MA: D.C. Heath & Co., 1971), 5
11. Louis W. Stern and Adel I. El-Ansary, *Marketing Channels,* op. cit., 415.
12. Janean Huber, "A New Breed," *Entrepreneur* (April 1993): 100.
13. Gabriella Stern, "Multiple Varieties of Established Brands Muddle Consumers, Make Retailers Mad," *The Wall Street Journal* (January 24, 1992): B1, B9.
14. Karen Blumenthal, "Wal-Mart Set to Eliminate Reps, Brokers," *The Wall Street Journal* (December 2, 1991): B1, B14.
15. Dana Milbank, op. cit., B1.
16. Materials for the Toys "R" Us example were adapted from the following sources: Joseph Pereira, "Toys "R" Us to Buy Stock for $1 Billion" *The Wall Street Journal* (January 12, 1994): A3, A5. Robert Neff, "Guess Who's Selling Barbies in Japan Now?" *International Business Week* (December 9, 1991): 85–86; "Toy Joy," *The Economist* (January 4, 1992): 56; "Japan's Next Retail Revolution," *The Economist* (December 21, 1991): 91–92. Paul Blustein, "Japan as Toyland: Urge to Pamper as Births Fall," *The Wall Street Journal Europe* (February 2, 1991).
17. For a comprehensive discussion of uses of existing channels by U.S. companies, see Erin Anderson and Annie T. Coughlan, "International Market Entry and Expansion vs. Independent or Integrated Channels of Distribution," *Journal of Marketing* (January 1987): 71–82.
18. "Chinese Fizz," *The Economist* (January 29, 1994): 65–66.
19. This discussion is adapted from D. Ford, "Buyer/Seller Relationships in International Industrial Markets," *Industrial Marketing Management* (May 1984): 101–112.

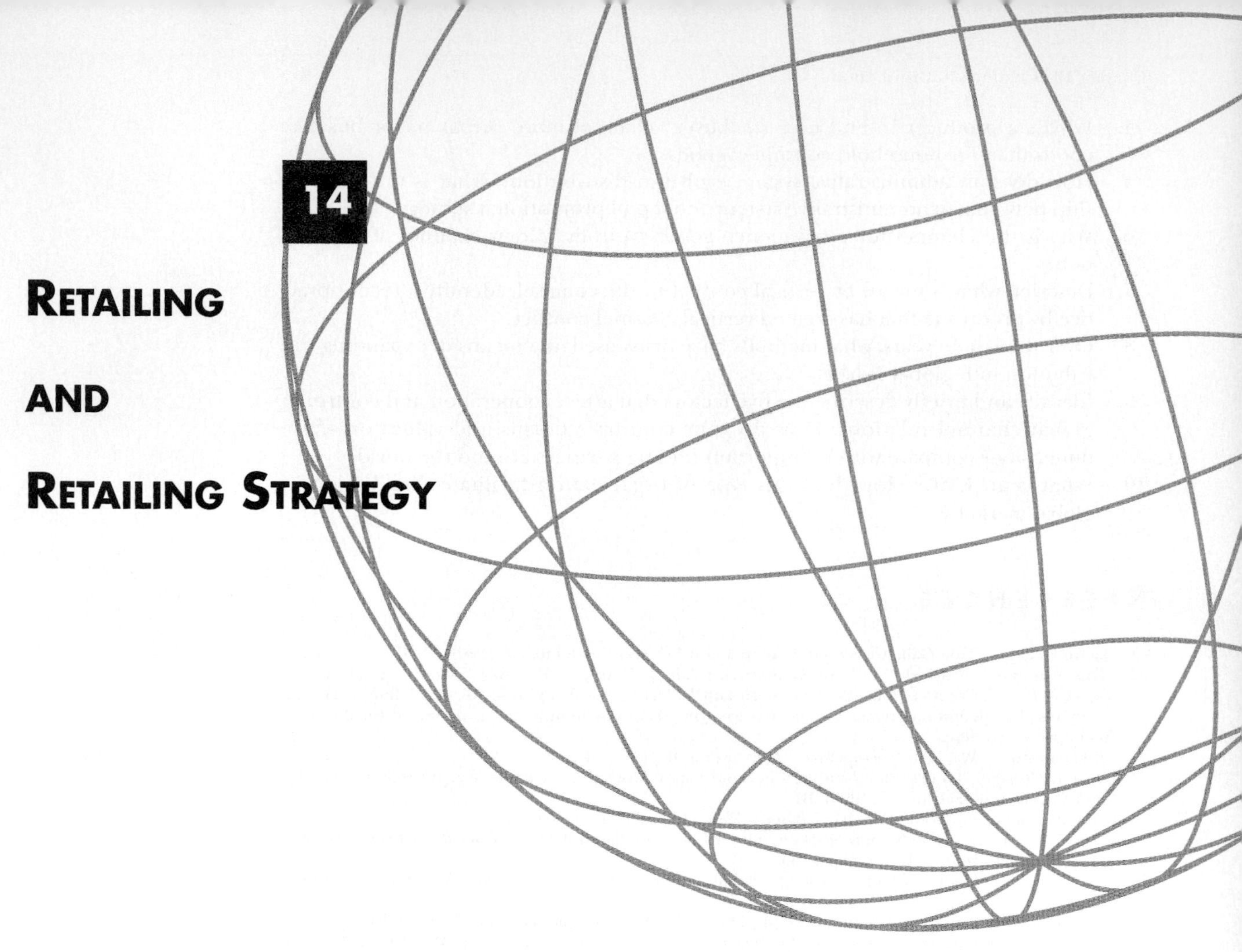

14

RETAILING AND RETAILING STRATEGY

AFTER STUDYING THIS CHAPTER, YOU WILL UNDERSTAND THAT:

1. Retailing brings the marketing concept to life at the very point where household consumers seek satisfaction.
2. Retailing strategy requires the development of a retailing mix not unlike the marketing mix prepared by producers.
3. Retailers establish competitive position based on the degree of merchandise specialization within the store and the added value they bring to the consumer's acquisition process.
4. The application of high technology and industry consolidation are two current trends that are having dramatic effects on the nature of retailing.
5. The level of economic development in different global markets is used to predict the degree of retail concentration likely to be found in those markets.

The proud names of retailing—Bonwit Teller, Bloomingdale's, Jordan Marsh, Macy's—have lost market share to the new power retailers—Home Depot, The Gap, Toys "R" Us, Dillard Department Stores, Nordstrom's, and the most powerful of all, Wal-Mart, now dominate retailing in the United States. Much of the explanation for the emergence of these new and powerful retailers lies with the fact that the leaders of these organizations have responded quickly and accurately to the new environment for retailing. Consumers have demanded more and better products and services at lower prices. The new leaders of retailing have created corporate cultures where motivated employees strive to serve customer needs at every opportunity. Identifying and serving customer needs at the retail level is the most visible sign of the marketing concept at work.

No corporate culture is more dedicated to the marketing concept than Wal-Mart, whose founder and leader, Sam Walton, before his death in 1992, expressed it to his employees in stunning simplicity: "Be an agent for consumers, find out what they want and sell it to them for the lowest possible price."[1] Sam Walton's down-home Arkansas version of the marketing concept has paid off. In 1991, Wal-Mart sales passed both Kmart and Sears, established leaders in American retailing, to claim the crown of retailing. In the relatively short span of 30 years, Wal-Mart has grown from a single dry-goods store to over 2,000 stores, over $65 billion in annual sales, and profits approaching $3.5 billion per year. And Sam Walton's vision was to continue that torrid pace. By the year 2000, he predicted his Wal-Mart chain would reach sales of $125 billion! Based on the most recent numbers, Sam Walton's Wal-Mart is actually ahead of that rigorous schedule he set in 1991.

Wal-Mart is one of the new "power retailers" that now dominate retailing in the United States.

The Role and Importance of Retailing

Wal-Mart and other power retailers have stunned their competitors by using creative and aggressive retailing strategies. The *role of retailing* is to fulfill the distribution requirements of manufacturers to provide goods to household consumers. But retailing is much more than simply physically moving products from the manufacturer to the household end user and fulfilling manufacturers' needs for distribution. An important aspect of the role of retailing is to follow through with a firm's plans regarding the marketing concept and its premise of providing customer satisfaction. As Chapter 13 pointed out, the retail level of the distribution system is uniquely suited to satisfy customers. J. C. Penney, the founder of the department store chain that bears his name, was fond of reflecting on what he called the golden three feet. That final space between the customer and the salesperson or the customer and the self-service display where the production, pricing, promotion, and distribution of goods meet their test. No matter how much satisfaction the producer of a consumer good builds into the product or how well that value is communicated through advertising to potential buyers, it is the retailer who either consummates or obstructs the sale. The fundamental **role of retailing** then is the manifestation of the marketing concept at the very point in time when the household consumer is about to make a purchase.

The **importance of retailing** can be measured at several levels: within the economic system, within business operations, and at the consumer level. At the broad economic system level, retailing is tremendously important to the economy of the United States. In 1992, nearly 2.5 million retail establishments generated $1.96 *trillion* in sales.[2] The massive expansion of the U.S. economy during the 1980s was fueled primarily by consumer expenditures at retail establishments. An appreciation of the size and importance of large retailing operations in the United States can be gained from Table 14-1, which displays the sales, profits, and number of employees for the ten largest retailers. Note that discount stores (Kmart and Wal-Mart), department stores (JCPenney and May Department Stores), and grocery retailers (Kroger and Safeway) dominate the list. The data in Table 14-1 reveal the enormous importance and power of the ten largest retailers in the United States. Together, these organizations alone generated $274 billion in sales or about 14 percent of the total retail sales annually in the United States. Further, their combined number of employees represents nearly a quarter of a billion jobs to the U. S. economy.

At the business operations level, the retailing network provides manufacturers with a critically important direct link to household consumers. The specialized distribution functions provided by retailers allow manufacturers to reach consumers with products in a highly efficient way. Retailers specialize in creating product and service assortments, they bulk-break large quantities into smaller quantities for consumer purchase, and they efficiently handle transactions with consumers. Furthermore, retail store personnel are specifically trained to serve household customers. Manufacturers could not perform these specialized retail distribution functions with the same efficiency. The result of these retailer activities is that the overall cost of distribution is reduced.

Retailer	Sales (in millions)	Percentage Change from 1992	Profits (in millions)	Profits as Percentage of Sales	Employees
Wal-Mart	$67,344.6	21.4%	$2,333.3	3.5%	520,000
Sears	54,873.4	-7.2%	2,374.4	4.3%	308,000
Kmart	34,156.0	-9.5%	-974.0	0%	344,000
Kroger	22,384.3	1.1%	-12.2	0%	190,000
JCPenney	19,578.0	2.6%	940.0	4.8%	192,097
Dayton Hudson	19,233.0	7.3%	375.0	1.9%	174,000
American Stores	18,763.4	-1.5%	247.1	1.3%	127,000
Safeway	15,214.5	.4%	123.3	0.8%	105,900
Albertson's	11,283.7	10.9%	339.7	3.0%	75,000
May Stores	11,020	-1.3%	711	6.4%	Department 113,000

Source: "Fortune's Service 500" *Fortune* (May 30, 1994): 214. Used with permission, *Fortune*, © 1994 Time, Inc. All rights reserved.

TABLE 14-1
Ten Largest Retailers in the United States Ranked by Total Sales for 1993

Finally, retailing is of paramount importance to consumers themselves. A greater variety of goods and services is available due to the activities performed at the retail system. If every manufacturer had to develop and maintain retail distribution facilities, far fewer products and far fewer retail locations would exist. The efficiency of the retail system, achieved through economies of scale and specialization, results in lower costs of operations than alternative forms of distribution. These lower costs are often passed on to consumers in the form of lower prices as retailers try to compete with one another. Finally, the evolution of the retail system has provided consumers with more precise satisfaction of their desires. As retailers have learned how to position themselves to provide greater satisfaction than their competitors, household buyers have become the beneficiaries of more and better products and services.

THE DYNAMIC NATURE OF RETAILING

Retailing in the United States is continuously adapting to changes in culture, economics, technology, and competition. These forces in turn shape the nature of retailing. The institutions and methods of retailing must be as dynamic as these influences from the external environment in order to meet ever-changing consumer expectations. Over time, some forms of retailing pass by the wayside: the variety store (e.g., W. T. Grant) is an example of a form of retailing institution that has disappeared from the American scene. Numerous theories of retail evolution and change have been proposed to explain and predict change in retailing institutions. We will consider three of the most viable theories in order to gain a better appreciation for the dynamic nature of retailing. These theories are the wheel of retailing, the retail accordion, and the retail life cycle.

THE WHEEL OF RETAILING

Professor Malcolm McNair, a retailing authority in the 1950s, proposed an explanation for the cyclical evolution of retail institutions that he likened to a wheel. The wheel of retailing theory suggests that new retail competitors always enter a market with low prices made possible by low operating costs. These low operating costs are made possible by low-status physical facilities and few services. As the new low-cost retailer prospers, competitors enter the market. In an effort to achieve a competitive advantage, services are added, prices rise, and the wheel "turns" leaving room at the bottom for new, low-cost retailers to enter the market.[3] This process continues over time as retailers strive to compete and achieve a competitive position in the market.

While the wheel of retailing theory is inadequate for explaining all aspects of evolution and change in retailing—such as catalog retailing and the development of the shopping mall—it does provide explanation for competitive dynamics at the low-end of the competitive structure. Validity for this theory can be seen in the emergence of retailers like Home Depot, 50-Off Stores, and Filene's Basement. As Kmart and Wal-Mart continue to enhance their operations with greater services and higher-quality merchandise, this has left an opening at the bottom end of the retailing market open for new competitors who can attract customers with lower prices. So, even though the wheel of retailing theory cannot explain all aspects of change, it provides useful insights for some aspects of retailing evolution.

THE RETAIL ACCORDION

The accordion theory of retail change highlights the tendency for retail institutions to start out as very general in their merchandise assortment and then gradually to become more specific only to return to greater generality. If a long-term view of retailing in the United States is taken, this accordion effect of general to specific to general merchandising can be witnessed. The general store of the early twentieth century carried a wide range of merchandise to meet the needs of the average household. Everything from food products to hardware to clothing was carried by these local merchants. As time passed and competitive pressures for differentiation increased, specialty stores emerged that carried a wide assortment of products within each of those lines—the clothing store, hardware store, and grocery store.

In modern times, we have become accustomed to the highly specialized retail outlet that caters to very specific customer needs. However, a tendency is emerging among American retail institutions to move back to the more general product collection. The desire for convenience and one-stop shopping has created superstores that carry appliances, clothing, and food products. Wal-Mart has plans for nearly 100 Wal-Mart Supercenters. These stores will carry the current Wal-Mart collection of goods plus a supermarket, complete deli, fresh bakery, portrait studio, dry cleaners, optical shop, and hair salon.

Perhaps the contemporary version of the retail accordion is the factory outlet mall. While this is not a single store as the original concept would suggest, factory outlet malls can have up to 60 specialty stores that, while each is very specific in its merchandise line, together they constitute a very general collection for consumer choice.

THE RETAIL LIFE CYCLE

The important distinction between the retail life cycle theory and the two preceding theories of retail change is that the retail life cycle theory attempts to identify the speed with which change occurs. This theory suggests that the pace of innovation in retailing accelerates over time within any particular retail form. The following are descriptions of the stages of the retail life cycle:[4]

- *Innovation Stage.* A radical departure occurs from the prevailing method of retail operations in the market. The innovation may center on cost, methods of operation, product assortment, or another innovation that attracts customers.
- *Accelerated Development.* This stage is characterized by growth in both sales and profits of the new form of retailing. The stage is also characterized by geographic expansion for the innovator of the format and the appearance of competitors that imitate the method.
- *Maturity.* This is the most significant stage in the life cycle in that competition is the most intense. The prevalence of competition makes this stage the most managerially challenging. Profits begin to decline, industry-wide, in the maturity stage.
- *Decline.* This stage can often be avoided or delayed by repositioning and adaptation on the part of competitors. But, an institutional form may, in fact, succumb to cultural, technological, or competitive changes and disappear from the market. Such may be the case with the "old style" department store characterized by Sears until the late 1980s. Sears has now adapted to market trends and demands with new merchandise and methods of operations.

These theories of retail change and evolution are valuable to managers as they attempt to predict and adapt to demands in the market. While no single theory exists to explain completely the dynamic nature of retailing, it is useful to rely on concepts such as these to help manage a firm's retail distribution decision making in rapidly changing markets.

CLASSIFICATION OF RETAILERS

From the need to understand and predict change in retailing, we will turn our attention to a description of the institutions that characterize the retailing environment.* To fully appreciate the strategic opportunities of retailing, a broad classification of retailers is useful. Classifying retail-

*The discussion of retailing and retailing strategies is restricted to goods and does not include services such as fast-food restaurants, health-care operations, or personal services. There are good reasons why services are discussed separately in the context of retailing. Services marketing is a unique area that requires significant adaptation of basic principles. Additionally, service "products" require a different form of retail distribution. For these reasons, services and services marketing are treated as a complete topic in Chapter 18.

ers allows for a view of retailing that highlights its diverse nature. Further, by concentrating on different aspects of the retailing process, we can begin to appreciate the strategic positioning that retailers achieve. Two different classification schemes are used to provide insights into the retailing system: durable goods versus nondurable goods and type of store.

DURABLE GOODS AND NONDURABLE GOODS

An advantage of classifying retailers based on whether they sell durable or nondurable goods is that this method of classification is used by the U.S. Department of Commerce. The Department of Commerce annually publishes comprehensive information on retail sales based on this classification method. Some of the information is outlined in Figure 14-1. Several important pieces of information are contained in Figure 14-1. One is the percentage of total retail sales generated by all retail outlets within the broad durable and nondurable goods category. While **durable goods** such as furniture, appliances, and automobiles are higher-priced items, note that they account for only 35.9 percent of all retail sales. **Nondurable goods** such as clothing and food constitute a much larger percentage of consumer expenditures at 64.1 percent of all retail sales. Another useful aspect of this classification approach is that the Department of Commerce breaks the durable and nondurable goods classification into specific store types using SIC codes (these are also indicated in Figure 14-1). For example, SIC code 53, general merchandise group stores, accounted for 12.6 percent of all retail sales in 1992. These are department stores, variety stores, and miscellaneous general merchandise stores like Dillard Department Stores and Woolworths. A final bit of information that can be gleaned from the Department of Commerce classification is the retail dollar sales volume generated by stores in each category. This is simply a matter of taking total retail sales for a year, in 1992 the total was approximately $1.962 trillion, and multiplying the percentage in a category to that total. As an example, apparel and accessory stores, SIC 56, accounted for 10.3 percent of all retail sales in 1992 or approximately $105 billion.

The only drawback of the durable and nondurable goods classification is that some stores are difficult to classify. Sears, for example, sells merchandise in both classes of goods and in several SIC codes within each classification. The durable and nondurable classification is valuable, however, for the broad perspective on retailing it provides. Inspection of these figures allows analysts to determine general trends in retail shopping behavior. However, it is valuable to proceed to a more specific breakdown of retail operators by using a more detailed classification scheme based on type of store. This classification further emphasizes the strategic positioning retailers try to achieve in the market.

TYPE OF STORE

From a marketing strategy perspective, it is more informative to establish a classification of retailers by type of store. The type of store classification is based on differences in merchandise offered, pricing strategy, and distribution methods. A useful classification of retailers by type of store includes six differ-

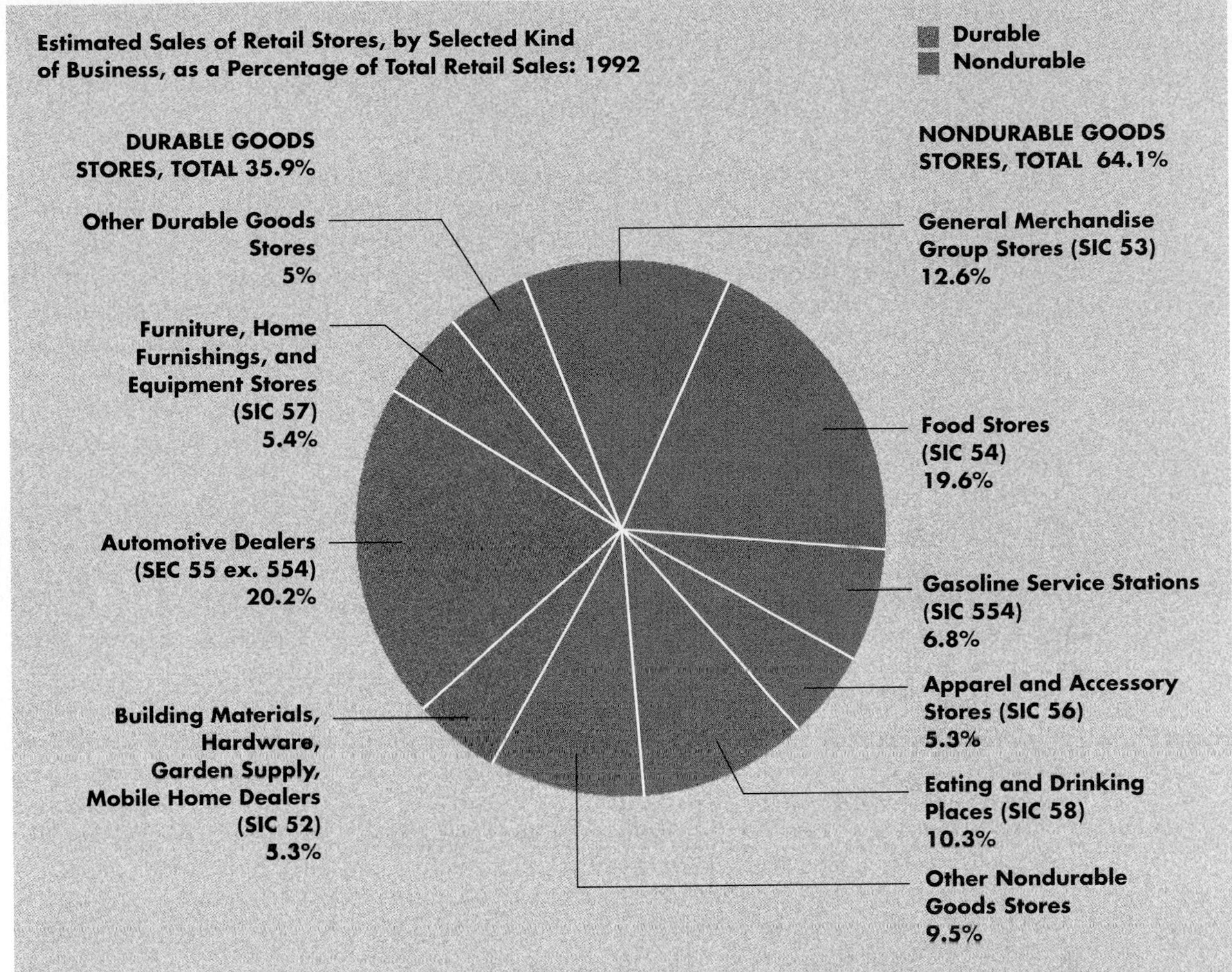

Source: U.S. Department of Commerce, Bureau of Census, *Current Business Reports: Monthly Retail Trade* (Washington, D.C.: U.S. Government Printing Office, January 1993): 4.

FIGURE 14-1
Classification of Retailers by Durable versus Nondurable Goods Proportion of Retail Trade 1992

ent categories: department stores, discount stores, supermarkets, specialty shops, convenience stores, and nonstore retailers.

Department Stores

The department store form of retailing began in Europe. By the mid-1880s, Wanamakers in Philadelphia, ZCMI in Salt Lake City, and Macy's in New York City were established in the United States. Today, department stores still account for nearly 10 percent of all retail sales. Department stores in the United States originally placed their operations in the center of major cities. Most have abandoned the downtown location, with the exception of downtown shopping malls, and have opted for suburban locations.

The **department store** type of retail operation is characterized by its wide offering of merchandise divided into departments throughout the store. They have a clientele that is predominantly made up of women. Department stores are distinguished from other types of retail stores by offering a considerable number of services including their own credit cards, layaway plans, clothing alterations, delivery, and ample parking. Department stores excel in providing consumers with expert sales help and a comprehensive assortment of goods, especially in the clothing category. In the final assessment, department stores are most potent at offering consumers satisfaction in the form of possession utility.

The department store type of operation has limitations as well. It is difficult for a large store to convey an atmosphere of warmth and personality found in smaller specialty shops. By definition, department stores assemble a collection of goods for broad target markets. As such, a department store may be viewed as too eclectic by shoppers seeking specific goods. And, active management of a department store is far removed from the point of sale. Motivating sales personnel is difficult for department store management without direct and frequent contact. A related issue is that department stores often employ low-paid, part-time clerks who are not particularly committed to the organization and typically do not provide excellent service.

Department stores are also plagued by high operating costs. Unless the organization can maintain high profit margins, the profitability and ultimately the survival of the firm are threatened. This is the circumstance currently facing Sears. Amid the retailing giant's attempts to switch to a brand-oriented, low-price strategy, administrative costs are gobbling up 32 cents of every sales dollar—nearly double the overhead rate of Wal-Mart Stores.

Despite the difficulties facing the traditional department store type of retailer, some are thriving. Primary among this group is Nordstrom's. Nordstrom's concentrates its product assortment on high-end men's, women's, and children's clothing. It rigorously trains store personnel to provide customer service at every opportunity. The stores are modern and stylish, and in-store displays are carefully designed to be attractive and appealing. The results are record sales and profit performance year after year. Nordstrom's maintains a net profit margin of 3.9 percent of sales despite providing expensive and extensive personal service to its customers.[5]

Discount Stores

Price has traditionally been used by retailers as a competitive strategy. The label "discount house" was attached to the type of retail operation that emerged immediately after World War II. The original discount houses advertised and sold brand name appliances at discounts as great as 40 percent below other outlets. The discount houses gradually added to their lines and eventually offered almost everything found in department stores. This class of retailer competed in the market with a low-status image and maintained low margins to offer consumers reduced prices.

Today, there are really three types of discount stores: general merchandise discount stores, so-called category killers, and warehouse clubs. The **general merchandise discount store** is defined as an outlet with over 10,000 square feet of selling space, carries both durable and nondurable goods, and maintains a cost and pricing structure lower than department stores. Prominent national competitors in the general merchandise discount store category are Kmart, Target Stores, and Wal-Mart. Sears has recently tried to move away from its traditional department store operation and reposition itself as a general merchandise discount store. Regional discounters of this type include Caldor, Fred Meyer, and Meijers Thrifty Acres.

General merchandise discount stores do not sell all their merchandise at prices significantly below department store prices. They often have price leaders but also have products with profit margins that are comparable to department stores. More demanding and market-wise consumers have forced these discounters to carry more brand names as opposed to the "off-brand" merchandise carried by the original discount houses. Further, the distinction between traditional department stores and general merchandise discount stores has become less defined in recent years. Large national discounters now offer many of the services, like credit and delivery, that the large department stores offer. The primary differences between these two classes of retailers lie with the self-service nature and minimal decor of discount stores as opposed to the stylish interior of the department store.

A comparison of profit margins between department stores and general merchandise discount stores for the years 1982 and 1988 appears in Table 14-2. The profit margins in 1992 for some prominent department and general merchandise discount stores also appear in Table 14-2. These data reveal the move by discounters to provide more services. Note that profit margins for the discounters have eroded dramatically over the ten-year period because of fierce competition and value-oriented consumers. Also note the counter trend in profits that has allowed department stores to increase their margins over time despite providing a wide range of services. Overall sales by discounters in the general merchandise category have continued to grow significantly during the 1990s, and by 1993 they accounted for 42 percent of all general merchandise sales in the United States.[6]

Stores in the second category of discount stores have been dubbed category killers. The category killer retail outlet gets its name from the marketing strategy employed. **Category killer** stores carry a very deep assortment of merchandise in one or only a few product categories at such low prices that they "kill" the competition with such complete product category coverage. An example of this type of store is Cohoes Specialty Stores. Cohoes Specialty

TABLE 14-2
Comparison of Profit Margins for Department Stores and General Merchandise Discount Stores

	Profit Margin as a Percentage of Sales		
	1982	1988	1992
Department Stores	3.21%	3.46%	
JCPenney			4.1%
May Department Stores			5.4%
Dillard Department Stores			4.8%
General Merchandise Discount Stores	4.05%	3.07%	
Wal-Mart			3.6%
Kmart			2.5%
Fred Meyer			2.1%

Sources: *Standard & Poor's Industry Surveys*, July 1983 for the 1982 data, R-125 and R-135; July 1991 for the 1988 data, R-98 and R-99. Information for individual stores 1992 data taken from "Fortune's Service 500," *Fortune* (May 31, 1993): 220–221.

Stores attracts high-income customers by stocking large inventories of high-quality name brand and even designer-label clothing: Calvin Klein shirts and slacks, Ralph Lauren suits, and even $400 per pair Italian shoes. Cohoes' prices are a minimum of 20 percent lower with 30 percent more sales per square foot than standard stores.[7] Another example of a category killer is Toys "R" Us. Toys "R" Us invented the toy supermarket in the late 1950s. Toys "R" Us outlets carry huge inventories of literally thousands of different toys. The firm takes a smaller mark-up, 30 percent, as opposed to the toy industry standard of 50 percent and passes most of the difference on to the consumer. Toys "R" Us sales have increased 185 percent in a recent five-year period while toy retailing sales in general have increased only 37 percent. Category killer stores can be found in a broad range of product categories: the Fleet Foot athletic shoes; IKEA, home furnishings and housewares; Home Depot, do-it-yourself home improvement materials; Tower Records; BizMart, office supplies; and Sportsmart, general sporting goods. The reason these stores compete so effectively is that consumers have learned they will find what they want at a low price with a minimum of hassles. Category killer stores gain their market power by providing consumers with the satisfaction of time utility. Products are kept in large inventory ready for purchase and a single shopping trip will ensure finding the item desired.

The **warehouse club** store in many ways is a reinterpretation of the general merchandise discount store except that the warehouse store is characterized by stark decor and even fewer services than the general merchandise discount store. The warehouse club was originally distinguished from other discounters by charging a nominal club membership fee of $10 to $25 although most have dropped the fee. This form of retailing has grown considerably since its inception. Current estimates put the number of warehouse club stores at 600, with total revenues exceeding $33 billion.[8] Wal-Mart's entry, Sam's, leads all competitors with 256 warehouse outlets and $12.5 billion in sales. The outlets in this category of retailing truly maintain their warehouse appearance. Products are typically stacked 20 feet high on metal racks or displayed in shipping cartons. The floors are concrete and the walls are often cinder block. Few amenities are provided to customers in the average warehouse club, but the low prices and wide assortment of items attract customers.

Supermarkets

Supermarkets differ in operations and, consequently, no recognized precise definition for this category exists. It is safe to describe **supermarkets** as large stores whose main product line is food items and consumer packaged goods. The method of operation is largely self service.

An important aspect of the recent evolution of supermarkets is the practice of *mixed merchandising* (often referred to as scrambled merchandising), which became prevalent in the 1970s. Since typical grocery retailers were only realizing a gross margin of about 3 percent on food and packaged household items, they began to "mix" their merchandise collection with products traditionally not found in the supermarket. Originally, auto products, stationary, and garden supplies provided supermarket retailers with gross margins of 20 to 40 percent to boost overall margins. More recently, video rentals, camera supplies, and flower shops have been added to further increase margins. Beyond increasing profit margins, these new lines of merchandise serve to increase store traffic and provide consumers with one-stop-shopping convenience. But, mixed merchandising is not just happening in grocery stores. Department stores are carrying computers, convenience stores are selling auto products and toys, and general merchandise discounters are selling cosmetics.

Competition in the supermarket category is fierce. Leading supermarket chains have modified their product lines to meet changes in demographic, sociocultural, and economic trends. Recent product line modifications designed to respond to consumer preferences include selling hot and cold prepared foods, in-store bakeries and fish markets, bulk food bins, and expanded pharmacy services. Vons Supermarkets in California have a Japanese chef preparing sushi, produce sections that offer three times as many fruits and vegetables as the average supermarket, glass-lined display ovens showing oversize muffins cooking, and a wine shop featuring 1,500 different selections. Vons stocks each of its 135 neighborhood supermarkets with a custom array of products for its local patrons. Each of these specialty departments contributes to higher margins for Vons and attracts customers.

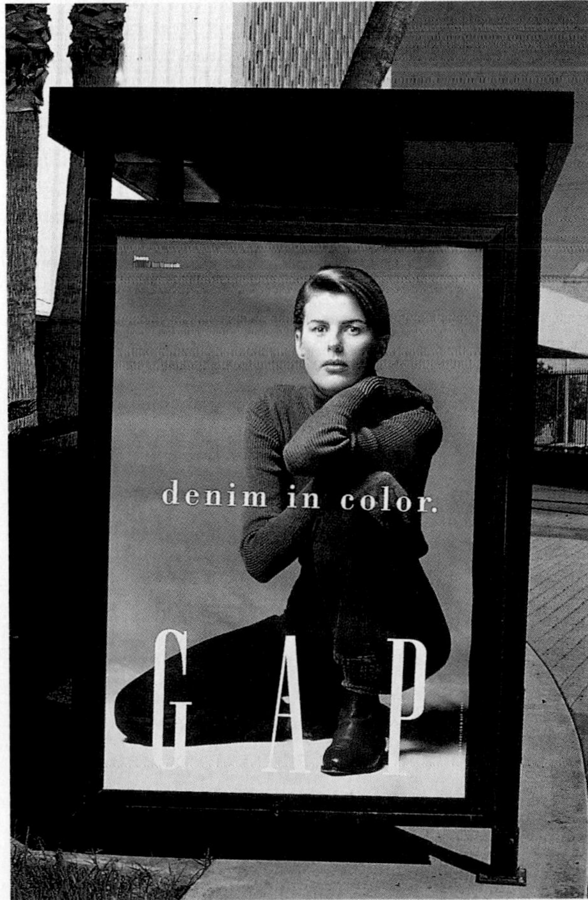

The GAP has emerged as one of the leading specialty shops in the retailing industry.

Specialty Shops

Florists, jewelers, bookstores, bakeries, meat markets, shoe stores, furniture stores, and men's and women's apparel stores are examples of specialty shops. **Specialty shops** carry a narrow but very deep assortment of goods in a particular product category. Specialty shops may carry precisely the same product collection as category killers but attract customers by offering service and style rather than reduced prices. (Note that specialty shops do not necessarily sell only specialty goods as such items were described in the consumer goods classification in Chapter 4.)

One of the most successful specialty shop chains of all time (although there have been some recent setbacks) is The Limited. Leslie Wexner, the founder and CEO of The Limited, has built a retailing empire around the concept of carefully segmenting the market and opening specialty shops to serve different segments. The Limited chain was originally conceived to serve the clothing needs of the growing number of women entering the work force in the 1970s. Wexner has since launched the Limited Express, Limited Too, Victoria's Secret, Lerner, Henri Bendel, Structure, and has acquired Abercrombie & Fitch. Each specialty chain targets a different, well-defined target segment of the market. Sales have nearly tripled from 1986 to 1993 to over $7 billion annually with profits still running at a stellar 6.6 percent of sales. Wexner offers an explanation for successful retailing in a compelling expression of the marketing concept: "The common thread among retailers who really are doing it right is that they realize the customer is the one calling the shots, not the other way around."[9]

Convenience Stores

Unless you've just arrived from another planet, you no doubt have had frequent contact with a convenience stores. Whether it's an early morning stop to get a cup of coffee on the way to class or a late-night craving for ice cream, convenience stores thrive on providing time and place utility to consumers. **Convenience stores** stock food items and frequently purchased household necessities and realize a competitive advantage based on location, easy movement through the store, and long hours of operation. They are typically small—about 1,500 to 3,000 square feet—compared to the average supermarket at 30,000 square feet.

During recent years, the gross operating profit of these stores was nearly 31 percent as compared to 19 percent for supermarkets. Consumers are, therefore, willing to pay about 12 percent for the time saving and convenience these outlets offer. Most convenience stores have entered into agreements with major gasoline refiners to provide customers with the added convenience of filling up while they grab a few items in the store.

Perhaps more than any other category of retailing, the convenience store is an illustration of identifying and taking advantage of an opportunity that arises when the competitive, cultural, and economic environments provide an opportunity. In the late 1960s, as long lines at supermarkets became tedious (competitive), consumers placed greater importance on time and convenience (cultural), and households became more affluent (economic), the convenience store emerged in the United States to accommodate the convergence of these influences. Now a multibillion dollar industry, the convenience store is a primary form of retailing in America.

Nonstore Retailing

It is somewhat of a misnomer to categorize nonstore retailing as a "type of store." **Nonstore retailing** includes all forms of direct retailing to household consumers that take place outside a retail store. However, the process of retailing to consumers from "stores without walls" adheres to the basic principles of effective retailing and therefore is considered here.

Most of the recent growth in nonstore retailing has come from telephone-order, mail-order, catalog, and direct-sales retailers. These forms of nonstore retailing realized 15 percent annual growth in sales during the 1980s.[10] Nonstore retailing also includes merchandise purchased by consumers through coin-operated vending machines and network (person-to-person) selling. In 1993, purchases by household consumers from all types of nonstore retailers approached $70 billion in the United States. Two types of nonstore retailing warrant detailed discussion: catalog shopping and in-home shopping.

Catalog shopping is the most important form of nonstore retailing. While overall growth in nonstore retailing has been significant, it is the catalog merchants who have realized the most spectacular rise in revenue generation. Catalog marketers are estimated to have achieved total sales of about $62 billion in 1993—a 12 percent increase over 1992.[11] L.L. Bean, Orvis, Land's End, C.O.M.B., and DAK are familiar names in the mail-order catalog market. Specialty retailers have recently adopted this method and are expanding the scope of catalog shopping to areas beyond the traditional apparel and electronics product groups. One of the most impressive retailers in this regard is MedCo Containment Services, which was acquired in 1993 by Merck, the pharmaceutical firm. Medco markets prescription drugs through the mail and has grown to a $1 billion company from revenues of $150 million in 1986. MedCo Containment concentrates on drugs that are taken for chronic ailments and are ordered regularly by mostly elderly consumers. Prescriptions can be filled at up to 40 percent below the cost of even discount pharmacies.

Catalog shopping is popular among consumers for a variety of reasons. First, the ease, convenience and leisurely pace of catalog shopping appeals to many consumers. Second, many nonstore retailers can sell the same merchandise found in traditional retail outlets at significantly lower prices due to lower overhead expenses and personnel costs. Finally, the catalog retailers have contributed to their own success by ensuring the satisfaction of customers with liberal return policies. There are drawbacks for the consumer, however. While time and place utility are high for catalog shopping, possession utility suffers. Typically, a catalog order will take five days to two weeks to arrive, although two-day express delivery is available at extra cost from most catalog merchants.

Some trends are emerging that may threaten the future of catalog shopping. First, as consumers become more environmentally aware and concerned, they ask to have their names removed from catalog mailing lists to save the enormous amount of paper used to print catalogs. Second, more and more states are attempting to implement legislation that would force catalog merchants to collect the appropriate state sales tax and forward these tax payments to state treasury coffers. Aside from raising the price of items by the percentage sales tax that would be charged, the cost of operations will rise as well to collect and then disburse the taxes. Finally, consumers are beginning to tire of having their names and addresses sold freely to catalog and direct-mail merchants. As more consumers request (or demand) that their names be removed from mailing lists, it will be more difficult for catalog merchants to effectively target households and then efficiently distribute their catalogs.

Aside from catalog shopping, **in-home shopping** through network sales, computer on-line services, and television shopping programs represents another major form of nonstore retailing. Tupperware, Avon, Mary Kay Cosmetics, and Amway are the premier network sales retailing organizations. Network retailers hold small gatherings or parties to present a line of health, beauty, or houseware items to friends and acquaintances. This form of retailing has the advantage of providing place utility to consumers. On the other hand, many consumers are now feeling like they don't have time to attend a gathering to order a product and would rather order by phone.

Television shopping programs reach out to armchair consumers for sales of over $2.5 billion annually. A study of these television shopping direct-response buyers indicates that they have more formal education and higher incomes than the average consumer.[12] Led by QVC network with 47 million subscribers and $1.07 billion in revenue and the Home Shopping Network with 60 million subscribers and $1.1 billion in revenue, this form of retailing is growing at 20 percent per year.[13] On-line computer shopping through subscription programs like Prodigy and America On-Line provide a new in-home shopping option for consumers. The success of such on-line systems remains to be seen.

All the types of retailing discussed in this section focus on one objective: to provide consumers with direct access to products. In that sense, the retail part of the distribution system serves manufacturers well. Let's turn our attention now to the way retailers themselves devise effective market and competitive strategies.

Retailing Strategy

The strategic planning in retailing is, in general, closely patterned after strategic planning for the marketing function. Retailers face the challenges of market segmentation and target marketing, developing a retailing mix, and establishing an effective competitive position. The distinguishing feature of strategic planning for retailing is that retail managers have a different perspective than marketing strategists at the manufacturer's level. The basis for this different perspective is that retailers occupy a position in the marketing process that is *within* the channel of distribution.This is very different from the manufacturer's position at the head of the channel. For example, a retailer is not responsible for stimulating demand for a particular brand (except during special promotions) but rather attempts to attract customers to the retail establishment. This does not mean that strategy planning and implementation are any less complex and challenging. Retailers must deal directly with the consumer at the point of purchase, which is one of the most formidable of all marketing tasks. Retailing strategy includes the following activities: identifying the target market, developing the retailing mix, and establishing a competitive position. These activities are depicted in Figure 14-2.

FIGURE 14-2
Retailing Strategy Decisions

IDENTIFYING THE TARGET MARKET

Much like their manufacturing counterparts, retailers engage in market segmentation analysis with the goal of identifying target markets. Retailers use the same approach to segmentation and target marketing as manufacturers. Demographic characteristics, geographic location, socioeconomic status, and life-style (psychographics), as described in Chapter 4, are common bases for identifying target markets in retailing. Pier 1, the home furnishings and accessories chain, has thrived recently by using a demographic targeting strategy that carefully tracks the fashion trends and preferences among shoppers between the ages of 35 and 50. Gottschalks often operates the only department store with brand name merchandise in small central California towns like Yuba City and Antioch, thus using a geographic basis for identifying target markets.[14] This retailer avoids the competitive climate of big cities like Los Angeles and San Francisco and opts instead to serve small city target markets.

Retailers like Gottschalks and Pier 1 follow the same painstaking, systematic processes that manufacturers do in making target market decisions. Target markets are evaluated on the basis of the nature of competition, consumer and market trends, and the firm's ability to compete effectively for consumer patronage. Secondary data sources are useful in providing composite profiles of retail shoppers. An example of this sort of broad description of retail target markets is shown in Table 14-3. Profiles like these are of general use in the strategic planning process for retailing and give a description of retail shoppers much like the VALS, whose typology divides Americans into life-style groups and was discussed in Chapter 4.

DEVELOPING THE RETAILING MIX

Retailers must create their own mix of operations. Just as a marketing mix is created for a brand, retail strategists must develop a **retailing mix** of physical facilities, merchandise, pricing, promotion, and service strategies. All of these factors will ultimately translate into the customer appeal for a retail operation and help establish the retailer's competitive position.

Physical Facilities

Decisions regarding the physical facilities focus on two different decisions: location and what are referred to as *atmospherics.* The location of a retail outlet

TABLE 14-3
Composite Profiles of Retail Shoppers

Agreeable Shoppers (22%)
Easy going consumers who are especially susceptible to advertising and are most likely to shop at discount stores.
- Lower-middle income
- 68 percent of this group are white
- More likely than average to enjoy TV, grocery shopping, and household work
- High brand loyalty in both the shopping and convenience goods categories

Practical Shoppers (21%)
Smart shoppers who research their purchases and look for the best "deal." Shop at stores that sell brand name clothing at discount prices.
- Mostly women
- Younger, better educated, middle income
- Consider remote control, video cameras, and CDs as "modern frills"
- 75 percent of this group consider the increased use of credit cards as a change for the worse
- Pay more attention to food labels
- Least brand loyal group

Trendy Shoppers (16%)
Impulse buyers who love to shop and stay up with the latest fads.
- Tend to shop at fashion boutiques
- Younger, unmarried, and politically liberal
- Low brand loyalty
- Fewer than 33 percent of shoppers in this group believe that America makes quality products or that American- made products satisfy consumers' tastes

Value Shoppers (13%)
Cost-conscious and traditional shoppers who tend to believe that the best products are those that have withstood the test of time. Often don't have the money to buy the very best.
- Shop at mid-priced department stores
- Middle income homemakers and retirees
- More likely to view shopping as a chore
- Care more about saving money than time and rarely buy on impulse

Top-of-the-Line Shoppers (10%)
These buyers place a premium on a brand's reputation for quality and believe they have the right to buy the very best.
- Shop at upscale department stores
- Oldest and highest median income group
- Believe foreign goods are better than American goods
- Less likely to enjoy browsing or window shopping
- Less inclined to want the latest consumer gadgets

Safe Shoppers (9%)
This group looks for familiar products that make them feel comfortable.
- Inclined to shop at well-known mass merchandise stores like Sears and Kmart.
- Most likely to be white and male
- Most likely to feel they have the same values as their parents
- Find shopping a chore
- Less confident than other groups in buying grocery products and pay little attention to food labels

Status Shoppers (5%)
Sometimes impractical in their buying practices.
- Fascinated with gadgets
- Buy designer-label products
- Youngest and most politically conservative group
- Second-highest median income group
- Most likely to own cordless phones, CD players, and answering machines
- Most likely to browse and buy on impulse

Source: Adapted from "Peter Hart's Showcase of Shoppers," *The Wall Street Journal* (August 19, 1989): B4. Based on research conducted by Peter D. Hart Research Associates. Reprinted by permission of *The Wall Street Journal*,

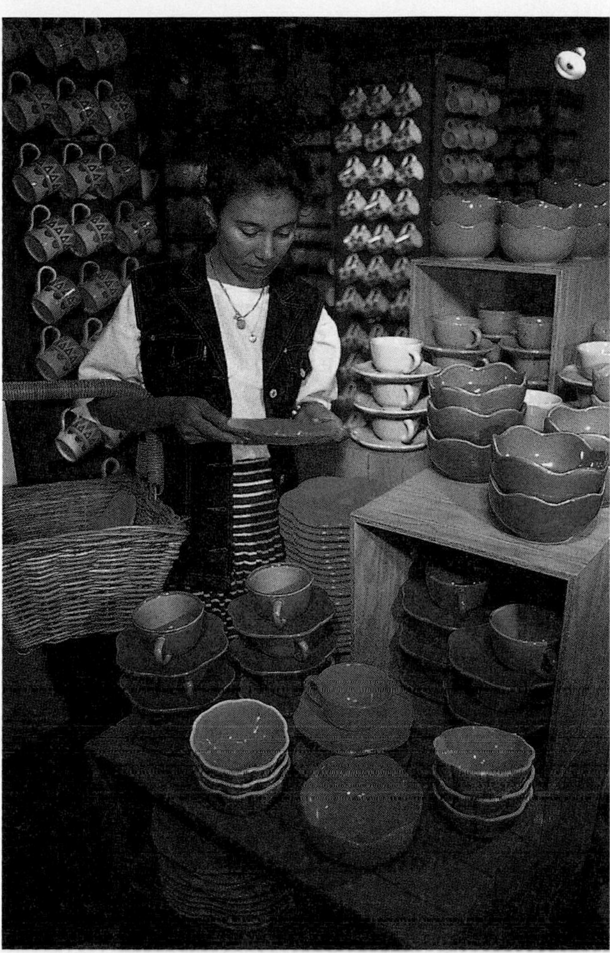

Pier 1 uses a specialized merchandise mix to attract shoppers.

is driven by the target market being pursued. Stores must be conveniently accessible for the targeted consumers. Remember that location is fundamental to providing place utility satisfaction. Beyond good access, a good location should also provide a retailer with good visibility as well. A retail outlet that is not visible from the street or clearly visible within a mall location will have a hard time attracting customers. The location must also be consistent with the image of the retailer. Placing an outlet in a part of town that does not match the quality of merchandise being carried will violate consumer perceptions of what is appropriate and will ultimately affect their desire to shop at the store. A location decision necessarily includes the choice of a free-standing store, a strip mall location, or an enclosed mall location. This feature of the location decision is affected both by the cost for the space as well as its ability to attract the target market. When mall locations are being evaluated, the nature of the other tenants in the mall is essential to the retailer's decision.

Atmospherics is that element of physical facility design that specifies the decor and amenities of the space. Robert Grayson, director of the 825 store Lerner chain, tries to exceed customer expectations when it comes to store atmosphere. His strategy is to "overshoot the customer in everything—style, ambiance, selection—except price, so that she doesn't want to shop anyplace else."[15] The flagship store in the Lerner chain, located in New York City, is luxurious, with polished marble floors, spacious private dressing rooms, and plush seating areas. A very different and distinctive ambience is created in the warehouse clubs. Here, shoppers want it to look and feel like they're getting a bargain. So, metal shelves, concrete floors, and 30-foot ceilings create the proper atmosphere. The overall purpose of atmospheric design is to create a physical shopping environment that is efficient, appealing, and satisfying to customers. Whether it be rock music, creative lighting effects, or dramatic displays, the in-store atmosphere does much to attract and satisfy shoppers.

Aside from the aesthetic appeal that can be created through atmospherics, interior store design can meet a wide range of customer desires and expectations. Consumers want to shop in retail outlets that are clean, well lit, and easy to move around in. They expect that merchandise will be easy to find and easy to inspect. This includes accessible shelves and racks and wide, comfortable aisles. In apparel stores, consumers will expect to be able to try on merchandise in comfortable and private dressing rooms. The point is that atmospherics relate to the overall physical environment shoppers encounter and it must be appealing and comfortable or it will detract from the quality of the shopping experience.

Merchandise Mix

The decision regarding what merchandise to carry in a retail outlet is effected by several criteria. First, the type of store being operated sets the boundaries for the breadth and depth of the product lines. Specialty shops that concentrate on one or a few product lines must create a merchandise mix that is deep in order to attract customers and meet shoppers' expectations for variety of choices within the specialty store format. Conversely, department stores and general merchandise discount stores will concentrate on a broad assortment of goods as the basis for customer appeal. Retailers must also take on decisions related to expanding or contracting the merchandise carried. JCPenney engaged in major contraction of merchandise lines when it decided to stop carrying major appliances, auto supplies, hardware, paint, and lawn and garden supplies.[16]

Second, and after the breadth and depth decision is made, the retailer must tailor the product collection to the taste and desires of the target market being pursued. In targeting the 18 to 35-year-old market, The Gap used to stock its shelves with all-cotton, no-frills clothing. But, in the last two years, the firm has determined that its target customers are upgrading their wardrobes. In response, The Gap now sells hats, handbags, flowing skirts, and linen slacks.[17] Finally, the cost of goods being sold is a major consideration in choosing particular items to carry in a store. Retailers will establish gross margin and net profit objectives for each product in stock.

A recent trend in merchandise strategy for retailers is to develop and sell their own brands. Chapter 8 discussed the house-brand strategy as a way for retailers to glean higher margins and free themselves from the control of manufacturers. Successfully developing an in-house brand has the added advantage of ensuring repeat patronage since the consumer can *only* buy the brand from one particular retailer. Long the province of grocery retailers, private label merchandise is now spreading to other product categories, particularly in the clothing industry. Designer label clothes have become so widely distributed and discounted that major retailers are turning to their own private labels as a way to bolster profit margins. Bargain Fifth Ave, Macy's, and specialty retailer Alcott & Andrews have developed private labels. The Gap brand clothing is now the second best-selling label in the United States.[18]

Price

Pricing has always been a way for one retailer to distinguish itself from another. As the earlier discussion of store classifications pointed out, general merchandise discount stores, some category killer stores, and warehouse clubs use pricing as the main strategy for attracting customers. Further, all types of retailers use reduced prices and sales to move excess inventory and generate cash flow.

The key to using price as an effective strategic tool in retailing is the same as it is in the marketing mix for manufacturers: price is but *one* of the costs considered by consumers. Consumers will make a decision to buy from a particular retailer on a variety of criteria including, but not restricted to, the price charged. Shopping at a convenience store for an item may cost a consumer 20 percent more for the product itself, but the time cost of shopping is reduced. You may buy an RCA television at a discount store, carry the item to your car, into the house, and set it up. Or, you could purchase the identical model at a department store, have it delivered, unpackaged, and set-up by the store's delivery personnel. The cost of the RCA television is likely to be significantly greater at the department store, but other costs are reduced. Retailers must balance the price against the services and amenities provided to a consumer. As the number and extensiveness of services are increased to satisfy shopper desires, prices must be increased. Similarly, if the atmospherics of the store are stylish and comfortable as opposed to stark and harsh, shoppers will pay a higher price.

Retailers are also beginning to have less flexibility in managing the price variable. Several manufacturers have instituted "anti-discounting" policies that restrict the extent to which retailers can cut the price on their brands. Prince Manufacturing and Specialized Bicycle Components both have cut off supply to retailers who discount their Prince rackets and Specialized mountain bikes. Kayser-Roth stopped shipping its sock line to Burlington Coat Factory outlets because of the retailer's off-price strategy.[19]

Retailers must be aware of the risks of using pricing as the primary strategic tool in their retailing mix. Retailers can suffer the same consequences as manufacturers when price is the featured appeal. It is too easy for competition to copy, and it can give consumers a commodity perception of the store. That is, the retailer has nothing distinctive to offer. Consider the dismal performance of Sears when it implemented its "Everyday Low Pricing" strategy in 1989. Shoppers were unimpressed. Store traffic increased insignificantly, revenues increased only slightly, and by 1990, net income had tumbled 40 percent.[20] The decline continued for Sears with losses approaching $4 *billion* in 1992. It appears that some moderation of the price emphasis had begun to save Sears by 1993 (see Table 14-1). On the other hand, those retailers known for their service to customers (and higher prices) like Nordstrom's and Dillard Department Stores are enjoying record profits and comfortable profit margins.

In summary, using price as a strategic tool in retailing depends on a variety of factors. First, the general pricing strategy must be consistent with the type of store the retailer operates. In stores that are replete with services and shopper amenities consumers will have to pay—and will expect to pay—higher prices for those services. Second, the market is in an era of value-oriented and price-conscious consumers. This does not mean *low* prices though. Remember that value is a judgment of how much is received for a given price. And, price consciousness means that consumers are scrutinizing prices but not necessarily choosing the lowest priced item.

Promotion

Retailers have the full complement of promotional tools at their disposal. Most retailers rely heavily on local advertising in newspapers and occasionally on television and radio. Retailers with national distribution, like Wal-Mart, can make effective use of mass media advertising. The media most heavily relied on by retailers are television, newspapers, radio, and billboards. Some national and regional operations can make use of magazines but this is relatively rare.

An important strategic consideration in the use of advertising is the extent to which a retailer uses institutional advertising versus product advertising. **Institutional advertising** focuses on the store or the chain itself. It is intended to develop name recognition and establish an image for the retailer. **Product advertising** features specific products. Product advertising can rely on messages that tout the availability of certain brands at the outlet or can feature prices much like newspaper advertising does.

Personal selling is a dominant promotional tool for many retailers. The shopping goods category of consumer products—appliances, home electronics, automobiles, clothing—depends on point-of-purchase contact with salespeople. Since consumers are using a shopping trip as an information gathering activity, the salesperson can be very effective. Again, the type of store and the retailer's decision regarding self-service within the store affect the extent to which personal selling plays an important role in promotion.

Retailers often rely heavily on sales promotion tactics. Coupons, discounts, inventory clearance sales, and special events attract the attention of shoppers. Each time ShopKo, a general merchandise discounter, opens a new store anywhere in the country, it holds a "Grand Opening Sale" event at every store in the chain and features discounts on selected merchandise. In retailing, as in individual product marketing, sales promotions must be used only to stimulate demand in the short term.

There are several distinct short-term purposes for sales promotion at the retail level. Sales promotions attract attention to the store and can increase store traffic. Cash flow can be increased in the short-run using sales promotion tactics. Finally, slow-moving merchandise can be featured with sales promotions to reduce inventories.

Services

Services are an important component in the retailing mix. It has already been emphasized that satisfying customers through time, place, and possession utility is manifest in large part by providing services. Since retailers rarely have exclusive rights to sell a manufacturer's brand, then differentiation must be achieved in other ways. Services often represent the basis for differentiation. Credit, delivery, installation, lay-a-way, alterations, and expert sales personnel all can form a foundation for differentiating one retailer's offering from another.

The importance of services to the retail shopper should not be underestimated. According to a study conducted by the U.S. Office of Consumer Affairs, between 37 and 45 percent of people who are unhappy with the service they receive do not complain—they simply shop somewhere else.[21] Consumer demands for services have motivated some retailers to make extraordinary efforts to satisfy consumer service needs. Consider the efforts of these organizations:[22]

- Dayton-Hudson has moved away from a maze layout floor design to a center aisle design to make it easier for customers to move through the store.
- At Childworld, the store has been rearranged into coordinated "learning centers" so buyers can examine and play with the toys. Management feels this will enable shoppers to shop more quickly.
- A new firm, Shoppers Express, is assisting large chains like A & P and Safeway by taking phone orders and delivering merchandise directly to a consumer's home or office.
- Montgomery Ward has authorized 7,700 sales clerks to approve checks and handle merchandise returns on their own. This eliminates the time taken with older procedures where floor manager approval was needed.

It is likely that more firms will have to comply with consumers' rising expectations for services. As service features become a point of competitive differentiation, retailers will either have to meet or exceed their competitors' service capability or end up losing market share.

ESTABLISHING A COMPETITIVE POSITION

Establishing a competitive position requires a retailer to consider the relationship between two fundamental aspects of retailing operations: value-added and merchandise specialization. Much of the strategic decision making in developing a retailing mix relates to the overall purpose of creating added value for customers. **Value-added** refers to the extent to which the product and the shopping experience are enhanced by actions of the retailer. Extended store hours, convenient location and parking, large inventories, credit, delivery, and customization are examples of basic value-added retailer activities. A retailer can also use value-added activities to establish a competitive position by having knowledgeable sales personnel, stylish in-store decor, and a prestigious location.

Value-added as a basis for competitive positioning is not restricted to the pursuit of *high* added value, however. At the other end of the spectrum, *low* added value through a lack of store features and retailer actions is just as effective in creating a distinct competitive position. Costco and BJs Warehouse Clubs are effectively positioned against competitive operations simply because they lack amenities and services but rather provide consumers with low prices.

Merchandise specialization is the other basis upon which retailers can pursue a distinct competitive position. **Merchandise specialization** specifies the breadth and depth of merchandise carried in a store. Category killer stores are a distinct shopping alternative for consumers because these types of outlets carry a comprehensive range of products within one or a few product categories. Shoppers are attracted to these stores because they are confident they will be able to find precisely what they're looking for in a single shopping trip.

Figure 14-3 graphically depicts the relationship between value-added and merchandise specialization as bases for competitive positioning. Note that an effective competitive position can be achieved either by emphasizing added value or merchandise specialization or by blending the two factors uniquely to create a distinctive position. Dillard Department Stores and JCPenney concentrate on high value-added retailing while killer category stores offer greater merchandise specialization. IKEA, the Swedish home furnishings retailer, is the extreme case of merchandise specialization with almost no value-added services provided to customers. The prices at IKEA are good and the furniture is stylish and durable. But customers at IKEA stores have to put up with long lines, little sales help, and the furniture is frequently out-of-stock or in transit. Customers often have to wait weeks to get their goods. The president of IKEA says simply, "If we offered more services, our prices would go up."[23] The high specialization and low value-added positioning strategy seems to be working for IKEA. Customers pack the stores and many rent trucks to haul home their purchases.

It is possible for a retailer to establish a position by pursuing *both* high value-added retailing and high merchandise specialization. Bergdorf Goodman is an example of such a retailer. Bergdorf has a prestigious Manhattan location. The store is adorned with antique furniture and towering floral arrangements. Each floor of the store is arranged as a series of salons with each featuring an exclusive designer label. Sales personnel cater to the whims of up-scale shoppers by allowing them to literally spend hours trying on one designer outfit after another.

At the other end of the spectrum, it is possible to occupy a competitive position by providing little added value or merchandise specialization. These are retailers that operate general merchandise discount stores but do not provide as many services or convenient locations. Examples of stores in this category are, again, the warehouse clubs. Each carries a broad range of merchan-

FIGURE 14-3
Competitive Positioning Based on Value-added and Merchandise Specialization

Value Added ↓ / Merchandise Specialization → (Low … High)			
High	JC Penney Dillard Department Stores	The Gap The Limited	Bergdorf Goodman Henri Bendel
	Wal-Mart Kmart	J. Riggins Contempo Casuals	7-11 Fleet Foot
Low	Costco BJs Warehouse	Kroger Safeway	Payless Shoe Source 50-Off Stores IKEA

Source: Adapted from a model appearing in William R. Davidson, Daniel J. Sweeney, and Ronald W. Stampfl, *Retailing Management*, 6th ed. (New York: John Wiley & Sons, 1988), 138.

dise from clothing through housewares to garden supplies and some food items but does not have much specialization within any line. The primary appeal is low prices and standardized items.

While few of us may be able to frequent shops like Bergdorf Goodman or may prefer more services than provided by Payless Shoe Source, the main point is that value-added retailing and merchandise specialization provide the foundational bases for retail competitive position. Whether the position is prestigious and exclusive based on these factors or spartan and common, the goal is to provide a competitively distinctive shopping option for consumers.

Trends in Retailing

Current trends in retailing will affect both the quality of the shopping experience for consumers and the cost of goods acquired in retail outlets. Two current trends fundamental to the retail industry will affect the nature of retailing in the future: the application of technology and industry consolidation.

The **application of technology** to retailing affects operations at several levels. Much of the technological innovation in retailing is invisible to the consumer. Automated distribution centers and satellite-link inventory re-order systems ensure products are on the shelf for consumer purchase but are not conspicuous in the shopping process. But more visible computer and communications technology is becoming a part of the shopping experience. Levi Strauss has installed "Jeans Screens" in several hundred retail outlets in the United States. The machines lead a customer through the product line and essentially fulfill the information provision role formerly played by a salesperson. Chevron and Phillips 66 have installed credit card controlled gas pumps in their corporate-owned stations. If a customer wants only gasoline, then no contact with personnel inside the store is necessary. A credit card can be used to completely control the operation of the pump and payment.

Home shopping channels have three new technological opportunities on the horizon that could maintain or even accelerate the 20 percent per year growth realized in recent years and significantly change the nature of retailing:

- Consumers are finding the newly improved infomercials more appealing and bought nearly $800 million worth of merchandise from them in 1993. This relatively inexpensive form of retailing could attract many more infomercial retailers.
- When 500-channel cable systems become accessible, some traditional retailers could have their own channels. Macy's has already announced it is launching its own 24-hour channel in the fall of 1994.
- As digital, interactive technology becomes a reality, viewers can ask TV retailers for specific information on items and place orders directly through the television. Nordstrom's believes that by 1998 it can offer its "personal shopper" services through television access.[24]

The trend toward **industry consolidation** in retailing is being led by the success of large general merchandise discounters, specialty retailers, and specialty discounters. Traditional discount stores are being overwhelmed by the new powerful discounters. Wal-Mart, Kmart, and Target are estimated to have generated 60 percent of the $90 billion general merchandise discount business in 1990.[25] During that same period, traditional discount houses such as Ames, Maxway, Gee Bee, Heck's, Alco, and Yellowfront Stores all filed for bankruptcy. Before them, Gold Circle, Mars Department Stores, and Times Square Stores went out of business. Recent mergers and acquisitions among the warehouse clubs have created a sort of consolidation. Wal-Mart has just purchased the 144-unit Pace Warehouse chain from Kmart, and Price Co. and Costco have merged in competitive response. By 1994, only 6 of the original 20 warehouse club operations in the United States were still in business.[26]

In the department store category, consolidation is taking place as well. Inefficient or poorly positioned department store retailers are failing. In their place, the most successful department store retailers are poised for buyouts. In 1991, the massive failure of Campeau Corp. put proud retailing names like Bloomingdale's and Abraham & Strauss on the auction block. The survivors of the department store shakeout are expected to be May Department Stores, Dillard Department Stores, and Nordstrom's, with an outside chance that The Limited, currently a specialty chain expert, will expand into the department store category.[27]

Consolidation of the industry may either be beneficial to consumers or end up increasing prices sharply in the years to come. Consolidation will allow the surviving competitors to take advantage of economies of scale and specialization. This will potentially lower the cost of operations—a cost savings that can be passed on to consumers in the form of lower prices. On the other hand, consolidation means fewer competitors. Fewer competitors can try to control the market and through such control steadily raise prices to increase profits. The only safeguard against such a steady increase in prices is that excess profits will attract new competitors and ultimately bring prices back down.

These two pervasive and very different influences on retailing will shape its future. While the ultimate impact of these trends is unknown, it is a certainty that retailers will need to monitor and comply with consumer desires in order to prosper. Consumers are more educated, more experienced, and more demanding. They can shift patronage from one retailer to another instantly. With this sort of power, consumers will dictate the nature of retail operations in the future.

Retailing in the United States serves important channel strategy opportunities and is a dynamic competitive market in its own right. At the global level of analysis, retailing takes on a very different flavor as cultures around the world have their own unique styles of retailing.

Retailing and Retailing Strategy: A Global Perspective

In the 1990s, the shop-till-you-drop and conspicuous consumption behavior of the Japanese consumer has waned and has given way to a passion for bargain-hunting. And this has triggered a quiet revolution within Japanese retailing. The nation's once mighty department stores are suffering a prolonged slowdown and facing fierce competition from a new breed of discount and specialty retailers, forcing them to refashion their entire approach to the business, as well as to start marking down prices. To compete with the discounters, Japan's high-end retailers face an expensive task of making major changes with their distribution systems and altering their pricing strategies. For starters, major department stores will have to reduce their inventory levels and breadth of product offerings. This will not be easy, given the corporate culture among retailers that if you're not carrying everything, you're not doing the job right. Mitsukoshi Ltd., for example, carries 1,800 different kinds of men's neckties!

Analysts point to Japan's complicated and expensive distribution systems as another source of the difficulties. Many department stores often directly lease out store space to suppliers and collect what amounts to rent from them. Because they are not responsible for unsold goods, department store executives greatly reduce their risk. However, the department store also gives control of its pricing in these cases to the manufacturer, who charges the highest price the market will bear. The solution, analysts say, is for stores to take responsibility for all of the goods they buy from wholesalers and manufacturers, without returning unsold goods. Since they are relieving the middle man of inventory risk, they can demand lower prices and pass the savings along to customers. Yet changing the distribution system presents another problem. Department store executives would have to do a much better job of tracking which products are selling. In North America and Europe, retailers commonly employ point-of-purchase computer systems to do this task. But in Japan, a country with a strong cultural tradition for using technology in business operations, such customer tracking systems in the retail industry are, surprisingly, still rare. The stores are poorly equipped to assess the purchasing patterns of consumers and thus their own purchasing risk in this changing environment. Still, retailers remain optimistic. Once they make these adjustments in pricing and inventory management, they point to favorable factors that will help them to remain profitable: A concentrated urban population, a wealthy household consumer sector, and a rapidly aging society that encourages its elders to shower youngsters with money and presents.[28]

This retailing example in Japan illustrates the global context of the retailing trends discussed in the last section of this chapter. Clearly, the quality of the experience demanded by consumers, the management of the costs of goods acquired, and the application or lack of technology are reshaping the nature of Japan's retailing industry, which is one of the most regulated and traditionally structured retail industries in the entire world. These trends are not just being observed in Japan. Throughout much of the world, the manifestation of the marketing concept is being demonstrated at the retail level through consumers' desire for better service, better goods, and more value through lower prices.

Global retailing patterns and the practices of doing business at the level of the individual consumer are as diverse as the countries in which they take place. In many respects, retailing as an institution accurately mirrors the prevailing social and cultural norms and government controls that influence the exchange processes in a market. For the global marketer, gaining insights into the economic, legal, social and cultural forces that shape retail activities is

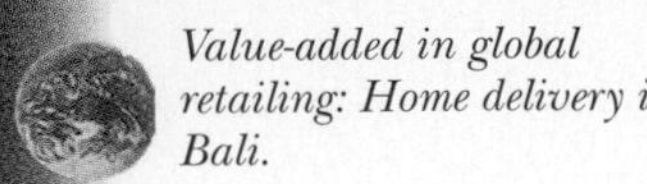

Value-added in global retailing: Home delivery in Bali.

analogous to developing an understanding of consumer behavior in that country. In Italy, small "mom and pop" stores still dominate the retail grocery industry, with an average of approximately 30 families supporting the typical grocery outlet. Italians' strong, traditional sense of community and neighborhood, coupled with laws that strongly protect small stores and make supermarket expansion a difficult and time-consuming process, help to explain this retail structure. Contrast this to the U.S. retail food shopping experience of driving a car to a large supermarkets and parking the car in an ample parking lot conveniently located to the store. Customers can do one-stop shopping in a large, well-stocked supermarket. What's more, the supermarket offers competitive prices resulting from economies of scale due to centralized purchasing and efficiencies in scale stemming from corporate investments in technology and training of personnel. Both retail systems deliver satisfactions to end users, albeit for totally different reasons. This North American model of grocery retailing is becoming more predominant in Europe as well. Table 14-4 summarizes the growth of superstores for several European countries.

Understanding how and why retailers create utilities to satisfy their customers and the forces that determine the nature of competition and cooperation between retailers are critical to developing retail strategies. The remaining portion of this chapter identifies key country-specific factors that influence global retailing and discusses the impact that global retailing strategies have on local retail markets.

RETAIL CONCENTRATION

In the early 1970s, published empirical studies suggested that the retail structure of a given country emerged from the development of the economic environment of the country. Using personal consumption expenditures, expendi-

TABLE 14-4
The Effect of Superstores on Other Retailers

Country	Superstores 1992 No. of Outlets	Superstores % Change from 1988	All Food Stores 1992 No. of Outlets	All Food Stores % Change from 1988
Austria	1,421	+50.2%	9,677	–12.0%
Belgium	89	N.A.	13,400	–6.9
Britain	723	+41.0	39,721	–20.6
France	902	+36.3	42,498	–11.8
Germany*	2,010	+27.5	66,030	–9.5
Italy	101	+100.2	142,200	–3.9
The Netherlands	40	+33.3	7,500	–22.1
Sweden	70	+45.8	7,181	–9.2
Switzerland	48	+20.0	6,800	–10.5

*Western half only.

Source: C. Rohwedder, "Europe's Smaller Food Shops Face Finis," *The Wall Street Journal* (May 12, 1993): B1. Reprinted by permission of *The Wall Street Journal*, © 1993 Dow Jones & Company, Inc. All rights reserved.

tures per capita, passenger car ownership, and geographic concentration of population, these studies concluded that supermarkets were more common and retail outlets much larger in countries with higher GNPs per capita.[29]

As a general statement, this relationship is true, and the data in Table 14-4 support this trend for the 1990s. Not only is the number of retail stores per capita in developing countries much greater than in developed countries, but, not surprisingly, the number of customers served is also much lower. Smaller retailers typically carry limited lines with limited variety and generally run inefficient operations, at least by Western management criteria. For international marketers, the problems of reaching and servicing outlets in this kind of retail structure are almost insurmountable. Retail outlets that are small in sales volume, scattered throughout a wide geographic area, and unorganized as a group characterize the retail structure in many developing countries. This structure creates a situation where the global marketer must rely on several layers of wholesalers in order to achieve market coverage. Alternatively, for the small local retailer, this less-organized and fragmented retail structure provides an advantageous environment for sustaining a niche in the market. Small shopkeepers can exploit the feelings of personal attention and service that they can offer relative to superstores. The success of upscale specialty stores that offer regional dishes, precooked foods, and longer opening hours is evidence that not all retail operations need to operate the same way. In particular, ethnic-run retailers operating in countries where shopping hours are not tightly regulated are flourishing, by exploiting the tradition of nighttime shopping.[30]

An additional managerial implication here has to do with what can be offered within this structure. Typically, manufacturers need to settle for just the distribution of their product and promotional or merchandising materials. Introducing innovative retailing practices typically involves persuasive communication to sell the concept and training of store owners or personnel to execute the program. In highly fragmented markets, this type of effort is a tremendous undertaking and likely to be cost prohibitive. This situation is very different from retail markets in more developed economies where a small number of retail organizations dominate the market. In the Netherlands for example, Albert Heijn Stores control roughly 70 percent of retail food sales. This concentration of coverage gives the firm a competitive strength that allows it to be the channel captain and negotiate the terms of trade directly with manufacturers.

But the level of economic development does not always explain the size or number of retailers. Japan's highly developed economy has long channels of distribution and is a market dominated by small retailers—roughly 132 retail outlets per 10,000 consumers, compared to half that amount in the United States and urban northern Europe.[31] This structure has developed and persisted through tradition and is also based on the cooperative nature of the relationships that retailers have with wholesalers and manufacturers. Japanese retailers have never had to bear any inventory risks because manufacturers offer generous rebates and cash-back offers on products that don't sell. Having always relied on local manufacturers to manage their inventories for them, few Japanese retailers know how to manage it themselves, and the opening example in this section clearly suggests that Japanese consumers are searching for alternative outlets that provide more satisfaction and value. With the upcoming reforms of the Retail Price Maintenance Act in Japan, these practices will become outlawed, which may contribute to the eventual restructuring of the retail industry during the 1990s. The reforms contained in the act not only eliminate rebates but also open up a legal environment more favorable to the development and expansion of larger retail outlets. As a result, smaller and relatively inefficient retailers will find it more difficult to compete, especially as European and American discount retailers gain entry into this market.

LEVEL OF RETAIL SERVICES

The level of services that retailers offer to manufacturers and customers is closely related to their size. Larger retailers finance and carry their own inventory, participate in cooperative promotional campaigns, and supply market information to the global marketer on a regular basis. In contrast, smaller retailers tend to depend on wholesalers (or manufacturer-sponsored wholesaler promotions) for credit and supplying promotional and merchandising displays.

The general attitude toward providing retail service to the consumer also varies greatly throughout the world. While consumers everywhere can all recall an unpleasant or less than optimal retail experience, it is not unfair to argue that the overall level of retail consumer service is highest in North America and Japan—it is also found in countries where labor costs are low and the traditional values for providing personal service are part of the culture. The highly competitive nature of retailing, coupled with rising consumer expectations helps explain this trend toward service in the United States and Japan. In many affluent consumer economies such as those of Western Europe, retail wages are low, the employment status of working in the retail sector is also low, and employee turnover is high. The problem of attracting and retaining skilled and committed workers is aggravated in countries where social welfare programs offer unemployment benefits that are competitive with the minimum wages offered in the retail industry. One of the great challenges for retailers in eastern Europe is going to be that of developing a service mentality among their employees. Service operators in the hotel, banking, and tourist markets will be among the first retailers to come in contact with global marketers who will offer competing services under their own company standards and proven retail formulas.

A final issue related to service at the retail level is the standardization of services across markets. In independently operated local retail situations, it's simply not feasible for a global marketer to attempt to train and motivate retailers to maintain the same high levels of customer service across countries. Like product quality, the quality of customer service is a subjective phenomenon that depends on the customer's perceptions. Global marketers can control the service and are more successful in introducing their own retail offerings through strategies when they own and operate their own outlets or expand into new markets via global franchising.

STRATEGIC GLOBAL RETAILING

There are two basic strategic options for achieving global retail distribution: corporate-owned stores and international franchising. The basic advantages and disadvantages of each as described earlier in the chapter apply to the global context. However, the global context provides unique opportunities and challenges that will be discussed here.

Corporate-owned Stores

Global expansion of **corporate-owned stores** can be triggered by a variety of different factors. In some cases, geographic proximity provides an obvious expansion route. Export situations in neighboring countries eventually develop into large enough operations to open and operate a retail outlet to serve the local market directly. Leonidas, the Belgium-based manufacturer and retailer of chocolates and bonbons, expanded with retail outlets in Holland after noting that Dutch chocolate lovers were driving to Belgium to buy their chocolates. Using a minimal amount of retail floor space, the company owns and operates very economical and profitable sales outlets in a number of shopping centers located in urban markets in Holland.

In other cases, a combination of political, economic, and legal developments open up new market opportunities for the expansion of corporate-owned retail outlets. For U.S. retailers, the signing of NAFTA, coupled with an economic resurgence in Mexico, has created new international opportunities. A shift in the attitudes of the Mexican government toward U.S. business has led to a reduction in tariff rates from over 100 percent to a maximum of 20 percent, and the real economic growth that Mexico has experienced in the past five years has enhanced the purchasing power of the middle class. While Mexico's new wealth probably won't benefit the 55 million who don't belong to the middle and upper classes, 30 million Mexicans have sufficient purchasing power and pent up demand for consumer goods. Affluent Mexicans are concentrated around the cities of Mexico City, Guadalajara, and Monterey,

simplifying the expansion plans of retailers, since operating in those three cities reaches 70 percent of the market. Table 14-5 summarizes the expansion plans of select U.S. retailers and marketers in Mexico for the 1990s.[32]

International Franchising

Franchising is a term with many connotations in business. For the purposes of this book, our discussion of **global franchising** will be limited to the context of private enterprise, where a franchise refers to a contractual association between a manufacturer, wholesaler, or service organization (the franchiser) and independent businesspeople who buy the right to own and operate one or more units in the franchise system (franchisees). Franchise systems are normally based on some unique product or service or on a method of doing business, a trade name, goodwill, or patent that the franchiser has developed.

Companies use franchises as an expansion strategy because it provides a relatively standardized business format to introduce in new market growth situations. As a method for market expansion at the retail level, franchising has proven to be a successful international strategy in such diverse markets as fast food, hotels, recreation, and business services. Firms may need to make minor adaptations in the company's marketing mix, but for the most part a successful retail formula is sold to the franchisee and implemented in a local market. For example, in Germany and France, McDonald's offers beer and wine respectively on their menus, since those beverages are so common to meal times in these countries. In Japan, Toys "R" Us has difficulty maintaining deep price discounts in part due to high distribution and real estate costs.

Host countries typically welcome franchises because they involve a contractual arrangement with local entrepreneurs right from the beginning.

TABLE 14-5
Expansion of Corporate-owned Retail Operations in Mexico by U.S. Retailers

Wal-Mart
Plans to open five warehouse clubs, called Club Aurrera, along with Cifra, Mexico's biggest retailer.

Price Co.
Teaming up with retailer Comercial Mexicana to launch two warehouse clubs outside of Mexico City.

Sears Roebuck
In Mexico since 1945, Sears will spend $150 million opening new stores and malls in Mexico. It is also renovating its old stores.

McDonald's
Has earmarked $500 million to open 250 new restaurants in Mexico by the year 2000.

Ford, GM, Chrysler
Exporting luxury models to Mexico and expanding auto dealerships, thanks to changes in auto import laws.

PepsiCo
Expanding its snack business by buying majority stake in Gamesa, Mexico's largest cookie maker.

Franchises also offer a high-standard, quality product or service in the local market, often at competitive prices since the franchise operation typically has economies of scale as a whole. Finally, apart from providing the good or service, franchising brings expertise and management skills to the host country's market. This tends to raise the level of competition and the level of expectations among clients. Ultimately this can lead to the overall improvement in the quality of retailing within the industry. Many challenges face franchisers. They need to be aware of government regulations and legal restrictions such as taxes and limitations of profit expatriation. Further, they must be able to find qualified personnel and suppliers in order to maintain the quality standards of the franchise. Finally, franchisers must adjust to a culture that most likely has different attitudes and values regarding the creation of utilities that provide satisfaction in the retail exchange. This will be the challenge for franchise operations in eastern Europe in particular over the decade of the 1990s.

GLOBAL RETAIL TRENDS AND OPPORTUNITIES

Retailing activities are closely linked to the unique behaviors of consumers in individual countries. As a result, **global retail trends and opportunities** will always show some diversity. Retail activities throughout the world may be viewed as more or less efficient as business operations and more or less convenient to consumers depending on the cultural values brought to the retail encounter. Unless companies have contractual arrangements with selective or exclusive retail outlets in a market, they will have little control over the activities of independent retailers. Relying on the knowledge and support of wholesalers is the most common approach to retail coverage, especially for small and medium-sized companies who export. For larger global firms, pursuing international expansion via franchising, joint ventures, or direct investment are the most common approaches to establishing a retail presence in foreign markets.

Political and legislative events have had a positive effect on global retailing in recent years. The reduction of tariffs and trade barriers and the freer movement of products and labor have made for more competitive markets in many regions of the world. Reforms in Japan's retail laws, the signing of regional trade zone treaties, the unification of markets in western Europe and the opening of markets in eastern Europe are all developments that will affect the way in which retail markets evolve. As competition increases and consumer expectations rise, global retail markets will continue to consolidate and become more efficient at supplying utilities that enhance satisfaction. Discount retailers in particular will continue to have a big impact throughout Europe, Latin America, and Asia. Sophisticated electronic point-of-purchase equipment and inventory control systems will continue to diffuse into retail markets, especially in Japan and Europe. Firms adopting these high-tech advances will eventually squeeze out many of the inefficient players in the market. It may be, though, that this technology will never equal the ability of the hundreds of thousands of small retail operations to reach so much of the world's population.

Key Terms and Concepts

Role of retailing
Importance of retailing
Durable goods
Nondurable goods
Department store
General merchandise discount store
Category killers
Warehouse club
Supermarket
Specialty shop
Convenience store
Nonstore retailing
Catalog shopping
In-home shopping
Retailing mix
Atmospherics
Institutional advertising
Product advertising
Value-added
Merchandise specialization
Application of technology
Industry consolidation
Global retail concentration
Corporate-owned stores (global)
Global franchising

Questions and Exercises

1. What is the role of retailing? How does it relate to what is called the "golden three feet?"
2. Of what use is the durable goods versus nondurable goods classification of retailers used by the U.S. Department of Commerce? What is the drawback of this classification scheme?
3. Find a category killer retail store in your local market area. What merchandise does the store sell and why do you consider it to be a category killer store?
4. What utilities does nonstore retailing provide that would help to explain its tremendous growth over the last decade?
5. What is the retailing mix? How does it differ from a producer's marketing mix?
6. Identify a store in your area that is not listed in Figure 14-3. Where would you place it in this value-added/merchandise specialization figure?
7. In what ways are retailers making use of new technologies. Have you seen new technology applied in any of the retail outlets you shop at?
8. Considering retailing in the global context, what is the relationship between economic development and retail concentration? Identify changing consumer preferences that help to explain the growth of discount retail operations throughout much of the world.
9. How do small, local retail services around the world find their niche and compete against large discounters?
10. What are the two primary ways of achieving global retail distribution?

References

1. Bill Saporito, "Is Wal-Mart Unstoppable?" *Fortune* (May 6, 1991): 58–59.
2. U.S. Department of Commerce, Bureau of the Census, Current Business Reports, *Monthly Retail Trade* (Washington, D.C.: U.S. Government Printing Office, January 1993), Table 1, p. 4.
3. Malcolm P. McNair, "Significant Trends and Developments in the Postwar Period," in *Competitive Distribution in a Free High-Level Economy and Its Implications for the University,* Albert V. Smith, ed. (Pittsburgh: University of Pittsburgh Press, 1958), 17.
4. This concept was proposed by William R. Davidson, Albert D. Bates, and Stephen J. Bass, "The Retail Life Cycle," *Harvard Business Review* (November–December 1976): 89.
5. Susan Caminiti, "The New Champs of Retailing," *Fortune* (September 24, 1990): 94.
6. Joseph Spiers, "Those Exuberant Consumers Will Soon Settle Down," *Fortune* (February 21, 1994): 19.
7. "Back on the Strip," *Forbes* (December 17, 1986): 35.
8. Howard Schlossberg, "Warehouse Club Owners Hope to Sign Everybody Eventually," *Marketing News* (September 13, 1993): 1, 10.
9. Susan Caminiti, *Fortune,* op. cit., 98.
10. *Standard & Poor's Industry Surveys* (April 1991), R-93.
11. Laura Loro, "Catalogers Foresee Happy Holidays," *Advertising Age* (October 25, 1993): S4.
12. Scott Donaton, "Home Shopping Audience Widens," *Advertising Age* (November 22, 1993): 19.

13. Laura Zinn, et al., "Retailing Will Never Be the Same," *Business Week* (July 26, 1993): 54.
14. Eva Pomice, "Stores for the 1990s," *U.S. News and World Report* (May 13, 1991): 52–53.
15. Susan Caminiti, *Fortune*, op. cit., 98.
16. "New Shine on a Tarnished Penney," *The New York Times* (April 23, 1989): 4.
17. Russell Mitchell, "The Gap Dolls Itself Up," *Business Week* (March 21, 1994): 46.
18. Russell Mitchell, "The Gap," *Business Week* (March 9, 1992): 58–64.
19. Paul M. Barrett, "Anti-Discount Policies of Manufacturers Are Penalizing Certain Cut Price Stores," *The Wall Street Journal* (February 27, 1991): B1, B3.
20. Gary Cohen, "Can Sears Recover?" *U.S. News and World Report* (May 13, 1991): 55–56.
21. Susan Caminiti, *Fortune*, op. cit., 98.
22. Eugene Fram, "The Time Compressed Shopper," *Marketing Insights* (Summer 1991): 36.
23. Jeffery A. Trachtenberg, "Ikea Furniture Chain Pleases with Its Prices, Not with Its Service," *The Wall Street Journal* (September 17, 1991): A1, A6.
24. Laura Zinn, op. cit. 55.
25. Joseph Pereira, "Discount Department Stores Struggle Against Rivals That Strike Aisle by Aisle," *The Wall Street Journal* (June 19, 1990): B1, B7.
26. See Bob Ortega, "Warehouse-Club War Leaves Few Standing, and They Are Bruised," *The Wall Street Journal* (November 18, 1993): A1; and Howard Schlossberg, op. cit., 10.
27. Jeffery A. Trachtenberg, "Retailers Face Cutbacks, Uncertain Future," *The Wall Street Journal* (August 29, 1989): B1, B2.
28. Materials for this example were taken from "Japan Stores Shed Old Ways," *International Herald Tribune* (February 24, 1993): 12; and "The World in Figures," *The World in 1994,* The Economist Publications, 1994, 94.
29. Johan Arndt, "Temporal Lags in Comparative Retailing," *Journal of Marketing* (October 1972): 40–45. Susan Douglas, "Patterns and Parallels of Marketing Structures in Several Countries," *MSU Business Topics* (Spring 1971).
30. Cacilie Rohwedder, "Europe's Smaller Food Shops Face Finis," *The Wall Street Journal* (May 12, 1993): B1.
31. "Japan's Next Retail Revolution," *The Economist* (December 21, 1991): 92.
32. Stephen Baker and S. Lynne Walker, "The American Dream Is Alive and Well—In Mexico," *International Business Week* (September 30, 1991): 54–55.

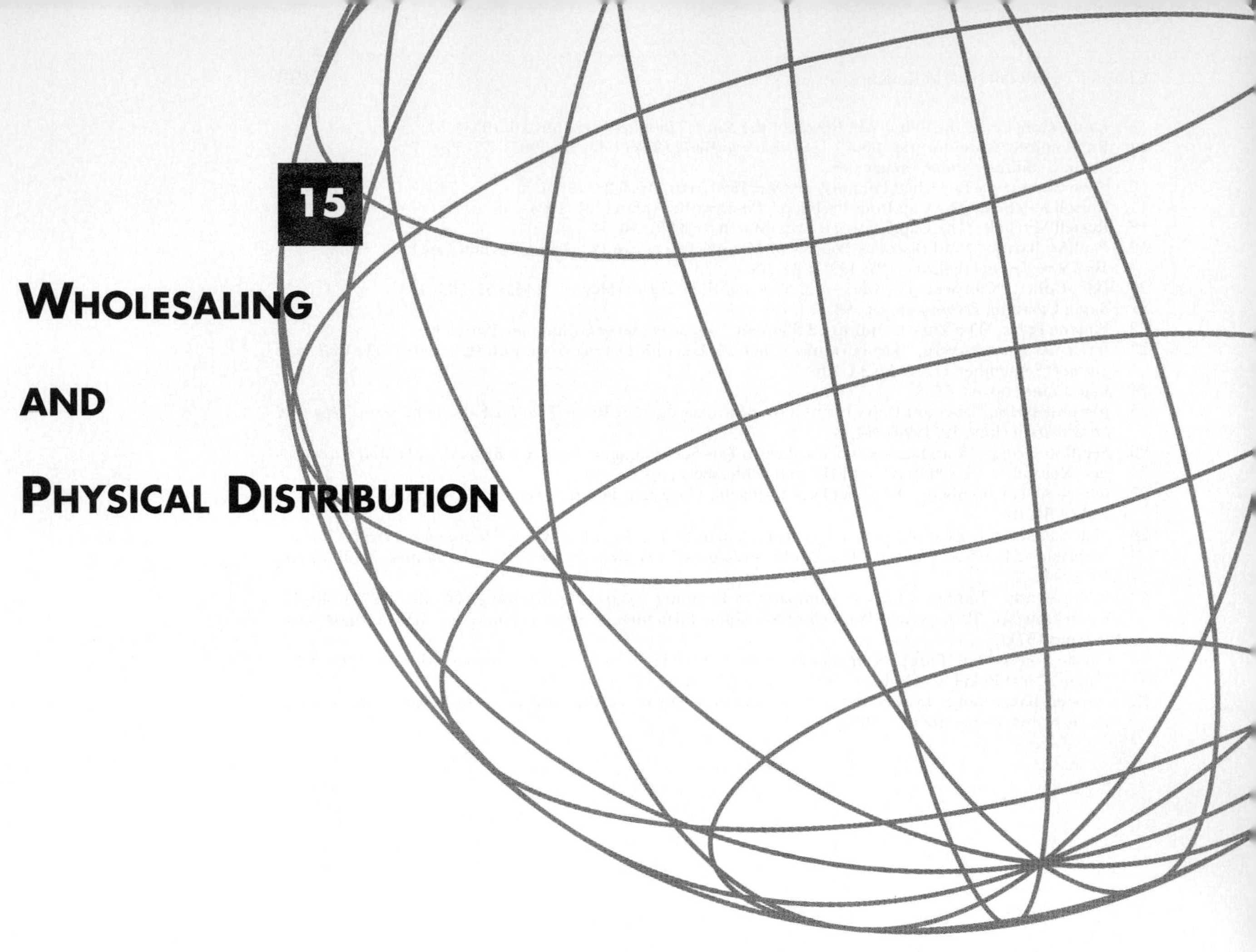

15

Wholesaling and Physical Distribution

AFTER STUDYING THIS CHAPTER, YOU WILL UNDERSTAND THAT:

1. Wholesalers carry out important activities in a channel of distribution that neither producers or retailers are particularly well suited to perform.
2. A broad range of wholesaling institutions are available to manufacturers and retailers to serve their channel needs.
3. Physical distribution is an integrated system of activities that is best viewed from a total cost perspective rather than an operating cost perspective.
4. Physical distribution activities have significant strategic impact on the entire channel of distribution because they can affect time and place utility.
5. In global markets, the level of competition and the cultural environment are key forces in determining the range and quality of wholesale services available.

Sean DeForrest, the CEO of American Lock & Supply, a $70 million a year security products wholesale operation, is looking for a competitive advantage and a secure place in the channel. A weak economy, competition from other wholesalers, and the growth of general merchandise discounters are eroding margins, and wholesalers like American Lock & Supply are looking for ways to increase productivity and service to make themselves indispensable in the channel. DeForrest decided to install a system so that any customer with a personal computer could dial into a central computer at American Lock & Supply, enter an order, and know within seconds when it would be shipped. This computer-to-computer connection has given the company a way to cut paper work and increase service to customers. DeForrest claims that, "Our output per person has gone up unbelievably. That has freed up salespeople to provide better service."[1]

The situation at American Lock & Supply reveals the trials and triumphs of wholesaling and physical distribution. Being positioned squarely in the middle of most channels of distribution presents wholesalers with the opportunity to provide important services to both producers and the next level in the channel, usually retailers. However, recall from the last chapter that *any* intermediary in the channel can be eliminated as long as the functions are maintained. Well, wholesalers are particularly vulnerable to the prospect of elimination. Because of this vulnerability, competition is fierce and demands from retailers for lower and lower prices are unrelenting. Further, producers and wholesalers don't always see eye-to-eye, as Chapter 13 pointed out, with respect to conflict in the channel. Despite these pressures, wholesaling is a $2.5 trillion industry in the United States and employs over six million people. This dollar volume of activity is testimony to the value-added contributed by wholesalers to not only the function of the channel but also to the entire marketing process.

This chapter will identify the value and importance of wholesaling and physical distribution within the channel as an integral part of the overall marketing process. And, the types of wholesalers and their activities will be discussed, as well as a system for physical distribution and the methods employed within that system. The concluding section in the chapter identifies the challenges and opportunities in wholesaling from a global perspective.

Definition and Importance of Wholesaling

Wholesaling, in the most fundamental sense, involves all sales transactions *except* those made to individuals or households for their personal consumption. **Wholesaling** is all sales of raw materials, the sale of business goods from one producer to another or from a distributor to a producer, the sale of import and export goods, and all sales to retailers.

The average wholesaling operation is not fronted with brilliant lights, nor are we dazzled with double-page spreads in national magazines advertising wholesalers' services. Wholesaling, in other words, is hardly a glamorous industry. But, despite the lack of glamour, wholesaling is an important activity in the channel of distribution. Wholesaling evolved in the channel of distribution and continues to exist because it serves an important role related to the nature of production and consumption. Goods are seldom consumed in the place they are produced. Nor are goods consumed at the rate they are produced. In geographic areas that have a comparative advantage for production, these same areas are rarely high in consumption for the goods being produced. To further complicate matters, the most efficient rates of production almost never coincide with the desired rate of purchase and consumption.

In light of these realities of production and consumption, some set of activities must be in place to ensure that the required assortment of products is at the place they are needed when they are needed. Since little, if any, naturally occurring coordination of production and consumption occurs, wholesalers have emerged to serve this coordination function for manufacturers, retailers, and business buyers. Wholesaling and wholesalers exist for the very important reason that there is a demonstrated need in a channel for a set of identifiable functions to be performed that suit neither manufacturers nor retailers particularly well.

The Activities of Wholesaling

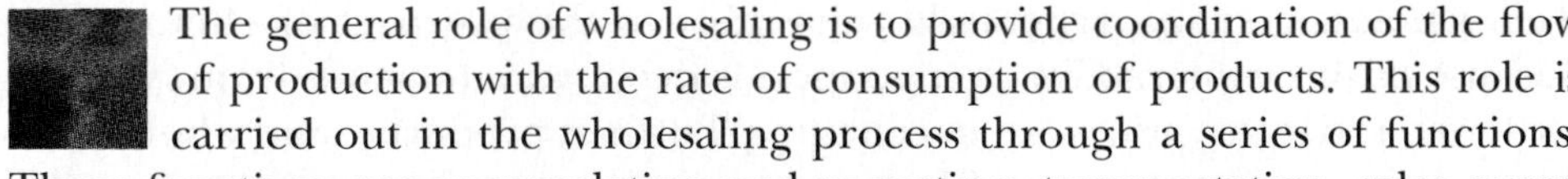

The general role of wholesaling is to provide coordination of the flow of production with the rate of consumption of products. This role is carried out in the wholesaling process through a series of functions. These functions are accumulation and re-sorting, transportation, sales coverage, merchandising, storage, and credit provision.

ACCUMULATION AND RE-SORTING

One of the most significant contributions of wholesaling is to economize the time and energy required to move goods by reducing the number of transactions associated with that movement. The goods of a single manufacturer are sold to many retailers and the goods sold by an average retailer are produced by many manufacturers. **Accumulation** is bringing together the goods of many manufacturers to a single location. **Re-sorting** is the process of putting together a collection of manufacturers' goods desired by retailers into single shipments. The wholesaler's role is to accumulate the merchandise from several manufacturers and then re-sort those goods to fill orders from retailers. When manufacturers concentrate their sales effort on a few wholesale accounts instead of literally hundreds of individual retail accounts, the number of orders processed and accounts served are greatly reduced. This is the kind of efficiency that was highlighted in Chapter 13 when the issue was raised as to why intermediaries exist.

Similar savings are realized by retailers through the accumulation and re-sorting activities performed by wholesalers. For example, if an average retail store carries 10,000 items manufactured by 200 different firms, the manager of such a store (or chain of stores) would have to try to make an intelligent selection from among all those product varieties and allocate time to sales representatives from all 200 manufacturers. By using a wholesaler, however, the retailer can rely on the specialized buying expertise of the wholesaler to sort through the range of selections and present options in a single, concise sales presentation. Illustration 15-1 demonstrates the wholesaler's capabilities in performing accumulation and re-sorting activities.

TRANSPORTATION

Wholesaling plays an important part in the **transportation** of goods from manufacturers to retailers. A single manufacturing firm may ship enough of its entire line to a wholesaler to serve several hundred retailers. Retailers necessarily need to have goods from several different manufacturers to serve the needs of their customers. Wholesalers are able to re-sort merchandise into an allotment ordered by each retailer from the stock of several different manufacturers (refer to Illustration 15-1 again). Through this function, large-volume shipments of merchandise are able to move both from manufacturers to wholesalers and again from wholesalers to retailers. These large volume shipments reduce the transportation cost per unit shipped—another instance of economies of scale being realized in the channel. In addition to the increased size of the shipment, the number of shipments are reduced by wholesalers at an accumulation and re-sorting point. In general, the transportation activities provided by wholesalers present another opportunity for lower cost and greater efficiency for both manufacturers and retailers.

SALES COVERAGE

For two very specific reasons, wholesalers have distinct advantages over manufacturers in performing the selling function, called **sales coverage.** First, wholesalers provide a maximum degree of market coverage of all types and sizes of retailers, which could not easily be achieved by a manufacturer. Every

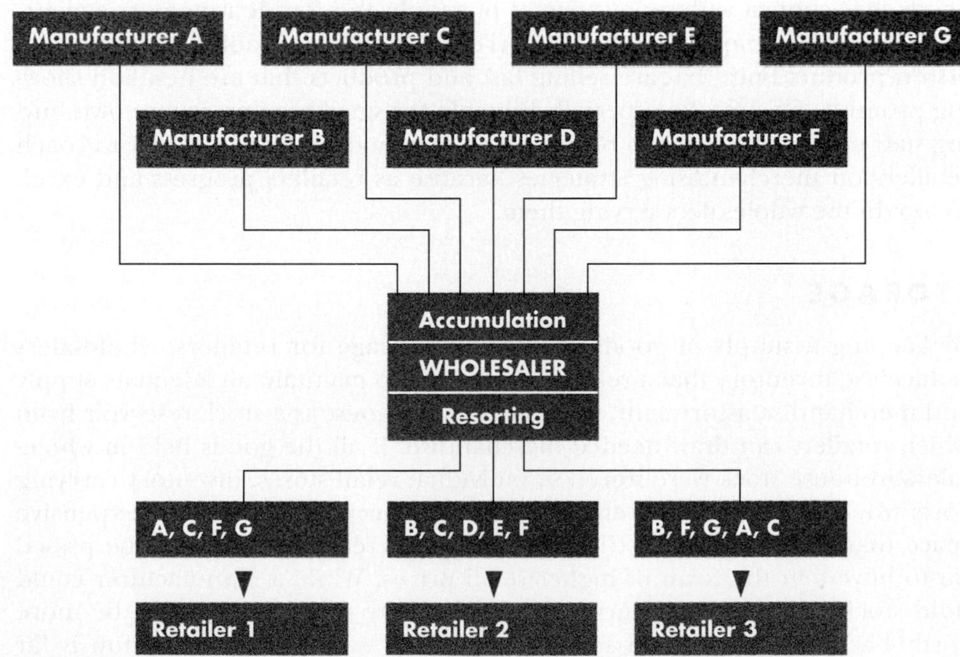

ILLUSTRATION 15-1
Accumulation and Re-sorting Activities Performed by Wholesalers

manufacturer wishing to sell directly to retailers would have to accept the time and expense related to developing and maintaining an entire sales force to sell a single or a few product lines *just* to retailers. Second, wholesalers and retailers have a common tie that could never develop between manufacturers and retailers. The prosperity and existence of both the wholesaler and the retailer are threatened by manufacturers that develop vertically integrated channel systems (see the discussion of *integrated channel systems* in Chapter 13). As such, wholesalers and retailers are motivated to work cooperatively to achieve combined success. In some instances, the pressures from channel integration have forced wholesalers into contractual agreements with retailers to form voluntary and cooperative chains.

The efficiency of a wholesaler's sales operation would be difficult for a manufacturer to match as well. When a wholesaler's sales representative calls on a small retailer, some sort of order is usually placed with the wholesaler because of the wide range of products the representative carries. This is in contrast to the narrow line of items a typical individual manufacturer's sales representative would have available. This makes it feasible for wholesale representatives to call on all forms of retail outlets and truly achieve complete coverage in a market area.

MERCHANDISING

Being out of stock is evidence of a failure in merchandising. Retailers experience out-of-stock conditions because insufficient amounts of the right type of merchandise are not ordered and supplied at the proper times. With a wholesaler's assistance, a retailer can identify the proper mix of merchandise and order small amounts of stock because a wholesaler makes it possible to reorder and get delivery at short intervals. In addition to this sort of **merchandising** assistance, the wholesaler, by virtue of being a specialist in certain classes of goods, has contact with many sources of supply and a wide range of retailers. Because of this unique view of the market, a wholesaler is able to advise retailers on product lines that are selling fast and products that are new and showing promise. This can be especially valuable for small retailers whose own buying staff cannot specialize in buying areas. It behooves the wholesaler to coach retailers on merchandising strategies because as retailers progress and excel, so too do the wholesalers serving them.

STORAGE

By keeping a supply of goods available in **storage** for retailers, wholesalers reduce the inventory that a retailer must carry to maintain an adequate supply and merchandise assortment. A wholesale warehouse is a stock reservoir from which retailers can draw needed merchandise. If all the goods held in wholesale warehouse stock were stored in individual retail stores, inventory carrying costs would soar because retailers generally occupy much more expensive space than do wholesalers. Ultimately, these increased costs would be passed on to buyers in the form of higher retail prices. While a manufacturer could hold stock for retailers or arrange storage near retailers, it would be more costly because the size and specialization of a wholesaler's operation is far more efficient than an operation any single manufacturer could devise.

Wholesalers assist retailers with merchandising decisions by tracking turnover of different product lines.

CREDIT PROVISION

On some occasions, a wholesaler will make a merchandise advance to a new retail business to help it get started. Wholesalers may also carry a running credit account for some customers. It would be difficult for manufacturers to perform this **credit** function as efficiently as it is performed at the wholesaling level. The organization, namely a wholesaler, that is at the scene of a retailer's activities and has direct contact with management can act with wisdom and insight in credit administration. Often a wholesaler will extend credit because of factors that a manufacturer far removed from the scene could not know. On occasion, not extending credit under certain circumstances could mean the failure of a retailer that otherwise would be successful. With credit, retailers may be able to carry a wider assortment with which to attract and serve a customer base. Further, credit in the merchandise area often allows retailers to spend precious funds for advertising, special promotions, or additional store personnel all of which may serve to stimulate demand and potentially increase sales. These indirect effects of merchandise credit provision by wholesalers can ultimately reward the wholesaler with greater revenue.

THE VALUE OF WHOLESALING

The activities of wholesaling just discussed highlight the value of wholesaling to the overall marketing process. The value of wholesaling stems from and contributes to the overall value of the entire distribution system. Recall that the value of distribution, itself, comes from the ability of distribution to create customer satisfaction by providing time, place, and possession utility. Wholesaling, by virtue of its position in the channel of distribution, makes a unique and valuable contribution to these utilities.

Time utility is created at the wholesale level by two of the activities performed by wholesalers: merchandising and storage. Merchandising services provided by wholesalers allow retailers to replenish stock of the right merchandise mix quickly and properly. The storage function of wholesaling ensures that adequate stock is held in the vicinity of retail demand. In general, having adequate stock of the right products when they are needed provides time utility to retailers through the wholesaling function.

A related benefit comes from a wholesaler's attempt to provide time utility. Typically, manufacturers can achieve economies in the production process if goods can be produced at an even rate throughout the entire year. However, as discussed earlier, household consumer sales vary throughout the year. By virtue of the wholesaler's storage and merchandising functions, manufacturers can produce at an even rate and rely on wholesalers to provide supply to retailers at the needed, and usually uneven, rate. This coordination effort on the part of wholesalers once again proves to be of benefit to both manufacturers and retailers.

Place utility is achieved through the storage and transportation activities. Retailers must rely on wholesalers for stock to be at the place where it is needed. The proximity of inventory storage and the ability to transport from the storage area create place utility. Finally, *possession utility* is created for retailers by virtue of the credit function and, again, the transportation (and delivery) function. Recall that providing possession utility depends on removing barriers that stand between a buyer and the desired goods. The capability of the wholesaling level of the channel to extend credit to retail buyers and then ship expeditiously to retailers' locations facilitate speed and ease of possession.

Wholesaling Institutions

Wholesaling institutions include "establishments or places of business primarily engaged in selling merchandise directly to retailers; to industrial, commercial, institutional, or professional users; or to other wholesalers; or acting as agents in buying merchandise for, or selling merchandise to, such persons or companies."[2] This is the official U.S. Department of Commerce definition of what a wholesaling institution is and to whom such institutions sell. For marketing strategy and planning purposes, it is important to realize that wholesale operations vary by size, activity, style of business, and types of services provided.

Table 15-1 identifies the principal types of wholesale institutions now counted by the U.S. Department of Commerce. With nearly half a million establishments and $2.5 trillion in sales, wholesaling is critical to economic activity in the United States. Notice that merchant wholesalers dominate both the number of establishments engaged in wholesale trade and account for the largest percentage of wholesale sales. Also notice that manufacturers with vertically integrated channel systems (listed as "manufacturers' sales branches/offices") who own and operate their own wholesaling operations account for nearly one-third of all wholesale activity even though these wholesale operations constitute less than 10 percent of the establishments. Based on the categories in Table 15-1, a description of the operations of each type of

TABLE 15-1 *Wholesale Trade in the United States*

Type of Operation	Percentage of Total Wholesale Establishments (total establishments: 469,829)	Percentage of Total Wholesale Sales (total sales $2,524,726,802)
Wholesale trade, total	**100.0%**	**100.0%**
Merchant wholesalers, total	**83.3**	**58.6**
Distributors and jobbers	76.5	44.5
Importers	3.8	8.9
Exporters	1.3	3.2
Grain elevators	1.2	1.3
Assemblers of farm products	0.5	0.7
Manufacturers' sales branches/offices	**7.7**	**31.0**
Merchandise agent wholesalers, total	**9.0**	**10.4**
Brokers	1.9	3.8
Commission merchants	1.4	1.3
Manufacturers' agents	5.2	3.9
Auction companies	0.3	0.9
Import agents	0.1	0.2
Export agents	0.1	0.3

Source: U.S. Department of Commerce, Bureau of the Census, *1987 Census of Wholesale Trade, U.S. Summary* (Washington, D.C.: U.S. Government Printing Office), Table 1.

wholesale institution is valuable. The descriptions that follow identify what services and activities different types of wholesalers perform. With this information, producers can choose the wholesaler who best fits the firm's needs for services within the channel.

MERCHANT WHOLESALERS

Merchant wholesalers are distinguished in the realm of wholesaling in that these institutions take title and ownership of the goods they sell. The broad class of merchant wholesalers includes two types of wholesale operations: full - service wholesalers and limited function wholesalers.

Full-Service Wholesalers

The typical **full-service** (also known as full-function) **wholesaler** performs a variety of services that benefit both manufacturers and retailers. Table 15-2 provides a useful summary of the value of full-service wholesalers by indicating the services provided both to manufacturers and to retailers. The full-service wholesaler's ability to provide these services comes not only from the unique position they occupy in the channel—between manufacturers and retailers—but also from the risk they assume through ownership of the products they handle. A further element of risk occurs when the full-service wholesaler extends credit to retail customers. Every business encounters bad debts and the credit provision practices by wholesalers are not free from this bad-debt risk.

There are three types of full-service merchant wholesalers. **Industrial distributors** are establishments that handle "a general line of industrial goods and

Services Provided to Manufacturers	**Services Provided to Retailers**
• Promotion to the next level in the channel—usually to retailers	• Purchase of items in quantities beyond the capability of the average retailer
• Direct purchase and ownership of stock providing immediate cash flow	• Through ownership of stock can arrange direct transfer of title
• Storage of inventory closer to next level in the channel	• Storage of inventory closer to end user
• Reduction of risk through ownership	• Assumption of part of the transportation costs
	• Provision of credit
	• Accumulation of stock variety and bulk breaking into smaller quantities

TABLE 15-2
Services Provided by a Full-Service Wholesaler

sell largely to industrial users—establishments dealing in a more or less complete line of materials and/or supplies for mines, factories, oil wells, public utilities, and similar industries."[3] Industrial distributors provide storage, sales personnel, delivery, order taking, credit, and often provide repair services. Wide-ranging sales coverage and repair services are possible in this category because the costs of such services are spread over a large number of products from many different manufacturers.

Farm product assemblers exist because there is a need to gather the output from many small farm producers and provide efficient transportation, storage, and distribution of farm goods. These wholesalers purchase directly from farmers and operate on a regional basis. Because of narrow margins in many farm product categories, it is unlikely that most small farm operations could survive without the services of farm product assemblers.

Finally, **importers and exporters** are full-service merchant wholesalers. Importers are establishments that buy primarily from foreign sources. They buy the stock outright and locate their own buyers. Often importers will sell to other wholesalers along with cultivating a retail customer base. Merchant wholesalers that are primarily engaged in selling to foreign markets are classified as exporters. Again, this group accepts the risk of stock ownership and must cultivate buyers in foreign markets. Like the importers, exporters often sell to wholesalers in a foreign market rather than directly to retail establishments.

Limited Function Wholesalers

Limited function wholesalers offer some but not all of the services of a full-service wholesaler. The main appeal of this category of wholesaler is lower cost. If a manufacturer or retailer is capable of performing some of the needed wholesale functions, then the services of a limited function wholesaler may be sufficient. There are four main types of limited function wholesalers: truck distributors, rack jobbers, drop shippers, and cash and carry wholesalers.

Truck distributors are distinguished by the fact that they combine sales and delivery functions. These wholesalers carry a limited assortment of fast-moving items of a perishable or semi-perishable nature. They are capable of providing a relatively limited amount of stock in storage—often only enough for one day's operation. The driver of the truck is also the sales representative and makes sales and deliveries at the same time. Such operations are among the most costly of all types of wholesaling because a truck is an expensive warehouse. Further, the sales representative makes relatively small sales per call. The cost is offset by a retailer's ability to get frequent, small orders of perishable items thus ensuring freshness for the retail customer. Snack foods, fresh coffee, dairy products, fruits, and vegetables are often carried by truck distributors. Grocery stores, restaurants, and convenience stores are the primary customers of this wholesale group.

Rack jobbers are merchant intermediaries who sell mainly through grocery stores and convenience food stores. This category of wholesaler is often referred to as a service merchandiser. Rack jobbers arrange with store owners for display space, which the jobber then supplies and maintains. As a rule, rack jobbers specialize in nonfood items and confine their sales to one brand in a product line such as drug items, household and kitchenware, toys, or inexpensive clothing items like socks, children's underwear, and women's hosiery. The success of a rack jobber is based on the ability to provide very small quantities and assume the risk and expense of maintaining in-store racks.

Drop shippers are wholesalers who buy and sell goods but do not store them. Rather, a drop shipper arranges for the shipment of goods directly from a producer to the buyer. This group of wholesalers often deals in goods that are graded and then sold by grade. These goods are sold in large quantities and stock is typically accumulated from several manufacturers. An example of a drop shipper operation is when a building contractor requires lumber of certain specifications. It is much easier for the contractor to buy from a drop shipper than to make all the arrangements. The drop shipper takes the order, finds lumber to meet the required specifications (often from several sources), and buys the lumber. Then, the drop shipper arranges for handling and shipment and monitors delivery to ensure that the contractor receives the right goods at the time and place desired. A drop shipper may never have direct contact with the goods, but bears all the risks of ownership and credit extension. Drop shippers do not, however, maintain inventory of any of the goods they buy and sell.

Cash and carry wholesalers sell primarily to retailers and do not provide credit or delivery services. The services provided by this group of wholesalers are accumulation and re-sorting of goods and maintenance of inventory. In this sense, these wholesalers provide precisely the services that drop shippers do not. Conversely, they do not accommodate their customers needs with respect to credit extension. Cash and carry wholesalers are most common in the food industry but can be found in a variety of product categories.

MERCHANDISE AGENT WHOLESALERS

Merchandise agent wholesalers are distinguished from merchant wholesalers by the fact that agent wholesalers do not take title to merchandise. The diversity and overlap of services provided by members of this group and the variability of operations makes distinct classifications difficult in this category of wholesale operations. However, the most widely accepted categorizations are merchandise brokers, purchasing agents and buying brokers, commission merchants, manufacturers' agents, food brokers, selling agents, auction companies, and import/export agents.

Merchandise brokers negotiate transactions rather than consummate sales. In a strict sense, merchandise brokers never take possession of goods or assume title. As such, they completely avoid the risks of price fluctuations, changes in market demand, or loss due to damage. Additionally, brokers do not handle invoices or extend credit to customers. Manufacturers who make use of merchandise brokers usually limit the brokers' powers regarding prices and payment terms and require confirmation from the principals involved in the transaction before approving a sale. Brokers are paid a commission based on the value of the merchandise. Merchandise brokers rarely develop long-term relationships with either buyers or sellers.

Merchandise brokers deal primarily in food, farm products, and are occasionally found dealing in some heavy industrial lines of goods. Because brokers avoid much of the risk of transactions in the way they conduct business, their fees are relatively low. Some high-volume brokers in this category handle their business from modest offices in their homes or even from hotel rooms. This is possible because the merchandise broker's most valuable asset is knowledge of market conditions, sources of supply, and a sense for when a deal can be negotiated.

Purchasing agents and **resident buyers** are unique in that they work for the *buyer* in a transaction rather than the seller as most brokers and agents do. Both of these types of wholesalers work most often in the dry goods, apparel, and general merchandise fields. Purchasing agents operate much like general brokers in that they negotiate deals on behalf of a buyer and work on a commission basis. Resident buyers are somewhat unique in that they specialize in certain lines of apparel and dry goods and maintain offices to serve their retail clients. When retail buyers go to market, they get product and price information bulletins from their resident buyers. Then, when it is not practical for a buyer to make a market trip, the resident buyer will often be able to buy the needed merchandise.

Commission merchants are not technically merchants because they do not take title to the goods they sell. They are distinguished among the group of agent wholesalers in that they take possession of the goods they handle, even though they do not take title. The most common type of commission merchant is found in large city vegetable and produce markets. They accept goods on consignment and try to sell them at the most favorable price and terms that can be negotiated.

Manufacturers' agents sell a part of the output of two or more manufacturers whose goods are noncompeting. Their principal duty is to locate potential buyers and perform the personal selling function. Some manufacturers' agents do, however, engage in warehousing activities. This group of agent wholesalers is found principally in business goods and durable consumer goods lines. Several features of the manufacturer's agent business are appealing to manufacturers. These agents restrict their activities to specified geographic areas. They handle only part of the output of two or more noncompeting but complementary manufacturers and are willing to accept strict policies regarding pricing. Finally, these types of agents generally have thorough knowledge of one or two industries that use the types of products in which they specialize. Suppliers to the automobile industry have traditionally used manufacturers' agents because such agents have contacts with the large auto firms that small manufacturers could not hope to cultivate individually.

Food brokers are not classified separately by the U.S. Department of Commerce but are always considered a distinct group by members of the trade. These agent intermediaries deal almost exclusively with grocery chains and food products. Many of the most familiar brands on the shelves of grocery stores are sold nationwide through food brokers. Quite often, these brokers handle from 20 to 30 different noncompeting items from many producers. The brokers distribute within clearly delineated geographic territories that are of sufficiently small size so that proper sales and service coverage can be achieved. The broad range of items carried by food brokers provides them with the economies of scale needed for high-level service to their clients.

Food brokers engage in a full range of distribution activities. They provide personal selling for their clients' products, set up store displays and sampling programs, assist retailers with promotions, and provide coverage of both wholesale and retail store buying offices. Food brokers are not, however, expected to store, deliver, or otherwise physically handle the goods they sell. Some brokers will maintain a small stock of each of the items they carry from which they can make emergency deliveries if a retailer runs short on inventory before a regular delivery arrives.

Selling agents are frequently confused with manufacturers' agents because they sell goods for clients on a commission basis. Selling agents are different, however, chiefly because of the scope of authority they are granted by the firms they represent. Whereas manufacturers' agents are limited in geographic coverage and policy-making authority, selling agents assume full responsibility for selling the entire output of one or more products for a client. This does not mean that they are granted authority for an entire product line of a manufacturer, but for certain product items they are give exclusive selling rights. Typically, selling agents handle the output of two or more manufacturers, and based on their market experience, chose the most desirable markets and selling methods. In most instances, selling agents perform such services as production scheduling, credit and collection of buyers' payments, and occasionally assist in product design.

Selling agents are well suited to handling the output of organizations that are highly skilled in production but have not become skilled or experienced in marketing. As a result, selling agents are often found in industries where many relatively small producers turn out products suitable for sale through many different kinds of retail outlets. The cotton and textile mills of the southern United States fit this description and are typically served by selling agents. Mill operators are often highly specialized production experts. Similarly, customers for fabric are often highly demanding in quality and design requirements. Selling agents are well suited to serving the needs of these buyers and sellers.

Auction companies are most frequently used in the distribution of leaf tobacco, livestock, fruit, and vegetables in the business market and real estate, antiques, and automobiles in the household consumer market. Auction companies are typically paid a commission on the goods sold, although some charge a flat fee. Almost all cigarette tobacco is sold from auction barns. In large terminal markets such as Chicago and New York a majority of the fresh produce is sold through auction companies. In rural market areas of the United States, livestock auctions account for an important portion of total livestock marketing.

Auction companies are among the oldest wholesaling establishments. They furnish the selling staff and in many instances the physical facilities where sales can take place. An auction is an excellent example of the free interplay of price-making forces at work. The quality of the goods, the amount of stock on hand, and expert judgment on the part of buyers competing for the goods all play a role in determining the price. But auctions are a rather cumbersome exchange process in that the buyers must physically inspect the goods and be on hand during the entire selling process. The utility embodied in telephone or electronic ordering is much greater than the auction process provides. Nevertheless, auctions remain fairly important to the sales volume of products that do not readily lend themselves to other forms of distribution.

Export agents confine their dealings to trade between firms in different countries. A principal type of export agent is the export management company (EMC). As discussed in Chapter 13, an EMC acts much like the export department in a firm. Its activities include foreign market research, identification of foreign market distributors, exhibition of a firm's products at relevant trade shows, and handling the documentation required for export of goods. An EMC handles several allied but noncompeting product lines from several manufacturers.

Another type of export agent is the manufacturers' export agent (MEA). This is an organization that operates in foreign markets much like manufacturers' agents operate in the U.S. market. This type of agent maintains operations in foreign markets and is relatively free to sell clients' products to any customers that can be located. Both types of export agents merely match buyers with sellers and typically do take possession or title to goods. Recently, however, more export agents have become involved in arranging financing for foreign buyers.

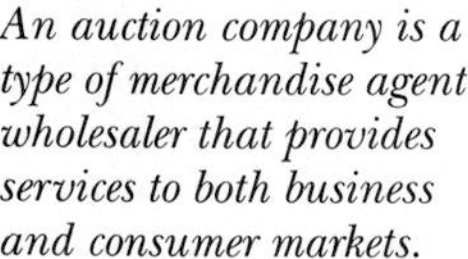

An auction company is a type of merchandise agent wholesaler that provides services to both business and consumer markets.

TRENDS IN WHOLESALING

There are two significant and related **trends in wholesaling:** fierce competition within the channel and industry consolidation. In 1994, gross profits in the wholesale industry were estimated to increase about 6 percent to nearly $430 billion. The gross profit margin wholesalers commanded increased slightly from prior years to 21.1 percent.[4] The increase in dollar profits and profit margin percentage have resulted from wholesalers carefully managing their operations in an era of fierce price competition and challenges from both the manufacturing and retailing positions in the channel. Retailers are demanding more price concessions and more manufacturers are establishing vertical marketing channels. Increases in productivity and service, like those instituted by American Lock & Supply, have reduced effects of these price and competitive pressures. Another example of a wholesaler that has achieved greater strength in the channel is United Stationers, Inc., the largest distributor of office supplies. United Stationers has had to face the challenge of discount retail office suppliers like Office Depot, Office Max, and Staples. In response to these competitive challenges, United Stationers has helped its independent retail dealers by increasing the merchandise mix to include furniture and computers. And, the wholesaler has also used overnight delivery to increase the effectiveness of its retailers.[5]

In response to such price and competitive pressures, another industry trend has emerged: consolidation. Wholesalers are merging and the industry is experiencing unprecedented consolidation. Many of the consolidated operations are resulting from publicly held companies replacing old family-owned firms. Larger operations allow greater economies of scale. The savings from large-scale operations will potentially bolster sagging profit margins. And, these larger operations can afford to adopt and take full advantage of new productivity enhancing technology. United Stationers has bought one of its largest competitors, Stationers Distributing Co., to achieve greater efficiency. McKesson, a large drug wholesaler, bought out a Canadian distributor, Provigo, Inc., to increase its buying power and competitive position.[6]

Beyond consolidation, wholesalers are responding to changing market conditions with a variety of growth-oriented strategies. Some of the more prevalent strategies are:

- Adding foreign product lines to their product collection, which often carry higher profit margins than domestically produced goods.
- Developing their own brands in standardized product categories to increase profit margins.
- Adopting a broader service role and performing some retail functions like catalog selling or operating wholesale club operations that sell directly to household consumers.
- Increasing certain manufacturer-type activities such as repackaging, first-stage processing, and fabrication. Activities like these would create form utility, which is not currently prevalent in most wholesaling operations.
- Diversifying into new or complimentary lines in an attempt to leverage current client relationships, current facilities, or systems use.

As you can see, many of the growth strategies initiated by wholesalers resemble vertical integration tactics. While wholesalers have not moved beyond establishing cooperatives with retailers (as discussed in Chapter 13) as an approach to integration in the market, adopting more retailer and manufacturer processes suggests that integration of functions, if not ownership of operations, is an emerging trend.

Much of what wholesalers can do to increase efficiency, productivity, and service relates to the physical distribution activities performed by wholesalers. We will turn our attention now to this aspect of the distribution process.

Physical Distribution

Physical distribution is the term used to describe activities related to having the right product at the right place at the right time in the right quantity at the right cost. In this sense, physical distribution, which is often referred to as **logistics,** is essential to the time and place utility aspects of the entire channel system. If this part of the distribution system fails to provide for the physical handling and flow of goods and services from the point of production to the point of consumption, then time and place utility are completely undermined. Good managers realize that quality is defined by both a good product *and* its availability where, when, and in the condition desired.[7]

Physical distribution is an area where significant opportunities abound to enhance customer satisfaction and create competitive advantages. One practicing logistics manager expressed these opportunities in physical distribution this way: "A well-managed and operated logistics network has the potential of adding value for the consumer even if a company's product is not significantly differentiated from that of its competitors."[8] Once again, we see the prominence of the value-added aspect of a component of the marketing system. The key to taking advantage of the opportunities embodied in physical distribution is to recognize and treat physical distribution as a system of activities.

The Physical Distribution System

It is important to conceive of physical distribution as a system of activities rather than considering physical supply activities as merely a series of discrete acts. A *system* of activities at this level of distribution is again best represented as a *flow* and the physical handling of material goods from point of origin to end user. This portrayal highlights that physical distribution activities must be handled from supplier to producer, from producer to wholesaler, from wholesaler to business user or retailer, and again from retailer to consumer. In other words, every intermediary in a channel will have challenges, opportunities, and activities associated with physical distribution.

From a strategic perspective, physical distribution provides a potent set of activities that can contribute to customer satisfaction *and* contain costs in a firm's quest to achieve competitive advantage. Two concepts form the basis for these contributions of physical distribution to the overall marketing process: the total package of values concept and the total cost concept.

TOTAL PACKAGE OF VALUES CONCEPT

Customers do not buy only the core or generic product. They buy goods that meet their needs when and where they are desired. In this sense, consumers will perceive value in a firm's offering based on both the features of the product *and* the services rendered. The physical distribution system is ideally suited to make contributions to the services associated with a product and thus help create a perception of value on the part of customers. Pursuing this opportunity is based on the development of a customer service level as part of a **total package of values concept** for the physical distribution system

Customer service level is a standard against which physical distribution performance can be measured. The earliest implementation of the standard was a measure of the time elapsed between the receipt of an order and the delivery of goods by the buyer. In modernized and sophisticated physical distribution systems, customer service level is operationalized through a variety of activities related to customer demands for service. Customer service level measures typically include the following factors:

- Time elapsed from receipt of an order to delivery of goods; this factor is often further broken down by product class, customer type, time of year, and geographic territory.
- Consistency in time elapsed and specification of allowable variance.
- Backorders as a percentage of total orders due to out-of-stock conditions.
- Specification of limits on order size and frequency (i.e., minimum order quantity per time frame).
- Order placement procedures, billing methods, order status information systems, and other procurement and order tracking policies and procedures.
- Return policy
- Accuracy of the system (i.e., percentage of orders filled, shipped, and billed properly).
- Number of and responsiveness to customer complaints.

Monitoring internal company records provides much of the information needed for these measures. Some of the signals that indicate a need for service level enhancement are increases in out-of-stock conditions, complaints of slow delivery, damaged goods, and increasing errors in order filling.

TOTAL COST CONCEPT

The value of a systems oriented approach to physical distribution is that it focuses attention on the effectiveness and efficiency of the whole system rather than on separate, isolated activities. In true systems fashion, maximum efficiency in one activity may not support and foster the performance of the entire system. For example, the sales force would prefer large inventories so that customer demands, no matter how out of the ordinary, could be responded to rapidly. Finance and accounting functions within the organization, however, would like to see minimal stock levels to reduce inventory costs. Similarly, the marketing department prefers fast order processing while finance would settle for a slow, inexpensive system for order handling and filling.

When a **total cost concept** is implemented as part of a physical distribution system, then each function in a firm must recognize that cost trade-offs within an area may be called for in order to minimize the cost of the overall system. Total cost, *not* the operating costs of each unit involved in the process, is the relevant level of analysis. So, the marketing department may have to accept smaller inventories and slower order processing than would be ideal for its purposes. The accounting and finance areas may have to accept larger inventories and more costly order processing procedures than they would consider most efficient for their purposes. The challenge for a physical distribution manager is to decide whether increased costs in one of the elements of the physical distribution system provide a sufficient increase in customer satisfaction to offset the added costs.

Components of a Physical Distribution System

With a total package of values and total cost concept perspective, the goal of a physical distribution system is to achieve the needed level of customer service at the lowest possible total cost. Note that total cost is subordinate to customer service level. Low total cost, per se, is not the goal but rather lowest *possible* total cost given a specified customer service level. In order to pursue customer service/total cost goals, an effective and efficient physical distribution system is built of several components: information system, order processing system, storage facilities, materials handling, inventory management and control, and transportation management. Each of these components must work together in the context of the total package of values and total cost concepts. We will consider each component separately to identify the unique contributions they make to customer service levels and cost efficiency. These components are depicted graphically in Illustration 15-2.

INFORMATION SYSTEM

An **information system** is needed for physical distribution to determine appropriate customer service levels, to forecast demand for inventory and locations, and to determine optimum modes of transportation and packaging requirements. A well-designed and carefully maintained information system provides the data base for the design, operation, maintenance and evaluation of a physical distribution system. One of the most elaborate information systems is maintained by Toys "R" Us. Toys "R" Us first accumulates and then re-sorts and redistributes over 18,000 different toy items to stores in its national distribution network. The key to managing such a huge volume and wide variety of toys is a centralized information system that is hooked to each cash register in every store. When a customer buys an item, the universal product code is scanned and the information sent to the central information system. With this information, management identifies quantities needed at each store and can maintain appropriate inventory levels on every item. This information system designed to aid the physical distribution process helps Toys "R" Us avoid out-of-stock conditions (and thus increase customer satisfaction) and reduce distri-

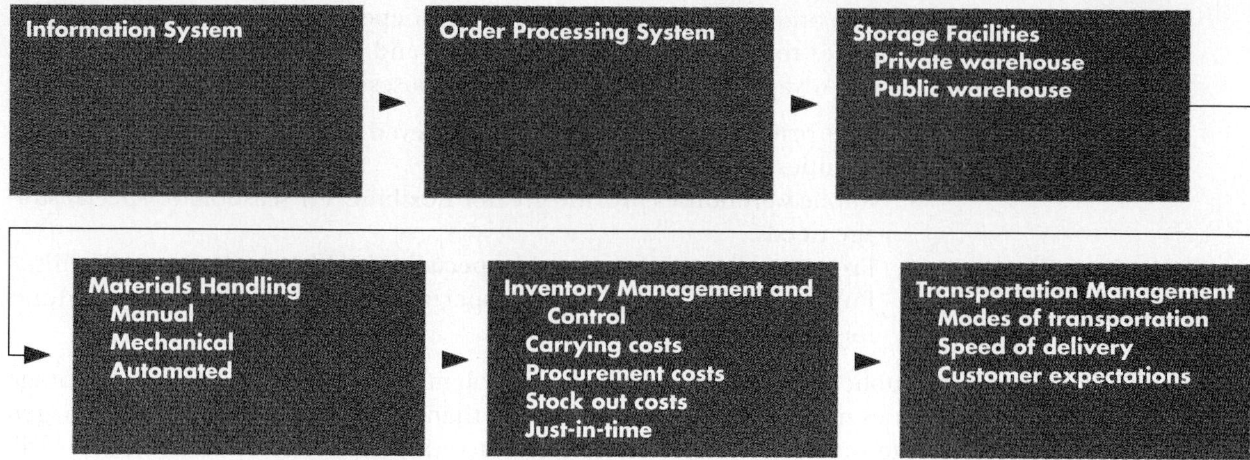

ILLUSTRATION 15-2
Components of a Physical Distribution System

bution costs. This, in turn, allows the firm to continue to sell toys well below manufacturers' suggested retail prices and competitors' prices.

ORDER PROCESSING SYSTEM

An **order processing system** includes all the activities involved in receiving, monitoring, and transmitting orders for the purpose of packing and shipping goods. Speed and accuracy in order processing have a direct effect on customer satisfaction. Slow or erratic order filling leads to customer frustration and increased costs to correct errors. Further, there are often excess transportation, re-stocking, and storage costs involved. Conversely, high-quality performance in order processing improves the competitive position of the firm. Recall the order processing system of the National Bicycle Company of Japan, which accepts customer orders directly from retail shops to the production facility. In two weeks, a customer has a completely customized bicycle. When properly designed and managed, an order processing system can be an excellent source of information—customer names and locations, order size and revenue by customer type, sales patterns by product type, sales patterns by geographic area and by sales person. This data improves production planning and inventory levels and help create more accurate demand forecasts—all of which can significantly reduce total cost.

Much of the advancement in order processing systems has come about because of advances in computer technology—in particular, the ability for computer-to-computer information transmission. The Gap clothing chain has recently opened a $75 million automated order processing and distribution center outside Baltimore that allows the firm to supply its New York City area stores daily instead of three times a week.[9]

STORAGE FACILITIES

For storage of inventory, firms can choose between private warehousing, public warehousing, or a combination of the two. **Private warehouses** are those that are owned and managed by firms that own the goods. **Public warehouses** are owned and operated by professional, independent warehousers who provide services to a number of different firms and are paid only for the services provided. Advantages of using public warehouses are:

- The firm that owns the goods is relieved of the investment in storage facilities.
- Public warehouses provide greater flexibility for seasonal or special storage needs.
- Professional management with specialized skills comes with the facility.
- Public warehouses often have specialized equipment and procedures for storage and handling.

Public warehouses may present problems for a firm, however. Such storage facilities may cost more per unit stored than a well-designed and well-managed private warehouse. There is no assurance that a public warehouse can or will meet the space and handling needs of a firm. Finally, it is often difficult to integrate public warehouses into a firm's total system of physical distribution.[10]

Small manufacturers prefer public warehouses because of the range of services provided. Storage can be accomplished in proper quantities and all arrangements related to receiving, handling, and shipping are carried out efficiently. Many public warehouses also provide clerical services, repackaging, traffic accounting and pre-payment of freight charges, and telephone answering for customers' sales forces. Organizations that maintain their own private warehouses tend to be larger operations. Sears, JCPenney, Kmart, and Wal-Mart all maintain their own large distribution centers. The regional centers maintained by these firms provide customized storage and shipping services suited to the unique method of operation each organization prefers. Wal-Mart has the most sophisticated system. The firm maintains 22 distribution centers throughout the United States averaging one million square feet each. With its own fleet of trucks, 2,500 drivers, and 16,000 employees in the distribution system, Wal-Mart does customized delivery to its stores to accommodate peak season, night, and accelerated deliver demands. [11]

Deciding between public and private warehousing for storage is based on the balance between customer service and total cost—goals that pervade decision making throughout the physical distribution system. The method of storage that reduces total costs, results in reduction of inventories, creates few stock outs and order-filling errors, and maintains customer service level objectives will be the storage method of choice.

MATERIALS HANDLING

Handling goods within a warehouse setting may seem like an obvious task: goods are stored in inventory until they are ordered. Well, the **materials handling** aspects of physical distribution are significantly more complicated and sophisticated than the average person might imagine. The costs of materials handling can be great enough that the firm that identifies opportunities for efficiency in materials handling can achieve a competitive advantage. Kids "R" Us provides an excellent example in this regard. Many of the firm's warehouses have completely automated materials handling systems. In one such

Modern materials handling systems increase efficiency and can contribute to competitive advantage.

warehouse, clothes items are moved on an overhead monorail system to the shipping area, sorted for shipment, and packed in containers of 1,000 items. Price tags and labels are attached to each garment before shipping. When a Kids "R" Us store receives these garments, they are priced, labeled, sorted, and ready to be displayed.[12]

The functions performed at the materials handling stage include receiving goods, labeling and sorting, dispatching to storage, holding, selecting goods from inventory, packing shipments, and dispatching shipments. In most instances, facilities will employ modern materials handling equipment, which either palletizes or otherwise has items arranged for mass movement. It is simply too costly to handle a large number of goods one item at a time.

Physical handling of items in a storage facility takes place in one of three ways:

1. In manual handling, human power is used and goods are moved by hand with the aid of hand trucks.
2. Mechanical handling uses mechanically powered devices such as forklift trucks and conveyors to move the goods with human thought required to select and route the items.
3. Automated handling employs mechanical devices to stack, pick out, and route the goods. These systems are controlled by computer programs and human control is only indirect.

The more the materials handling process can move away from manual handling, the more cost savings can be incurred. Food wholesalers, for example, have been able to lower their gross margins from around 12 percent in the 1970s to about 3 percent today. More efficient materials handling systems are largely responsible for making this decrease in margin possible.

INVENTORY MANAGEMENT AND CONTROL

During the decade of the 1980s, inventories needed to support consumer and business sales were slashed by about $40 billion. This across-industry inventory reduction was accomplished by reducing inventory carrying costs through just-in-time inventory systems, automated storage and retrieval systems, and such mundane-sounding efforts as warehouse design and location of goods within warehouses that facilitate order filling and shipping. The most important impact of these improved systems has been to make better use of employees. A major component of the enhanced efficiency of **inventory management and control** has been employee participation in planning and providing employees with responsibility and authority.[13]

While great progress has been made, much opportunity for even greater efficiency lies in this area of physical distribution. An examination of the nature of inventory costs and the reasons for maintaining inventory reveals the basis for inventory management approaches and control systems. We can examine the nature of inventory by specifying the inventory costs: carrying costs, procurement costs, and stock-out costs.

Carrying costs are those costs incurred by holding an item in inventory over time. It is estimated that carrying costs as a percentage of total inventory costs average about 20 to 25 percent, although the range is 14 to 43 percent of total inventory costs. A critical decision facing a firm is the balance between having inventory on hand to provide customer service versus the costs incurred by carrying inventory. Inventory carrying costs are calculated as the sum of interest on the capital expenditure to purchase the inventory, protection against damage or deterioration provided by proper warehousing and storage, handling costs, taxes, and insurance.

Procurement costs, which are also referred to as order costs, consist of keeping records of inventory levels and determination of order points. *Order point* is the level of inventory at which a reorder is placed to replenish stock. Other costs charged as procurement costs include the selection of suppliers, office expenses to prepare requisitions and process payments, and the cost of maintaining inventory records.

Stock-out costs are the costs associated with not having an item available when it is ordered by a customer. Stock-out costs are difficult to measure from an opportunity costs standpoint. However, the actual costs include cost of back ordering, excess cost in special ordering, excess cost of express shipments, canceled orders, and lost customers.

Maintaining proper inventory levels and containing inventory costs can provide tremendous strategic impact within a channel. Remember that inventory plays an important part in providing time and place utility satisfaction. However, the strategic impact of inventory levels can be extremely costly due to the types of costs just identified. In an effort to realize the strategic potential of inventory yet effectively contain costs, the concept of just-in-time inventory has been supported. **Just-in-time inventory (JIT)** is the process of providing an amount of inventory that is matched as closely as possible to the quantities ordered by customers at the times customer orders are received. The goal of JIT systems is to minimize inventory carrying costs without incurring substantial stock-out costs. The ideal is to have almost no inventory in storage, but rather to receive new shipments of goods "just-in-time" to ship those goods to fill customer orders. Advances in demand estimation procedures and more restrictive ordering policies have made just-in-time inventory a workable approach to inventory cost management.

TRANSPORTATION MANAGEMENT

Transportation is the link between sources of supply and points of demand throughout the distribution channel. As such, decisions regarding physical transport of goods can have significant effects on time and place utility in the system. If transportation to the demand site is rapid, then replenishment of stock is also rapid and the requirements of time and place utility are served. These strategic implications of transportation, however, often are secondary to the cost factors of transportation. Because transportation often represents the single largest expense in many physical distribution systems, cost considerations often dominate **transportation management** decision making.

The major transportation alternatives are rail, truck, air, water, and pipeline. The features of each transportation option are highlighted in Table 15-3. The differences among these **modes of transportation** and the decision regarding which to use must take into consideration a variety of factors, which, again, highlights the nature of physical distribution as a *system* of activities. Within the context of cost, therefore, two systems-oriented criteria must be considered in making transportation decisions: speed of delivery and customer expectations.

Speed of delivery will affect inventory levels that are required at both the origin of distribution and the destination. The increased delivery time that results from slow transportation modes will require customers to carry greater inventory levels. Since stocks cannot be replenished quickly in the context of slow distribution, customers want to avoid stock-out conditions and will hold greater inventory. The cost savings of slower modes of transportation must be weighed against higher inventory carrying costs. Conversely, if customers have emergency needs for stock, speed of delivery is the priority and the cost of transportation is of little consequence.

Customer expectations for delivery time affect speed of transportation and, subsequently, the cost of transportation. If customers have come to expect and demand frequent and short deliveries of stock, then the transportation system must be managed to fulfill these expectations. If a customer is accustomed to long lead times in the delivery process, then lower cost, slower modes of transportation can be used. In general, both the speed of delivery and customer expectations must be weighed against the transportation costs, inventory costs, and the cost of stock-outs. If the risks of poor customer service are great, then more expense in transportation may have to be incurred to achieve strategic customer service objectives.

Wholesaling and physical distribution decisions in the domestic market require careful analysis and a broad systems view of the process. When this phase of distribution must be managed for global market needs, managers must reassess the entire system in order to make effective decisions. We will turn our attention now to the challenge of wholesaling and physical distribution in the global context.

TABLE 15-3
Key Features of Major Modes of Transportation

Mode of Transportation	Key Features
Rail	Large capacity and weight/size capability
	Good access to major market areas
	Low cost per unit
	Varying reliability
	Slow speed
Truck	Moderate capacity and weight/size capability
	Flexibility to reach any destination point
	Moderate cost per unit
	Good reliability
	Good speed of delivery—1 to 5 days
Air	Large capacity, limited weight/size capability
	Direct access limited to major markets
	Highest cost per unit
	Varying reliability
	Highest speed
Water	Large capacity and weight/size capability
	Very limited direct access to markets
	Very low cost per unit
	Slowest speed
Pipeline	Very high capacity for limited commodities
	Limited access points
	Lowest cost per unit
	High reliability

Wholesaling and Physical Distribution: A Global Perspective

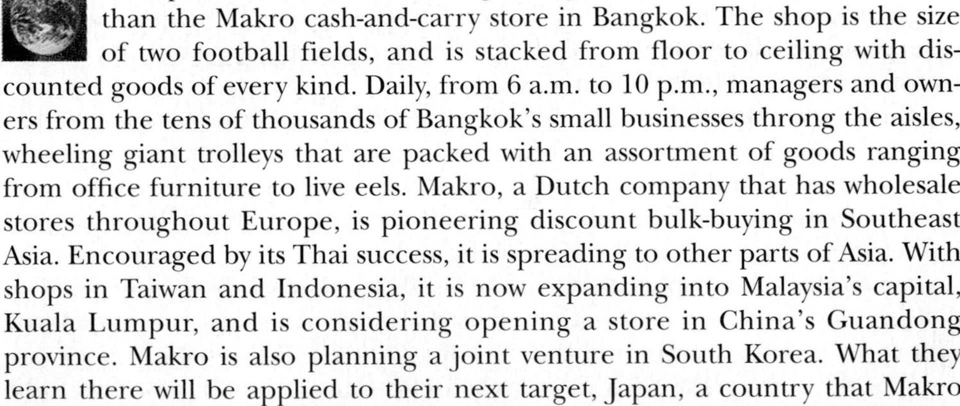

Few spectacles illustrate Asia's growing consumer culture more vividly than the Makro cash-and-carry store in Bangkok. The shop is the size of two football fields, and is stacked from floor to ceiling with discounted goods of every kind. Daily, from 6 a.m. to 10 p.m., managers and owners from the tens of thousands of Bangkok's small businesses throng the aisles, wheeling giant trolleys that are packed with an assortment of goods ranging from office furniture to live eels. Makro, a Dutch company that has wholesale stores throughout Europe, is pioneering discount bulk-buying in Southeast Asia. Encouraged by its Thai success, it is spreading to other parts of Asia. With shops in Taiwan and Indonesia, it is now expanding into Malaysia's capital, Kuala Lumpur, and is considering opening a store in China's Guandong province. Makro is also planning a joint venture in South Korea. What they learn there will be applied to their next target, Japan, a country that Makro believes has a retail and distribution structure similar to Korea's. [14]

How did Makro do it? In Thailand the company was helped by an alliance with Charoen Pokphand, a local conglomerate that opened doors, especially those of Thai manufacturers'. Eighty-five percent of Makro's products come from local manufacturers. Demand from small shopkeepers is responsible for the rest. In most parts of Southeast Asia, "mom and pop" stores are captives of the big distribution companies, which dictate the selection of goods to be sold. Makro gives these retailers the chance to bypass traditional distributors and buy their own choice of goods, in bulk, and at lower prices. Inevitably, the company's success is attracting rivals. Three new competitors modeled on Makro's approach to serving retailers have opened shops in Thailand. An additional threat to Makro comes from the other side of the supply chain—the growing sophistication of Southeast Asia's retailing market. By 1995, Bangkok will contain one million households with an income of $10,000 a year, up from just 160,000 such households in 1986. Analysts predict that the number of department stores in Bangkok will rise from 86 to more than 115 by 1996. Such an increase in the supply of stores could undermine the small shopkeepers who are Makro's lifeblood.[15]

Both at the beginning of this chapter and in the section "Trends in Wholesaling," the focus of the discussion has been on the fierce competition that characterizes activities in the U.S. wholesale sector. In fact, in industrialized and developing markets throughout the world the emerging trend toward vertical integration has put competitive pressures on wholesalers from both the producer and retail levels in the channel causing them to improve operations in order to increase efficiencies and lower margins. As the Makro example illustrates, within global markets the level of competition and the evolving cultural environment are key forces in determining the range and quality of wholesale services offered. Additionally, the nature and structure of the retail markets targeted by manufacturers will influence the choice and number of wholesalers used.

THE GLOBAL SCENE IN WHOLESALING

Both the range and quality of services provided by wholesalers are strongly influenced by the amount of competition in a local market. In highly competitive industrialized markets, competition is the force that drives the level of services provided by wholesalers. For small and medium-size companies, the choice of an overseas wholesaler may be left to their own exporter, such as the export management company operator discussed in Chapter 13. These export companies have already developed foreign channel relationships and are usually capable of assessing whether a wholesaler is needed for a market and, if so, which ones to choose. For example, if distribution activities are highly competitive and the retail structure in a foreign market is well organized, any of a number of competing wholesalers may be suitable for the company's efforts. Alternatively, if the retail segment is disorganized and highly fragmented, the exporter may need to rely on the services of many levels of wholesalers in order to achieve market coverage. Whatever the situation, unless the manufacturer's domestic exporter takes legal possession of the goods being exported, there likely will be a contractual agreement with the foreign exporter. For this reason alone, it is advisable for companies wishing to enter foreign markets to take an active role in selecting intermediaries.

For a small fee, the U.S. Department of Commerce will provide secondary sources of information that identify potential intermediaries and give a general assessment of their reliability as well as a profile of their existing product lines.[16] An on-site visit is the next step that is the most effective way to assess the potential for a good working relationship with a wholesaler. Being there helps an export/marketing manager understand which distribution channels are being used and why. Interviewing end users and retailers is an important aspect of these efforts, since they may offer a different perspective on the wholesale structure as well as identify alternative wholesalers for consideration. Once a shortlist has been developed, an in-depth analysis would be done in order to understand the wholesaler's approaches and methods. This assessment would include identifying their major customer groups and the competing lines they carry and determining their ability and interest in providing the marketing services that the company needs to meet its marketing objectives.

Entering into a contract requires the counsel of a lawyer in the intermediary's market. Conditions relating to services expected, lack of performance, exceptional costs, or termination differ greatly from one country to another and need to be clearly specified. Switching distributors can be disruptive to a firm's marketing efforts, can lead to stock-out situations and lost sales, and can involve other financial penalties. Compensation fees for terminating a contract, which are awarded because of the intermediary's efforts to build market share, can be high (as much as two years' commission fees). In countries where wholesalers have informal agreements about shared markets, or in countries where the wholesaler is part of a company that dominates the channels of distribution, finding an alternative approach to supplying customers may be difficult.

In countries where competition is lacking at the wholesale level, the established wholesalers may be nothing more than a necessary intermediary that has to be used in order to gain market access. The efficiencies (or inefficiencies) of their operation or the range and quality of related services they provide (or don't provide) may have no bearing on the margins they charge in distributing goods. In developing markets, importers and wholesalers may have monopolies or exclusive arrangements within an industry due to social or political connections. In such cases, services such as extending credit, shipping, on-time delivery, and market research information may be inefficiently carried out or nonexistent.

Despite their importance to the market efficiency of developing countries, wholesaling as a profession is often held in low esteem. Developing countries are often characterized by scarcity of goods, and the economic emphasis is on production rather than distribution. Further, in many of these countries, wholesaling activities are dominated by foreigners or ethnic minorities. As a result of this, the wholesale trade can be insular and the local population often looks on wholesalers with suspicion and fear that they are being exploited by their presence rather than benefiting from the services provided. This bias is very often unfair, since wholesalers in many developing countries play a key role in handling imports and in financing the flow of goods between producers and retailers. In much of Africa, for example, the wholesale and retail trade is dominated by Indians who run efficient operations in competitive environments and accept low margins. In Indonesia and the Philippines, ethnic Chinese dominate the wholesale and retail trade, offering highly competitive services relative to the operations of the local populations.

GLOBAL PHYSICAL DISTRIBUTION MANAGEMENT

Reliable sources of supply and rapid delivery often outweigh considerations of price in competing for customers in the global market. This being the case, the physical distribution of goods and services, or **global physical distribution management,** is becoming more important as a strategic tool in international marketing. As is often the case when moving from a domestic to a global setting in marketing, the basic elements of the discussion may remain the same; it's just that the complexity of execution goes up. Such is the case in managing the six components of an effective and efficient physical distribution system in the global context. Four elements of the system in a global setting have significant issues associated with them and will be highlighted here: information systems, storage facilities, inventory, and transportation.

Information Systems

Access to global information systems is no longer the luxury of large multinational corporations. It has become a necessity for all international marketers and is an integrating element in the activities of global warehousing, transportation, and inventory management. Just as multinational firms use global communication systems for daily management of foreign currency exchange risk and the redistribution of foreign exchange based on the needs of their subsidiaries around the world, companies of all sizes use communication systems to optimally manage the so-called global pipeline to supply customers around the world. Checking on the status of goods as they cross national borders, querying international and local carriers, faxing the numerous documents relating to banking, insurance, tariffs, and duties, and checking inventory levels around the world in anticipation of upcoming production runs provide just a small glimpse of the communications needs that are met through global information systems. For some wholesalers, the technical knowledge that the firm possesses is its key competitive advantage. Fleming Companies, a large American grocery store distributor, uses a strategy of licensing its distribution system software to Japanese and Korean distributors to build its ties abroad. As was discussed in Chapter 14, Japan in particular is lagging in inventory management systems, and the licensing of Fleming's distribution technology is the first step to expanding their grocery sales.[17]

Storage Facilities

Basic decisions with respect to warehousing have to do with the size of the facility and the country of location. In most instances, these decisions will be based on where the firm's customers are (both current and future) and what level of customer service is needed. Multinational firms with global marketing efforts may select a regional warehouse to serve a number of markets. For example, Apple Computer's European production facility is in Ireland where the company enjoys access to a large, highly trained technical work force. The computers are shipped to the Netherlands by truck for warehousing and further distribution for the rest of Western Europe. Sales to African countries are also shipped from Holland via air freight. Air shipments to Africa are safer than surface methods, and the relatively high price of the computers makes the higher shipping costs a smaller percentage of total costs. Such speedy delivery significantly increasing the perception of value-added to African clients. In most industrialized countries, full-service warehouse facilities are available, which offer not only modern storage facilities, but also transportation services, freight forwarding, insurance, and customs brokerage. If prompt and reliable delivery is key to maintaining customer satisfaction, then having a full-service warehouse in the local market may be necessary.

In many less-developed countries, or in regions of the world with political instability, storage facilities are limited, often unreliable, or not available at all. In such cases, a regional warehouse that serves an extended market may be sufficient. For example, Athens, Greece, provides warehousing services for many companies serving the Middle East. Its location, modern port facilities, and cosmopolitan atmosphere make it an ideal compromise for companies who do not have facilities in the Middle East or who do not choose to take on the risk of storage in the region. Free Trade Zones also offer regional warehousing options to global shippers. **Free Trade Zones (FTZs)** are specially designated areas within a country to which companies ship products for storage, sorting, assembly, or repackaging without paying taxes or custom duties. Only when the products leave the FTZ to be sold in the country do they become subject to local tariffs and duties.

Inventory

International marketing typically involves great distances, more intermediaries, and other delays in transportation time such as document checks at border crossings. Given these variables, the company is more likely to have proportionally larger quantities of products in transit at any given time than in a domestic market situation. These factors all serve to increase working capital and extend the amount of time for accounts receivable. How often to order and how much to order are decisions that are inversely related in global inventory management. If too many orders are placed in a given accounting period, ordering costs go up. Alternatively, if large quantities are shipped at one time, the total number of orders is reduced (and subsequently, costs of processing orders), savings from bulk shipping may be gained, but carrying costs in inventory will rise. Company-owned integrated channels are typically better equipped to deal with these issues compared to a company that has to deal with independently owned channel members. Integrated channel members are more willing to take a surplus inventory during periods of high inflation or unfavorable exchange rates, since transfer pricing practices within the global company allow them to optimize inventory costs. Independent channel members have their own policies, pricing objectives, and ideas of how to allocate their storage space and manage their inventory.

Transportation Considerations

Transportation decisions focus on the methods for shipping both internationally and locally within a foreign market. These choices will be influenced by the nature of the product, the availability of different transportation modes, the infrastructure of the country, the costs of different methods, and the level of customer service desired (i.e., whether delivery is routine or urgent). For high-value products with high inventory costs, total distribution costs will be lower if a faster, albeit more expensive, transportation method such as air

The most common method of transportation for shipping products to international markets is by boat.

freight is used. For perishables and seasonable products where timing is critical to the products' acceptance, a fast and reliable method may be the only option. For example, fresh-cut flowers are flown from the Netherlands to America on KLM's daily flights to New York, Chicago, and Los Angeles.

By far, the most common transportation method in international trade is via water. Apart from the efficiencies of bulk shipments via supertankers and super-cargo ships, many ports offer access to large markets. If you draw a radius of just 750 miles around Rotterdam, the world's busiest port in terms of tonnage, you will encompass a market approximately the same size as the population of the United States. Australia is another market where 80 percent of the country's population lives along the coastal front. The major drawback to large port cities is most often found in developing countries where internal transportation systems are insufficiently developed to handle the delivery capacity of large ocean vessels. Even when global companies can be efficient with their international shipping, poorly maintained roads and rail systems inland can cause bottlenecks in local distribution efforts.

The preceding issues describe the nature of wholesaling and physical distribution when the context is the global marketplace. As in the United States, these two areas are realizing change. The tremendous expansion of global trade since the end of World War II has created a growth market for global export offices, wholesalers, and shippers. While global trade continues to grow, the trends in global wholesaling are following the trends in the United States. Particularly in highly competitive, industrialized markets the trend is toward consolidation of wholesale and shipping activities. By merging together import offices, freight forwarders, wholesale companies, and retail outlets, these new operations have greater economies of scale and provide more competitive service. Perhaps most important to their own long-run survival, the larger operation enhances their importance in the total global distribution system, which ultimately improves their bargaining power and their cooperative relationships with large multinational firms that have their own global distribution networks. For example, the American VWR Corporation, a wholesaler of laboratory equipment, was pulled into expanding globally by the Du Pont Corporation, one of VRW's key customers. Du Pont wanted VWR to expand into Canada citing Du Pont's desire to deal with as few suppliers as possible as a way to having greater control and efficiency in maintaining their corporate quality programs with suppliers.[18]

In terms of global opportunities for wholesalers and physical distribution companies, a tremendous need exists for innovative, customer-oriented channel members and efficient and effective companies to move both imported and domestically produced goods and services to the marketplace. Expanding consumer markets in Asia, Latin America, and eastern Europe coupled with the needed development of antiquated port facilities and general improvements in infrastructure are forces that will shape global wholesaling and physical distribution activities into the next millennia.

Key Terms and Concepts

Wholesaling
Accumulation
Re-sorting
Transportation
Sales coverage
Merchandising
Storage
Credit
Merchant wholesalers
Full-service wholesalers
Industrial distributors
Farm product assemblers
Importers and exporters
Limited function wholesalers
Truck distributors
Rack jobbers
Drop shippers
Cash and carry wholesalers
Merchant agent wholesalers
Merchandise brokers
Purchasing agents
Resident buyers
Commission merchants
Manufacturers' agents
Food brokers
Selling agents
Auction companies
Export Agents
Trends in wholesaling
Physical distribution
Logistics
Total package of values concept
Customer service level
Total cost concept
Information system
Order processing system
Private warehouses
Public warehouses
Materials handling
Inventory management and control
Carrying costs
Procurement costs
Stock-out costs
Just-in-time inventory (JIT)
Transportation management
Modes of transportation
Global physical distribution management
Free trade zones (FTZs)

Questions and Exercises

1. Explain how the wholesaling functions of accumulation and re-sorting provide an important service to both producers and retailers.
2. The entire channel of distribution provides time, place, and possession utility. How does wholesaling make a contribution to these utilities and ultimately to customer satisfaction?
3. What is the main appeal of the limited function wholesaler? In order to make effective use of a limited function wholesaler, what must producers and retailers be prepared to do?
4. Find a full-service wholesaler in your area and identify how this wholesaler provides services to both manufacturers and retailers.

5. What are the two significant trends that have emerged in wholesaling? What types of strategies are wholesalers using to increase growth?
6. Why is physical distribution a system of activities in the true sense of the phrase?
7. What is the total package of values concept related to physical distribution? What role does customer service level play in this concept?
8. What two systems-oriented factors should be considered in the context of the cost of transportation?
9. Describe how the structure of competition and evolving consumer markets change the level and quality of services offered by wholesalers in global markets.
10. How is physical distribution different in global markets from what can be expected in the U.S. domestic market?

REFERENCES

1. Joseph Weber, "It's Like Somebody Had Shot the Postman," *Business Week* (January 13, 1992): 82.
2. U.S. Department of Commerce, Bureau of the Census, *1982 Census of Wholesale Trade,* 1 (Washington, D.C.: U.S. Government Printing Office), iii.
3. Ibid.
4. Richard A. Melcher, "Cut Out the Middleman? Never," *Business Week* (January 10, 1994): 96.
5. Ibid., 96.
6. Joseph Weber, "On a Fast Boat Anywhere," *Business Week* (January 11, 1993): 94; and Richard Melcher, *Business Week,* op. cit., 96.
7. Hirotaka Takenchi and John A. Quelch, "Quality Is More Than a Good Product," *Harvard Business Review* (July–August 1983): 139–145.
8. Howard Gochberg, "Logistics Can Be an Integral Part of the Value Equation," *Marketing News* (September 30, 1991): 17.
9. Russell Mitchell, "The Gap," *Business Week* (March 9, 1992): 61.
10. Joe Douress, "Public Warehouses," *Global Trade* (August 1987): 24.
11. *Wal-Mart Annual Report 1993,* 2–3.
12. "Kids "R" Us Takes a Merchandising Approach," *Chain Store Age* (January 1987): 180.
13. John J. Ettorre, "Next Step in Warehouse Efficiency Pondered by Distribution Experts," *Traffic World* (April 7, 1987): 39.
14. "Makro-Economics" *The Economist* (September 25, 1993): 80–81.
15. Ibid.
16. The U.S. Department of Commerce provides reports such as *Trade Opportunities Program (TOP),* the *Foreign Trade Index (FDI),* and *World Traders Data Report (WTDR).* Source: U.S. Department of Commerce (Washington, D.C.: U.S. Government Printing Office).
17. Joseph Weber, *Business Week* (January 11, 1993): op. cit.
18. Ibid.

SECTION FOUR

Managing the Marketing Process:

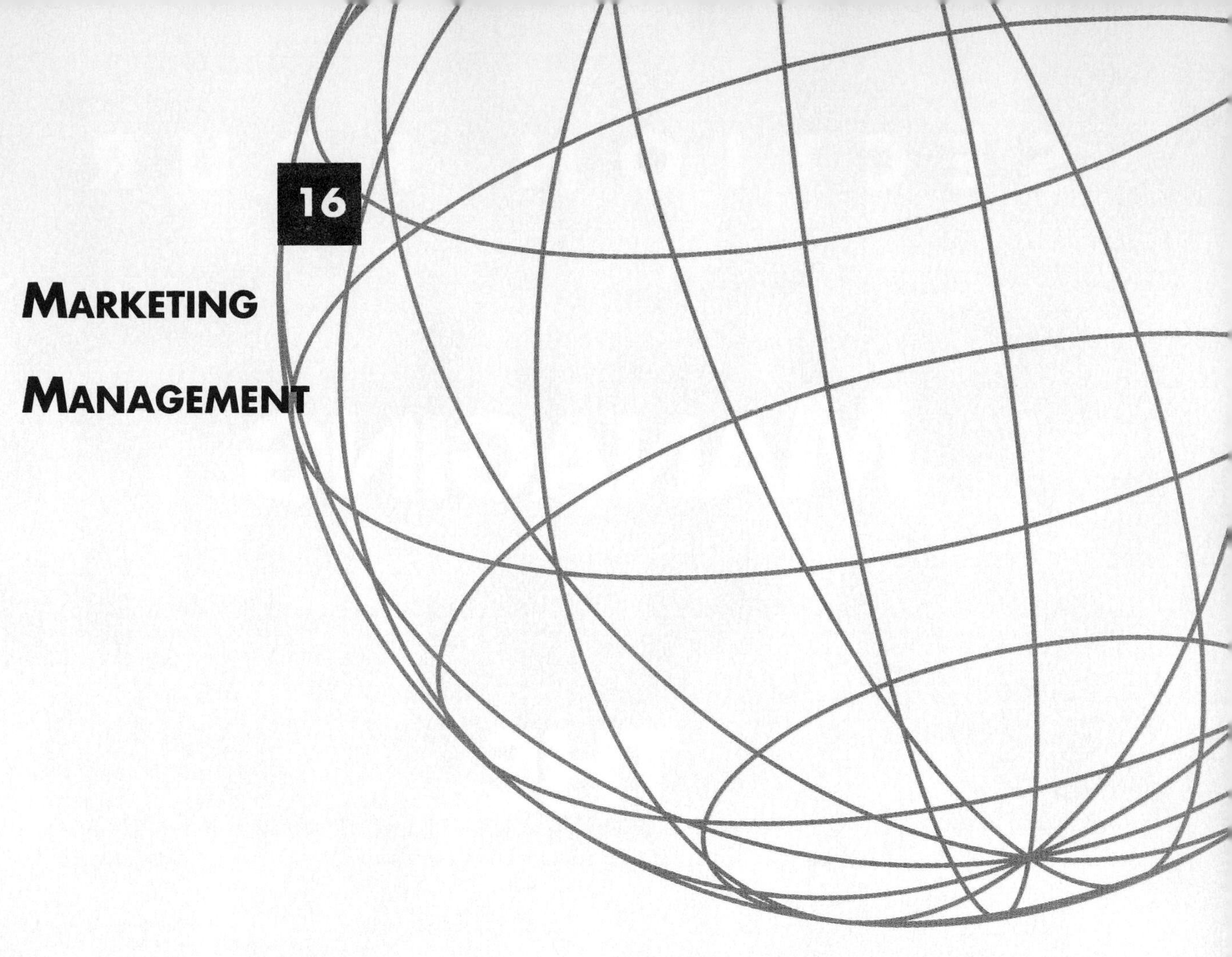

16

Marketing Management

AFTER STUDYING THIS CHAPTER, YOU WILL UNDERSTAND THAT:

1. The role of marketing management is to provide a guiding mechanism for strategic marketing decision making.
2. Managers must evaluate an organization's resources and then set sales, profit, and market objectives based on resource strengths.
3. Marketing strategy decisions at the marketing management level include identifying market opportunities, selecting target markets, and establishing market position.
4. Managers may rely on several traditional models of marketing management to provide a framework for decision making.
5. New trends in corporate management, including total quality management (TQM), horizontal structures, reengineering, and the virtual corporation, affect the way marketing management activities are carried out.

A Tale of Management Challenges

By the start of the 1980s, Harley-Davidson, the last U.S. motorcycle maker, had seen its share of the super-heavyweight motorcycle market drop from 75 percent in 1973 to less than 25 percent. Quality in the production process was so poor that more than half the cycles produced came off the assembly line missing parts and were delivered to dealers inoperable. The big Harleys leaked oil, vibrated excessively, and were hard to start. Performance couldn't touch the new "bullet bikes" arriving from Japan with their breath-taking acceleration and silky smooth transmissions. Harley loyalists were still willing to get their hands greasy to fix the big bikes and to modify their performance, but new buyers who were fuelling the growth in the motorcycle market had no intention of doing so. Needless to say, Harley-Davidson faced a huge management challenge. As Vaugn Beals, chairman of Harley-Davidson, put it, "We were being wiped out by the Japanese because they were better *managers*. It wasn't the robotics, or culture, or morning calisthenics and company songs—it was professional managers who understood their business and paid attention to detail."[1]

Beals devised a long-range plan to win customers and bring Harley-Davidsons back to prominence in the motorcycle market. The important change would be to upgrade performance with a new generation of engine designs. But this transition would take up to ten years. Harley needed solutions much sooner to survive. Those solutions came in the form of marketing management decisions to implement short- and intermediate-term strategies:

- "Willie G." Davidson created a series of cosmetic styling changes. In the five years before Harley could bring the new engines on line, he introduced a succession of new models—*Super Glide, Low Rider, and Wide Glide*—that emulated the look of the choppers Harley fanatics were putting together themselves. With a decal here and a paint strip there the new models were a huge success.
- Beals and several managers toured a Honda assembly plant and came away knowing their manufacturing techniques were woefully outdated and costly. A manufacturing team introduced a just-in-time inventory program in the firm's Milwaukee engine plant. Huge inventories and elaborate materials handling systems were eliminated with the program. The result was an increase in quality and a reduction in costs.
- In marketing, management shifted its focus away from trying to compete with the Japanese across several product lines and concentrated on developing the big-bike segment. In 1983, the company formed the Harley Owners Group (HOG) to develop a closer relationship with customers. Shortly afterward, a $3 million demonstration campaign was initiated called SuperRide, which invited bikers to visit any of the company's 600 dealers for a ride on a new Harley.

The Role of Marketing Management

In 1984, Harley-Davidson sales were a mere $294 million, which produced a profit of only $2.9 million. By 1993, sales had soared to over $1.2 billion and profits approached $75 million. Harley-Davidson has

Harley-Davidson has recaptured leading market share with a variety of marketing management strategies

not only survived, but has prospered and grabbed nearly 50 percent market share in the super-heavy weight market. The leaders of the firm *managed* Harley-Davidson out of crisis: corporate resources were focused on an identifiable target market segment, marketing and manufacturing were integrated to contain costs, programs to attract customers and support dealers were initiated, and strategies for the short- and long-term target market development were conceived and implemented.

As this episode in the history of Harley-Davidson highlights, the role of marketing management in an organization is to provide a mechanism for guiding marketing strategy development and implementation. No firm can compete effectively without performing basic tasks in the marketing mix: product development, pricing, distribution, and promotion. But, the difference between a firm that achieves mediocre results and a firm that prospers is often based on how much emphasis is placed on the *management* of marketing activities. Marketing management is critical to making the marketing process prominent in a firm. As the marketing process is granted unique status through focused management attention, the precision and impact of marketing activities increases.

This chapter will demonstrate that *managing* marketing activities rather than simply implementing marketing tasks has a tremendous impact on the competitive strength and profitability of a firm. Marketing management involves specialized management efforts. A highly useful and well-articulated definition of marketing management is:

The analysis, planning, implementation, and control of programs designed to create, build, and maintain mutually beneficial exchanges and relationships with target markets for the purpose of achieving organizational objectives. [2]

This definition highlights several aspects of the **role of marketing management.** When marketers manage, they perform activities to bring about desired exchanges between the firm and its target markets—both trade customers and final users. Marketing managers know that exchange doesn't just happen spontaneously. Instead, these exchanges must be managed with care and finesse. At Harley-Davidson, managers provided proof of the importance of marketing management in an organization. These managers *analyzed* problems with current products and marketing programs, *planned* new product designs (through engine and styling changes), *implemented* the changes by focusing on a specific product/target segment (the super-heavyweight market), and *controlled* the process by making sure that strategies were being carried out at the dealer level.

This perspective on marketing management highlights the need to manage marketing *activities* from initial market analysis and research through customer satisfaction after the purchase. To this traditional view, however, we need to add the dimension of managing *people.* Activities in the marketing process are, after all, carried out by people. This requires that marketing managers become excellent people managers, not just activity managers. Firms are recognizing the power and potency of the human factor in the management process. At General Electric, widely credited with helping shape the nature of contemporary American management style, sweeping changes are being implemented to take advantage of the human factor. The dynamic and visionary CEO of General Electric, John F. Welsh, Jr., believes that the twenty-first century manager will forgo many traditional methods for new duties such as counseling groups, providing resources for them, and helping them to think for themselves. Welch believes, "We're going to win on our ideas, not by whips and chains."[3] In other words, the management system must recognize the value of its human resource as well as establish a sound management structure for decision making. This issue will be discussed later in greater detail as it relates to management systems, in particular, the concepts of horizontal structure, reengineering, total quality management (TQM), and the "virtual" corporation.

The Primary Tasks of Marketing Management

Marketing managers are charged with the responsibility to make decisions that guide the overall marketing effort. To this point in the text, we have examined the full complement of activities associated with marketing from the analysis of the external environment through physical distribution. The **primary tasks of marketing management** focus on the effective use of human and financial resources to coordinate all the activities in the marketing process. The ultimate goal of managing the marketing process is to create the greatest impact in the market with limited resources. The primary tasks of marketing management are as follows:

- Evaluating corporate resources
- Setting objectives
- Organizing the marketing effort
- Establishing marketing strategy
- Formulating the marketing mix
- Forecasting sales
- Controlling and evaluating the marketing function
- Implementing corrective action

EVALUATING CORPORATE RESOURCES

Managers must honestly evaluate and be fully aware of the resource strengths and weaknesses of the organization in order to effectively manage the marketing process. Under conditions of great resource strength, managers can pursue strategies that would not be possible under conditions of weak or marginal resources. Marketing managers will evaluate the status of the following resources, which can provide either opportunities or constraints in decision making:

- *Financial Resources.* Cash on hand and cash flow patterns.
- *Capital Resources.* Production facilities, office space and location, communications networks.
- *Human Resources.* Managerial skills, current labor capability, availability of specialized labor, sales force size and capability.
- *Research and Development Resources.* Facilities, personnel, work-in-progress, patents (pending and expiring).
- *Sources of Supply Resources.* Availability and certainty of materials needed for production, vendor contracts.
- *Market Resources.* Strength of distribution systems, strength of brands, strength of promotional programs.

These resources represent the corporation's "asset base" upon which management must rely in managing the marketing process. These resource areas must be carefully evaluated to determine the strengths and weaknesses of the firm and will affect decision making and overall management of the marketing process. Strengths within a resource area provide managers with strategic opportunities for competitive advantage. Table 16-1 shows the kinds of strategic opportunities that can result from resource strength in each area. Overall, taking an inventory of corporate resources allows marketing managers to assess the range of potential available. As an example of seizing an opportunity based on market resource strength, one of the compelling reasons for Marion Laboratories' merger with Merrill-Dow Pharmaceuticals was the relatively weak international distribution network Marion had in place. Merrill-Dow, on the other hand, was already well-positioned internationally, and the merger created a new firm with significantly greater market resources in the area of distribution than its competitors.

TABLE 16-1 *Strategic Opportunities Created by Corporate Resource Strengths*

Resource Strength	Strategic Opportunities
Financial	Acquire new products, initiate promotional programs
Capital	Cost advantages in production, speed of information
Human	Sales force deployment and coverage
Research and development	Product development, patent protection
Sources of supply	Exploit unique sources for market advantage
Market	Product line and mix extensions

SETTING OBJECTIVES

Setting objectives is a two-stage process. First, marketing managers assist in the objective-setting process for the whole corporation. Many factors—financial, environmental, human, and marketing—are considered when a firm's overall objectives are set. Recall the discussion in Chapter 1 in which the process of marketing within a business organization was identified as part of the overall corporate process. Broad-based corporate objectives focus on the types of businesses the corporation will pursue, revenue growth, profitability, return on investment, and corporate image. Second, objectives must be set for the marketing process specifically. Marketing objectives must be consistent with and support corporate objectives. Again, recall from Chapter 1 that marketing objectives flow from and contribute to overall corporate objectives. In addition, objectives set at the corporate level may significantly impact the range and focus of marketing objectives. Remember that Procter & Gamble's *corporate objective* of globalization was the driving force behind the *marketing objectives* for its *Oil of Olay* brand product design and global marketing strategy. To help ensure consistency with and support of corporate objectives, marketing objectives should have the following characteristics:[4]

- Objectives must be clear and concise so the possibility of misinterpretation is minimized.
- Objectives should be provided in written form to avoid the possibility of objectives "evolving" as results are being realized.
- Specific results anticipated in key areas should be identified.
- The time frame over which objectives will be pursued must be specified. Short-term objectives can be stated quarterly to annually. Long-term objectives are specified for three to five years or longer.
- Objectives should be measurable. Standardized units of measurement such as dollars, unit volume, percentages, rank, number of accounts, and the like provide quantitative benchmarks.
- Objectives should be realistic in relation to the corporate resources available.

Using these guidelines, marketing managers will set objectives in one or more of the following areas: sales objectives, profit objectives, and market objectives. **Sales objectives** reflect the fundamental purpose of the marketing process within the organization, which is revenue generation. Sales objectives can be stated in total dollars or in total units produced and sold. Sales objectives can also be stated in relative terms using percentage change objectives from period to period. **Profit objectives** can be stated in a variety of ways to reflect an emphasis on dollar profits: total profits, profit per unit, or gross profit versus net profit. Profit objectives are also often stated in relative terms as a percentage of sales, as a percentage of return on investment, or as a change in profit from period to period. **Market objectives** can relate to literally any area of the marketing mix. New product introduction, price maintenance levels, promotional campaigns, and development of trade relationships can all be the subject of market objectives. The most common, broad-based market objective specifies the market share a firm believes it can capture in a product area. Market share is a measure of the firm's performance relative to competition and market conditions. In many ways, it is the most relevant and revealing statement of objective a firm can use. Table 16-2 gives examples of objectives following the guidelines for setting objectives. From Table 16-2, you can see that often it is necessary to state objectives for *both* sales and profits. The reason is that sales must not be pursued without regard for profitability. It is easy to envision a circumstance where the pursuit of sales is undertaken without regard to costs. Managers might be so motivated to achieve sales objectives that profits are sacrificed. To avoid such a circumstance, objectives are stated in both areas.

Finally, once marketing objectives are stated, they must be communicated to members of the organization who will be directly responsible for achieving the objectives. If objectives are not communicated effectively, they cannot serve as a motivating and directive force in the organizational effort.

ORGANIZING THE MARKETING EFFORT

One of the most challenging marketing management tasks is to develop an efficient and effective organizational structure for implementing marketing activities. While several new concepts of effective organization have recently been proposed (and will be discussed later in the chapter), two typical management organizational structures are shown in Figures 16-1 and 16-2. Figure

TABLE 16-2
Statements of Objectives

Area	Example Statements of Objectives
Sales objectives	a. Achieve sales of $500,000 during fiscal third quarter. b. Sell 200,000 units during fiscal third quarter. c. Increase sales 10% in dollars from prior year period.
Profit objectives	a. Realize total net profit of $2.5 million on product line A during fiscal year. b. Maintain gross profit margin of 15% per unit. c. Increase profits 6% in dollars from prior year period.
Market objectives	a. Increase brand name awareness 20% among 18 to 25 year old women over the next six months. b. Introduce one new product into national distribution during fiscal year. c. Achieve customer satisfaction rating of 85% during fiscal year.

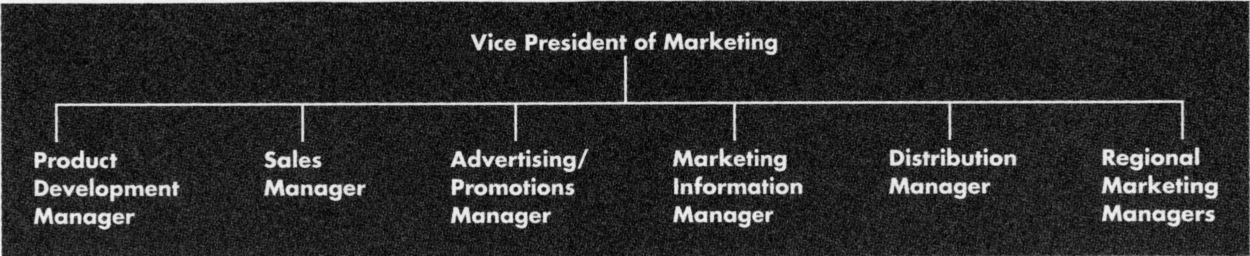

FIGURE 16-1
Functional Marketing Organizational Structure

16-1 portrays an organization that revolves around marketing functions. New product development, sales, advertising and promotions, marketing information, and distribution are typical functions isolated for specific management attention. Notice that to the far right of Figure 16-1, the positions titled "Regional Marketing Managers" are indicated. Several firms are establishing such positions to deal with high-volume or unique markets. For example, many consumer product firms have assigned regional marketing managers to Southern California to track the large hispanic market there. These managers customize all areas of their firms' marketing mixes for this target market, which has distinctive demand characteristics. Overall, firms that employ a functional marketing organizational structure have a relatively small product mix of similar or related products. As an example, Apple Computer, while it has a sophisticated and complex group of products, would rely on a functional structure for marketing because functional area decisions would be about the same for all products in the mix.

The second organizational structure, shown in Figure 16-2, depicts an organization in which product or brand managers are used. Packaged goods companies with extensive product lines and broad product mixes rely on this sort of organizational structure. Product/brand managers may be given all or some of the responsibility for the products or brands they have under management. Such responsibilities relate to product design, materials purchasing, packaging, pricing, media scheduling, sales force management, and trade relations. Typically, product/brand managers will have several assistants who spe-

FIGURE 16-2
Product/Brand Manager Organizational Structure

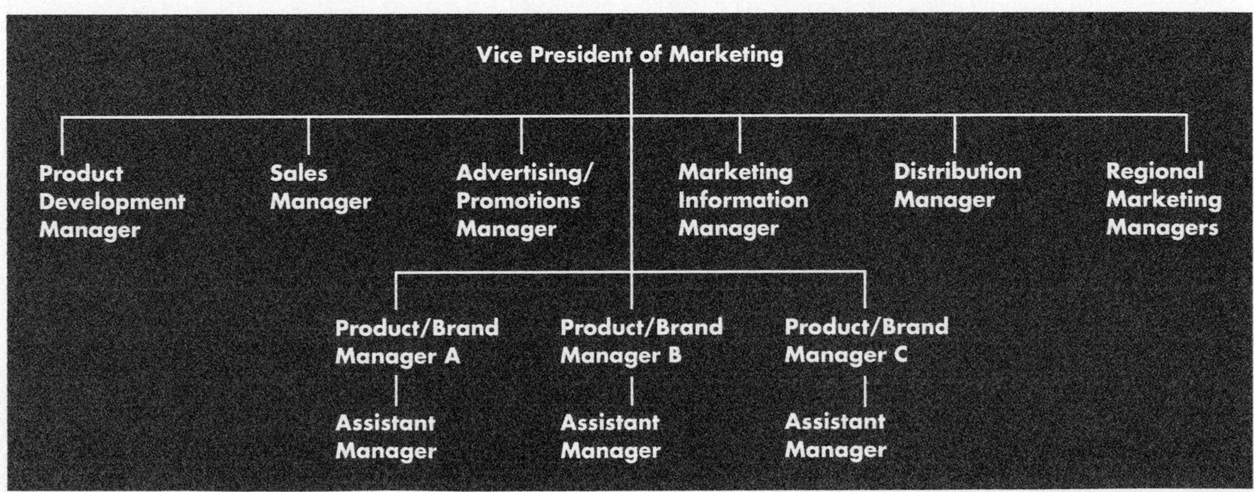

cialize in several of the functions managed. Procter & Gamble pioneered this sort of structure in the 1920s and it remains the primary organizational format in the firm. Recently, however, P & G has begun to restructure its traditional product/brand management approach. A "category manager" has been inserted into the system who has greater spending power and decision-making authority to respond more quickly to changing market conditions. Another new position in the P & G structure is "product supply manager" who works with representatives from manufacturing, engineering, distribution, and purchasing to cut product development time.

It should be noted that in the current era of reengineering corporate operations, the brand manager organizational structure itself has come under heavy scrutiny. Several packaged goods firms like Pillsbury and Unilever are replacing old-style structures with multifunctional teams organized around product groups rather than brands. These multifunctional teams include representatives from marketing, sales, engineering, and production to better manager products from inception through final sale.[5]

ESTABLISHING MARKETING STRATEGY

Of the many tasks undertaken by marketing managers, establishing marketing strategy is perhaps the most important and difficult. Basically, *all* the topics covered throughout the text describe the tasks involved in setting marketing strategy, which gives some indication of the size and complexity of this stage in marketing management. After managers have set objectives and decided on an organizational structure, they must focus their daily attention on the process of strategy planning. Three activities are involved in establishing marketing strategy: managers must identify opportunities, select target markets, and then determine product positioning.

Identifying Opportunities

Identifying opportunities depends primarily on an astute assessment of the external environment as discussed in Chapter 2. As management identifies trends in the demographic, social/cultural, economic, competitive, technological, regulatory, and physical environments, an assessment of the firm's capabilities can be judged against these potential opportunities. The task of identifying opportunities is greatly aided by a MkIS that employs environmental scanning systems and marketing research data. The evaluation of information will focus on trying to find market opportunities and/or product opportunities.

Motorola has assessed the technological environment and has planned for the future. Engineers and marketing strategists at Motorola believe that in the not too distant future, each of us will be carrying a communicator the size of a credit card that will allow us to tap into our office computers for files, to check our e-mail, and to make phone calls halfway around the world.[6] The firm controls a network of 66 satellites that will allow for voice, paging, data, and fax transmission through totally wireless communication. In a different approach to the task of identifying opportunities, management at Mattel, Inc., has expanded the *Barbie* line of dolls and doll clothing to a Barbie-style line of girl-sized costumes, bed sheets, and accessory items.[7] Mattel wants to develop *Bar-*

bie's appeal to girls aged seven to eleven with ties to the doll many of them played with years before.

As management seeks opportunities, two factors narrow the search. First, corporate resources limit the types of opportunities a firm can pursue. Mattel's potential for expanding into the children's clothing line would have far less potential without the market resource strength of the *Barbie* brand name within the segment the firm plans to pursue. The second limiting factor are the corporate objectives. The objectives of the firm may define the type of business(es) it should be in and may also include statements relating to growth and the use of external debt, for example. These factors may bar managers from considering certain types of growth opportunities.

Selecting Target Markets

The second step in setting marketing strategy involves selecting a target market. This decision is based on the identification of favorable opportunities in the prior stage. Target market selection depends on the market segmentation process as described in Chapters 4 and 5 with respect to both the household consumer and business markets. Recall that the process of market segmentation breaks large and diverse markets into segments that are more homogeneous. The target identified must be large enough to sustain the expenditures needed to cultivate it and provide the firm with an appropriate profit.

In Chapters 4 and 5, procedures for identifying target markets were described. It is the marketing manager's task to take those descriptions and select a target or targets to be pursued. For example, segmentation studies may indicate that the microcomputer market includes four basic business segments: managers, salespeople, administrative staff, and production staff. Two of the segments, managers and salespeople, are quite similar with respect to their needs, attitudes, and use of microcomputers. The other two segments are quite different. In this situation, the marketing manager must decide whether a standardized marketing mix will be appropriate for the manager and sales force segments. If so, these two segments can be grouped together and a **combining strategy** can be used. If not, completely separate programs will be developed for each along with individual marketing programs for the staff and production user target segments.

Determining Product Positioning

Following target market selection is the development of the product positioning strategy. Within an array of competitive products on the market, the marketing manager must identify a niche for the product. Product positioning has both internal and external dimensions. Internally, the products a firm markets must have a unique position relative to one another to avoid the problem of "cannibalization." *Cannibalization* occurs when a firm's products are not viewed by consumers as significantly different from each another and merely take sales from one another rather than from competitors. Recall from Chapter 7 the problems IBM had with positioning the *PCjr* microcomputer and how it cannibalized sales from IBM's own PCs rather than taking sales from the *Apple IIe*. Externally, a product must be positioned against competitive products. The challenge of external positioning is to locate a unique, unoccupied spot in the market by providing satisfaction to consumers in a manner no competitor can match. A marketing manager must evaluate the functional, emotional, or benefits of use values the product provides as a basis for external positioning.

FORMULATING THE MARKETING MIX

Formulating the marketing mix means blending the right amount of promotion and distribution coverage with the an appealing price and product design. The marketing mix is designed to provide a satisfying offering to potential customers in the target market. Ideally, managerial decisions regarding the marketing mix will provide a firm with a differential advantage over competing firms. **Differential advantage** means that from a competitive standpoint, a firm's market offering has at least one unique aspect that gives it a strong position in the market with respect to achieving customer satisfaction and loyalty.

One mix variable or several in combination can form the basis for differential advantage. When Ford Motor Company's *Taurus* took over as the best selling car in the United States from the *Honda Accord* in 1992, it was a matter of several marketing mix factors combining to create differential advantage. The *Taurus* had more safety and performance features (air bag and V-6 engine), lower price, and more intensive promotion.[8]

The marketing mix is formulated by the marketing manager and a marketing team with knowledge about corporate resources, the target market, and the concept of differential advantage in mind. Several factors create an effective marketing mix—these will be considered next.

Consistency

A key dimension of an effective marketing mix is that all elements of the mix must be consistent and supportive. To most consumers, mink coats and fine jewelry would be totally out of place in a general merchandise discount warehouse outlet. The products and the outlet must be consistent with one another in image and price range. It is particularly important that promotional programs be consistent with other elements of the marketing mix. Advertising messages that promise more than a product can deliver set the firm up for problems with dissatisfied customers. Similarly, advertisements that look amateurish detract from the image of the product and the firm. Marketing managers need to keep in mind that consistency must be evaluated from the consumer's perspective. What is viewed as appropriate and consistent evolves and changes and is generally in a state of flux. The discussion in Chapter 14 of scrambled merchandise at the retail level—adding nontraditional products to a store's merchandise mix—is evidence of the changes that can occur relative to consistency in the marketing mix.

Feasibility

In order to effectively implement a marketing mix, it must be feasible. For a small office-furniture manufacturer to propose a national television campaign is not likely to be feasible. Using low prices as a differentiating factor for a 24-hour convenience store is also probably not feasible in that the high costs associated with providing time and place utilities cannot be properly supported with low prices. Misconceptions about advertising and personal selling commonly lead to impractical approaches. Expecting advertising campaigns or personal selling efforts to make up for weaknesses in other areas of the mix is not reasonable and simply not feasible.

Matching Target Market Expectations

A key element in designing an effective mix is that the nature of each mix variable must match target market expectations. The product must have the features that are desired, and the price must be viewed as appropriate. Distribution needs to meet consumer demands for time, place, and possession utilities. With regard to promotion, functional, emotional, or benefits of use information must be provided depending on consumer desires for particular types of information. Similarly, if the target relies on the input of salespeople, plans for an appropriate personal selling effort must be in place. The manager's ability to determine features of each element in the mix that match target market expectations is heavily dependent on information from the MkIS and past experiences with the target segment. Recall that products can actually be priced too low and not match market expectations for a "reasonable" price.

FORECASTING SALES

Forecasting sales has important implications for the marketing process and the other activities in an organization. A sales forecast relates directly to managers' primary responsibilities for the marketing process itself: revenue generation and profits. And, other corporate operations such as production and finance (cash flow) are dependent on the marketing manager's ability to accurately forecast sales for future periods so that material supplies and inventories can be managed as efficiently as possible. While managers would prefer to forecast sales before this point in the process, it is really not possible or appropriate. An evaluation of resources, establishment of objectives, determining organizational structure, setting strategy, and identifying target markets all have to be undertaken before a realistic forecast can be made. A variety of methods are available to forecast sales. These include jury of executive opinion, top-down forecast, sales force composite estimates, trend projections, and leading indicators.

Jury of Executive Opinion

Jury of executive opinion depends on the speculative judgment of seasoned executives in the firm. Although it may not employ highly scientific calculations, it does allow for well-informed subjective assessments of factors such as competition, changes in consumer taste, the effects of the economy, or even labor union activities. Leaders of various parts of the organization will submit their estimate of the increase (or decrease) in sales for coming periods. These estimates are aggregated by marketing managers to produce an overall sales forecast. Rarely is jury of executive opinion the sole basis for a sales forecast, but it still remains a frequently used technique.

Top-Down Forecast

Top-down forecasting requires an estimate of what total industry sales would be under various levels of marketing effort across the industry. Such an estimate explicitly recognizes the marketing activities of all competitors in the industry. Working with this figure, marketing managers then forecast the firm's potential market share given different industry levels of effort. Market share is the percentage of total industry sales the firm anticipates it can capture. In using a top-down forecast, a manager typically relies on total industry sales estimates provided by economists or industry trade associations. The manager will then determine the relative strength of the firm's marketing program compared to competition. The computation of a sales forecast in this manner emphasizes the notion that sales result from effective overall marketing strategy.

Sales Force Composite Estimate

Sales force composite estimate is also referred to as *build-up sales forecasting*. It relies on members of the sales staff to make projections for sales in their individual territories or product lines. Management will then simply aggregate these projections and "build up" a sales forecast. The technique works particularly well for firms selling to business markets where there may be a limited number (in comparison to consumer markets) of potential buyers. One risk with this method is "low-ball" estimates being provided by salespeople. Since many firms use quotas as a basis for commission or bonus payments, salespeople may not want to contribute to the inflation of quotas by providing overly optimistic sales estimates. Another problem with this technique is that it can be very slow and cumbersome, especially in firms with a large sales force.

Trend Projections

Trend projections in sales depend on historical data from either overall industry sales patterns or the firm's own sales data. Trends can be predicted on a quarterly or annual basis. The trend line can be constructed using units sold or dollar volume. To employ a trend projection, managers will simply establish a percentage rate of change for different periods. The rate of change will then be used to calculate a trend line, and projections to future periods are estimated along this trend line. The problem with trend projections is that they are purely quantitative and implicitly assume that environmental influences will affect sales in the future in precisely the same way they have affected sales in the past. To combat this problem, trend lines are reconstructed regularly in an attempt to accommodate the most recent influences on sales. Figure 16-3 shows how sales over the first nine months of a year can be used to create a trend line to forecast sales for the remaining three months.

Leading Indicators

In situations where a firm's sales are heavily dependent on the general health of the economy, fundamental economic indicators can provide a basis for sales forecasting. **Leading indicators** such as housing starts, unemployment, consumer price index, or changes in consumer debt may relate directly to a firm's ability to cultivate future sales. Automobile companies, appliance manufacturers, and home furnishings firms can make use of a leading indicators approach to sales forecasting.

The accuracy of any particular sales forecasting technique is a critical concern. As stated earlier, sales forecasts produced by marketing managers have

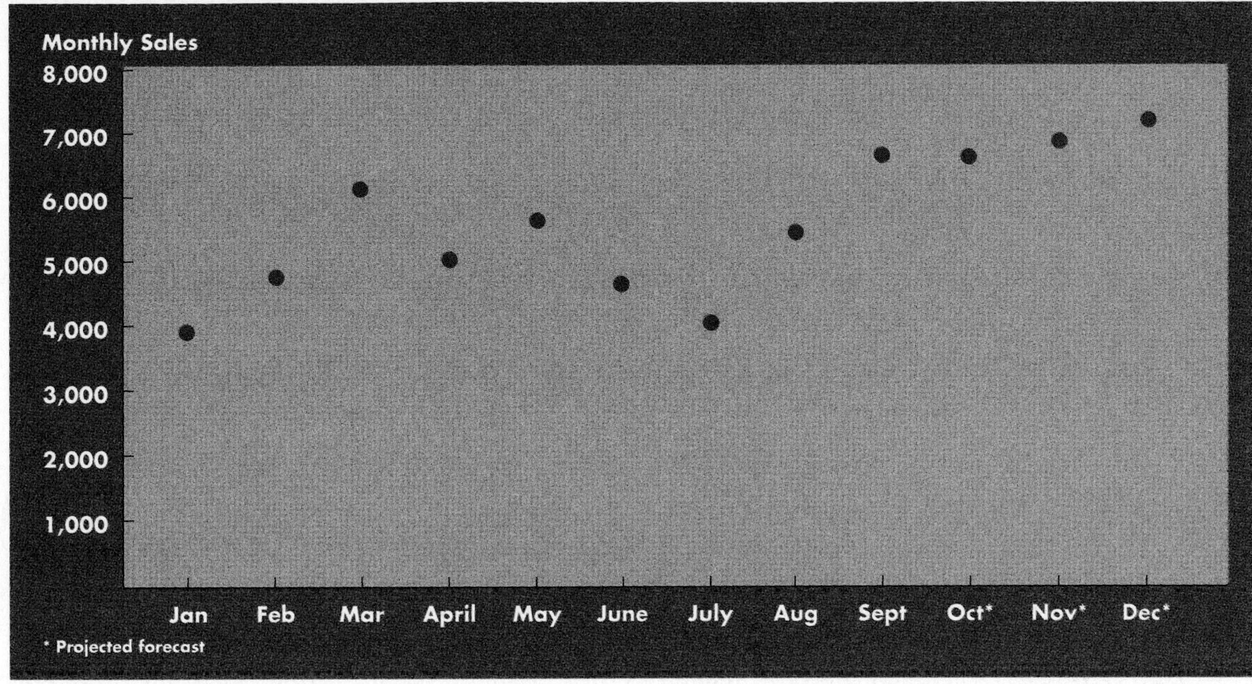

FIGURE 16-3
Trend Projection as a Sales Forecasting Technique

ramifications throughout the firm. Firms often rely on quantitative techniques to forecast sales.[9] This does not necessarily mean that quantitative techniques are superior or preferred to more judgmental methods like sales force estimates or jury of executive opinion. Rather, every manager must determine which sales forecasting method is best suited to the firm's particular circumstance and managerial expertise.

CONTROLLING AND EVALUATING THE MARKETING FUNCTION

The marketing manager's job is not finished when marketing activities are designed and implemented. In many ways, the most formidable tasks remain, which are controlling and evaluating the marketing function. Through control procedures, the manager tries to ensure that the marketing plan brings to fruition corporate and marketing objectives. Additionally, evaluating performance allows the manager to fine tune components of the system.

Establishing Performance Standards

The control and evaluation process begins with establishing performance standards. Based on the firm's stated objectives, performance standards represent an expected level of performance against which actual performance can be judged. The most general performance standard is overall sales revenue specified by month or quarter. Other, more specific standards can be established for product lines, geographic regions, market share, or even individual sales representatives. Performance standards must be realistic relative to the resources devoted to implementation. Managers that continually expect employees to work harder with fewer resources create an untenable and demoralizing situation. People in functional areas that are challenged with high performance standards must have resource endowments that are consistent with the challenge.

Controlling Performance

Control over activities and the performance of personnel is truly difficult to achieve. Most firms are really only in control of the *planning* of marketing activities, and the *implementation* is carried out by people and institutions outside the firm and thus beyond the control of marketing managers. Consider the important activity of retail display of a product. Display relates directly to a monthly sales performance standard. If retail operators do not provide proper display for a product or maintain needed inventory, then performance will be compromised and sales standards will not be achieved. In addition to retail operators, marketing managers must contend with distributors, transportation firms, advertising agencies, the media, and various other external facilitators also beyond the direct control of the organization.

How then does the firm control performance? Part of the answer lies in the speed with which a manager has access to comprehensive information. The ability to quickly and accurately monitor all marketing activities will shorten the time needed to implement corrective action. Next, for those personnel who are directly implementing marketing activities, such as sales representatives, weekly updates on activities and restructuring of tasks by management can contribute to controlling performance. Many firms issue laptop computers to salespeople in order to gain information as quickly as possible. The most important element of control, however, is to devise strategies at the outset that are inherently more controllable. For example, as the discussion in Chapter 13 pointed out, shorter channels of distribution are more controllable. Similarly, when external facilitators are essential to implementing marketing strategies, greater control over their activities is achieved by specifically defining their roles in the operation. Finally, for firms well endowed with resources, control of the system can be achieved by stimulating demand so strongly among end users for the firm's product (i.e., using a pull strategy) that external facilitators find it in their best interest to execute a strategy according to the firm's desires.

Evaluating Performance

Evaluation of system performance takes place at two levels. **Micro-evaluation** evaluates the performance of specific factors within the marketing mix and customer satisfaction measures. The following are examples of typical micro-evaluation criteria:

- Product
    - Number of units returned
    - Number of product failures
    - Sales by product line
    - Number of customer complaints
- Price
    - Variability at wholesale and retail

Management of valuation of marketing processes depends on timely, reliable data from the field.

Consumer perception of price
Margin earned per unit
Contribution to profit by product line

- Distribution
  - Units shipped per time period
  - Units delivered in good condition
  - Number of out-of-stock occurrences
  - Inventory levels
  - Time lag between order and delivery
  - Order size
  - Distribution costs per unit
- Promotion
  - Reach and frequency of advertising
  - Audience recall of advertising
  - Performance of the sales force
  - Promotion costs per unit sold
  - Demand effects of sales promotion
- Customer Satisfaction
  - Product satisfaction
  - Service satisfaction
  - Overall satisfaction

Beyond the micro-evaluation that isolates each variable in the marketing mix, a more traditional and easily implemented evaluation is macro-evaluation. **Macro-evaluation** focuses on more broad-based measures such as total sales, market share, or profits. Frequently, firms will use total-dollar sales volume as a sole evaluation criterion. This represents the broadest measure of performance and is easily judged against prior years. It may not be fully revealing, however. A firm's sales may grow at 10 percent in a quarter while overall industry sales have grown 18 percent. Further, increased sales volume may have been achieved by sacrificing profits.

An alternative to total sales as a macro-evaluation is market share. Market share as a criterion has the advantage of being a relative standard as mentioned previously. A firm's sales may have actually decreased in a quarter, but the firm could still experience an increase in market share. This would indicate that the firm is outperforming competitors in a declining market.

Finally, profits can be used as an evaluation standard. Attention is paid to both total revenue and costs in using the profit measure. This sort of analysis highlights the efficiency of the system. Profit figures can be generated for individual products, full product lines, or total profits across all operations.

An alternative for firms to consider is to combine a micro and macroset of evaluation criteria in what is called a **marketing audit.**[10] This approach to evaluation dissects every component of the marketing process and reevaluates objectives, strategies, tactics, and activities both internal and external to the firm. The marketing audit is commendable by virtue of its comprehensiveness. It may be difficult for many firms to implement a full-fledged marketing audit, however. The expense and time required to properly conduct a marketing audit would be beyond the means of many organizations.

IMPLEMENTING CORRECTIVE ACTION

The final task for marketing managers is to implement corrective action. The evaluation of performance will identify areas where activities are not achieving objectives. Depending on the nature of the deficiencies, the manager has three choices for corrective action. First, personnel can be replaced to infuse the organization with people who can perform to the established standards. Second, the organization for the marketing process can be changed in an attempt to increase the potency of marketing activities. Finally, objectives can be adjusted to more realistically reflect the capabilities of the firm. Consider the actions of Harley-Davidson in the scenario presented at the beginning of the chapter:

1. Personnel can be replaced: Vaugn Beals was appointed CEO, "Willie G." Davidson was assigned to develop new models.
2. Organizational structure can be changed: Production methods were redesigned.
3. Objectives can be adjusted: Harley focused on the super-heavyweight market.

In order to deal with the sales and profitability crises facing Harley-Davidson, the firm implemented all three corrective actions to rejuvenate sales, market share, and profitability. Figure 16-4 graphically depicts the primary tasks of marketing management as they have been discussed here. Notice that the tasks build on one another and that corrective action is directed at the planning and implementation levels. It is at these stages where corrective adjustments will affect the operations of the system.

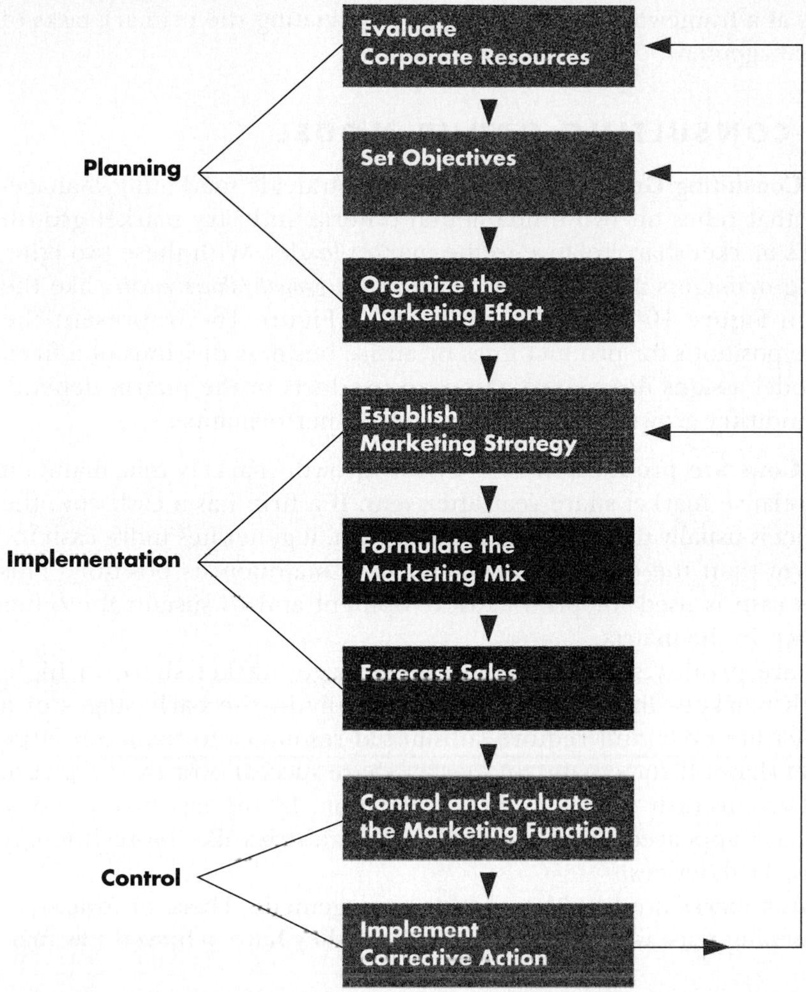

FIGURE 16-4
The Primary Tasks of Marketing Management

TRADITIONAL MARKETING MANAGEMENT MODELS

The primary tasks of marketing management identify areas in which managers concentrate their efforts to guide the marketing process. But the preceding section simply identifies these tasks. Marketing management decisions form the foundation of a firm's *strategies* in the marketplace. As an aid to decision making, marketing managers will often rely on management models that focus on one or more important factors in strategic decision making across all the task areas just discussed. Just as the product life cycle and diffusion of innovation concepts can improve decision making in the product area of the marketing mix, marketing management models can improve management of the entire marketing process. Several models of marketing management are available to assist managers. The management models discussed here have served as a framework for managers in various industries for many years. It is worth describing these models to see how managers can rely on them as a framework for initiating and evaluating the primary tasks of marketing management.

BOSTON CONSULTING GROUP MODEL

The **Boston Consulting Group** (BCG) **model** is a strategic marketing management model that relies on two fundamental criteria: industry market growth and the firm's market share relative to the market leader. With these two criteria, marketing managers in a firm can construct a *growth/share matrix* like the one shown in Figure 16-5. The four sectors in Figure 16-5 represent the growth/share positions for product lines or entire business divisions of a firm. The BCG model assigns descriptive names to products in the matrix depending on their industry growth/relative market share performance:

- **Cash Cows** are products in slow or low growth markets that maintain high relative market share year after year. If a firm has a cash cow, the product is usually the market leader. In turn, it generates more cash for the firm than the expenditures needed to maintain its position. This excess cash is used for product development and to sustain the other products in the matrix.
- **Stars** are products that have captured large market share in high-growth markets. Star products are normally in the early stages of a product life cycle and require substantial resources to maintain large market share. If stars maintain market share success over the long run, they become cash cows for the organization. In the last two decades, stars have appeared in high technology industries like biotechnology and medical devices.
- **Question marks** are troublesome for management. These products are not keeping pace with competition in that they have achieved low mar-

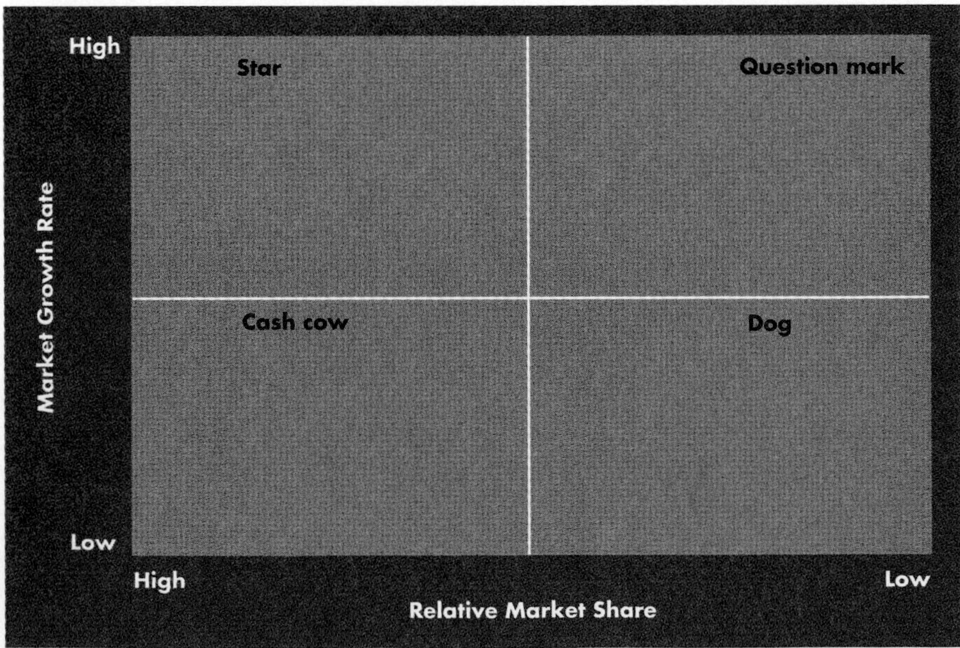

FIGURE 16-5
Boston Consulting Group Model

ket share in a fast growing market. A firm must decide whether it wants to commit the financial and human resources to turn a question mark into a star. The main problem with question marks is that they require large resource commitments to keep up with competitors in fast-growing markets but are not generating the kind of cash (due to low market share) like the competitors' products.

- **Dogs,** with low market share in slow-growth markets, typically generate very little profit and may be incurring losses for the firm. Dogs must be evaluated for the contribution they make to the firm. In many cases, dogs simply contribute revenues toward overhead. Firms that manage dogs should seriously consider dropping them from the portfolio.

An analysis of Sony Corp., the Japanese electronics giant, would suggest that this firm manages several cash cows, at least one dog and one question mark, and no stars. Sony's engineering and manufacturing (televisions and video/audio hardware) and music entertainment (formerly CBS records) divisions appear to be cash cows. Both are in slow-growth markets but hold relatively strong market shares. The firm's Columbia Pictures division is clearly a dog with less than 10 percent market share in a slow-growth market. The question mark for Sony is its electronic publishing division, which is working on technologies to combine text, images, and sound on compact disks.

The BCG model provides managers with a framework for tracking the health and potential of products. Many products begin as stars or question marks and eventually become cash cows or dogs. Managers can use this model to determine resource allocations for various product lines and develop strategies needed to maintain the health of a product and prevent it from achieving dog status.

GENERAL ELECTRIC MODEL

The **General Electric model** is actually an outgrowth and adaptation of the BCG model. GE used the Boston Consulting Group model but felt that single criteria for market position and growth were inadequate to fully reflect the stature and potential of a product or entire corporate division. GE enlisted the services of the consulting firm McKinsey & Company to come up with a model that uses multiple measures to specify **market attractiveness** and the firm's current **competitive position.** The following are the types of measures typically used to rate market attractiveness and competitive position in the GE Model.

Market Attractiveness	*Competitive Position*
Overall market size	Current market share
Annual market growth rate	Product quality
Seasonal nature of demand	Brand reputation
Cyclical nature of demand	Price competitiveness
Competitive intensity	Distribution strength
Capital requirements	Production strength
Gross profit margins	Sales force effectiveness
Distribution availability	Managerial skill
Promotional requirements	Financial strength
Rate of technological change	
Political and legal barriers	

FIGURE 16-5
General Electric Model

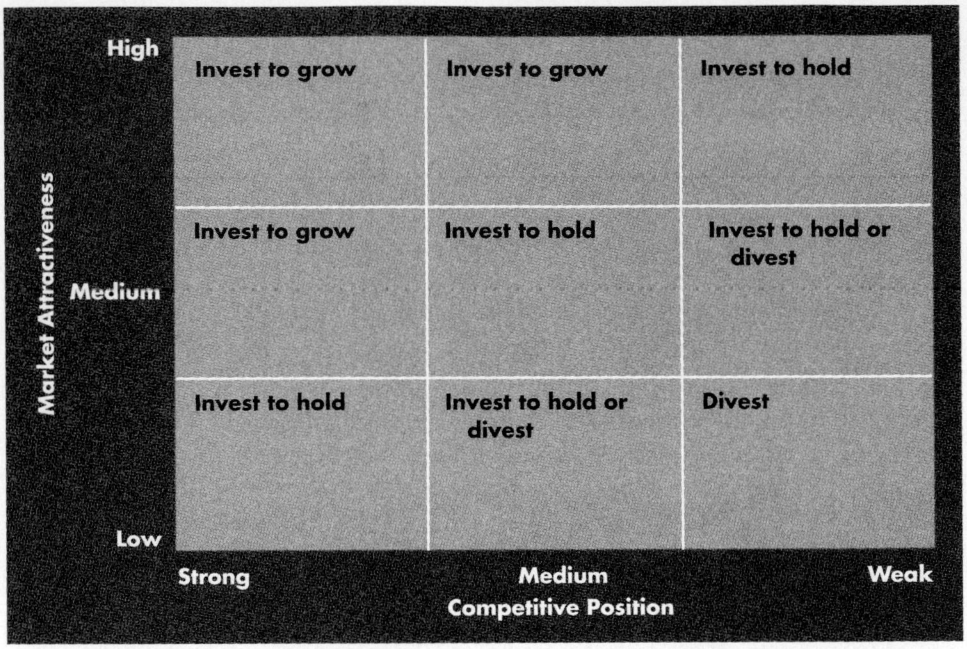

Market Attractiveness	Strong	Medium	Weak
High	Invest to grow	Invest to grow	Invest to hold
Medium	Invest to grow	Invest to hold	Invest to hold or divest
Low	Invest to hold	Invest to hold or divest	Divest

Competitive Position

Factors in each area are rated and evaluated by managers. These ratings are then used to place products within cells in the matrix shown in Figure 16-6. The main thrust of the GE approach is to identify products or whole divisions that warrant investment for growth or to hold competitive position versus those that warrant no investment and should be divested. When a product is in a market that is highly attractive and rates high on competitive position, it warrants investment of the firm's resources. Conversely, a product in an unattractive market with a poor competitive position should be divested. Products that fall in the middle cells should be supported and maintained. The GE model improves on the BCG model by virtue of its greater specificity and focus on resource allocation strategy.

PRODUCT/SEGMENT GROWTH MODEL

The BCG and GE models concentrate on the management of a firm's current stable of products. The **product/segment growth model** concentrates on identifying opportunities for revenue growth both with the firm's existing products and with new products. Displayed in Figure 16-7, this model demonstrates that, in a very real sense, every opportunity facing a firm for revenue generation depends on the nature of the product and the nature of the market segment. A firm will be dealing with either *existing products* or *new products* and will be trying to generate revenues from either *existing segments* or *new segments.* These product/segment variations present the firm with four basic opportunities for growth:

- **Market Penetration.** Marketing existing products to existing segments is simply the attempt by a firm to do a better job in its current marketing activities. Sales growth in this area comes about either because the

		Segments	
		Existing	New
Products	Existing	Market penetration	Market development
	New	Product development	Diversification

FIGURE 16-7
Product/Segment Growth Model

entire industry is experiencing growth or the firm is taking market share away from competition in a stable or declining market. Expanding the distribution system geographically or increasing the number of outlets (i.e., increasing the intensity of distribution) are common strategies for bringing about growth through market penetration. Another common strategy is to motivate current users to use the product more frequently. When the Florida Citrus Growers Association used the campaign, "Orange juice isn't just for breakfast anymore," the goal was to get current segments to use the current product more frequently—a market penetration strategy. Market penetration is considered the least risky, although not the most creative, approach to growth because no product changes are required nor will new users be sought.

- **Market Development.** Marketing existing products to new segments is also a relatively low-risk approach to growth. A firm invests little, if any, money in product development. Rather, the attempt here is to seek out new segments to which current products can be marketed. Johnson & Johnson successfully used this strategy in marketing its baby shampoo to adults. Coca-Cola was unsuccessful using this approach in trying to market *Tab* (traditionally targeted to women) to men.
- **Product Development.** The advantage of this growth strategy is that a firm is marketing to existing segments with which it already has experience and a good reputation. These buyers should have a favorable predisposition toward the firm and its products. A new product benefits from these prior successes in that satisfied customers will more readily try a new product from the same firm. Procter & Gamble has used this strategy successfully in bringing out a series of flanker brands: *Ivory Shampoo and Conditioner, Liquid Tide, Folgers Instant Coffee.* Minute Maid has not been as successful with this strategy in introducing a carbonated orange beverage.
- **Diversification.** Diversification is by far the most expensive and risky route to revenue growth. The firm takes on the challenge developing new products and marketing to new segments with whom management may have no experience. Diversification can lead some firms far astray from their primary businesses. When communications giant ITT acquired the Sheraton Hotel chain, it ventured into a business and competitive environment with which its management had literally no experience. Diversification need not be so radical, however. Toyota Motors stuck with one of its primary businesses when it introduced the *Lexus* line of automobiles. The product was totally new and designed to

One strategy for growth is to sell existing products in new markets. Here, GM vans are being loaded for shipment to overseas markets.

appeal to a luxury/performance segment with which Toyota had not dealt before.

Table 16-3 lists several examples of firms that have pursued growth with one of the product/segment growth strategies. One of the key features of the product/growth model that distinguishes it from the BCG model and the GE model is that it is much more marketing-oriented and much more focused on *growth.* Both the BCG and GE models concentrate on the *management process,* per se, with growth being a by-product of the management structure.

TABLE 16-3
Examples of Product/Segment Growth Strategies

Growth Strategy	Examples
Market Penetration	Tabasco Sauce promoted for use in hamburgers and other recipes
	A.1. Steak Sauce promoted for use in restaurants
	Arm & Hammer Baking Soda promoted as deodorizer for refrigerators
Market Development	Kellogg's Frosted Flakes promoted to adult users
	Wal-Mart opens stores in large, metropolitan markets
Product Development	Memorex puts its name on VCRs and audio cassette players
	Mars introduces ice-cream bars
Diversification	Lego, the toy maker, is building a theme amusement park in California
	Matsushita Electric Industrial Co. buys MCA Records
	Williams Cos. feeds fiber optic cable through its obsolete oil/gas pipelines

The models presented here provide managers with alternative frameworks within which the primary tasks of marketing management can be organized. Each has a slightly different approach and emphasis. Whether managers rely on one of these models or not, it is important that some guiding framework toward the challenge of revenue growth be adopted within an organization. Otherwise, the primary tasks of marketing management become unrelated tasks with no overall guide to implementation. Under this condition, efficiency and effectiveness are much more difficult to achieve.

Trends in Management Systems

The three management models just discussed exemplify the traditional sort of model on which managers can rely. The search for techniques to enhance the effectiveness of managerial decision making regularly produces new proposals for management systems. Recently, several trends in management systems have emerged that affect the process of marketing management. These management trends have caused firms to completely change the way an entire organization is managed and the way marketing activities are carried out. The results have often been pervasive and dramatic, if not always positive. While many management trends have emerged, the most significant are: total quality management, horizontal structures, reengineering, and the virtual corporation.

TOTAL QUALITY MANAGEMENT (TQM)

In the early 1990s, a philosophy of management called "total quality management" gained popularity. Its origins are traced to the ideas of U.S. quality experts W. Edwards Deming and Joseph Duran and highlighted by such programs as the Malcolm Baldrige National Quality Award in the United States. **Total quality management (TQM)** is defined as "managing the entire organization so that it excels in all dimensions of products and services that are important to the customer." [11] As the definition states, this philosophy concentrates on quality as a primary component of the organization's drive for competitive advantage. Marketing decision making is directly effected by such a system because quality is a component of product/service design and can be an important decision-making criterion employed by potential buyers.

The TQM model goes beyond product and service quality, however, and suggests that a highly structured system of management that emphasizes mechanisms like control and punitive action stifles people and ultimately hinders an organization's attempt to produce quality products and services. Rather, the organization that views *all* its employees as critical, creative resources will be much better able to pursue quality in every activity and through every decision. Some of the key tenets of TQM are:

1. Every employee has creative skill and talent that can be beneficial to the organization, and employees should be empowered with decision-making responsibility and authority.
2. An organization must engage in parallel and *simultaneous* decision making rather that *hierarchical* decision making. Functions like marketing

and production must work together and simultaneously to create solutions rather than waiting for one another and engaging in reactive decision making.

3. An organization must replace a control mentality and structure with one that nurtures creativity and cross-functional participation in decision making.
4. Speed and quality are the essential dimensions of competitive advantage and should constitute the overriding objectives of the organization.

The underlying premises of TQM are attractive. Speed and quality are essential to the concept of TQM as they are to product development (review Chapter 7) and the efforts by firms like Honda to cut development time and use speed as a strategic tool. And, the argument that rigid and hierarchical organizational structures suppress creativity and limit an organization's potential is a believable proposition. But, firms are discovering that the concept of TQM has some practical hazards that make complete implementation difficult. Specifically, TQM as a management approach can be compromised by the following:

1. Not all employees are capable of or desire to be empowered. Many employees, even at middle-management levels are content to make contributions to the organization by following rather than leading.
2. It can be difficult to motivate employees to embrace corporate objectives over their own personal or career objectives. Effective implementation of TQM requires that corporate goals be placed ahead of personal goals.
3. Effective implementation of TQM procedures presumes effective and swift communication within an organization in order for functional areas to operate simultaneously rather than hierarchically. Many organizations are unable to establish effective and rapid communications networks essential to the success of a TQM system.
4. Implementation of a total quality system requires its own sort of bureaucracy, which itself can bog down the organization from the standpoints of both cost and speed of decision making.[12]

While TQM is an appealing philosophy, it remains to be seen whether it can be effectively implemented across complex organizations. Some firms, like Motorola, have had tremendous success with a TQM approach to management. Many other firms, however, have experienced almost insignificant quality increases when compared to the massive scale of the firm's quality effort.[13]

HORIZONTAL MANAGEMENT STRUCTURE

The horizontal corporation may be the most radical of the new management systems being touted. A **horizontal management structure** is defined as managing *across* an organization rather than in a top-down, hierarchical fashion by identifying key processes and creating teams to manage them. The main premise of horizontal management structure borrows a dimension from TQM: the downward, hierarchical authority of an organization must be dismantled to take advantage of all corporate resources. In place of vertical authority, a new horizontal system is proposed that organizes a firm around processes rather than tasks. Such a horizontal structure is said to eliminate a task orientation and focus company resources on customers instead. Figure 16-8 shows how marketing activities would be managed in a horizontal structure. Compare this arrangement to the traditional marketing structures depicted in Figures 16-1 and 16-2.

The following are the seven key elements of a horizontal structure management system:[14]

1. *A Process Organizational Structure.* Create a structure around processes rather than tasks. The entire company can be built around three to five core processes. A process owner is assigned to each.
2. *Horizontal Structure.* Levels of supervision should be kept to a minimum by combining tasks within processes. The hierarchical nature of the organization should be flattened to resemble the activities in Figure 16-8.
3. *Team Management.* Teams rather than managers will run processes. Each team is held accountable for performance within processes.
4. *Customer Satisfaction Drives Performance.* Do away with old measures of performance like stock appreciation or profitability and use customer satisfaction instead—profits will follow if customers are satisfied.
5. *Team Performance Rewards.* The evaluation and pay system should emphasize team not individual performance. Encourage the development of multiple skills rather than specialization.
6. *Maximum Supplier, Customer, Employee Contact.* Employees must have direct and frequent contact with suppliers and customers. Find in-house teams where suppliers and customers can be participants.
7. *Inform and Train All Employees.* Employees must be trusted with critical data and important decisions. Include *all* employees, not just leaders.

The horizontal structure, like others, is intended to increase the speed and efficiency of activities and decision making. So far, it has met with considerable success. AT&T Network Systems Division has reorganized all of its 130 activities

FIGURE 16-8
The Flow of Activities in a Horizontal Marketing Structure

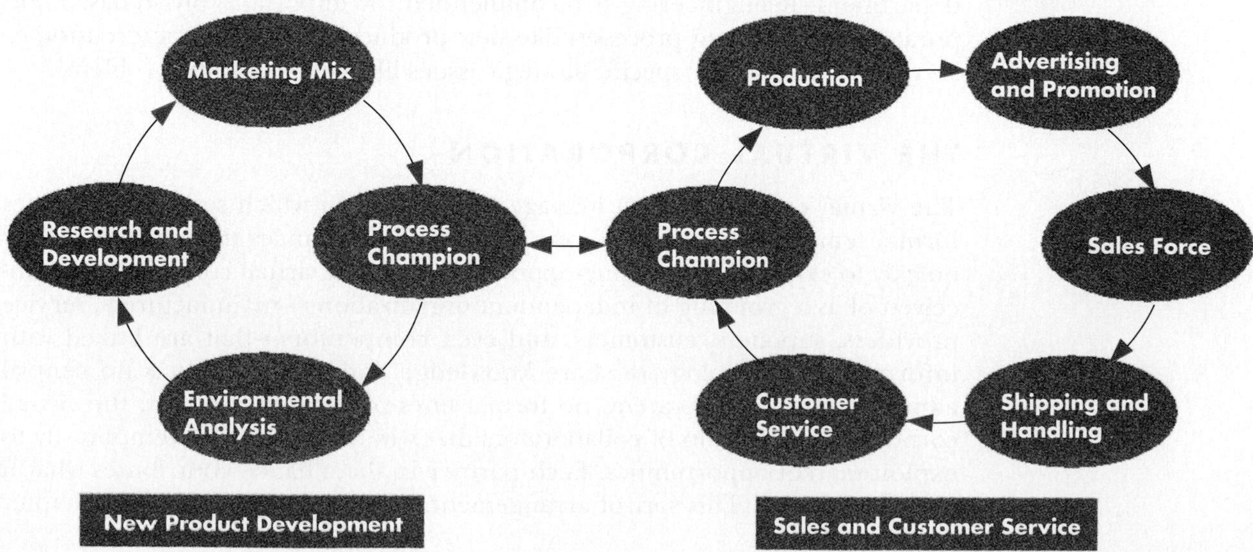

around 13 core processes and employee bonuses are based on customer satisfaction evaluations. Kodak has eliminated several vice-president level positions and uses self-directed teams to manage the areas instead. Finally, Xerox now handles its new product development through multi-disciplinary teams that work in a single process structure rather than vertical or even simultaneous functions.[15]

REENGINEERING

Reengineering as a management imperative is similar to the horizontal structure system with one major exception. Reengineering focuses on the redesign of processes within an organization just as the horizontal system does. But, reengineering is not restricted to any particular redesign of processes. Rather, the entire organization is scrutinized from top to bottom to search for opportunities for improvement. **Reengineering** is defined as "the radical redesign of business processes to achieve major gains in cost, service, or time."[16] Changing processes to achieve productivity or effectiveness gains does not distinguish reengineering from either TQM or a horizontal structure. There are, however, two distinctive aspects of reengineering. First, reengineering examines the organization from the outside in and designs it around customers' needs. The key question to be asked is, "If we could start this company from scratch, how would it be designed?" Second, reengineering promotes strong leadership from the top, the COO or CEO leads the organization. This is completely different from either TQM or a horizontal structure.

Several firms have had tremendous success with reengineering. Union Carbide has used reengineering to cut $400 million out of the fixed costs of its operations over a three-year period. GTE reengineered its customer service operations from the outside in and created "customer care centers." Before reengineering, customers had to deal with three different departments for line problems, billing questions, and special services. After reengineering, GTE has a single customer contact process where effectiveness is judged by how many times a problem can be solved without passing the customer on to another department. Reengineering is recommended for important, broad-based corporate and marketing processes like new product development and customer service rather than for specific strategic issues like cost or quality problems.[17]

THE VIRTUAL CORPORATION

The **virtual corporation** is a management system in which several companies form a temporary network of joint ventures and alliances that come together quickly to exploit fast-changing opportunities.[18] The virtual corporation is conceived of as a grouping of independent organizations—manufacturers, service providers, suppliers, customers, and even competitors—that are linked with information technology to share knowledge and skills. There is no central administration, no hierarchy, no formal lines of authority. Rather, the virtual corporation is a group of collaborators that will come together temporarily to exploit market opportunities. Each partner in the alliance contributes what it is best at doing. (This sort of arrangement is highlighted in the next chapter on global marketing management with an example of Toshiba Electronics global alliances.) The key features of a virtual corporation management arrangement are:

1. *Excellence.* Each partner in a virtual corporation alliance brings a core competence to the collaboration. In this way, each function and process can be world class caliber.
2. *Technology.* Global information networks will allow participants to create electronic links for sharing expertise and knowledge. Information superhighways could create electronic contracts without legal ties.
3. *Opportunism.* The partnerships are temporary and created to exploit a specific market opportunity. Once the opportunity disappears, the alliance will likely disappear as well.
4. *Trust.* The fate of each partner is dependent on the other. Trust is a key dimension in the successful performance of a virtual corporation.
5. *No Borders.* The collaboration among customers, suppliers, producers, and competitors breaks down borders between organizations.

The virtual corporation concept has its critics, but it also has brought together some of the most prominent names in the corporate world. AT&T used Marubeni Trading Co. to establish a relationship with Matsushita Electric Industrial Co. to expedite the production of notebook computers, which were designed by a fourth partner, Henry Dreyfuss Associates. Corning, Inc., has 19 partnerships that account for nearly 13 percent of the firm's earnings. Former rivals IBM, Apple, and Motorola have created an alliance to develop an operating system and microprocessor for a new generation of computers, the *Power PC.*

Once again, this proposed corporate management system would have pervasive effects across the marketing systems of the firms involved. Product development speed and efficacy, customer service, sales effectiveness, and price levels all can be directly affected. The future of the virtual corporation vision is unknown. While it is conceptually intriguing, there are definite obstacles. The information technology is not quite in place; firms have never had to trust each other to the degree that this proposal calls for; and there may need to be changes in regulations related to antitrust and intellectual property before virtual corporations can actually be formed.[19]

MARKETING MANAGEMENT: A GLOBAL PERSPECTIVE

By now you have become accustomed to a discussion at this point of the global issues associated with a topic area. Successful cultivation of world-wide markets is by far the most formidable challenge faced by marketing managers. An organization's resources are pressed to their limits when foreign markets become the focus of the marketing effort. Because of the complexity and extensiveness of the marketing management tasks in global marketing, the entire next chapter, Chapter 17: Marketing Management: A Global Perspective, is devoted entirely to these issues.

Key Terms and Concepts

Role of marketing management
Primary tasks of marketing management
Sales objectives
Profit objectives
Market objectives
Combining strategy
Differential advantage
Jury of executive opinion
Top-down forecast
Sales force composite forecast
Trend projections
Leading indicators
Micro-evaluation
Macro-evaluation
Marketing audit
Boston Consulting Group model
Cash cow
Star
Question mark
Dog
General Electric model
Market attractiveness
Competitive position
Product/Segment Growth Model
Market penetration
Market development
Product development
Diversification
Total quality management (TQM)
Horizontal management structure
Reengineering
Virtual corporation

Questions and Exercises

1. What short-term marketing strategies did Harley-Davidson implement while it was developing the long-term strategy of redesigned engines?
2. How would you describe the role marketing management plays in an organization? How is this role related to the overall role of marketing in an organization as it was described in Chapter 1?
3. Financial, capital, and human resources are clearly related to a firm's strength, but do research and development, sources of supply, and market resources affect a manager's ability to manage the marketing process?
4. Distinguish between sales, profit, and market objectives that a manager may set for the marketing process.
5. Identify the role of an MkIS in a firm when marketing managers undertake the tasks of establishing market strategy and formulating the marketing mix.
6. Describe the top-down and build-up methods of sales forecasting. What is another name for the build-up method?
7. Do you think a micro-evaluation or a macro-evaluation is more valuable to marketing managers in assessing the performance of the marketing system? Why?
8. Examine the annual report of a large, multinational firm. Annual reports are available in most university libraries or from campus placement offices. Categorize the firm's products (or divisions) according to the Boston Consulting Group model which specifies cash cows, stars, question marks, and dogs. Do you think this firm has a good stable of products? Does the firm need to change?
9. How is the Product/Segment Growth Model more specifically focused on revenue growth than the BCG and GE models?
10. Describe the differences and similarities between TQM, horizontal management structure, reengineering, and the virtual corporation as management systems.

References

1. Points in the discussion of Harley-Davidson are taken from "How Harley Beat Back the Japanese," *Fortune* (September 25, 1989) 155–164.
2. Philip Kotler, *Marketing Management: Analysis, Planning, Implementation and Control,* 4th ed. (Englewood Cliffs, NJ: Prentice-Hall, Inc., 1980), 22.
3. Thomas A. Stewart, "GE Keeps Those Ideas Coming," *Fortune* (August 12, 1991): 41–49.
4. Adapted from Robert E. Stevens, David L. Loudon, and William E. Warren, *Marketing Planning Guide,* (Binghamton, NY: The Haworth Press, Inc., 1991), 130–131.

5. Brian Dumaine, "P & G Rewrites the Marketing Rules," *Fortune* (November 6, 1989): 35–48; and "Death of a Brand Manager," *The Economist* (April 9, 1994): 71–72.
6. Thomas Stewart, "Welcome to the Revolution," *Fortune* (December 13, 1993): 66.
7. Pauline Yoshihashi, "Mattel Shapes a New Future for Barbie," *The Wall Street Journal* (February 12, 1990): B1, B5.
8. Jacqueline Mitchell and Neal Templin, "Ford's *Taurus* Passes *Honda Accord* as Bestselling Car in a Lackluster Year," *The Wall Street Journal* (February 7, 1993): B1.
9. For a good summary of sales forecasting techniques see Donald S. Tull and Del I. Hawkins, *Marketing Research,* 6th ed. (New York: Macmillan Publishing Company, 1990), Chapter 21.
10. For a full description and discussion of the factors in a marketing audit, see Philip Kotler, *Marketing Management: Analysis, Planning, Implementation, and Control,* 7th ed. (Englewood Cliffs, NJ: Prentice-Hall, Inc., 1991), Chapter 26.
11. Richard B. Chase and Nicholas J. Aquilano, *Production and Operations Management: A Life Cycle Approach,* 6th ed. (Homewood, IL: Richard D. Irwin, Inc., 1992), 186–187.
12. "The Cracks in Quality," *The Economist* (April 18, 1992): 69–70.
13. See Gilbert Fuchsberg, "Baldrige Awards May Be Losing Some Luster," *The Wall Street Journal* (April 19, 1993): B1; and Gilbert Fuchsberg, " 'Total Quality' Is Termed Only Partial Success," *The Wall Street Journal* (October 1, 1992): B1.
14. John Bryne, "The Horizontal Corporation," *Business Week* (December 20, 1993): 76–81.
15. Ibid., 78–79.
16. Thomas Stewart, "Reengineering the Hot New Management Tool," *Fortune* (August 23, 1993): 42.
17. Ibid., 42.
18. The definition of the virtual corporation and the discussion in this section adapted from John A. Bryne, et al., "The Virtual Corporation," *Business Week* (February 8, 1993): 99–102.
19. John A. Bryne, "The Futurists Who Fathered the Ideas," *Business Week* (February 8, 1993): 103.

17

Marketing Management: A Global Perspective

AFTER STUDYING THIS CHAPTER, YOU WILL UNDERSTAND THAT:

1. Fundamentally, the role of the marketing manager of a firm in a global environment is the same as in a domestic environment. The environment is just more complex and dynamic.
2. A perspective that examines how companies and industries develop and sustain competitive advantage, not just comparative advantage, in global markets is critical to understanding global competition in the 1990s.
3. Multinational corporations have unique abilities in developing and executing global corporate strategies, which then influence the development of marketing strategies.
4. Global strategies influence the organizational structure within firms and the organizational structure itself influences global strategy development. The current trend is to develop global strategies based on strategic alliances and partnerships among firms rather than outright ownership of all operations.
5. As countries develop parity with respect to technology, product quality, and manufacturing costs, the role of marketing will become even more important for achieving and sustaining competitive advantage in global markets.

Competition and Interdependence in Our Global Village

Spoken with true "Star Trek" enthusiasm, Iridium's CEO Bob Kinzie previews the company's mission: "We're bringing dial-tone to places no dial-tone has gone before." A subsidiary of Motorola, the American telecommunication equipment manufacturer, Iridium plans to spend over $4 billion launching a telephone service that will use 66 "low earth orbit" satellites to let customers use pocket-phones to call to and from anywhere on the earth's surface. Apart from the technological marvel of a seamless worldwide telephone system, the company also faces the formidable task of accomplishing their goals in a market thick with six other international competitors who will also compete using satellite technology, plus a host of "terrestrial" telephone networks who will be using wireless cellular telephones to compete in the mobile telephone market.

Just as falling prices, continual advances in computing power, and increasing ease of use have led to the expansion of the personal computer market in the early 1990s, similar developments have stimulated sales of mobile phones. Ten years ago, the cellular-telephone business barely existed. In 1991, two-thirds of mobile phone sales in America were for phones in autos. In 1994, two-thirds of mobile-phone sales are of units that fit into jacket pockets, and over 30 million units are in use in some 70 countries (see Figure 17-1 for a summary of world mobile-telephone subscribers). Miniaturization processes have cut the internal volume of the average cellular phone by a factor of 1,000 in little more than a decade, while the average costs to consumers has fallen from $2,500 in 1986 to $390 in 1994, with cost projected to be around $100 by 1998. Falling prices have clearly meant greater market penetration for the cellular market. In the mid-1980s, the average household income of a cellular

Motorola's "flip-phone" is one of the leading products in the fast growing global cellular telephone market.

FIGURE 17-1
World Mobile-Telephone Subscribers

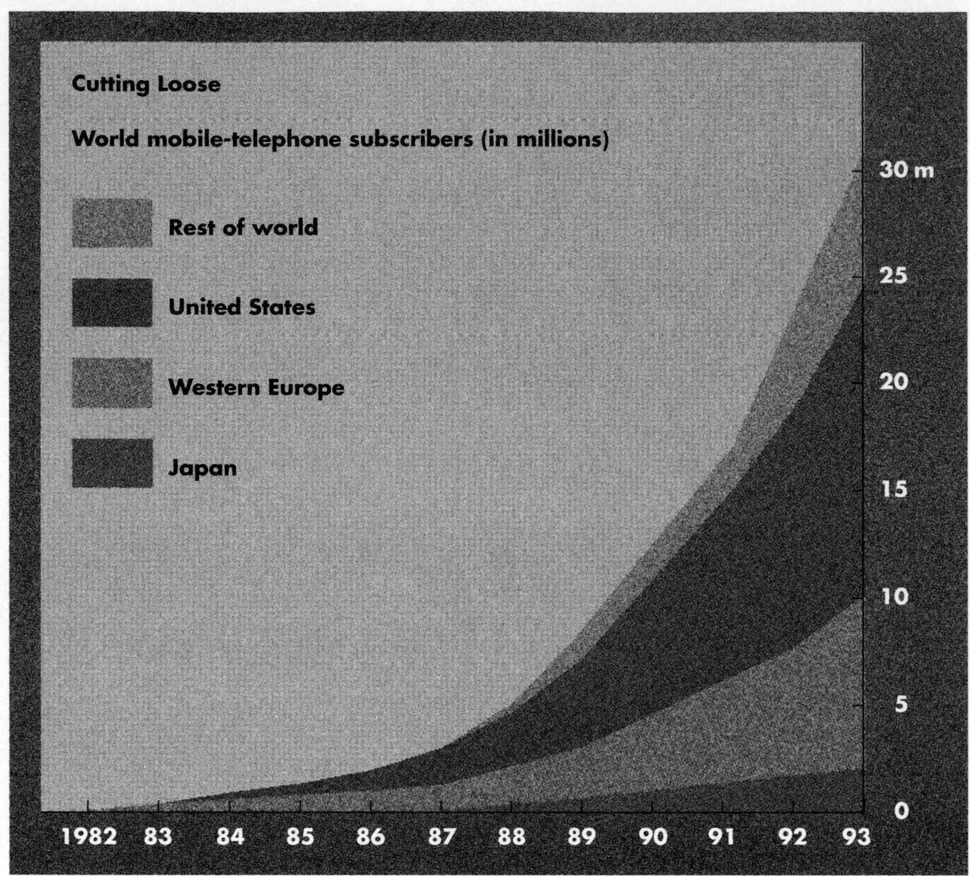

Source: *The Economist: A Survey of Telecommunications* (October 23, 1993): 5.

phone user was $14,500. By 1998 however, cellular phones may be owned by people with average household incomes of around $600! By then, three-quarters of the world's countries will have at least one cellular network, and the global total of subscribers is projected to exceed 100 million.

In order for any of the satellite companies to offer service, they must first get an allocation from governments around the world for frequencies in the radio spectrum. In March of 1992, the World Administrative Radio Conference, an assembly of the world's radio-wave regulators, reserved one group of frequencies for voice transmissions and another group of frequencies near the FM range for electronic message transmissions. In addition to seeking approvals from local agencies such as the Federal Communications Commission, these companies must also convince individual governments around the world (most of whom still reserve all voice telephony for state-owned monopolies) to open their markets to new competition.

Lined up against Iridium for a voice allocation permit are Globalstar, a $1.5 billion project using a system of 48 satellites developed by Loral and aerospace companies; Aries and Ellipso consortia of smaller firms; and TRW, a defense contractor that has already built a satellite-telephone system for the U.S. Pentagon. Two firms are already operating in the market. Inmarsat, a large and unwieldy treaty organization controlled by 71 telephone companies that are mostly government owned. This well-established firm enjoys free access to a huge amount of the radio spectrum and doesn't pay taxes or duties in many of the countries where it operates. Inmarsat is looking to expand beyond its current market of supplying communications to ships and into the bigger market for mobile communications on land. The other would-be competitor in this market is Orbcomm, part of Orbital Sciences, a Virginia-based company that makes launch vehicles and other space paraphernalia.

To keep costs down, Iridium plans to build small satellites for $13 million each—one tenth the current cost in relation to weight of the cheapest traditional satellites. Much of the cost of current satellites comes from trying to reduce the failure rate to as low a level as possible—which means using the best components and lots of backup systems. Lockheed, which is in charge of building Iridium's satellites, may find this a significant challenge since they are more accustomed to the technical high standards but financially forgiving world of government contracting. Lockheed's challenge is all the greater because Iridium requires new technologies for low-orbit satellites rather than older technologies that are relatively cheaper.

To support just its operating and financing costs, estimated to be $1 billion for the first two years of service, Iridium needs to find a large market. One long-term target that is politically appealing at this stage, is the prospect of serving eastern Europe and other developing country economies that have decrepit, land-based telephone systems. Even today, half the world's population lives more than two hours away from a telephone. By eliminating the need to install costly cables and microwave transmitters, the new telephones could be a boon to the remote and poor regions of the earth. At roughly half the cost of installing copper wiring to a subscriber, the economics of wireless telephone systems are appealing to countries whose consumers are desperate for extra telephone lines. But more immediately, Iridium and its rivals expect early users to be globe-trotting, First-World businesspeople. In terms of product launch, they will concentrate first on the lucrative American market. The company's marketing research forecasts look optimistic. If operations commence in 1997 as planned, Iridium hopes to have 1.8 million subscribers by the year 2001 and 3.2 million by 2006. Apart from the number of users, Iridium's forecasts of usage rates are also optimistic. Today, the average American mobile-telephone bill is $72 a month while Iridium hopes for monthly averages of $100 to $150. Even with the first satellite phones costing roughly $3,000 per unit, and with charges of $3 per minute, the company is convinced they will find a market. "The top 2 percent are heavy users, and those are the ones we'll be attracting first," argues Iridium's CEO.

To enhance resource allocations and spread risks, Iridium and the other competitors are bringing in foreign firms as investors and suppliers. Apart from Motorola's 34 percent interest, Iridium's investors include America's Sprint, Raytheon, and Lockheed corporations, and Nippon Iridium Corporation, a consortium of 18 Japanese companies including Sony, Mitsubishi, and Kyocera. Loral hopes to attract European investors for Globalstar by using European hardware suppliers—Alcatel, Alenia, and Aerospatiale (which already owns 49 percent of the company's satellite-making subsidiary). Iridium has hired British Aerospace, Deutsche Aerospace, and France's Matra Marconi to help Lockheed with its satellites. Japan's KDD and Hong Kong's Hutchinson Whampoa are interested in buying stakes as well. All of these alliances may be good politics and are undoubtedly financially necessary, but they also increase the administrative and control aspects of putting together the system. Getting the best engineering at low cost is difficult enough even in a tightly organized homogeneous group.

Finally, the companies not only need government permission to operate, but they also need government support to build a large base of subscribers, collect bills, and fulfill their potential. Instead of serving users directly, Iridium and Globalstar plan to let local telephone companies bill customers and take a percentage of the call revenues collected by the local company.[1]

Iridium's strategic plans provide an up-to-date example of the complexities and challenges of operating a global firm in the 1990s. The subsidiary of a large multinational, Iridium is developing a consortium of investors and business partners who also serve as suppliers, contractors, and political liaisons in the various countries where Iridium seeks permissions to operate. With these investors and partners, the firm plans to spend large amounts of money to develop cutting-edge technology in order to offer a service that doesn't even exist yet to a global market! Management activities involve R&D coordination with multiple partners and suppliers. There are international and national regulatory agencies to deal with, a clear element of competition between firms who want to enter this new market, plus an element of both competition and cooperation in negotiations with governments around the world who control the local telephone markets. Marketing research is needed to estimate worldwide market potential, suggest product launch strategies, and convince investors of the eventual payoff of participating is this high-tech global venture. Clearly, marketing management is one of the critical managerial activities at work in this project. Iridium is undoubtedly a technology-based company, but it is also a company with a global market vision.

MARKETING MANAGEMENT'S GLOBAL RESPONSIBILITIES

For Iridium and for any firm operating in the international environment, the central **responsibilities of global marketing management** are to determine the firm's overall global goals and objectives and to shape the organization to achieve those goals and objectives. Marketing's responsibility is to contribute insight, knowledge, forecasts, and programs that lead to superior perceived value by consumers in global markets, and ultimately, to maximize long-term corporate profitability. Marketing may not be dominant in the management culture in companies like Iridium, but it is a marketing management perspective that necessarily guides an organization in bringing new and innovative products to market. Regardless of whether a company views its market as one single global market, as regional markets, or as individual country markets, the role of the global marketing manager is to provide a mechanism for guiding marketing strategy and implementation in those markets.

Before beginning the discussion of the specific managerial tasks related to planning, organizing, and controlling marketing activities in international marketing, it is worthwhile to briefly review the nature and structure of contemporary global markets. Understanding the dominant trends in global business will provide a clearer basis for appreciating the complexities and challenges of developing and executing marketing management strategies and tactics in the global context. The following sections review two interrelated developments in world trade that have had a significant impact on the nature of global competition and marketing: the rise of multinationals within the triad of Europe, Japan, and America; and the tremendous increase in the use of strategic alliances and joint ventures as strategic tools in global competition.

MULTINATIONALS AND THEIR COMPETITIVE ADVANTAGE

Throughout the chapters in this text, the "Global Perspectives" sections have advocated a broad view of selling products to customers around the world and have highlighted the unique aspects of marketing activities in the global context. While many small and medium-size companies are highly successful in developing global marketing strategies, the dominant share of global business belongs to the world's large multinational corporations (MNCs). Apart from the competitive strengths that arise from their sheer size and financial resources, **MNCs have unique abilities** to exploit their strengths gained in one nation in order to establish a position in another. MNCs not only export, but they compete in markets abroad via their foreign subsidiaries.

While no nation in the world is economically independent, some groups of nations are more economically interdependent on each other than others. The roughly 900 million relatively affluent consumers that comprise the triad countries of Japan, Europe, and North America make up less than 25 percent of the world's population, but account for approximately 70 percent of the value of all world trade. Table 17-1 identifies the top ten importing countries in the world, which account for 62 percent of the total world's imports.[2]

TABLE 17-1
World's Top Ten Importers, 1990

Country	Value in $ Billions	% Share of World Imports
United States	$517	14.3%
Germany*	356	9.9%
Japan	235	6.5%
France	234	6.5%
Britain	223	6.2%
Italy	182	5.0%
Holland	126	3.5%
Canada	124	3.4%
USSR (CIS)	121	3.3%
Belgium/Luxembourg	120	3.3%

*Unified Germany

Sources: GATT, OECD.

Further, most of the world's large corporations have their headquarters in one of the triad countries. Table 17-2 gives an overview of the top 500 global companies based on sales revenues and distributed by industry and region. Notice that 449 of the top 500 companies for these selected industries have their headquarters in one of the Triad countries.[3] In a recent study of the top global corporations based on market value of the company, only 15 out of the top 500 companies were headquartered outside of the Triad countries.[4]

TABLE 17-2
Largest Companies in the World by Industry and Country

Industry	Europe	U.S.	Japan	Major Company
Aerospace	5	10	0	Boeing
Apparel	0	2	0	Levi Strauss Ass
Beverages	5	4	3	PepsiCo
Building materials, glass	8	4	3	Saint-Gobain
Chemicals	18	14	12	E.I. Du Pont
Computers, office equipment	2	9	6	IBM
Electronics, electrical equipment	11	16	15	General Electric
Food	18	19	11	Philip Morris
Forest and paper products	6	12	5	Int. Paper
Industrial and farm equipment	11	7	9	Mitsubishi Ind.
Jewelry, watches	0	0	2	Citizen Watch
Metal products	6	5	7	Pechiney
Metals	14	6	8	IRI
Mining, crude-oil production	3	0	0	Ruhrkohle
Motor vehicles and parts	14	9	18	General Motors
Petroleum refining	12	14	8	Exxon
Pharmaceuticals	10	11	4	Johnson & Johnson
Publishing, printing	3	4	2	Matra-Hachette
Rubber and plastic products	4	2	3	Bridgestone
Scientific, photo control equip.	1	7	2	Eastman Kodak
Soaps, Cosmetics	4	3	2	Procter & Gamble
Textiles	1	0	5	Toray Industries
Tobacco	2	3	1	RJR Nabisco Holdings
Toys, sporting goods	0	0	2	Nintendo
Transportation equipment	2	0	0	Kvaerner
Top 500 companies:				
United States: 161				
Europe: 160				
Japan: 128				
Other: 51				

Source: Adapted from "Global 500," *Fortune* (July 26, 1993): 62–72.

MOVING FROM COMPARATIVE ADVANTAGE TO COMPETITIVE ADVANTAGE

Trade statistics such as those in Table 17-1 describe the flow of goods and services among nations. It is important to remember that while governments can and do directly influence the environment in which business activities takes place, nations don't trade, companies do. A number of theories have been devised to explain why goods and services are traded internationally, including investment theories, the international product life cycle (discussed in Chapter 7), and the theory of comparative advantage.

The theory of **comparative advantage and its underlying assumptions** are the basis for most other theories of world trade and provide a useful starting point for a discussion of not only global trade, but global competition. Briefly, the theory of comparative advantage explains international trade flows between nations by examining a country's "factor endowments." Factor endowments are resources such as land, labor, and capital. By specializing in those industries in which a country's firms are relatively more productive and importing those goods and services in which its firms are less productive than foreign rivals, a country can raise total productivity for the entire economy. To help illustrate this point a comparison of import and export figures for Japan is given in Table 17-3. Japan exports very little food, raw materials, or fuels, but imports large amounts of these items. By contrast it imports relatively few motor vehicles or other machinery but does export them. These figures illustrate the principle of comparative advantage: as a country, Japan is exporting what it is good at making and importing what it is less good at making.[5]

Comparative advantage theory was proposed by the economist Ricardo over 200 years ago and assumes that companies do not enjoy benefits derived from economies of scale, that labor and capital do not move between nations, that companies have equal access to technology, and that products are undifferentiated. The MNCs of the twentieth century violate all of these assumptions—they source supplies where they need to, exchange good ideas between subsidiaries and move management talent, set up off-shore production plants,

TABLE 17-3
Japan's Trade by Category, 1990.

Category	Exports in $ Billions	Imports in $ Billions
Foodstuffs	1.6	31.6
Raw Materials	1.9	28.5
Fuels	1.3	56.7
Chemical Products	15.9	16.0
Motor Vehicles	51.0	6.4
Other Machinery and Transport Equipment	150.3	31.5
Other Manufactures	60.3	57.9
Miscellaneous	4.6	6.2

Source: OECD; Japanese Ministry of Finance.

and develop global marketing programs to sell differentiated products and services in all markets simultaneously. Certainly, easy access to capital has played a key role in these developments. Electronic international money flows for purely financial transactions during a single week would be sufficient to finance total world trade for an entire year—more than $2,000 billion dollars per week![6] Thus, while the theory of comparative advantage has been very useful in helping explain the flow of goods and services between countries with specific factor endowments, it does not explain how firms or industries within a country can sustain such an advantage in competitive global markets over time.

A theory of **competitive advantage and how to sustain it** in global markets is evolving and includes a number of complex interrelationships between a country and the firms conducting business in that country. Using the perspective of competitive advantage, rather than the economist's favorite concept of comparative advantage, management expert Michael Porter makes the argument that globalization and technological change have made traditional ways of gauging comparative advantage, such as the costs of labor and raw materials, less important. What matters now are the abilities to innovate and to develop clusters of competitive companies in particular industries.[7] The following three examples illustrate the underlying notions of competitive advantage at the country, industry, and firm level.

Certainly, differences in culture, values, history, and economic structures will contribute to a country's economic successes. For example, Taiwan's economic and social transformation from an agrarian to an industrialized society in roughly 35 years is due to a number of factors. Most important was the determination of the citizens of Taiwan to survive and prosper on the island following the communist revolution on the mainland in 1949. The strong work ethic of the Chinese, coupled with the political and economic support from the United States, as well as heavy investments from other industrialized countries combined to make Taiwan a country with a strong export strategy and yearly trade surpluses. From 1950 through the 1970s, Taiwan's comparative advantage was in its highly disciplined, low-cost labor force. In the late 1970s Taiwanese companies and foreign multinationals began heavily investing in R&D facilities. Now, Taiwanese companies sustain their competitive position by producing high technology—high value-added products. With per capita income levels similar to Greece and Spain, Taiwan is no longer the low-wage production site it was 30 years ago. Taiwanese firms now source their own low-cost labor with off-shore production platforms in the mainland Chinese province of Guangdong.[8]

Even in countries with strong natural resource endowments (a fundamental assumption under the theory of comparative advantage), using a competitive advantage perspective can often provide a better understanding of competing in global markets. Colombia, with its close proximity to North America, a temperate climate, long equatorial days, low labor costs, and rich soil has seen their exports of cut flowers triple in the past ten years to over $315 million. The number of large growers has tripled to over 400, as has the acreage under cultivation. Still, the country's share of global exports has not risen above 10 percent, a distant second to Holland's 60-percent market share, and the Colombian growers are largely unprofitable. While the Colombian flower industry has pursued a niche at the low end of the market and competes purely on price, their Dutch rivals have invested heavily in research to produce better flowers and have spent heavily to develop efficient distribution systems. Bogota's airport, the main outlet for Colombia's flowers, has only one runway in use and no refrigeration facilities. Nearly all the exported flowers are flown to Miami, and then they must be reshipped north or west. As Miami serves as the main hub for Latin American flights, bottlenecks are frequent, and the price is paid in freshness of the flowers. In contrast, the Dutch produce higher priced and higher margin flowers and fly them in specially designed refrigerated containers daily to a number of "gateway" destinations such as New York, Chicago, and Los Angeles. In spite of much higher labor costs, an unforgiving North Sea climate, and longer transportation logistics, the Dutch flower growers sustain their competitive advantage over rivals who would be predicted to have comparative advantage.[9]

Early in this chapter it was asserted that MNCs have the unique ability to exploit their strengths gained in one nation in order to establish a position in another. Let's consider one final example that illustrates this point but does not focus on the presence or absence of factor endowments; instead it focuses on the competitive advantages which are gained by being a global player. The world's six biggest accountancy firms are in the top rank in virtually every country in the world except where they are barred by law. Yet auditing and accounting are intensely local practices requiring detailed knowledge of local rules and regulations. Arthur Andersen or Price Waterhouse ought not, in theory, to have an advantage over domestic competitors except with multinational clients, which, though large, are almost always a minority. Why, then, have these firms become such successful multinationals and so well established in local markets? One answer may lie in their related businesses such as consulting, in which they have special skills. Another explanation may be their ability to provide, organize, and install information technology. Yet these characteristics are not enough to explain such widespread dominance. *Reputation,* the power of the corporate brand name, clearly plays a key role. The market for accounting and auditing is an imperfect market: buyers lack the information to tell a good accountant from a bad one or find it costly to find out. They seek out a highly reputable accountant's brand name as a means to convince others about their own worth, especially in relationship to potential investors and creditors, who are similarly short of local information. In this example, the equity of having a strong global brand name coupled with the hiring of locals who meet the firm's high standards (personnel are in fact the key "product" offering in many professional service organizations) provide the firm's competitive advantage.[10]

In summary, many business observers believe that the ability of a work force to continually make improvements in productivity and efficiency and make the best of new technologies provide a country and its firms the best competitive advantage. Wealth in raw materials, the foundation of innovation two centuries ago, barely matters anymore. MNCs secure long-term contracts with reliable suppliers of raw materials and they also source commodities on very short notice through the highly efficient "spot" markets that operate 24 hours a day. Proximity to affluent markets matters less as transport costs fall relative to the value of the goods and as MNCs forge joint ventures to gain efficient market entry. A demanding local market is nice, but it can be replaced by still more demanding foreign markets. Technologies diffuse and become quickly standardized. Creating an environment where the intangible, vital qualities of innovative thinking and productive skills can operate is a critical and relatively nontransferable asset.

Marketing management's role in sustaining a company's competitive advantage is to provide direction and vision to the company in all their markets. This is accomplished by analyzing markets, developing market forecasts, and generating and implementing strategies that differentiate their company's offerings in selected market segments around the world—in short, using a global marketing perspective as an integrating tool in all management planning, organizing, and controlling activities. In many respects, MNCs are in the best position to make use of this perspective. By virtue of their size and scope of activities, they are already actively pursuing markets with a global perspective. Size is not the only criterion however—the Dutch Flower Growers example makes that point clear. What matters is the philosophy of providing continuous innovation and improvements in business operations in order to satisfy clients' needs! Many small and medium-size companies succeed in global competition as well and a discussion of their strategies will follow later in this chapter.

Global Joint Ventures and Strategic Alliances

Global competition has become a team sport. Since the beginning of the 1980s, world markets have been characterized by the trend of companies to form and operate in alliances and cooperative ventures. In the United States, cooperative agreements outnumber fully owned foreign subsidiaries by a factor of at least four to one, and since the 1980s U.S. firms have formed over 2,000 agreements with European corporations.[11] Japan's powerful *Keiretsu* structure and South Korea's *Chaebol* organizations are further examples of stable alliances of companies who create **cooperative advantage** by closely linking their suppliers, manufacturers, financing, and marketing activities together for long-term strategies of market conquest.

Typically, it is large multinational corporations that seem the most inclined to enter into strategic alliances. Within these strategic alliance networks, firms create global oligopoly market structures that involve complex relationships based on the coexistence of both cooperative and competitive interests. Figure 17-2 illustrates the network of alliances for the multinational electronics giant, Toshiba. While a number of these alliances involve sharing in the risks and costs of R&D projects, other alliances are formed to share established technology and marketing efforts and to supply a range of products that extends from gargantuan power plant equipment and refrigerators for households to the most elaborate memory chips.[12]

Before identifying the major forces behind the trend toward strategic alliances and discussing the advantages and disadvantages of the approach, consider the following example of how alliances can be used as a powerful strategy for global marketing.

FIGURE 17-2
Toshiba's Network of Alliances

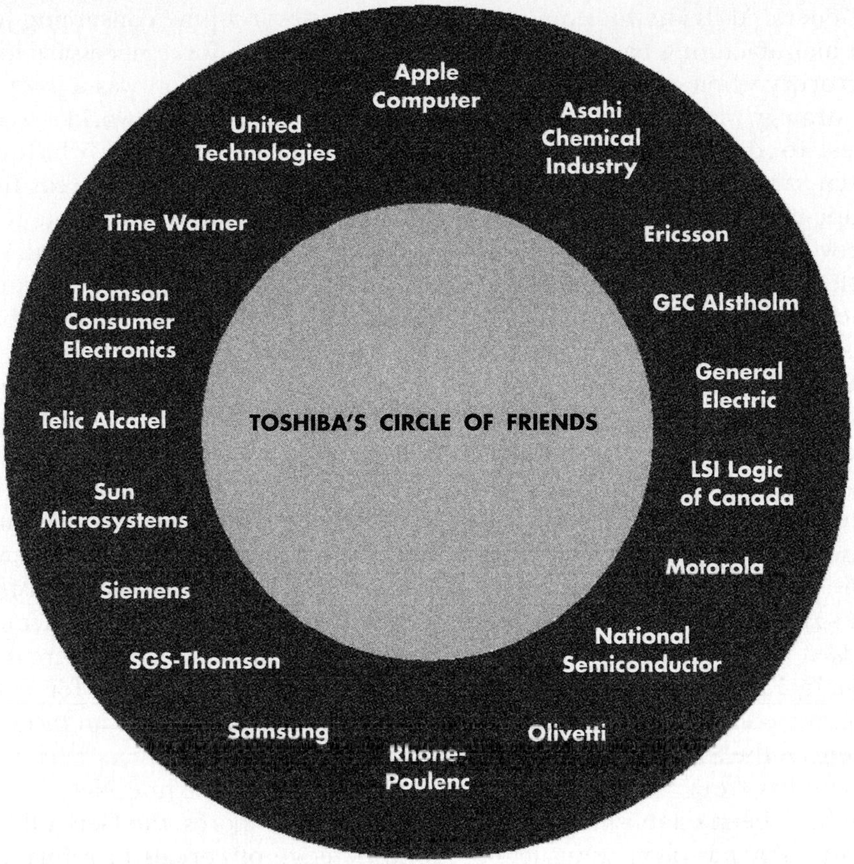

TOSHIBA'S CIRCLE OF FRIENDS

Apple Computer
Asahi Chemical Industry
Ericsson
GEC Alsthom
General Electric
LSI Logic of Canada
Motorola
National Semiconductor
Olivetti
Rhone-Poulenc
Samsung
SGS-Thomson
Siemens
Sun Microsystems
Telic Alcatel
Thomson Consumer Electronics
Time Warner
United Technologies

Source: Brenton R. Schleuder, "How Toshiba Makes Alliances Work," *Fortune* (October 4, 1993): 116.

A GLOBAL FOOD FIGHT

Ready-to-eat breakfast cereal is one of the most profitable and competitive of all consumer businesses. Kellogg, the $5.2 billion-a-year maker of *Corn Flakes, Rice Crispies,* and *Frosted Flakes,* sells these brands and others in 130 countries around the world and earns 35 percent of its profits outside the U.S. market. It owns about 50 percent of the total market share in Europe having built the market from scratch in the U.K. during the 1920s and expanding to the European continent in the 1950s. Although this business uses relatively cheap and easy-to-source commodities as its raw materials, it is both capital and marketing intensive (making corn flakes involves a lot of high-tech processes and machinery!). Firms need production economies of scale and must develop high-volume sales in order to have sufficient margins for profit.

General Mills, in partnership with the European giant Nestlé, are teaming up and have announced business goals of achieving a 20 percent market share by the end of the decade. The alliance, called Cereal Partners Worldwide (CPW) is the food industry's first major joint venture designed to be a global business. Several European countries are experiencing a cereal boom, with the volume consumed growing at a rate of 30 percent per year. Forecasts are for a $6.5 billion market by the year 2000, making cereal the fastest-growing food category in Europe.

General Mills knew it would be extremely costly and time consuming to set up a manufacturing base and support the massive sales force necessary to call on grocery wholesalers and retailers worldwide. The solution was a joint venture strategy with an established European partner. Nestlé, the world's second-largest food company (Philip Morris is the largest), with $36.5 billion in annual sales and operations in more than 100 countries, was a great fit. In Europe it had everything General Mills lacked—a well-known corporate name, a network of production plants, and a powerful distribution system. What Nestlé lacked was a strong name in breakfast cereal brands. The company launched a few cereals in the mid-1980s, including *Chocapic,* a chocolate-based cereal, but none has been successful in competing with Kellogg's brands.

The alliance had an inescapable logic. General Mills would provide the knowledge in cereal technology, including some of its proprietary manufacturing equipment, its line of well-known brands, and its sophistication in marketing and promoting cereal to consumers. Nestlé would provide the corporate name on the box, access to retailers, and the production capacity in Europe that would be converted to making General Mill's cereals. The announcement of the alliance has already frightened one competitor out of the business. Ranks-Hovis-McDougall, a relatively small British cereal maker, had acquired *Shredded Wheat* from RJR Nabisco in 1989, and was the third-largest cereal producer in Britain. Rather than competing in the upcoming battle for market share, the company sold out to CPW giving the new joint venture an instant 15 percent of the $1 billion British market.

Benefits from the joint venture are already visible. While Nestlé's sales force have been establishing shelf space in European stores, the General Mill's side of CPW has been using its unique knowledge of cereals to reformulate *Chocapic,* Nestlé's relatively unsuccessful cereal to give it a softer texture. Also, instead of a windmill-like figure on the box, which was not particularly appealing to European children, advertising specialists from General Mills in the United States created a hyperactive cartoon hound. The character will appear in TV ads that will be generic enough so that various European languages can be dubbed into them at little extra cost. Furthermore, as part of an exclusive agreement to supply food for Euro Disneyland, which opened near Paris in 1992, Nestlé has rights to use Walt Disney characters on its products throughout Europe and the Middle East. These well-known figures will likely appear on CPW's cereal boxes in the near future. Finally, the alliance's managers like their global prospects. In Asia, Africa, and Latin America, CPW should have a tactical advantage over Kellogg because Nestlé is a food powerhouse in those markets, while Kellogg has only cereal.

For General Mill's, the greatest risk in the alliance might be the global corporate strategy that Nestlé follows of preferring to own their companies outright. Within the past decade, Nestlé has acquired the American milk producer Carnation, the British food giant Roundtree, and France's *Perrier Water.* General Mills would seem to make a nice addition to Nestlé's group of high-margin food businesses. While General Mill's current price/earning ratio of 21 gives them a good defense against a takeover, the American company included a "stillstand" agreement in the formation of CPW, which excludes the company from operating in North America and bars Nestlé from selling cereal in North America for ten years should CPW be dissolved.[13]

General Mills and Nestlé have entered into a joint venture agreement to develop and sell products in global markets.

PROS AND CONS IN BUILDING GLOBAL ALLIANCES

In the global context, the competitive advantages of firms reside more in their ability to create, acquire, and coordinate the use of resources across national boundaries than in the outright possession of individual assets. In recent years, two factors have been the major forces behind the growth of **strategic alliances**:[14]

1. *The Globalization of Markets.* Homogenization of consumer life-styles for many consumer product categories, and the continued trend of standardized practices in business markets creates a need for more flexible structures and new forms of organizations in order to enable firms to compete successfully on a worldwide basis.
2. *Technological Advances.* Technological advances lead to major changes in the traditional competitive advantages of a firm. Increases in costs and uncertainty of R&D programs cause firms to share the risks of new product development. Technology also shortens a product's life cycle both domestically and internationally, and market-based alliances allow for rapid access to global markets.

Table 17-4 presents the results of a survey of 4,182 alliances that were made in the 1980s. The right half of the table strongly suggests that the three reasons most commonly cited for alliances were to gain access to a market, to exploit complementary technologies, and to reduce the time taken for innovation.[15] Finally, Figure 17-3 provides one final example of the increasing need to form alliances in order to share risks and effectively compete in markets where no one company has the resources or the knowledge to go it alone. As the telecommunications, computer, and media industries merge, both the risks of developing those new markets and the potential payoffs for being successful in them are tremendous. Actually, as of 1994, no one is even certain what these new products and markets will entail, or how they will evolve! One

	Number of Alliances	Main reason for alliance, % of total High-cost risks	Lack of financial resources	Technological compatibility	Reduced innovation time-span	Basic R&D sharing	Market access/ structure	Technology monitoring/ market entry
Biotechnology	847	1	13	35	31	10	13	15
New materials technology	430	1	3	38	32	11	31	16
Information technology	1,660	4	2	33	31	3	38	11
Computers	198	1	2	28	22	2	51	10
Industrial automation	278	nil	3	41	32	4	31	7
Microelectronics	383	3	3	33	33	5	52	6
Software	344	1	4	38	36	2	24	11
Telecommunications	366	11	2	28	28	1	35	16
Other	91	1	nil	29	28	2	35	24
Automotive	205	4	2	27	22	2	52	4
Aviation/defence	228	36	1	34	26	nil	13	8
Chemicals	410	7	1	16	13	1	51	8
Consumer electronics	58	2	nil	19	19	nil	53	9
Food and beverages	42	1	nil	17	10	nil	43	7
Heavy electric/power	141	36	1	31	10	4	23	11
Instruments/medical technology	95	nil	4	35	40	2	28	10
Other	66	35	nil	9	6	0	23	8

Source: Hagedoorn and Schakenraad, Maastricht Economic Research Institute in Innovation and Technology.

TABLE 17-4
Strategic Alliances by Sector and Effects of Technology

thing is certain: Global alliances will be the only way to compete in this new global market of information and entertainment.

While many alliances concentrate on R&D projects, the General Mills/Nestlé deal is an example of a strategic alliance wherein several value-added activities, such as the combination of R&D, production, and marketing, motivate the formation of the new company. The CPW example illustrates many of the advantages that accrue to inter-firm agreements: co-opting competition (i.e., the British manufacturer of *Shredded Wheat*); sharing of the large investments needed for specific activities such as production or marketing; rationalization of production and efficiencies of scope (i.e., European cereal production and standardizing the advertising campaign for *Chocapic*); and access to complementary resources (General Mill's strong brand names and Nestlé's strong corporate name and global channels of distribution).

The predominant view in the 1990s seems to be that firms will continue engaging in alliances as they continue to recognize and accept that there are limits to what they can achieve efficiently both in terms of their scale and scope when operating alone. In spite of this growing trend, not all strategic alliances will work out the way they were planned! Cultural differences in management styles, poor communications among the partners regarding clearly

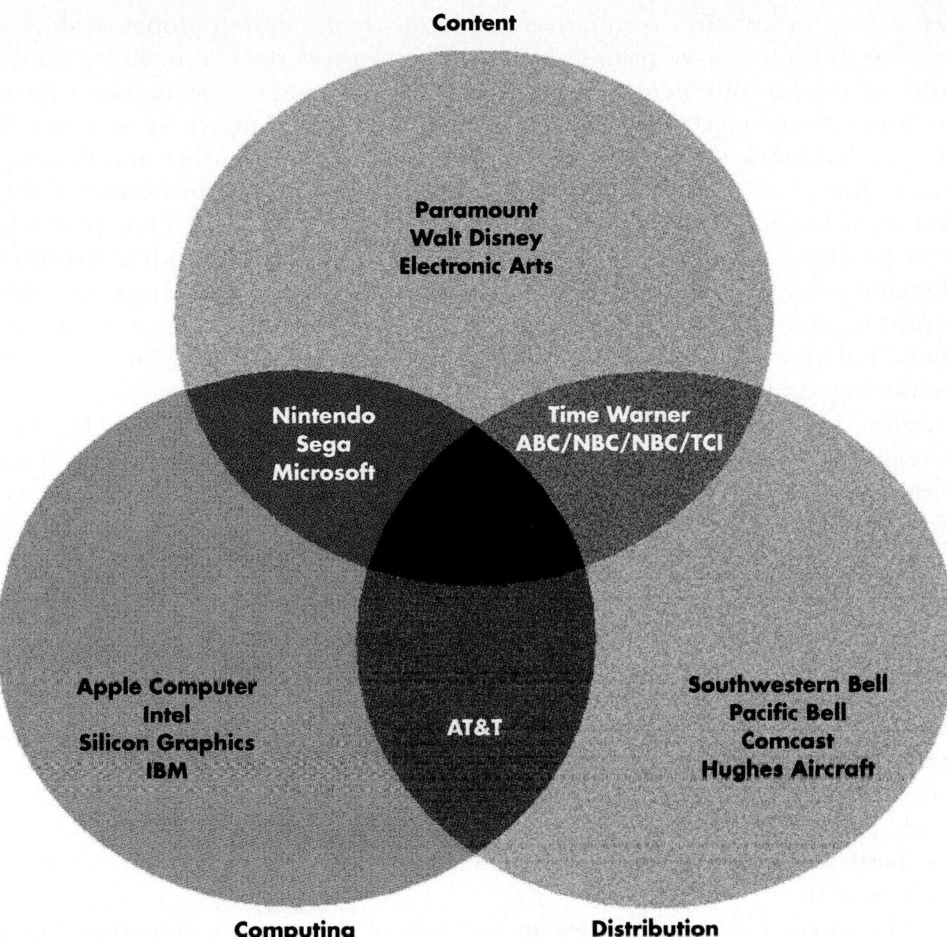

FIGURE 17-3 *Alliances in the Telecommunications Industry*

Source: Salomon Brothers, "Feeling for the Future: A Survey of Television," *The Economist* (February 12, 1994): 7.

defined goals of the alliance, and opportunism may lead to the demise of strategic alliances. Other risks include the misappropriation of technological know-how, the loss of control over operations, and the risk that a partner may become a stronger competitor. In global markets, the potential for conflict arises because firms are often cooperating with some partners in one network or market, while they compete with them in other networks or markets.[16]

Planning and Organizing for Global Markets

Immediately following the Iridium example at the start of this chapter, the claim was made that marketing management's responsibility is to contribute insight, knowledge, forecasts, and programs that lead to superior value as perceived by consumers in global markets and, ultimately, to maximize long-term corporate profitability. The key words that make this definition unique are "global markets." The majority of firms develop international plans for separate and distinct markets, while a relatively small number of companies plan globally and treat the world as one single market. This difference in orientation is important, since truly integrated global strategies involve different assumptions about doing business relative to firms whose international involvement is to follow an export strategy or some other form of international marketing. A fundamental point of difference in approach is that **global marketing strategies** view the world as one market and develop marketing plans that concentrate on cross-cultural similarities instead of differences. Reebok and Nike are global firms in the sense that their products and promotional programs appeal to athletes sharing similar product demands. Adjustments in their channels strategies and pricing strategies in different markets will reflect local conditions, but do not detract from their fundamental view of concentrating on cross-cultural similarities. **International marketing strategies,** on the other hand, are based on the premise of cross-cultural differences and the strategies and tactics are guided by the belief that foreign markets require their own culturally adapted marketing efforts. Many food manufacturers that have global operations can still be seen as international in their approach, given that they make adjustments in all aspects of their marketing programs in order to accommodate local tastes and consumption patterns.

Also, strategic planning for global markets or regional markets will have an influence on the organization's structure. When companies have one large national market and a number of smaller foreign markets, an international division may be formed to handle foreign marketing. If nations or regions have highly different marketing needs, the use of national subsidiaries may be the best way to organize in order to tailor the marketing mix and make it work. Alternatively, when markets are perceived as relatively homogeneous, the basis for planning may be global and organized on a worldwide product division basis.

The music industry provides an example of product segmentation and a global approach to strategic planning. Table 17-5 shows the six major record companies that together account for 80 percent of the $22 billion dollar global music market.[17] Notice that, apart from indicating the extremely global nature of the music industry, all of the parent companies are either multimedia giants like Time/Warner, Thorn, and Bertelsmann/BMG or major manufacturers of consumer electronic products such as Sony, Philips, and Matsushita/MCA (Thorn is also in this industry, but is small relative to the other three companies). All of these global companies have the financing, distribution, and marketing strength to create and maintain global markets. Organizationally, they all treat music as a separate division and all of them use strategies of global, rather than market by market, product launches in introducing new products. The media companies see music as one of their core business offerings within their total product line, while the electronics firms see their music companies as a complementary strength, and as strategically important software to drive the sales of their new technology hardware developments.

GLOBAL STRATEGIES FOR GLOBAL FIRMS

Global marketing strategies are clearly the trend with large MNCs, although this approach is tempered by the awareness that all firms have limitations: that technology has become so advanced and that markets have become so com-

TABLE 17-5
Global Music Companies and Their Labels

Company	Music Labels
Time Warner (USA)	Atlantic Elektra Sire Warner Bros.
Sony (Japan)	CBS Def Jam Epic
Philips/Polygram (the Netherlands)	A&M Island Polydor
Thorn EMI (U.K.)	Virgin Music Capitol Chrysalis EMI Records SBK
Bertelsmann/BMG (Germany)	Arista RCA
Matsushita/MCA (Japan)	Geffen MCA Motown

plex that a large global firm simply can't expect to be best in all business activities anymore. Even without absolute homogeneity in global markets, standardization of strategies is sought across markets. For these firms, the issue is not whether to go global, but how to tailor the global marketing concept to fit each business and how to make it work.[18] Many large MNCs use the conceptual frameworks of the product life cycle or the Boston Consulting Group and GE models (discussed in Chapters 8 and 16) in developing their global strategies. Management consultant Michael Porter offers advice for developing a global approach to marketing strategy:[19]

- Sell worldwide, not just in a home market. International sales are viewed not as incremental business but as integral to strategy. Global marketing involves strategies that establish international brands and controlling global channels of distribution and other elements of the marketing mix.
- Locate marketing activities in other nations in order to make use of local advantages, to facilitate local market penetration, to offset disadvantages in home markets.
- Operating in a number of international markets is not the same as having a global strategy. Global strategies entail integration, coordination, and cooperation among the company's subsidiaries. These activities are necessary in order to gain the benefits of economies of scale and learning, to enjoy the benefits of market acceptance that comes from a consistent brand reputation, and to serve international buyers.

Table 17-6 provides an overview of corporate strategy for Canon, a large, multinational Japanese firm that described itself in 1990 as being in the

Years	1950	1960	1970	1980	1990
1. General					
a. Product	Camera	Camera-related products	Image products	Image and information products	Image, information and communication products
b. Market	Home market	Exporting	Foreign direct investment	Multinational enterprise	Multinational enterprise
2. Core technology	Optical Fine mechanical	Electronics Physics Chemistry Fine Optical	Software System Material technology Communication	(Same as 1970)	Biotechnology Energy technology
3. Product mix	Still camera Movie camera Lens	EE camera Reflex camera Calculator	Copier Facsimile Laser printer Word processor	Office automation Video Word processor Electronic fitting	Audio-visual products UA FA system Information service
4. Production	One plant	Multiple plants	Foreign direct investment	Optimum production domestic and overseas	Optimum worldwide production location
5. Sales channel				(Same as 1970)	System integration Customer-oriented system
a. Domestic	Outside wholesaler	Construction of direct sales channel	Strengthening direct sales channel		
b. Overseas	Outside agency	Construction of direct sales channel			
6. Personnel	Recruiting	Training	Utilization of human resources	Enhancement of creativity	Enhancement of entrepreneurial spirit
7. Organizational structure	Functional	Preparation of product division	Product divisions	Group divisions	Global management system
8. Sales (billion yen)	0.4	4.2	44.8	240.7	900.0
9. Long-range planning		1st long-range plan Construction of resource structure for diversification	2nd long-range plan (1968–1972) (Diversification, Expansion of production capacity and sales channel) 3rd long-range plan (1973–1977) (To image industry, to knowledge products. Development of multinational management)	Excellent company plan (1976–1981) 1000 billion plan (1979–1989 + Medium-range plan 2nd Excellent plan (1982–1986) (Strengthening Canon group, creative new product development capability, strengthening resource structure.)	Global company plan (1988–1992) (To global company, to information industry)

Source: Reprinted with permission from *Long Range Planning,* Volume 25, Toshio Nakahara and Yutake Isono, "Strategic Planning for Canon: The Crisis and the New Vision," 1992, Pergamon Press Ltd.

TABLE 17-6
The Strategies of Canon: 1950–1990

"image, information, and communication products businesses."[20] The strategic themes in the table can be described as "internationalization" and "diversification." These themes are also reflected in the company's name changes over the years. In 1937 the company was called Precision Optical Industries; in 1947, the name was changed to Canon Camera, Inc., and in 1969, the name changed to its current Canon, Inc. As you move from left to right in the table, notice the expansion and diversification of products and divisions, the increases in foreign investments, and the evolving organizational structure. With over 35 years of strategic global planning experience, Canon has also developed a list of **failure factors in strategic planning** that they believe impede the successful execution of global planning. While the list comes from Canon's own observations, the points made could be relevant and useful to any global company.

1. Hasty conclusions are reached in the analysis of environmental assumptions about social, economic, political, technological, and international situations.
2. Top management does not possess a clear managerial belief or vision.
3. The planning staff drew up the plan without confirming top management's intentions.
4. Excessive focus is placed on numbers resulting in a lack of clear priorities and overall balance.
5. A collection of departmental plans has been compiled but it lacks a corporate viewpoint. Oftentimes, the planning staff works alone without the participation of line departments.
6. The planning staff monopolizes information necessary for planning.
7. Upon completion of the plan, it is filed away with no effort to disseminate it to the whole organization.
8. Analysis, assessment, and feedback are not properly carried out to identify the gaps between the plan and actual performance.[21]

BENEFITS OF A GLOBAL MARKETING APPROACH: THE CASE FOR STANDARDIZATION

Although the benefits of a global approach to marketing based on efforts to standardize the marketing mix have been discussed throughout the preceding chapters, they can be summarized here. The most obvious benefits of **global standardization** are the economies of scale in production and marketing. Being able to plan and execute production runs based on global demand estimates and developing one basic strategy for product launches greatly reduces both manufacturing costs and the use of managerial time. When CPW produces cereals for its various European markets, the production runs will be done in bulk and the actual packaging of the cereals will be systematically organized at the assembly line to account for packages with different language requirements. Distribution costs will be shared by other CPW or Nestlé products destined for the same wholesaler or retailers in various countries. By having one uniform cartoon character for advertising, quality standards will be consistent, quantity discounts for air time can be negotiated on Pan European Satellite networks, and relatively inexpensive voice-overs can be used in different markets. Transfer of experience and knowledge through improved integration of marketing activities is also a frequently mentioned benefit of standardization efforts. The accumulated expertise of multinationals allows them to be efficient and effective in launching brand extenders as well as complementary product lines. Not only does unique knowledge aid in the marketing efforts of global companies, but recognition of their brand names and their uniform global image accelerates new product introductions and acceptance.

It is important to acknowledge that the success of standardization efforts will depend upon two key factors. The first factor is the firm's ability to implement the programs within the company. Organizational structure, the new orientation needed by personnel, and the company culture will all influence standardization efforts. The second factor that is a potential barrier to standardization has to do with the external environment in which the company operates and includes the channel structure and political and legal issues.

THE CASE FOR CUSTOMIZATION IN INTERNATIONAL MARKETING

International marketing strategies are based on the premise of cross-cultural differences, and the strategies and tactics are guided by the belief that foreign markets require their own culturally adapted, customized marketing efforts. Proponents of the **customization** approach argue that the trend toward global competition and global strategies should not be confused with a trend toward global product offerings. In short, global competition does not necessarily imply global products.[22] Companies that follow a course of customizing marketing strategies for each market do so for a variety of reasons. In some cases, the historical development of strategy is coupled with strong management personalities and the evolution of the company's organizational structure. The overwhelming reason for following this course is the firm's belief that customizing the marketing mix is their best strategy to differentiate themselves in the market from competitors and to serve their clients.

Arguing that products should be tailored to fit the individual needs of customers in different countries hits right at the heart of the marketing concept. While global marketing management views the world as one market and develops marketing plans that concentrate on cross-cultural similarities instead of cross-cultural differences, there is certainly substantial evidence to the contrary. The recent growth in nationalism in Europe, the renewed pride in ethnic origins all over the world, and a return to extreme religiosity all suggest a trend toward heterogeneity rather than homogeneity in global markets. In practice, strategies of pure standardization or pure customization are simply not feasible. The important perspective to have here is to know to what extent standardization should (and can) be used and how far it should be taken. For example, McDonald's sells a standard franchise formula worldwide, yet they are savvy enough to make modifications in the menus they offer around the world. The uniform global image that the company enjoys stems from its consistently high standards of business operations and offering high perceived value—not from offering the identical menu and identical tastes in their food products. Minor modifications in all of the elements of the marketing mix in order to best respond to important differences in global markets is the optimal middle ground in the standardization-customization debate.

ALTERNATIVE MARKET ENTRY STRATEGIES FOR INTERNATIONAL MARKETERS

Developing plans for global or international marketing involves first and foremost a philosophical commitment from the company's management. Once domestic and international market opportunities have been identified, managers must be prepared to allocate resources among those various opportunities. In prioritizing the firm's goals and objectives, firms evaluate potential return on investment and various opportunity costs. Decisions will be made to commit money, management time and talent, and production runs to foreign markets. Some companies approach foreign opportunities by making a minimal commitment and investment, limiting their activities to infrequent exporting, and concentrating their resources on domestic business operations. Other companies choose to make larger investments of capital and management talent in order to cultivate and maintain a long-term operation in foreign markets. Either approach may be appropriate for a given company and profitable if done correctly.

Regardless of a firm's size, it can develop foreign markets. Once the commitment to go international has been made, the company must evaluate an entry strategy. The responsibility of the marketing manager is to guide the company's decision-making process by analyzing market potential and assessing the degree of marketing involvement and commitment necessary for the firm to successfully compete in foreign markets. A variety of entry strategies can be considered in going international. The choice or evolution of choices over time will depend on the company's strengths and weaknesses, its commitment to operating in foreign markets, and the characteristics of the markets in which the firm chooses to compete. The basic choices are exporting, licensing and franchising, joint ventures, consortia, and direct foreign investment.

Exporting

Entering the foreign market by exporting from the home country offers the lowest level of commitment and risk and the least amount of marketing control for the exporter. Many firms are **casual exporters,** responding to unsolicited or infrequent orders from abroad. These firms see exporting as extra revenue and an opportunity to absorb overhead. While this level of commitment minimizes risk, it also minimizes opportunity since a lack of a sustained marketing effort will unlikely lead to future sales.

Firms can also be **active exporters** and make a higher level of commitment to exporting while still minimizing risks. While large multinationals account for the bulk of the $400 billion in U.S. exports revenues, the majority of exporters are small companies, and the trend in the past decade for increased exporting activities continues to come from small and middle-sized companies. Maturing U.S. markets and competition from large U.S. firms as well as from foreign competitors are forcing small companies to pursue export strategies. The biggest areas of growth in the 1990s has come from companies in the medical products, scientific instruments, environmental systems, and consumer goods sectors, where thousands of small companies have carved niches.[23] A number of factors have contributed to America's increase in exports from small companies. Fax machines, express mail services, and international 800 telephone numbers have greatly improved the ability of small firms to be in contact with their clients and have reduced the costs of going global. Telecommunication services also allow small U.S. exporters to send e-mail messages to their distributors, allowing even small suppliers to have worldwide contacts and a network of distributors. Finally, the expansion of U.S. credit card companies allows foreign customers to buy products over the telephone with their credit cards. Setting up export departments that take advantage of these opportunities created by improvements is a more conscious and systematic approach to exporting and recognizes exporting activities as a regular and increasingly important source of revenue.

Licensing and Franchising

Licensing is another approach for gaining access in foreign markets without large capital outlays. The parent company or licensor grants rights to use a patent, trademark, or technological process in foreign markets. Licensing is a favorite form of entering foreign markets, especially for small and medium-sized companies who own patented processes or other legally protected unique knowledge. Large firms also generate considerable revenues from licensing of technology (i.e., Philips), and trademarks (i.e., The Disney Corporation and the National Football League). The critical aspect of licensing is to choose foreign business partners who have the requisite capabilities to successfully use or market the licensor's assets. It is typically the home company's responsibility to retain some measure of control to ensure that the corporate or brand image in the licensee's market are maintained with high quality standards.

International franchising is a rapidly growing form of entry strategy for companies in many markets and this trend is likely to continue. Franchise systems are normally based on some unique product or service, or on a method of doing business, a trade name, goodwill, or patent that the franchiser has developed. Companies use franchises as an expansion strategy because it provides a relatively standardized business format to introduce in new market growth situations. As a method for market expansion, franchising has proven to be a successful international strategy in such diverse markets as fast food, hotels, recreation, car rentals, and business services. A more detailed discussion of international franchising was provided in Chapter 14.

Joint Ventures

Joint ventures is another global strategy that has increased dramatically in the past ten years. In Europe alone, the number of mergers, acquisitions, and other forms of strategic alliances made by Europe's 1,000 leading companies leapt from 303 in 1986–1987 to 622 in 1989–1990. Many of these mergers were national mergers and primarily were seen as a defensive strategy for the competitive and legal changes that took place in European markets following unification of eastern and western Europe in 1993. In the 1990s, the number of international mergers exceeded local mergers, and these deals generally can be construed as offensive strategies. The clear benefits that global companies enjoy from joint ventures was discussed in detail earlier in this chapter. For the small and medium-size firm, joint ventures are also an attractive entry strategy in global marketing and often are motivated by the firm's limited amount of capital or personnel or when local tariffs and trade barriers are so high that local partnership is the most effective way to gain market access.

Pepsi has entered into a joint venture agreement as a way to cultivate the market in Mexico.

Consortia

A consortium is a broad form of a joint venture, typically involving a large number of participants or investors. Usually, one firm acts as the lead firm, or a corporation may be newly formed that serves as the holding company for the consortium members and is otherwise legally independent of its originators. Global projects that are large scale use a consortium strategy for pooling financial and managerial resources and to spread risks. Some business experts argue that the 1990s will be dominated by vast multi-company alliances, coined "relationship enterprises," that will be formed to handle big, complicated projects.[24] The Iridium example at the beginning of the chapter is typical of a **consortia** venture. Motorola, the parent company, hopes to sell off 85 percent of Iridium to other investors while retaining a leadership role in the company's future market developments. Small and medium-size companies can buy into consortia not only for investment purposes but also as a strategy to secure their role as a qualified subcontractor to the larger project.

Direct Foreign Investment

When the demand justifies the investment and when firms believe that local production will help ensure success in a market as well as in subsequent export markets, then **direct foreign investment** may be a viable market entry strategy. For large multinationals, this strategy is the logical extension of their efforts for global expansion. Traditional reasons for direct foreign investment have been to capitalize on low-cost labor, avoid high import taxes, reduce transportation costs, gain access to raw materials, or gain entry into other markets. More recent motives for direct foreign investment have to do with global investment strategies of large multinationals who acquire companies in their core or complementary businesses (see Table 17-4 for examples) or with political and economic pressures from the host government to encourage the foreign company to produce locally (i.e., the decision of Japanese car manufacturers to open plants in the U.S. market).[25]

Global Structures for Organizing and Control

While many successful global and international companies have developed effective strategies and tactics to serve foreign markets, almost all companies experience difficulties in formulating and implementing an organizational structure that allows their business operations to work at optimal efficiency. A global firm's organization is primarily comprised of the functional management elements of the company and its management personnel, which includes their varying cultural values and managerial styles. The company assigns tasks and responsibilities among its various business units, and as interactions and interdependencies develop among people, functions, and units, they must be organized and managed—not a simple task in a dynamic and diverse global business operation!

DEGREE OF CENTRALIZATION

There are nearly as many organizational structures as there are companies, but most fit into one of three general categories: centralized organizations, regional structures, or decentralized organizations. Regardless of whether the context for doing business is domestic or global, a company's managerial philosophy regarding *control* will influence the choice of organizational structure it adopts. In global marketing, however, additional factors affect decisions regarding structure and control. One crucial factor is whether or not the firm has the managerial talent to deal with the complexities inherent in global markets. A practical issue that must be considered is the physical distance that separates countries and management. Even with modern telecommunications and transportation systems, greater distance usually means an increase in both time and expense as well as the potential error in communications that affect the company's operations.

A **centralized structure** is used by firms that choose to exercise a high degree of control in planning, implementation, and monitoring activities. In this situation, all records and information flow to a central headquarters, and decisions for all business units are either made or approved in the home office. For example, in companies where management talent with a global view is scarce, then an international division with strong links to the home office is the best way to concentrate scarce managerial expertise for international operations.

When strong differences in international markets exist that make individualized strategies necessary, then a global company may use a **regional structure.** Regional managers are given full responsibility in order to adapt product and service offerings and business operations to regional market conditions. For example, in the textbook publishing industry, global publishers typically use regional structures to distinguish between English and non-English speaking markets. This approach comes not only from the unique needs of their customers with respect to language, price, and book contents, but because the structure of the retail book trade varies in different regions of the world. Campus bookstores in North America allow for efficient distribution and payment between publishers and channel members. In other regions of the world, bookstores may be scattered throughout the city, specialize in certain disciplines or serve specific faculties, and have other practices regarding inventory control and payment.

A **decentralized structure** is adopted by a company whose philosophy is simply to operate in decentralized fashion using competent managers who are given full responsibility for operations. Here, managers are in direct contact with their own markets and operations, but typically they lack a broad company view, which can lead to loss of economies of scale and inefficiencies of operations. Companies with highly diverse portfolios of businesses adopt this type of structure and are often organized along divisional lines with each SBU responsible for its own operations.

ORGANIZATIONAL SIZE AND ORGANIZATIONAL COMPLEXITY

For small and medium-size companies with an active export operation, organizational structure is relatively uncomplicated since one manager or department can typically handle the export activities. As foreign revenues grow, regional sales or export managers may be hired who are physically present in foreign markets, calling on channel members, introducing new products, and providing local service. As international marketing expands beyond this export level, organizational structures become more complex and may include foreign subsidiaries and international divisions. Typically, the structure of an international division looks similar to the structure of the domestic operation.

If a company has narrow product lines and global demand for the product is highly similar (for example, producers of heart pacemakers), then the company often chooses a **functional organizational structure.** Marketing is one of the functions, along with R&D, engineering, and finance. Knowledge and experiences in marketing are concentrated since market needs are highly similar, which tends to reduce operating costs. The key disadvantage to this structure is that management at headquarters tends to react slowly to differences that develop in local markets.

When companies have both broad and deep product lines, they typically are organized into a **product division structure** representing the firm's major products. Marketing strategies for the different divisions are developed and coordinated centrally, although tactical adjustments are made in different markets around the world. Canon, Inc., provides a good example of this structure with their seven divisions—cameras, business copying machines, image systems, computer peripherals, computer and information systems, chemical products, and optical products. These product divisions are all centrally located in Japan, where globally standardized marketing strategies are developed. These general plans are then disseminated to their strategically important sales organizations such as Canon Sales Co. (Japan), Canon U.S.A., and Canon Europe N.V., where adjustments to the local market situations are made. The literature on organizational structure and multinationals is extensive, and, in fact, no definitive set of rules applies for choosing the best structure for marketing management activities in the global context.[26] However, some general guidelines do emerge from the literature, and among them are the following:

- Corporations using a worldwide product-division structure have grown faster than those using a regional structure.

- The greater the diversity of product lines, the more likely it is that an American company will manage its foreign business through worldwide product divisions.
- The availability and depth of management resources influences structure. A geographic division requires a large number of broad-gauged managers with considerable general management experience. Worldwide product divisions provide the widest scope and latitude for individual decision making and local adaptation.
- Geographic divisions can concentrate most efficiently on developing close relationships with national and local governments. Worldwide product divisions do not fare as well in this regard.[27]

DEVELOPING A GLOBAL CONTROL SYSTEM

Chapter 16 identified and discussed a variety of control processes that can be used to establish performance standards and evaluate marketing performance. While the global marketing manager essentially has the same set of controls to work with, the implementation of a **global control system** can become extremely complex. Multinationals are by their very nature widespread, multicultural, and subject to a variety of managerial styles. This rich diversity is an asset, but also it is the source of the problem in developing and implementing control systems. Rapidly shifting macro forces such as changes in political and economic factors, new and unfriendly legislation, or new competition all have an influence on the relevancy and effectiveness of control systems and the evaluation process. Even in relatively stable market situations, there will always be unique country and cultural differences between operating units that will conflict with the corporation's control objectives.

While the strategic importance of having a global marketing information system in place was discussed in Chapter 3, its specific uses in the control process should be stressed here once again. Global information systems cannot only monitor the global environment and aid the firm in assessing markets for eventual goal setting and strategy development, they are also critical to the review process and serve to monitor performance in different product-markets and geographic areas. Complex environments require sophisticated information systems that store up-to-date and relevant information from a number of sources. Having data that are easily accessible and easy to relate to data from other market areas sounds simple enough, but it is nonetheless a complicated task for a number of reasons. Apart from the technical challenge of moving data across systems, there are the management issues such as which information to collect and share and which data to use as criteria for evaluating performance.

GLOBAL MARKETING MANAGEMENT CHALLENGES FOR THE 1990S

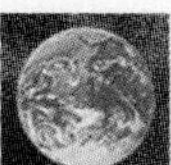

The emerging growth and power of markets in the Asian Pacific, the growing economic stability and rise of the middle classes in Latin America, the continuing political turmoil in the Middle East and the changes in the economic and competitive strengths of North America in the past decade are all events that create a highly dynamic and unpredictable environment for decision making. For companies, managers, and students of business there has never been a more exciting and challenging period to cultivate and develop a global perspective for the purposes of planning and decision making.

In Europe, the decade of the 1990s will certainly be viewed and remembered as one of the most politically, socially, and economically turbulent decades in modern history. While western Europe continues to move toward political and economic integration, eastern Europe and the Commonwealth of Independent States are struggling to unravel problems stemming from decades of planned economies. Consumers in these countries not only have painfully few products and services available, they still have painful choices to make regarding the allocation of their scarce resources in developing a market economy that meets their domestic demand and allows them to compete globally. It is clear that the roughly 390 million citizens in this part of the world have made a historic choice for what they consider to be a preferred state of affairs, and that is the choice for free market economies. At the macro level, marketing's challenge is to be the mechanism that allocates a country's resources among its citizens and provides consumers with the desired products, at the right time, in the right place, and at affordable prices.

To close this chapter, consider the comments of J. M. Juran, the noted American quality-control consultant, made at a conference in Tokyo in 1990. Surveying an audience of mostly Japanese executives who have used his total-quality-control (TQM) methods to humble their U.S. competitors, he declared that America is about to bounce back. In the 1990s, he said "made in the USA" will become a symbol of world-class quality again. Even if the United States doesn't actually catch Japan, he expects big gains in competitiveness. "When 30 percent of U.S. products were failures versus 3 percent for Japan, that was an enormous difference. But at failures of 0.3 percent and 0.03 percent, it'll be difficult for anyone to tell."[28] At the micro level, marketing's challenge is to contribute insight, knowledge, forecasts, and programs that lead to superior perceived value by consumers in global markets and, ultimately, to maximize long-term corporate profitability. As global companies move toward technological and manufacturing parity and increasingly high levels of product quality, marketing management's role in developing strategies to sustain competitive advantage will become increasingly important.

Key Terms and Concepts

Responsibilities of global marketing management
Unique abilities of MNCs
Comparative advantage and its underlying assumptions
Competitive advantage and how to sustain it
Competitive advantage
Factor endowments
Strategic alliances
Global marketing strategies
International marketing strategies
Failure factors in strategic planning
Global standardization
Customization
Casual exporters
Active exporters
Licensing
International franchising
Joint ventures
Consortia

Direct foreign investment
Centralized structure
Regional structure
Decentralized structure
Functional organizational structure
Product division structure
Control systems

Questions and Exercises

1. Outline the likely international product life cycle for Iridium's global markets. What types of marketing problems would you anticipate the company to encounter in launching the product in developing country markets?
2. Consider the following statement: "Marketing may not be the dominant management culture in a company such as Iridium, but it is the managerial perspective which guides the organization in its plans to bring new and innovative products to market." What possible managerial roles can marketing play in high-tech global firms such as Iridium?
3. Discuss the benefits to a multinational company should they develop and execute a global marketing strategy.
4. What is the fundamental difference between a global marketing strategy and an international marketing strategy? To what extent does the size of a firm influence the choice of one approach or the other? What market conditions would encourage a company to use an international strategy perspective?
5. Select a country from the Triad Markets and develop a list of products or industries in which that country has comparative advantages in trade and competitive advantages in business strategies.
6. Pick a global industry and discuss how important the strategy of competition through cooperation is for that industry.
7. *The Wall Street Journal* regularly features articles on exporting activities and global factors that influence exporting. Scan through a number of back issues within the past six months, and identify the external environmental factors that increase export sales for American firms or firms from other countries.
8. Discuss the role that a firm's global strategy has on the design of it's organizational structure. How do width and depth of product lines influence organizational structure?
9. Identify and discuss a number of macro and micro issues that make the implementation of control systems such a complex undertaking for the global company.
10. Work up your own list of global marketing challenges for the 1990s. Identify the factors that make the topics on your list challenging. Are there differences in the nature of marketing challenges for companies situated in different countries of the world? Why?

References

1. Adapted from the following sources: G. Christian Hill, "Motorola Asks FCC to Bar Comsat from Phone Field," *The Wall Street Journal* (October 28, 1993): B9; "A Survey of Telecommunications," *The Economist* (October 23, 1993): 1–24; "Beam Me Up Scottie," *The Economist* (March 28, 1992): 75–78; and "Phones into Orbit," *The Economist* (March 28, 1992): 16.
2. "Japan's Troublesome Imports," *The Economist* (January 11, 1992): 57.
3. "Fortune Guide to the Global 500," *Fortune* (July 26, 1993): 62–72.
4. "The Global 1000," *Business Week* (July 15, 1991): 43.
5. "Japan's Troublesome Imports," *The Economist* (January 11, 1992): 57.
6. "Heading for European Monetary Union," speech by Mr. T. A. Meys, member of the board of directors, ABN/AMRO Bank, Amsterdam, November 26, 1991.
7. For a thorough, scholarly, and managerial discussion of sustaining global competitive advantage, see Michael E. Porter, *The Competitive Advantage of Nations* (London: The Macmillan Press Ltd., 1990).

8. Pete Engardio and Lynne Curry, "The Fifth Tiger Is on China's Coast," *International Business Week* (April 6, 1992): 22–24.
9. "Fallow Ground," *The Economist* (October 23, 1993): 86.
10. "Creatures of Imperfection," in *A Survey of Multinationals, The Economist* (March 27, 1993): 9.
11. Farok J. Contractor and Peter Lorange, eds., *Cooperative Strategies in International Business* (New York: Lexington Books, 1989).
12. Brenton R. Schlender, "How Toshiba Makes Alliances Work," *Fortune* (October 4, 1993): 116–120.
13. Christopher Knowlton, "Europe Cooks Up a Cereal Brawl," *Fortune* (June 3, 1991): 175–179.
14. Philippe Gugler, "Building Transnational Alliances to Create Competitive Advantage," *Long Range Planning*, 25, no. 1, 97.
15. "A Survey of Multinationals: Everybody's Favorite Monsters," *The Economist* (March 27, 1993): 20.
16. For an additional discussion of the advantages and pitfalls of global alliances, see: "A Survey of Multinationals: Everybody's Favorite Monsters," *The Economist* (March 27, 1993); Jordan D. Lewis, *Partnerships for Profit: Structuring and Managing Strategic Alliances,* (New York: The Free Press, 1990); James B. Treece, et al. "The Partners," *Business Week* (February 10, 1992): 38–43.
17. "Mystery Dance," *The Economist* (February 22, 1992): 67; Mark Maremont, "Richard Branson Clears the Runways," *Business Week* (March 23, 1992): 27.
18. John A. Quelch and Edward J. Hoff, "Customizing Global Marketing," *Harvard Business Review* (May–June 1986): 59–68.
19. Porter, op. cit., 583.
20. Toshio Nakahara and Yutaka Isono, "Strategic Planning for Canon: The Crisis and the New Vision," *Long Range Planning* 25, no. 1 (1992): 66.
21. Adapted from Nakahara and Isono, op. cit., 71.
22. Jagdish Sheth, "Global Markets or Global Competition," *Journal of Consumer Marketing* (Spring 1986): 9–11.
23. William J. Holstein and Kevin Kelly, "Little Companies, Big Exports," *International Business Week* (April 13, 1992): 18–22. For a thorough discussion of export strategies, see Subbash C. Jain, *Export Strategy* (Westport CT: Greenwood Press, Inc., 1989).
24. "A Survey of Multinationals: Everybody's Favorite Monsters," *The Economist* (March 27, 1993): 23.
25. "The Business of Europe," *The Economist* (December 7, 1991): 41–42.
26. For an interesting discussion on the political motives for direct foreign investment, see Carla Rapoport, "The Big Split," *Fortune* (May 6, 1991): 38–46; Alan Murray and Urban C. Lehner, "U.S., Japan Struggle to Redefine Relations as Resentment Grows," *The Wall Street Journal* (June 13, 1990): A1, A8, 23. Also see Christopher A. Bartlett, "Building and Managing the Transnational: The New Organizational Challenge" in M.E. Porter, ed., *Competition in Global Industries* (Boston: Harvard Business School Press, 1992), 367–401.
27. Adapted from James F. Bolt, "Global Competitors: Some Criteria for Success," *Business Horizons* (January–February, 1988): 34–41.
28. Otis Port and John Carey, "The Quality Imperative: Questing for the Best," *Business Week* (December 2, 1991): 18.

SECTION FIVE

SPECIAL ASPECTS OF THE MARKETING PROCESS

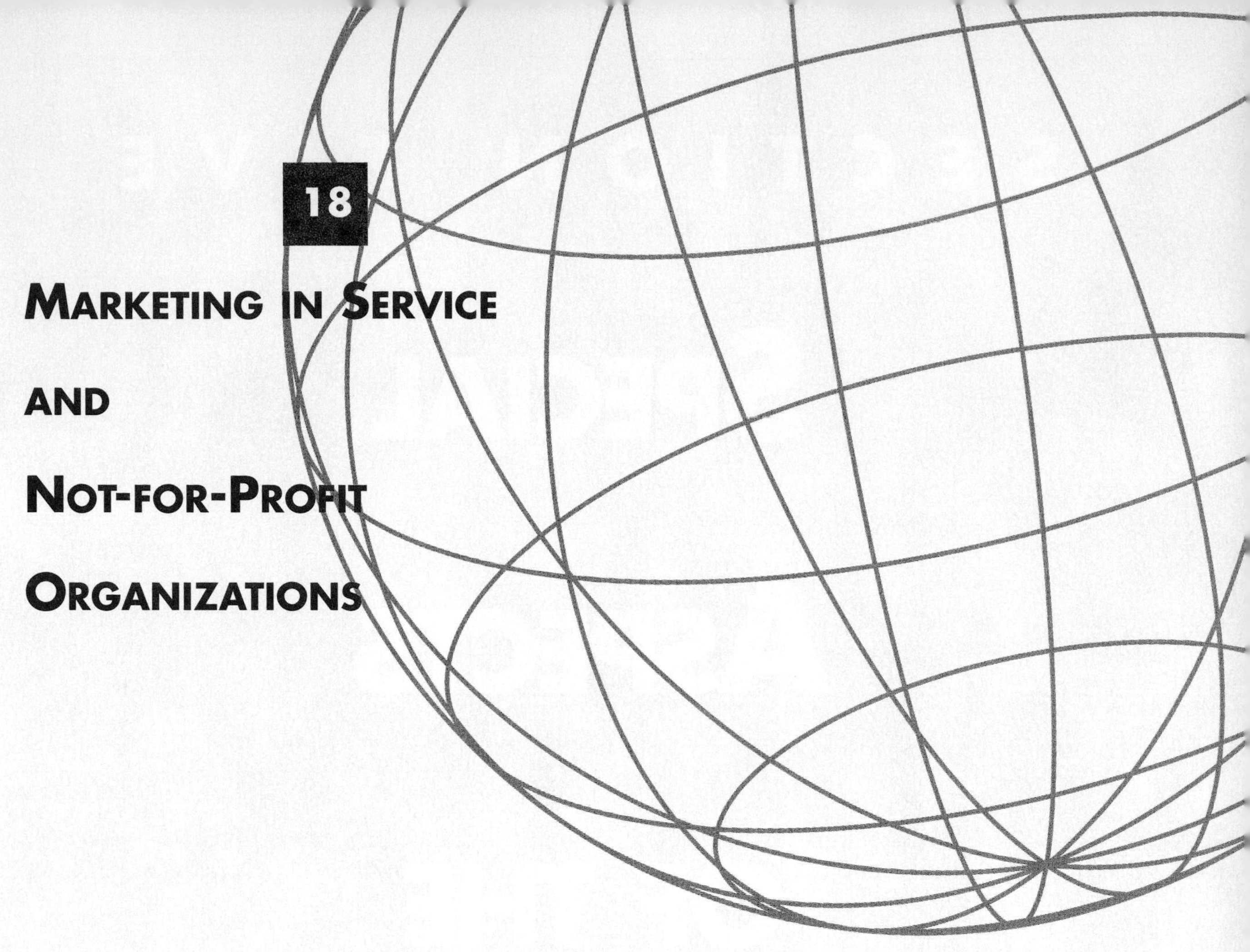

18

Marketing in Service and Not-for-Profit Organizations

AFTER STUDYING THIS CHAPTER, YOU WILL UNDERSTAND THAT:

1. The United States has a service economy in which over half of annual GNP and nearly three-quarters of total employment come from services.
2. Important differences between marketing tangible products and marketing services require a complete reexamination of the marketing mix variables.
3. Consumer behavior is different in the services market because of the unique nature of services.
4. Designing a marketing mix in not-for-profit service organizations poses interesting and formidable challenges.
5. In the global context, there are trade barriers to the global marketing of services that relate directly to the unique characteristics of services.

In days gone by, a trip to the arena to see a basketball or hockey game was a true sports outing. You could always get a ticket in the upper levels for about $5. Hot dogs were a buck, peanuts fifty cents, and the vendors who hawked the stands had been doing this for most of their adult lives. The fold-down seats got harder by the quarter, and the score board, amazingly, simply gave the score. Times have changed. Today, the *real* sports fan watches a contest from a luxury suite—lounging on a leather couch. Caterers wheel in tasty treats including caviar. The score board is a video-display board that provides instantaneous replays, interesting shots of crowd action, and the obligatory score of the contest. Should the live action be lacking, a multi-screen sports bar is just down the hall. For these amenities and additional options, the price of a sports outing has risen slightly. A luxury suite from which modern sports events can be watched runs from a paultry $40,000 per season in Salt Lake City's Delta Center to a somewhat pricier $190,000 in the newly remodeled Madison Square Garden—in other words, from about $900 per basketball game to see the Utah Jazz to about $4,000 per game to see the Knicks play in Madison Square Garden. Welcome to the world of big-time sports entertainment and big-time services marketing.[1]

While this example highlights the pampering that services can deliver, services and services marketing represents a broad range of activities. From high level corporate consulting to having your personal auto cleaned and washed, services pervade our daily lives. And, over the last 25 years, service and not-for-profit organizations that traditionally have not relied on marketing technology have turned to marketing as a way of enhancing their growth. Throughout their existence, service and not-for-profit organizations have, by necessity, used marketing techniques. Every business, whether it markets a service or product for a profit or not, must develop the product or service, price it, deliver it to users, and stimulate demand in the marketplace through promotion—the basic tasks of marketing. Not until recently, however, have service and not-for-profit organizations *recognized* that marketing is an inescapable activity in any business. Historically, the typical service organization has felt that professional standards and adherence to principles were the only requirements for survival and success. This attitude has caused the demise of many worthwhile and socially relevant organizations.

This chapter will discuss the nature of marketing in service organizations—both the profit-seeking service firm and the not-for-profit service organization. Technically, both types of organizations could be discussed under the broad category of services. But, there are important distinctions between the two when it comes to marketing planning and strategy implementation. The first part of the chapter will point out the importance and nature of services generally, whether the context is a for-profit organization or a not-for-profit organization. Then the profit-oriented and not-for-profit versions of services marketing are discussed to point out the important differences in marketing applications between them. The chapter concludes, as always, with a global perspective on the significant issues and challenges related to marketing services.

The Importance of Services

The **importance of services** can be measured in many ways. Services affect the quality of life in both corporations and consumer households. Services have become valuable and valued across a wide range of industries and in households throughout the United States. Consider these contemporary examples:

- H&R Block and other income tax preparation services now complete over half of all personal income tax forms in the United States.
- Medco Containment Services, a division of Merck Pharmaceuticals, is helping corporations hold down heath-care costs by offering cut-rate prescriptions by mail. The firm sends drugs through 1,023 corporations, unions, and health maintenance organizations that cover 25 million people and reduces drug costs by as much as 40 percent.
- FileNet produces imaging technology that allows firms to electronically scan paper documents and convert the information into digital images, which can be stored on optical disks. Pacific Mutual Life Insurance Co. estimates it will save $8.4 million over the next five years by using FileNet technology.
- In Chicago, Personalized Services will walk your dog or take the kids to little league or wait in line for theater tickets. In New York City, if your plants need to be watered or your dry cleaning needs to be picked up, call Busy Body Helpers.
- Andersen Consulting, the management consulting firm, has 22,765 professional staff working out of 151 offices in 47 countries. In 1993, they served nearly 5,000 different business and professional organizations with consulting services and generated over $3 billion in revenue.[2]

All of us, both in our business and personal lives, would find it difficult (and maybe quite unpleasant) to give up the services that are now so prevalent in the U.S. economy. Tasks that are either too complicated (tax preparation), totally beyond our ability (medical care), or simply too unpleasant (washing widows) can be taken care of by highly trained service providers. Aside from

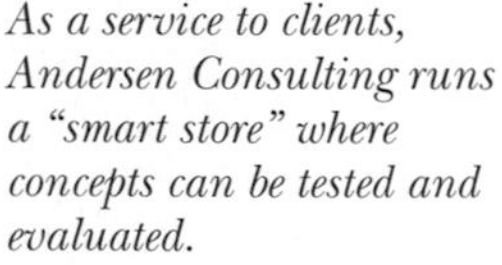
As a service to clients, Andersen Consulting runs a "smart store" where concepts can be tested and evaluated.

being highly effective in performing services, it's usually true that service providers are more efficient and save us either time or money or both.

Another measure of the importance of services is the role they play in the economy of the United States. Service industries are an important and integral part of the U.S. economy. As shown in Figure 18-1, the service segment of the economy is growing at a faster rate than the product sector. The reaction of many businesspeople to this phenomenon was best summed up by one executive when, in the late 1960s, he exclaimed, "70 percent of [GNP] growth is supposed to be in services and 30 percent is supposed to be in products; and I want to be in on that 70 percent."[3] Well, this executive's prediction has nearly become a reality. As the data in Table 18-1 show, in 1970, the United States was a manufacturing economy. By 1980, services as a proportion of GNP had surpassed goods production. And by 1990, services accounted for over 50 percent of GNP while goods production had slipped below 40 percent.

A further indication of the importance of services, especially to marketers, is illustrated in Table 18-2 and Figure 18-2. As you can see, since 1970, spending on services has progressively increased as a proportion of total personal consumption expenditures. In fact, it was in 1985 that for the first time spending on services by households exceeded the *combined* spending for durable and nondurable goods. By 1990, the proportion of services expenditures was beyond 53 percent of total household spending versus 46.6 percent for spending on durable and nondurable goods combined. Put another way, out of every dollar spent by consumers, 53 cents are spent on services.

Table 18-3 and Figure 18-3 demonstrate another broad aspect of the importance of services to the U.S. economy. Total employment in service-related industries, including government, approached three-quarters of the total labor force in 1990. It is important to recognize that while nearly 75 percent of workers in the United States are engaged in providing services, services account for only just more than half of total GNP. The disparity in these figures relates to the well-publicized fact that service jobs pay far less per worker than manufacturing jobs. It is possible that the gap in the proportion of the

FIGURE 18-1
Services as a Proportion of GNP in the United States (in billions of current dollars)

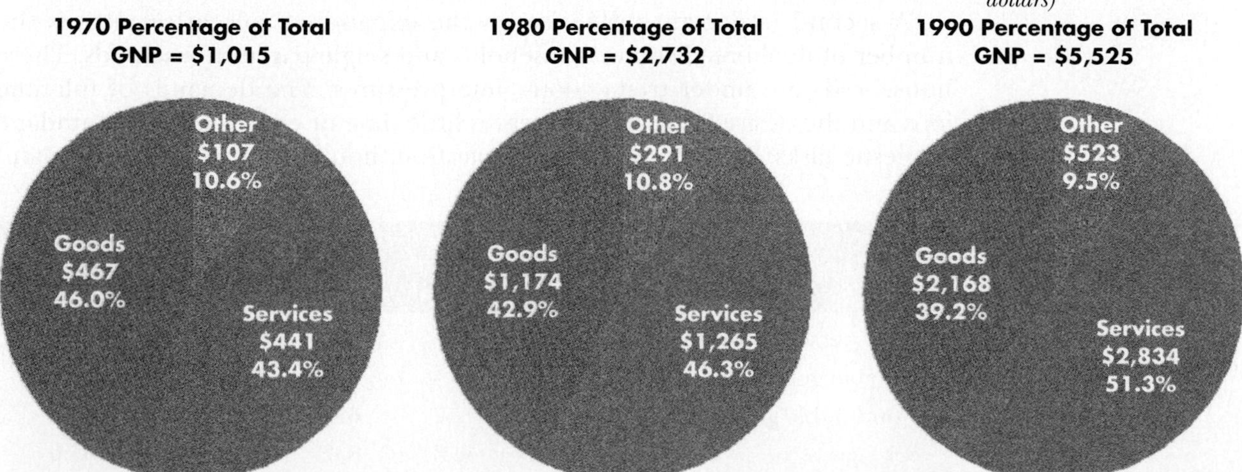

Source: U.S. Department of Commerce, Bureau of the Census, *Statistical Abstract of the United States* (Washington, D.C.: U.S. Government Printing Office, 1992): 430, Table 676.

TABLE 18-1
Services as a Proportion of GNP in the United States (billions of current dollars)

	1970	Percent of total	1980	Percent of total	1990	Percent of total
GNP	$1015	100%	$2732	100%	$5525	100%
Goods	467	46.0	1174	42.9	2168	39.2
Services	441	43.4	1265	46.3	2834	51.3

Source: U.S. Department of Commerce, Bureau of the Census, *Statistical Abstract of the United States* (Washington, D.C.: U.S. Government Printing Office, 1992): 430, Table 676.

labor force and services' contribution to GNP will widen even further in the years to come. This is due to the labor-intensive nature of services and the difficult (though not impossible) challenge of increasing productivity in labor-intensive tasks.

Finally, some of the largest and most profitable corporations in the United States are service organizations. In fact, the 500 largest service firms in the United States earned a combined $93.7 billion in profits in 1993 while the 500 largest industrial firms managed only $62.6 billion in profits.[4] Table 18-4 lists the largest service organizations in the United States by service category. Notice that some of these firms generate an enormous amount of revenue with very few employees while others need a very large labor force. This aspect of different services is discussed in the next section.

The data in these tables and figures are a few of the many quantifiable ways to illustrate the increasing role that services play in the U.S. economy. This expanding role of services has been called a service revolution. Evidence suggests strongly that this service revolution has been spawned as a consequence of an increasingly affluent society: as people grow more affluent, they have a greater desire, need, and ability to pay for various services. The basic explanation for this is that, as people become more affluent, they substitute pleasant activities for less pleasant activities. However, the less pleasant activities (cleaning the house or car or computing income tax) must still be accomplished. Therefore, people use some of their growing affluence to pay others to perform the less pleasant but nevertheless necessary tasks.

A second important influence on the expanding role of services is the number of dual breadwinner households and single-parent households. These households are under tremendous time pressures. The demands of full-time jobs and the desire for recreation leaves little time or enthusiasm for mundane domestic tasks. This includes tax preparation, house cleaning, lawn care, and

TABLE 18-2
Expenditures on Services as a Proportion of Total Personal Consumption in the United States (billions of current dollars)

	1970	Percent of total	1980	Percent of total	1990	Percent of total
Total personal consumption	$640	100%	$1733	100%	$3743	100%
Durable goods	86	13.4	219	12.6	466	12.4
Nondurable goods	270	42.2	681	39.3	1218	32.8
Services	284	44.3	832	48.0	2059	55.0

Source: U.S. Department of Commerce, Bureau of the Census, *Statistical Abstract of the United States* (Washington, D.C.: U.S. Government Printing Office, 1992): 428, Table 673.

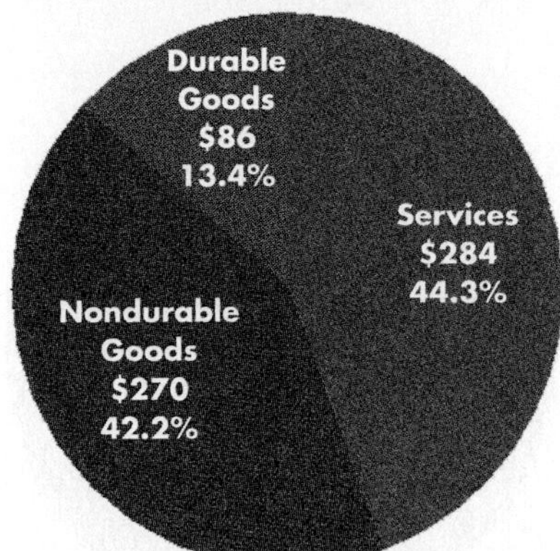

1980 Percentage of Total
Total personal consumption = $1,733

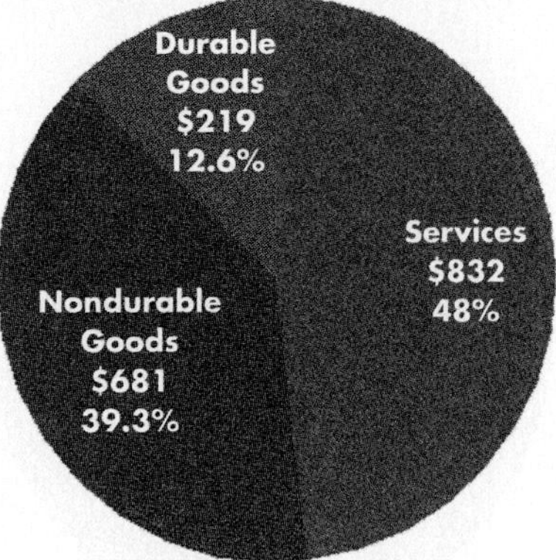

1990 Percentage of Total
Total personal consumption = $3,743

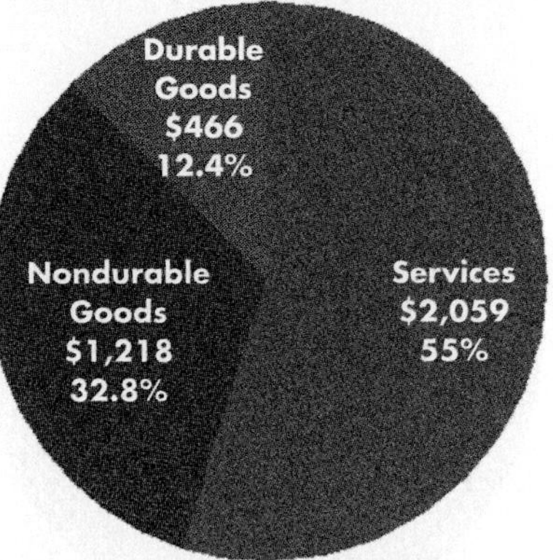

Source: U.S. Department of Commerce, Bureau of the Census, *Statistical Abstract of the United States* (Washington, D.C.: U.S. Government Printing Office, 1992): 428, Table 673.

FIGURE 18-2
Expenditures on Services as a Proportion of Total Personal Consumption in the United States (in billions of current dollars)

the like. Further, many of these households have children and require extensive child-care services. There is no indication that either the number of dual breadwinner households or single-parent households will decline in the near future. This means that the demand for services will remain strong.

Because of the pervasiveness and importance of services, it is important to understand this major force in the market. To further appreciate the services area, we will turn our attention to the nature of services. First, a classification of services is provided and then a strategic perspective is added through a discussion of the unique characteristics of services.

The Nature of Services

To understand services marketing, the distinction between a pure service and a product-related ancillary service must be clearly recognized. A product, as we have discussed it throughout this text, is a complex bundle of satisfactions perceived to hold value by a prospective buyer. We saw

TABLE 18-3
Employment in Goods and Services Industries (in thousands)

		1970		1980		1990	
		Number employed	Percent	Number employed	Percent	Number employed	Percent
Goods:	Agriculture, construction, mining, manufacturing	29,544	37.5%	32,500	32.7%	33,264	28.2%
Services:	Business services, personal services, entertainment, recreation professional, public administration	49,134	63.5	66,803	67.3	84,650	71.8

Source: U.S. Department of Commerce, Bureau of the Census, *Statistical Abstract of the United States* (Washington, D.C.: U.S. Government Printing Office, 1992): 396, Table 632.

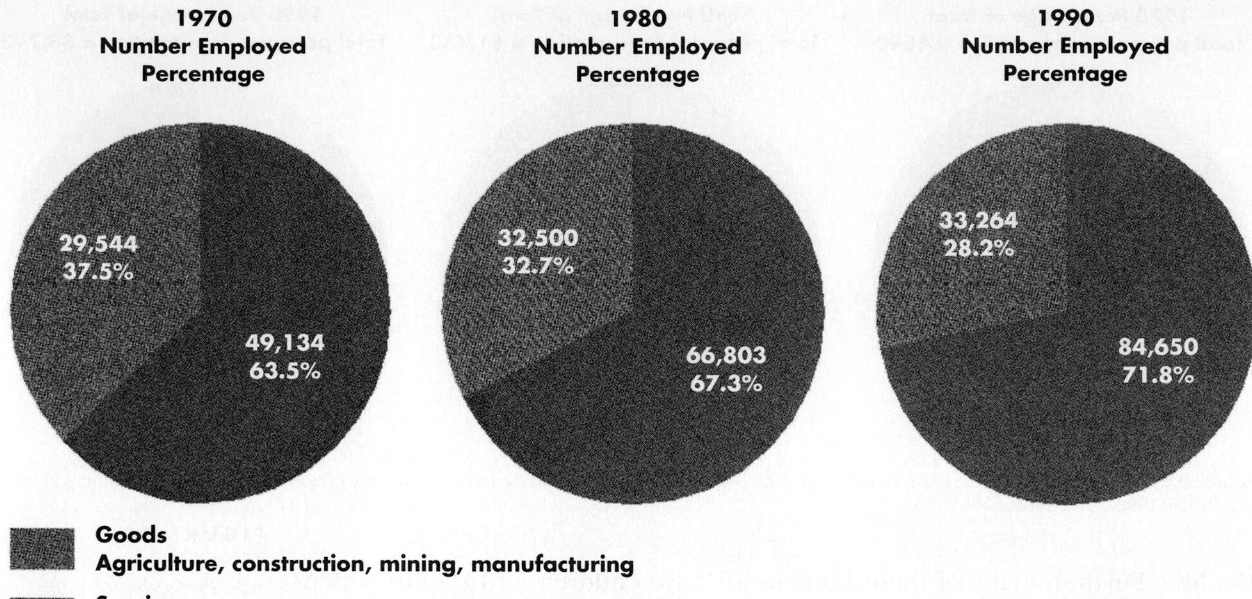

Source: U.S. Department of Commerce, Bureau of the Census, *Statistical Abstract of the United States* (Washington, D.C.: U.S. Government Printing Office, 1992): 396, Table 632.

FIGURE 18-3
Employment in Goods and Services Industries (in thousands)

in Chapter 1 and again in Chapter 4 that a product can include functional, emotional, and benefits of use attributes that potential buyers find appealing. And, many products are augmented with various services during and after a sale.

The relationship between products, products that are augmented with services, and pure services can be represented through use of the continuum depicted in Figure 18-4. Note that the end points of the continuum represent pure product and pure service. At the far left, pure products like salt, laundry detergent, and motor oil are tangible products and require no services in purchase and use in the household. Moving to the right toward the center of the continuum, some products are tangible but require services such as installation, training for proper use, or warranty service after the sale. Automobiles and microcomputers are prominent examples of products at this point on the continuum. In the center are products that are relatively equal parts of tangible product and intangible service. In additional to the examples given in Figure 18-4, auto repair and maintenance services fit this category. To the right of center, products become less tangible and more strictly service in substance. Financial services may be accompanied by receipt of a stock certificate, but the value of the exchange really lies with the professional advice received. Finally, pure services, exemplified at the far right, are the most intangible of all. There may be benefits perceived by the buyer, but the service does not provide any physical product.

DEFINITION OF SERVICES

With Figure 18-4 as a framework and foundation, it is possible to define services in a manner that distinguishes these market offerings from products. **Services** are activities, benefits, or satisfactions offered for sale where buyers and

TABLE 18-4 *The Largest Service Organizations in the United States in Selected Service Categories*

Service Category	Company	Sales (Millions)	Number of Employees
Diversified Service	AT&T	$67.15	308,700
	Fleming	13.09	23,300
	Supervalu	12.56	42,000
	MCI	11.92	36,235
	McKesson	11.67	14,000
Commercial Banking*	Citicorp	216.57	81,500
	BankAmerica	186.93	79,225
	NationsBank	157.68	57,463
	Chemical Bank	149.88	41,567
	J.P. Morgan	133.88	15,193
Retailing	Wal-Mart	67.34	520,000
	Sears	54.87	308,500
	Kmart	34.15	344,000
	Kroger	22.38	190,000
	JCPenney	19.57	192,097
Transportation	United Parcel	17.78	286,000
	AMR	15.81	118,900
	UAL	14.51	83,400
	Delta Air Lines	11.99	73,533
	CSX	8.94	47,063
Utilities	GTE	41.57	117,000
	BellSouth	32.87	95,084
	Bell Atlantic	29.54	73,600
	NYNEX	29.45	76,164
	Pacific Gas	27.16	23,000

*Figures under "sales" for commercial banking organizations represent total assets rather than sales.

Source: Adapted from "The Service 500," *Fortune* (May 30, 1994): 200–218. Used with permission, Fortune Copyright 1994. All rights reserved.

sellers exchange value for value but there is no exchange of tangible goods involving a transfer of title. Observe the three important aspects of this definition. First, a marketing exchange occurs—that is, each party is giving up something of value to gain something of value. Second, the value being acquired by the purchaser is an activity, benefit, or satisfaction. Finally, an exchange of title for a tangible good does not take place. A tangible good may be used to provide a service, such as air travel or hotel accommodations, but the buyer does not acquire title to a good after use of the service.

FIGURE 18-4 *Goods-Services Continuum*

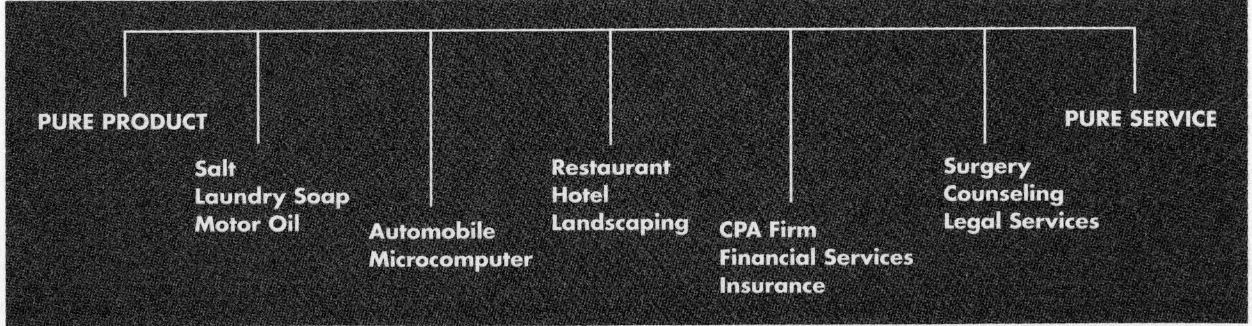

Examples of services are amusement parks, movie theaters, concerts, hotels, public utilities, advertising agencies, hairstyling shops, repair and maintenance firms, financial institutions, and professional service providers such as doctors and attorneys. But simple examples can limit the perspective on the scope of services. It is useful to examine a classification of services to fully appreciate the breadth of this category of goods.

CLASSIFICATION OF SERVICES

While classification schemes have limitations, it is valuable to provide a perspective on the breadth and depth of service offerings available. More importantly, a well-conceived classification can give insights into consumer behavior toward services. As we will see later in the chapter, with such insights, marketers can do a better job of both developing a service offering and then devising a marketing mix for the service.

Classification of services can be done in many ways. Common classification criteria include type of seller, type of buyer, buying motives, buying practices, characteristics or attributes, and degree of government regulation. A useful synthesis of these classification criteria, which provides further insight into the nature of services, follows.[5]

The first basis for classifying services relates to the *target customer* for whom the service has been developed. Some services are totally or primarily for household consumers; other services are targeted toward businesses, not-for-profit institutions, or governments. Examples of consumer services include life insurance, radio broadcasts, dry cleaning, and personal care services such as those provided by hairstylists. Examples of services provided primarily to business, institutional, or government customers include consulting, advertising, accounting, and maintenance services.

A second category in the classification of services is based on whether the services are *human or machine-centered.* Human-centered services are those in which the benefit to the user of the service comes primarily from highly labor-intensive services. Massage, swimming instruction, or cleaning services fall into this category. Machine-centered services include household utilities and all types of transportation (airline travel) and communication (telephone) services where contact with humans, while important, is incidental to gaining the value the service has to provide. Machine-based and human-based services are going through a transition though. New technologies are redefining the human-centered nature of many services. For example, Taco Bell is experimenting with an automated ordering terminal in several of its outlets that would eliminate the need for a customer to interact directly with servers.

A third basis for service classification is the *skill and formal training* required of the service provider. Some service providers, such as doctors, lawyers, and consultants, require extensive professional training. Other services require less specific skill and almost no formal training. Lawn care, window cleaning, and janitorial services are examples. Of course, some service providers fall somewhere in the middle of these dichotomies: watch repair, computer repair, and plumbing services are examples. Illustration 18-1 is an advertisement for a financial advisory firm that provides specialized corporate business services.

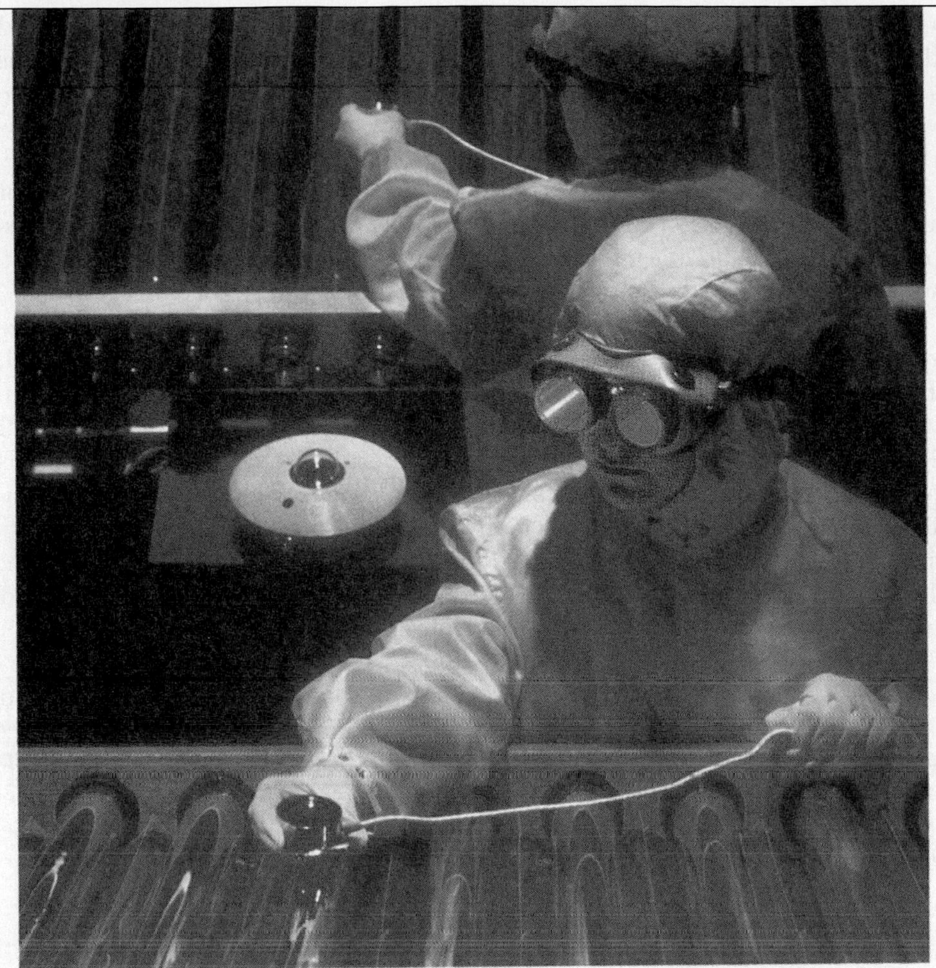

IF YOU THINK HIGH TECHNOLOGY REQUIRES INNOVATION,
IMAGINE INSURING IT. Advanced scientific disciplines like solar cell technology and genetic engineering are exploding with possibilities. And fraught with hidden risks. The professionals at AIG Companies who underwrite these and other specialty risks possess a much-sought-after talent: the ability to evaluate the unknown and assess businesses on the cutting edge of technology. Over the years we've developed the necessary rational skills and intuitive talents to a degree most others have not. It's part of why AIG is a global organization known for its innovative insurance solutions. Particularly when dealing with endeavors as complex as capturing the energy of the sun.

AIG
WORLD LEADERS IN INSURANCE AND FINANCIAL SERVICES.
American International Group, Inc., Dept. A, 70 Pine Street, New York, NY 10270.

ILLUSTRATION 18-1
Corporate service organizations provide specialized expertise to business customers.

Services can also be classified in terms of whether they are *profit-oriented or not-for-profit-oriented.* Profit-oriented services are those that have fueled the growth of GNP in the United States cited earlier and include such firms as Federal Express (package/document delivery), United Airlines (air transport), and Chubb Insurance (business and household insurance). Not-for-profit service organizations include a variety of artistic, philanthropic, and educational organizations. Opera, symphony, theater, and dance organizations as well as museums make an important contribution to the culture and the overall quality of life in the United States. They are heavily dependent on government support and the generosity of donors for their continued existence. United Way, March of Dimes, the Salvation Army, and literally thousands of small, community-based organizations provide much needed care to the disabled, the poor, and the elderly. Finally, universities and private schools are important educational organizations in the not-for-profit service category.

Services can also be classified with respect to the *degree of government regulation.* Some service providers, such as utility companies, are highly regulated, while other service providers rely primarily on self-regulation. Highly regulated organizations include the public utilities and mass transit providers. Still high in regulation but somewhat less than the prior examples are hospitals and insurance companies. The government provides some degree of regulation when it requires a license for many trades so contractors, plumbers, electricians, and beauty care providers are subject to some government regulation. The vast majority of service providers are not directly government regulated and include catering, lawn care, sports teams, and films.

Finally, services can be classified by *degree of customer contact.* In some services, no contact is made with the customer at all—an automated car wash and a radio station are two examples. In other cases, direct and intimate contact with the customer is essential—hair care and medical services are two very different examples. There are, of course, varying degrees of contact. Hotel services, airline travel, and financial services require some contact and then the service is provided via other means.

UNIQUE CHARACTERISTICS OF SERVICES

Several **unique characteristics of services** distinguish these market offerings from traditional, tangible products. With a full understanding of how services can be unique on several dimensions, a marketing decision maker can appreciate the distinctive values services represent to consumers in the market. The characteristics of services that are important to fully understand and appreciate are the intangibility of services, services are consumed when produced, the consumer participates in the production of services, services are perishable, variable levels of quality are found in services, and services involve higher perceived risk on the part of buyers.

Intangibility

The fundamental difference between products and services is their **intangibility.** Services cannot be touched, felt, or even tried out by a buyer before purchase. And, no exchange of title (ownership) occurs when a purchase is made. This feature of services translates into unique motives for decision making for both buyers and sellers. Buyers must rely on surrogate indicators of quality in trying to judge services. Often, the reputation of the service provider or length of time in business are used as a basis for judgment in the absence of hard, physical evidence. Recommendations from friends, relatives, and acquaintances also play a greater role in the judging of services. For sellers, there is a need to try to make tangible what is intangible. This is why many service providers furnish a certificate along with the service. As examples, veterinarians often provide a portfolio for the family pet's documents, and lawn maintenance firms will leave a notice on the door that the lawn has been treated. In both of these cases, the consumer needs evidence of the service just provided because no tangible evidence exists. Another example of providing tangible evidence of service quality and value is when service providers—such as hairstylists and auto repair technicians—display certificates of training or awards for performance. This communicates to customers in a tangible way that the service (represented by the human provider) is of high quality.

Consumed When Produced

Production and consumption of services take place simultaneously. For example, consider the physician giving a physical examination or a commercial airline flying passengers across the country. The service is actually being **consumed when produced.** This clarifies the claims made throughout the chapter that there is not an exchange of title involved in service encounters. A consumer does not "own" a service in a traditional sense. A consumer will benefit from the service encounter with an entertaining evening at the theater, time saved from an airline trip, or being cured of an illness. But when a service is consumed as it is produced, it is *experienced* rather than owned.

Consumer Participation in Production

Related to the simultaneity of production and consumption is the fact that services require **consumer participation** in production for a service to be provided. In several cases the consumer's actual presence is necessary as in the physician and airline examples. Even without actual physical presence, however, consumers participate in every service production. Attorneys and accountants need information from clients to provide legal and tax services. Hotels, entertainment events, and auto repair shops are dependent on consumers' participation in the production of the service. Without consumers, these organizations would literally have nothing to do: hotels would have no tenants to serve, theater halls would be empty, and the auto mechanic would be greeted by an empty garage each morning.

Perishability

The perishability of services is related to the fact that services cannot be stored in inventory as tangible products can. An empty airline seat or vacant hotel room is a lost service opportunity. Physicians and dentists often charge for missed appointments because the service opportunity was available only at that time.

Because services cannot be stored like the output of a production line where products lie in inventory awaiting demand, several tactics can be used to try to alleviate the problem of missed service opportunities.[6] One example is differential pricing during off-peak demand periods. Utility and telephone companies use this tactic in their pricing structures. Large commercial users of electricity and natural gas are given substantial rate discounts if they can channel their consumption to off-peak demand hours. Consumers can realize substantial savings on long-distance calls by placing the calls on weekends or during evening hours when commercial use has decreased and the phone companies have more capacity. Another form of trying to smooth demand for services is requiring an advanced reservation. Advanced reservation systems are common among many service organizations (airlines, hotels, repair services, or even entertainment centers) in an attempt to use service times efficiently and reduce the effect of not being able to keep an inventory of the service.

The perishability of services is linked closely to the issue of the labor intensity of services. One of the fundamental difficulties of services marketing is having personnel available at the precise point in time the service is demanded. For those many services that are dependent on direct contact between provider and consumer, the fleeting nature of the supply of services (or the perishability) makes coordination between supply and demand a difficult task. The labor scheduling issue is another reason service firms implement strategies that attempt to spread demand more evenly over time.

Variability

Because of the labor-intensive nature of services and the minimal capital investment associated with getting into many service businesses, there often is a large degree of heterogeneity and **variability** in the quality of the service provided. Physicians, consultants, entertainers, and tax analysts will all provide a unique version of the service based on differences in their backgrounds, training, and personalities.

Even in those service areas where large capital expenditures are required, such as airlines, hotels, or auto repair, great variability in output is a hallmark in these industries as well, because the activities of personnel ultimately shape the quality of the service. As we will see shortly, this human factor in service provision affects not only the true quality of the service but also consumer perception of the service regardless of the actual level of quality.

Higher Perceived Risk

Given the intangible, perishable, and variable nature of services, it is not surprising that both household consumers and business buyers perceive higher risks in selecting services. Without tangible features and standardized criteria, the task of evaluating service alternatives becomes even more difficult for consumers than evaluating tangible products. Service firms are therefore heavily dependent on factors that can enhance the reputation and image of the organization in the mind of potential buyers. The number of years a firm has been in business, guarantees for services provided, and tangible manifestations of the service (for example, a certificate, written guarantee, or portfolio of service records) aid buyers in relating to the value of a firm's offering.

The unique characteristics of services and the resultant higher perceived risk all contribute to an increased probability of cognitive dissonance. Buyers can experience high degrees of anxiety in the post-purchase phase of the decision process for services because of the difficulty associated with evaluation. In addition, many services are characterized by high-involvement decision making. A new hairstyle, care for the family pet, or an important medical procedure all can produce anxiety. The medical profession is trying to deal with this aspect of the services they provide. In a recent study it was discovered that 25 percent of U.S. patients switched physicians at least once during the prior year because the doctor made them feel uncomfortable or didn't relieve their anxiety.[7] On the other hand, it was also discovered that when medical patients received follow-up care by phone, those patients reduced their annual medical costs by an average of 28 percent.[8] It appears that not only can anxiety be addressed with post-purchase contact from the service provider, but the quality and impact of the service, at least in the medical area, may be increased.

THE MARKETING MIX FOR PROFIT-ORIENTED SERVICE ORGANIZATIONS

The unique characteristics of services make the marketing challenge in the service sector interesting and difficult. As one noted author points out, "When you ask prospective customers to buy promises—as all service-oriented firms do—you must provide metaphorical reassurances of quality and industrialize the service delivery process."[9] This section will consider each variable in the marketing mix and the way in which decision making must be carried out to increase the probability of success of the service offering.

Recall at this point that the discussions here apply to both profit-oriented and not-for-profit organizations. Also, be aware that service organizations, profit oriented or not, face the same environmental influences as discussed in Chapter 2. And, service marketers use marketing research techniques (Chapter 3) make market assessments, market segmentation, differentiation, and positioning decisions (Chapters 4 and 5), and analyze buyer behavior (Chapter 6) using the same methods as product marketers. The significant adaption from product marketing comes in the development of marketing mix strategies. In services marketing, the conception of the mix actually has to be expanded to accommodate the unique characteristics of services and consumer behavior toward services. We will turn our attention now to this adapted marketing mix for services.

SERVICE DEVELOPMENT AND MANAGEMENT

Service development and management are as important for the service marketer as product development and management are for the product manufacturer. Service development refers to the process of continued enhancement of the service offering through modification or innovation. Service management refers to the day-to-day activities necessary to ensure that the service achieves the objectives outlined by management for target market penetration, revenue generation, and profitability.

A service offering is changed and adjusted for several reasons. The primary reason is that the external environment has changed fundamentally. For example, ski resort operators have to cope with the reality that in the 1960s, 70 percent of the skiers were under 35 years old and annual skier visits to resorts were growing at double-digit rates. But, in the 1990s, less than 50 percent of skiers are under 35 and the majority have kids and mortgages and retirement to worry about. In addition to these demographic and life-style changes, resort operators have to contend with environmentalists who are concerned about overdevelopment of natural landscapes. The response to these changes in the external environment is that resorts are merging to maintain the quality of the skiing experience. In 1980, there were 845 ski areas. In 1992, there were 529 with firms like the Japanese-owned Kamori Kanko Co. buying resorts like Steamboat Springs in Colorado and Heavenly Valley in California.[10]

Identifying an opportunity in the competitive environment is a second important reason for developing or modifying service offerings. American Express recognized a competitive opportunity to extend its service offerings by initiating a travel management service for major corporations. The service combines the operations of American Express' Travel Related Services with the American Express Credit Card operations to provide firms with services in handling travel expense management—from booking travel to charging expenses and accounting for expenses.[11]

Assessment of the broad demographic, social, and cultural environments provide important information assessing opportunities for service development or expansion. As alluded to earlier, the desire for convenience and the importance of time in the U.S. culture have fueled the expansion of services in the economy over several decades. These influences, combined with the greater number of women in the workforce, have created a wide range of opportunities in child care, clothing care, domestic help, personal care, and food away from home services.[12]

SERVICE-PLACE INTERFACE

In addition to standard marketing mix factors, service providers must recognize the need to manage a **service-place interface.** That is, consumers will often relate their perception of satisfaction and value of the service to the *place* at which it was provided as much as to the quality and value of the service itself. Managers of service operations must therefore recognize that there are many interactions consumers encounter in the consumption of a service regarding the place where the service is provided. Aside from the service the consumer is paying for, place factors include the people involved in providing the service, the atmosphere of the delivery area, and the physical appearance of the delivery area. These factors make tangible for a consumer what is intangible about insurance, estate planning, a restaurant meal, or a haircut. Rude employees, a shabby office, and an uncomfortable atmosphere are reflections, accurate or not, of the quality of the service itself.

PRICING OF SERVICES

Because the standardization of services is difficult, considerable variation in pricing exists. Consider the example of two women's hairstylists. One stylist may charge higher prices than another stylist for the same service because of factors such as reputation, experience, quality of work, or even professional background (European training, for example) of the individual providing the service. Also, many service markets are comprised of several small suppliers of services. A large number of small businesses providing a service increases the competitive pressure in the market. And competitive pressures tend to keep prices fairly similar. A laundromat with washers set for three quarters a load will attract more customers than one with washers set for four quarters. However, as the importance of the service to the individual increases and as nonstandardized services are demanded, price variations will result. Prominent attorneys retained by clients involved in criminal trials are frequently able to ask for and receive fees that are much larger than the norm. Or, a laundromat with high-speed, large-capacity washers that is open 24 hours may be able to get that extra 25 cents per load.

Regardless of the type of service, methods for setting prices are eventually the same as for product pricing. Prices can be set on the basis of cost, on the basis of demand, or on the basis of competition. Frequently, a combination of two or three of the methods is used. Typically, prices are set to cover costs, to provide a profit, and to be competitive with other service providers in the marketplace.

Finally, in the area of service pricing, government regulations and public opinion are perhaps of greater importance than in product marketing. Formal government regulation of pricing occurs in government-sponsored but privately owned public utilities. The local power company, telephone companies, and the mass transit system all provide necessary and vital services. Various economic reasons exist for granting public utilities monopoly rights. However, because the monopolies are allowed to exist, prices are regulated.

DISTRIBUTION AND DELIVERY OF SERVICES

This is another area where services require an adaptation to the standard set of variables in the marketing mix. The channel of distribution for services is necessarily very short and direct. The reason for this is that service production and delivery are performed simultaneously. This aspect of services was discussed earlier and is evident in medical care, air transportation, and entertainment.

The direct nature of delivery for services is one reason large-scale concentration in the service industries has not occurred until now. The direct nature of many services has inhibited the use of intermediaries. However, there are exceptions to this. Airlines are in the transportation business, and users of the service must eventually come into direct contact with these service providers. However, airlines have employed independent intermediaries—travel agents—to arrange reservations and write tickets thus lengthening the channel.

Aside from the fundamentally short nature of distribution channels for services, there are strategic opportunities in this area as there are in product distribution. Creative thinking and implementation can offer service marketers many new ways to distribute their services. A bank that uses 24-hour automatic teller machines is a good example. An example in the not-for-profit area is the use of mobile units by public libraries to make their services available to more members of society. Franchising has been used extensively in many areas of service marketing as a way to keep service operators close to customers in a short channel. The hotel and motel field is a good example. Ramada Inns provide lodging for business and pleasure travelers. Each Ramada Inn is independently owned and operated but in accordance with a franchise agreement. Of course, the fast-food industry is the best example of franchise distribution in the services area.

Finally, innovations in the distribution of services result from delivery to the user's location. Traditionally, many service providers such as insurance and real estate agents have practiced delivery of their service to the user's location. More innovative and recent service deliveries include veterinary care, physical fitness training, and auto windshield repair.

PROMOTION OF SERVICES

The promotion of services like the promotion of products is an important factor in determining whether the service offering will be successful. However, service promotion presents some unique problems. These problems, in part, revolve around the intangibility of the service.

As already mentioned, intangibility of services means that a service lacks physical form or substance. When General Motors advertises an automobile or when Procter & Gamble advertises a detergent, the actual physical product can be illustrated, displayed, and even demonstrated. In promoting a service, the actual product cannot be so easily visualized. For example, what does life insurance protection look like?

Because of the intangible nature of many services, the benefit of the service is frequently emphasized in the promotional program. For example, New York Life Insurance Company emphasizes the primary benefit of financial security in its advertising program. This benefit is presented and emphasized in many effective and creative ways from a comfortable retirement to financing children's education. American Express emphasizes the quality of its service with its advertised motto: "Membership has its privileges." The firm then demonstrates these privileges in its advertising with scenes of luxury and recreation. Illustration 18-2 is an example of a service organization stressing benefits in its advertising.

A second emphasis in promotion relating to the intangible nature of services is the importance of the reputation of the service provider. Potential purchasers cannot inspect the actual product or can do so only with some difficulty. Consequently, the reputation of the service provider is critical to success. Reputation is, to some degree, related directly to the quality of the service provided. The service provider, however, can influence his or her reputation by effectively using promotion.

Traditionally, certain types of service providers were ethically or legally prevented from engaging in formal promotional activities other than through the use of an office sign, business card, and through selling their services through the process of community involvement. However, taboos preventing physicians, dentists, attorneys, and other professionals from advertising themselves and their services are changing. Attorneys can now use various promotional methods but only in restricted ways. Additionally, some states have passed laws that will allow physicians to advertise their services.

PROMOTION-DISTRIBUTION-PRICE INTERFACE

Another adaptation in the nature of the marketing mix for services is the interrelationship of promotion, distribution, and price in the service area. This is referred to as the **promotion-distribution-price interface.** When a service provider communicates with a potential or current user of a service, in

Meetings.
Deadlines.
Rush hour.
Someday
you'll just
sail away.

Your tomorrows depend on the consistent performance of your long-term investments. And that's why investors have made Kemper one of America's largest asset managers. For over forty years, the Kemper Family of Mutual Funds has been dedicated to the kind of steady, long-term performance that builds tomorrows today. Ask your financial representative or call Kemper Mutual Funds at 1-800-KFS-8600, ext. 75.

Kemper MUTUAL FUNDS

We're Building Tomorrows Today℠

Before you invest in a fund, carefully read the brochure and prospectus for more complete information, including management fees and expenses.
Fund performance cannot be guaranteed and will fluctuate. ©1994 Kemper Financial Services, Inc. 219600

NAT-72C 1/94

ILLUSTRATION 18-2
Many consumer service organizations stress benefits of use in their advertising due to the intangible nature of their market offerings.

many cases the place where the communication is occurring is also the place where distribution occurs and the price of the service is being incurred. Consider a visit to a financial consultant. The consultant talks about the various services available (promotion), delivers the advice sought (distribution), and collects a commission (price). In a variety of circumstances, when a service provider promotes a service and converts a person into a customer, promotion, distribution, and pricing occur simultaneously. This unique relationship between marketing mix variables focuses attention on the individual and the setting within which the service encounter takes place. As pointed out earlier, because of this interaction, service personnel and the atmospherics of the service facility are often used by consumers as surrogate indicators of service quality.

To this point, the discussion of services has focused on aspects of services that are universally applicable to both the profit oriented and not-for-profit service organization. Both types of organizations make important contributions to overall economic activity and employment in the United States. The market offerings of each have the characteristics unique to services discussed earlier. However, the services offered by not-for-profit organizations pose interesting and unusual challenges for marketing. We will discuss the area of marketing in not-for-profit organizations now.

Marketing in Not-for-Profit Organizations

A **not-for-profit organization** is defined as any public or private institution involved in providing a market offering without the purpose of making a profit. Strictly speaking, not-for-profit organizations fall into the general category of service organizations. But, these organizations are being discussed separately because marketing the services offered by a not-for-profit organization poses some unique and formidable challenges. Often, the topic of marketing in not-for-profit organizations is discussed under a heading like "nonbusiness organizations." This is truly an inappropriate description. Not-for-profit service marketers are businesspeople of the highest order. They engage in planning, capital management, personnel management, and are challenged daily by the pressures of a complex business environment. For our purposes, therefore, we will consider the not-for-profit organization a true business, albeit one that does not pursue the profit objective.

The relevance of marketing in the context of not-for-profit organizations was highlighted many years ago by a landmark article entitled, "Broadening the Market Concept."[13] The article stirred controversy (and still does) among marketing analysts and practitioners. The authors proposed that marketing is truly a broad societal activity that encompasses more than merely commercial enterprises. Further, not-for-profit organizations of all types are argued to be performing marketing tasks whether managers in these organizations are aware of the marketing process and its tactics or not.

Once again, the distinctions between marketing in not-for-profit organizations and commercial product marketing are essentially the same as the distinctions between product marketing and services marketing discussed in the last section. The intangibility, consumer participation in production, variability, and perishability are all characteristics of not-for-profit service offerings. There are, however, significant differences between profit-oriented service firms and the not-for-profit service organizations with regard to the nature of the marketing mix.

The Marketing Mix in Not-for-Profit Organizations

The list of not-for-profit organizations is lengthy and diverse. Public not-for-profit organizations include federal, state, and local governments; museums;

public transportation modes; and park services. The list of private not-for-profit organizations is nearly endless. Artistic, religious, hobby, health care, athletic, legal, political, scientific, educational, and philanthropic organizations are just a few categories. Often, these firms have important and admirable objectives and few resources with which to pursue them. Further, the challenges they face in the marketing mix are, in many ways, more formidable than those facing profit-oriented service firms.

Service Development and Management

As in the profit-oriented service organization, the not-for-profit service marketer must develop and manage the service being offered. In most cases, though, the decision makers who are responsible for marketing decisions in not-for-profit-organizations are not able to adjust the service in response to consumer preference in an effort to increase its market potency. This is a significant departure from every concept of marketing strategy discussed throughout this book. Decisions regarding the attributes of the service in the not-for-profit setting are generally reserved for those people in the organization who represent the artistic or philanthropic purpose of the organization. Hospital physicians, college professors, and religious leaders must adhere to professional standards and philosophical guidelines in determining the nature of the service rather than consumer desires and preferences. For example, the Boston Symphony could amplify each instrument, use a laser light show and pyrotechnics, and try to compete with a rock group for patronage. Altering the service offering of the Boston Symphony in this way might provide market viability, but it is not likely to meet with the approval of the organization's artistic director. But, there are times when the philosophical becomes highly marketable as well. When Pete Townshend, leader of the rock group The Who, adapted his rock opera *Tommy* for the Broadway stage, it was a huge, Tony Award–winning success. This is a case where an artistic performance was so well suited to the times that it was not only artistically successful but financially successful as well.

Given the potential restrictions on developing services in not-for-profit organizations, marketers have addressed this area of the marketing mix by concentrating on developmental efforts such as market segmentation analysis, differentiation, and positioning. The marketability of the service can be increased by trying to identify the highest potential number of customers who share the values and intentions of the organization.[14] Without being able to make substantive changes in the service, the best approach not-for-profit service marketers can take is to fully understand what features of a service are most appealing to what specific segments of the market and try (without violating philosophical standards) to provide those features.

Distribution

Distribution is another difficult area for marketers in a not-for-profit context. Many organizations (for example, universities, hospitals, museums) serve client-customers from a fixed location. When location is not a factor that can be changed or expanded, it is difficult, although not impossible, to strategically enhance the delivery system to accord the time, place, and possession utilities that distribution often can provide buyers. A university can make scheduling more compatible with student needs, a hospital can have satellite locations, and a museum can put collections on tour. These represent attempts to overcome the generally fixed nature of the distribution variable. Further, those factors that relate to retail patronage motives, such as parking convenience, hours of operation, and decor, can be manipulated to increase consumer satisfaction stemming from distribution.

The barriers to using the distribution variable to greatest advantage have to do with the inability of most organizations to have multiple locations, to store the product (perishability), and to bear the costs of an elaborate delivery system. Some surprising and creative uses of the distribution factor have resulted in increased market effectiveness. In 1991, the U.S. government began an experiment designed to streamline the welfare system. Welfare recipients in Baltimore, Maryland, were issued white plastic cards with which they could access their welfare benefits through automatic teller machines (ATMs) throughout the city. This alternative distribution system for cash and food stamps is intended to reduce fraud and administrative waste.[15] This is an example of a marketing strategy that can increase the efficiency of an organization's operations.

Pricing

Several aspects of the character of not-for-profit organizations make pricing decisions difficult. First, because most not-for-profit organizations are serving the public welfare, break-even and low-cost pricing is an inherent goal. The revenues generated, donations, and grants must all be factored into a final pricing decision.

Second, it is very difficult for many not-for-profit organizations to reduce the cost of operations through increased productivity. To have musicians play faster or health-care providers rush clients through would be compromising professional standards or just plain silly. Certainly, adding more performances or more health-care personnel are options, but variable costs are then increased and overall cost is adversely affected. Recently, innovative staffing schemes and consolidation of facilities have produced significant productivity gains in both hospitals and universities.[16] This may signal a new era in not-for-profit organization productivity and pricing flexibility.

Finally, many public not-for-profit organizations do not price their products at all. Welfare agencies, parks and recreation systems, and city and state development agencies deal in free services (at the point of delivery and consumption). As such, these organizations concern themselves with the cost of operations rather than pricing decisions.

What must be recognized in the pricing scheme for not-for-profit organizations is that customers, donors, or patrons will still perceive costs in dealing with the organization. Recall the discussion in Chapter 1 and again in Chapter 9 that the price of a product, or in this case a service, is only one of many costs perceived by potential customers. In this sense, not-for-profit organizations are, just like producers and profit-oriented service providers, challenged to recognize and reduce all forms of cost perceived by potential customers. If a museum has inconvenient hours, little parking, and poorly informed volunteers, then its customers are being asked to incur a great deal of cost even though there may be no admission charge to visit the facility.

Promotion

Of the marketing mix variables, promotion is the most accessible and fully functioning strategic tool available to not-for-profit organizations. The mass media are required and willing to run public service announcements. Newspapers seek relevant public interest articles. Volunteers from the community engage in personal selling. These activities in combination with conventional paid-for advertising allow not-for-profit organizations to communicate with the market. Illustration 18-3 is a good example of promotion by the American Heart Association to attract volunteers.

Administrators in not-for-profit organizations struggle with the difficult decision of how much money and human effort should (or can) be diverted from service provision to demand stimulation. Hospitals compete for patients with highly stylized advertising campaigns. Philanthropic organizations like the March of Dimes and the United Way use advertising to raise funds. Other organizations like Mothers Against Drunk Driving use advertising to try to deter socially unacceptable or dangerous behaviors like substance abuse.

Promotion is potentially of great value to the not-for-profit organization. As demand is stimulated, revenues can be increased, cash-flow benefits gained, and the cost of capital allocated over larger numbers of people serviced. However, much of the efficiency of promotional vehicles is lost as very specialized segments are pursued.

THE VALUE OF MARKETING TO NOT-FOR-PROFIT ORGANIZATIONS

The preceding discussion illustrates that not-for-profit organizations face unique challenges in marketing decision making. But it should be realized that the **value of marketing to not-for-profit organization** is enormous. Not-for-profit organizations,

- Are providing services and can market those services in a fashion similar to profit-oriented firms.
- Can develop brands, slogans, and identifiable benefits to offer the market.
- May be subject to a product life cycle and the advantages and disadvantages of the cyclical nature of the market offering.
- Must differentiate their offering for social and economic success.
- Must monitor quality of the delivery process and environment to ensure customer satisfaction.

Further, marketing techniques and knowledge can have a tremendous impact on the success and viability of a not-for-profit organization. Prime examples in this regard are arts organizations and health-care providers. Performing arts organizations were some of the first not-for-profit groups to turn to marketing techniques to improve the viability of symphonies, ballets, opera companies, theater companies, and dance companies. Arts organizations were drawn to marketing tactics by virtue of needing to increase revenues by attracting larger audiences, increasing donations from patrons, and improving the efficiency of operations. Marketing techniques have proved to be directly

ILLUSTRATION 18-3
Of the marketing mix variables, promotion is the most accessible and fulfilling strategic tool available to not-for-profit organizations.

Remember When "Play" Was More Than A Button On The VCR?

Remember jump rope? Kickball? Tag? They're still great ways for kids to have fun and establish life-long exercise habits that help lower their risk of heart disease as adults. Good reasons to push the "off" button and send them out to play. *You can help prevent heart disease and stroke. We can tell you how. Call 1-800-AHA-USA1.*

American Heart Association

applicable to arts organizations because segmentation, pricing, distribution, and promotion decisions are required. Further, as arts administrators have become more fully aware of consumer motivations for patronizing the arts, they have been able to build a larger group of loyal patrons and donors.

To date, arts administrators have applied marketing techniques to improve programs related to season ticket subscription campaigns, fund raising, and special promotions for the sale of wares (souvenirs and organization paraphernalia). One important contribution marketing can make to the arts is to ease their dependence on philanthropic funding. As arts organizations can continue to build solid marketing programs and generate greater revenues to fund their own activities, the arts in the United States can be better ensured of survival.

Health-care providers have turned to marketing due to a variety of pressures. Rising costs, innovative programs that need exposure, and changing consumer attitudes have required that hospitals and other health facilities use marketing tactics to either enhance their operations or to try to simply remain in operation.[17] Hospitals no longer find themselves in the luxurious position of being able to define their service in strictly medical terms. Just as business decision makers have, hospital administrators have had to cope with environmental influences such as competition and changing cultural trends (lower birthrates, for example).

Hospitals are attempting to define aspects of their services according to community desires and needs while still retaining the medical standards for the features of the service. Further, many hospitals are establishing marketing positions within their administrative personnel structures to take better advantage of the benefits of an organized marketing strategy. Researchers in marketing are also contributing to the health-care field by providing analyses of the marketing tasks associated with this unique application.[18]

Overall, marketing can contribute to the success of not-for-profit organizations in two basic ways. First, the technology of marketing can help an organization achieve its philosophical, professional, or philanthropic goals by helping the organization effectively deliver its service to the intended recipients. In this sense, the organization is aided in fulfilling its objectives and its charter. But also, marketing can make an important contribution to the efficiency of the organization. Since most not-for-profit organizations are long on goals and short on funding, this is an important contribution to their success and perpetuation.

Marketing in Service and Not-for-Profit Organizations: A Global Perspective

Less than ten years ago, United Parcel Service (UPS) had only a small international presence in the global package distribution market. Today, UPS has become a leader in this market having reengineered its business operations to speed packages through overseas customs barriers in over 186 countries and territories around the world. The key to their rapidly expanding success story is a company-wide international shipment processing system (ISPS), coupled with a long-term commitment to reengineering business processes, system enhancement, innovative technology, and employee training.

The ISPS program has created a way for the company to transmit information about each day's shipments hours or even days before the packages physically arrive at their destination. Up-to-the-second tracking of any size package from the most remote location is the ultimate key to success in the highly competitive international freight business. For example, when a shipment from the United States is still far from Hong Kong, the invoice data are keyed into ISPS at the export location, fed directly into UPS's information service center in New Jersey, and then transmitted to its operation center in Hong Kong. Customs clearance documents are prepared on computer, and the UPS or third-party agent presents the appropriate documents to customs officials, who then decide which packages need to be inspected and which can be pre-cleared. Operation center employees use laser scanners at the import and export locations to identify transit packages and final destination packages, including those that are not pre-cleared by customs. This scanner information is then passed from the local area computer network at the location to the system mainframe in New Jersey. As UPS's client companies continue to move toward just-in-time delivery practices, having a courier who can combine global transportation networks with computerized shipment control allows UPS to be an important strategic partner in their clients' logistics management activities.

From a company that has admitted to under investing in computing and networking in the early 1980s, UPS is aggressively investing in state-of-the-market technologies to develop and sustain their global competitive advantage in this service category. Expenditures in equipment and methods have grown by more than $250 million in five years and the number of ISPS employees has expanded by more than 400 percent. UPS is heavily committed to this new investment in their business operations: "We have not only changed our technology, we've changed the focus of our business. Efficiently moving and sorting information is now as important as efficiently moving and sorting packages."[19]

Investing in technology to develop global competitive advantage in the offering of UPS's services only tells part of this service story. The other part of the UPS service story comes from Andersen Consulting, the global management consultant company that helped UPS formulate and implement their global strategy. Anderson Consulting in itself is a compelling example of a global service. In particular, Andersen's knowledge in putting together integrated information systems on a global scale was critical to UPS's strategy. As mentioned at the beginning of the chapter, making use of 151 offices in 47 countries allows Andersen to offer comprehensive consulting services, ranging from competitive industry analysis and strategy formulation, marketing and sales planning, operations planning, organization and change management, and information technology strategy and implementation.[20] The strong trend of globalization of business services goes hand in hand with the globalization of markets that has been discussed throughout this book. Global advertising agencies, consulting, accounting and insurance firms, financial and banking service companies, transportation companies, and suppliers of global communications networks are all critical services used by multinational firms to enhance efficiencies of scope, standardize operations, and gain economies of scale. Even small, export-only operations rely heavily on these business services, (see Chapter 17).

Having a key service partner in global operations with whom the company can closely coordinate planning and implementation of activities is only part

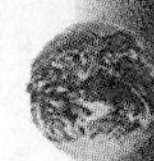

of the strategic basis for cultivating the market for services globally. Cultural factors such as language, business customs, and norms for behavior in business negotiations are critical aspects of global service transactions. Global service providers can offer a consistent global strategy and operational format to their clients, yet, due to the inseparable nature of the production and consumption of many services, they can also customize their efforts in local markets when necessary.

THE IMPACT OF SERVICES ON THE GLOBAL ECONOMY

Estimates are that by the year 2020, the largest industries in the world will be travel and tourism, telecommunications, and health care—all service industries that utilize high technology and costly capital goods.[21] Travel and tourism (T&T) is already the largest industry in the world by virtually any economic measure, including gross output, added value, capital investment, employment, and tax contributions. Consider the following factors related to this **globalization of business services**:

- In 1994, T&T generated over $3.4 trillion in gross output. This is greater than the GNP of every country in the world except for the United States and Japan. T&T also contributed more than $655 billion in tax revenues to local, regional, and national governments.
- T&T's gross output includes over $1.2 trillion in purchases of goods and services from other industries, such as fuel or food and beverages. It also accounts for 10.9 percent of all consumer expenditures and 6.9 percent of government spending. It is difficult to accurately estimate the indirect effects, but the increases in sales, jobs, investment, and taxes are believed to be at least equal to its direct effects.
- T&T employs more than 183 million people world-wide, or roughly one in 10 employees, making it the world's largest employer. In the United States, T&T employment is more than three times the employment in electronics, textiles, or agriculture, and more than ten times the employment in auto or steel.[22]

Because different countries use different reporting and classifications systems with respect to services, it is difficult to measure services' true contribution to world trade. Figure 18-5 gives an indication of the importance of marketing commercial services globally for the top ten service countries in the world. **Direct services** are traded directly between countries and are recorded in balance of payment ledgers. If a technical service company from the United States obtains a contract from a Mexican firm, the fees paid will be recorded as a service transaction in the balance of payments for both nations. **Indirect services** are services linked with a physical good and are captured in the costs of the good itself in the record of payments. For example, when a U.S. manufacturer of radar equipment for airports gets a contract in Morocco, the installation costs and after-sales service contract will be recorded in the total purchase price of the radar system, which is classified as a good rather than a service. Indirect services are not recorded separately in national income accounts, which means that the importance of services in world trade is underestimated.

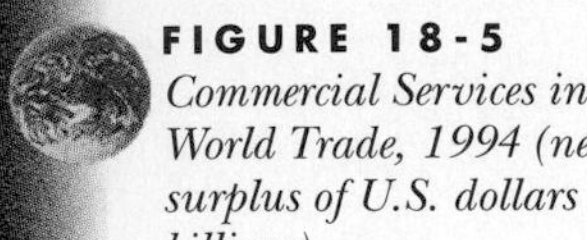

FIGURE 18-5
Commercial Services in World Trade, 1994 (net surplus of U.S. dollars in billions)

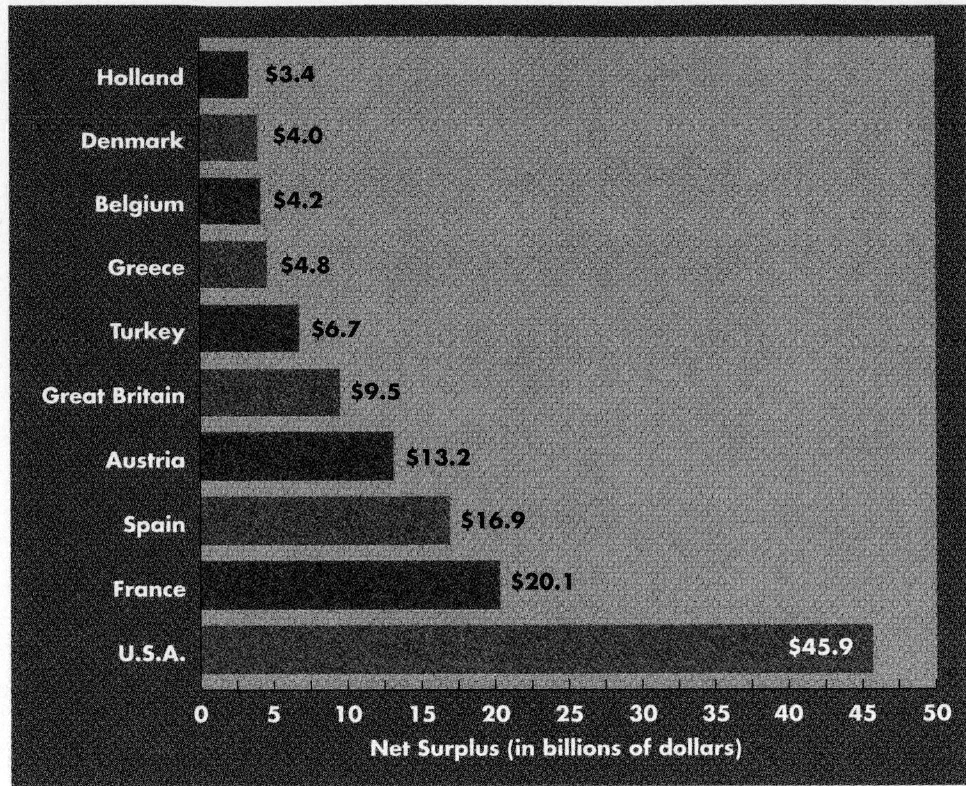

Source: *The World in Figures,* The Economist's Publications, 1993, 104.

As a general rule, for countries where service is important to the economy, such as in the OECD countries, services tend to be a high value-added market offering. That is, services carry high prices and margins because of the high value they represent to clients or customers who use the services. Accounting and financial services, consulting, information processing, and telecommunications are examples of **high value-added services.** Worldwide demand for these kinds of services is highly competitive and represents the real growth opportunity in global markets in the coming decades.

There is a widely held view that having **essential services** in **developing countries** in the infrastructure is the key to further economic development. Heavy capital investments in transportation networks, hospitals, banking and financial institutions, and telecommunications are necessary for other forms of economic development. The government of the new Republic of Ukraine's commitment "to move straight into the twenty-first century" by signing a $1 billion joint venture contract with AT&T and the Dutch PPT to build a cutting-edge telephone system for their new country is an example of developing essential services in order to stimulate economic growth.[23] The service industry is also an important sector in developing countries where labor costs are low and unemployment levels are high. A small service organization such as a kiosk or shoe repair shop can be started with considerably less capital than is needed for a manufacturing plant. These operations in the informal sector may be relatively inefficient (many service operations are characterized as

such), but that is not really the point. More important is absorbing unemployment, providing a means for livelihood, and making a positive contribution to the economic and social system.

TRADE BARRIERS TO GLOBAL SERVICE MARKETING

Service activities often take place in politically and economically sensitive sectors, and because of this, **global trade barriers in services marketing** tend to be more restrictive than barriers for the marketing of goods. The inseparability of services is one characteristic that poses both political and economic problems. A U.S. firm providing consulting or telecommunication services to the state-run oil industry in Libya will not be as welcome as a French or Italian firm providing the same services. Further, services tend to be labor intensive, and the loss of sales to a foreign competitor may have a significant direct and indirect impact on local employment. Finally, some service sectors such as aviation, insurance, banking, financial services, and telecommunications are partially or wholly owned by governments and are viewed as critical industries in a country's economy.

Given both the inseparability and perishability of services, geographic distance can pose special problems for global service providers. In trading global services, mobility of either the supplier or the buyer or both is required. If the service is immobile and is inseparable from its provider, then the buyer must come to the service provider. Tourist destination managers must inform buyers of the availability of the service and persuade buyers that their offerings make it worthwhile for the buyer to come there. For example, ski resort operators in Colorado have been successful in marketing their resorts to British skiers by developing packages in cooperation with airlines and hotels that make an American ski holiday price competitive with a European ski holiday. In some cases, bringing both supplier and buyer together in a third location is the key to marketing the service. American business schools offer high value-added (read "expensive" here) executive management seminars in London for European managers who come for long weekends of study. Convenient air connections from both North America (suppliers) and the Continent (buyers), modern telecommunications equipment for keeping in touch with the home office, and the cosmopolitan atmosphere of London make it an optimal choice for this service exchange.

Often, it is new technological advances that provide a solution to the problems of distance in service exchanges. Fiber-optic telecommunication systems can transmit photos as well as sound and data and have linked together the world's medical community and greatly enhanced the ability for professional consultations in medical cases. American Express's worldwide system of ATMs, which provide 24-hour service, is another example of using technological processes to establish competitive advantage and enhance customer service by eliminating the element of perishability in the service opportunity.

Finally, technology can be used to circumvent trade barriers. The most common example would be using worldwide banking and financial services for the optimal sourcing of capital loans. These machine-centered services, where contact with humans is incidental to realizing the value of the service, can reach around the globe. Technology will continue to have a dramatic impact on the trading of global services, particularly in the expanding telecommunications industry. For example, International Discount Telecommunications (IDT) avoids having to deal with the bureaucracy of gaining access to markets and host government permissions by providing their clients the service of international calls through a call-you-back system in the United States. IDT's clients are each given a number that gets them through to a node in Hackensack, New Jersey, when they call from outside the United States. After one ring, the client hangs up. The node is programmed to recognize the caller and rings the client back within three seconds. The client is then able to make international telephone calls through the American long-distance carrier that the client chooses. The three big American carriers, AT&T, MCI, and Sprint, are fierce competitors and therefore charge much less for international calls than the monopoly and quasi-monopoly utilities that provide the telephone service in many other countries. Soon, even the major American telecommunication carriers will face additional global competition that will come from technological advances. A new breed of telecommunication carriers will soon appear in the market, exploiting the differential between the high individual charges made by established carriers to their clients, and the cheap price that can be charged by leasing an international circuit that uses fiber-optical cables. These new "call resellers" will sell small chunks of their capacity on their leased lines to other users. They are in fact the exact entrepreneurial equivalent of charter airline operators of the 1970s. With the operational costs of a fiber-optic cable call between Europe and the United States dropping to less than 3 cents per minute, these service providers will help bring down the traditionally high telephone charges across the world.[24]

GLOBAL FRANCHISING FOR SERVICE MARKETERS

The global section in the retailing chapter (Chapter 14) discusses the importance of international franchising as the fastest-growing market entry technique for the marketer of international services. Its appeal to service marketers stems from the fact that what gets marketed internationally is an entire management system and retail formula. Successful franchises have worked out superior management operations that give them competitive advantages in operations, and over the years this has increased their companies' brand recognition and acceptance. Striving for consistently high-quality standards and reducing the heterogeneity of the service offering through well-formulated business operations is a key characteristic of a successful franchise operation. The global traveler's decisions for hotels, car rentals, financial services, courier services, and restaurants can be greatly simplified if the franchise operation's name means the same quality of service worldwide. One of the key challenges for success in global franchise operations will be to cultivate a high-level professional service attitude among employees in countries where service expectations have traditionally been low.

PUBLIC AND NOT-FOR-PROFIT MARKETING IN THE GLOBAL CONTEXT

Marketing thought and practices in the public and not-for-profit sectors around the world are highly divergent. As a general observation, there are

Pizza Hut is one of many U.S. franchises that is prospering in international markets.

many countries throughout the world whose political and socioeconomic philosophies lead them to different goals and priorities for the public and not-for-profit services they offer their citizens. As a result of this, global marketing practices in this sector are difficult to compare.[25]

Another general observation is that marketing practices in this sector are more readily accepted in the United States than in other countries of the world. This should not be confused with the level of services or the reach of services offered. Many countries in the world have a stronger socialist orientation relative to the United States, regarding the well-being of their citizens. As mentioned earlier in the chapter, many not-for-profit organizations in the United States are "long on goals, and short on funding" and have recognized that marketing can contribute to the efficiency of the organization. In other countries where stable budgets for public and not-for-profit programs provide an atmosphere of ensured continuity, the need for marketing may be less urgent or less recognized. In many public and not-for-profit sectors throughout the world, marketing has a bad image and is a misunderstood managerial philosophy.[26] Typically, organizations in this sector are managed by personnel with little or no marketing or professional management training, and the sector worldwide often can be characterized as operating in a rigid, and bureaucratic environment. As such, the nature of marketing in the global context of public and not-for-profit organizations is often underdeveloped and sparsely applied.

Key Terms and Concepts

Importance of services
Definition of services
Classification of services
Unique characteristics of services
Intangibility
Consumed when produced
Perishability
Variability
Service-place interface
Promotion-distribution-price interface
Not-for-profit organizations
Value of marketing to not-for-profit organizations

Globalization of business services
Direct services
Indirect services
High value-added services
Essential services in developing economies
Global trade barriers in services marketing

Questions and Exercises

1. Define service products and distinguish them from standard products.
2. What external environmental factors have contributed to the proliferation of profit-oriented service organizations in the United States?
3. Identify five household consumer services and five corporate (business) services. Why would consumers and business pay for these services rather than perform the activities themselves?
4. Why is it that over 70 percent of the U.S. labor force is classified as engaging in services production, but only about half of GNP in the United States is produced by services industries?
5. Why is it so difficult to increase productivity in service organizations?
6. Why are services considered perishable? How do some firms deal with the perishable nature of their service offerings?
7. Visit a not-for-profit service organization in your town. Ask the people in the organization how they use marketing techniques and what are the organization's most difficult marketing challenges.
8. The intangibility of services has the potential to affect consumer satisfaction. What techniques can a firm use to make service output more tangible for consumers?
9. What do you speculate will be the most important global service products over the next several decades? Are firms in your country well positioned to provide these services? Make use of the concept of competitive advantage to formulate your response to this question.
10. Why is it that the application of marketing in public and not-for-profit services organizations is more prevalent in the United States than in other parts of the world?

References

1. John Heylar, "Game? What Game? Arenas Emphasize Ambiance and Amenities to Entice Fans," *The Wall Street Journal* (March 20, 1991): Bl.
2. Examples taken from Eva Pomice, "Shaping Up Services," *U.S. News and World Report* (July 22, 1991): 42–44; Susan Benway et al., "Presto! The Convenience Industry: Making Life a Little Simpler," *Business Week* (April 27, 1987): 86; and Ronald Henkoff, "Inside Andersen's Army of Advice," *Fortune* (October 4, 1993): 78.
3. K. W. Bennett, "Service Industries," *Iron Age* (June 12, 1969): 78.
4. Data cited in "The Service 500," *Fortune* (May 30, 1994): 200.
5. This classification of services is adapted from a long-standing framework offered by John M. Rathmell, *Marketing in the Service Sector* (Cambridge, MA: Winthrop Publishers, Inc., 1974), 10. For a very different approach to classifying services that highlights different aspects of the nature of services see Christopher Lovelock, *Services Marketing* 2nd ed. (Englewood Cliffs, NJ: Prentice-Hall, Inc., 1991): 25–37.
6. Earl Sasser, "Match Supply and Demand in Service Industries," *Harvard Business Review* (November–December 1976): 133.
7. Sonia L. Nazario, "Medical Science Seeks a Cure for Doctors Suffering from Boorish Bedside Manner," *The Wall Street Journal* (March 17, 1992): B1, B10.
8. Ron Winslow, "House Calls by Phone Seen Improving Care," *The Wall Street Journal* (April 1, 1992): B1, B6.
9. Theodore Leavitt, "Marketing Intangible Products and Product Intangibles," *The Cornell HRA Quarterly* (August, 1981): 37.
10. Sandra D. Atchison and Mark Maremont, "On the Acquisition Trail," *Business Week* (December 6, 1993): 72.

11. Associated Press, "Credit Card Losses Push American Express into Travel Management for Corporations," *Salt Lake Tribune* (April 1, 1992): B 5.
12. Haracio Soberon-Ferrer and Rachel Dardis, "Determinants of Household Expenditures for Services," *Journal of Consumer Research,* 17 (March, 1991): 385–397.
13. Philip Kotler and Sidney J. Levy, "Broadening the Marketing Concept," *Journal of Marketing* 33, no. 1 (January 1969): 10.
14. For a comprehensive discussion of strategic decision areas for not-for-profit organizations see Richard J. Semenik, "State of the Art of Arts Marketing," *Advances in Nonprofit Marketing,* 2, Russell Belk, ed. (Greenwich, CT: JAI Press, 1987): 99–124. 15. Timothy Noah, "Welfare Recipients Collect Benefits with ATM Cards," *The Wall Street Journal* (April 10, 1991): B1.
16. See the discussions in Robert Tomsho, "Columbia Hospital Is Expanding, One Market at a Time," *The Wall Street Journal* (December 4, 1992): B5; and Alan Deutschman, "Why Universities Are Shrinking," *Fortune* (September 24, 1990): 103–108.
17. Pamela Sebastian, "Pleasing Hospital Patients Can Pay Off," *The Wall Street Journal* (May 13, 1993): B1.
18. Several articles on health-care marketing issues appear in *Advances in Nonprofit Marketing,* 4 (Greenwich, CT: JAI Press, 1993), Richard J. Semenik and Gary J. Bamossy, eds. Also, the *Journal of Health Care Marketing* (American Marketing Association) is published quarterly and contains articles on marketing issues.
19. Compiled from: "All Strung Up," *The Economist* (April 17, 1993): 72 and "The Art of Shipping," *Outlook* 2, (Chicago, IL: Andersen Consulting, 1992): 10–11.
20. "Strategic Services: Creating the Future" (Chicago, IL: Andersen Consulting, 1992).
21. Jagdish Sheth, excerpted from speech at seminar on "Teaching Global Marketing," Georgetown University, Washington, D.C., June 30, 1991.
22. Compiled from "Travel and Tourism: A Special Report from the World Travel and Tourism Council,", *WTTC,* Brussels, 1993, and Wharton Econometric Forecasting Associates, reported in "Travel and Tourism in the World Economy," *American Express Annual Report,* 1991, 16.
23. "Telefoonorder van Oekraïne voor PTT," *De Telegraaf,* Amsterdam, January 10, 1992, T7.
24. Jim Chalmers, "Tumbling Phone Bills," "The World in 1994," *The Economist* (1994): 101; Michael Galen, et al., "Rome to Bonn via New Jersey," *International Business Week* (April 13, 1992): 42–43; "The Miracle of Hackensack," *The Economist* (February 15, 1992): 69.
25. See Seymour H. Fine, *Social Marketing: Promoting the Causes of Public and Nonprofit Agencies* (Needham Heights, MA: Allyn and Bacon, 1990). In particular Chapters 3 and 5 discuss the American and European sectors.
26. Gary Bamossy, "The Public and Not-for-profit Sector in The Netherlands" in Seymour H. Fine, ed., *Social Marketing: Promoting the Causes of Public and Nonprofit Agencies* (Needham Heights, MA: Allyn and Bacon, 1990): 56–67.

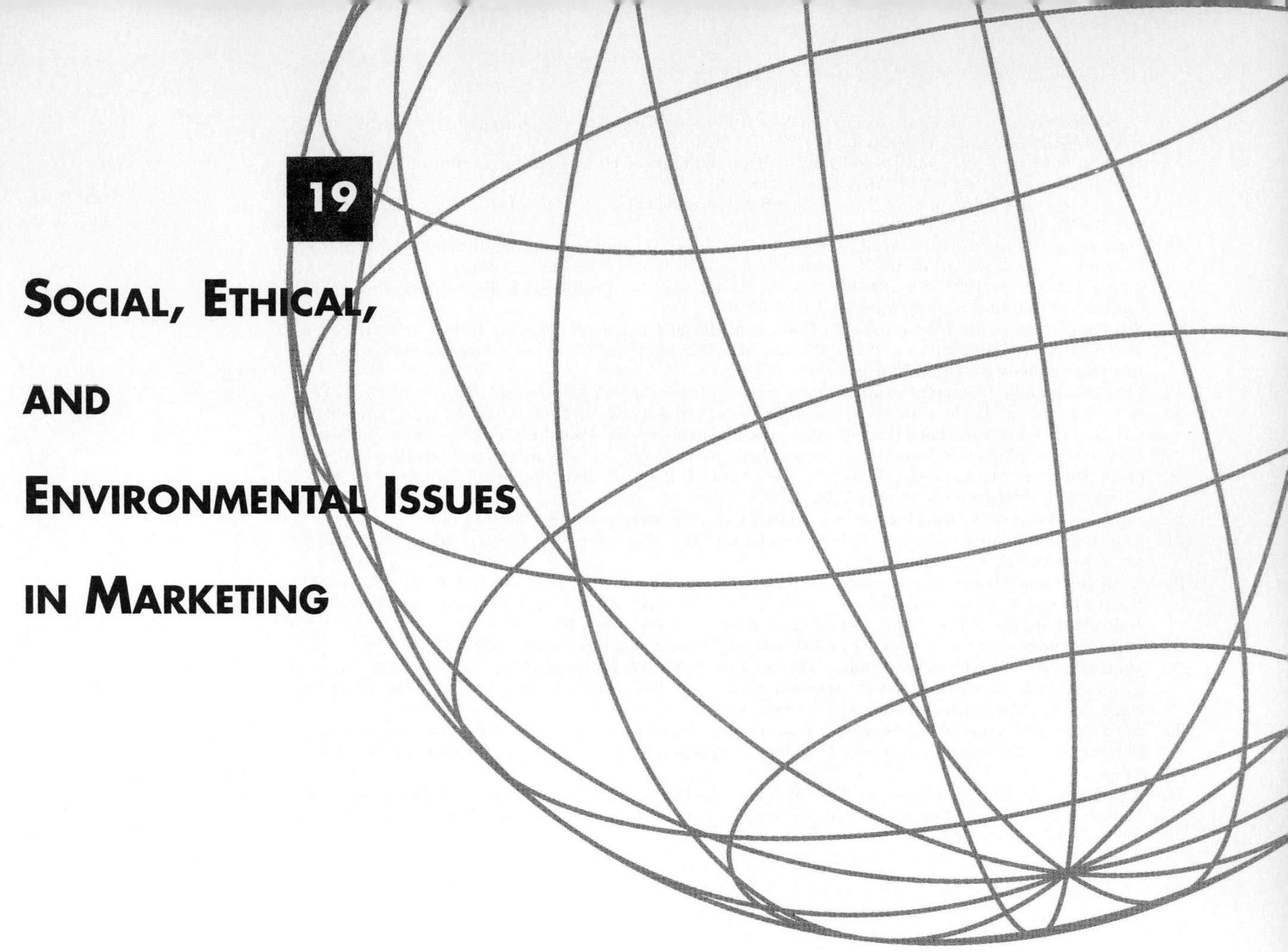

19

Social, Ethical, and Environmental Issues in Marketing

AFTER STUDYING THIS CHAPTER, YOU WILL UNDERSTAND THAT:

1. The social, ethical, and environmental performance of firms in many industrialized countries, including the United States, must be judged in a context that includes significant government regulations.
2. Consumer information and consumer education are two completely different approaches to keeping consumers fully informed about products and services.
3. Consumerism and the marketing concept can exist side-by-side because of a lack of precision in executing marketing strategies and tactics.
4. Marketing, as a social and economic process, has great potential in contributing to the solution of various social and environmental challenges.
5. Social, ethical, and environmental issues in the global context are made more complicated by varying standards of appropriate and acceptable corporate behavior across cultures.

The topics discussed in the text so far have been complex and challenging. But none are more complex and challenging than the social, ethical, and environmental issues that face marketers today. Like other social and economic processes, marketing practices have created some good, bad, and terrible social, ethical, and environmental situations:

The good:

- McDonald's Corp. has started to work with the Environmental Defense Fund in a major effort to reduce the solid waste produced at its 11,000 restaurants by more than 80 percent over the next few years.
- American Savings Bank has increased its loans in low income neighborhoods from 1.1 percent of the company loans in 1991 to 10.5 percent in 1993.
- Levi Strauss announced that it would stop buying garments from 30 Chinese contractors because the firm became aware of pervasive human rights violations.[1]

The bad:

- The leading firm in the rental furniture business has been accused of using high pressure sales tactics on unsophisticated consumers to rent more furniture than they can afford at exorbitant fees. A VCR, for example, with a retail value of $289.98 was rented for 18 months for a total rental fee of $1,003.56.
- A well-known chemical company in the United States is accused of knowingly selling faulty breast implants for cosmetic surgery.
- Parents have protested the use by PBS stations of fundraising pledge drives during "Barney the Dinosaur" programming. Parents claim that the appeals tantalize children with toys and tapes and represent a violation of FTC rules on advertising during children's shows.[2]

The terrible:

- A manufacturer of firearms has had direct reports of 600 accidental firings of one of its handgun models. Forty deaths have been reported, hundreds of lawsuits have been filed, but the company has never made an attempt to recall the weapons.
- A firm that dominates the specialized area of motion-picture research has been accused by former employees of falsifying results and in some cases outright manufacturing of information that it sells to Hollywood studios for several million dollars a year.
- A pharmaceutical firm offers free Caribbean vacations to doctors if the doctors agree to sit in on a few lectures about new products the firm has developed.[3]

These examples highlight that organizations, in the normal course of business, can be quite sensitive and responsive to their social, ethical, and environmental responsibilities to the community. These examples also show that some firms are so focused internally on revenues and profits, that their marketing practices can be predatory and irresponsible. The eighteen chapters in the text thus far have presented the marketing process in its most favorable light: how marketing performs an important role in a firm to help it achieve the goals of revenue generation and profits. Now that you understand a great deal about marketing as a business tool, it is necessary to step back and examine the process from a broader perspective—a social responsibility perspective. What good does and can marketing do? What are the problem areas? How can firms be both profitable and socially responsible at the same time? These are some of the most difficult challenges marketers face.

This chapter raises *issues* in the truest sense. It also raises controversies that should make you think about and debate the very nature of the marketing process. These issues and controversies are critical to your understanding of marketing because, more than any other business discipline, marketing affects individuals lives and has an impact on society as a whole. Because of what marketing and its decision makers are capable of doing—influencing behavior and channeling limited resources—marketers must retain a perspective on the social as well as competitive impact of their decisions. In both a business and a very personal sense, marketing decision makers have a responsibility to society that, in itself, makes these issues relevant.

Social, ethical, and environmental issues in marketing range from very broad circumstances to very specific acts with considerable overlap. Many of the social issues raised in this chapter pose ethical dilemmas as well. Environmental issues can be both social and ethical. An attempt is made to provide a balanced view of the issues. Many marketing activities do and should come under watchful scrutiny. On the other hand, many marketing practices do and can have a very positive societal and environmental impact. Every effort has been made to address considerations on both sides of every issue.

Marketing, Regulation, and a Free-Enterprise Economy

At the outset of a discussion of social, ethical, and environmental issues relating to marketing, it is important to establish the proper context for these discussions. Recall that marketing was not the brainstorm of gray-flannel-suited, Madison Avenue schemers. To reinforce the discussions in Chapter 1, a marketing process will naturally emerge in industrialized societies from a need for efficient and effective movement of goods to and through a marketplace to the citizenry. The fundamental basis for the existence of the marketing function is both economic and social. Products that are centrally located and produced in large quantities typically cost less and are more easily obtained. In a **free-enterprise economy,** a process such as marketing is implicitly required. And, the competitive aspects of a free enterprise system motivate firms to strive for competitive advantage at every opportunity. Much of what constitutes competitive advantage lies within the parameters of the marketing function: superior product design, efficiency that keeps prices low, attractive distribution, and compelling promotion.

In our society, however, it must be recognized that the economy of the United States functions only partially on the principles of free markets. The complex nature of an industrial state has brought about regulations and government intervention. The result is that a **mixed economy** has evolved where restrictions and guidelines have been imposed on fundamental economic exchange processes. Marketing has progressed and evolved simultaneously with the economy. It now functions as part of a somewhat free, partly socialistic, and heavily regulated economy.

Marketing exerts a useful and important influence on the economy of the United States. It is, however, vastly different from its natural form. Marketing has evolved to be a pervasive process that must face many difficult challenges in trying to meet both consumer and government demands. This means that beyond the challenge of identifying consumer needs and desires, marketing decision makers must produce products that address those needs *and* do so within the constraints of the many government regulations listed in Chapter 2.

The result of this more-regulated version of free enterprise is that the marketing process must move much more slowly. For example, when a pharmaceutical company develops a new drug product, it may take up to ten years to gain Food and Drug Administration approval of the drug. Only after the FDA approves a drug is mass distribution of the product possible. Under circumstances such as these, there is a limit to how responsive to society the marketing process can be in a firm.

So, as we consider the performance of marketing on social, ethical, and environmental dimensions, keep in mind that the overall process of marketing and the individual firm's use of marketing techniques are affected by the broader context: a free-enterprise economic system regulated by government intervention.

Social Issues

Social issues have to do with aspects of the marketing process that affect individuals in a society but are not strictly ethical in nature. Rather, as marketers go about their business in a completely legal manner, there is controversy surrounding the basic nature of the marketing process. Much of the controversy in the area of social issues has to do with the subjective position one takes on the value of marketing as a process, per se. The primary social issues in marketing have to do with consumer information and education, consumerism, whether marketing creates needs, and marketing to the poor, the elderly, and children.

CONSUMER INFORMATION AND EDUCATION

As marketing practices have become more widespread, demands for consumer education and information have grown as well. The issues involved in this area relate to how much information is useful to consumers and how that information should be provided. It is important to make a clear distinction between consumer information and education because they are totally different forms of information and the ways to satisfy demands in each area are, therefore, also different.

Consumer information is the provision of facts and description of goods and services through advertising, labeling, warranties, consumer reports, and other information vehicles. The marketing process is held directly responsible for content of information that appears in many of these sources. The difficult issue to address in this area is the *type of information* that should be provided to consumers. The basic criticism of marketing with respect to consumer information is that marketer-controlled sources of information frequently carry very little, if any, actual product information. What critics mean by "actual product information" are functional features and performance results. But, as pointed out in Chapter 6 on consumer and business buying behavior, in many instances consumers are buying more than a physical, tangible material good with purely functional value. When a buyer is seeking satisfaction of a motivating need, the functional attributes of a product may be secondary in both the information search and the choice process. What becomes relevant to the consumer is information relating to the need-satisfying characteristics of the product and this information often comes in the form of emotional or benefits of use information. It is true that these types of messages carry little actual product information as it is narrowly defined to be functional features and performance information. That is because the consumer is *not seeking* product information of that type. The *relevant* information for the buyer is that information that relates to the criteria being used to judge the satisfaction potential of the product.

As an example of the complexity of this problem, in the early 1970s, it was believed that providing consumers with unit-pricing information in grocery stores would lead to more informed consumer choice since it would allow direct price comparisons (usually on a per-ounce basis) between competitive products. After great expense in institutionalizing a unit-pricing program nationwide, various estimates indicate that only 30 percent of consumers use the information. Both government and marketing proponents of the unit-pricing strategy have learned the expensive lesson that consumers employ a multitude of information cues in the choice process, and price, as a bit of functional feature information, is only one type of information that may be relevant. If consumers are to retain the controlling position in product choice, then a firm is required to provide the information desired by consumers. There are times when the relevant information does not include facts about functional product features.

If the argument is forwarded that consumers *should use* only functional product information in the choice process, then the issue is not one of consumer information but one of **consumer education**—training consumers to recognize and use objective information about functional product features, performance results, and warranties as the basis for choice. This sort of prescription for consumer decision making goes beyond the boundaries of what is appropriate for firms to undertake. Firms are not in a position to decide for consumers what they should or should not use as information. Rather, consumer education should rightfully fall to public service groups.

The implementation and success of consumer education would require two significant changes in the development of consumer behavior. First, rather than having people learn the consumption process through doing or from family upbringing, formal programs would need to be implemented in the educational system. Courses in grade schools and high schools could teach students how to identify significant product differences based on performance, use, and warranties. The second necessary change in the process may not be easy to implement or even rationalize. Based on the premise that consumers *should not* use information related to nonfunctional product attributes, the second requirement for effective consumer education is to suggest to consumers that they suppress their basic human tendencies for psychological and sociological need satisfaction through product acquisition and use. The problem here is that it seems unreasonable to expect that consumers can cease to be human beings during the product choice process. Such a proposal obviously is unworkable.

The reasonable approach to informed consumer choice is one that integrates both consumer information and consumer education. An approach where functional feature information about products is made readily available to consumers and formal consumer education programs alert consumers to the fact that many products have a component of emotional appeal that they may or may not choose to respond to. In this fashion, control of the choice process is retained by the individual buyer, and he or she is free to engage in decision making as an individual.

THE COST OF MARKETING

Many criticisms of marketing focus on the charge that the marketing process costs too much. It is easy to verify that the costs of the marketing process *are* high. If the total cost of product research and development, primary and secondary market research, pricing and price determination, channel development and physical distribution, retailers' expenses and margins, promotion, and public relations are charged as marketing expenses, then marketing costs would exceed manufacturing costs of most products. This would seem to be a heavy financial burden for consumers to bear. There are, however, several conditions related to the **cost of marketing** that should be considered when judging whether these marketing costs are too high.

First, it is difficult to accurately assess the value of marketing versus its costs. It is hard for consumers to estimate how much it is worth in dollars and cents to have a large variety of products from which to choose. And, what does it mean to consumers in monetary terms to have products conveniently located, for a store to have convenient shopping hours, or for products to come in different forms and package sizes, and to pay by check or credit card? Each of these aspects of the marketing process have become firmly established in business operations. Consumers have demonstrated a desire to have and a willingness to finance convenience, variety, and service. Whether having these market utilities costs too much or too little is almost impossible to determine. But it is true that the cost of marketing has increased in recent years because of demands placed on the system by consumers. Consumer demands for credit, delivery, repair, installation, and liberal return policies are expensive services to provide. Certainly, if a business operated on a cash-only basis, refused to make refunds, and had no service staff, the cost of doing business would be reduced appreciably. Consider, however, how unattractive this type of service would be to the contemporary consumer. Perhaps the strongest argument for the viability of a marketing practice is that it survives and proliferates. The test of market survival indicates consumer approval of various marketing efforts.

A second issue related to marketing costs is that of efficiencies created by marketing that result in actual cost reductions. Stimulating large quantity demand can create cost benefits from economies of scale that must be deducted from marketing costs. Exactly what are these savings? This, again, is difficult to determine. Efficiencies also accrue to the consumer as products are readily available and in the proper form for use and satisfaction. This saves consumers time and expense in the search process.

Third, the costs of marketing must also be considered within the context of the benefits to society that the process generates. As Chapter 1 pointed out, it can be argued that a high and rising material standard of living is a valid social objective. As such, marketing can be instrumental in facilitating the attainment of this goal. By providing the distribution of goods and information concerning product availability, marketing directly contributes to the standard of living enjoyed by a society. And, the competitive environment in an economy stimulates product improvements and technological advances. Again, the marketing process contributes to the drive for market success of a product.

Finally, a discussion of the costs of marketing must address the question of whether the system responds quickly enough to consumer desires. On this point, the efficiency of the process is questionable. There are reasons for this type of inefficiency. For firms that are truly consumer oriented, the desires expressed by consumers must be verified and then built into product features. This process can be lengthy and costly. The cost of an error in market assessment is even more costly; so firms proceed cautiously and, yes, slowly. Also, there are those organizations that simply have not adopted the marketing concept as a business philosophy and, in fact, do not respond at all to consumer desires. This type of firm has a high probability of failure in the marketplace, however, and is likely to suffer the consequences of being unresponsive to consumer desires.

The issue of marketing costs is a complex one. Based on the issues raised here and the lack of techniques for accurately measuring marketing productivity, the best that can be hoped for is that there is an appreciation for positive and negative aspects of marketing costs. Marketing will always cost the consumer something. It is necessary, however, that the marketing process add value in the marketplace above and beyond the costs it generates.

CONSUMERISM

Consumerism is difficult to separate from other issues in marketing. Consumer movements historically have been related to social, environmental, and ethical issues. However, consumerism is a social process and in that sense is most appropriately discussed as a social issue. Central to consumerism are actions affecting the marketing process and the activities of corporations designed to respond to consumer demands.

In the history of consumerism, the 1960s marked an era when consumers were most vocal and visible. Consumer discontent at that time culminated in then President John F. Kennedy's issuance of a statement of **consumer rights.** These rights were stated as follows:

1. The consumer has the right to safety.
2. The consumer has the right to be informed.
3. The consumer has the right to choose.
4. The consumer has the right to be heard.

Value-conscious consumers scrutinize the practices of business organizations more than ever before.

President Kennedy's call for consumer rights raised public consciousness and resulted in several actions that have had a great impact on marketing as a societal process: the passage of more legislation intended to aid the consumer, the creation of consumer protection agencies at both the federal and state level, and the implementation of class action suits. Each of these actions provides consumers with increased power in the marketplace and additional influence on firms in cases of dissatisfaction.

The truth, however, is that in the last two decades consumer action groups have made few inroads and have struggled to hold the gains of the 1970s. Due to a rise in consumer materialism during the 1970s and 1980s and conservative, pro-business political regimes, consumer groups have had to settle for negotiated compromises and few major gains in consumer protection. Without public support for their issues, consumer groups have experienced an erosion of political power. In light of such limited public concern, these groups have turned their attention to basic "pocketbook" issues such as telephone and power rates rather than mass marketed product issues. However, the 1990s seems to be the beginning of a return to greater consumer awareness and activism. The excesses of the 1980s are being rejected. The value consciousness of modern consumers, discussed throughout the text, is bringing more suspicion and scrutiny of firms and their marketing practices. It will be interesting to see whether the years ahead bring greater cooperation or conflict between consumers and corporations.

A final general consideration in the area of consumerism is the apparent philosophical contradiction between consumerism and the marketing concept. On the surface, it would seem that consumerism and the marketing concept should not exist side by side. If firms are trying to understand and satisfy consumer desires and provide value, then there should be little if any conflict. Actually there are several reasons why consumerism and the marketing concept exist at the same time. First, because of the diversity of human interests and desires, it is virtually impossible to design and market a product geared to every individual's unique desires. Firms attempt to design and market products that meet a range of needs so that economies of scale in production and distribution can be achieved. Such a product does not, therefore, exactly fulfill the needs of any one individual perfectly, but rather meets the needs of a mass market. Second, a firm must try to develop products and services that satisfy market demands within reasonable cost parameters. Certainly each of us would value and find satisfying the craftsmanship, durability, safety, and service that are inherent in a Rolls Royce automobile. Few of us, however, are willing or able to pay $160,000 for these product features. To make products accessible to the mass market and competitively viable, products are often less than the absolute best they can be.

The diversity of human desires and the need to make products available to the masses make consumerism and the marketing concept strange bedfellows. The appropriate view of this area is that consumers and corporations must continue to develop a more effective dialogue so that consumer satisfaction and value continue to be enhanced.

DOES MARKETING CREATE NEEDS?

A common cry among critics is that marketing creates needs and makes people buy things they don't need or want. This is a volatile issue. In considering this claim, there are several factors a thoughtful analysis should include.

A good starting point is to reexamine the basic human motivators that provide the catalyst for the consumer decision-making process (Chapter 6). Recall that in the first stage of consumer decision making, three basic forms of need recognition can motivate product search. These search motivators can be classified as fairly insignificant as in an out-of-stock condition, or functional when a more important need arises (e.g., (transportation need), or psychological and sociological, which produces an emotional need (the need for esteem, status, affiliation, or self gratification, as examples). With regard to the practical out-of-stock condition and functional needs, the criticism of marketing is somewhat less intense. Consumers engage in the routine restocking of items and may be drawing upon firmly established and frequently used decision criteria. The third category is often cited as the dastardly practice of marketing. Close examination of emotional motivators for product search, however, suggests that these are basic human needs far beyond the control of marketing. Humans will find these needs emerging at different periods of their individual life experiences. The search for satisfaction of these needs many times leads people to the marketplace. Firms, in turn, will devise (or portray) products capable of satisfying these needs. The need for love and belonging may be manifest in new clothes, a new hairstyle, or a club membership.

Needs are fundamental to human beings and cannot be created by marketing tactics. The legitimate social issue regarding human needs and the marketing process is not whether marketing creates needs, but rather whether marketers appeal to these needs in devious and questionable ways. The adolescent consumer provides a good example of questionable appeals. At this delicate stage of human development, the typical young adult's need state is dominated by the overwhelming urge to gain acceptance, love, and an assurance of belonging. Products can easily be portrayed as useful in gaining the desired acceptance. The essence of these messages then can simply be: If you don't use this product you won't be as popular as you could be. The firm using this type of appeal would receive high marks for providing a young decision maker with relevant information. The need to be popular is one of the most relevant and urgent motivations in an adolescent's life. However, is it appropriate to prey on or appeal to this need with such brute force that conflict is created? Herein lies the essence of marketing and its relationship to needs.

On a higher conceptual plane, marketing and need satisfaction must be considered as they affect human achievement. Our consumer-oriented society has come to value many products that provide prestige and status simply because of their rarity or excessive cost. Thus, it may be possible to simply *purchase* prestige or status in the marketplace. In a less industrialized society lacking a proliferation of products and the mass communication to publicize their existence, the achievement of status and prestige has to be *earned* rather than purchased. Our affluent industrialized society may act as a deterrent to behavior that generates esteem and prestige.

A final point of consideration regarding the ability of marketing to create needs relates to the rate of success of new products. About eight out of ten new products fail. If marketing had the powerful effect that some critics attribute to it, certainly the failure rate would be much lower. Products could be eased into the marketplace with little difficulty and would enjoy instant success. The consumer is simply too intelligent to buy just anything. Because, as has been pointed out, consumers possess cognitive faculties for evaluating a product's pertinence and usefulness, products fail because they do not fulfill the needs and demands of consumers. Thus, marketing cannot create needs.

MARKETING TO THE POOR, THE ELDERLY, AND CHILDREN

The young, the old, and the poor represent special populations in the United States that have suffered from abuses in marketing practices. Some of the effects on these consumer groups are unintentional. Other effects are the result of unethical business practices. Each of these segments of society has its own unique problems relating to the social issues of marketing.

Marketing to the Poor

One of the casualties of a mass-consumption society is the poor. Low-income consumers struggle to maintain a reasonable living while engulfed in the allure of all kinds of goods and services. The poor are isolated in urban ghettos and rural pockets of poverty. Ethnic groups and the elderly make up a large part of their number. Aside from welfare legislation and minority hiring practices, few efforts have been directed at the consumption problems of low-income consumers. There are and have been, however, both conscious and inadvertent abuses of the poor stemming from the marketing process.

No other area of marketing has suffered more from unethical practices than consumer credit in low-income areas. Preying on the low-income consumers' lack of education and their desire for an improved standard of living, poverty-area credit merchants have, in the past, been found to use illegal and fraudulent enticements to lure the low-income consumer. Bait-and-switch tactics, easy-credit terms, and shoddy merchandise are examples of the abuses that have plagued low-income consumers.[4]

Another issue regarding low-income consumers and the marketing process relates directly to the basis upon which unethical merchants are capable of exploiting the poor through credit enticement. Simply because the poor are isolated sociologically does not mean that psychologically they do not have the same needs and desires as their affluent counterparts. The human urgings for belonging, prestige, esteem, and dignity are irrepressible, as the discussions of motivators in Chapter 6 point out. Low-income consumers are not immune to these desires and like everyone else are aware of products on the market that directly address their needs. Unfortunately, many of these products are designed for and marketed to affluent consumers. The result is, because of financial incapacity, low-income consumers cannot afford to buy these goods, and anxiety results. The impoverished consumer is then put in a position of trying to cope with the reality that these sources of satisfaction are beyond his or her means. The stress is especially difficult for low-income parents as they try to cope with demands of their children—demands that have been stimulated by advertising for products like toys or clothes.

In many cases, marketers that are attempting to provide want-satisfying products for one target market, unintentionally have been the source of stress for the poor. This is not a devious plot on the part of marketers to expose the poor to products they can't afford and that actually don't satisfy their current needs. Rather, the products are appealing to low-income consumers because the consumers aspire to rise above their current state. The imperfections of mass media and mass distribution systems expose low-income consumers to products that were designed for a totally different segment.

Marketing to the Elderly

The elderly of the United States many times suffer from the dual liability of being old and poor. To the marketing system, the old may represent an unattractive market segment. They are sometimes viewed as having limited financial means and a restricted range of product desires. As such, products are not designed or marketed to meet their unique needs, except for very specialized products. When the elderly are also poor, they suffer from the same market-place hazards discussed in the previous section.

It is not only the impoverished elderly who suffer market abuses, however. Those older citizens who have managed to establish reasonable financial security are often the target of fraudulent investment schemes. Elderly couples have been bilked of life savings by real estate and precious metal schemes.

In the next 30 years, the population of people in the United States between ages 60 and 69 years old will swell to over 20 percent of the population. This group of "new old" will, in fact, dominate the population and represent the mass market. Furthermore, unlike their counterparts of the 1970s and 1980s—many of whom were products of immigration, the Depression, and lack of education—the new old will be more educated, more secure financially, and more market wise. The state of knowledge regarding decision criteria and product values of the elderly can be described as minimal at this point. The marketing discipline must research this group if marketers are to be able to serve the elderly effectively with products and services.

Marketing to Children

Several social issues revolve around marketing to children. In the 1970s the United States Senate held hearings on the practices of cereal manufacturers. The arguments were that, through compelling television advertising, children were being "sold" breakfast foods that were not nutritious and that nutrition information was not being made available to children. The FTC considered issuing regulations for television advertising to children (known as the "Kid Rule"), but the proceedings were concluded in 1981 with no action being taken. The courts felt that no operational solution had emerged from the hearings. The advertising issue regarding children is a persistent one. Critics have attempted to get all television advertising to children banned, claiming that young children cannot distinguish fact from fantasy. Thus, advertising is alleged to be responsible for shaping a warped perception of reality.

The marketing issues associated with children will likely persist throughout the cultural and technological evolution of the United States. As long as children are viewed as inexperienced consumers, they will always be considered in need of protection from various aspects of the marketing system. We will discuss later in the chapter issues associated with marketing ethics that again address this special population.

ETHICAL ISSUES

Ethics are moral standards and principles against which behavior is judged. Honesty, integrity, fairness, and sensitivity can all be included in the broad definition of ethical behavior. Much of what is judged to be ethical or unethical comes down to subjective judgment. Few hard and fast rules and guidelines exist. Certainly, outright deception through blatant lies constitutes dishonest and therefore unethical behavior. But what is ethical and unethical is not always so clear.

To help clarify the nature of ethics in a business context, a continuum of ethics philosophies is provided in Figure 19-1.[5] At the left end of the continuum, the "buyer beware" philosophy represents the ethics environment. This position asserts that profit maximization is a firm's prime directive and decision making is subject only to legal constraints. In the middle of the continuum, firms are sensitive to attempts by industry organizations like trade associations and professional organizations that suggest standards of ethical behavior. At this point in the continuum, many firms will adopt their own corporate code of ethics. At the far right of the continuum is the "seller beware" philosophy. This position asserts that consumer satisfaction and well-being is placed ahead of the success of the firm. Clearly, a position somewhere in the middle of the continuum is the most workable. And, realistically, the central position just described is most representative of the current climate of business and marketing ethics.

In business generally and in marketing in particular, the issue of ethics is critically important—and complex. The claim has been made that there is a

Philosophy	Buyer Beware	Corporate Sensitivity	Seller Beware
Emphasis	Profit maximization	Adherance to ethical codes	Total customer satisfaction

Source: Adapted from "An Ethics Continuum," offered by N. Craig Smith in "Ethics and the Marketing Manager," in N. Craig Smith and John A. Quelch, *Ethics in Marketing* (Homewood, IL: Richard D. Irwin, Inc., 1993), 21. Used with permission.

FIGURE 19-1
A Contimuum of Ethics Philosophies

"new crisis in business ethics."[6] Economic sluggishness, corporate downsizing, and intense competitive pressures are all cited as influences contributing to questionable and sometimes plainly criminal corporate behavior in the United States. In an effort to succeed and excel, subordinates fudge sales figures, abuse a competitor, or shortchange a customer. The charge has been leveled that 20 to 30 percent of corporate managers in the United States have written deceptive internal memos.[7] Marketing has more than its fair share of ethical dilemmas and challenges. As the corporate function that is responsible for revenue generation, perhaps more pressure is placed on marketing and marketing people than on any other functional area in a firm.

We will consider the ethical issues related to marketing by structuring the discussing along the lines of several primary marketing activities: product issues, pricing issues, promotion, and marketing research. Remember that ethics is a matter of judgment and conscience with few absolutes. The following discussion raises issues that necessitate contemplation.

PRODUCT ISSUES

Several ethical issues in marketing revolve around the product variable. Factors relating to product safety, packaging, planned obsolescence, and the nutritional content of food products are the most cri-tical.

Product Safety

The National Commission on Product Safety annually reports that 600 household products in 400 product categories pose serious safety hazards to users. The top 20 products on the annual list include several frequently purchased and widely used items such as cleaning agents, bicycles, liquid fuels, power lawnmowers, and space heaters. The estimates of annual injury from household product use are staggering. Each year approximately 40 million Americans will be injured seriously enough to require some form of treatment.

The product, the user, and the way in which the product is used are all part of the safety problem. Each of these variables of product application is capable of being solely responsible for an accident. The Consumer Product Safety Commission itself identified stairs as one of the most hazardous product categories. The stairs themselves represent a recognizable use-risk to consumers. The incidence of accident, however, is only partly due to the inherent hazard posed by stairs. Consumer use of the product is a significant contributing factor. Legislation and other forms of government intervention can solve only part of the product-safety problem. The informed use of products by consumers is a significant element in reduced hazard risk.

Firms in the United States are doing better on the product safety issue. Part of the reason is that product safety has become much more valued in the consumer choice process. Another part of the reason, quite honesty, is that many firms fear that more rigorous safety standards will be imposed by the government anyway. For example, Ford, GM, and Chrysler have increased the overall safety of their cars and minivans to such an extent that American-made vehicles now dominate the top ten list of safest vehicles.[8]

Packaging

The ethical issue related to packaging is the extent to which product packages are deceptive in suggesting the quantity available. What critics are claiming is that in recent years firms have "downsized" packages while maintaining the same price without informing consumers. The result is claimed to be a means of raising prices in such a way that consumers are unaware they are paying more for less.[9] Examples include the traditional 6 1/2-oz. tuna can is now a 6 ⅛-oz. can; the package of 88 disposable diapers now holds only 80 diapers; toilet tissues makers have cut a roll from 350 sheets to 300 sheets. Without changing the price, these new packages represent 5.8 percent, 9.1 percent, and 14.2 percent increases respectively.

Firms respond with the argument that the weight or amount is clearly marked on the package and that unit pricing is clearly marked on most grocery store shelves. Critics counter-argue these points by saying that most consumers rarely check numbers so precisely and the changes are, therefore, nearly invisible. Other firms are saying that their downsizing is merely the application of modern technology that allows greater yields from smaller amounts of product. *Lipton Tea* and *Brim Coffee* packages both have been downsized recently but contain the same number of servings as the old, larger packages. The issue is being dealt with in New York in the courts. Under a proposed law, any firm that downsizes would be required to put a notice on the label that reads "reduced," "decreased," or "less."

Planned Obsolescence

Planned obsolescence is the allegation that a manufacturer will cause its product to become obsolete before it really needs to be replaced. Planned obsolescence can take two forms. **Planned style obsolescence** is a strategy whereby a producer attempts to influence buyers' perceptions of acceptable appearance in a product category. Although most style obsolescence is associated with fashion apparel, automobiles, furniture, and even electronic equipment can be subject to the influence. The other form of alleged planned obsolescence is functional obsolescence. **Functional obsolescence** charges that producers keep important product improvements off the market because such improvements would make current successful products unattractive. For years the rumor has circulated that Detroit really has a carburetor that can get 100 miles per gallon! That rumor is no doubt false, but it exemplifies the type of functional planned obsolescence suspected by some.

While it is impossible to estimate the extent or deliberateness of planned obsolescence, corporations have a variety of responses to critics' challenges.

First, manufacturers argue that consumers like change and that change is essential to maintaining competitive advantage. Second, new functional features may be withheld from the market if they have not been adequately tested. Finally, new materials may be used in product production due to lower costs or new production techniques, and this itself may render some products obsolete.

Food Products and Nutrition

In an attempt to appeal to consumer taste and maximize profit, it is argued that processed food being marketed to consumers lacks essential nutritional value. Due to attempts at cost saving in the production and distribution of food and consumer visual and taste preference, many foods contain artificial ingredients that satisfy both consumers' desires and business motives. Dyes are used to restore product color and enhance the attractiveness of foods like meat and produce. "Pseudoplasticity agents" are added to products like salad dressings to make them pour more smoothly, keep them from separating, and aid in the production process. Other agents add crispness, firmness, balance, and "zing" to foods. These agents in foods are more often added to appease superficial consumer desires rather than to address human nutritional needs. Nutritionists argue that food manufacturers have the technology to add back only about one-third of the nutrients that are lost in food processing.[10] The result is that processed foods have narrowed the dietary range of consumers and represent a potential, long-term health hazard.

A related issue involves health claims being made by marketers about the health benefits of low-cholesterol and low-sodium foods. Firms are using words such as *light* (or *lite*) to describe calories or cholesterol content. These firms have been challenged in court to defend the health implications of their labelling. Similarly, several cereal companies are being sued for overstating the nutritional benefits of their cereals.[11]

PRICING ISSUES

The ethical issues in pricing are derived almost entirely from legal restrictions on pricing practices. The pure ethical issue in pricing was covered under packaging in the prior section where hidden price increases can be initiated through imperceptible reductions in package size. The ethical/legal pricing issues focus on practices that affect consumer buyers directly or pricing tactics that affect competition and business buyers. Those practices that affect consumers are bait-and-switch pricing and price fixing. Bait-and-switch pricing is the most blatant of the unethical pricing practices. **Bait-and-switch pricing** is a tactic whereby a firm advertises a very low-priced item (the "bait") to get customers into the store, and then salespeople try to "switch" customers to a higher-priced item by claiming to be out of the low-priced advertised product. **Price fixing** is a similar tactic in that the primary intent is to maintain an artificially high price to customers and undermine the positive price effects of competition. Price fixing occurs when firms in an industry collude to set prices at a certain level. Price fixing can occur by agreements between manufacturers or by arrangements made between manufacturers and their trade channel partners. In the trade arrangement, distributors and retailers agree not to discount the manufacturers' items so that margins and profits can be maintained at artificially high levels. Bait-and-switch pricing and price fixing are outlawed by the Federal Trade Commission Act and Sherman Act.

The ethical pricing issues in the business market fall in the categories of unfair pricing practices and price discrimination. **Unfair pricing** results when a firm (or firms) price products very low, sometimes below cost, to drive competitors out of the market. Then, when marginal competitors are eliminated, prices are increased—often above the original levels. While such practices are illegal under the Sherman Act, it is often difficult to determine whether firms are merely competing aggressive or unethically establishing low prices to restrict competition. **Price discrimination** occurs when a manufacturer sells similar trade customers similar products at different prices. The practice first emerged in the 1940s when manufacturers over-zealously tried to lure large chain stores and offered prices well below those being offered to other retailers in the market. Such price differentials are not restricted if a manufacturer can prove that it costs less to serve one customer than another. Price discrimination is an illegal act under the Robinson-Patman Act, but there are ethical considerations relative to the fairness of treatment of one customer versus another.

PROMOTION

The ethical issues related to promotion are some of the most volatile. Mostly because abuses in advertising are so conspicuous and widely publicized. With respect to advertising, there is no defense for deception in advertising. The practice is simply unacceptable as a market mechanism. The difficulty regarding this issue, however, is to determine what is deceptive. The manufacturer who claims the firm's laundry product can remove grass stains is subject to legislation and punishment if the product cannot perform the task. The manufacturer who claims to have the "best laundry detergent in the world," however, is free from legislative mandate. The use of absolute superlatives like "number 1" or "best in the world" is called **puffery** and is considered completely legal. The courts long ago ruled that consumers recognize such claims as obvious commercial hype and therefore not deceptive.

A related issue is that it is impossible to legislate against emotional appeals to beauty or prestige because these claims are unquantifiable. Since these types of appeals are legal, then the ethics of such appeals fall into a gray area. Beauty and prestige, it is argued, are in the eye of the beholder and such appeals are neither illegal nor unethical.

Other ethical issues in advertising relate to the use of sex and the portrayal of stereotypes in advertisements. Sex in advertising has long been criticized. The use of sex in advertisements is seen to contribute to a decline in morals. It is claimed that mass media accentuation of sex endorses promiscuity. Stereotyping of women and ethnic groups is another charge leveled at advertising. The critics note that women are portrayed as housewives, mothers, or sex objects; ethnic groups, they say, have been relegated to stereotypical roles in advertising themes. Firms and advertising agencies are sensitized to the emotionalism surrounding these issues and have attempted to show both women and ethnic group members in a wide range of activities and situations.

One of the most complex and controversial areas of ethical concern is the advertising of alcohol and cigarettes. Several practices by cigarette and alcoholic beverage manufacturers have come under heavy scrutiny. These firms have been charged with targeting adolescents with both packaging strategies and advertising campaigns.[12] Critics have also called into question targeting ethnic and minority groups with products and advertising. Similarly, the tobacco and beer brewing industry have been the target of boycotts over their sponsorship of college and professional sporting events. These industries answer their critics with the counter-claim that the advertising targets smokers and drinkers of legal age and that any appeal to underage consumers is merely a matter of the imprecision of media scheduling.[13] The firms argue that they have no intention of illegally selling products to minors. Several pieces of legislation have appeared before Congress for consideration and it remains to be seen whether ever-greater advertising restrictions will be placed on these industries.

While most of the ethical controversy swirls around advertising, it is not the only area of promotion that is challenged. Personal selling, because of the direct contact between a firm and its customers, is an area where the ethics of individual salespeople are often tested. Firms have long engaged in the practice of "wining and dining" customers and prospective customers. Gifts and free travel have also been used as enticements to try a new brand or product. In a recent study of such practices in the pharmaceutical industry, 82 percent of the doctors surveyed felt that drug companies were trying to buy their business. While few in the study had difficulty with the practice of giving away free samples for trial use, others called into question gifts and offers for research funding that have reached as high as $38,315.[14]

MARKETING RESEARCH

The ethical issues in marketing research have mostly to do with invasion of privacy and the accuracy of reporting research results. Some of the privacy issues are no more severe than the nuisance created by being stopped in a shopping mall or called away from the dinner table to answer some marketing research questions. Others are more problematic, however, like the use of two-way mirrors or hidden microphones to gather data on unsuspecting consumers. But more serious issues abound. Consider the practice of physicians and pharmacists who are opening up their patient records to data collectors that sell them to pharmaceutical companies that need data on how their products are being prescribed and used.[15] Physicians and pharmacists say their disclosures don't invade patients' privacy because the patients' names are deleted before the data is handed over to the collection firm. Critics argue that customers of all types, including medical patients, have a right to have their private transactions with a firm kept private at all levels of specificity.

The other major ethical issue that has emerged in marketing research is the bias and distortion that has crept into an increasing number of research efforts. It is argued that many so-called marketing research studies are little more than vehicles for pitching products. An example is a recent study sponsored by the disposable diaper industry in which the question was asked:

It is estimated that disposable diapers account for less than 2 percent of the trash in today's landfills. In contrast, beverage containers, third-class mail, and yard waste are estimated to account for about 21 percent of the trash in landfills. Given this, in your opinion, would it be fair to ban disposable diapers?

Not surprisingly, 84 percent of the respondents answered "no" to this question.[16] Critics claim that under the guise of independent research, biased studies are being offered as proof of product performance, public opinion, and consumer preferences. What is worse is that the news media are publicizing such studies without examining methodology. When broadcast nationally over major news networks, the studies acquire an air of legitimacy and truth. Again, in an effort to gain competitive impact, firms would seem to have crossed over ethical boundaries.

Every individual, through upbringing and life experiences, develops a personal code of ethics. In a corporate setting, that personal code may be in conflict with activities of the firm. Each of the marketing decision areas holds the potential for ethical or moral conflict. Unethical marketers do exist and will continue to practice their brand of marketing. Deceptive advertising, shoddy products, and fraudulent schemes will exist as long as unethical and immoral people exist. The marketing system will be troubled by unethical practices as long as society itself is burdened by people with a lack of ethics. For your reference, the "Code of Ethics of the American Marketing Association" is provided in Illustration 19-1.

Environmental Issues

Massive oil spills, toxic waste, chlorofluorocarbons (CFCs) depleting the earth's ozone layer, overfull solid-waste disposal facilities, air and water pollution alerts—are we burying and choking ourselves in the by-products of consumption? We may very well be and citizens of the United States are starting to express concern about **environmental issues**. A *New York Times/CBS News* poll asked the public to agree or disagree with the statement: "Protecting the environment is so important that requirements and standards cannot be too high, and continuing environmental improvements must be made regardless of cost." In September of 1981, 45 percent agreed and 41 percent disagreed with that statement; in June 1989, 79 percent agreed and 18 percent disagreed. In a rare show of unity, liberals and conservatives and Democrats and Republicans expressed concern for the environment in equal numbers.[17]

Firms are beginning to recognize the threat to the environment that the by-products of production and consumption are causing. Many have taken steps—some dramatic and innovative—to try to deal with environmental problems. Consider the following recent efforts:[18]

- By the year 2000, Du Pont will be out of the $750 million-a-year CFC business in which it currently holds the leading market share. In addition, the firm is spending $50 million a year on environmental projects beyond what the law requires. The CEO is making zero pollution a stated company goal.

Code of Ethics

Members of the American Marketing Association are committed to ethical, professional conduct. They have joined together in subscribing to this Code of Ethics embracing the following topics.

Responsibilities of the Marketer
Marketers must accept responsibility for the consequences of their activities and make every effort to ensure that their decisions, recommendations, and actions function to identify, serve, and satisfy all relevant publics: customers, organizations, and society.

Marketers' professional conduct must be guided by:
1. The basic rule of professional ethics: not knowingly to do harm;
2. The adherence to all applicable laws and regulations.
3. The accurate representation of their education, training, and experience; and
4. The active support, practice, and promotion of this Code of Ethics.

Honesty and Fairness
Marketers shall uphold and advance the integrity, honor, and dignity of the marketing profession by:
1. Being honest in serving consumers, clients, employees, suppliers, distributors, and the public;
2. Not knowingly participating in conflict of interest without prior notice to all parties involved; and
3. Establishing equitable fee schedules including the payment or receipt of usual, customary, and/or legal compensation for marketing exchanges.

Rights and Duties of Parties in the Marketing Exchange Process
Participants in the marketing exchange process should be able to expect that
1. Products and services offered are safe and fit for their intended uses;
2. Communications about offered products and services are not deceptive;
3. All parties intend to discharge their obligations, financial and otherwise, in good faith; and
4. Appropriate internal methods exist for equitable adjustment and/or redress of grievances concerning purchases.

It is understood that the above would include, but is not limited to, the following responsibilities of the marketer:
In the area of product development and managment,
- disclosure of all substantial risks associated with product or service usage;
- identification of any product component substitution that might materially change the product or impact on the buyer's purchase decision.
- identification of extra cost-added features.

In the area of promotions,
- avoidance of false and misleading advertising;
- rejection of high-pressure manipulations or misleading sales tactics;
- avoidance of sales promotions that use deception or manipulation

In the area of distribution,
- not manipulating the availability of a product for purpose of exploitation;
- not using coercion in the marketing channel;
- not exerting undue influence over the resellers choice to handle a product.

In the area of pricing,
- not engaging in price fixing;
- not practicing predatory pricing;
- disclosing the full price associated with any purchase.

In the area of marketing research,
- prohibiting selling or fund raising under the guise of conducting research;
- maintaining research integrity by avoiding misrepresentation and omission of pertinent research data;
- treating outside clients and suppliers fairly

Organizational Relationships
Marketers should be aware of how their behavior may influence or impact on the behavior of others in organizational relationships. They should not demand, encourage, or apply coercion to obtain unethical behavior in their relationships with others, such as employees, suppliers, or customers.
1. Apply confidentiality and anonymity in professional relationships with regard to privileged information;
2. Meet their obligations and responsibilities in contracts and mutual agreements in a timely manner;
3. Avoid taking the work of others, in whole, or in part, and represent this work as their own or directly benefit from it without compensation or consent of the originator or owner;
4. Avoid manipulation to take advantage of situations to maximize personal welfare in a way that unfairly deprives or damages the organization of others.

Any AMA member found to be in violation of any provision of this Code of Ethics may have his or her Association membership suspended or revoked.

Source: American Marketing Association.

ILLUSTRATION 19-1
Code of Ethics of the American Marketing Association

- Federal regulations require replacement or improvement by 1998 of all underground storage tanks. Minnesota Mining & Manufacturing has decided to comply by 1993 at a cost of $80 million.
- In 1990, McDonald's began asking customers to dispose separately of polystyrene packaging in selected outlets. The material is recyclable.
- Intel Corporation spent three years and 20,000 hours testing replacements for CFCs that are used in its manufacturing process for computer chips. Since 1989, the firm has cut CFC use by 90 percent. In addition, Intel recycles 1100 tons of paper, 240 tons of cardboard, and 225 tons of metal annually.

Much of what firms are doing with regard to the natural environment has been dubbed "green marketing." **Green marketing** refers to the fact that firms are promoting their efforts to protect the environment by eliminating toxic materials from production and using recyclable or reusable materials in products and packages. Procter & Gamble engages in green marketing by providing the following information on all boxes of *Bold* and *Tide* laundry detergent:

- This package is designed to reduce solid waste in the environment.
- The box is smaller than conventional detergent packages.
- The box is made from recycled paper.
- The scoop is coded for ease of recycling
- The cleaning agents in *Bold* (*Tide*) are biodegradable.
- *Bold* (*Tide*) is safe for washers and septic tanks.
- This product requires less energy to produce and deliver than conventional detergents.
- This *Bold* (*Tide*) formula contains no phosphorus.

The information on the *Bold* and *Tide* boxes addresses recycling, energy consumption, solid-waste disposal, and water pollution. The strong evidence of consumer concern for the environment has led many firms other than P & G to produce and distribute products that are "environmentally friendly." One study estimates that 26 percent of all new household product launches in 1990 boasted that they were either ozone-friendly, recyclable, biodegradable, compostable, or some other "shade of green." But, since FTC guidelines were issued setting the suggested guidelines for environmental claims, the number of such claims made by marketers for new products has fallen to just 11 percent of all new product introductions. [19] But critics are claiming that many of the green marketing efforts touted by manufacturers are simply attempts to join the environmental bandwagon and appeal to renewed consumer concern as a way to sell more products. One maker of garbage bags that claimed they were degradable in landfills was sued by seven states because the bags don't fully break down if covered. Reusable diaper firms are claiming superiority over disposable diapers that will ultimate clog landfills; on the other side, one research group claims it would take 9,620 gallons of water per child per year to wash the reusable variety.[20]

What is truly "green" and helpful for the environment is not a clear issue. Ultimately, the development of products and production methods that actually are less harmful and more friendly to the environment and succeed in the marketplace will be fostered by three forces. First, consumers will have to act on their expressed concern and be willing to pay more for products that are designed to reduce pollution or otherwise address environmental issues. Products of this type generally require more expensive materials and production procedures. Second, leaders of major corporations will have to embrace the idea of green marketing as a primary corporate objective. While there is some evidence that some corporate leaders have done so, such as the CEO of Du Pont, a much larger movement would be needed to significantly affect the environment. Finally, and perhaps the most motivating for many firms, if there is a positive effect on profitability, firms will be more inclined to follow an environmentally sound set of practices. While this may be too much to hope for, it can happen. 3M has learned that its environmental controls have led to cost savings. By reusing solvents that were once emitted into the atmosphere or replacing a volatile solvent with a water-based one, the need for costly pollution control equipment has been eliminated saving the firm over $1 billion since 1975. Similarly, Allied Signal Corp. has discovered that by using sophisticated waste-water treatment equipment, the water by-products from its plants not only exceed environmental standards, but are being used in the least wasteful and most cost-effective manner.[21] Firms that have made extraordinary efforts in the area of the environment were recognized for their efforts recently by *Fortune* magazine. These environmental leaders in the United States are listed in Table 19-1.

The discussion here points out that environmental issues are complicated. Firms must balance the social responsibility of concern for the environment against primary business goals of revenue generation and profitability. To accept and adopt extraordinary concern for the environment and place the firm at a devastating competitive disadvantage violates the charter of the corporation and the trust of employees and stockholders. On the other hand, being good environmental citizens is a responsibility firms and their leaders need to accept as necessary—not just a threat from pending legislation. To accept such a responsibility, the CEO of Pacific Gas and Electric offers the follow guidelines to firms with a concern for their environmental policies:[22]

1. Make environmental considerations and concerns part of any decision you make, right from the beginning. Don't think of it as something extra you throw in the pot.
2. Develop an internal cadre of environmentalists. They have minds of their own and will advocate things. They may not get everything they want, but there certainly are occasions where they prevail.
3. Put someone on your board to help you factor-in environmental issues.
4. Do these things because they are the right thing to do, not because somebody forces you to do them.

FUTURE CHALLENGES

The social and environmental challenges facing the United States are abundant and formidable: education, health care, pollution, energy shortages, and substance abuse and dependency. Recall from the macro-marketing discussion in Chapter 1 that the process of marketing, by its very nature, has the potential to make important contributions to the solutions for social problems. In a general sense, since much marketing knowledge

TABLE 19-1
America's Top Ten Environmental Champions

Company	Examples of Environmental Achievements
AT&T	Lowered air emissions 81 percent in past 5 years. Recycles 60 percent of office paper used.
Apple Computer	Reduced toxic emissions 97 percent between 1987 and 1992. New Macintosh Color Classic has "sleep" mode that lowers energy consumption 50 percent.
Church & Dwight	Made first phosphate-free detergent in 1970. Cut already low release of toxic chemicals 45 percent from 1989–1992.
Clorox	Reduced toxic releases to 519 pounds in 1991, lowest in its industry. Eliminated 8.2 million pounds of virgin material from packaging in 1992 by using recycled materials.
Digital Equipment	Eliminated use of CFCs before international deadline. Reduced releases of toxic chemicals 55 percent.
Dow Chemical	Toxic releases are lowest in industry. First to put environmental officer on board of directors.
H.B. Fuller	Lowered toxic releases 53 percent from 1989 to 1991. Nearly eliminate underground chemical storage tanks from operations.
IBM	Publishes comprehensive environmental annual report. Recycles 61 percent of solid waste.
Herman Miller	Uses only tropical wood from well-managed sustainable forests in furniture manufacturing. Has reduced solid waste in manufacturing 80 percent since 1982.
Xerox	Remanufactures one million unserviceable parts each year. Reusable packaging saves 10,000 tons of waste annually.

Source: Adapted from Faye Rice, "Who Scores Best on the Environment," *Fortune* (July 26, 1993). Used with permission.

and technology is designed to shape and predict behavior, this knowledge can be used to help enhance efforts to solve the social and environmental problems currently plaguing the United States. Just as importantly, much of marketing's contribution lies with increasing the efficiency of operations. The education and health-care challenges facing the United States are, in part, exasperated by high costs and would be greatly aided by marketing technology that can increase efficiency. More specific social and environmental contributions can be considered as well.

In the area of education, firms like IBM, AT&T, and Apple Computer are donating millions of dollars in equipment and thousands of hours of personnel time to help grade schools, high schools, and colleges implement the use of computer and communications technology in the classroom. The goal of these firms is not simply to expose young people to computer hardware and thus cultivate a future market. Rather, the goal is to enhance the learning environment and make U.S. students competitive with their global counterparts. What's more, this sort of technology can increase the ability of a single teacher to effectively and efficiently assist students with their individual learning needs.

Developing recycling systems is one of the contributions that marketing can make to environmental challenges. Here, old Nike shoes await recycling.

In the area of health-care, marketing technology would seem to have a major contribution to make to improving the system and reducing costs. In a major assessment of the U.S. health-care system, *Fortune* magazine identified several key areas where the system needs to be changed in order to truly function effectively and efficiently.[23] Several of these areas relate directly to technology and practices used primarily by the marketing discipline:

- Create data bases for access to information on medical ministrations—drugs, surgery, tests—for more effective treatment of patients.
- Initiate programs and procedures to more effectively communicate with patients regarding prevention techniques patients can engage in to save the system money. Low-back pain, early stage breast cancer detection, and mild hypertension videodiscs are early attempts in this regard.
- Use market segmentation tactics to more efficiently deploy limited resources and utilize health-care personnel and facilities more efficiently.

Pollution problems and a general public concern for the environment will continue to pressure marketing organizations into devising products and manufacturing procedures that are more ecologically sound. Product packages that are recyclable and product materials that are biodegradable are examples that were provided earlier. Also, marketing techniques can be used to help alter consumer behavior so that wasteful consumption can be reduced. The returnable bottle is a good example, although marketing practitioners continue to wage the war against consumers' desires for convenience versus the environmental value of returnable packages.

More firms are taking on a wide range of pollution problems by altering corporate operations. As an example, consider the efforts of Occidental Petroleum Corporation:[24]

- OXYChem division reduced toxic emissions by 10 percent in 1991 and will reduce emissions by 50 percent by 1996. This division also expanded its plastics recycling commitment by initiating construction of a facility that will be able to process up to 40 million pounds per year of the most common household plastic containers.
- OXY USA installed equipment to recycle and purify more than half a million gallons per day of water produced by oil production operations. The reclaimed water reduces the amount of fresh ground water needed for operations.
- During 1991, Occidental Petroleum Corporation committed $257 million to environmental matters related to ongoing operations and another $149 million in reserves for remediation expenses related to past operations and disposal sites.

Another social/environmental issue in which marketing has the potential to make a legitimate contribution is in the area of changing to alternative sources of energy. As this country faces the threat of severe energy shortages, marketing can take part in two major aspects of solving the problem. First, marketing tactics can be used to stimulate behaviors aimed at conserving energy. Promotional techniques can promote consumer awareness of steps that can be taken to save energy, such as driving at reduced speeds, insulating their homes, and reducing consumption of heating fuels. Also, attempts to stimulate the use of mass transit and car pooling can be facilitated by marketing tactics. Using the concepts of consumer choice criteria discussed in Chapter 6, we can try to change consumers' attitudes about using their personal vehicles. Second, when plentiful and affordable energy alternatives are made feasible, marketing can aid in the introduction of these energy sources to society. The introduction of new products has long been the responsibility of the marketer, and these techniques can be used to alleviate the problems that will come from switching to new forms of energy.

But the challenges in switching consumers to alternative energies will be formidable because of compromises in technology and that sacred consumer value—convenience. An example is the electric car. The best estimates are that an electric vehicle will cost anywhere from $1,350 to $20,000 more than the average traditional gas-powered car. And, the maximum drive time is limited to 90 minutes or even less if the headlights, heater, or air conditioner are operated. *Then,* the vehicle will have to be recharged for eight hours.[25] Higher cost and less utility—not exactly the value contemporary consumers are demanding. Consumers will have to hold environmental concerns quite dear to overcome these compromises in basic consumption values.

Finally, the problem of alcohol and drug abuse in the United States is no secret. Again, marketers' skills in influencing behavior can act as a strong positive force in addressing this national disgrace. Media organizations have already come forward to join in the battle against drug abuse. In a single year, $45 million in free media time was donated to the "Cocaine—The Big Lie" and "Just Say 'No' to Drugs" campaigns.[26] Tactics in target marketing and promotional strategy have high potential for identifying high-risk groups and then targeting these groups for persuasive communications that can help change attitudes and behaviors. Illustration 19-2 shows a campaign sponsored by the Advertising Council, an advertising industry trade organization, which is trying to alert parents to the risk and prevalence of teenage drug use.

ILLUSTRATION 19-2
The techniques of marketing can try to help cure social ills.

Source: The Advertising Council, Inc.

The future challenges in the area of ethics are formidable, indeed. One reason is that changes in marketing can only progress as fast as changes in the general corporate culture related to ethics. As long as U.S. firms are short-term, quarterly results oriented, there will be an inordinate amount of pressure on individuals. This "bottom line" attitude will aggravate rather than alleviate the ethical dilemmas that face marketing and all other corporate personnel. When corporations decide that individuals are more important than profits and long-term success is better than short-term profitability, the ethical dilemmas facing U.S. managers will be lessened.

Social, Ethical, and Environmental Issues: A Global Perspective

In Chapter 1, which deals with the role and purpose of marketing and then again in Chapter 17, on global marketing management, we discussed the sometimes conflicting but always interrelated forces of competition and interdependence. These are the two dominant market forces that set the basic agenda for global business and provide an underlying framework for marketing activities with organizations. We raise the issue again here because these forces strongly influence the nature of social, ethical, and environmental issues in the global context. As companies try to develop and sustain competitive advantage in the global marketplace, they constantly do so within a complex framework of competition and negotiations involving other companies, regulatory agencies, and other governments, all of which bring their own set of values and norms to the process.

Earlier in this chapter, it was argued that marketing in the United States functions in a somewhat free, partly socialistic, and sometimes heavily regulated economy. This description is even more accurate when considering the global business environment. At the broad societal level, it is the rich diversity of political and economic market structures and market conditions that provide opportunities for trade and allow global companies to exploit their strengths, knowledge, and advantages gained in one nation in order to establish a position in another. Given the complexities of developing and executing global business strategies, a discussion of global marketing's impact on social, ethical, and environmental issues as separate and distinct issues would be cumbersome. Issues tend to blur and take on different meanings when discussed across markets and cultures. Complicating the discussion of these issues even further is the profound problem of attempting to exert or apply one particular culture's standards of what constitutes ethical and socially acceptable behavior across the diverse cultures of the world. [27] For example, the environmental issues facing the developed and developing countries are not always the same, and their proposed solutions have different implications for different parties. Developed countries tend to give priority at home to those environmental problems that harm health and wealth. The pollution caused by affluence—smog-causing chemicals from cars, municipal solid waste, and smoke from burning fossil fuels such as coal, oil, and gas—is viewed as much less urgent than worldwide threats to the environment. Having brought their most acute country-specific environmental problems under control, industrialized nations have increasingly turned their attention to those environmental problems that cross international boundaries, such as acid rain and global warming. For developing nations, different priorities make sense for other reasons. A developing country may deliberately decide to pay less attention to protecting its own environment than to other types of investment. When faced with a choice between cleaner air and less poverty, many poor countries will accept more pollution than will a rich country, in exchange for more economic growth. If a developing country has the choice between investing in smoke stack scrubbers on power stations to prevent acid rain or building hospitals, it will build hospitals first. And it will make more sense to persuade local industry to dump its toxic waste with reasonable safety than to persuade it to treat the waste to the same levels that American companies are required to do.

Rather than treating social, ethical, and environmental issues in the global context as separate topics, this section will try to integrate all three issues within the framework of competition and interdependence. This approach is consistent with the book's efforts to take a global perspective in analyzing issues. It is also intended as a useful exercise in reducing the tendency that we all have of using our self-reference criteria in our orientation and analysis of complex issues.

PLAYING THE TARIFF GAME FOR POLITICS AND PROFITS

It may seem odd to reintroduce the topic of tariffs in this chapter. The reason it is reintroduced here is that the evolution of trading frameworks between nations and the detailed "rules of the game" for trade are forged between countries. While countries sign treaties and trade arrangements, there is no doubt that the process is strongly influenced by lobbying activities of companies in a particular industry who have a vested interest in influencing the rules of trade. Obviously, shaping the rules of trade is of tremendous strategic importance to global firms and industries since the rules dictate the subsequent behavior of the individual players in a particular market or region.

Increasingly, trade measures are being used by countries or groups of countries to try to influence what happens beyond their own jurisdictions. For example, between 1940 and 1960 the United States signed two multilateral environmental treaties; between 1960 and 1979 it signed ten more and in the 1980s an additional eleven. [28] Without doubt, these treaties signaled the United States as a world leader in setting environmental policy, although strong support for environmentalism is clearly present in western Europe and other developed economies such as New Zealand. One direct effect of this increased awareness and importance for environmentalism is the stimulation of the young and expanding worldwide industry for environmental technology. The industry's worldwide sales are estimated at $200 billion, and the most dynamic sectors are materials recycling, waste management, water purification and conservation, sewage treatment, and air pollution control. [29] Unfortunately, these treaties also have had the effect of restraining trade, not only between the United States and its partners, but, because of the wording of the United States treaties, there is also restraint of trade between other pairs of trading countries as well. The effect of environmental issues on international trade is not large in economic terms as yet, although it is becoming a top priority as a topic of discussion that will undoubtedly affect the future behavior of firms in their global activities. As international environmental agreements proliferate, they will inevitably include clauses on trade. In the following discussion, the emphasis tends to be on industries that shape the process of negotiat-

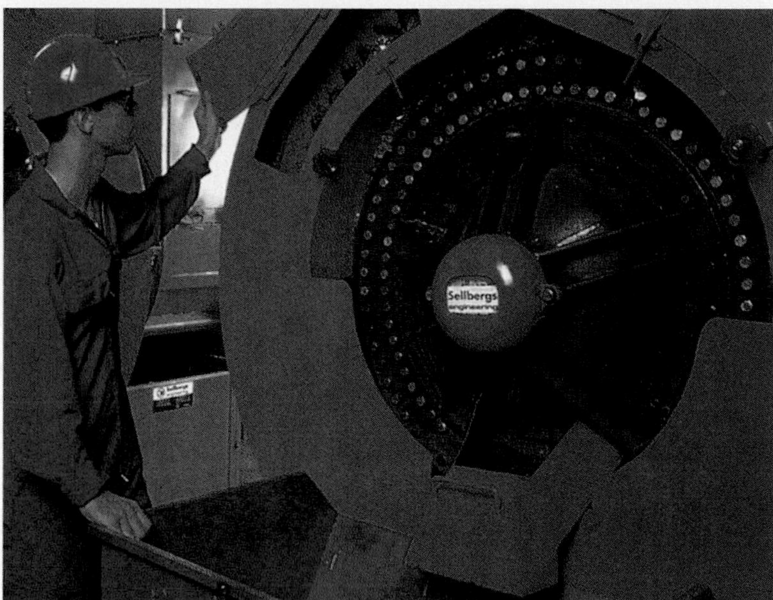

Solid waste disposal systems like this one being engineered by WME Technology is a key future social challenge for marketers.

ing trade terms and on the behavior of firms within the macro marketing environment that they helped to create.

Tariffs as Negotiating Chips

In the broadest sense of world trade, countries engage in the negotiation of trading arrangements to reach a number of political as well as economic goals. Just as channel captains use their power in the channel to negotiate for the best possible terms of trade in relationships with suppliers, countries use their political and economic influence to negotiate a number of trade issues to reach the best terms for their country as a whole. Often, it is the influence of individual industries on the negotiation process rather than the behavior of any one particular firm that affects trading relations, not only for that industry but for other industries as well. For example, almost every developed country's government generously protects and subsidizes farm production. The resulting surpluses of output then have to be sold at artificially high prices making a mockery of international market mechanisms. The cost to developed country taxpayers and consumers is heavy. A recent estimate by economists at the Organization for Economic Cooperation and Development (OECD) put the cost at more than $200 billion a year. Figure 19-2 summarizes the costs per person for agricultural subsidies for a number of industrialized nations.[30] In particular, the United States has demanded far-reaching reforms of the European Union's Common Agriculture Policy (CAP), a policy that is generally acknowledged as the paragon of farm-trade lunacy.

Using Tariffs for Profits

Peter Sutherland, the new director-general of GATT, has issued an interesting pamphlet on the costs of trade protection. Its title is "Trade, the Uruguay Round, and the Consumer," but its subtitle better conveys its tone, The Sting:

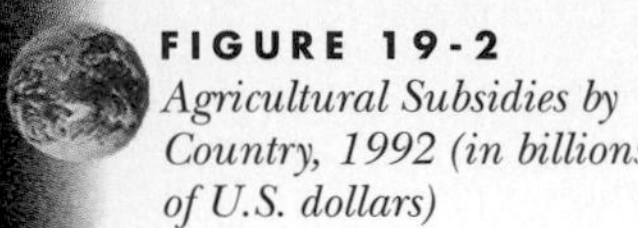

FIGURE 19-2
Agricultural Subsidies by Country, 1992 (in billions of U.S. dollars)

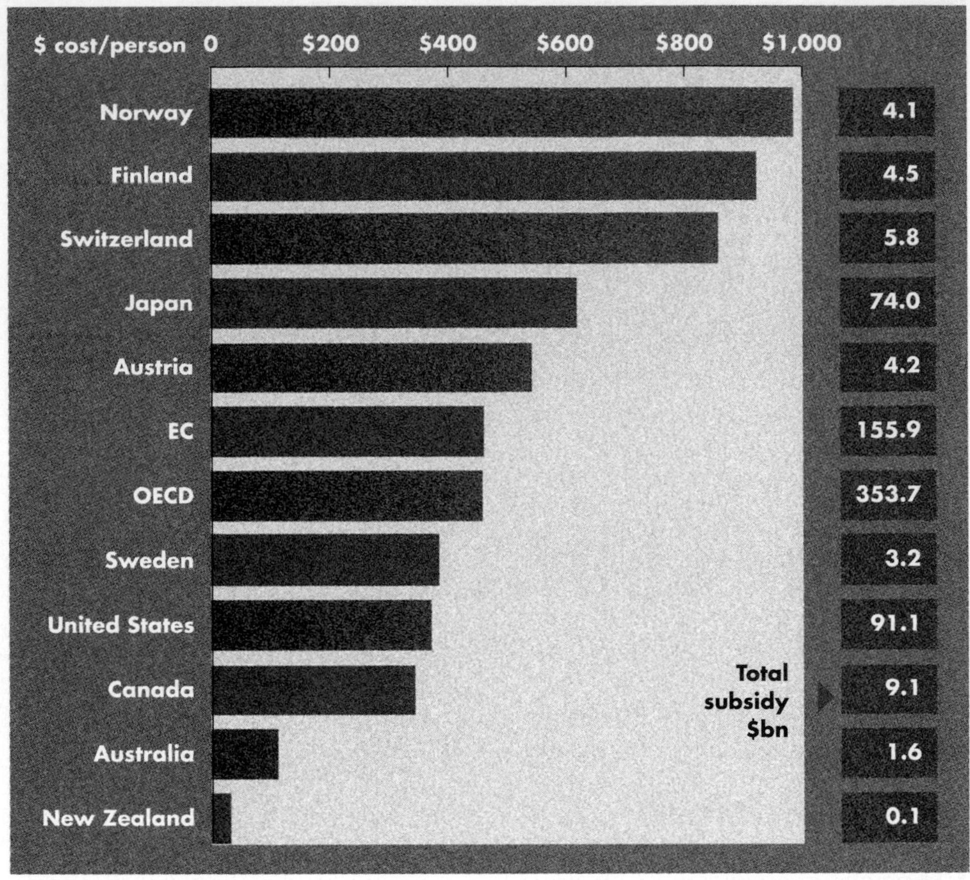

Source: Permission granted from *The Economist* (August 21, 1993): 49.

How Governments Buy Votes on Trade with the Consumer's Money." While Figure 19-2 points out the costs per consumer on agricultural subsidies, the pamphlet goes on to single out other industries. The restrictions on Japanese car imports have forced British and American buyers to pay much higher prices; restrictions on imports of textiles and clothing that come from the Multifiber Arrangement cost a typical family in the United States $200 to $420 per year, $220 in Canada, and up to $130 per family in Great Britain.[31]

Most common among the many traditional arguments for imposing tariffs are protection of the home market as a way of encouraging development of domestic industry and discouragement of **dumping** (not allowing foreign products to be sold in host markets for a lower price than they are sold in the producer's home market). While there are market situations in which these arguments have been validly applied, in many instances in world markets tariffs have long outlived their original intent. Removing these tariff and quota restrictions via the Uruguay Round of GATT and subsequent treaties will ultimately increase competition and significantly improve prices, choice, and quality for consumer products across the board. Tariffs and restrictive quotas not only have an impact on consumer markets and prices. Japan's photocopier makers face duty problems in Europe and their case is just one of literally thousands that clearly illustrate the themes of competition and interdependence played out under unfair and inappropriate terms. In 1986, the European Commission imposed a heavy 20 percent duty on Japanese photocopy machines on the grounds that the Japanese were dumping these machines—selling them at a lower price in Europe than in Japan. Japanese firms spent five years disputing the commission's arithmetic before the European court but lost the case in March 1992. Correctly calculated or not, European businesses have had to pay more for their copiers ($523 million more per year for their machines than they would have paid if the duties had been imposed). Meanwhile, the big European copier manufacturers have used the duties to increase their profits rather than their market shares with domestic market share of European copiers barely moving up from 29 percent in 1986 to 31 percent in 1990. In this case, it would seem that duties served not only to compromise customer value, but also to compromise their own long-term market potential by using unfair tariffs to take inflated profits.

Ironically, the two firms lobbying the hardest to have the duties renewed, Britain's Rank Xerox and Italy's Olivetti, both have close links with Japanese copier makers. Olivetti makes machines with Canon in a joint venture factory in northern Italy. These "European" photocopier models attract no duty. Even more oddly, Rank Xerox holds a 20 percent share of the Japanese copier market via Fuji Xerox, a $4.6 billion joint venture with Fuji Film. Because Fuji Xerox does not export to Europe, the duties do not sour Rank Xerox's relationship with its Japanese partner. But the venture makes nonsense of the underlying argument for duties—in this case, that European firms need to be compensated for their inability to penetrate the Japanese market. Europe's small copier manufacturers are even more dependent on Japanese help. Gestetner, a British office products supplier in which Ricoh owns 29 percent, sells only copiers made by Ricoh and Mita, another Japanese firm. Afga-Gavaert buys machines from Minolta and Canon. As Rank Xerox's submission to the commission clearly demonstrates, making copiers is cheaper in Japan![32]

Using and Abusing Regulations

In many countries, the regulatory environment is organized in such a manner as to either hinder or provide opportunity for trade and competition. Companies monitor these regulatory environments and comply with the letter of the law on a country-by-country basis. If countries have lower requirements on purity levels for chemicals and pesticides in agricultural use, then manufacturers produce products for those markets. If established products no longer meet the evolving standards for product safety in one land, then inventory may be shifted to countries where the products do meet the codes. If a "dolphin-friendly" tuna catch is not an issue for consumers in Europe, then global manufacturers don't make it an issue either. These marketing activities are perfectly legal and are done to take advantage of an existing regulation before the environment (potentially) changes to a less favorable one.[33]

While these examples illustrate the alertness of multinationals in using existing regulations to gain competitive advantage, there are also examples of regulation abuse in global marketing. In several industries, the separation between government interests and private enterprise is difficult to discern creating situations where companies can optimally influence the competitive environment via regulations. For example, in spite of spectacular growth in telecommunications globally, many competitors are at a disadvantage due to the composition of the regulatory agencies that determine the industry's growth and standards. For example, Intelsat, the consortium of national telephone companies, has a virtual monopoly on the transmission of satellite signals between continents. Under treaty rules that the consortium designed, they have the right to veto potential competitors should they decide that a new rival might do "significant economic harm, or interfere with Intelsat's own broadcasts."[34]

By the time these anti-competitive types of arrangements are arbitrated, much of the competitive advantages will have already accrued to the firms who have had the favorable position. In other cases, the anticipation of pending legislation is reason to have concern over marketing developments. For example, pending environmental standards for products have the same effects as other product standards: they make trade a bit more complicated and arduous. In 1992, Germany passed legislation requiring companies to take back and recycle most of their packaging. Officials argued that there was nothing discriminatory about this, since the obligation applied equally to German and to foreign firms (or their German distributors). But the impact is certainly likely to disrupt trade if for no other reason than the fact that foreign competitors will have to go through much greater effort and expense to retrieve their product packages for recycling. Now, in cooperation with the German auto industry, the government is designing legislation to require the auto industry to take back and recycle its products at the end of the vehicles' useful lives. German car companies have for some years been devising recycling techniques, and an obligation to retrieve and recycle cars would be easier for German manufacturers to meet than for foreign competitors.

VALUE SYSTEMS IN GLOBAL MARKETING

Thus far, our treatment of social, ethical, and environmental issues in global markets has tried to steer clear of making any value judgments about the "correctness" of a global firm's behaviors, concentrating instead on identifying and discussing the imperfect framework in which firms find or create latitude for operating in a social, environmental, and social context. There are many instances in which the rules for ethical conduct are not at all agreed upon by competitors in global business. For example, **bribery** has been clearly proven to be an effective and extensive form of promotion in international marketing. For U.S. firms, bribery of foreign government officials or political parties is illegal under the 1977 Foreign Corrupt Practices Act. Given that bribery is illegal, that should make the decision process fairly simple: don't engage in illegal acts. However, bribery is not illegal in some countries where U.S. firms conduct business. In some cultures it is an acceptable, common, and expected practice consistent with the value systems of the culture. Many non–U.S. firms that compete in global markets are not forbidden to use bribes and thus enjoy a competitive advantage over U.S. companies. Finally, the law itself is ambiguous. Bribery can take an endless variety of forms, so the firm will often be uncertain whether or not a particular payment could be construed as illegal. It would be simple if honesty were always the best, and most profitable, policy.

Other ethical issues in global marketing for the 1990s have to do with establishing priorities, a process that is always value-laden. Consider the tobacco industry's global strategies as an example. From a strictly strategic and managerial perspective, aggressive marketing in developing countries and eastern Europe by companies such as Philip Morris, R. J. Reynolds, and BAT makes perfect sense. Their home markets are declining as more consumers perceive the negative health effects of smoking. As a result of these negative business trends at home, coupled with the opening up of eastern European markets, these companies are moving into new market opportunities where pent-up demand for their products is high. With 700 billion cigarettes being sold annually in eastern Europe, the market size is 40 percent larger than that of the United States. Figure 19-3 summarizes per capita cigarette consumption for a number of countries throughout the world.

These new markets are being exposed to companies that have tremendous financial reserves, a long-term view of developing markets, and decades of experience in executing sophisticated marketing programs for promoting and

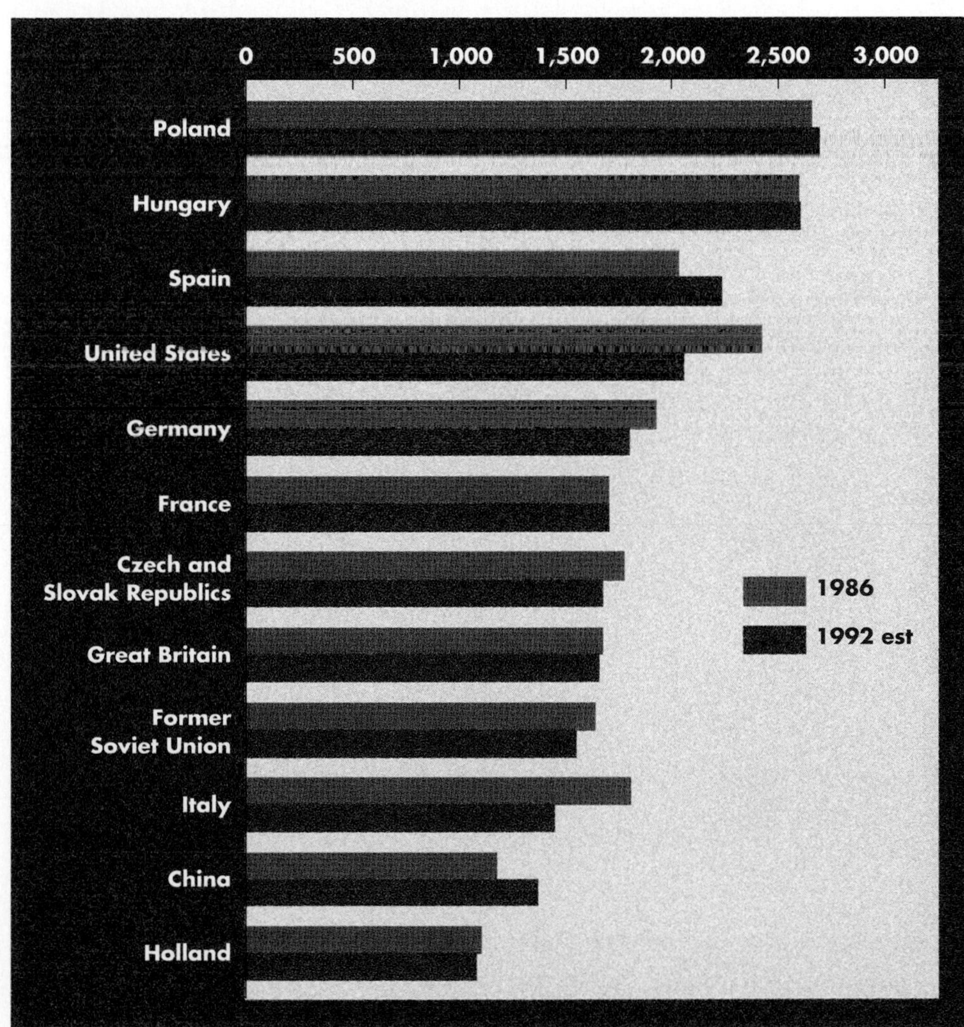

Source: "Tobacco in Eastern Europe," *The Economist* (August 21, 1993): 55.

FIGURE 19-3
Cigarette Consumption per Capita by Country, 1986 and 1992

distributing cigarettes. While tobacco companies' strategic business moves are easy to explain, there are lingering ethical controversies related to marketing to these new markets with respect to health issues and the use of scarce foreign exchange reserves. Smoking remains socially acceptable throughout eastern Europe and the few health lobbies that exist are unpopular with cash-strapped governments. In 1992, tobacco taxes raised $990 million in Poland, $380 in the Czech Republic, and $310 million in Hungary—sums that these financially troubled governments can't overlook.[35]

Finally, in terms of **value systems in global marketing,** the West (and in particular the United States) can be seen as a net exporter of popular culture. Western symbols in the form of images, words, and brand names have been broadcast to all corners of the world via the global media. Figure 19-4 summarizes the lop-sided trade in entertainment products between America and the European Union. This influence is eagerly sought by many consumers who have learned to equate Western life-styles and the English language with modernization and sophistication. Two admittedly value-laden criticisms of these activities are worth considering. First is the **cultivation effect,** which suggests that consumers take from the mass media an *image* of how the Western world

FIGURE 19-4
European Community Trade with the United States in Entertainment Products, 1988–1992 (in billions of dollars)

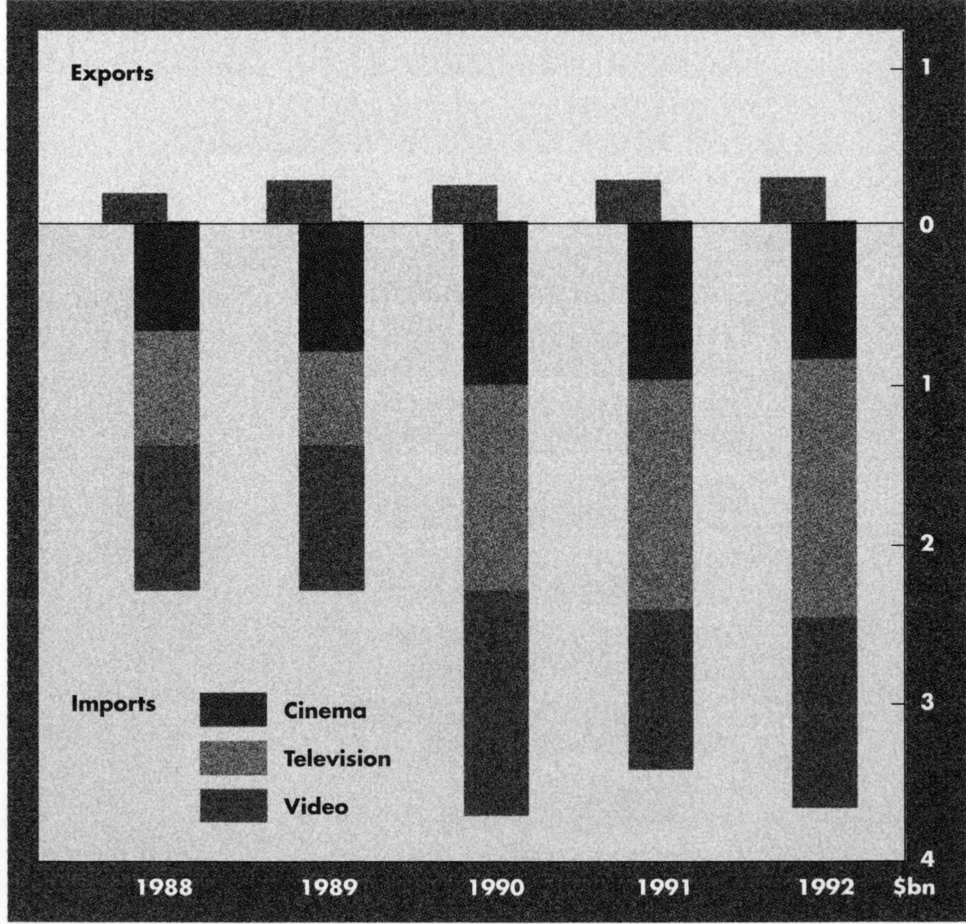

Source: IDATE, *The Economist* (September 25, 1993): 41.

really is. Images in media are often exaggerated in intensity, relative to common everyday experiences, and this leads to the cultivation of beliefs that the portrayals are more common in everyday life than they really are. As a result, advertising creates and stimulates unreasonable expectations for Western (affluent) products in consumer markets such as Asian and eastern European countries where limited buying power could be better directed toward purchasing local products. A second concern is that promoting Western pop culture is "Americanizing" local cultures. That is, as cultures incorporate Western objects and symbols into their traditional culture, the meanings of these objects are transformed and adapted to the detriment of the local cultural values.

In spite of the shortcomings of marketing practices in the global context, it is, no doubt, a system that will survive and proliferate. Perhaps the easiest way to view the value of marketing in relation to the costs of marketing is to think about the costs of living in an economic system where marketing forces have not been used to allocate goods and services. The pent-up demand and the severity of black markets in eastern Europe serve as testimony to the value of a marketing-oriented economy in spite of all its many imperfections.

Key Terms and Concepts

Free-enterprise economy
Mixed economy
Consumer information
Consumer education
Cost of marketing
Consumerism
Consumer rights
Does marketing create needs?
Marketing to the poor, the elderly, and children
Ethics
Planned style obsolescence
Functional obsolescence
Bait-and-switch pricing
Price fixing
Unfair pricing
Price discrimination
Puffery
Green marketing
Environmental issues
Dumping
Bribery
Abusing global regulations
Value systems in global marketing
Cultivation effect

Questions and Exercises

1. How does the context of a free-enterprise, mixed-economic system affect the perspective of social, environmental, and ethical issues in marketing?
2. Distinguish between consumer education and consumer information. Which of these two is a firm responsible for and which is beyond the scope of corporate responsibility?
3. What benefits to the consumer create a balance against the costs of marketing activities?
4. Why is it that consumerism and the marketing concept can exist simultaneously?
5. Why can't marketing create needs? Use your knowledge of consumer behavior in arguing that marketing cannot create needs.
6. Do you believe firms engage in planned obsolescence? Do you have a personal experience you can describe?
7. What can firms do to address the significant environmental issues of the day? Give a current example of a positive and beneficial activity by a firm that directly addresses an environmental issue.
8. Why is product safety such a complex ethical issue in marketing? Have you ever encountered an ethical dilemma of a marketing type?

9. How do the forces of competition and interdependence shape the nature of social, environmental, and ethical issues in the global context?
10. How is it that the "rules of the game" can change from global market to global market? What are the ethical implications for competitors of this phenomenon?

REFERENCES

1. See Frank Edward Allen, "McDonald's Launches Plan to Cut Waste," *The Wall Street Journal* (April 17, 1991): B1; Amy Barrett, "Talk about Doing Well by Doing Good," *Business Week* (December 6, 1993); and Steve Kaufman, "Overall Overhaul at Levi," *The Arizona Republic* (December 23, 1993): D6.
2. See Alix M. Freedman, "A Marketing Giant Uses Its Sales Prowess to Profit on Poverty," *The Wall Street Journal* (September 9, 1993): A1; John A. Byrne, "The Best-Laid Ethics Programs . . ." *Business Week* (March 9, 1992): 67–69; Mary Lu Carnevale, "Parents Say PBS Stations Exploit Barney in Fund Drives," *The Wall Street Journal* (March 19, 1993): B1.
3. See Erik Larson, "Gun Often Fires If Dropped, but Firm Sees No Need for Recall," *The Wall Street Journal* (June 24, 1993): A1; Richard Turner and John R. Emshwiller, "Movie-Research Czar Is Said by Some to Sell Manipulated Findings, *The Wall Street Journal* (December 17, 1993): A1; *Time* (March 18, 1991): 70.
4. Little seems to have changed over many years with respect to exploitation of the poor. An early treatment of the problem appears in David Caplovitz, *The Poor Pay More* (New York: The Free Press, 1967); more recently the sorts of abuses were discussed in Alix Freedman, *Fortune*, op. cit., A1.
5. This continuum is an adaptation of an ethics continuum suggested by N. Craig Smith, "Ethics and the Marketing Manager," in N. Craig Smith and John A. Quelch, *Ethics In Marketing* (Homewood, IL: Richard D. Irwin, Inc., 1993), 21.
6. Kenneth Labich, "The New Crisis in Business Ethics," *Fortune* (April 20, 1992): 167–176.
7. Ibid., 167.
8. Bruce Ingersoll, "Big Three Cars Get High Marks in Safety Study, *The Wall Street Journal* (December 1, 1992).
9. John B. Hinge, "Critics Call Cuts in Package Size Deceptive Move," *The Wall Street Journal* (February 5, 1991): B1, B6.
10. Carole Christopher, "The Case Against Fortifying Foods," *Community Nutrition Institute Weekly*, 10, no. 28 (July 10, 1980): 4–5.
11. Mark Lander, "Suddenly, Green Marketers Are Seeing Red Flags," *Business Week* (February 25, 1991): 74, 76.
12. See, for example, Ronald Alsop, "Cigarette Packs Look Flashier to Attract Younger Smokers," *The Wall Street Journal* (April 30, 1987): 29; and Kathleen Deveny, "Joe Camel Ads Reach Children Research Finds,". *The Wall Street Journal* (December 11, 1991): B1, B6.
13. Kevin Goldman, "Coors Ads Try Not to Attract Teen-Agers," *The Wall Street Journal* (November 10, 1992): B10.
14. Associated Press, "80 Percent of Doctors Say Drug Firms Try to 'Buy' Business," *Salt Lake Tribune* (April 3, 1992): A1.
15. Michael W. Miller, "How Drug Companies Get Medical Records of Individual Patients," *The Wall Street Journal* (February 27, 1992): A1, A6.
16. Cynthia Crossen, "Studies Galore Support Products and Positions, but Are They Reliable?" *The Wall Street Journal* (November 14, 1991): A1, A8.
17. David Kirkpatrick, "Environmentalism: The New Crusade," *Fortune* (February 12, 1990): 46.
18. Ibid., 44. Information on Intel's pollution control and recycling efforts can be found in the firm's *Third Quarter Report 1992.*
19. Jaclyn Fierman, "The Big Muddle in Green Marketing," *Fortune* (June 3, 1991): 91; and Howard Schlossberg, "Report Says Environmental Marketing Claims Level Off," *Marketing News* (May 24, 1993) 12.
20. Jaclyn Fierman, *Fortune*, op. cit., 91.
21. David Kirkpatrick, *Fortune* (February 12, 1990): 48; and Myron Magnet, "The New Golden Rule of Business," *Fortune* (February 21, 1994): 62.
22. David Kirkpatrick, *Fortune*, op. cit., 48
23. See Edmund Faltermayer, "Let's *Really* Cure the Health System," *Fortune* (March 23, 1992): 46–58.
24. Information obtained from, *1991 Annual Report: Occidental Petroleum Corporation*, 25.
25. Alex Taylor, III, "Why Electric Cars Make No Sense," *Fortune* (July 26, 1993): 126.
26. Joanne Lipman, "Media and Advertising Firms Join Forces to Launch Major Anti-Drug Campaign," *The Wall Street Journal* (March 5, 1987): 29.
27. For a more thorough treatment of culture's influence on norms and values, see: Marshall H. Segall, et al., *Human Behavior in Global Perspective: An Introduction to Cross-Cultural Psychology* (Boston: Allyn and Bacon, 1990); and Mike Featherstone, *Global Culture: Nationalism, Globalization and Modernity* (Newbury Park: Sage Publications, 1990).
28. For an excellent discussion on the impact of the environment on world trade, see: "A Survey of the Global Environment," *The Economist* (May 30, 1992).
29. *The Commerzbank Report on German Business and Finance*, October 1993, and "Viewpoint," *The Economist* (October 23, 1993): 74.

30. "Guilty on All Counts," *The Economist* (August 21, 1993): 49; "Free Trade's Fading Champion," *The Economist* (April 11, 1992): 71–72. See also Lester Thurow, *Head to Head: The Coming Economic Battle Among Japan, Europe, and America* (Boston: William Morrow Publishers, 1992).
31. "Trade, the Uruguay Round, and the Consumer: The Sting: How Governments Buy Votes on Trade with the Consumer's Money." GATT, 1993; "Guilty on All Counts," *The Economist* (August 21, 1993): 49.
32. "Copy Cats," *The Economist* (April 18, 1992): 70.
33. See N. Craig Smith, *Morality and the Market: Consumer Pressure for Corporate Accountability* (London: Routledge Press, 1990).
34. "Intelsat Upon," *The Economist* (February 22, 1992): 65.
35. Richard W. Stevenson, "Western Tobacco Goes East" *The International Herald Tribune* (November 13, 1993): 9; "Tobacco in Eastern Europe," *The Economist* (August 21, 1993); Barry Newman, "The Marlboro Man Gets Bushwacked by an Old Red Foe," *The Wall Street Journal* (September 24, 1993): A1.

Acknowledgments

For permission to reproduce the photographs/advertisements on the pages indicated, acknowledgment is made to the following:

page 4 © Sunshine
9 © Todd Buchanan
11 L.L. Bean, Inc.
18 Courtesy Cadillac
25 © SIPA Press/Sunshine
43 General Motors
48 © John Mantel/SIPA Press
56 © Ed Kashi
73 © Kenneth L. Resen
78 © John Madere
90 © R. Danktoff/Sunshine
395 © Sunshine
114 © 1994 BMW of North America, Inc.
119 © 1991 Infiniti Division of Nissan Motor
125 © Sunshine
128 © Sunshine
135 © Brownie Harris
153 Compaq Computer Corp.
154 © Tom Tracy/Tony Stone Images
158 © George Hunter/Tony Stone Images
163 ©Martin Rogers/Tony Stone Images
171 © Sunshine
175 U.S. Trust
184 Courtesy of Campbells Soup Company
191 Courtesy Pitney Bowes
196 © Laski/Sunshine
213 Courtesy Ford Motor Company
223 © James Schnept Photography
238 © Greg Girard/Contact/Woodfin Camp & Associates
242 © Chris Usher 1992
248 Featured with permission of Buick Motor Division
253 © Visa U.S.A., Inc., (1992). All Rights Reserved. Reproduced with the permission of Visa U.S.A., Inc.
276 © Marc Chaumeil
286 Courtesy of Southwest Airlines Co.
298 © Ken Kerebs/DOT
310 © R. Daukloff/Sunshine
315 © Sunshine
317 Courtesy Inter-Continental Hotels
336 © 1993David Graham/Black Star
347 Reproduced with permission of Saab Cars USA
370 Featured with permission of Buick Motor Division
383 © Peter Freed
391 © Sara Lee Corporation
402 © Frank Herholdt/Tony Stone Images
413 © 1992 Steve Winter/Black Star
420 © 1992 Robb Kendrick
427 © Charles Gupton/Tony Stone Images
438 © Jeff Zaruba
443 © Tom Tracy
460 © Ron McMillian/Gamma Liaison
463 © Sunshine
477 Outdoor Advertising Association of America, Inc.
483 © Martyn Goddard
492 © Patrick Frilet/Sunshine
505 © 1994, John Harding
512 © 1990 Tom Sobolik/Black Star
519 © 1992 Chris Usher
527 © Roger Tully/Tony Stone Images
534 © Nick Helsh
554 © Stephen Ferry/MATRIX
563 © Caroline Parsons/Gamma Liaison
575 © Susan May Tell/SABA
585 © Tom Tracy
596 © John S. Abbot
603 Courtesy of American International Group, Inc.
611 © 1994 Kemper Financial Services, Inc.
623 © Sunshine
633 © Barth Falkenberg
648 © Bud Lee

INDEX

A

H

N

O

P

T